Instant
Access
Databases

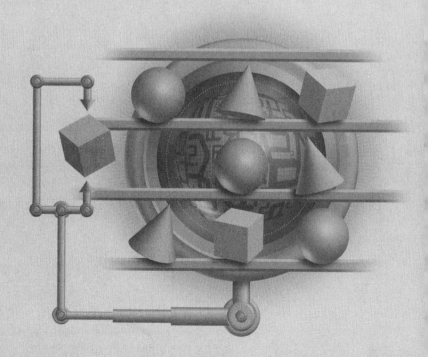

Instant
Access
Databases

Greg Buczek

McGraw-Hill
New York   San Francisco   Washington, D.C.
Auckland   Bogotá   Caracas   Lisbon   London
Madrid   Mexico City   Milan   Montreal   New Delhi
San Juan   Singapore   Sydney   Tokyo   Toronto

Osborne/**McGraw-Hill**
2600 Tenth Street
Berkeley, California 94710
U.S.A.

For information on translations or book distributors outside the U.S.A., or
to arrange bulk purchase discounts for sales promotions, premiums, or
fund-raisers, please contact Osborne/McGraw-Hill at the above address.

Instant Access Databases

1234567890 CUS CUS 01987654321
Book p/n 0-07-213075-X and CD p/n 0-07-213074-1
parts of
ISBN 0-07-213076-8

Publisher
Brandon A. Nordin

Acquisitions Coordinator
Paulina Pobocha

**Vice President &
Associate Publisher**
Scott Rogers

Cover Design
William Chan

Acquisitions Editor
Rebekah Young

Production
MacAllister Publishing Services, LLC

Project Manager
Dave Nash

Dedication

This book is dedicated to Truth, Knowledge and Remembrance, from these ideals flows Compassion, Understanding and Acceptance.

Contents at a Glance

Contents

Acknowledgments

I wish to acknowledge and thank Joyce Buczek for her tremendous support and assistance during this project. I would also like to thank Michael Adams, my technical editor, and Rebekah Young, my editor at McGraw-Hill.

In addition, I must thank my gracious readers who have contacted me and provided me the enthusiasm to continue to write. Their frequent kind words and support have made many long days worthwhile.

Book Structure

This book is divided into three sections: Access Programming Basics, Instant Access Databases, and Advanced Topics. The first section, "Access Programming Basics," introduces you to the different ways for setting up your database so that it is easier to develop with . This section also introduces you to events.

The bulk of the book is the second section, "Instant Access Databases." This section presents complete Access 2000 databases that you can find on the accompanying CD-ROM. A discussion is presented for each database. First, you will see how the database works through a walk-through. Then each table is defined, as is each field, with a discussion on relationships and special property values. After that, you will find a discussion on all the code that makes up the database used on the forms and reports.

The third section of the book, "Advanced Topics," will show you how to port your data to the Internet and create add-ins.

Final Note

As you are reading, reviewing, and playing with the database applications presented in this book, always think about how you could modify the database to satisfy a different need. Don't pass by one database because you think you will never use it. Open your mind and think about how you could mold it for your own needs.

SECTION 1

Access
Programming
Basics

CHAPTER 1

Intro to Access

Creating Efficient and Effective Access Databases

One of the things overlooked by many developers when working with Access is the basics of database design. This book will begin with a review of what you can do from the beginning to make your development work easier in the long run.

First, we will look at creating tables, the different data types and their properties. We will also look at the properties of tables themselves. Then we will discuss relationships. We will define what they are and how you can graphically manage relationships in your database through Access.

Creating Tables

Access comes with a wizard that helps you create some basic tables, but most of the time the wizards fall far short of taking you to the end result needed by your database applications. In this section of the chapter, we will go past the wizards and look at creating tables from scratch.

Field Names and Description

To create a new table from scratch in Access, you begin by selecting "Create a Table in Design View" from the Tables tab of the Database Window. When you do that, Access opens a new blank table-in-design view like the one displayed in Figure 1-1. You also can open an existing table-in-design view by selecting the table from the Tables tab and then pressing the Design Button.

The grid at the top of the Design view is used for supplying the name, type and description of your field. Once you enter a field and its type, you can then enter the properties for that field at the bottom of the form.

A field name can be up to 64 characters. You can even use spaces and special characters, but you shouldn't because even though Access allows this, many other databases don't. If you need to convert your database to a different type in the future, that will be just another problem to deal with. Instead of using spaces, use mixed case. For example, instead of calling your field this:

    First Name

call it:

    FirstName

and you will avoid complications at conversion.

Figure 1-1

The Table Design View

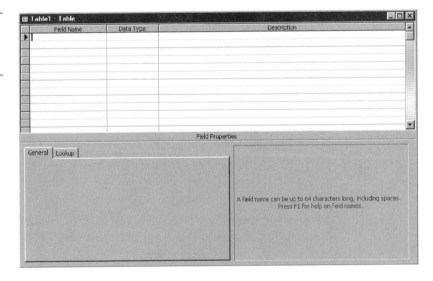

After you enter the name for a field, select its type. Various types are reviewed in the next section.

The third column for a field provides space for you to enter a description for your field. This can be used in two ways. First, you can use it to document your work by providing text here that supplies special information about a field such as what it is used for, why you created it or an explanation beyond its name. You can provide text here that supplies special information about a field, like what it is used for, why you created it, or an explanation beyond its name.

The other reason to use a description is that whatever text you enter here is displayed in the status bar when the user is entering data into this field in the table. The value is also placed on the status bar by default when the user is entering data into this field through a form.

Data Types

When you select the Data Type column for a field, you see a list of 10 different types, one of which is not really a data type at all. These Data Types are summarized in Table 1-1.

Text Data Type

The Text data type should be used for specific pieces of information that are of a predictable length. For example, a person's name, a phone number, the serial number on a product or the name of a building would be Text Data Types.

The field contains a property called Field Size, where you set the maximum number of characters that the user can enter into the field. The value can be set to a maximum of 255. This means that a Text field cannot be longer that 255 characters, so it would not be a good choice for something like a description.

Memo Data Type

If you need to go beyond the 255-character limitation of a Text field you can use a Memo field. A Memo field would allow the user to enter free-flowing text such as a note or a description.

A Memo field is actually stored within the record as a pointer to a place in the database where the text is outside of the table itself. The field cannot be indexed.

Data Type	Description
Text	Used to store characters and or numbers of a small to medium length.
Memo	Used to store extended text information.
Number	A numeric value. Has a variety of subtypes.
Date/Time	Used to store a date, time or date and time.
Currency	Used to store dollar amount. A specialized sub-type of a number.
AutoNumber	Used to create a unique value for each record for the field in a table.
Yes/No	Used to create a Check Box field that can have a value of True or False.
OLE Object	Stores insertable objects such as pictures, sound or movies.
HyperLink	A special text field that stores a link and a caption for the link.
Lookup Wizard	Not a data type, provides the ability to link tables together and/or create combo boxes.

Table 1-1

Data Types

Number Data Type

You use the number data type to store a numeric value that is not being used to store money. When you select that type, it has a special property called Field Size that you set to the type of number you want to use. Table 1-2 displays the different sub-types you can select through the Field Size property.

Date/Time Data Type

The Date/Time data type is used to store a date or a time or both a date and a time. This field is ideal for any date in your database such as a birth date, an order date or a modification date. Internally, dates are stored as a number. So even if you only display or enter a two-digit year, Access stores a four-digit year.

	Data Type	Description
Table 1-2 Number Data Types	Byte	A whole number, no fraction, in the range of 0 to 255.
	Integer	A whole number, no fraction, in the range of -32,768 to 32,767.
	Long Integer	A whole number, no fraction, in the range of approximately +/− 2.1 billion.
	Single	Stores a number and its fraction for up to 7 decimal places.
	Double	Stores a number and its fraction for up to 15 decimal places.
	Replication ID	Stores a Global Unique Identifier, which is a 16-byte hexadecimal number.
	Decimal	Stores a number and its fraction for up to 28 decimal places.

Currency Data Type

The Currency data type is used to store money information. The field would be good for order totals, salaries or product prices. A Currency field has a whole number portion and can have from 0 to 4 decimal places.

AutoNumber Field

As you look through the databases in this book, you will see that almost all the tables have a field that is an AutoNumber field. An AutoNumber field is a special number field. The value of this field cannot be edited and when a new record is added to a table, the field is automatically populated with a unique value.

Thus, the field is well-suited for being a primary key. You can only have one field in a table that is an AutoNumber field. An AutoNumber field can be set up in three ways as displayed in Table 1-3.

Yes/No Data Type

The Yes/No data type enables you to create a field that has two states, True and False. When you create a field of this type, it appears as a check box in the Table view or on a form. Fields like TaxExempt, OpenAllNight and IncludeInMailingList are ideal candidates for this type of field.

Data Type	Description
Long Integer - Increment	Stored as a Long Integer and, as a new record is created, the number is increased by one.
Long Integer - Random	Stored as a Long Integer and, as a new record is created, a random number is used.
ReplicationID	Instead of a Long Integer, the value is stored as a Global Unique Identifier.

Table 1-3

AutoNumber
Data Types

OLE Object

An OLE Object field enables you to store an insertable object into a record. This type of field is ideal for including a picture, sound or movie with a record. You can even use it to store Word documents, Excel spreadsheets or any other insertable object that is installed on the user's computer.

A field of this type is stored like a Memo field. The data is not stored with the record. Instead, a pointer to where the data is located in the database is stored. When you select this type for a field, the user can right-click on the field in the Table view and select Insert Object to see the Insert Object dialog displayed in Figure 1-2.

The user can select to create a new file. If so, the application that goes with the type is opened and the user can then create the object. When the application is closed, the object becomes part of the record in the database. Another option is to select a file that contains the object the user wants to insert by selecting the Create From File option.

Hyperlink Data Type

The Hyperlink Data Type is a special type of Text field. It contains two text values: one is the text to display and the other is where to go when the text is clicked like the link on a Web page.

This data type is used for fields like WebSite, EmailAddress or even a link to a file. To create a field of this type, the user can just type in a Web address and click it. Or the user can right-click on the field and choose Hyperlink/Edit Hyperlink to see the Edit Hyperlink dialog displayed in Figure 1-3.

Figure 1-2

The Insert Object
Dialog

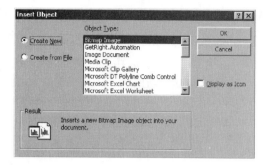

Figure 1-3

The Edit
Hyperlink Dialog

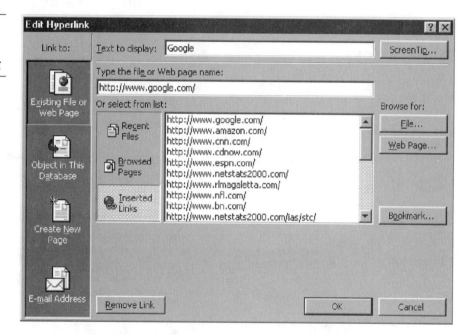

From this dialog, text can be entered to display with the link and enter
the link itself, or select it from a variety of lists. Note that the user can
also link to an object in the current database or have Access create a new
email message by clicking on the field.

Lookup Wizard

The Lookup Wizard is not really a Data Type. Instead, it walks you
through a wizard that produces a field with a combo box. The combo box
can contain a list of fixed values or values from another database table.

The wizard starts automatically when you select this type and move off that column. When you do that, you see the first page of the wizard displayed in Figure 1-4.

If you select the first option on this page of the wizard, Access prompts you for the name of the table that has the fields that you want to display in the combo box and the names of the fields you want to display in that list. If you select the second option and press Next, you see the second page of the wizard displayed in Figure 1-5.

Here you enter a list of values that you want to appear in the combo box. As you will see later in this chapter, you can also set a property so that the user can only select a value from the list you include.

Primary Keys

A primary key is a field or group of fields used to uniquely identify a record. The value in the field or fields is not repeated throughout the table. A primary key is to verify that the record you are referring to is the same record over time.

For example, suppose that you have an Employees table and a Dependents table, and you have an employee, Julie Smith, who has a dependent named Ami Smith. Now suppose you hire a new employee whose

Figure 1-4

The Lookup
Wizard page 1

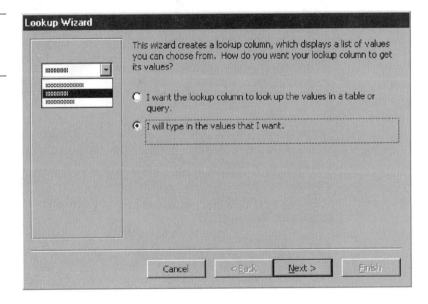

name is also Julie Smith. If you used the employee's name as the link between the two tables, you no longer know which employee the dependent goes with.

Instead, you should add a new field such as EmployeeID that you create as an AutoNumber field. The field would be the primary key and would provide a way for the relating records to stay related because no record will have an EmployeeID repeated. To make a field the primary key, select the field or fields, and then from the menu, select Edit/Primary Key.

Indexes

Indexes provide a way for you to tell Access that a field or group of fields will be used to sort or search records in a table. When you tell Access this, it maintains a separate list of fields sorted by the field or fields that you select as an index.

Indexes do help to speed up queries, but they can slow down adds and updates because Access has to manage the values in both the data table and the index table. You should use indexes where appropriate, but don't overuse them.

Figure 1-5

The Lookup
Wizard page 2

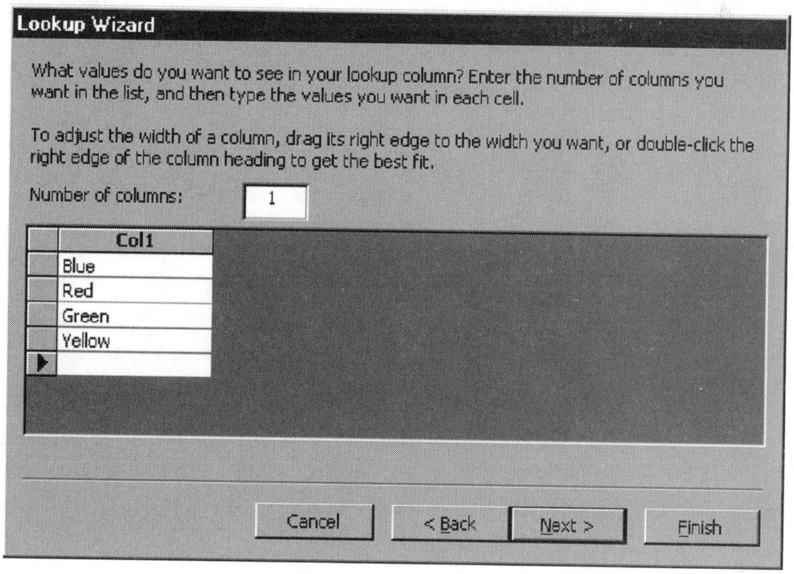

Figure 1-6

The Indexes
dialog

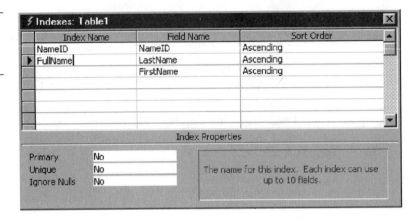

You can create indexes in two ways. One way is through the indexed property. Select a field and in the property portion of the Design view, change the indexed property to Yes (Duplicates OK), Yes (No Duplicates) or No.

But suppose that you want to index more than one field. For example, you may find that you are frequently sorting records or searching records by last name followed by first name. To index multiple fields, use the Index dialog, which you can view by selecting View/Indexes from the Access menu. That dialog is displayed in Figure 1-6.

You can use this dialog to manage all the indexes in the table or to create an index that is based on more than one field. Here, you see an index called FullName. The first field of the index is the LastName field. In the next row you see that the Index Name column is blank, which means that it is part of the index that is above it. So the FirstName field is the second field in the index.

Field Properties

Format Property

The Format property provides a way for you to specify how the data in this field should be displayed as it is entered. Depending on the Data Type you chose, you will see different choices here. For dates, you see a variety of date formats. For numbers, you see a variety of number formats.

You can also enter your own format. Say, for example, that you want dates displayed in a format like this:

`12/01/2002`

You could enter this value in the format property:

`mm/dd/yyyy`

The two mm say that I want to see a two-digit month followed by a "/" character and a two-digit date. Then we have another "/" character followed by the four-digit year.

Now, suppose that you want this number:

`1.1`

to appear in this format:

`000,001.10 WS`

You would use this format:

`000,000.00" WS"`

The zeros indicate that a number must appear. The comma and period are the number and decimal separators. Follow that with the text WS.

The benefit of setting this up properly at the beginning is that when creating a query, report or form that uses this field, it will inherit that property. This is true for many of the properties discussed in this section.

Input Mask Property

The Format property controls how the data looks after it is entered. The Input Mask property controls how the data looks as the user is typing data into the field. It also controls what the user can type into the field.

You can use the Wizard by clicking on the "..." to the right of the property to use one of the standard Input Masks. You could also create your own.

Here's an example of an Input Mask:

`!(999) 000-0000;0;_`

The Input Mask is made up of three parts. Each part is separated by a semicolon. The first part is the mask itself. This defines what is seen as the user enters the data and what can be typed into the field. The second part can be a 0 or a 1. If it is a zero, the mask is to be stored with the data.

If it is a 1, only the data will be stored. By entering a 0, a phone number will be stored like this:

```
(565) 222-2222
```

If you enter a 1, the same data will be stored like this:

```
5652222222
```

The third part of the mask indicates what characters the user sees in the placeholder fields. So when the user enters a blank field with the above mask, the following is seen:

```
(__) __-____
```

Caption Property

As discussed earlier in this chapter, spaces and special characters should be avoided when naming fields. But when displaying the field on a form or report, the user needs to see the spaces and special characters. The Caption property provides a way to supply the readable name of the field. The value put in this property is used for the label when the field is added to a Form or Report.

A field with this name:

```
FirstName
```

would have this caption:

```
First Name
```

Default Value Property

The Default Value property provides a way to supply an initial value for a field when a new record is added to the table. This can speed up and ease data entry.

For example, suppose you have a State field for your employees. If your company has a single location, then most of the employees probably live in the same state. If your company was in New Mexico, this value could go in the Default Value property for the State field:

```
"NM"
```

But something dynamic can also be put in the Default Value property, for example, a HireDate field. In this example, the HireDate value is the current date. To accomplish this, enter this in the Default Value property:

```
=Date()
```

Date is a function that returns the current system date. Therefore, the current day's date would appear in a new record.

Another example is a DueDate field that should be set initially to one month past the current date. Enter this in the Default Value property:

```
=DateAdd("m",1,Date())
```

The function used here is called DateAdd. It takes three parameters. The first is the unit of time to be added, the "m" indicates months. The second parameter is the number of months we want to add, in this case 1. The last parameter indicates the date to add to. In this case, the current date.

The same function is also used to subtract from a date. Say that you wanted the default value to be three months in the past. You would enter this into the Default Value property:

```
=DateAdd("m",-3,Date())
```

So the same function is used. Just add a negative number to achieve the subtraction.

Validation Rule Property

The Validation Rule property is used to limit which values the user could enter into a field. For example, suppose you had a salary field and that salary at your company should be in the range of $20,000 and $200,000. You could enter this in the Validation Rule property:

```
>=20000 And <=200000
```

So the number entered must be at least 20,000 and must be no more that 200,000. Using this property will help keep your data accurate, because it will not allow the user to enter a value that is way out of range.

You also could use the property to limit dates. For example, a date entered into a field must be within the last 20 years. You would use this value:

```
>=DateAdd("yyyy",-20,Date())
```

In this example, the value must be greater than the date 20 years before the current date.

Validation Text Property

When you use the Validation Rule property, you also should use the Validation Text property. Violating this rule results in a message box with whatever text you have entered into this property that lets the user know what is wrong. So if the date rule placed in the last section was violated, put this text for them to see in the Violation Text property:

```
The date entered needs to be within the last 20 years.
```

If you don't put anything in the Validation Text property and the rule is violated, the user will see a standard Access message with the rule itself in it, like the one shown in Figure 1-7. Most users would not understand this.

Required Property

The Required property is used to indicate whether a field in a table is required or not. If the property is set to Yes, an error message lets the user know that a value must be entered in the field.

Allow Zero Length Property

The Allow Zero Length property can also be set to Yes or No. The action of this property has to do with whether the user can remove text from a text field and replace it with nothing. If the value of this property is set to No, the user cannot remove a text entry without replacing it with some text.

Figure 1-7

The Default
validation
violation message

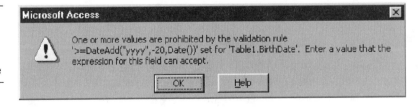

Lookup Properties

The properties section for a field has two tabs. We have focused thus far on the General Properties tab. The other tab is for the Lookup Properties. Figure 1-8 shows the Lookup Properties tab.

The first property on the tab toggles each of the other properties shown in this tab. The property, Display Control, indicates the type of control you want displayed when this field is included on a form or when it is displayed in Table view.

The property has three values: text box, list box and combo box. If the property is set to a text box, the field is displayed as a text box and the other properties are not visible. Otherwise, you can set the other properties and the user sees a list of some kind when the field is selected.

The Row Source type and Row Source property are used in tandem. Selecting Value List for the Row Source property displays a set of fixed values that you enter into the Row Source property for this field. If you enter this:

```
"Blue";"Red";"Green";"Yellow"
```

Those color names appear on their own lines in a combo box. Note that a semi-colon separates each value. The Row Source property also can be

Figure 1-8

The Lookup
Properties tab

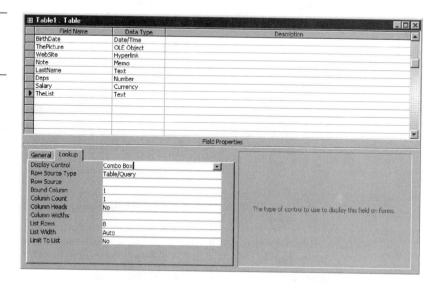

set to Table/Query. That enables you to display a list made up of values from another table. You then could set the Row Source property to this value:

```
Select TheColors from ShirtColors
```

Now the user would see whatever text was entered in a field called The Colors in a table called ShirtColors.

The Rows Source Type property can also be set to Field List. When you do this, you then select the name of a Table whose field names you want to appear in the list for this field through the Row Source property.

You can include more than one field in the list portion of a combo box through the Lookup properties. Suppose, for example, that you wanted to display the full name of an employee, but you also wanted to store his or her ID in this field. You would choose Table/Query for the Row Source Type property and enter a value like this in the Row Source property:

```
Select EmpID, LastName, FirstName from Emps
```

Even though you could display all three fields, you can only store one with the table. The one to store would be the primary key, the EmpID field. To do this, set the Bound Column property to 1 because EmpID is the first field outputted by the SQL syntax.

You also would need to adjust the Column Count property to indicate the number of columns that you wanted to display in the combo box. If you wanted all three, set this property to 3 and the Column Widths property to:

```
1";1":1"
```

This would display each field with one-inch width.

If instead you wanted to display the name of the employee without the ID, but still store the ID, you would still set the Bound Column property to 1. Set the Column Count to 2 and place this in the Column Widths property:

```
0";1":1"
```

The Column Heads property determines whether the names of the fields in the list portion of a combo box will be seen. If you set this property to Yes, it will; otherwise, it won't.

The List Rows property is set to the maximum number of rows that you want displayed in the list portion of the combo box. The Limit to List property is used to determine what action to take if the user enters a value that is not in the list. If you set the property to Yes, the user must select one of the items in the list. If you set it to No, the user can enter any value in the field.

Table Properties

The Table itself also has properties. If you right-click in the Design view of a table and select Properties, you will see the Table Properties dialog displayed in Figure 1-9. A few of these properties are worth noting and are discussed in this section.

Description Property

The Description property for a table is a place for you to put whatever text you want. Here you could put information about who created the table, when it was created and what it is for.

Validation Rule Property

We saw in the last section of this chapter that the Validation Rule property enables you to limit the input for a field. But sometimes a rule goes beyond a single field and needs to be based on a value in another field.

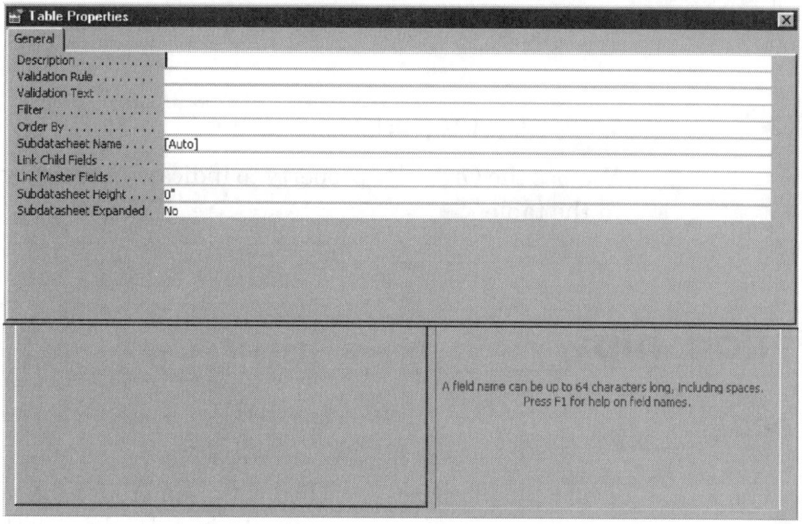

Figure 1-9

The Table Properties dialog

If you had a table with a StartDate field and an EndDate field, you would probably want the start date to be before or equal to the end date. To accomplish this you would need a Table Validation rule set to this value:

```
[StartDate] <= [EndDate]
```

Now the user will get an error if the start date is after the end date. Notice the brackets around the text StartDate and EndDate. This indicates that those are field names, not just text.

Validation Text Property

The Validation Text property is set to a message that you want to appear when the user violates the table-level validation rule. If you used the above property, you could place this text in the Validation Text property:

```
The Start Date must not be after the End Date.
```

Filter Property

You can use the Filter property to define a sub-set of records that you want to appear when the table is opened. For example, if you wanted to show only the records in the employee table that had a salary of at least $50,000, you could put this in the property:

```
[Salary] >= 50000
```

Order By Property

You use the Order By property to indicate the sorting order for the records in the table.

Relationships

Defined

Typically, databases are filled with numerous tables. Many of these tables relate to each other. For example, in a database with an Employees table and a Departments table, the tables would relate to each other; they are not isolated. They have something in common—an employee works in a department and that department is listed in the Departments table.

You can have three different kinds of relationships. The first is a one-one relationship, in which one record in one table relates directly to one record in another table and vice versa. An example of this is an Employees table and a SignificantOther table. For insurance purposes, you may allow an employee to be covered along with his or her significant other. At any one time, an employee can have a single significant other covered and a significant other would be related to just one employee. The result is a one:one relationship.

One of the most common relationships is a one-to-many relationship. An Employees table and a Departments table relate in a one-to-many relationship. Each employee belongs to a single department, but each department can have many employees in it.

The third type of relationship is a many-to-many relationship. An Instructors table and a Courses table provide a good example of a many-to-many relationship. Each instructor can teach many courses and each course can be taught by many instructors. When you have such a relationship, you need a third table that is in a one-to-many relationship with both of the other tables. To take this example further, you need a table called something like InstructorCourses. That table would be in a one-to-many relationship with the Instructors table and the Courses table.

Relationships Dialog

Access provides a way for you to graphically work with the relationships between your tables. This is done through the Relationships dialog. Select Relationships from the Toolbar and then select the tables you want to include in the Relationships window. When you do that, the Relationships dialog is shown, as displayed in Figure 1-10.

In this example, three tables have been created. One is an Employees table, Emps. Another is a Significant Others table, SOs; and the third is a Timesheets table. The Emps table relates to the other two tables through the EmpID field. To establish these relationships, drag information from the EmpID field in the Emps table to the EmpID field in the other tables. When this is done, Access draws a line between the tables like those shown in Figure 1-11.

Now double-click on any of the relationship lines and further define the relationships through the dialog displayed in Figure 1-12.

Figure 1-10

The initial view of the Relationships dialog

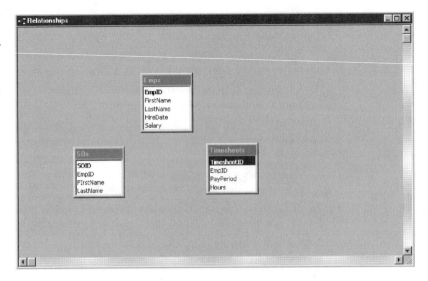

Figure 1-11

The Relationships dialog with relationships in place

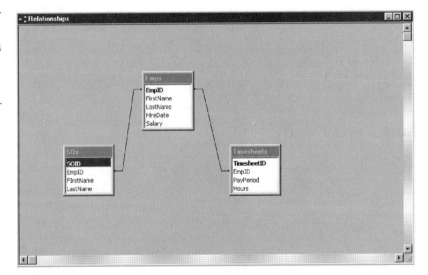

Figure 1-12

Edit
Relationships
dialog

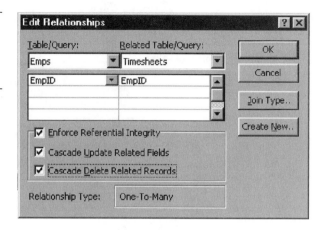

Probably the most important thing you can do through this dialog is to set the referential integrity for the relationship. If referential integrity is enforced, no records can be in the child table without records in the parent table. In this example, by turning on referential integrity, a timesheet cannot be created for an employee that doesn't exist.

Also, select cascade updates. If this option is on, any changes made in the ID of the parent record will propagate to the related ID in the child record(s). Cascade delete is the other referential integrity option. If it is checked when you delete the parent record, all of the child records are deleted as well. You can also use the Join Type option to select which records you want to display when the two tables are displayed together in a query.

Summary

It is most important to think about all the things discussed in this chapter as you are defining your tables and the relationships. If you do, creating queries, forms, and reports will go much smoother because they will use the properties and initial values we have discussed.

CHAPTER 2

Access Programming Techniques

Beyond Wizards

Through wizards, Access makes it pretty easy to create a form or a report. As you develop with Access, however, you will quickly find that wizards are a good starting point, but your solution needs to go well beyond them.

In this chapter, we will go beyond wizards and take a closer look at Forms and Reports. First we will review some of the properties of forms, reports, and controls. Then we will take a look at the code window and review the events of forms, reports and controls. The chapter ends with a discussion of the Data Access Objects.

Designing Forms, Reports, and Controls

Sections

As you design a form that has more than a few fields, you will find that you just can't fit all the fields on the form. One way you can deal with this is by using sections and page breaks. Take a look at Figure 2-1.

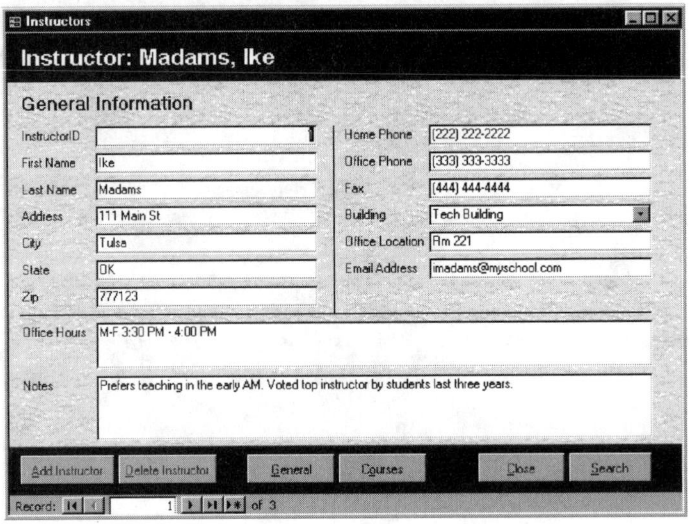

Figure 2-1

The first page from a two-page form

The form displays information about instructors from a school database. The basic form was initially created using a wizard, but all the fields could not be placed evenly on a single page of the form. So a second page was added to the form, using a Page Break control to add more space to the form. The second page of this form is displayed in Figure 2-2.

A Page Break control is available on the Toolbox. All you do is drag it to the place on the form where you want the page break to be. Then add buttons to your form that provide a way to get to each of the different pages.

On this form, the General and Courses buttons perform this task. The General button takes the user to the first page of the form and the Courses button takes the user to the second page of the form. This is done with just one line of code. Later in this chapter, how to use the DoCmd object in code will be discussed, but here is the line of code that takes the user to the first page of the form:

```
Private Sub Command33_Click()
  DoCmd.GoToPage 1
End Sub
```

and the code that takes the user to the second page of the form:

```
Private Sub Command34_Click()
  DoCmd.GoToPage 2
End Sub
```

Figure 2-2

Page two of the
sample form

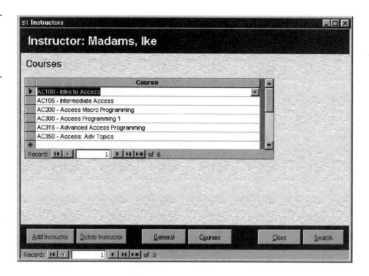

Note that the code is in a click event. Therefore, the code fires when the user clicks on the command button or presses Enter while it has the focus. The code then uses the GoToPage method of the DoCmd object to send the user to a page on the form. The specific page desired is stated in the parameter of the method, that is, the 1 shown in the first code block and the 2 shown in the second code block.

Notice that on each of the two pages of the form the same information is at the top and bottom, the header and the footer. This form is similar to a Web page with frames. A top section called the Header section stays fixed and contains some general information about the record. A middle section called the Detail section displays the bulk of the information about the record, and that section changes based on the page view. Then the Footer section contains our navigational aids or buttons. These sections can be turned on and off by selecting Form Header/Footer from the View menu. You can even add page headers and footers to a form.

These types of sections are typically needed on a report. Frequently, you will want to display a piece of information at the top of the first page of the report, such as the name of the report. That section is called the Report Header.

Sometimes you'll want information displayed at the end of a report. Maybe you want to show the total number of records or the summation of field. You would place that information in the Report Footer section.

Each page also has its own header and footer section. In the Page Header section, you would usually put the name of the fields being displayed. In the Page Footer section, you would frequently put the report date and the page number.

Also on a report, it is sometimes necessary to group information by fields. For example, if you are displaying items ordered by customers, you may want to group the information by the customer's name. You could then add a group header and a group footer to your report. The group header displays the name of the customer, and the group footer displays the total cost and quantity of items ordered. Take a look at the design view of the form displayed in Figure 2-3.

This report has report and page footers and headers. The report header displays the title of the report, while the page header displays the field names for the fields listed in the next section, the Detail section. The Detail section also contains two sub-reports. After that the Page Footer section displays the current date and time as well as the current page number. Then after that is the Report Footer section. Notice that it has been shrunk down in size since nothing is displayed in that section. To turn on or off these sections, select View from the menu and then Report Header/Footer or Page Header/Footer.

Figure 2-3

Design view of a report

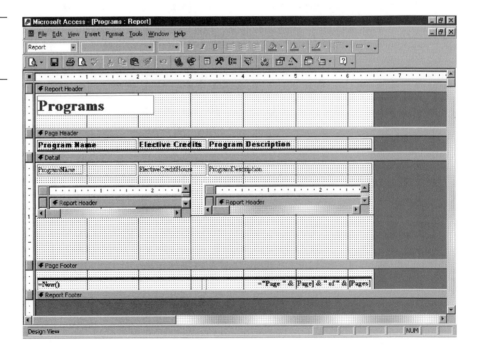

Group headers and footers are added through a different mechanism. From the View menu, select Grouping and Sorting. You should then see the dialog displayed in Figure 2-4.

The Sorting and Grouping dialog provides a way for you to manage grouping and group sections for your report. First, select the field that you want to sort by in the Field column. Then you select how you want the field sorted. At the bottom of the section, indicate whether you want to use a group header and footer. Also enter how you want to group the field and how you want the grouped data displayed.

Form Properties

In this section, some of the lesser-known and important properties of a form are reviewed. To view the properties of a form, enter the Design view of the form. Note the little box in the upper-left corner of the form, which is where the horizontal and vertical rulers meet. Right-click on that box and select Properties.

Record Source Property

The fields on a form are bound to a table in the database. The specific table that they are bound to is the name of the table listed in the Record Source property. You can also place a query in this property to include only certain fields, to include only certain records, or to limit the records displayed. For example, take a look at this this SQL statement:

```
Select FirstName, LastName form Emps Where LastName Like 'B*' Order By LastName
```

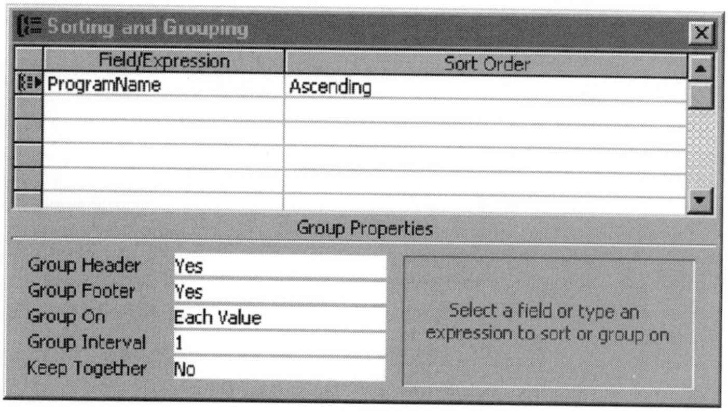

Figure 2-4

The Sorting and
Grouping Dialog

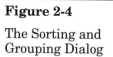

Only the first and last name fields from the Emps table appear. Only those last names that start with a B are included. The records are sorted by last name.

Filter Property

The Filter property enables you to limit the records that are displayed on the form when it is first opened. An entry like this:

```
[Salary] > 20000
```

would only show records that had a salary greater than $20,000 when the form was opened.

Allow Filters

When a user views your form, he or she can turn on his or her own filters to limit the records that are shown. If you do not want to allow them to do this, set the Allow Filters property to No.

Default View

When a user opens your form, he or she typically sees just a single record. But take a look at Figure 2-5.

In this form, the user sees three records on the form at the same time, because the Default view of the form has been changed to Continuous Forms. This type of view shows the form as repeating for each record in

Figure 2-5

The Continuous
Forms view

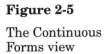

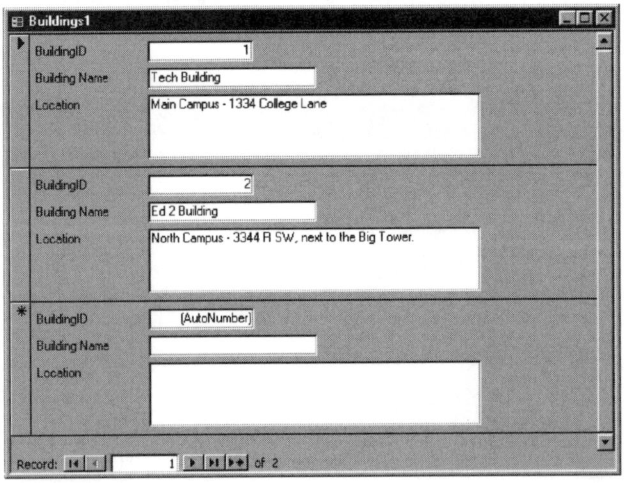

the table. The property can also be set to Single View, which is the default. It shows the one normal record on a form. The property can also be changed to Datasheet view to enable the user to see the data on the form in grid format like the Datasheet view of a table.

Views Allowed Property

A user who plays around with the menus in Access can quickly discover that he or she can view the data as Continuous, Single, or Datasheet by selecting those options from the menus. You can also limit what can be selected with the Views Allowed property. By default, the property is set to both, which enables any of the three views. You can, however, limit the view to datasheet by setting the property to Datasheet. If you set the property to Form, the user can view the data as a single form or continuous forms.

Allow Edits, Allow Deletions, and Allow Additions Properties

Sometimes you need to limit which type of data activity you want to allow a user to perform through your form. You can limit the user's action through the Allow Edits, Allow Deletions, and Allow Additions properties.

If you set the Allow Edits to No, the user cannot edit existing records through this form. If you set Allow Deletions to No, the user cannot delete records, and if you set the Allow Additions property to No, the user cannot add any new records.

Data Entry Property

Another way that you can control the action a user can take through a form is by using the Data Entry property. If you set this property to Yes, the user can add new records and can edit records that have been added since the form was opened. Once the form is reopened, the added records or any other records are hidden.

Record Locks

If you are working with a database that will have more than one user changing the data at the same time, it is important that you know about record locking. Record locking refers to what action you want Access to take if more than one user is editing a record at the same time.

You control that behavior through the Record Locks property. The default for the property is No Locks. This enables more than one user to edit the same record at the same time. When the second person saves his or her changes, a message appears, letting them know that someone else changed the record.

Another value you can set this property to is All Records. This basically locks the entire table from anyone else editing, adding, or deleting records in the underlying table. The lock is released when the form is closed.

A less restrictive locking can be achieved by setting the property to Edited Records. This locks a page of records when any field is edited, which prevents another person from editing the record currently being worked on. A page in Access is 4,000 bytes of data. So, if each of your records are 1,000 bytes, locking one page or editing one record actually locks four records.

Record Selectors, Navigation Buttons, and Dividing Lines Properties

You can control the look of the form through the Record Selectors, Navigation Buttons, and Dividing Lines properties. If you set the Record Selectors property to No, the user does not see the bar to the left of a record that enables them to highlight an entire record. If you set the Navigation Buttons property to No, the user does not see the arrows at the bottom of the form that enable them to scroll through the records. The purpose of the Dividing Lines properties is to determine whether you see the lines between the form and the navigation section.

For most of the forms in the sample databases in this book, the Record Selectors and Dividing Lines properties are set to No. If you are using a form as a dialog form that does not directly link to the fields in the database, you set the Navigation Buttons property to No.

Report Properties

This section examines some helpful and lesser-known properties of a report that are different from those reviewed in the Form Properties section. As with a form, you view the properties of a report by right-clicking on the small box in the upper-left corner of the report in Design view.

Page Header and Page Footer Properties

The Page Header and Page Footer properties are used to indicate whether or not to display the header and footer sections on a report. By default, the property is set to All Pages. This prints the section on all the pages of a report. If you set the property to Not with Rpt Hdr, the section is not printed on the page that the report header is printed. If you set the property to Not with Rpt Ftr, then the section is not displayed on the page that the report footer is displayed. If you set the property to Not with Rpt Hdr/Ftr, the section is not displayed on the page where the report header or the report footer is displayed.

Force New Page

Some of the sections of a report have a property called Force New Page. This property is used to indicate the layout action around the section of the report. The default for this property is None, which does not force any page breaks before or after the section prints. If you set the property to Before Section, however, a new page of the report appears before the section. If you set the property to After Section, a new page appears in the report after the section. You can also set the property to Before & After, which forces a new page before and after the section of the report.

Control Properties

This section reviews some of the properties of the common controls that you can add to your form through the Toolbox. To view the properties of a control while in Design view of a form or report, right-click on the Control and Select properties. Note that most of these properties are only available for some of the controls.

Control Source Property

Most of the controls that you add to a form or report can be bound to a field in the underlying table of the form or report. When it is said that a field is bound, that means that the field displays the data for a field in the database. As the user changes that data, the underlying fields are updated. The Control Source property is used to determine which field the control will display.

Status Bar Text Property

Sometimes the field name or the field caption does not tell the user enough information about the field for him or her to be able to enter the data correctly. You can provide the user with more information, however, through the Status Bar Text property. Whatever text you place in this property is displayed in the status bar when the field has the focus.

Enter Key Behavior

Based on the type of field, you may want the Enter key to take one action or another. For example, when the user presses the Enter key in a field such as a First Name, you want the focus to move to the next field such as the Last Name field. In a field like Notes or Comments, however, you may want an Enter key to display a new line.

You can set this behavior through the Enter Key Behavior property. If the property is set to Default, then Access uses the default Access behavior for the field. Typically, it moves it on to the next field on the form. If you set the property to New Line in Field, a new line is added at the point the Enter key is pressed in the field.

Enabled and Locked Properties

The Enabled and Locked properties control the data changes that can be made to the data in the control. By default, Enabled is set to Yes and Locked is set to No, which enables the user to edit the data in a field.

If Enabled is changed to No, the data in the field is still displayed, but it is grayed out and the user cannot highlight the text. If the Locked property is set to Yes, the data is not grayed out, but it still cannot be edited. The user can, though, highlight and copy the locked text.

Tab Stop and Tab Index Properties

Typically, when a user works with your form, he or she uses the Tab key to move from field to field. The order that dictates where the user goes as they tab from field to field is referred to as the Tab Order. You can easily modify this order through the Tab Order dialog displayed in Figure 2-6.

You can select this dialog through the View menu. The dialog enables you to drag and drop the order in which a field occurs in the Tab Order list.

You can also control this behavior through the Tab Stop and Tab Index properties. First, remove a control from the Tab Order by setting the Tab Stop property to No. The Tab Index property is used to indicate the order in which the control appears in the Tab Order.

ControlTip Text

Many programs use a device that displays a yellow box that displays some brief text when a user moves the cursor over a field. That box is sometimes called Balloon Help, Tool Tip Text, or, in Access, ControlTip Text. Whatever text you place in this property is displayed when the user hovers the cursor over the control.

Figure 2-6

The Tab Order
dialog

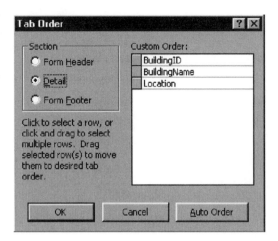

Creating Code

As you are learning to write code in your Access application, you can use
a couple of tricks to help you generate code and learn which code takes
which action. This section looks at a couple of these techniques and also
reviews the code window.

Creating Code Through a Wizard

One of the ways you can learn a little about coding is through a Command
Button control wizard. Go into the Design view of a form and take a look
at the Toolbox. One of the buttons on the Toolbox shows a magic wand and
if you move your cursor over it, it says Control Wizards. Make sure that
button is pressed. Then add a button to your form. When you do so, you
will see the dialog displayed in Figure 2-7.

The Command Button wizard writes code for you that you want to fire
when the button is pressed. You can select from a variety of actions. Here
you want the button to undo the changes made to a record. Select the
action you want to take and continue with the wizard, supplying it with
text or an icon that you want to appear on the button. Also assign the button with a name.

Figure 2-7

The Command
Button Wizard

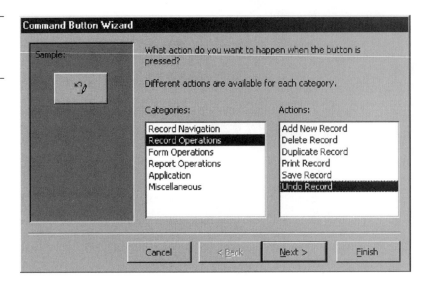

Access then adds the button to your form with the code needed to take the action. To see the code that takes the selected action, right-click on the button in Design view and select Build Event. Access then opens Visual Basic Editor and shows you the code that performs the selected action.

For the Undo Record action selected in this example, it produced this code:

```
Private Sub Command15_Click()
      On Error GoTo Err_Command15_Click
      DoCmd.DoMenuItem acFormBar, acEditMenu, acUndo, ,
acMenuVer70
Exit_Command15_Click:
 Exit Sub
Err_Command15_Click:
 MsgBox Err.Description
 Resume Exit_Command15_Click
End Sub
```

The important line of code is this line:

```
DoCmd.DoMenuItem acFormBar, acEditMenu, acUndo, , acMenuVer70
```

This is the line that removes the record changes. The rest of the code is error-handling code.

Learning Through Macros

Another way that you can learn how to write code in Access is by converting a macro to code. If you know how to create macros, you can use a simple wizard to export your macro to code.

For example, suppose you want to know how to generate a message box and then open a form in code. You know how to do it in a macro but are not sure what it should look like in code. You can then create a macro like the one displayed in Figure 2-8.

The first line of the macro displays the message box and the second line opens a form. Save your macro by selecting Save As to see the dialog displayed in Figure 2-9.

Enter a name that you want to save the code as and then change the As Combo box to a module. Press OK, select whether you want comments and error handling, and press Convert. Now, from the Database window, switch to the Modules tab and double-click on the code module you just created to see the code that was generated in the Visual Basic Editor.

Here's the code that was generated to do the previous example:

```
'---------------------------------------------------------------
' SampleMacro1
'
'---------------------------------------------------------------
Function SampleMacro1()
On Error GoTo SampleMacro1_Err
 Beep
 MsgBox "This is a sample meaage.", vbExclamation, "The Caption"
 DoCmd.OpenForm "Buildings", acNormal, "", "", , acNormal
SampleMacro1_Exit:
 Exit Function
SampleMacro1_Err:
 MsgBox Error$
 Resume SampleMacro1_Exit
End Function
```

Before the message box, make a beep sound:

```
Beep
```

Then a message box is displayed:

```
MsgBox "This is a sample message.", vbExclamation, dd"The Caption"
```

and open a form through code:

```
DoCmd.OpenForm "Buildings", acNormal, "", "", , acNormal
```

Figure 2-8

Sample macro to
be converted to
code

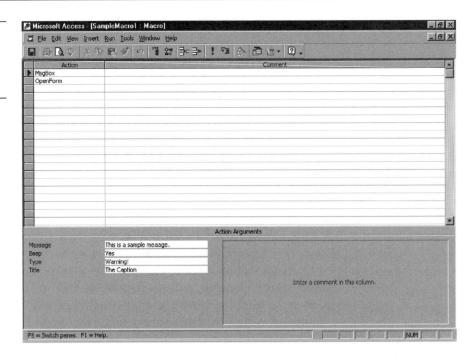

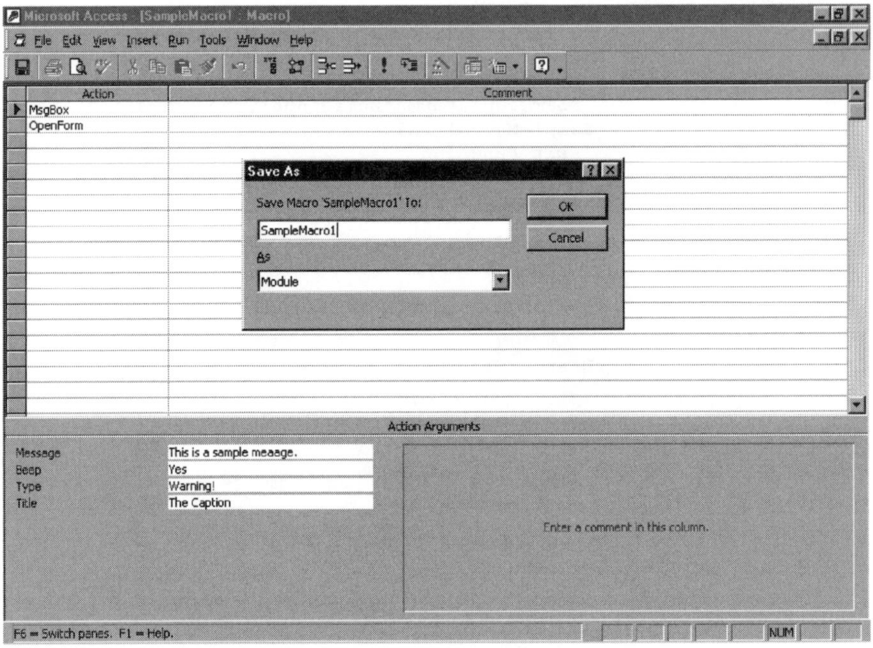

Figure 2-9

Exporting a
macro to a code
module

Visual Basic Editor and the Code Window

Take a look at Figure 2-10. When you are working with code in Access, use the Visual Basic Editor. You can view the code window or other parts of the Visual Basic Editor by right-clicking on any control on a form or report and selecting Build Event followed by Code Builder. You can also view the Visual Basic Editor by selecting Module.

First look at the code window displayed in the Visual Basic Editor, the one with the code. Notice the two drop-downs at the top of that window. One says CommandAdd and the other says Click. These drop-downs indicate where you are located in the code. The first is the object you are looking for in the code, in this case for a button called CommandAdd. The other indicates which event you are looking at for that object. In this case, it is the code for the Click event, which fires when the button is pressed.

Now look at the window in the upper-right portion of the Visual Basic Editor. It is the Project Explorer. It lists all the Forms, Reports, and Code modules in your database application that have code associated with them. You can double-click on any of these items in the Project Explorer to view their code window.

Figure 2-10

Visual Basic
Editor and the
Code Window

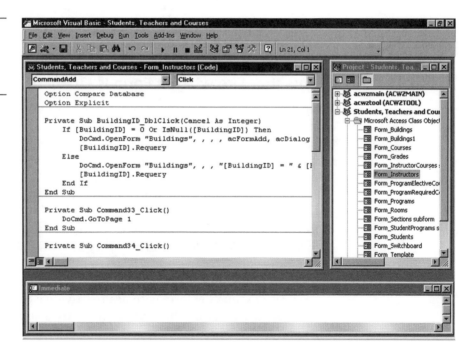

At the bottom of the Visual Basic Editor is a third window called the Immediate Window. This window is helpful when you are debugging your code. You can use it to evaluate an expression. For example, suppose your code was not working correctly. You suspect the problem has to do with the value in a field called Salary. While you were debugging, you could type this:

```
?[Salary]
```

in the Immediate Window to see the value of that field for the current record.

Events

Events provide you with a place to put code that you want to fire when something occurs. For example, in the last section, you saw the Click event of a Command button. The code in that event fires whenever the Command button is pressed. Other events fire when a user types in a text box or when they open a form. This section looks at some of the Form, Report, and Controls events.

Form Events

Events that Fire when a Form Is Opened

When you first open a form, the following events fire in the following order: Open, Load, Resize, Activate, and Current. The Open event fires before the first record is displayed, so it enables you to take some action before working with the data. You can use this event to cancel the form loading.

The next event that fires when a form first opens is the Load event. This event fires after the first record on the form is displayed.

Next, the Resize event fires. This event also fires anytime the user changes the size of the form and enables you to take some action based on that change.

After that, the Activate event fires. This event fires with the data, but it also fires anytime the form becomes reactivated. So, if you were to click on another form and come back to this form, the Activate event would fire again.

Finally, the Current event fires. This event fires when a form is loaded, but it also fires anytime the user changes to a different record. It enables you to format some fields or labels based on the values of some other fields.

Events that Fire when a Form Is Closed

When you close a form, the following events fire: Unload, DeActivate, and Close. The Unload event fires when the form is being closed, but it fires before the form itself is closed from the screen. With this event, you have the opportunity to cancel the close action. The DeActivate event fires when the form loses the focus. It not only fires when the form is closed, but it also fires when you leave the form by clicking on another form. Finally, the Close event fires when the form is closed and when the form is no longer visible on the screen.

Deleting Record Events

When the user deletes a record, three different events are activated. First, the Delete event fires. This event occurs before the record is deleted in any way and provides a way for you to cancel the record deletion. Next, the BeforeDelConfirm event fires. This event fires after the record is marked for deletion, but before the user sees a message box confirming that they want to delete the record. The last event that fires is the AfterDelConfirm event, which is activated after the user sees the confirmation dialog box.

Inserting Records Events

Two events fire at the Form level when records are added to a table. The first is the BeforeInsert event. This event actually fires after the user goes to a new record and places the first piece of data in the record but before the record is actually added to the database. After the record has been inserted into the database, the AfterInsert event fires.

Updating Record Events

When you update a record, similar events fire. Before the record is updated, the BeforeUpdate event fires. The AfterUpdate event fires after the changes have been committed to the database.

Report Events

Events that Fire when a Report Is Opened

Just two events fire when a Report is opened: the Open event and the Activate event. The Open event fires before any data on the Report is displayed and enables you to cancel the form from opening. After that, the Activate event fires. This event fires after data is displayed on the report. The event also fires when you click on another form or report and return back to this report.

Events that Fire when a Report Is Closed

When you close a form, two events also fire. First, the DeActivate event fires. This event still has the data on the report when it fires. The event also fires when the report loses the focus by clicking on another form or report.

After that, the Close event fires. This event fires when the report has disappeared from the screen and the data is no longer available.

NoData Event

If the report the user is opening does not have any data that can be displayed, the NoData event fires. You can use this event to inform the user of the problem, make changes to the database, or simply close the report.

Page Event

The Page Event fires each time a new page in a report is being created by Access, but the event fires before the page is actually printed.

Control Events

Mouse Events

When the user takes an action on a control with his or her mouse, a variety of events fire. When the user clicks on a control, the Click event fires. This event is most useful on a Command button. When the user double-clicks on a control, the DblClick event fires, but you can take even deeper action involving the mouse with the MouseDown, MouseUp, and Mouse-Move events. When the user presses a mouse button, the MouseDown event fires before the user releases it. The MouseUp button fires after the user releases the mouse button. The other event, MouseMove, fires when the user moves the mouse over a control without clicking on it.

Keyboard Events

Every time the user types a single keystroke on a control, three events fire: These events are the KeyDown, KeyPress, and KeyUp events. The KeyDown event fires before the user sees the character on the screen. The KeyUp event fires when the user releases a key. These two events fire with most characters, such as the Home, Insert, and Function keys.

The KeyPress event also fires before the user sees the character on the screen. The event receives, as a parameter, the ASCII value of the character typed in.

The events enable you to modify the characters typed in before the user sees them or to take action based on the data in a control after the key has been released. For example, the following code placed in the KeyPress event would convert everything that is typed in to upper case:

```
KeyASCII = Asc(UCase(Chr(KeyASCII)))
```

This code placed in the KeyPress event prevents the user from typing in any character except for a, b, or c:

```
If Instr("abc",Chr(KeyASCII)) = 0 then
        Beep
        KeyASCII = 0
End If
```

Instr is a function that looks for a string within a string. Here you are looking for the character that the user typed, in the allowable characters of a, b, or c. If the character is not found, Instr would return a 0:

```
If Instr("abc",Chr(KeyASCII)) = 0 then
```

In that case, beep at the user:

```
Beep
```

and turn the character he or she typed in into a Null character, which essentially throws the character away:

```
KeyASCII = 0
```

Focus Events

When the user enters a control by tabbing to it or clicking on it, two events fire. First, the Enter event fires. This event actually fires before the control gets the focus. Then, once the control actually does have the focus, the GotFocus event fires. You can use these events to make changes to the data as the user enters a control. For example, if you put this code in the GotFocus event of a text box called Text1:

```
Text1.SelStart = 0
Text1.SelLength = Len(Text1.Text)
```

All the text in the text box will be highlighted.

When the user leaves a field either by tabbing out of it or by clicking on some other control, two other events fire. First, the Exit event fires. This event actually fires before the control actually loses the focus. This event is where you can put some special validation code to check to see if some value follows a rule from some other table. You can then cancel the user leaving the field so he or she can make a correction based on your rule. After that event fires, the LostFocus event fires after the control has actually lost the focus.

Change Event

Each time the user changes the text in a text box or changes the selection in a combo box, the Change event fires. You could use this event to have code that runs based on the status of the text in a field.

Data Access Objects

In almost every database application used in this book, the database is manipulated in one way or another through code. In fact, most of the code you write in your database applications will probably involve changing the data in the database. The method used in this book to access the data in the database through code is using *Data Access Objects* (DAO).

If you are in a new database and want to use DAO, you need to make a reference to a DAO library. From the Visual Basic Editor, select View/References. You should then see the References dialog displayed in Figure 2-11.

Figure 2-11

The References
dialog

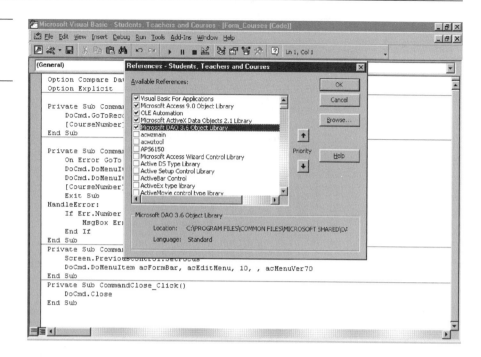

Scroll through the References dialog until you find the entry:

```
Microsoft DAO 3.6 Object Library
```

Check that item, or a version close to it if you don't have 3.6, and press OK. You can now create the objects needed to connect to the database through code.

The first object you need when connecting through code to a database is a Database object. Here you create an object called MyDB that is of the Database class of the DAO library:

```
Dim MyDB As DAO.Database
```

To connect that database to the current database that you have open in Access, you just need to do this:

```
Set MyDB = CurrentDb
```

For some of the queries seen in this book that can add or update records, all you need is a Database object. To update a record in a database, use the Execute method of the Database object created earlier like this:

```
MyDB.Execute "Update tblEmps set Salary = 50000 Where EmpID = 10"
```

This code updates a field called Salary in the table called tblEmps to the new value 50,000 for an employee with the ID 10. You often need to retrieve data from the database, which can be done with a recordset object. Here you create an object called RSUsers that is of the Recordset class of the DAO library:

```
Dim RSUsers As DAO.Recordset
```

You can then use the OpenRecordset method of the Database object to return records from a table in the database:

```
Set RSUsers = MyDB.OpenRecordset("Select FirstName, LastName form
tblEmps", _
        dbOpenSnapshot)
```

The object RSUsers now contains all the first and last names from a table called tblEmps. Most of the time when you have a Recordset object; you are just looking at data, not changing it. That's why the dbOpen-Snapshot parameter is used. It returns a low-overhead, read-only copy of the data. You can now access the data in a record with code like this:

```
x = RSUsers("FirstName")
```

SECTION 2

Instant Access Databases

CHAPTER 3

Employees

ON THE CD:

Employees.mdb

Employee Testing.mdb

Job Application.mdb

Databases to Manage Employees

In this chapter, we will look at three databases used to support the management needs of employees. First, we will look at the Employees database. This database tracks basic employee information, as well as sick and vacation time for the employee. Second, we will look at the Employee Testing database which provides the interface for creating and scoring the tests that employees take and scoring those tests. Then, we will look at the Job Application database. This database provides an employer with a tool for gathering information on potential employees.

The first database we will look at is the Employees database. This tool would be used by a manager or a human resources department to track information about an employee. As you review this database, pay close attention to the code used to display the number of hours of sick and vacation time that the employee has. Also note the use of validation rules in some of the date fields.

Sample Walk-through

When the user first enters the Employees database, he or she sees the menu shown in Figure 3-1. The menu form enables the user to access any of the forms and reports used in the database. The main form is the Employees form. The first page of this form is displayed in Figure 3-2.

The Employees form is made up of five pages. The Page Break control is used to separate each page of information. The footer of the form contains buttons that the user presses to go to the different pages of the form.

The first page is the General page. Here the user supplies the basic information about the employee. When the user presses the Notes button, the second page of the form is displayed as in Figure 3-3.

Figure 3-1

Employees Menu form

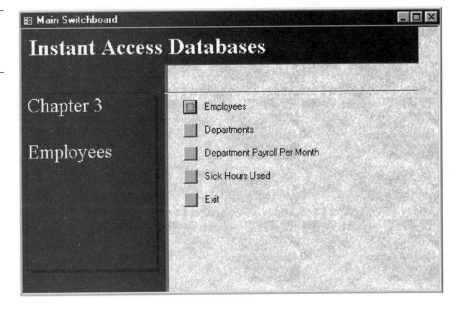

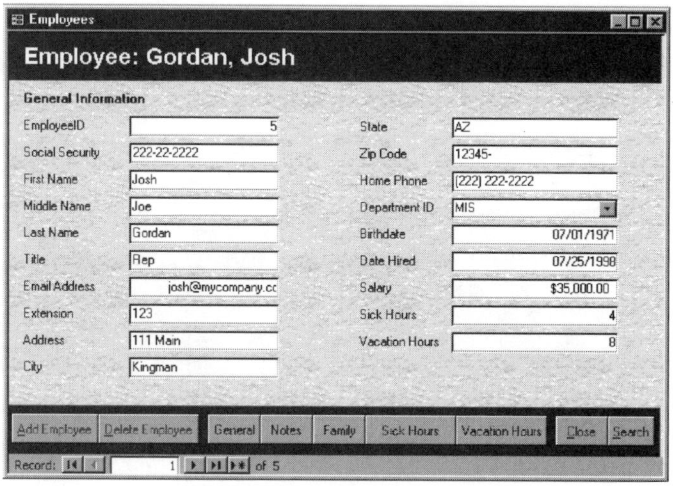

Figure 3-2

General page of the Employees form

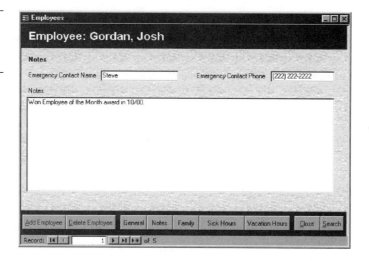

Figure 3-3

Notes page of the Employees form

Notice the header of the form. It displays the name of the current employee through use, regardless of the page of the form. The Notes page enables the user to enter extended notes about the employee, as well as emergency contact information.

When the user clicks on the Family button, the third page of the form is displayed as in Figure 3-4. The Family page contains a sub-form that enables the user to enter all the information for all the family members of

Figure 3-4

Family page of
the Employees
form

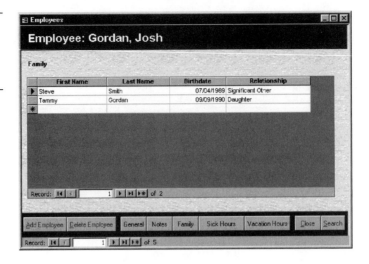

the employee. Note that the combo box for the Relationship field is set up as a self-populating list, so whenever a new item is entered into this field, it becomes part of the list for the next employee entered.

When the user presses the Sick Hours button, the page displayed in Figure 3-5 appears. The Sick Hours page contains a sub-form where entries are made whenever the employee uses some of their sick time. On the bottom of the page, the user sees summary information about the sick hours.

The last page of this form is accessed through the Vacation Hours button and is displayed in Figure 3-6. On this page, the user sees all the vacation time used by the employee and the number of hours in total that have been used, acquired, and are remaining. These values are calculated based on when the employee was hired and how many hours he or she earns per month.

The other form in this application is the Departments form which is displayed in Figure 3-7. The Departments form enables the user to manage the names of the departments, and it also displays the total yearly salary requirements for that department.

The database contains two reports. The first report is the Department Payroll Per Month, which is shown in Figure 3-8. This report shows the total amount of payroll each department has to pay on a monthly basis. The other report in this database is the Sick Hours Used report. That summary report is displayed in Figure 3-9.

Figure 3-5

Sick Hours page
of the Employees
form

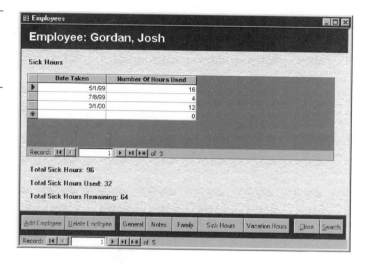

Figure 3-6

Vacation Hours
page of the
Employees form

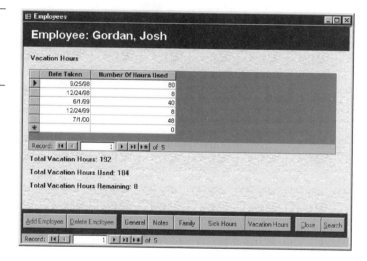

As with the last report, the Sick Hours Used report groups the information by the name of the department. It then displays the total number of sick hours used for each of the departments by the employees in that department.

Figure 3-7

Departments form

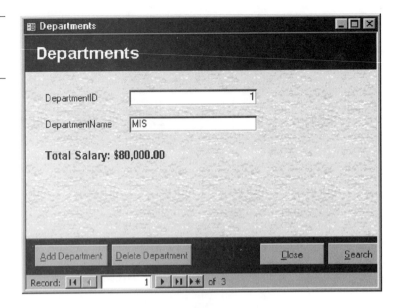

Figure 3-8

Department Payroll Per Month report

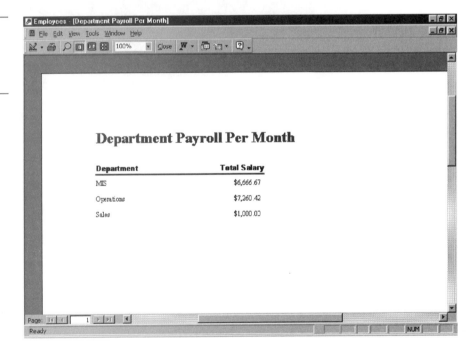

Figure 3-9

Sick Hours Used
report

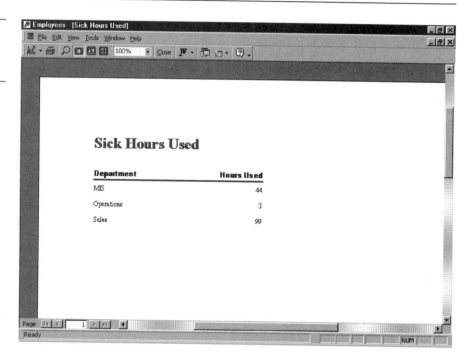

Table Definitions and Relationships

Employees Table

The Employees table is the top-level table in the database. The table
relates to all the other tables in the database. It relates directly to the
Departments table in a one-to-many relationship. Each of the departments can have numerous employees, but each employee works for a single department.

EmployeeFamily Table

The EmployeeFamily table stores the information about the family members of the employee. The table is in a one-to-many relationship with the
Employees table. Each of the employees can have many family members,
but each family member is associated with a specific employee.

SickHoursUse Table

The SickHoursUse table stores the dates and amounts of sick time used by an employee. The table is in a one-to-many relationship with the Employees table. Each record goes with one employee, but each employee can have many entries of sick time use.

VacationHoursUse Table

The VacationHoursUse table stores the occasions when an employee has used some of his or her vacation time. The table is in a one-to-many relationship with the Employees table.

Departments Table

The Departments table stores the names of the departments for which an employee can work. This information is then used on the Employees form.

Field Specifications

Employees Table

The field specifications for the Employees table are displayed in Table 3-1.

The EmployeeID field is the primary key for the table. It is an Auto-Number field so the user cannot modify the data in this field, and it is entered as a unique value.

The EmailAddress field has an Input Mask entered to ease Data Entry:

```
?????????????????"
```

The first part of the pattern, with the question marks, indicates that the user can enter any text. The string in quotes is then appended to whatever they enter. Therefore, in this pretend scenario, the domain name for this company is mycompany.com. This domain name is always added to the end of the employees email address. The second parameter "0", indicates that the user wants to store the mask with the data. If the user did not, a one would replace the zero. The third parameter indicates the place holder character used when entering data into this field.

The DepartmentID field is a foreign key that links this table to the Departments table. It is displayed as a combo box with the following value in the Row Source property:

```
SELECT [Departments].[DepartmentID], [Departments].[DepartmentName] FROM Departments;
```

Field Name	Field Type	Notes
EmployeeID	AutoNumber	Primary Key
SSN	Text	Length = 50
FirstName	Text	Length = 50
MiddleName	Text	Length = 50
LastName	Text	Length = 50
Title	Text	Length = 50
EmailAddress	Text	Length = 50
Extension	Text	Length = 30
HomeAddress	Text	Length = 255
HomeCity	Text	Length = 50
State	Text	Length = 20
Zip	Text	Length = 20
HomePhone	Text	Length = 30
DepartmentID	Number	Type = Long, Foreign Key
BirthDate	Date/Time	
HireDate	Date/Time	
Salary	Currency	
SickHoursPerMonth	Number	Type = Long
VacationHoursPerMonth	Number	Type = Long
EmergencyContactName	Text	Length = 50
EmergencyContactPhone	Text	Length = 50
Notes	Memo	

Table 3-1

Employees Table Field Specifications

The ID of the department is stored with the record, but the user sees the name of the department.

The BirthDate field stores the date that the employee was born. It has the following validation rule:

```
<=DateAdd("yyyy",-15,Date())
```

The date entered must be less than the data derived in this line of code. The code uses the DateAdd function, which adds a value to a date. The value that needs to be added is in years. This value is indicated by "yyyy". The amount to be added is -15, which means that the value is actually being subtracted. The date to subtract from is the current system date, Date(), so the birth date of the employee must be at least 15 years ago. If the rule is violated, the user sees this entry:

```
The person must be at least 15 years old to work for this company.
```

The person must have been hired within the last 60 years since the Validation Rule property for the HireDate is set to this value:

```
>=DateAdd("yyyy",-60,Date())
```

If an older value was entered, the user sees this message:

```
The person must have been hired during the past sixty years.
```

The Salary field has a validation rule so that it is at least $8,000:

```
>=8000
```

The SickHoursPerMonth and the VacationHoursPerMonth fields must be a positive number since this rule is placed in the Validation Rule property for those fields:

```
>=0
```

EmployeeFamily Table

The field specifications for the EmployeeFamily table are displayed in Table 3-2.

Table 3-2	Field Name	Field Type	Notes
EmployeeFamily Table Field Specifications	EmployeeFamilyID	AutoNumber	Primary Key
	EmployeeID	Number	Type = Long, Foreign Key
	FirstName	Text	Length = 50
	LastName	Text	Length = 50
	BirthDate	Date/Time	
	Relationship	Text	Length = 50

The EmployeeFamilyID field is the primary key for this table. The EmployeeID field is a foreign key that links this table to the Employees table. The Relationship field is displayed as a combo box. Take a look at the *Structured Query Language* (SQL) used in the Row Source property for that field:

```
SELECT [EmployeeFamily].[Relationship] FROM EmployeeFamily;
```

The values in the list are retrieved from this same field. As the user enters a new value into this list, it automatically becomes part of the list for future entries.

SickHoursUse Table

The field specifications for the SickHoursUse table are displayed in Table 3-3. The SickHoursUseID uniquely identifies each of the records in this table. The EmployeeID field is a foreign key that links this table to the Employees table.

Table 3-3

SickHoursUse Table Field Specifications

Field Name	Field Type	Notes
SickHoursUseID	AutoNumber	Primary Key
EmployeeID	Number	Type = Long, Foreign Key
DateTaken	Date/Time	
NumberOfHoursUsed	Number	Type = Integer

VacationHoursUse Table

The field specifications for the VacationHoursUse table are displayed in Table 3-4. The VacationHoursUseID field is the primary key for the table. The EmployeeID field is a foreign key that links this table to the Employees table.

Departments Table

The field specifications for the Departments table are displayed in Table 3-5. The DepartmentID field is the primary key for this table. The DepartmentName field stores the name of the department.

Table 3-4	Field Name	Field Type	Notes
VacationHoursUse Table Field Specifications	VacationHoursUseID	AutoNumber	Primary Key
	EmployeeID	Number	Type = Long, Foreign Key
	DateTaken	Date/Time	
	NumberOfHoursUsed	Number	Type = Integer

Table 3-5	Field Name	Field Type	Notes
Departments Table Field Specifications	DepartmentID	AutoNumber	Primary Key
	DepartmentName	Text	Length = 50

Forms

Switchboard Form

The Switchboard form is used to navigate through the forms and reports in the Employees database. It was created using the Switchboard wizard, which is accessible within Access through the Tools/Database Utilities/Switchboard Manager menu item. Only the look and design of the form produced with that wizard have been altered.

Employees Form

The code on the Employees form needs to supply the functionality of the Footer button. It also displays the name of the current employee in the header and calculates the vacation and sick hours summary information.

The first code block fires when the user presses the Add Employee button:

```
Private Sub CommandAdd_Click()
    DoCmd.GoToRecord , , acNewRec
    [EmployeeID].SetFocus
End Sub
```

The GoToRecord method of the DoCmd object enables you to navigate through the form's underlying recordset. Here, the constant acNewRec indicates that the user wants to move to a new record:

```
DoCmd.GoToRecord , , acNewRec
```

Then, move the insertion point to the EmployeeID field:

```
[EmployeeID].SetFocus
```

The next code block fires when the Delete Employee button is pressed:

```
Private Sub CommandDelete_Click()
    On Error GoTo HandleError
    DoCmd.DoMenuItem acFormBar, acEditMenu, 8, , acMenuVer70
    DoCmd.DoMenuItem acFormBar, acEditMenu, 6, , acMenuVer70
    [EmployeeID].SetFocus
    Exit Sub
HandleError:
    If Err.Number <> 2501 Then
        MsgBox Err.Number & " " & Err.Description
    End If
End Sub
```

Be cautious of errors in this procedure. This first statement tells the compiler to go to a line of code labeled HandleError if an error occurs:

```
On Error GoTo HandleError
```

Then delete the current record:

```
DoCmd.DoMenuItem acFormBar, acEditMenu, 8, , acMenuVer70
DoCmd.DoMenuItem acFormBar, acEditMenu, 6, , acMenuVer70
```

If the record deletion is successful, the code flows here. Move the insertion point to the detail section of the form:

```
[EmployeeID].SetFocus
```

Then leave this procedure:

```
Exit Sub
```

If an error occurs, the code flows here:

```
HandleError:
```

Then check to see if the error was a known problem that occurs when the user cancels the record deletion:

```
If Err.Number <> 2501 Then
```

If it is some other error, the message is displayed:

```
MsgBox Err.Number & " " & Err.Description
```

When the user presses the General button, the General page of the form appears, which is the first page:

```
Private Sub Command40_Click()
    DoCmd.GoToPage 1
End Sub
```

When the user presses the Notes button, the second page of the form appears which includes the Notes section:

```
Private Sub Command41_Click()
    DoCmd.GoToPage 2
End Sub
```

The GoToPage method is used to send the user to that second page. The user is sent to the third page, as indicated by the parameter 3, when the user presses the Family button:

```
Private Sub Command42_Click()
    DoCmd.GoToPage 3
End Sub
```

When the user presses the Sick Hours button, the GoToPage method of the DoCmd object is used to display the fourth page of this form:

```
Private Sub Command43_Click()
    DoCmd.GoToPage 4
End Sub
```

The Vacation Hours button sends the user to the fifth page of this form:

```
Private Sub Command44_Click()
    DoCmd.GoToPage 5
End Sub
```

The next code block fires when the Search button is pressed:

```
Private Sub CommandSearch_Click()
    Screen.PreviousControl.SetFocus
    DoCmd.DoMenuItem acFormBar, acEditMenu, 10, , acMenuVer70
End Sub
```

When the user presses the Search button, it is assumed that he or she wants to search the field that was being viewed prior to pressing this button. This line of code returns the focus to that field:

```
Screen.PreviousControl.SetFocus
```

Then use the DoMenuItem method to open the Access Search Dialog:

```
DoCmd.DoMenuItem acFormBar, acEditMenu, 10, , acMenuVer70
```

The next code block fires when the user presses the Close button. It closes the form:

```
Private Sub CommandClose_Click()
    DoCmd.Close
End Sub
```

The code also needs to display the name of the employee in the header and the summary information about the sick and vacation hours used by the employee. The code in the Current event takes that action:

```
Private Sub Form_Current()
    Dim MyDB As DAO.Database
    Dim RSTotalSickUsed As DAO.Recordset
    Dim TotalSick As Long
    Dim RSTotalVacationUsed As DAO.Recordset
    Dim TotalVacation As Long
    Label16.Caption = "Employee: " & [LastName] & ", " & [FirstName]
    If IsNumeric([EmployeeID]) Then
        Set MyDB = CurrentDb
        Set RSTotalSickUsed = MyDB.OpenRecordset("Select Sum([NumberOfHoursUsed]) " _
            & "As TheNum from SickHoursUse where EmployeeID = " _
            & [EmployeeID], dbOpenSnapshot)
        Label50.Caption = "Total Sick Hours Used: " _
            & Format(RSTotalSickUsed("TheNum"), "General Number")
        If IsDate([DateHired]) And IsNumeric([SickHoursPerMonth]) Then
            TotalSick = DateDiff("m", [DateHired], Date) * [SickHoursPerMonth]
            Label49.Caption = "Total Sick Hours: " & Format(TotalSick, "General Number")
            Label51.Caption = "Total Sick Hours Remaining: " _
                & Format(TotalSick - RSTotalSickUsed("TheNum"), "General Number")
        Else
```

```
                Label49.Caption = "Total Sick Hours: "
                Label51.Caption = "Total Sick Hours Remaining: "
        End If
        Set RSTotalVacationUsed = MyDB.OpenRecordset("Select Sum([NumberOfHoursUsed]) " _
                & "As TheNum from VacationHoursUse where EmployeeID = " _
                & [EmployeeID], dbOpenSnapshot)
        Label53.Caption = "Total Vacation Hours Used: " _
                & Format(RSTotalVacationUsed("TheNum"), "General Number")
        If IsDate([DateHired]) And IsNumeric([VacationHoursPerMonth]) Then
                TotalVacation = DateDiff("m", [DateHired], Date) * [VacationHoursPerMonth]
                Label52.Caption = "Total Vacation Hours: " & Format(TotalVacation, " _
                & "General Number")
                Label54.Caption = "Total Vacation Hours Remaining: " _
                        & Format(TotalVacation - RSTotalVacationUsed("TheNum"), "General Number")
        Else
                Label52.Caption = "Total Vacation Hours: "
                Label54.Caption = "Total Vacation Hours Remaining: "
        End If
    Else
        Label50.Caption = "Total Sick Hours Used: "
        Label49.Caption = "Total Sick Hours: "
        Label51.Caption = "Total Sick Hours Remaining: "
        Label53.Caption = "Total Vacation Hours Used: "
        Label52.Caption = "Total Vacation Hours: "
        Label54.Caption = "Total Vacation Hours Remaining: "
    End If
End Sub
```

The code needs to make a connection back to this database:

```
Dim MyDB As DAO.Database
```

and retrieve information on the number of sick hours used:

```
Dim RSTotalSickUsed As DAO.Recordset
```

This variable stores the total amount of sick hours earned:

```
Dim TotalSick As Long
```

and this one retrieves from the database the total number of vacation hours used:

```
Dim RSTotalVacationUsed As DAO.Recordset
```

and a variable to store the total amount of vacation hours earned:

```
Dim TotalVacation As Long
```

Then set the label in the header so it displays the name of the employee:

```
Label16.Caption = "Employee: " & [LastName] & ", " & [FirstName]
```

Before entering the summary hours information, make sure that you are on a valid employee record:

```
If IsNumeric([EmployeeID]) Then
```

If so, connect to the current database:

```
Set MyDB = CurrentDb
```

and retrieve the total number of sick hours used by this employee:

```
Set RSTotalSickUsed = MyDB.OpenRecordset("Select Sum([NumberOfHoursUsed]) " _
    & "As TheNum from SickHoursUse where EmployeeID = " _
    & [EmployeeID], dbOpenSnapshot)
```

Then display that value in one of the labels:

```
Label50.Caption = "Total Sick Hours Used: " _
        & Format(RSTotalSickUsed("TheNum"), "General Number")
```

Next, make sure that you have a hire date and a value in the Sick-HoursPerMonth field:

```
If IsDate([DateHired]) And IsNumeric([SickHoursPerMonth]) Then
```

If so, calculate the total number of sick hours earned, by deriving the number of months the employee has been with the company and multiplying that value by the number of hours they earn per month:

```
TotalSick = DateDiff("m", [DateHired], Date) * [SickHoursPerMonth]
```

Then enter that value into a label on the form:

```
Label49.Caption = "Total Sick Hours: " & Format(TotalSick, "General Number")
```

Also calculate and display the total number of sick hours remaining:

```
Label51.Caption = "Total Sick Hours Remaining: " _
        & Format(TotalSick - RSTotalSickUsed("TheNum"), " _
        & "General Number")
```

If the hire date is empty or a value did not appear in the Sick-HoursPerMonth field, nothing is displayed in these labels:

```
Label49.Caption = "Total Sick Hours: "
Label51.Caption = "Total Sick Hours Remaining: "
```

Next, retrieve the total number of vacation hours used by this employee:

```
Set RSTotalVacationUsed = MyDB.OpenRecordset("Select Sum([NumberOfHoursUsed]) " _
        & "As TheNum from VacationHoursUse where EmployeeID = " _
        & [EmployeeID], dbOpenSnapshot)
```

Then enter that value into a label. Note the use of the Format function. It displays the number with appropriate comma separators:

```
Label53.Caption = "Total Vacation Hours Used: " _
            & Format(RSTotalVacationUsed("TheNum"), "General Number")
```

Then make sure a hire date and a value in the VacationHoursPerMonth field are entered:

```
If IsDate([DateHired]) And IsNumeric([VacationHoursPerMonth]) Then
```

If so, the total number of vacation hours earned can be calculated:

```
TotalVacation = DateDiff("m", [DateHired], Date) * [VacationHoursPerMonth]
```

Then display that value in a Label:

```
Label52.Caption = "Total Vacation Hours: " & Format(TotalVacation,
"General Number")
```

Then display the total number of vacation hours remaining:

```
Label54.Caption = "Total Vacation Hours Remaining: " _
            & Format(TotalVacation - RSTotalVacationUsed("TheNum"), _
            "General Number")
```

If the HireDate field or the VacationHoursPerMonth field are invalid, the code flows here and you clear the labels:

```
Label52.Caption = "Total Vacation Hours: "
Label54.Caption = "Total Vacation Hours Remaining: "
```

If the EmployeeID field was not valid, the code flows here and you clear all the summary labels:

```
Label50.Caption = "Total Sick Hours Used: "
Label49.Caption = "Total Sick Hours: "
Label51.Caption = "Total Sick Hours Remaining: "
Label53.Caption = "Total Vacation Hours Used: "
Label52.Caption = "Total Vacation Hours: "
Label54.Caption = "Total Vacation Hours Remaining: "
```

Departments Form

The code on the Departments form provides the functionality for the Footer buttons. It also displays the summary salary information for the department.

The first code block fires when the Add Department button is pressed:

```
Private Sub CommandAdd_Click()
    DoCmd.GoToRecord , , acNewRec
    [DepartmentName].SetFocus
End Sub
```

Start by moving the record pointer to a new record:

```
DoCmd.GoToRecord , , acNewRec
```

Then move the focus to the DepartmentName field:

```
[DepartmentName].SetFocus
```

This next code block fires when the Delete Employee button is pressed:

```
Private Sub CommandDelete_Click()
    On Error GoTo HandleError
    DoCmd.DoMenuItem acFormBar, acEditMenu, 8, , acMenuVer70
    DoCmd.DoMenuItem acFormBar, acEditMenu, 6, , acMenuVer70
    [DepartmentName].SetFocus
    Exit Sub
HandleError:
    If Err.Number <> 2501 Then
        MsgBox Err.Number & " " & Err.Description
    End If
End Sub
```

Start with an error-handling line:

```
On Error GoTo HandleError
```

and then delete the current record:

```
DoCmd.DoMenuItem acFormBar, acEditMenu, 8, , acMenuVer70
DoCmd.DoMenuItem acFormBar, acEditMenu, 6, , acMenuVer70
```

Then move the focus to the detail section:

```
[DepartmentName].SetFocus
```

and leave the procedure:

```
Exit Sub
```

If an error occurs, the code flows here:

```
HandleError:
```

Check to see if the error was due to the user canceling the record deletion. If it was, that error does not need to be shown:

```
If Err.Number <> 2501 Then
```

But any other error message is displayed to the user:

```
MsgBox Err.Number & " " & Err.Description
```

The next code block fires when the Search button is pressed:

```
Private Sub CommandSearch_Click()
    Screen.PreviousControl.SetFocus
    DoCmd.DoMenuItem acFormBar, acEditMenu, 10, , acMenuVer70
End Sub
```

Start by using the SetFocus method to move the focus to the control that had the focus before this button was pressed:

```
Screen.PreviousControl.SetFocus
```

Next, open the Access Search Dialog:

```
DoCmd.DoMenuItem acFormBar, acEditMenu, 10, , acMenuVer70
```

The other button on the footer is the Close button. It uses the Close method to close the current form:

```
Private Sub CommandClose_Click()
    DoCmd.Close
End Sub
```

The other code block is in the Current event of the Form object. It fires anytime the record pointer moves and is used to display the summary payroll information.

```
Private Sub Form_Current()
    Dim MyDB As DAO.Database
    Dim rs As DAO.Recordset
    If IsNumeric([DepartmentID]) Then
        Set MyDB = CurrentDb
        Set rs = MyDB.OpenRecordset("Select Sum([Salary]) as TheSum " _
            & "From Employees Where DepartmentID = " _
            & [DepartmentID], dbOpenSnapshot)
        Label28.Caption = "Total Salary: " & Format(rs("TheSum"), "Currency")
    Else
```

```
              Label28.Caption = "Total Salary: $0.00"
       End If
End Sub
```

The user needs to connect to this database:

```
Dim MyDB As DAO.Database
```

and retrieve data from it:

```
Dim rs As DAO.Recordset
```

Then make sure a valid department record is displayed:

```
If IsNumeric([DepartmentID]) Then
```

If so, connect to the database:

```
Set MyDB = CurrentDb
```

and retrieve the total amount of salary for this department:

```
Set rs = MyDB.OpenRecordset("Select Sum([Salary]) as TheSum " _
        & "From Employees Where DepartmentID = " _
        & [DepartmentID], dbOpenSnapshot)
```

That value is displayed in a label:

```
Label28.Caption = "Total Salary: " & Format(rs("TheSum"), "Currency")
```

If the department is not a valid record, clear the value in the label:

```
Label28.Caption = "Total Salary: $0.00"
```

Reports

Department Payroll Per Month Report

The Department Payroll Per Month report displays the total amount of payroll for all the employees in each department. The report is based on the Department Payroll Per Month query, which has the following SQL syntax:

```
SELECT Departments.DepartmentName AS Department, Sum([Salary]/12) AS [Total Salary]
FROM Departments INNER JOIN Employees ON Departments.DepartmentID = Employees.DepartmentID
GROUP BY Departments.DepartmentName;
```

The query combines data from the Departments table with data from the Employees table. The records are grouped by the name of the department, and the sum of the salary divided by 12 for each department is displayed. The 12 is used to convert the salary format from year to month.

Sick Hours Used Report

The Sick Hours Used report displays the total number of sick hours used in each department. The report is based on the Sick Hours Used query which has the following SQL syntax:

```
SELECT Departments.DepartmentName AS Department,
Sum(SickHoursUse.NumberOfHoursUsed) AS [Hours Used]
FROM (Departments INNER JOIN Employees
ON Departments.DepartmentID = Employees.DepartmentID) INNER JOIN SickHoursUse ON
Employees.EmployeeID = SickHoursUse.EmployeeID GROUP BY Departments.DepartmentName;
```

This query combines data from three tables; the Departments table links to the Employees table, which links to the SickHoursUse table. The records are grouped by department, and the sum of the sick hours used is returned from the query.

Employee Testing Database

The next database to review in this chapter is the Employee Testing database. This database enables a user to create tests that can be taken through the database by an employee. The tests are then scored and stored in the database.

Sample Walk-through

When the user first enters the database, the menu shown in Figure 3-10 is displayed. The menu form enables the user to access any of the components of the database. If the Tests button is selected, the form in Figure 3-11 is displayed.

The Tests form has two pages. The first page is the General page, and it displays the basic information about the test. If the user clicks on the Questions button, the page of the form shown in Figure 3-12 appears.

Figure 3-10

Menu from the
Employee Testing
database

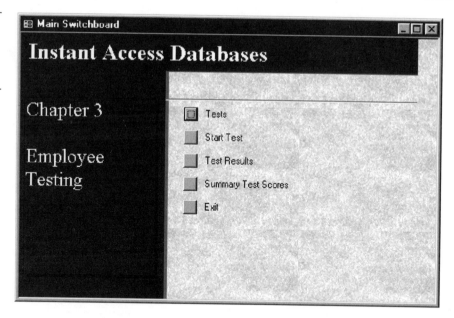

Figure 3-11

General page
from the Tests
form

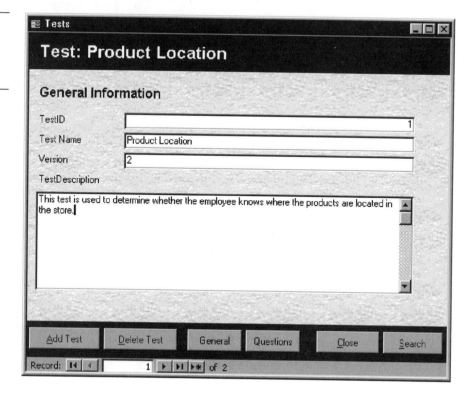

Figure 3-12

Questions page of
the Tests form

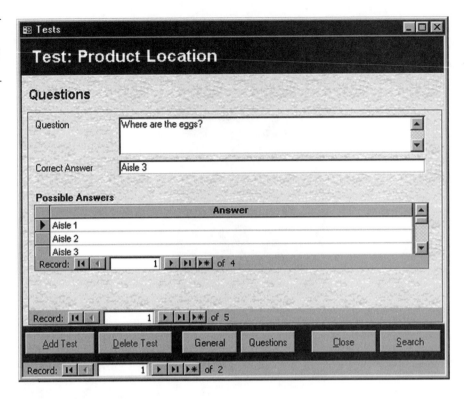

The Questions page, the second page, contains a sub-form that lists all the questions included on this test. Here the user could add another question, as well as the correct answer to that question. Then in the sub-form of the Questions sub-form, the user enters all the possible answers for this question. The correct answer needs to match one of these entries.

Once the user has completely created a test, someone can take the test by pressing the Start Test button on the main menu. When this button is pressed, the form shown in Figure 3-13 is displayed.

On this page, the user enters the requested employee information and then selects the test they are to take. The code then adds that information to the database and opens the test form shown Figure 3-14.

Once this form appears, the user allows the employee to begin the test. The form is presented as a dialog so the employee cannot, at this point, access any other part of the database. If the form is closed, the entire database closes. Once the employee has completed the test, a message box

Figure 3-13

Start Test form

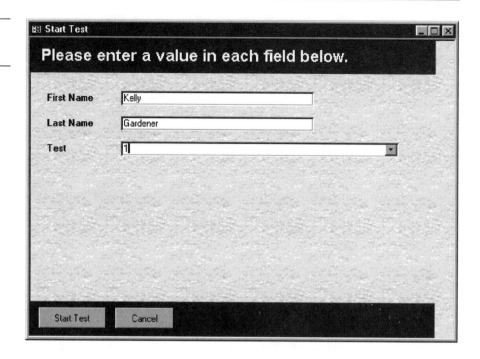

Figure 3-14

Test form

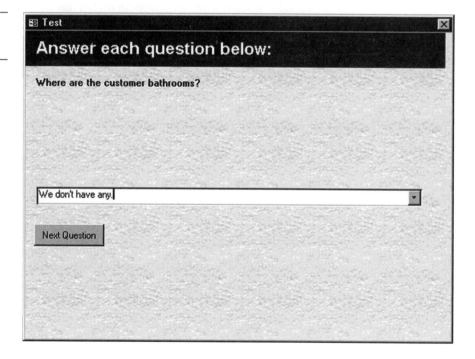

Figure 3-15

Test Results form

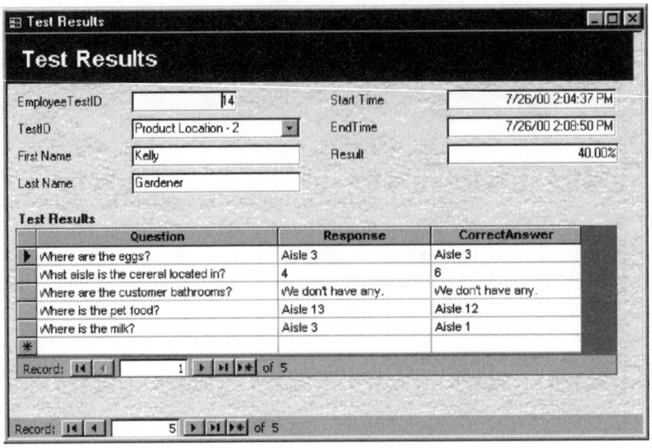

reveals the test results. The database then closes. The user can return to the database to view the employee's score through the Test Results form shown in Figure 3-15.

The Test Results form shows the information about the employee and the results of their test. In a sub-form, the user can see all the answers selected by the user and the correct answer for each question.

The database application also has a report called Summary Test Scores which is displayed in Figure 3-16. The report shows the total number of people that have taken the test and the average score on each test.

Table Definitions and Relationships

Tests Table

The Test table is the top-level table in the database storing information about the tests. It relates to many of the other tables in the database.

Questions Table

The Questions table stores information about each of the questions. The table is in a one-to-many relationship with the Tests table. Each test can have many questions, but each question goes with a single test.

Figure 3-16

Summary Test
Scores report

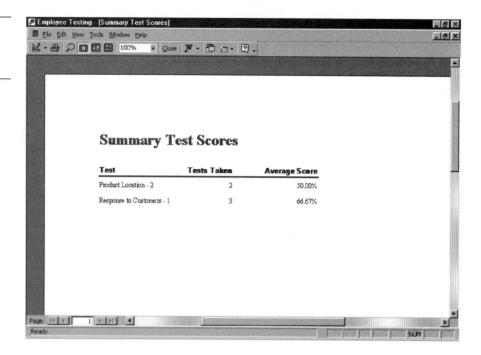

Answers Table

The Answers table stores all the possible answers for each of the questions. The table is in a one-to-many relationship with the Questions table since each question can have many possible answers.

EmployeeTests Table

The EmployeeTests table stores information about the employee taking the test and summary information about the results of that test. The table relates to the Tests table in a one-to-many relationship. Each test can be taken by many employees, but each record in this table is for a single test.

Responses Table

The Responses table stores the answer selected by the employee for each question. The table relates to the Questions table in a one-to-many relationship since each question can be answered by different employees. It also relates to the EmployeeTests table in a one-to-many relationship.

Each of the responses is for a specific question, but many questions are asked on a test.

Field Specifications

Tests Table

The field specifications for the Tests table are displayed in Table 3-6. The TestID field is the primary key for this table. The field is an AutoNumber so it is automatically populated when a new record is added to the table.

Questions Table

The field specifications for the Questions table are displayed in Table 3-7. The QuestionID is the primary key for this table. The TestID field is a foreign key and links this table to the Tests table.

Answers Table

The field specifications for the Answers table are displayed in Table 3-8. The AnswerID is the primary key for this table. The QuestionID links this table to the Questions table. The Answer field stores one of the possible answers that goes with this question.

Table 3-6

Tests Table Field Specifications

Field Name	Field Type	Notes
TestID	AutoNumber	Primary Key
TestName	Text	Length = 50
Version	Text	Length = 50
TestDescription	Memo	

Table 3-7

Questions Table Field Specifications

Field Name	Field Type	Notes
QuestionID	AutoNumber	Primary Key
TestID	Number	Type = Long, Foreign Key
Question	Text	Length = 255
CorrectAnswer	Text	Length = 100

Field Name	Field Type	Notes
AnswerID	AutoNumber	Primary Key
QuestionID	Number	Type = Long, Foreign Key
Answer	Text	Length = 100

Table 3-8

Answers Table Field Specifications

EmployeeTests Table

The field specifications for the EmployeeTests table are displayed in Table 3-9. The EmployeeTestID is the primary key in this table. The TestID field is a foreign key that links this table back to the tests table.

The StartTime field is populated in code, and it stores the date and time that the test started. The EndTime field is also populated in code and stores the time that the test ended. The Result field stores the percentage of questions that the employee answered correctly on the test.

Field Name	Field Type	Notes
EmployeeTestID	AutoNumber	Primary Key
TestID	Number	Type = Long, Foreign Key
FirstName	Text	Length = 50
LastName	Text	Length = 50
StartTime	Date/Time	
EndTime	Date/Time	
Result	Number	Type = Single

Table 3-9

EmployeeTests Table Field Specifications

Responses Table

The field specifications for the Responses table are displayed in Table 3-10. The ResponseID is the primary key for this table. Each of the responses connects with a particular employee, so the EmployeeTestID field is a foreign key that links this table to the EmployeeTests table.

Each of the responses also connects with a particular question. The QuestionID field provides the link to the question through the Questions table.

Field Name	Field Type	Notes
ResponseID	AutoNumber	Primary Key
EmployeeTestID	Number	Type = Long, Foreign Key
QuestionID	Number	Type = Long, Foreign Key
Response	Text	Length = 100

Table 3-10

Responses Table
Field
Specifications

Forms

Switchboard Form

The Switchboard form is used to navigate through the forms and to report in the Employee Testing database. It was created using the Switchboard wizard, which is accessible within Access through the Tools/Database Utilities/Switchboard Manager menu item. Only the appearance and design of the form produced with that wizard have been altered.

Tests Form

The code on the Tests form provides the functionality for the Footer buttons and the label in the header of the form.

When the user clicks on the Add Test button, this code block fires:

```
Private Sub CommandAdd_Click()
    DoCmd.GoToRecord , , acNewRec
    [TestName].SetFocus
End Sub
```

Start by moving the record pointer onto a new record:

```
DoCmd.GoToRecord , , acNewRec
```

Then move the focus to the TestName field so the user can start entering data:

```
[TestName].SetFocus
```

When the user presses the Delete Test button, the next code block fires:

```
Private Sub CommandDelete_Click()
    On Error GoTo HandleError
    DoCmd.DoMenuItem acFormBar, acEditMenu, 8, , acMenuVer70
    DoCmd.DoMenuItem acFormBar, acEditMenu, 6, , acMenuVer70
    [TestName].SetFocus
    Exit Sub
HandleError:
    If Err.Number <> 2501 Then
        MsgBox Err.Number & " " & Err.Description
    End If
End Sub
```

Start with an error handler:

```
On Error GoTo HandleError
```

Next, delete the current record:

```
DoCmd.DoMenuItem acFormBar, acEditMenu, 8, , acMenuVer70
DoCmd.DoMenuItem acFormBar, acEditMenu, 6, , acMenuVer70
```

If no error occurs, move the focus to the TestName field:

```
[TestName].SetFocus
```

and leave this procedure:

```
Exit Sub
```

If an error occurs, the code flows here:

```
HandleError:
```

Then check to see if the error that occurred was due to the user canceling the record deletion:

```
If Err.Number <> 2501 Then
```

If it wasn't, show the error to the user:

```
MsgBox Err.Number & " " & Err.Description
```

When the user clicks on the General button, he or she needs to return to the first page of the form. This is done through the GoToPage method of the DoCmd object:

```
Private Sub Command33_Click()
    DoCmd.GoToPage 1
End Sub
```

When the user clicks on the Questions button, he or she needs to return to the second page of the form:

```
Private Sub Command34_Click()
    DoCmd.GoToPage 2
End Sub
```

The next code block fires when the user clicks on the Search button:

```
Private Sub CommandSearch_Click()
    Screen.PreviousControl.SetFocus
    DoCmd.DoMenuItem acFormBar, acEditMenu, 10, , acMenuVer70
End Sub
```

When the user presses this button, it is assumed that he or she wants to search the field on the form that was being viewed before clicking this button. This line of code sends the focus back to that field:

```
Screen.PreviousControl.SetFocus
```

Then open the built-in Access Search Dialog:

```
DoCmd.DoMenuItem acFormBar, acEditMenu, 10, , acMenuVer70
```

The last code block for the Footer buttons closes the form when the Close button is pressed:

```
Private Sub CommandClose_Click()
    DoCmd.Close
End Sub
```

The header of the form needs to display the name of the current test, and it needs to update every time the record pointer moves. The current event that fires whenever the record pointer moves and is used here to update the header label:

```
Private Sub Form_Current()
    Label16.Caption = "Test: " & [TestName]
End Sub
```

Start Test Form

The code on the Start Test form sets up the database so a new test can be taken. The code that does this fires when the Start Test button is pressed:

```
Private Sub CommandStart_Click()
    Dim MyDB As DAO.Database
    Dim RSID As DAO.Recordset
    Dim RSQuestions As DAO.Recordset
    Dim CurrentTime As Date
    Dim TheFirstName As String
    Dim TheLastName As String
    Dim TheTest As Long
    txtFirstName.SetFocus
    TheFirstName = txtFirstName.Text
    txtLastName.SetFocus
    TheLastName = txtLastName.Text
    ComboTest.SetFocus
    TheTest = IIf(IsNumeric(ComboTest.Text), ComboTest.Text, 0)
    If TheFirstName = "" Then
        MsgBox "You need to enter a first name for the person taking the test!"
    ElseIf TheLastName = "" Then
        MsgBox "You need to enter a last name for the person taking the test!"
    ElseIf TheTest = 0 Then
        MsgBox "You need to select a test name!"
    Else
        Set MyDB = CurrentDb
        CurrentTime = Now
        MyDB.Execute "Insert Into EmployeeTests (TestID, FirstName, LastName, " _
            & "StartTime) values (" _
            & TheTest & ", " _
            & """" & TheFirstName & """, " _
            & """" & TheLastName & """, " _
            & "#" & CurrentTime & "#)"
        Set RSID = MyDB.OpenRecordset("Select EmployeeTestID from EmployeeTests " _
            & "Where StartTime = #" & CurrentTime & "#", dbOpenSnapshot)
        Set RSQuestions = MyDB.OpenRecordset("Select QuestionID from Questions " _
            & "Where TestID = " & TheTest, dbOpenSnapshot)
        Do Until RSQuestions.EOF
            MyDB.Execute "Insert into Responses (EmployeeTestID, QuestionID, " _
                & "Response) " _
                    & " values (" _
                    & RSID("EmployeeTestID") & ", " _
                    & RSQuestions("QuestionID") & ", " _
                    & """No Response"")"
            RSQuestions.MoveNext
        Loop
        DoCmd.OpenForm "Employee Test", , , , , acDialog, RSID("EmployeeTestID")
        DoCmd.Close
    End If
End Sub
```

Connect to the database:

```
Dim MyDB As DAO.Database
```

and retrieve the ID of the employee's test just added:

```
Dim RSID As DAO.Recordset
```

Also retrieve all the questions for the test selected:

```
Dim RSQuestions As DAO.Recordset
```

This variable stores the current system date and time:

```
Dim CurrentTime As Date
```

Two others for the name of the employee entered:

```
Dim TheFirstName As String
Dim TheLastName As String
```

One more is used to store the ID of the test selected:

```
Dim TheTest As Long
```

Start by moving the focus to the first name field:

```
txtFirstName.SetFocus
```

so the value entered by the user can be retrieved:

```
TheFirstName = txtFirstName.Text
```

The same is done for the last name:

```
txtLastName.SetFocus
TheLastName = txtLastName.Text
```

and for the test selected by the user:

```
ComboTest.SetFocus
TheTest = IIf(IsNumeric(ComboTest.Text), ComboTest.Text, 0)
```

Then make sure that the user entered a first name:

```
If TheFirstName = "" Then
```

If a first name was not entered, inform the user of the problem:

```
MsgBox "You need to enter a first name for the person taking the test!"
```

Then make sure a last name was entered:

```
ElseIf TheLastName = "" Then
```

If not, prompt the user with a different message:

```
MsgBox "You need to enter a last name for the person taking the test!"
```

Do the same for the test selected by the user:

```
ElseIf TheTest = 0 Then
    MsgBox "You need to select a test name!"
```

If all the information is entered, the code flows here:

```
Else
```

and a connection to the database is opened:

```
Set MyDB = CurrentDb
```

Then set a temporary variable to the current system date and time:

```
CurrentTime = Now
```

Insert a new employee test record with the values entered by the user on this form and the temporary time variable:

```
MyDB.Execute "Insert Into EmployeeTests (TestID, FirstName, LastName, " _
    & "StartTime) values (" _
    & TheTest & ", " _
    & """" & TheFirstName & """, " _
    & """" & TheLastName & """, " _
    & "#" & CurrentTime & "#)"
```

The ID for the record just added needs to be retrieved so that it can be passed on to the Test form. Retrieve it here, based on the time that the record was added to the database:

```
Set RSID = MyDB.OpenRecordset("Select EmployeeTestID from EmployeeTests " _
    & "Where StartTime = #" & CurrentTime & "#", dbOpenSnapshot)
```

Next, retrieve a list of all the questions that are on the test that the user is taking:

```
Set RSQuestions = MyDB.OpenRecordset("Select QuestionID from Questions " _
    & "Where TestID = " & TheTest, dbOpenSnapshot)
```

Then start a loop in order to process each of the questions for the test:

```
Do Until RSQuestions.EOF
```

Use the question and the ID for the test to create a new record for the question in the Responses table, which is where the response made by the employee will be stored. Note that the value of the response is initially set to the test "No Response":

```
MyDB.Execute "Insert into Responses (EmployeeTestID, QuestionID, Response) " _
    & " values (" _
    & RSID("EmployeeTestID") & ", " _
    & RSQuestions("QuestionID") & ", " _
    & """No Response""")"
```

Move on to process the next question:

```
RSQuestions.MoveNext
Loop
```

Then launch the Employee Test form. It opens as a dialog so the employee can enter any other part of the database. Pass the ID for this employee's test to that form:

```
DoCmd.OpenForm "Employee Test", , , , , acDialog, RSID("EmployeeTestID")
```

and close this form:

```
DoCmd.Close
```

Employee Test Form

The code on the Test form displays each of the questions and answers and scores the test when the user has finished. A couple of variables need to be available for different procedures on this form. The variables are therefore declared in the General Declarations section.

```
Private MyDB As DAO.Database
Private RSQuestions As DAO.Recordset
Private RSAnswers As DAO.Recordset
Private RSCurrentTest As DAO.Recordset
```

A connection to the database is needed:

```
Private MyDB As DAO.Database
```

A Recordset to store all of the questions on this test:

```
Private RSQuestions As DAO.Recordset
```

The answers for each question:

```
Private RSAnswers As DAO.Recordset
```

and the ID of the current test:

```
Private RSCurrentTest As DAO.Recordset
```

When the form first loads, you need to set up these variables and display the first question on the test.

```
Private Sub Form_Load()
    Set MyDB = CurrentDb
    Set RSCurrentTest = MyDB.OpenRecordset("Select TestID from EmployeeTests " _
        & "Where EmployeeTestID = " & Me.OpenArgs, dbOpenSnapshot)
    Set RSQuestions = MyDB.OpenRecordset("Select QuestionID, Question " _
        & "From Questions Where TestID = " & RSCurrentTest("TestID"), " _
        & "dbOpenSnapshot)
    Set RSAnswers = MyDB.OpenRecordset("Select Answer from Answers " _
        & "Where QuestionID = " & RSQuestions("QuestionID"), dbOpenSnapshot)
    LabelQuestion.Caption = RSQuestions("Question")
    ComboAnswer.RowSource = ""
    Do Until RSAnswers.EOF
        ComboAnswer.RowSource = ComboAnswer.RowSource & RSAnswers("Answer") _
            & ";"
        RSAnswers.MoveNext
    Loop
    ComboAnswer.Requery
End Sub
```

Start by connecting through code to the current database:

```
Set MyDB = CurrentDb
```

Then retrieve the ID of the test that the employee is taking:

```
Set RSCurrentTest = MyDB.OpenRecordset("Select TestID from EmployeeTests " _
    & "Where EmployeeTestID = " & Me.OpenArgs, dbOpenSnapshot)
```

and all the questions on that test:

```
Set RSQuestions = MyDB.OpenRecordset("Select QuestionID, Question " _
    & "From Questions Where TestID = " & RSCurrentTest("TestID"), dbOpenSnapshot)
```

Next, retrieve all the possible answers for the first question on the test:

```
Set RSAnswers = MyDB.OpenRecordset("Select Answer from Answers " _
    & "Where QuestionID = " & RSQuestions("QuestionID"), dbOpenSnapshot)
```

Then display the text of the current question in a label:

```
LabelQuestion.Caption = RSQuestions("Question")
```

and clear the combo box that will store the possible answers:

```
ComboAnswer.RowSource = ""
```

Then start a loop in order to process each of the possible answers for the current question:

```
Do Until RSAnswers.EOF
```

Each answer is added to the combo box through its Row Source property:

```
ComboAnswer.RowSource = ComboAnswer.RowSource & RSAnswers("Answer") _
    & ";"
```

Then move on to process the next possible answer:

```
    RSAnswers.MoveNext
Loop
```

Finally, repopulate the combo box so it shows all the possible answers:

```
ComboAnswer.Requery
```

When the user presses the Next Question button, process their answer for the current question, and then either display the next question or score the test.

```
Private Sub CommandNext_Click()
    Dim RSTheResult As DAO.Recordset
    ComboAnswer.SetFocus
    MyDB.Execute "Update Responses set Response = " _
        & """" & ComboAnswer.Text & """ Where EmployeeTestID = " & Me.OpenArgs _
        & " And QuestionID = " & RSQuestions("QuestionID")
    RSQuestions.MoveNext
    If RSQuestions.EOF Then
        Set RSTheResult = MyDB.OpenRecordset("SELECT " _
            & "Sum(IIf([Response]=[CorrectAnswer],1,0)) AS TotalCorrect, " _
            & "Count([Response]) AS TotalCount FROM Questions " _
            & "INNER JOIN Responses ON Questions.QuestionID = Responses.QuestionID " _
            & "WHERE Responses.EmployeeTestID = " & Me.OpenArgs)
```

```
        MyDB.Execute "Update EmployeeTests set EndTime = #" & Now _
            & "#, Result = " & RSTheResult("TotalCorrect") / RSTheResult("TotalCount") _
            & " Where EmployeeTestID = " & Me.OpenArgs
        MsgBox "Test Complete. You scored " & RSTheResult("TotalCorrect") _
            & " out of " & RSTheResult("TotalCount") & " correct."
        DoCmd.Close
    Else
        Set RSAnswers = MyDB.OpenRecordset("Select Answer from Answers " _
            & "Where QuestionID = " & RSQuestions("QuestionID"), dbOpenSnapshot)
        LabelQuestion.Caption = RSQuestions("Question")
        ComboAnswer.RowSource = ""
        Do Until RSAnswers.EOF
            ComboAnswer.RowSource = ComboAnswer.RowSource & RSAnswers("Answer") _
                & ";"
            RSAnswers.MoveNext
        Loop
        ComboAnswer.Requery
        ComboAnswer.Text = ""
    End If
End Sub
```

One more Recordset object that will be used to score the test is needed:

```
Dim RSTheResult As DAO.Recordset
```

Start by moving the focus to the answer combo box:

```
ComboAnswer.SetFocus
```

Then update the employee's response for this question in the database based on the selection he or she made:

```
MyDB.Execute "Update Responses set Response = " _
    & """" & ComboAnswer.Text & """" Where EmployeeTestID = " & Me.OpenArgs _
    & " And QuestionID = " & RSQuestions("QuestionID")
```

Then move on to the next question of the test:

```
RSQuestions.MoveNext
```

and check if any more questions remain:

```
If RSQuestions.EOF Then
```

If all questions have been answered, score the test. Start by retrieving the total number of questions on the test and the total number of the employee's responses that match the correct answer:

```
Set RSTheResult = MyDB.OpenRecordset("SELECT " _
    & "Sum(IIf([Response]=[CorrectAnswer],1,0)) AS TotalCorrect, " _
    & "Count([Response]) AS TotalCount FROM Questions " _
    & "INNER JOIN Responses ON Questions.QuestionID = Responses.QuestionID " _
    & "WHERE Responses.EmployeeTestID = " & Me.OpenArgs)
```

Next, update the employee's test record by entering his or her score and the time that the test ended:

```
MyDB.Execute "Update EmployeeTests set EndTime = #" & Now _
    & "#, Result = " & RSTheResult("TotalCorrect") / RSTheResult("TotalCount") _
    & " Where EmployeeTestID = " & Me.OpenArgs
```

Then show the results to the employee:

```
MsgBox "Test Complete. You scored " & RSTheResult("TotalCorrect") _
    & " out of " & RSTheResult("TotalCount") & " correct."
```

and close this form:

```
DoCmd.Close
```

If the last question was not the last question on the test, the code flows here:

```
Else
```

Retrieve the answers for this question:

```
Set RSAnswers = MyDB.OpenRecordset("Select Answer from Answers " _
    & "Where QuestionID = " & RSQuestions("QuestionID"), dbOpenSnapshot)
LabelQuestion.Caption = RSQuestions("Question")
```

Then clear the combo box:

```
ComboAnswer.RowSource = ""
```

and start a loop in order to process each of the possible answers:

```
Do Until RSAnswers.EOF
```

Each answer is added to the combo box:

```
ComboAnswer.RowSource = ComboAnswer.RowSource & RSAnswers("Answer") _
    & ";"
```

Then loop to the next record:

```
    RSAnswers.MoveNext
Loop
```

and repopulate the combo box:

```
ComboAnswer.Requery
```

Finally, clear the text in the combo box since it will still have the last answer entered by the user:

```
ComboAnswer.Text = ""
```

When the employee closes this form, either by finishing the test or by clicking on the "X," he or she should not be able to enter the rest of the database. Therefore, the Unload event is used to close the database when this form closes:

```
Private Sub Form_Unload(Cancel As Integer)
    CloseCurrentDatabase
End Sub
```

Report

Summary Test Scores Report

The Summary Test Scores report displays the average score received on this test and the number of people who have taken the test. The report is based on the Summary Test Scores query, which has the following syntax:

```
SELECT EmployeeTests.TestID AS Test,
Count(EmployeeTests.EmployeeTestID) AS [Tests Taken],
Avg(EmployeeTests.Result) AS [Average Score]
FROM EmployeeTests GROUP BY EmployeeTests.TestID;
```

The records are by the test. The name of the test is returned as is the count of those taking the test and the average of the Result field.

Job Application Database

The Job Application database provides the interface for a company to collect information about potential employees that are applying for a job. The database is really a database within a database.

First, the database stores information on potential employees. But the questions that the potential employee answers on the application are based on questions stored in another table. So instead of a form with questions on it, it is a form where you enter the questions that you want to appear on the application.

Sample Walk-through

When the user first enters this database, they are taken straight to the main form in which the application is displayed, as shown in Figure 3-17. The entry form into the database is the Application form. The user creates new application types on this form, and gives the application a name and describes it. The user then supplies a list of all the questions that should be asked on this application.

When the user wants to allow a potential employee to fill out an application, or the user is entering the data, he or she presses the "Add an Employee Application" button. This button displays the form shown in Figure 3-18.

The Create Employee Application form takes the potential employee, one question at a time, through the list of questions associated with the type of application being completed. As each question is completed, the potential employee presses the Next Question button and sees the next question on this same form.

Figure 3-17

Application form

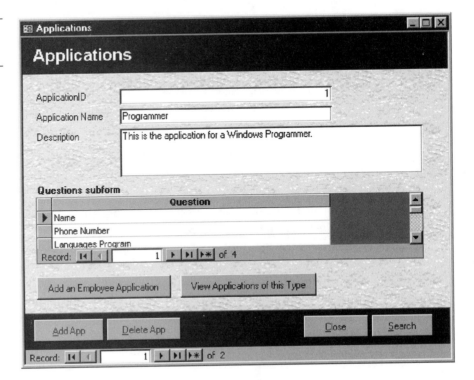

Figure 3-18

Create Employee
Application form

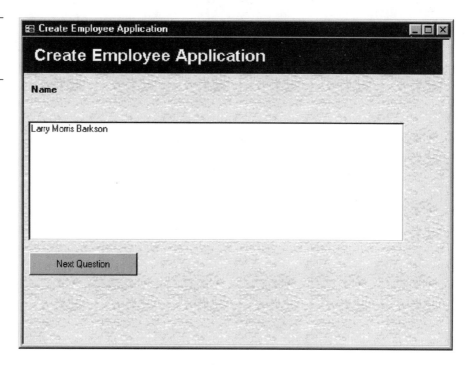

Then, by pressing the "View Applications of this Type" button, the user can view the content of application filled out by potential employees.

When this is done, the report shown in Figure 3-19 is displayed. This report includes all the information for all the potential employees who filled out the type of application that they are currently working with.

Table Definitions and Relationships

Applications Table

The Applications table stores the top-level information about the applications themselves. This is not the information about a potential employee but is information about an application.

ApplicationQuestions Table

Each of the applications has questions on it. The text of those questions is stored in the ApplicationQuestions table. The table relates to the Applications table in a one-to-many relationship.

Figure 3-19

Employee
Applications
report

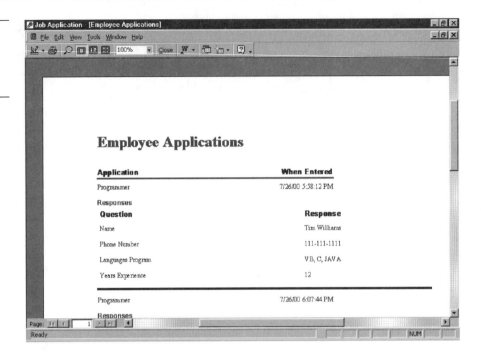

EmployeeApplications Table

The EmployeeApplications table stores the top-level information about an employee who is filling out an application. The table relates to the Applications table in a one-to-many relationship.

Responses Table

Each response made by a potential employee to one of the questions on an application is stored in the Responses table. The table relates to the EmployeeApplications table in a one-to-many relationship.

Field Specifications

Applications Table

The field specifications for the Applications table are displayed in Table 3-11. The ApplicationID field is the primary key for the table. The rest of the fields store information about the application.

Table 3-11	Field Name	Field Type	Notes
Applications Table Field Specifications	ApplicationID	AutoNumber	Primary Key
	ApplicationName	Text	Length = 50
	Description	Memo	

ApplicationQuestions Table

The field specifications for the ApplicationQuestions table are displayed in Table 3-12. The ApplicationQuestionID is the primary key for the table. The ApplicationID field is a foreign key that links this table to the Applications table. The Question field stores the text of the question.

Table 3-12	Field Name	Field Type	Notes
ApplicationQuestions Table Field Specifications	ApplicationQuestionID	AutoNumber	Primary Key
	ApplicationID	Number	Type = Long, Foreign Key
	Question	Text	Length = 255

EmployeeApplications Table

The field specifications for the EmployeeApplications table are displayed in Table 3-13. The EmployeeApplicationID field uniquely identifies each record in the table.

The ApplicationID field links this table to the Applications table. The WhenEntered field stores the date and time that the application was completed.

Table 3-13	Field Name	Field Type	Notes
EmployeeApplications Table Field Specifications	EmployeeApplicationID	AutoNumber	Primary Key
	ApplicationID	Number	Type = Long, Foreign Key
	WhenEntered	Date/Time	

Responses Table

The field specifications for the Responses table are displayed in Table 3-14. The ResponseID is the primary key for this table. The EmployeeApplicationID field links this table to the EmployeeApplications table in a one-to-many relationship. The question field stores the text of the question asked and the Response field stores the text of the response supplied by the potential employee.

Table 3-14	Field Name	Field Type	Notes
Responses Table Field Specifications	ResponseID	AutoNumber	Primary Key
	EmployeeApplicationID	Number	Type = Long, Foreign Key
	Question	Text	Length = 255
	Response	Memo	

Forms

Applications Form

The code on the Applications form supplies the functionality for the buttons on the form. When the user clicks on the "Add an Employee Application" button, the following code block fires:

```
Private Sub Command30_Click()
    If IsNumeric([ApplicationID]) Then
        DoCmd.OpenForm "Create Employee Application", , , , , , [ApplicationID]
    End If
End Sub
```

When the user presses this button, a new employee application is added. To do this, you need to pass on to that form the type of application that should be used. But before that is done, make sure that that value is actually valid:

```
If IsNumeric([ApplicationID]) Then
```

If it is, open the Create Employee Application form and pass to it the type of application that should be used through the OpenArgs parameter:

```
DoCmd.OpenForm "Create Employee Application", , , , , , [ApplicationID]
```

The next code block fires when the user clicks on the "View Applications of this Type" button:

```
Private Sub Command31_Click()
    DoCmd.OpenReport "Employee Applications", acViewPreview, , "[ApplicationID] = " _
        & [ApplicationID]
End Sub
```

The code uses the OpenReport method to open the Employee Applications report. The report is filtered so that only those applications that are of the current type are displayed:

```
DoCmd.OpenReport "Employee Applications", acViewPreview, , "[ApplicationID] = " _
    & [ApplicationID]
```

When the user presses the Add button, the next code block fires:

```
Private Sub CommandAdd_Click()
    DoCmd.GoToRecord , , acNewRec
    [ApplicationName].SetFocus
End Sub
```

First, move the record pointer to a new record:

```
DoCmd.GoToRecord , , acNewRec
```

Then move the focus to the first data entry field on the form:

```
[ApplicationName].SetFocus
```

When the user presses the Delete button, the next code block fires:

```
Private Sub CommandDelete_Click()
    On Error GoTo HandleError
    DoCmd.DoMenuItem acFormBar, acEditMenu, 8, , acMenuVer70
    DoCmd.DoMenuItem acFormBar, acEditMenu, 6, , acMenuVer70
    [ApplicationName].SetFocus
    Exit Sub
HandleError:
    If Err.Number <> 2501 Then
        MsgBox Err.Number & " " & Err.Description
    End If
End Sub
```

Start by telling the compiler that errors that occur in this procedure are handled:

```
On Error GoTo HandleError
```

Then, delete the current record:

```
DoCmd.DoMenuItem acFormBar, acEditMenu, 8, , acMenuVer70
DoCmd.DoMenuItem acFormBar, acEditMenu, 6, , acMenuVer70
```

and move the focus back to the detail section:

```
[ApplicationName].SetFocus
```

Then leave this procedure:

```
Exit Sub
```

If an error did occur in this procedure, the compiler breaks the code to this point:

```
HandleError:
```

Then check to see if the error that occurred was due to the user canceling the record deletion:

```
If Err.Number <> 2501 Then
```

If it wasn't, display the error number and the message in a message box:

```
MsgBox Err.Number & " " & Err.Description
```

When the user clicks on the Search button, the next code block fires:

```
Private Sub CommandSearch_Click()
    Screen.PreviousControl.SetFocus
    DoCmd.DoMenuItem acFormBar, acEditMenu, 10, , acMenuVer70
End Sub
```

Start by moving the focus to the control that had the focus prior to the user clicking on the Search button:

```
Screen.PreviousControl.SetFocus
```

Then display the Search dialog:

```
DoCmd.DoMenuItem acFormBar, acEditMenu, 10, , acMenuVer70
```

When the user presses the Close button, use the Close method to close this form:

```
Private Sub CommandClose_Click()
    DoCmd.Close
End Sub
```

Create Employee Application Form

The code on the Create Employee Application form processes each of the questions asked to the potential employee. The form is not bound to any table. Instead, the code displays the text of the questions and stores the responses entered.

To provide this functionality, some form-wide variables and objects that are placed in the General Declarations section are needed.

```
Private MyDB As DAO.Database
Private RSQuestions As DAO.Recordset
Private EmpAppID As Long
```

This first is a Database object:

```
Private MyDB As DAO.Database
```

The next is a Recordset object that stores the text of the questions that need to be asked:

```
Private RSQuestions As DAO.Recordset
```

One variable stores the ID of the employee application on which you are working:

```
Private EmpAppID As Long
```

When the form first loads, you need to set up these variables and display the first question.

```
Private Sub Form_Load()
    Dim RSID As DAO.Recordset
    Dim CurrentDT As Date
    Set MyDB = CurrentDb
    CurrentDT = Now
    MyDB.Execute "Insert Into EmployeeApplications (ApplicationID, WhenEntered) " _
        & "values (" _
        & Me.OpenArgs & ", " _
        & "#" & CurrentDT & "#)"
    Set RSID = MyDB.OpenRecordset("Select EmployeeApplicatationID from " _
        & "EmployeeApplications Where WhenEntered = #" _
        & CurrentDT & "#", dbOpenSnapshot)
```

```
        EmpAppID = RSID("EmployeeApplicatationID")
        Set RSQuestions = MyDB.OpenRecordset("Select Question from ApplicationQuestions " _
            & "Where ApplicationID = " & Me.OpenArgs, dbOpenSnapshot)
        lblQuestion.Caption = RSQuestions("Question")
        txtResponse.SetFocus
        txtResponse.Text = ""
End Sub
```

An additional Recordset object in this procedure is needed:

```
Dim RSID As DAO.Recordset
```

and a variable to store the current system time:

```
Dim CurrentDT As Date
```

Then connect our database object to the current database:

```
Set MyDB = CurrentDb
```

and set the time variable to the system date and time:

```
CurrentDT = Now
```

Then add a new employee application based on the type of application that is to be used:

```
MyDB.Execute "Insert Into EmployeeApplications (ApplicationID, WhenEntered) " _
    & "values (" _
    & Me.OpenArgs & ", " _
    & "#" & CurrentDT & "#)"
```

Now retrieve the ID for the record just added, in order to use it when adding the responses to the database:

```
Set RSID = MyDB.OpenRecordset("Select EmployeeApplicatationID from " _
    & "EmployeeApplications Where WhenEntered = #" _
    & CurrentDT & "#", dbOpenSnapshot)
```

Then place that ID in a form-wide variable:

```
EmpAppID = RSID("EmployeeApplicatationID")
```

Next, retrieve all the questions that are used for this application:

```
Set RSQuestions = MyDB.OpenRecordset("Select Question from ApplicationQuestions " _
    & "Where ApplicationID = " & Me.OpenArgs, dbOpenSnapshot)
```

Then put the text of the first question in the label:

```
lblQuestion.Caption = RSQuestions("Question")
```

Set focus to the response text box:

```
txtResponse.SetFocus
```

and clear it out:

```
txtResponse.Text = ""
```

When the user clicks the Next Question button, store the response for the current question in the database and display the next question.

```
Private Sub CommandNext_Click()
    txtResponse.SetFocus
    MyDB.Execute "Insert Into Responses (EmployeeApplicatationID, " _
        & "Question, Response) values (" _
        & EmpAppID & ", " _
        & """" & lblQuestion.Caption & """, " _
        & """" & txtResponse.Text & """)"
    RSQuestions.MoveNext
    If RSQuestions.EOF Then
        MsgBox "That is the end of the application."
        DoCmd.Close
    Else
        lblQuestion.Caption = RSQuestions("Question")
        txtResponse.Text = ""
    End If
End Sub
```

Start by setting focus to the response text box:

```
txtResponse.SetFocus
```

and use our form-wide database connection to store the user's response in the database:

```
MyDB.Execute "Insert Into Responses (EmployeeApplicatationID, " _
    & "Question, Response) values (" _
    & EmpAppID & ", " _
    & """" & lblQuestion.Caption & """, " _
    & """" & txtResponse.Text & """)"
```

Then move on to the next question:

```
RSQuestions.MoveNext
```

and make sure there is a next question:

```
If RSQuestions.EOF Then
```

If no questions remain, let the user know that he or she is finished:

```
MsgBox "That is the end of the application."
```

and close the form:

```
DoCmd.Close
```

Otherwise, display the text of the next question:

```
lblQuestion.Caption = RSQuestions("Question")
```

and clear the previous response:

```
txtResponse.Text = ""
```

Report

Employee Applications Report

The Employee Applications report shows the details for applications filled out by potential employees. It is based directly on the EmployeeApplications table. The report contains a sub-report called Responses. This sub-report lists all the responses for the potential employee on the application.

CHAPTER 4

Company Management

ON THE CD:

PO.mdb

Equipment Check Out.mdb

Databases to Solve Internal Business Needs

In this chapter, we will look at two databases that are used by companies to meet specific internal needs. The first is the Purchase Order database, which provides the functionality needed to enable employees to submit and review purchase order requests. The other database in this chapter is the Equipment Check Out database. This database tracks when equipment is being used and by whom.

Purchase Order Database

The Purchase Order database enables employees to make and review the statuses of purchase order requests. The database application uses security to differentiate between employees and managers. Each group has different forms and reports to meet their specific needs.

Sample Walk-through

Securing the Database

The Purchase Order database has different forms and reports that are used by employees and managers. Thus, security is used in this application to monitor who is using the database and what the user should be able to do.

On the CD for this chapter, you will find the database as usual, but you will also see an MDW file. This is an Access Work-group file and it contains login information for all users in this database application. It was created using the MS Access Workgroup Administrator, which you should find a shortcut to in the Office subfolder of your MS Office folder. When you double-click on that shortcut, you will see the tool shown in Figure 4-1.

To create a new workgroup file, click on the Create button. When you do, the dialog shown in Figure 4-2 appears.

Figure 4-1

The Workgroup Administrator

Workgroup Administrator

Name:

Company:

Workgroup   C:\PROGRAM FILES\MICROSOFT OFFICE2000\OFFICE\SYSTEM.MDW

Your workgroup is defined by the workgroup information file that is used at startup. You can create a new workgroup by creating a new information file, or join an existing workgroup by changing the information file that is used at startup.

[Create...]   [Join...]   [Exit]

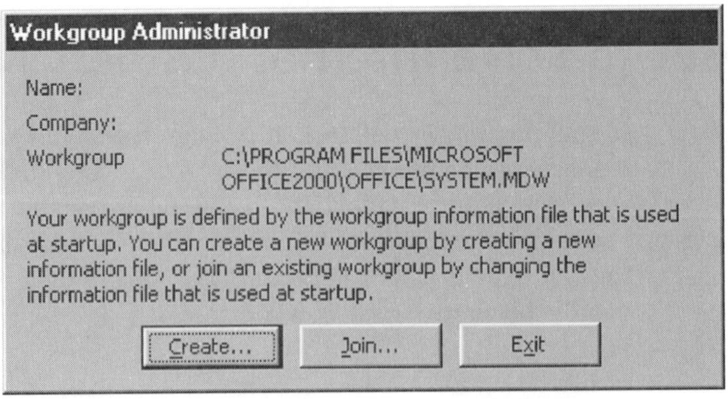

Figure 4-2

Creating a
workgroup file

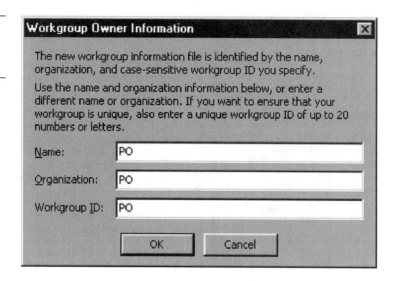

After you enter the information in this dialog, you are then asked to supply a file name for the workgroup file. Once that is selected, you have created your workgroup file and have joined it. The term join means that this is now the default security file you will use whenever you open Access or any Access database. Remember the name of the original workgroup file that you used so you can return to it at a later date if you need to move back to a non-secure environment.

NOTE:
Since the workgroup file is provided on the CD of this book, you don't need to recreate it. You can just use the Join button to join it.

Once you have created a new workgroup file, you need to make some changes to the accounts contained in it to make it secure. To do this, start Access and select the User and Group Accounts menu item displayed in Figure 4-3.

Figure 4-3

Selecting User
and Group
Accounts

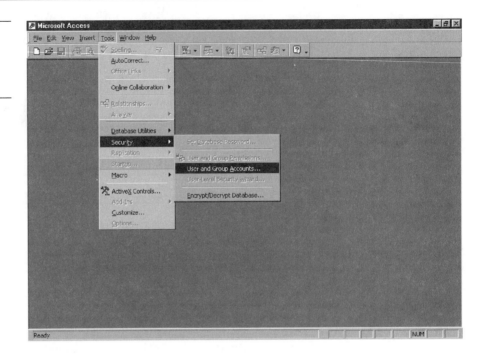

You now need to add a new database administrator. This is done so that
you can get rid of the default administrator. To do so, press the New button and provide the information for the new user. Then add the user to the
Admins group, as shown in Figure 4-4.

Here the new administrator is called Manager and has been added to
the Admins group as well as the Users group. All users belong to the
Users group.

Next, you need to log in as the new administrator in order to make further changes, but this can't be done until you give the old administrator a
password. Without a password in the Admin account, Access assumes that
you aren't using security and does not open the database with a login
screen. So, go to the Change Logon Password tab and supply the Admin
with a password, as shown in Figure 4-5. Note that the old password for
the Admin user is blank.

Figure 4-4

Adding a new
user

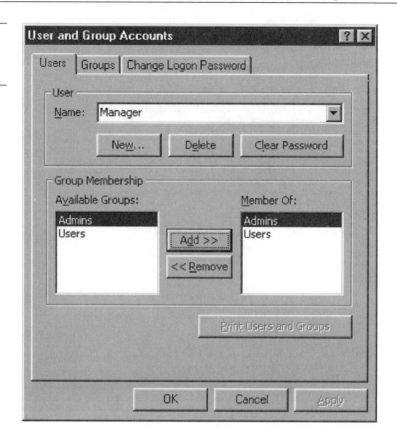

Now you need to restart Access and return to the User and Group
Accounts dialog without opening a database. When this is done, Access
prompts you for a user name and password. You'll need to enter in as the
manager, which currently doesn't have a password. Select the Change
Logon Password tab and supply the manager with a password, as shown
in Figure 4-6.

As with any newly created account, the manager's current password is
blank. In the workgroup file for this database, the manager is given the
password Manager.

Once again, restart Access and enter the User and Group Accounts dialog. When you do, you are prompted to log in. Log in now as the new
administrator with the password, as shown in Figure 4-7.

Figure 4-5

Supplying a
password to the
Admin user

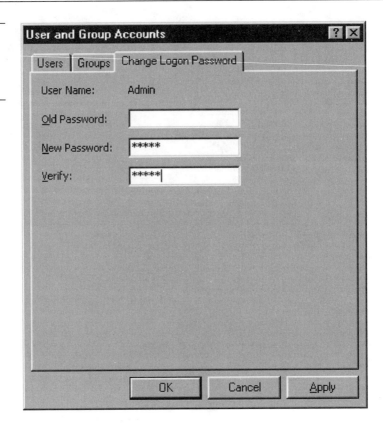

The next problem is the fact that the original administrator, Admin, still has full privileges on any database you create with this workgroup file. This shouldn't be allowed since it is a default account and provides anyone with easy access into your application just by opening the database with the default workgroup file. To do this, select the Admin user on the Users tab and remove it from the Admins group, as shown in Figure 4-8. Note that you cannot remove the Admin user from the Users group and that Access does not enable you to delete the Admin account.

Now you can create the new database that should be secured. Since you are currently logged in as the new administrator, that account will own this new database. After the new database has been created, you need to select the User and Group Permissions menu item displayed in Figure 4-9.

Figure 4-6

Supplying a
password for the
manager

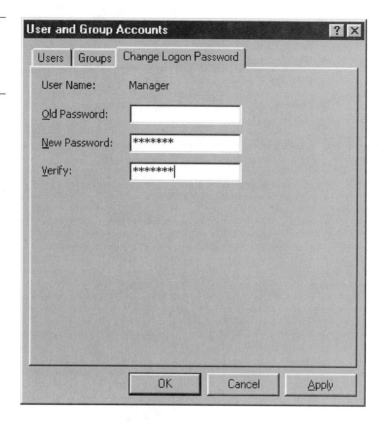

Now, remove the permissions from the Users group. Remember that by
default all users belong to this group, which by default has full access to
all the tables, forms, reports, and other objects in the database application. You could provide only limited access to users, but they would still
have full capabilities because they belong to the users group.

To prevent this, select the Groups list on the Permissions tab and then
select Users. Then remove all privileges from the group for every object in
your database, as shown in Figure 4-10. Here their permissions are being
removed from the database, but the group also needs its permissions
revoked from all the objects in the database.

To make your database really secure, you must perform one final step.
You need to encrypt it. If you don't encrypt your database, an individual

Figure 4-7

Logging in as the new administrator

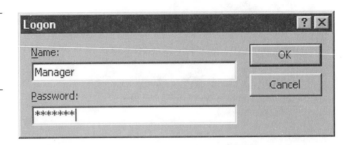

Figure 4-8

Removing the Admin from the Admins group

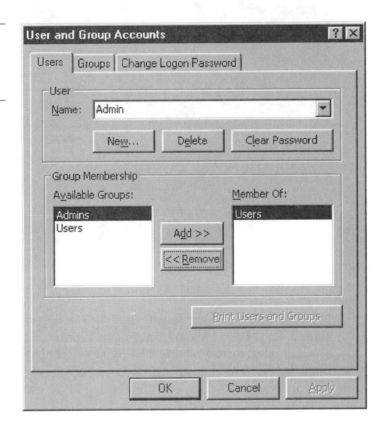

could open the database in a text editor and view its data. To encrypt your database, close it and select the Encrypt/Decrypt Database menu item shown in Figure 4-11. Access then prompts you for the name of the database to encrypt and what you want to call the encrypted database.

For this specific database, a couple more steps are taken. A new group called DBUsers has been created. This group is to be used by the employees to provide them with access to the basic functions of the application.

Figure 4-9

Selecting the
User and Group
Permissions
menu item

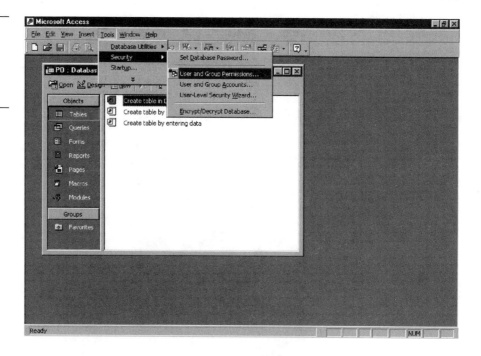

The group is given permission only to the tables, forms, macros, and reports that enable them their basic functionality.

Then each employee needs to be added as a user. Two have been added to this workgroup, J.J. and Sarah. Both of their passwords are left blank, and they are then added to the DBUsers group. Each of these employees, as well as the manager, must appear as a record in the Employees table that is looked at later in this chapter.

The Employee's View of the Database

When an employee enters the Purchase Order database, he or she sees the Users Menu shown in Figure 4-12.

Here the user can enter a new purchase order by pressing the first button. This form is displayed in Figure 4-13.

The form only enables the user to enter new purchase order requests. The Employee field is automatically populated so that it shows the name of the current user. The field is locked so the user cannot change it. The When Requested field is also locked. Once the user enters the request, he or she cannot change or delete it.

Figure 4-10

Removing
permissions from
the Users group

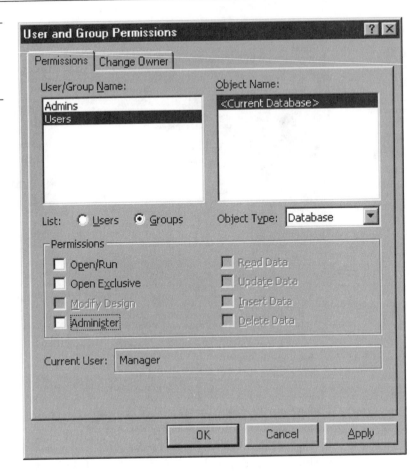

Users can, however, view any of their requests by pressing the Your
Purchase Orders button on the Users Menu form. This form is displayed
in Figure 4-14.

The Your POs form opens and displays only the users' requests. All the
fields are locked so the users can only see their requests. This gives them
the opportunity to see if the manager has reviewed the request and what
the decision is. If the user presses the Preview Report button, he or she
sees a report for this current purchase order, as shown in Figure 4-15.

Figure 4-11

Selecting the
Encrypt/Decrypt
menu item

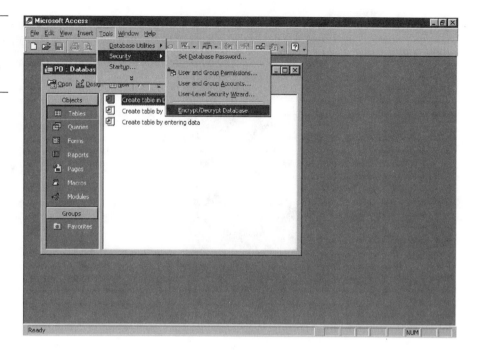

The Manager's View of the Database

When the manager enters the database, he or she sees a different menu
than what the employees see. This menu is displayed in Figure 4-16.

The manager actually has the permission to do anything in the database, and the Manager account is the owner of the database. The main
role of the manager is to process the purchase order requests, which is
done by pressing the Pending POs button. The manager then sees the
form shown in Figure 4-17.

The form displays only those requests that currently have the status of
Pending. The manager can then provide decisions on them.

The Manager Menu also enables the manager to work with employee
records. This is done through the Employee form shown in Figure 4-18.

Each of the employees that can log into the database application needs
to have an Employee record. This data is used to automatically fill in the
Employee field on the PO Request form.

Figure 4-12

Users menu

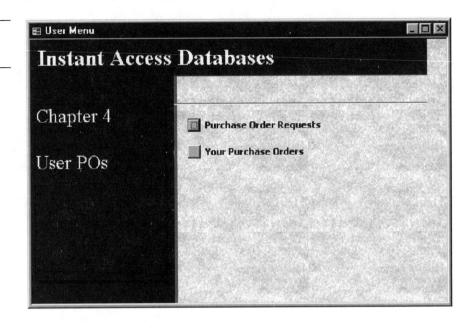

Figure 4-13

PO Request form

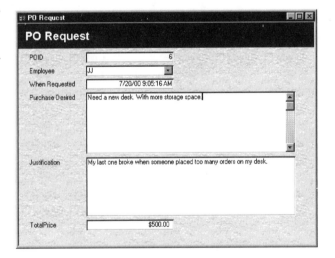

Figure 4-14

Your POs form

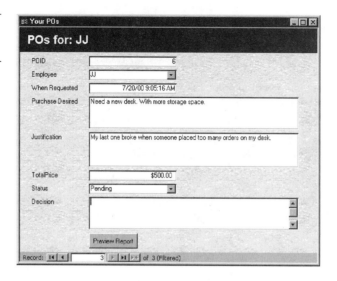

Figure 4-15

A purchase order report

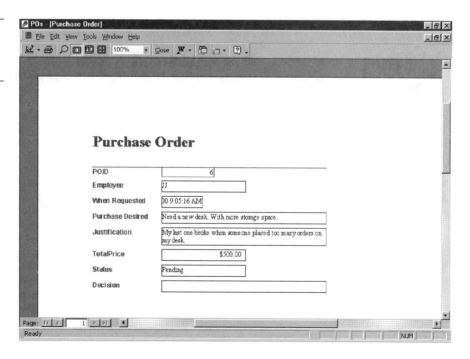

Figure 4-16

The Manager
Menu form

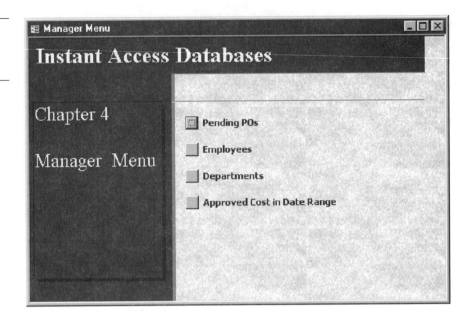

Figure 4-17

The Pending POs
form

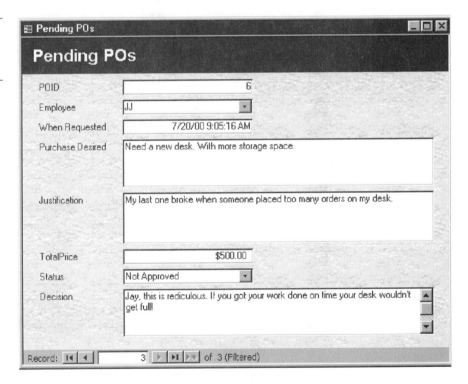

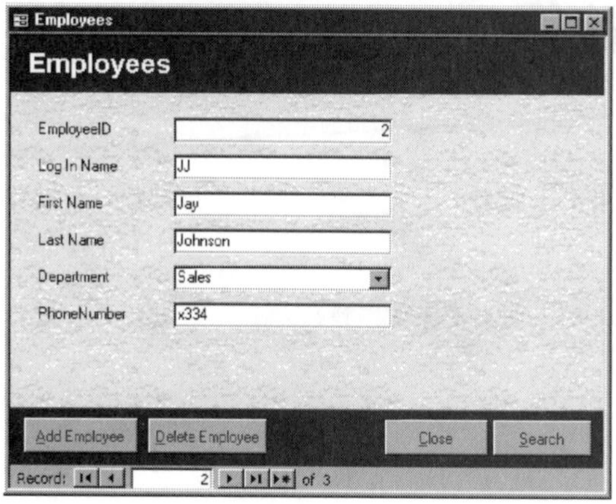

Figure 4-18

The Employee form

Each of the employees is from a specific department. The manager can add, view, edit, and delete departments through the Department form displayed in Figure 4-19.

The department information is then used on the summary report "Approved Cost in Date Range" to display the amount of approved purchase orders per department. This report is displayed in Figure 4-20.

When the manager first opens the report, he or she is asked for a date range when the requests must have been made. Thus, the manager can see the amount of approved purchases on a weekly, monthly, or quarterly basis, or in any other date range.

Table Definitions and Relationships

POs Table

The POs table is the top-level table in the database. It stores all the information about a purchase order request. The employee enters some of this information and the manager enters the rest of it.

Employees Table

Each of the employees that can log into the database must have a record in this table, which stores all the information about the employees. The table is in a one-to-many relationship with the POs table. Each employee can make many requests, but a single employee submits each request.

Figure 4-19

The Departments form

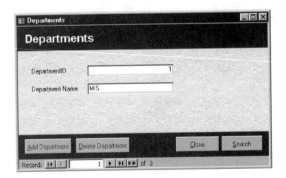

Figure 4-20

The Approved Cost in Date Range report

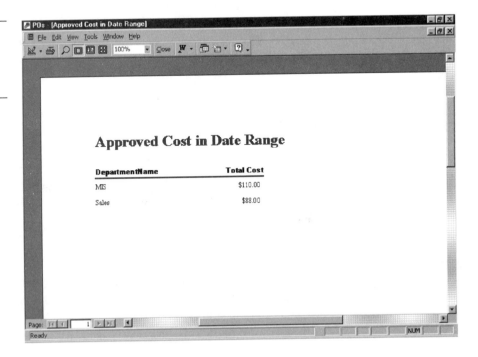

Departments Table

The Departments table stores the names of the departments used in the Employees table. It has a one-to-many relationship with the Employees table. Each employee belongs to a single department, but each department can have numerous employees.

Field Specifications

POs Table

The field specifications for the POs table are displayed in Table 4-1. The POID field is the primary key for the table, uniquely identifying each record. In code, the Employee field is automatically set to the user who is currently logged into the database. The field is a foreign key that links this table to the Employees table.

The WhenRequested field has the following value in the Default Value property:

```
Now()
```

so it is set to the current system date and time.

The Status field has a default value of Pending. It is displayed as a combo box and has the following values listed in it:

```
"Pending";"Approved";"Not Approved"
```

	Field Name	Field Type	Notes
Table 4-1	POID	AutoNumber	Primary Key
The POs Table Field Specifications	Employee	Text	Length = 50, Foreign Key
	WhenRequested	Date/Time	
	PurchaseDesired	Memo	
	Justification	Memo	
	TotalPrice	Currency	
	Status	Text	Length = 50
	Decision	Memo	

The Limit to List property is set to Yes, so the manager must choose one of those values.

Employees Table

The field specifications for the Employees table are displayed in Table 4-2. The EmployeeID field is the primary key and is automatically populated when a new record is added to this table since the type is AutoNumber. The LogInName field must match the exact login name used by this user to enter the database.

The DepartmentID field is a foreign key that links this table to the Employees table. The field is displayed as a combo box and has the following SQL text in its Row Source property:

```
SELECT [Departments].[DepartmentID], [Departments].[DepartmentName] FROM Departments;
```

The bound column is the ID of the department, but the manager would see the name of the department when he or she is selecting a value from this list.

Departments Table

The field specifications for the Departments table are displayed in Table 4-3. The DepartmentID field is the primary key for the table. The DepartmentName field stores the name of the department.

	Field Name	Field Type	Notes
Table 4-2	EmployeeID	AutoNumber	Primary Key
The Employees Table Field Specifications	LogInName	Text	Length = 50
	FirstName	Text	Length = 50
	LastName	Text	Length = 50
	DepartmentID	Number	Type = Long, Foreign Key
	PhoneNumber	Text	Length = 50

	Field Name	Field Type	Notes
Table 4-3	DepartmentID	AutoNumber	Primary Key
The Departments Table Field Specifications	DepartmentName	Text	Length = 50

Forms

Entering the Application

Typically, when a user enters one of your databases, you show them some sort of menu. Selecting that form in the Startup dialog box for the database application usually does this. In the Purchase Order database, however, you need to display a different form based on who is logging into the database. Another way to take an action when your application starts is by creating a macro and calling it AutoExec. When you open a database in Access, it always first checks to see if the database contains a macro with that name. If it does, then Access runs that macro.

In this database, you have such a macro. It does one thing; it runs a procedure that you have defined in a code module. The action in the macro is set to

```
RunCode
```

This action enables you to launch a function that is in one of your code modules. The Function Name parameter for this macro action is set to

```
OnDBOpen ()
```

which is the name of a function located in a module called PublicProcs. That function has the following code:

```
Public Function OnDBOpen()
    If Application.CurrentUser = "Manager" Then
        DoCmd.OpenForm "Manager Menu"
    Else
        DoCmd.OpenForm "User Menu"
    End If
End Function
```

The procedure is created as a function, even though it doesn't have a return value since that is required for the RunCode macro action. Use the

CurrentUser method of the Application object to retrieve the login name of the current user and check to see if that user is the manager:

```
If Application.CurrentUser = "Manager" Then
```

If it is, display the Manager Menu form:

```
DoCmd.OpenForm "Manager Menu"
```

Otherwise, the User Menu form is opened:

```
DoCmd.OpenForm "User Menu"
```

User Menu Form

The code on the User Menu form provides access to the Employees section of the database application. When the user clicks on the Purchase Order Requests button, the OpenForm method is used to open the PO Request form:

```
Private Sub Command23_Click()
    DoCmd.OpenForm "PO Request"
End Sub
```

When the user clicks on the Your Purchase Orders button, he or she is taken to the Your POs form:

```
Private Sub Command25_Click()
    DoCmd.OpenForm "Your POs"
End Sub
```

Manager Menu Form

The code on the Manager Menu form provides the manager with access to the forms and report for their management of the Purchase Order database. When the manager presses the Pending POs button, he or she is taken to the Pending POs form:

```
Private Sub Command23_Click()
    DoCmd.OpenForm "Pending POs"
End Sub
```

The next button on the form uses the OpenForm method to take the manager to the Employees form:

```
Private Sub Command25_Click()
    DoCmd.OpenForm "Employees"
End Sub
```

The third button uses the OpenForm method of the DoCmd object to take the manager to the Departments form:

```
Private Sub Command27_Click()
    DoCmd.OpenForm "Departments"
End Sub
```

The last button on the form uses the OpenReport method to show the Approved Cost in Date Range report in preview mode:

```
Private Sub Command29_Click()
    DoCmd.OpenReport "Approved Cost in Date Range", acViewPreview
End Sub
```

PO Request Form

The code on the PO Request form places the name of the current user logged in to the Employee field:

```
Private Sub Form_BeforeInsert(Cancel As Integer)
    [Employee] = Application.CurrentUser
End Sub
```

This is done in the BeforeInsert event of the form, which fires before a new record is inserted into the table. The code uses the CurrentUser property of the Application object to retrieve the name of the current user:

```
[Employee] = Application.CurrentUser
```

Your POs Form

The Your POs form has two code blocks. The form should only display the requests made by the current logged-in user. The Open Event of the Form object contains the code block that takes this action:

```
Private Sub Form_Load()
    Me.AllowFilters = True
    Me.Filter = "[Employee] = """ & Application.CurrentUser & """"
    Me.FilterOn = True
    Me.AllowFilters = False
    Label16.Caption = "POs for: " & Application.CurrentUser
End Sub
```

You don't want to allow the user to change the filters because that would permit him or her to remove the filter and see all the requests. Thus, set it to default at False. However, you also need to filter the form so that only those records that belong to this user are displayed. To do this, first change the AllowFilters property so that filtering is allowed:

```
Me.AllowFilters = True
```

Then set the filter so that only those records for the logged-in employee are displayed:

```
Me.Filter = "[Employee] = """ & Application.CurrentUser & """"
```

Now turn on the following filter,

```
Me.FilterOn = True
```

and remove the ability to use filters:

```
Me.AllowFilters = False
```

Last, place the name of the current user in the caption of this form:

```
Label16.Caption = "POs for: " & Application.CurrentUser
```

The other code block fires when the Print Report button is pressed:

```
Private Sub Command28_Click()
    DoCmd.OpenReport "Purchase Order", acPreview, , "[POID] = " & [POID]
End Sub
```

The OpenReport method of the DoCmd object is used to open the report named Purchase Order in preview mode, displaying the contents of the current purchase order:

```
DoCmd.OpenReport "Purchase Order", acPreview, , "[POID] = " & [POID]
```

Pending POs Form

The Pending POs form is used by the manager to process any pending purchase orders. The first code block fires when the form is first opened:

```
Private Sub Form_Open(Cancel As Integer)
    If Application.CurrentUser <> "Manager" Then
        Cancel = True
    End If
End Sub
```

For added protection, make sure that the person opening this form is the manager:

```
If Application.CurrentUser <> "Manager" Then
```

If it isn't, cancel the loading of the form:

```
Cancel = True
```

The other code block fires when the form is loaded:

```
Private Sub Form_Load()
    Me.Filter = "[Status] = ""Pending"""
    Me.FilterOn = True
End Sub
```

Set the filter so that only those records with a status of Pending are displayed:

```
Me.Filter = "[Status] = ""Pending"""
```

Then turn on that filter:

```
Me.FilterOn = True
```

Departments and Employees Forms

The Departments and Employees forms have nearly identical code, so they are discussed here collectively. Both forms have code that fires when the Add, Delete, Search, and Close buttons are pressed. The first code block fires when the Add button is pressed:

```
Private Sub Command17_Click()
    DoCmd.GoToRecord , , acNewRec
    [DepartmentName].SetFocus
End Sub
```

The GoToRecord method is used to move the record pointer to a new record:

```
DoCmd.GoToRecord , , acNewRec
```

Then set the focus to the DepartmentName field so the user can start entering data:

```
[DepartmentName].SetFocus
```

The next code block fires when the Delete button is pressed:

```
Private Sub Command18_Click()
    On Error GoTo HandleError
    DoCmd.DoMenuItem acFormBar, acEditMenu, 8, , acMenuVer70
    DoCmd.DoMenuItem acFormBar, acEditMenu, 6, , acMenuVer70
    [DepartmentName].SetFocus
    Exit Sub
HandleError:
    If Err.Number <> 2501 Then
        MsgBox Err.Number & " " & Err.Description
    End If
End Sub
```

Start by telling the compiler that you will trap errors that occur by having the code flow to a label called HandleError:

```
On Error GoTo HandleError
```

Then delete the current record:

```
DoCmd.DoMenuItem acFormBar, acEditMenu, 8, , acMenuVer70
DoCmd.DoMenuItem acFormBar, acEditMenu, 6, , acMenuVer70
```

If the record deletion succeeds, set the focus back to the detail section:

```
[DepartmentName].SetFocus
```

and exit this procedure:

```
Exit Sub
```

If an error occurs, the code flows here:

```
HandleError:
```

Ignore the error that occurs if the user cancels the record deletion,

```
If Err.Number <> 2501 Then
```

but any other error message is displayed:

```
MsgBox Err.Number & " " & Err.Description
```

The next code block fires when the Search button is pressed:

```
Private Sub Command19_Click()
    Screen.PreviousControl.SetFocus
    DoCmd.DoMenuItem acFormBar, acEditMenu, 10, , acMenuVer70
End Sub
```

Start by moving the focus back to the last control, which is the field the user wants to search:

```
Screen.PreviousControl.SetFocus
```

Then open the Access Search dialog:

```
DoCmd.DoMenuItem acFormBar, acEditMenu, 10, , acMenuVer70
```

The last code block fires when the Close button is pressed. It uses the Close method of the DoCmd object to close the current form:

```
Private Sub Command20_Click()
    DoCmd.Close
End Sub
```

Reports

Purchase Order Report

The Purchase Order report displays the contents of a purchase order. The report is not based on a query, but instead is based directly on the POs table. The report is accessed by the user pressing the Report button on the Your POs form. When the user does so, the report is filtered so that only the current purchase order is displayed.

The Approved Cost in Date Range Report

The Approved Cost in Date Range report displays the total dollar amount for all the approved purchase orders in a given date range that are grouped by the name of the department. The report is based on the Approved Cost in Date Range query, which has the following SQL syntax:

```
SELECT Departments.DepartmentName, Sum(POs.TotalPrice) AS [Total Cost]
FROM POs INNER JOIN (Departments INNER JOIN Employees
ON Departments.DepartmentID = Employees.DepartmentID)
ON POs.Employee = Employees.LogInName
WHERE (((POs.WhenRequested)>=[Start Date] And (POs.WhenRequested)<=[End
Date]) AND ((POs.Status)="Approved")) GROUP BY Departments.DepartmentName;
```

Three tables are needed for this query. The POs table is joined to the Employees table, which is joined to the Departments table. Since the Start Date and End Date fields are not known fields in this table, Access prompts the user for those values.

Equipment Check Out Database

The Equipment Check Out database enables users to reserve equipment that is a shared resource in a company. The database application makes sure that the user's request for a piece of equipment does not interfere with someone else's reservation.

As you review this database, note the use of the Calendar control and think about how you might use it to enhance your own database applications. Also note that the code is used to make sure the equipment can be reserved during the requested time. Look closely at the SQL used to generate the Equipment Status report.

Sample Walk-through

When the user first enters the Equipment database application, the menu shown in Figure 4-21 appears.

Figure 4-21

The Equipment Check Out menu

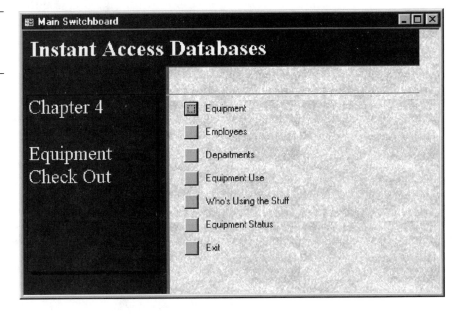

From this menu, the user can access all the forms and reports used in this application. The heart of the application is in the Equipment form, which is displayed in Figure 4-22.

The Equipment form has three pages. The first page is the General page and enables the user to enter the basic information about the equipment. If the user clicks on the Grid button, he or she sees the second page, shown in Figure 4-23.

The Grid page lists the reservations that have been made for this equipment. The records in the grid cannot be edited or added to. To check out equipment, the user must go to the Calendar page, which is displayed in Figure 4-24.

The Calendar page is where the users check out equipment. Here they use the Calendar objects to select the start and end dates of their requests. They also enter the name of the person who is checking the equipment out and any note for this request.

When the user presses the Reserve button, the code ensures that the end date is after or the same as the start date and that the user has selected an employee. The code also makes sure that no one else has this

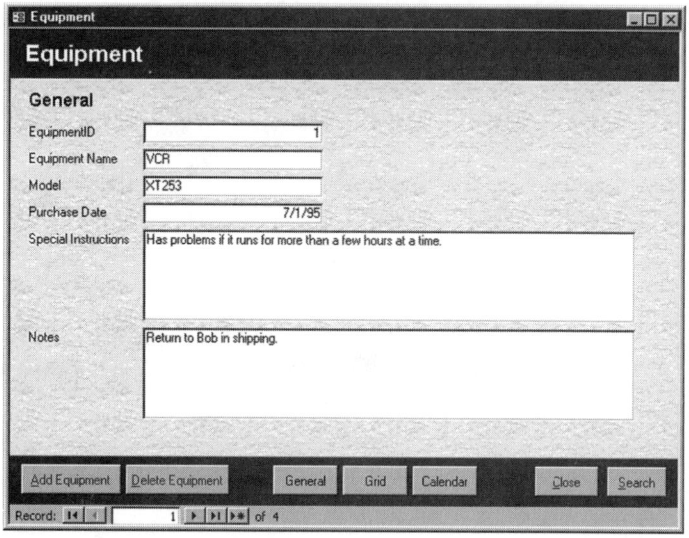

Figure 4-22

The General page from the Equipment form

Figure 4-23

The Grid page
from the
Equipment form

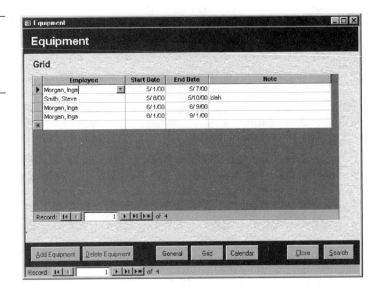

Figure 4-24

The Calendar
page from the
Equipment form

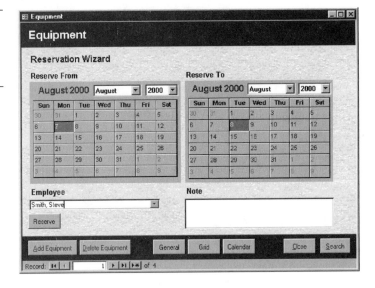

equipment reserved during the requested time period. If someone else has the equipment checked out in the timeframe selected, the message displayed in Figure 4-25 is shown.

If the user enters valid dates, then his or her request is added for this equipment and it appears on the Grid page. The names listed in the Employee combo box are entered through the Employees form displayed in Figure 4-26.

From the Employees form, the user can add, edit, delete, and view the employee records. Each of the employees belongs to a specific department. The department names are managed through the Departments form shown in Figure 4-27.

The user also has three forms that can be selected from the menu. The first is the Equipment Use report shown in Figure 4-28.

The Equipment Use report is a summary report that shows the total number of days that a piece of equipment has been checked out. Managers could use this report to gauge the need for additional purchases.

The next report accessible through the Menu is the Who's Using the Stuff report, displayed in Figure 4-29. This report groups the checkout

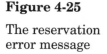

Figure 4-25

The reservation error message

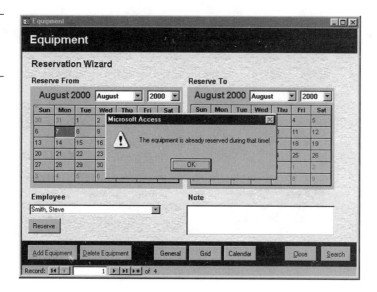

Figure 4-26

The Employees
form

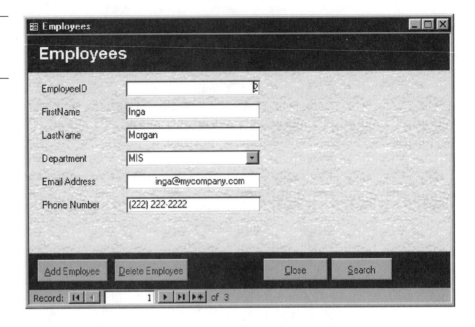

Figure 4-26

The Employees
form

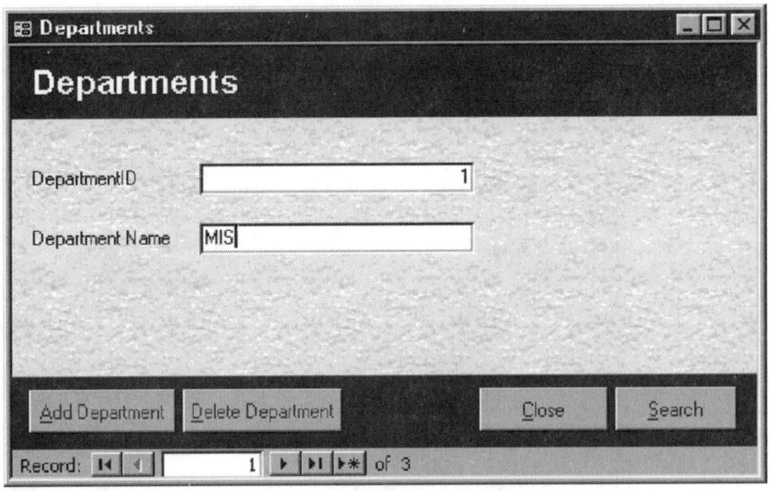

Figure 4-27

The Departments
form

Figure 4-28

The Equipment Use report

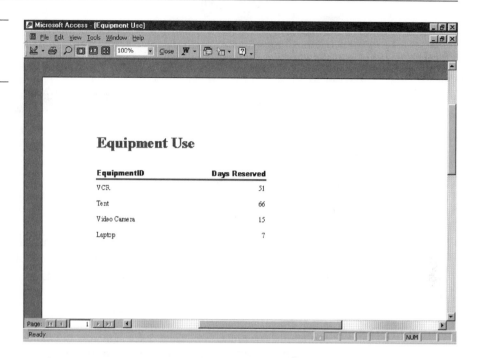

Figure 4-29

The Who's Using the Stuff report

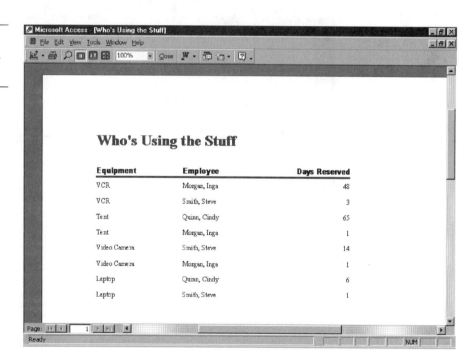

information first by the name of the equipment and then by the employee. It also shows how many days each employee has used each piece of equipment. The last report is called Equipment Status and is shown in Figure 4-30.

This Equipment Status report shows the status of the equipment. If the piece of equipment is checked out, the report shows whom has the equipment. Otherwise, the report shows the equipment as available.

Table Definitions and Relationships

Equipment Table

The main table in this database is the Equipment table. This table stores the general information about a piece of equipment. It relates directly or indirectly with all the other tables in the database.

Figure 4-30

The Equipment Status report

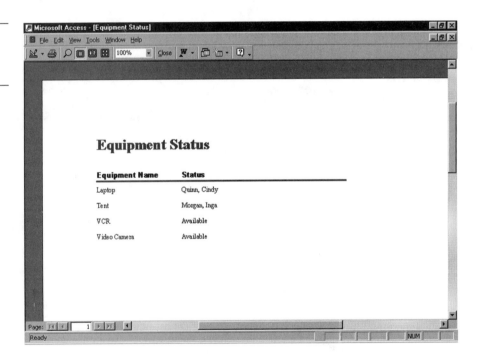

Employees Table

The Employees table stores the basic information about each of the employees. This information is then used to indicate whom a piece of equipment is checked out to.

CheckOuts Table

Each employee can check out more than one piece of equipment, and each piece of equipment can be checked out by many employees. This means that you have a many-to-many relationship. The CheckOuts table acts as the go-between table, satisfying this many-to-many relationship. The Checkouts table is in a one-to-many relationship with both the Equipment table and the Employees table.

Departments Table

The Departments table stores the names of the departments used in the employee records. The table is in a one-to-many relationship with the Employees table. Each employee works for a specific department, but each department can have many employees.

Field Specifications

Equipment Table

The field specifications for the Equipment table are displayed in Table 4-4. The EquipmentID field is the primary key for the table since it uniquely identifies each record. The rest of the fields store the basic information about the equipment.

Table 4-4

The Equipment Table Field Specifications

Field Name	Field Type	Notes
EquipmentID	AutoNumber	Primary Key
EquipmentName	Text	Length = 50
Model	Text	Length = 50
PurchaseDate	Date/Time	
SpecialInstructions	Memo	
Notes	Memo	

Employees Table

The field specifications for the Employees table are displayed in Table 4-5. The EmployeeID field is the primary key for the table. The DepartmentID field acts as a foreign key, linking this table to the Departments table. The field is displayed as a combo box since the Display Control property is set to Combo Box. The Row Source property contains the following SQL text:

```
SELECT [Departments].[DepartmentID], [Departments].[DepartmentName] FROM Departments;
```

Table 4-5

The Employees Table Field Specifications

Field Name	Field Type	Notes
EmployeeID	AutoNumber	Primary Key
FirstName	Text	Length = 50
LastName	Text	Length = 50
DepartmentID	Number	Type = Long, Foreign Key
EmailAddress	Text	Length = 50
PhoneNumber	Text	Length = 50

The first field is bound, so the ID of the department is stored in the database, but the name of the department is what the user sees. To ease data entry, the EmailAddress field has the following input mask:

```
!???????????????"
```

This mask enables the user to enter the first part of the email address, which proceeds the domain name of the company, so the user doesn't have to type out the company name every time.

CheckOuts Table

The field specifications for the CheckOuts table are displayed in Table 4-6. The CheckOutID field is the primary key for this table.

Table 4-6	Field Name	Field Type	Notes
The CheckOuts Table Field Specifications	CheckOutID	AutoNumber	Primary Key
	EquipmentID	Number	Type = Long, Foreign Key
	EmployeeID	Number	Type = Long, Foreign Key
	StartDate	Date/Time	
	EndDate	Date/Time	
	Note	Memo	

The EquipmentID field is a foreign key that links this table to the Equipment table, while the EmployeeID field links this table to the Employees table. These two fields together satisfy the many-to-many relationship between the Equipment and Employees tables.

You only want a date entered in the date fields, without a particular time. Therefore, the following Input Mask is used to limit the data entry to just the date in the StartDate and EndDate fields:

```
99/99/00;0;_
```

Departments Table

The field specifications for the Departments table are displayed in Table 4-7. The DepartmentID field is the primary key for the table, while the DepartmentName field stores the name of the department.

Table 4-7	Field Name	Field Type	Notes
The Departments Table Field Specifications	DepartmentID	AutoNumber	Primary Key
	DepartmentName	Text	Length = 50

Forms

Switchboard Form

The Switchboard form is used to navigate through the forms and reports in the Equipment Checkout database. It was created using the Switchboard Wizard, which is accessible within Access through the Tools/Database Utilities/Switchboard Manager menu item. Only the look and layout of the form produced by that wizard have been altered.

Equipment Form

The code on the Equipment form provides the functionality for the footer buttons and enables the user to check out equipment. When the user presses the General button, he or she is taken to the first page of the form using the GoToPage method of the DoCmd object:

```
Private Sub Command33_Click()
    DoCmd.GoToPage 1
End Sub
```

The next code block fires when the user clicks on the Grid button. It sends the user to the second page of the form, which contains the subform showing the equipment checkout history:

```
Private Sub Command34_Click()
    DoCmd.GoToPage 2
End Sub
```

When the user wants to check out a piece of equipment, he or she first presses the Calendar button. The code behind the Click event of that button uses the GoToPage method to take the visitor to the third page of this form:

```
Private Sub Command35_Click()
    DoCmd.GoToPage 3
End Sub
```

The next code block fires when the user clicks on the Add button:

```
Private Sub CommandAdd_Click()
    DoCmd.GoToRecord , , acNewRec
    [EquipmentName].SetFocus
End Sub
```

Start by moving the record pointer to a new record:

```
DoCmd.GoToRecord , , acNewRec
```

Then set the focus to the EquipmentName field so the user can start entering data:

```
[EquipmentName].SetFocus
```

The next code block fires when the Delete button is clicked:

```
Private Sub CommandDelete_Click()
    On Error GoTo HandleError
    DoCmd.DoMenuItem acFormBar, acEditMenu, 8, , acMenuVer70
    DoCmd.DoMenuItem acFormBar, acEditMenu, 6, , acMenuVer70
    [EquipmentName].SetFocus
    Exit Sub
HandleError:
    If Err.Number <> 2501 Then
        MsgBox Err.Number & " " & Err.Description
    End If
End Sub
```

Start by telling the compiler that you will process errors that occur in this code block:

```
On Error GoTo HandleError
```

Then delete the current record:

```
DoCmd.DoMenuItem acFormBar, acEditMenu, 8, , acMenuVer70
DoCmd.DoMenuItem acFormBar, acEditMenu, 6, , acMenuVer70
```

If the deletion is successful, the code flows here and you return the focus to the detail section of the form:

```
[EquipmentName].SetFocus
```

Then exit the procedure:

```
Exit Sub
```

If an error were to occur, the code would flow here:

```
HandleError:
```

Then make sure that the error isn't due to the user canceling the record deletion:

```
If Err.Number <> 2501 Then
```

Any other error is displayed to the user in the form of a message box:

```
MsgBox Err.Number & " " & Err.Description
```

When the user presses the Search button, the Click event of that button fires:

```
Private Sub CommandSearch_Click()
    Screen.PreviousControl.SetFocus
    DoCmd.DoMenuItem acFormBar, acEditMenu, 10, , acMenuVer70
End Sub
```

When a user wants to search a field, he or she selects that field and then presses the Search button. So the field you need to search is the field where the user was last. You can return to that field by using the SetFocus method of the PreviousControl object:

```
Screen.PreviousControl.SetFocus
```

Then open the Access Search dialog:

```
DoCmd.DoMenuItem acFormBar, acEditMenu, 10, , acMenuVer70
```

The last code block uses the Close method of the DoCmd object to close this form when the Close button is pressed:

```
Private Sub CommandClose_Click()
    DoCmd.Close
End Sub
```

The last code block on this form fires when the user presses the Reserve button. The code makes sure the checkout request is valid. If it is, it adds the request to the database. Otherwise, the problem is reported to the user.

```
Private Sub Command49_Click()
    Dim MyDB As DAO.Database
    Dim rs As DAO.Recordset
    Dim TheNote As String
    Dim TheEmployee As String
    txtNote.SetFocus
    TheNote = txtNote.Text
    ComboEmployee.SetFocus
```

```
TheEmployee = IIf(IsNull(ComboEmployee.Column(0)), 0, ComboEmployee.Column(0))
If CDate(CCFrom.Value) > CDate(CCTo.Value) Then
    MsgBox "The From Date must be before the To Date.", vbExclamation
ElseIf IsNull(TheEmployee) Or TheEmployee = 0 Then
    MsgBox "You must select an employee to check the equipment out to.", vbExclamation
Else
    Set MyDB = CurrentDb
    Set rs = MyDB.OpenRecordset("Select CheckOutID from CheckOuts " _
        & "Where ([StartDate] <= #" & CCFrom.Value _
        & "# and [EndDate] >= #" & CCFrom.Value & "# " _
        & "and [EquipmentID] = " & [EquipmentID] & ") or " _
        & "([StartDate] <= #" & CCTo.Value _
        & "# and [EndDate] >= #" & CCTo.Value & "# " _
        & "and [EquipmentID] = " & [EquipmentID] & ")", dbOpenSnapshot)
    If rs.EOF Then
        MyDB.Execute "Insert Into CheckOuts (EquipmentID, EmployeeID, " _
            & "StartDate, EndDate, [Note]) Values (" _
            & [EquipmentID] & ", " _
            & TheEmployee & ", " _
            & """" & CCFrom & """, " _
            & """" & CCTo & """, " _
            & """" & TheNote & " "")"
        CheckOuts_subform.Requery
        MsgBox "Reservation placed!", vbInformation
    Else
        MsgBox "The equipment is already reserved during that time!", vbExclamation
    End If
End If
End Sub
```

You also need a Database object:

```
Dim MyDB As DAO.Database
```

and a Recordset object to retrieve data from this database:

```
Dim rs As DAO.Recordset
```

This variable temporarily stores the value of the note entered for this checkout request:

```
Dim TheNote As String
```

The following one stores the employee selected for this request:

```
Dim TheEmployee As String
```

To retrieve the text in the note text box, you need to set the focus of that control:

```
txtNote.SetFocus
```

Then you can set your temporary variable to that value:

```
TheNote = txtNote.Text
```

You need to do the same for the Employee combo box:

```
ComboEmployee.SetFocus
```

You want to retrieve the ID, not the name, of the employee selected, so you can't use the Text property. Instead, use the columns collection and retrieve the value in the first column. But if the user has not selected a value, this field has a value of null, so check to see if the value in the combo box is null. If it is, set your temporary variable to a 0; otherwise, it is set to the value of the employee's ID:

```
TheEmployee = IIf(IsNull(ComboEmployee.Column(0)), 0, ComboEmployee.Column(0))
```

Next, make sure that the from date entered is before or the same as the end date:

```
If CDate(CCFrom.Value) > CDate(CCTo.Value) Then
```

If it isn't, report the problem to the user:

```
MsgBox "The From Date must be before the To Date.", vbExclamation
```

Next, make sure the user has selected an employee for the checkout request:

```
ElseIf IsNull(TheEmployee) Or TheEmployee = 0 Then
```

If he or she hasn't, use a message box to inform the user of the problem:

```
MsgBox "You must select an employee to check the equipment out to.", vbExclamation
```

Otherwise, connect to the current database:

```
Set MyDB = CurrentDb
```

Now look in the database for any checkout records that overlap the user's current request for this specific piece of equipment. Note carefully the placement of the parentheses in the Where clause:

```
Set rs = MyDB.OpenRecordset("Select CheckOutID from CheckOuts " _
    & "Where ([StartDate] <= #" & CCFrom.Value _
    & "# and [EndDate] >= #" & CCFrom.Value & "# " _
    & "and [EquipmentID] = " & [EquipmentID] & ") or " _
    & "([StartDate] <= #" & CCTo.Value _
    & "# and [EndDate] >= #" & CCTo.Value & "# " _
    & "and [EquipmentID] = " & [EquipmentID] & ")", dbOpenSnapshot)
```

Then check to see if you found any overlapping records. If you did, the EOF flag will not have been on since the record pointer would be pointing to a matching record:

```
If rs.EOF Then
```

If no interfering record is found, add the user's request to the database:

```
MyDB.Execute "Insert Into CheckOuts (EquipmentID, EmployeeID, " _
    & "StartDate, EndDate, [Note]) Values (" _
    & [EquipmentID] & ", " _
    & TheEmployee & ", " _
    & """" & CCFrom & """, " _
    & """" & CCTo & """, " _
    & """" & TheNote & " "")"
```

Then repopulate the CheckOuts subform so that it contains the record that was just added:

```
CheckOuts_subform.Requery
```

and inform the user that their request was entered:

```
MsgBox "Reservation placed!", vbInformation
```

Otherwise, inform the user of the problem with the dates he or she selected:

```
MsgBox "The equipment is already reserved during that time.", vbExclamation
```

The Equipment form contains a subform called CheckOuts. This contains one additional procedure that fires when the Employee field is double-clicked:

```
Private Sub Employee_DblClick(Cancel As Integer)
    If IsNull([EmployeeID]) Or [EmployeeID] = 0 Then
        DoCmd.OpenForm "Employees", , , , acFormAdd, acDialog
        [Employee].Requery
    Else
```

```
            DoCmd.OpenForm "Employees", , , "[EmployeeID] = " & [EmployeeID], , acDialog
            [Employee].Requery
        End If
End Sub
```

The code links this form to the Employees form, so you can check to see if an employee was selected in the current record:

```
If IsNull([EmployeeID]) Or [EmployeeID] = 0 Then
```

If none has been selected, open the Employees form in Add mode:

```
DoCmd.OpenForm "Employees", , , , acFormAdd, acDialog
```

After the user is done with that form, the code flows back here and you can repopulate the Employee combo box:

```
[Employee].Requery
```

If a value is present in the Employee field, open the Employees form and filter it so that the selected employee is displayed:

```
DoCmd.OpenForm "Employees", , , "[EmployeeID] = " & [EmployeeID], , acDialog
```

Then repopulate the Employee combo box:

```
[Employee].Requery
```

Employees and Departments Forms

The Employees and Departments forms contain similar code, so they are presented in this section collectively. Both contain code blocks that fire when the footer buttons are pressed.

The first code block fires when the Add button is pressed:

```
Private Sub CommandAdd_Click()
    DoCmd.GoToRecord , , acNewRec
    [FirstName].SetFocus
End Sub
```

Start by moving the record pointer to a new blank record:

```
DoCmd.GoToRecord , , acNewRec
```

Then move the focus so the user can start entering data without taking any further action:

```
[FirstName].SetFocus
```

The next code block fires in the Delete button's Click event:

```
Private Sub CommandDelete_Click()
    On Error GoTo HandleError
    DoCmd.DoMenuItem acFormBar, acEditMenu, 8, , acMenuVer70
    DoCmd.DoMenuItem acFormBar, acEditMenu, 6, , acMenuVer70
    [LastName].SetFocus
    Exit Sub
HandleError:
    If Err.Number <> 2501 Then
        MsgBox Err.Number & " " & Err.Description
    End If
End Sub
```

Start with an error handler statement:

```
On Error GoTo HandleError
```

Then move on to delete the current record:

```
DoCmd.DoMenuItem acFormBar, acEditMenu, 8, , acMenuVer70
DoCmd.DoMenuItem acFormBar, acEditMenu, 6, , acMenuVer70
```

After the record deletion, move the focus back to the detail section:

```
[LastName].SetFocus
```

Now exit this procedure:

```
Exit Sub
```

This label is where the code flows if an error occurs:

```
HandleError:
```

You then display an error message:

```
If Err.Number <> 2501 Then
        MsgBox Err.Number & " " & Err.Description
End If
```

When the user clicks on the Search button, the next code block fires:

```
Private Sub CommandSearch_Click()
    Screen.PreviousControl.SetFocus
    DoCmd.DoMenuItem acFormBar, acEditMenu, 10, , acMenuVer70
End Sub
```

Start by moving the focus to the last field the user was at before pressing the Search button:

```
Screen.PreviousControl.SetFocus
```

Then load the Access Search dialog:

```
DoCmd.DoMenuItem acFormBar, acEditMenu, 10, , acMenuVer70
```

The last code block on both of these forms fires when the user presses the Close button. It uses the Close method to unload this form:

```
Private Sub CommandClose_Click()
    DoCmd.Close
End Sub
```

Reports

Equipment Use Report

The Equipment Use report displays summary information that indicates the number of days a piece of equipment was checked out. The report is based on the Equipment Use query that has the following syntax:

```
SELECT CheckOuts.EquipmentID,
Sum(DateDiff("d",[StartDate],[EndDate])+1)
AS [Days Reserved] FROM CheckOuts
GROUP BY CheckOuts.EquipmentID;
```

The query sums the number of days between the start date and the end date to determine the total number of days that the equipment was in use.

Who's Using the Stuff Report

The Who's Using the Stuff report displays the number of days each employee has used each piece of equipment. The report is based on the Who's Using the Stuff query that has the following syntax:

```
SELECT CheckOuts.EquipmentID AS Equipment, CheckOuts.EmployeeID AS
Employee, Sum(DateDiff("d",[StartDate],[EndDate])+1) AS [Days Reserved]
FROM CheckOuts GROUP BY CheckOuts.EquipmentID, CheckOuts.EmployeeID
ORDER BY CheckOuts.EquipmentID,
Sum(DateDiff("d",[StartDate],[EndDate])+1) DESC;
```

As with the past report, the query sums the number of days between the start and end dates. Here the resulting records are grouped first by the equipment and then by the person using the equipment.

Equipment Status Report

The Equipment Status report displays the current status of a piece of equipment. That status is either the name of the person who has the equipment checked out or that it is available.

The report uses two queries to produce the desired output. The first is the Checked Out Equipment query:

```
SELECT CheckOuts.CheckOutID, CheckOuts.EquipmentID,
CheckOuts.EmployeeID,
IIf([StartDate]<=Date() And [EndDate]>=Date(),[LastName] & ", "
& [FirstName],False) AS [Currently Checked Out]
FROM Employees INNER JOIN CheckOuts
ON Employees.EmployeeID = CheckOuts.EmployeeID
WHERE (((IIf([StartDate]<=Date() And
[EndDate]>=Date(),[LastName] & ", " & [FirstName],False))<>"0"));
```

This query joins together the Employees and CheckOuts tables. Notice the use of the immediate If statement, the IIF:

```
IIf([StartDate]<=Date() And [EndDate]>=Date(),[LastName] & ", " & [FirstName],False)
```

The first parameter of this function checks to see if the current date falls between the checkout dates. If it does, the function returns the name of the person who has the equipment checked out. Otherwise, the function returns a 0. Then in the Where clause, you limit the output so that only those records that have the item currently checked out are returned.

This query is then used by the Equipment Status query, which joins it together with the Equipment table in this SQL statement:

```
SELECT Equipment.EquipmentName,
IIf([Currently Checked Out]="0","Available",[Currently Checked Out]) AS Status
FROM Equipment LEFT JOIN [Checked Out Equipment]
ON Equipment.EquipmentID = [Checked Out Equipment].EquipmentID;
```

Note the use of the LEFT JOIN. This means that you will see all the Equipment records even if they don't have a match in the Checked Out equipment query. In fact, you will use that information in the Status output field:

```
IIf([Currently Checked Out]="0","Available",[Currently Checked Out]) AS Status
```

Here you check to see if the Currently Checked Out record for this piece of equipment has no match, as indicated by a 0 value. If that is the case, the Status output field will contain the text "Available." Otherwise, it contains the name of the person who has the equipment checked out.

CHAPTER 5

Databases for Managing Networks

ON THE CD:

Software Documentation.mdb

Code Library.mdb

Software - Hardware Profiles.mdb

Keeping Track of Software and Hardware

In this chapter, we will look at three database applications that can be used by a company to track and manage their software and hardware.

First, we will look at the Software Documentation database. The database enables the user to manage information about code, bugs in applications, and documentation for customers. Then we will look at the Code Library database. Developers can use this database to store code blocks to be used by other developers in other applications.

The third database we will review is the Software - Hardware Profiles database. This database can be used by Network Administrators to track the software and hardware located on the computers in their network.

Software Documentation Database

In this chapter, we will start by reviewing the Software Documentation database. This database enables users to manage information about software in three ways. The first is by enabling developers to manage notes about code. The second is through the tracking of bugs found in an application. Third, the user also can manage notes of customers about applications that could be used to create an instruction guide.

Sample Walk-through

When the user first enters the application, he or she sees the form displayed in Figure 5-1.

Figure 5-1

Software
Documentation
entry form

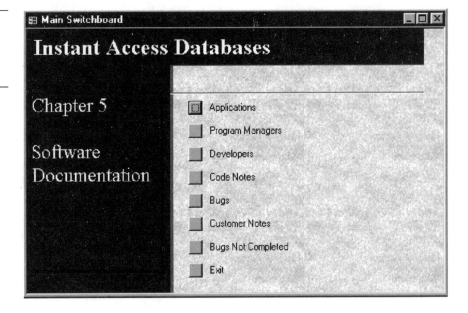

The Startup properties are set for this application so that the menu form automatically opens whenever the database is opened in Access. From this form, the user can select to go to any of the forms or reports in the application.

If the user were to press the Applications button, he or she would see the form displayed in Figure 5-2.

Each of the sections of documentation that are entered into the other parts of this database is based on an application. This form is used to manage those applications. The user would enter information about the application as well as the Program Manager for the application.

That field links to the Program Managers form so the user can see the extended information about a program manager. The Program Managers form is also available through the menu screen and is displayed in Figure 5-3.

From the Program Managers form the user can add, edit, delete and view the different program managers that are in charge of applications.

The next form available through the menu is the Developers form displayed in Figure 5-4.

Figure 5-2

Applications form

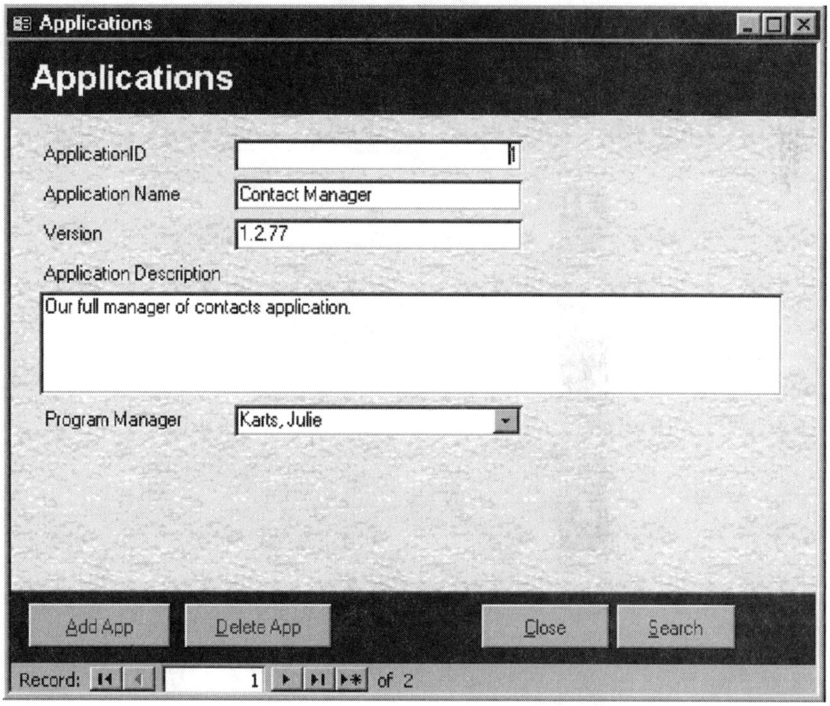

Figure 5-3

Program Managers form

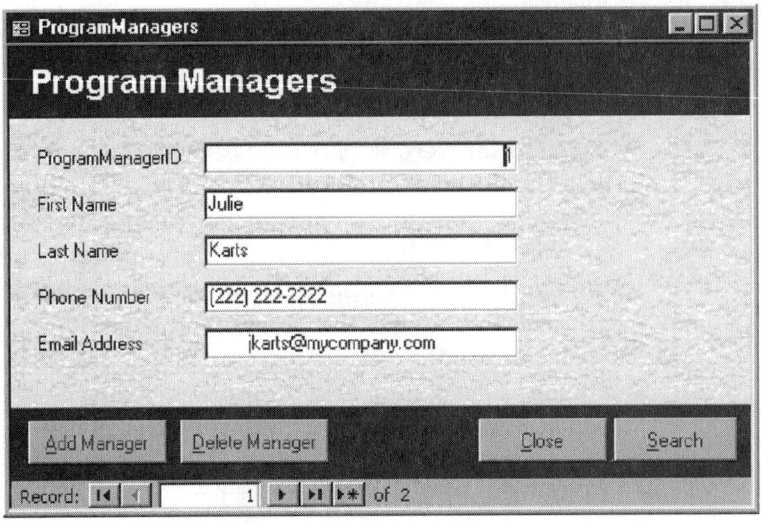

Figure 5-4

Developers form

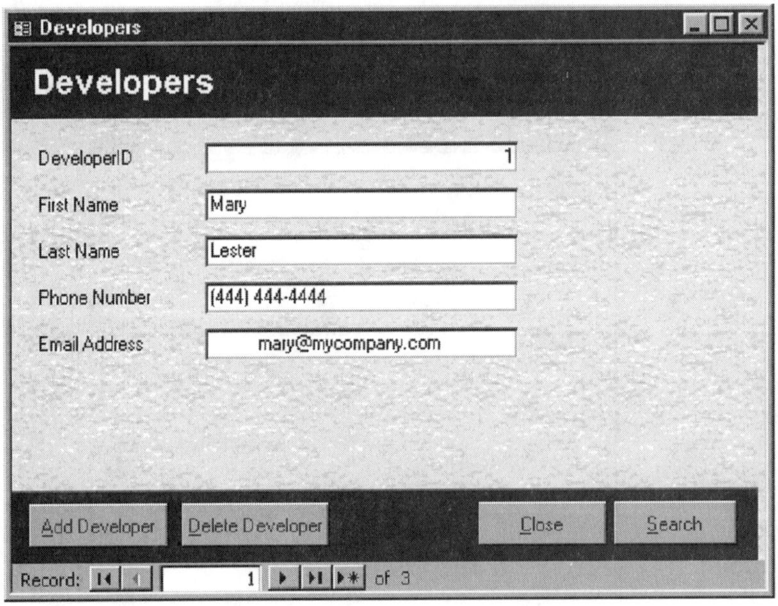

Developers in this database application are used to keep track of who has entered notes and who is responsible for fixing a bug. This form is used to manage information about developers.

The next form viewable through the menu is the Code Notes form, which is displayed in Figure 5-5.

The Code Notes form enables a developer to track documentation information about the code in her projects. The When Entered and Last Modified fields are locked so that the user cannot change these values. Instead, the When Entered field is set to the current date and the Last Modified field is set to the current date and time whenever the record is modified.

The next form that the user can select from the menu is the Bugs form. The first page of that form is displayed in Figure 5-6.

The Bugs form is divided into three pages. The first page is the General page. This page enables the user to enter general information about the bug. The Application and Assigned To fields link to the Applications and Developers forms, respectively, when the field is double-clicked. The bug can fall under a fixed list of statuses contained in the Status field.

Figure 5-5

Code Notes form

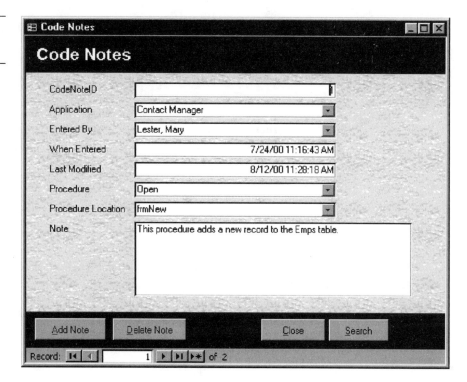

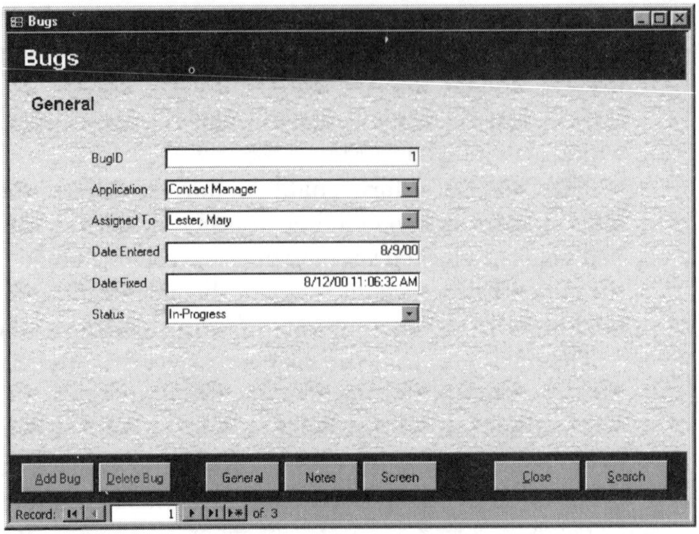

Figure 5-6

General page of
the Bugs form

Figure 5-6

General page of
the Bugs form

When the user selects the Notes button, he sees the Notes form shown in Figure 5-7.

The Notes page provides the person reporting a problem with a place to enter information on the bug he found. Then underneath that, the developer can add her own notes relating to the problem.

The last page of the form is shown in Figure 5-8.

The Screen Dump page provides the person reporting the problem with a place to insert a picture related to what he saw when the error occurred. The user can press the Print Screen button on the keyboard when an error message appears. He then can paste that picture into the record here to provide the developer with better information about the nature of the problem.

The other form available to the user is the Customer Notes form, which is displayed in Figure 5-9.

The Customer Notes form provides a way for the user to track notes to be used to produce a booklet or instruction manual for an application. The sequence number field is used to determine the order of the notes in a report that the user can view by pressing the Report button.

When the user presses the Report button, he or she sees the report shown in Figure 5-10.

Figure 5-7

Notes page of the
Bugs form

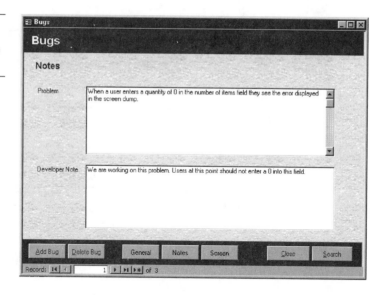

Figure 5-8

Screen Dump
page

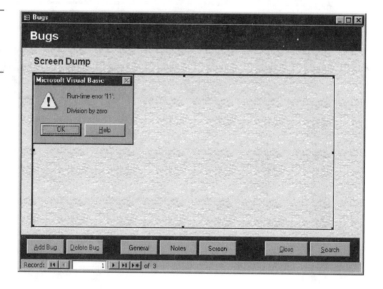

Figure 5-9

Customer Notes form

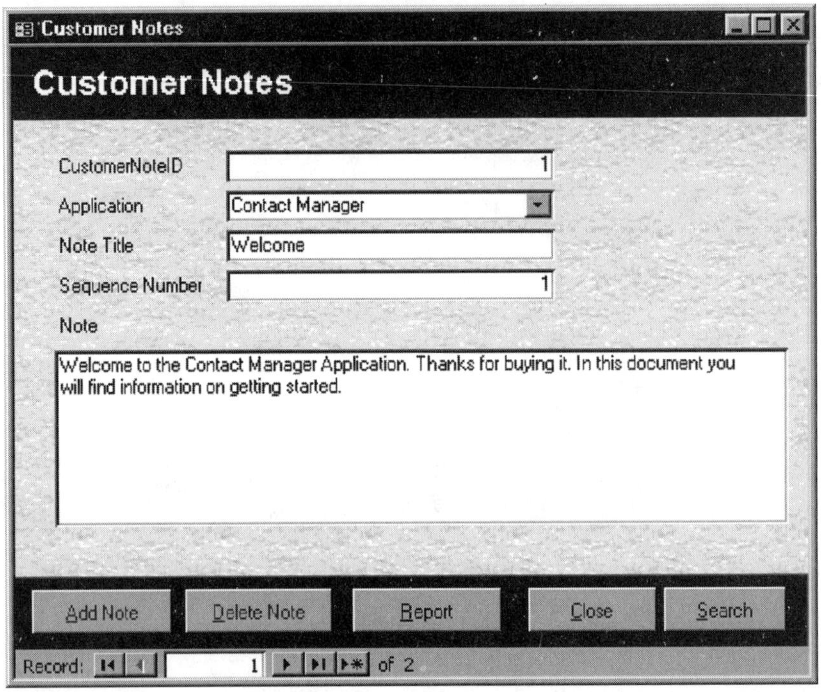

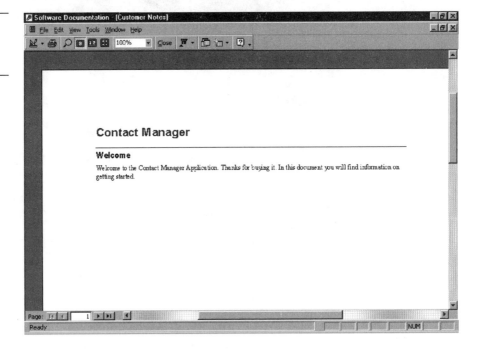

Figure 5-10

Customer Notes Report

The report displays all the notes for the application that is currently selected on the Customer Notes form. The report shows the information, so that each note starts on its own page. The report can be used to supply the customer with an information book or guide.

The other report is called Bugs Not Completed and is accessible through the menu. That report is shown in Figure 5-11.

The Bugs Not Completed report shows information on any bug that is not marked with a status of Complete. The records are grouped first by the application, then by the developer who is in charge of the application. The report also shows the number of days that have passed since the bug was reported.

Table Definitions and Relationships

Applications Table

The Applications table stores information about each application. That information is then linked to many of the other tables in this database.

Figure 5-11

Bugs Not
Completed report

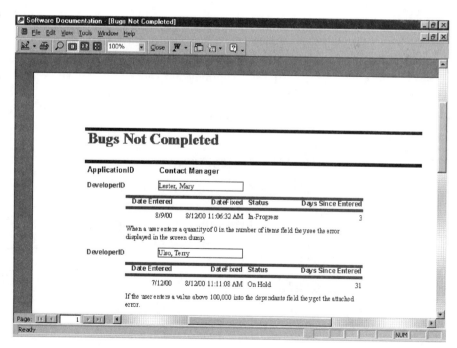

The table is in a one-to-many relationship with the ProgramManagers table. Each of the program managers can manage many applications, but each application can have only one program manager.

ProgramManagers Table

Program managers in this application are people who are in charge of an application. The ProgramManagers table stores that information.

Developers Table

Each of the bugs and codes notes goes with a specific developer. The Developers table stores the information about those developers.

CodeNotes Table

The CodeNotes table stores information about the code notes entered by developers. The table is in a one-to-many relationship with the Applications table. Each note goes with one application, but each application can have many notes. The table is also in a one-to-many relationship with the Developers table. Each note is entered by one developer, but each developer can enter many notes.

Bugs Table

The Bugs table stores the information on the different problems that have been reported by an application. The table is in a one-to-many relationship with the Applications table and the Developers table. Each of the bugs goes with a single application, and a single developer is assigned to fix the bug. Each application and developer can have many bugs associated with their records.

CustomerNotes Table

The last table in the database is the CustomerNotes table. The table stores notes about applications that are meant for the user of an application. The table is in a one-to-many relationship with the Applications table. Each note goes with a specific application, but each application can have many notes.

Field Specifications

Applications Table

The field specifications for the Applications table are displayed in Table 5-1.

Table 5-1	Field Name	Field Type	Notes
Applications Table Field Specifications	ApplicationID	AutoNumber	Primary Key
	ApplicationName	Text	Length = 50
	Version	Text	Length = 20
	ApplicationDescription	Memo	
	ProgramManagerID	Number	Type = Long, Foreign Key

The ApplicationID field is the primary key for this table. It is automatically populated when a new record is added to this table since it is an AutoNumber field. The ProgramManagerID field is a foreign key that links this table to the ProgramManagers table. The field is displayed as a combo box. It has the following value in the Row Source property:

```
SELECT [ProgramManagers].[ProgramManagerID],
[LastName] & ", " & [FirstName] AS Expr1 FROM ProgramManagers
ORDER BY [LastName] & ", " & [FirstName];
```

The user will see the name of the program manager, but the ID of the manager is stored in this field.

ProgramManagers Table

The field specifications for the ProgramManagers table are displayed in Table 5-2.

The ProgramManagerID field is the primary key for this table. The EmailAddress field has the Input Mask property set to make it easier for the user to enter email addresses:

```
!??????????????"
```

Table 5-2	Field Name	Field Type	Notes
ProgramManagers Table Field Specifications	ProgramManagerID	AutoNumber	Primary Key
	FirstName	Text	Length = 50
	LastName	Text	Length = 50
	PhoneNumber	Text	Length = 50
	EmailAddress	Text	Length = 50

The assumption is that the user works at a company where all the email addresses of the employees end in the extension "@mycompany.com." The user has to enter the first part of the email address and the rest is appended to what she types in. The parameters in the mask are separated by a semicolon. The first parameter is the mask itself. The question marks mean that the user can enter any letter or nothing. The second parameter says that the user wants to store the mask with the field in the database. The third parameter refers to the character that should be displayed as the user is entering data in this field, the placeholder character.

Developers Table

The field specifications for the Developers table are displayed in Table 5-3.

The DeveloperID field is the primary key for the table. The EmailAddress field has an input mask like the one used in the EmailAddress field of the ProgramManagers table.

Table 5-3	Field Name	Field Type	Notes
Developers Table Field Specifications	DeveloperID	AutoNumber	Primary Key
	FirstName	Text	Length = 50
	LastName	Text	Length = 50
	PhoneNumber	Text	Length = 50
	EmailAddress	Text	Length = 50

CodeNotes Table

The field specifications for the CodeNotes table are displayed in Table 5-4.

Table 5-4

CodeNotes Table Field Specifications

Field Name	Field Type	Notes
CodeNoteID	AutoNumber	Primary Key
ApplicationID	Number	Type = Long, Foreign Key
DeveloperID	Number	Type = Long, Foreign Key
WhenEntered	Date/Time	
LastModified	Date/Time	
Procedure	Text	Length = 50
ProcedureLocation	Text	Length = 50
TheNote	Memo	

The CodeNoteID field is the primary key for this table. The ApplicationID field is a foreign key that links this table to the Applications table. The field is set to be displayed as a combo box, because the Display Control property has that value. The Row Source property is set to this SQL statement:

```
SELECT [Applications].[ApplicationID], [Applications].[ApplicationName]
    FROM Applications;
```

The user will see the name of the application, but the ID of the application is stored in this field.

The DeveloperID field links this table to the Developers table. It also is displayed as a combo box with this text in the Row Source property:

```
SELECT [Developers].[DeveloperID], [LastName] & ", " & [FirstName] AS Expr1
FROM Developers;
```

The ID of the developer is the bound column because the Bound Column property is set to 1. The Column Widths property is set to

```
0";1"
```

so that the user does not see the bound column. Instead, she sees the second field in the SQL statement, which is the concatenation of the developer's last name with their first name. That is also how the records listed are sorted.

The Procedure field stores the name of the procedure that the note goes with. Since the values entered are likely to be used again, the field is displayed as a combo box with a self-populating list, so the user sees all the previously entered values in the list portion of the combo box. The Row Source property is set to this value:

```
SELECT [CodeNotes].[Procedure] FROM CodeNotes ORDER BY [CodeNotes].[Procedure];
```

The ProcedureLocation field is also a self-populating combo box.

Bugs Table

The field specifications for the Bugs table are displayed in Table 5-5.

The BugID field is the primary key for this table. The ApplicationID is a foreign key that links this table to the Applications table. The field is displayed as a combo box with the following value in the Row Source property:

```
SELECT [Applications].[ApplicationID], [Applications].[ApplicationName]
FROM Applications;
```

The ID of the application is the bound column, but the user sees the name of the application.

	Field Name	Field Type	Notes
Table 5-5	BugID	AutoNumber	Primary Key
Bugs Table Field Specifications	ApplicationID	Number	Type = Long, Foreign Key
	DeveloperID	Number	Type = Long, Foreign Key
	DateEntered	Date/Time	
	DateFixed	Date/Time	
	Status	Text	Length = 50
	Problem	Memo	
	DeveloperNote	Memo	
	ScreenDump	OLE Object	

The DeveloperID field is also a foreign key. It links the table to the Developers table. It is also displayed as a combo box with the following value in the Record Source property:

```
SELECT [Developers].[DeveloperID], [LastName] & ", " & [FirstName]
AS Expr1 FROM Developers;
```

The ID of the developer is the bound column, so it is stored with the record. The name of the developer is displayed in the list portion of the combo box.

The DateEntered field has the following in the Default Value property:

```
Date()
```

Therefore, the initial value of the field is the current system date.

The Status field is displayed as a combo box. It shows a list of static values, since the Row Source Type property is set to

```
Value List
```

The Row Source property has the following value:

```
"Assigned";"In-Progress";"On Hold";"Rejected";"Fixed"
```

The Limit to List property is set to Yes, so the user must select one of these values for the Status field.

The ScreenDump field is an OLE Object field, so the user can put a picture into it.

CustomerNotes Table

The field specifications for the CustomerNotes table are displayed in Table 5-6.

Table 5-6

CustomerNotes Table Field Specifications

Field Name	Field Type	Notes
CustomerNoteID	AutoNumber	Primary Key
ApplicationID	Number	Type = Long, Foreign Key
NoteTitle	Text	Length = 50
SequenceNumber	Number	Type = Long
TheNote	Memo	

The CustomerNoteID field is the primary key in this table. The ApplicationID field is a foreign key that links this table to the Applications table. The field is displayed to the user as a combo box and has this value in the Row Source property:

```
SELECT [Applications].[ApplicationID], [Applications].[ApplicationName]
FROM Applications;
```

The SequenceNumber field stores the order in which this note should appear when printing a report for all the customer notes for a particular application.

Forms

Switchboard Form

The Switchboard form is used to navigate through the forms and reports in the Software Documentation database application. It was created using the Switchboard wizard, which is accessible within Access through the Tools/Database Utilities/Switchboard Manager menu item. Only the look and design of the form produced with that wizard have been altered.

Applications Form

The code on the Applications form provides the functionality needed for the footer buttons and also links to the Program Managers form.

When the user clicks on the Add App button, this code block fires.

```
Private Sub CommandAdd_Click()
    DoCmd.GoToRecord , , acNewRec
    [ApplicationName].SetFocus
End Sub
```

Start by using the GoToRecord method of the DoCmd object to move the record pointer to a new record:

```
DoCmd.GoToRecord , , acNewRec
```

Then move the focus to the ApplicationName field so the user can start entering data:

```
[ApplicationName].SetFocus
```

When the user clicks on the Delete App button, the next code block fires.

```
Private Sub CommandDelete_Click()
    On Error GoTo HandleError
    DoCmd.DoMenuItem acFormBar, acEditMenu, 8, , acMenuVer70
    DoCmd.DoMenuItem acFormBar, acEditMenu, 6, , acMenuVer70
    [ApplicationName].SetFocus
    Exit Sub
HandleError:
    If Err.Number <> 2501 Then
        MsgBox Err.Number & " " & Err.Description
    End If
End Sub
```

Watch for an error, because a known one that you want to skip can occur:

```
On Error GoTo HandleError
```

Then delete the current record:

```
DoCmd.DoMenuItem acFormBar, acEditMenu, 8, , acMenuVer70
DoCmd.DoMenuItem acFormBar, acEditMenu, 6, , acMenuVer70
```

If the record deletion is successful, the code flows here and the focus is moved back to the detail section of the form:

```
[ApplicationName].SetFocus
```

Exit the procedure:

```
Exit Sub
```

If an error were to occur, the code flows here:

```
HandleError:
```

Then check to see if the error that occurred was due to the user canceling the record deletion:

```
If Err.Number <> 2501 Then
```

If that wasn't the problem, display information about the error to the user:

```
MsgBox Err.Number & " " & Err.Description
```

The next code block fires when the Search button is pressed.

```
Private Sub CommandSearch_Click()
    Screen.PreviousControl.SetFocus
    DoCmd.DoMenuItem acFormBar, acEditMenu, 10, , acMenuVer70
End Sub
```

Start by moving the focus back to the control that had the focus before this button was pressed:

```
Screen.PreviousControl.SetFocus
```

Then open the Access Search dialog:

```
DoCmd.DoMenuItem acFormBar, acEditMenu, 10, , acMenuVer70
```

When the user presses the Close button, the Close method of the DoCmd object is used to close this form:

```
Private Sub CommandClose_Click()
    DoCmd.Close
End Sub
```

When the user double-clicks on the ProgramManagerID field, the next code block fires.

```
Private Sub ProgramManagerID_DblClick(Cancel As Integer)
    If [ProgramManagerID] = 0 Or IsNull([ProgramManagerID]) Then
        DoCmd.OpenForm "Program Managers", , , , acFormAdd, acDialog
        ProgramManagerID.Requery
    Else
        DoCmd.OpenForm "Program Managers", , , _
            "[ProgramManagerID] = " & [ProgramManagerID], , acDialog
        ProgramManagerID.Requery
    End If
End Sub
```

First, check to see if the ProgramManagerID field is blank:

```
If [ProgramManagerID] = 0 Or IsNull([ProgramManagerID]) Then
```

If it is, assume the user wants to add a new record. The Program Managers form is opened in add mode as a dialog:

```
DoCmd.OpenForm "Program Managers", , , , acFormAdd, acDialog
```

Because it is opened as a dialog, the code stops at that line until the user is done with that form. Therefore, the combo box is repopulated after the user is done with that form:

```
ProgramManagerID.Requery
```

If the ProgramManagerID field contains a value, the code flows here:

```
Else
```

Assume that the user wants to see information on the program manager that she has selected:

```
DoCmd.OpenForm "Program Managers", , , _
    "[ProgramManagerID] = " & [ProgramManagerID], , acDialog
```

After she has finished with that form, the combo box is repopulated:

```
ProgramManagerID.Requery
```

Program Managers and Developers Forms

The Program Managers and Developers forms have almost identical code. Both forms provide the functionality needed for the footer buttons. When the user presses the Add button, the first code block fires.

```
Private Sub CommandAdd_Click()
    DoCmd.GoToRecord , , acNewRec
    [FirstName].SetFocus
End Sub
```

Start by using the GoToRecord method and pass to it the parameter that indicates a desire to move to a new record:

```
DoCmd.GoToRecord , , acNewRec
```

Then set the focus to the first field in the detail section of the form:

```
[FirstName].SetFocus
```

The next code block fires when the Delete button of the footer is pressed.

```
Private Sub CommandDelete_Click()
    On Error GoTo HandleError
    DoCmd.DoMenuItem acFormBar, acEditMenu, 8, , acMenuVer70
    DoCmd.DoMenuItem acFormBar, acEditMenu, 6, , acMenuVer70
    [FirstName].SetFocus
    Exit Sub
HandleError:
    If Err.Number <> 2501 Then
        MsgBox Err.Number & " " & Err.Description
    End If
End Sub
```

Start by telling the compiler that errors will be handled:

```
On Error GoTo HandleError
```

Next, delete the current record:

```
DoCmd.DoMenuItem acFormBar, acEditMenu, 8, , acMenuVer70
DoCmd.DoMenuItem acFormBar, acEditMenu, 6, , acMenuVer70
```

and set the focus to the first field in the detail section of the form:

```
[FirstName].SetFocus
```

Then leave this procedure without flowing into the error code:

```
Exit Sub
```

If an error occurs, the code flows here since this label is indicated in the error statement:

```
HandleError:
```

Check for a known error that occurs if the user cancels the record deletion:

```
If Err.Number <> 2501 Then
```

Any other error is displayed to the user in the normal way as a message box that shows the error number and type:

```
MsgBox Err.Number & " " & Err.Description
```

If the user presses the Search button, the next code block fires.

```
Private Sub CommandSearch_Click()
    Screen.PreviousControl.SetFocus
    DoCmd.DoMenuItem acFormBar, acEditMenu, 10, , acMenuVer70
End Sub
```

Assume that the field that the user wants to search was the field she was on before selecting the Search button. Start by setting the focus back to that field:

```
Screen.PreviousControl.SetFocus
```

Open the Access Search Dialog:

```
DoCmd.DoMenuItem acFormBar, acEditMenu, 10, , acMenuVer70
```

The other procedure on these two forms closes them when the Close button is pressed:

```
Private Sub CommandClose_Click()
    DoCmd.Close
End Sub
```

Code Notes Form

The code on the Code Notes form links this form to the Applications and Developers forms. It also sets the value for the LastModified field and provides the functionality for the footer buttons.

```
When the user double-clicks on the ApplicationID field, the first code blocks fires.
Private Sub ApplicationID_DblClick(Cancel As Integer)
    If [ApplicationID] = 0 Or IsNull([ApplicationID]) Then
        DoCmd.OpenForm "Applications", , , , acFormAdd, acDialog
        ApplicationID.Requery
    Else
        DoCmd.OpenForm "Applications", , , _
            "[ApplicationID] = " & [ApplicationID], , acDialog
        ApplicationID.Requery
    End If
End Sub
```

The code block links this form to the Applications form based on the value in the ApplicationID field. First, check to see whether that field is blank:

```
If [ApplicationID] = 0 Or IsNull([ApplicationID]) Then
```

If it is, assume the user wants to add a new record to the Applications table:

```
DoCmd.OpenForm "Applications", , , , acFormAdd, acDialog
```

Then repopulate the ApplicationID field so the new application entered by the user will now be visible:

```
ApplicationID.Requery
```

If the ApplicationID field contains a value, the code flows here:

```
Else
```

Open the Applications form and display the information on the current selected application:

```
DoCmd.OpenForm "Applications", , , _
    "[ApplicationID] = " & [ApplicationID], , acDialog
```

The user may have made changes to that application, so repopulate the ApplicationID field:

```
ApplicationID.Requery
```

The form also links to the Developers form when the DeveloperID field is double-clicked:

```
Private Sub DeveloperID_DblClick(Cancel As Integer)
    If [DeveloperID] = 0 Or IsNull([DeveloperID]) Then
        DoCmd.OpenForm "Developers", , , , acFormAdd, acDialog
        DeveloperID.Requery
    Else
        DoCmd.OpenForm "Developers", , , _
            "[DeveloperID] = " & [DeveloperID], , acDialog
        DeveloperID.Requery
    End If
End Sub
```

Check to see if the DeveloperID field is blank:

```
If [DeveloperID] = 0 Or IsNull([DeveloperID]) Then
```

If it is, open the Developers form in Add mode:

```
DoCmd.OpenForm "Developers", , , , acFormAdd, acDialog
```

and then repopulate the DeveloperID combo box:

```
DeveloperID.Requery
```

If the DeveloperID field contains a value, open the Developers form to show the information for the developer selected:

```
DoCmd.OpenForm "Developers", , , _
    "[DeveloperID] = " & [DeveloperID], , acDialog
```

and then repopulate the combo box:

```
DeveloperID.Requery
```

Whenever a record is added or changed, update the LastModified field so that it contains the current system date and time. This can be done through the BeforeUpdate event of the Form object, which fires before a changed record is committed to the database.

```
Private Sub Form_BeforeUpdate(Cancel As Integer)
    [LastModified] = Now
End Sub
```

Here, use the Now function, which returns the current system date and time:

```
[LastModified] = Now
```

When the user presses the Add Note button, the next code block fires.

```
Private Sub CommandAdd_Click()
    DoCmd.GoToRecord , , acNewRec
    [ApplicationID].SetFocus
End Sub
```

Start by moving the record pointer to a new record:

```
DoCmd.GoToRecord , , acNewRec
```

and then set the focus to the ApplicationID field:

```
[ApplicationID].SetFocus
```

When the user presses the Delete Note button, the next code block fires.

```
Private Sub CommandDelete_Click()
    On Error GoTo HandleError
    DoCmd.DoMenuItem acFormBar, acEditMenu, 8, , acMenuVer70
    DoCmd.DoMenuItem acFormBar, acEditMenu, 6, , acMenuVer70
    [ApplicationID].SetFocus
    Exit Sub
HandleError:
    If Err.Number <> 2501 Then
        MsgBox Err.Number & " " & Err.Description
    End If
End Sub
```

Watch for a known error:

```
On Error GoTo HandleError
```

and then delete the current record:

```
DoCmd.DoMenuItem acFormBar, acEditMenu, 8, , acMenuVer70
DoCmd.DoMenuItem acFormBar, acEditMenu, 6, , acMenuVer70
```

If the record was deleted without error, the code flows here. Set the focus back to the detail section of the form:

```
[ApplicationID].SetFocus
```

and exit this procedure:

```
Exit Sub
```

If an error occurred, the code flows here:

```
HandleError:
```

Then check to see if the user pressed the No button when asked to confirm the record deletion:

```
If Err.Number <> 2501 Then
```

That error is skipped, but any others are displayed to the user through a message box:

```
MsgBox Err.Number & " " & Err.Description
```

When the user presses the Search button, the next code block fires.

```
Private Sub CommandSearch_Click()
    Screen.PreviousControl.SetFocus
    DoCmd.DoMenuItem acFormBar, acEditMenu, 10, , acMenuVer70
End Sub
```

The code uses the SetFocus method of the PreviousControl object to return the focus to the control that last had the focus. The PreviousControl object is an object of the Screen object.

```
Screen.PreviousControl.SetFocus
```

Then the built-in Access Search dialog is opened:

```
DoCmd.DoMenuItem acFormBar, acEditMenu, 10, , acMenuVer70
```

The other code block on this form closes this form when the Close button is pressed:

```
Private Sub CommandClose_Click()
    DoCmd.Close
End Sub
```

Bugs Form

The code on the Bugs form enables the user to navigate through the pages on the form. It also links to the Applications form and the Developers form.

When the user clicks on the General button, he or she needs to be taken to the first page of the form. This is done through the GoToPage method of the DoCmd object:

```
Private Sub Command28_Click()
    DoCmd.GoToPage 1
End Sub
```

When the user clicks on the Notes button, he wants to see the Notes page of the Bugs form. This information is on the second page of the form:

```
Private Sub Command29_Click()
    DoCmd.GoToPage 2
End Sub
```

When the user presses the Screen button, he or she is taken to the Screen Dump page by using the GoToPage method and passing to it the parameter of 3 for the third page:

```
Private Sub Command30_Click()
    DoCmd.GoToPage 3
End Sub
```

When the user double-clicks on the ApplicationID field, he is taken to the Applications form:

```
Private Sub ApplicationID_DblClick(Cancel As Integer)
    If [ApplicationID] = 0 Or IsNull([ApplicationID]) Then
        DoCmd.OpenForm "Applications", , , , acFormAdd, acDialog
        ApplicationID.Requery
    Else
        DoCmd.OpenForm "Applications", , , _
            "[ApplicationID] = " & [ApplicationID], , acDialog
        ApplicationID.Requery
    End If
End Sub
```

Check to see if the ApplicationID field is blank:

```
If [ApplicationID] = 0 Or IsNull([ApplicationID]) Then
```

If it is, open the Applications form in Add mode:

```
DoCmd.OpenForm "Applications", , , , acFormAdd, acDialog
```

and repopulate the list portion of the combo box:

```
ApplicationID.Requery
```

If it isn't, open the Applications form and have it filtered so that only the data for the current application is displayed:

```
DoCmd.OpenForm "Applications", , , _
    "[ApplicationID] = " & [ApplicationID], , acDialog
```

Then repopulate the ApplicationID combo box:

```
ApplicationID.Requery
```

If the user double-clicks on the DeveloperID field, she is taken to the DeveloperID form:

```
Private Sub DeveloperID_DblClick(Cancel As Integer)
    If [DeveloperID] = 0 Or IsNull([DeveloperID]) Then
        DoCmd.OpenForm "Developers", , , , acFormAdd, acDialog
        DeveloperID.Requery
    Else
        DoCmd.OpenForm "Developers", , , _
            "[DeveloperID] = " & [DeveloperID], , acDialog
        DeveloperID.Requery
    End If
End Sub
```

If the DeveloperID field is blank:

```
If [DeveloperID] = 0 Or IsNull([DeveloperID]) Then
```

assume the user wants to add a new developer:

```
DoCmd.OpenForm "Developers", , , , acFormAdd, acDialog
```

After the user is done with the Developers form, repopulate the DeveloperID field:

```
DeveloperID.Requery
```

If the field is not blank, assume the user wants to see the extended information for this developer:

```
DoCmd.OpenForm "Developers", , , _
    "[DeveloperID] = " & [DeveloperID], , acDialog
```

The user may have made changes to the data on the Developers form, so repopulate the DeveloperID combo box:

```
DeveloperID.Requery
```

Customer Notes Form

The code on the Customer Notes form provides the functionality for the buttons in the footer of the form. The code also makes sure that the sequence number entered is unique for this application and it links to the Applications form.

When the user clicks on the Add Note button, the first code block fires.

```
Private Sub CommandAdd_Click()
    DoCmd.GoToRecord , , acNewRec
    [ApplicationID].SetFocus
End Sub
```

Start by moving the record pointer to a new record:

```
DoCmd.GoToRecord , , acNewRec
```

and return the focus to the ApplicationID field so the user can start entering data:

```
[ApplicationID].SetFocus
```

If the user clicks on the Delete Note button, the next code block fires.

```
Private Sub CommandDelete_Click()
    On Error GoTo HandleError
    DoCmd.DoMenuItem acFormBar, acEditMenu, 8, , acMenuVer70
    DoCmd.DoMenuItem acFormBar, acEditMenu, 6, , acMenuVer70
    [ApplicationID].SetFocus
    Exit Sub
HandleError:
    If Err.Number <> 2501 Then
        MsgBox Err.Number & " " & Err.Description
    End If
End Sub
```

Tell the compiler that if an error occurs, the code should flow to the label HandleError:

```
On Error GoTo HandleError
```

and then delete the current record:

```
DoCmd.DoMenuItem acFormBar, acEditMenu, 8, , acMenuVer70
DoCmd.DoMenuItem acFormBar, acEditMenu, 6, , acMenuVer70
```

Return the focus to the detail section:

```
[ApplicationID].SetFocus
```

and leave this procedure:

```
Exit Sub
```

The code flows here if an error occurs:

```
HandleError:
```

Filter out any error due to the cancellation of the record deletion:

```
If Err.Number <> 2501 Then
```

Any other error message is displayed in a message box:

```
MsgBox Err.Number & " " & Err.Description
```

If the user clicks on the Report button, the next code block fires.

```
Private Sub Command28_Click()
    DoCmd.OpenReport "Customer Notes", acViewPreview, _
        , "[ApplicationID] = " & [ApplicationID]
End Sub
```

The OpenReport method of the DoCmd object is used to open the report called Customer Notes in preview mode and filter it so that just the records from the current application are displayed in the report:

```
DoCmd.OpenReport "Customer Notes", acViewPreview, _
    , "[ApplicationID] = " & [ApplicationID]
```

If the user clicks on the Search button, the next code block fires.

```
Private Sub CommandSearch_Click()
    Screen.PreviousControl.SetFocus
    DoCmd.DoMenuItem acFormBar, acEditMenu, 10, , acMenuVer70
End Sub
```

Assume the user wants to search the last field he was on:

```
Screen.PreviousControl.SetFocus
```

Then open the Access Search dialog:

```
DoCmd.DoMenuItem acFormBar, acEditMenu, 10, , acMenuVer70
```

The last code block fires if the user presses the Close button. It closes the current form:

```
Private Sub CommandClose_Click()
    DoCmd.Close
End Sub
```

When the user double-clicks on the Application field, open the Applications form:

```
Private Sub ApplicationID_DblClick(Cancel As Integer)
    If [ApplicationID] = 0 Or IsNull([ApplicationID]) Then
        DoCmd.OpenForm "Applications", , , , acFormAdd, acDialog
        ApplicationID.Requery
    Else
        DoCmd.OpenForm "Applications", , , _
            "[ApplicationID] = " & [ApplicationID], , acDialog
        ApplicationID.Requery
    End If
End Sub
```

First, check to see if the field is blank:

```
If [ApplicationID] = 0 Or IsNull([ApplicationID]) Then
```

If it is, the Application form is opened in Add mode:

```
DoCmd.OpenForm "Applications", , , , acFormAdd, acDialog
```

Repopulate the list portion of this combo box:

```
ApplicationID.Requery
```

If the field isn't blank, assume the user wants to see the information on the current application:

```
DoCmd.OpenForm "Applications", , , _
    "[ApplicationID] = " & [ApplicationID], , acDialog
```

Then reload the data in the combo box:

```
ApplicationID.Requery
```

When the user selects an application and enters a sequence number for this record or changes those values, verify that the sequence number is not is use for this application. If it is, the user is given the opportunity of bumping up all the sequence numbers at and above the one he or she entered. This allows the record just entered to be placed in the middle of an existing sequence without having to change all the values for the other records.

The code that does this is in the Exit event of the ApplicationID and the SequenceNumber fields.

```
Private Sub SequenceNumber_Exit(Cancel As Integer)
    Dim MyDB As DAO.Database
    Dim rs As DAO.Recordset
If [ApplicationID] <> 0 And [SequenceNumber] <> 0 Then
        Set MyDB = CurrentDb
        Set rs = MyDB.OpenRecordset("Select CustomerNoteID from CustomerNotes " _
            & "Where [CustomerNoteID] <> " & [CustomerNoteID] _
            & " And [ApplicationID] = " & [ApplicationID] _
            & " And [SequenceNumber] = " & [SequenceNumber], dbOpenSnapshot)
        If Not rs.EOF Then
            If MsgBox("The sequence number entered is in use for " _
                & "this application. Would you like to bump up all " _
                & "sequence numbers? Selecting No will allow you to change the " _
                & "Sequence Number.", vbQuestion + vbYesNo, "Sequence Number") _
                = vbYes Then
                    MyDB.Execute "Update CustomerNotes set " _
                        & "[SequenceNumber] = [SequenceNumber] + 1 " _
                        & "Where [ApplicationID] = " & [ApplicationID] _
                        & " And [SequenceNumber] >= " & [SequenceNumber]
            Else
                    Cancel = True
            End If
        End If
    End If
End Sub
```

Connect to this database:

```
Dim MyDB As DAO.Database
```

and retrieve data:

```
Dim rs As DAO.Recordset
```

Then check to see if values have been entered in the ApplicationID and SequenceNumber fields:

```
If [ApplicationID] <> 0 And [SequenceNumber] <> 0 Then
```

If so, connect through code to the current database:

```
Set MyDB = CurrentDb
```

and check to see if any other records that are using the sequence number for this application exist:

```
Set rs = MyDB.OpenRecordset("Select CustomerNoteID from CustomerNotes " _
    & "Where [CustomerNoteID] <> " & [CustomerNoteID] _
    & " And [ApplicationID] = " & [ApplicationID] _
    & " And [SequenceNumber] = " & [SequenceNumber], dbOpenSnapshot)
```

If one is found, the EOF flag will not be set, because data is returned:

```
If Not rs.EOF Then
```

In that case, ask the user whether he or she would like to bump all the sequence numbers up to fit this new record into place:

```
If MsgBox("The sequence number entered is in use for " _
    & "this application. Would you like to bump up all " _
    & "sequence numbers? Selecting No will allow you to change the " _
    & "Sequence Number.", vbQuestion + vbYesNo, "Sequence Number") _
    = vbYes Then
```

If she wishes to take that action, increment all the sequence numbers at and above the number entered by one:

```
MyDB.Execute "Update CustomerNotes set " _
    & "[SequenceNumber] = [SequenceNumber] + 1 " _
    & "Where [ApplicationID] = " & [ApplicationID] _
    & " And [SequenceNumber] >= " & [SequenceNumber]
```

If the user does not want to bump the records up, he or she can leave this field:

```
Cancel = True
```

Reports

Customer Notes Report

The Customer Notes report shows all the notes for an application so that they can be printed as a booklet or manual. It is based directly on the CustomerNotes table. When the report is called through the Customer Notes form, only those records from a specific application are reported.

Bugs Not Completed Report

The Bugs Not Completed report displayed information on all the bugs that are not marked as being solved. The report is based on the Bugs Not Completed query, which has the following SQL syntax:

```
SELECT Bugs.ApplicationID, Bugs.DeveloperID, Bugs.DateEntered,
Bugs.DateFixed, Bugs.Status,
DateDiff("d",[DateEntered],Date()) AS [Days Since Entered], Bugs.Problem
FROM Bugs WHERE Bugs.Status="Assigned" Or Bugs.Status="In-Progress"
Or Bugs.Status="On Hold";
```

The query returns a calculated field, which is the number of days that have passed since the bug was reported. The DateDiff function returns that difference in days.

The Where portion of the query limits the records returned, so that only those with the specified status are returned.

Code Library Database

The next database that will be reviewed in this chapter is the Code Library application. This database enables the developer to store his code blocks in a single library, making them easier to locate at a later date. The code in this application automatically saves all versions of code blocks, and provides the developer with an easy way of placing the data onto the Windows Clipboard.

Sample Walk-through

When the user first enters the Code Library application, she sees the menu form displayed in Figure 5-12.

The menu enables the user to work with any of the forms and the one report in the database application. When the user presses the Code Blocks button, he or she is taken to the main form in the database that is displayed in Figure 5-13.

The Code Blocks form is divided into three pages. The first page is the Code page, which displays the code block itself as well as some general information about the code. The user can press the "Copy Code to Clipboard" button to copy the code block onto the Windows Clipboard, enabling her to easily use the code in her own application.

If the user presses the Old button, they see the Previous Versions page shown in Figure 5-14.

Whenever the user changes the code block, an old version of the code block is saved. That way the user can always look at old versions of the code to see the history of code changes. The Previous Versions page shows the old versions of the code block.

The other page of this form is displayed in Figure 5-15.

Figure 5-12

Menu form for
the Code Library
database
application

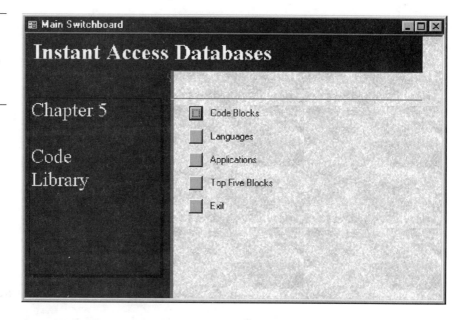

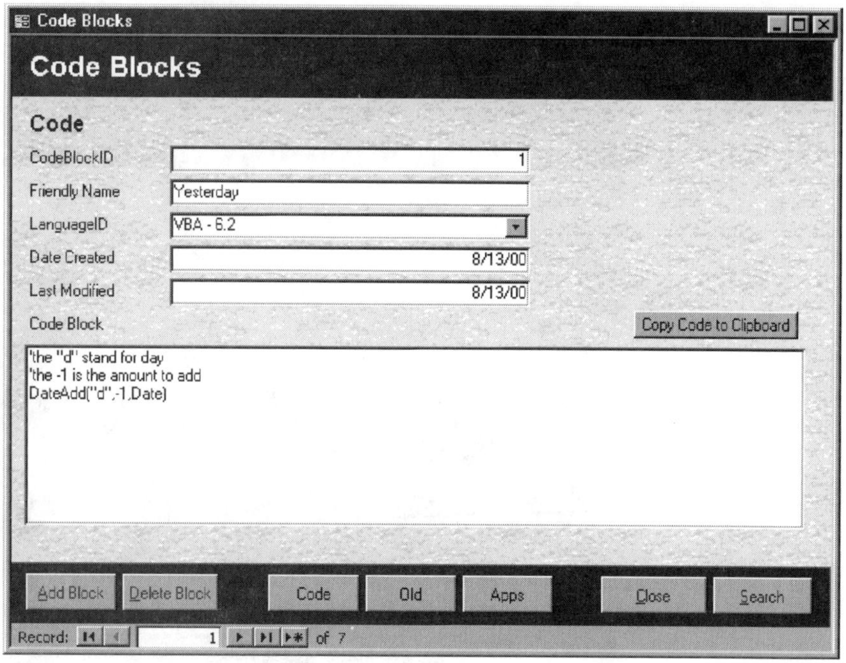

Figure 5-13

Code page from
the Code Blocks
form

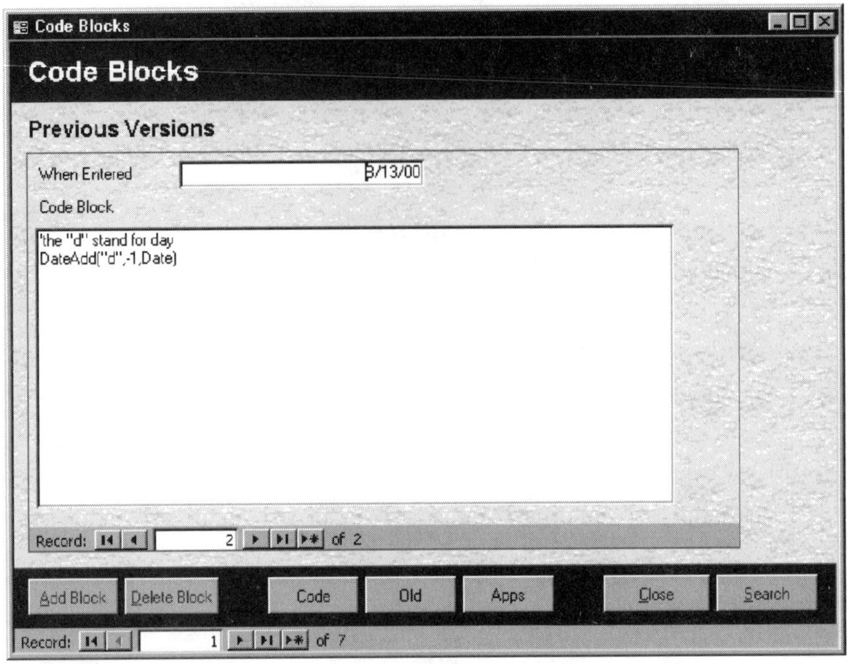

Figure 5-14

Previous Versions page from the Code Blocks form

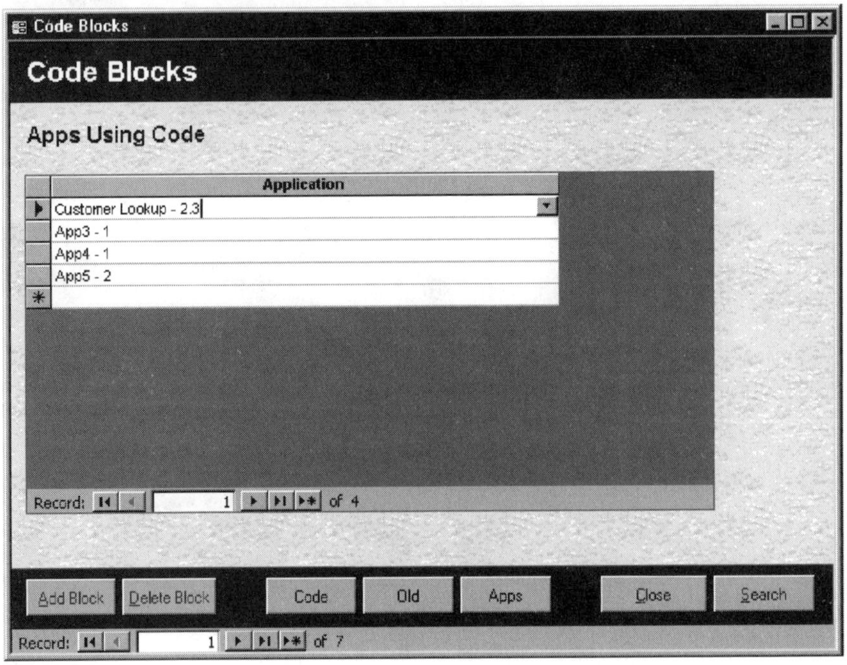

Figure 5-15

Apps Using Code page of the Code Blocks form

The Apps Using Code page enables the user to select the applications that have this code in use.

Two other forms are part of this database application. They both are accessible through the menu. The first is the Languages form, which is displayed in Figure 5-16.

Each of the code blocks is written in a specific language. Information about those languages is managed through the Languages form. The user could use this form to store specific requirements about a group of code based on a language or a sub-set of a language.

The other form available through the menu is the Applications form, shown in Figure 5-17.

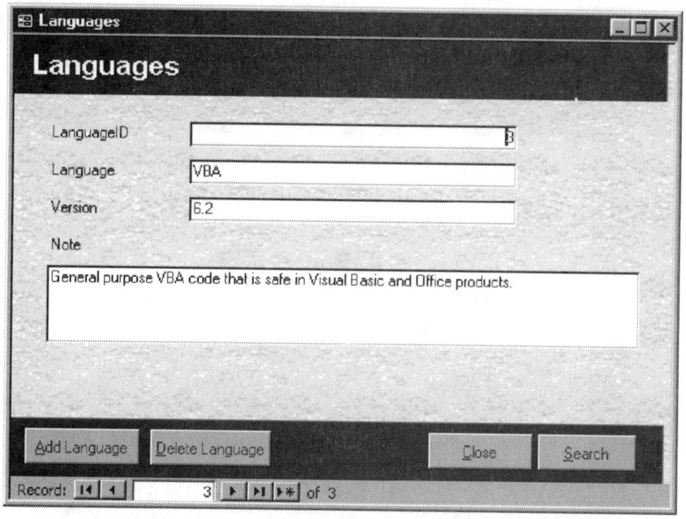

Figure 5-16

Languages form

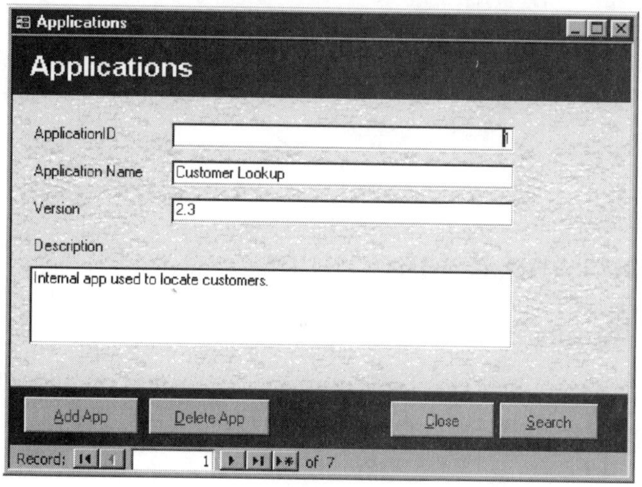

Figure 5-17

Applications form

Each of the code blocks can be used in numerous applications as you saw on the Apps Using Code page of the Code Blocks form. From this form, the user can manage information about those applications.

The database has one report called Top Five Blocks. This report is displayed in Figure 5-18.

This report displays the most popular code blocks, based on the total number of applications that are using the code block. As you see, when you look at the syntax of the SQL statement that this report is based on, the query limits the results so that only the five code blocks with the most applications using it are displayed.

Figure 5-18

Top Five Blocks report

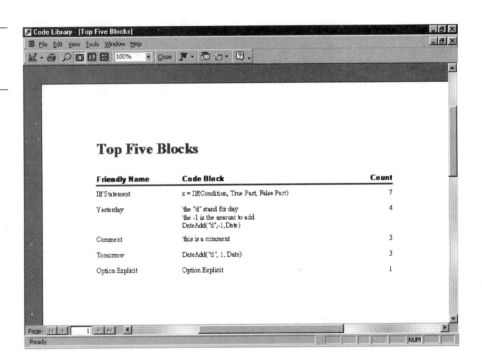

Table Definitions and Relationships

Applications Table

The Applications table stores the information about the applications that can use the code blocks.

Languages Table

The Languages table stores the data about the programming languages that are in use with the code blocks. The information is entered on the Languages form and is selected on the Code Blocks form.

CodeBlocks Table

The CodeBlocks table stores all the top level information about the code blocks. The table is in a one-to-many relationship with the Languages tables. Each of the code blocks is written for a specific language, but each of the languages can have many code blocks associated with it.

CodeBlockApps Table

The CodeBlocks table and the Applications table are in a many-to-many relationship. Each of the code blocks can be used in many applications and each of the applications can use many of the code blocks. To satisfy this relationship, a connecting table is needed. The CodeBlockApps table fills that rule. It is in a one-to-many relationship with both the CodeBlocks table and the Applications table.

OldCodeBlocks Table

Every time the user modifies a code block, the old version is saved in the OldCodeBlocks table. The table is in a one-to-many relationship with the CodeBlocks table. Each old block goes with an existing code block, but each code block can have numerous old versions.

Field Specifications

Applications Table

The field specifications for the Applications table are displayed in Table 5-7.

The ApplicationID field is the primary key for this table. It uniquely identifies each of the records in the table and is automatically populated with a unique value when a new record is added to this table. The rest of the fields store information about the application.

Table 5-7	Field Name	Field Type	Notes
Applications Table Field Specifications	ApplicationID	AutoNumber	Primary Key
	ApplicationName	Text	Length = 50
	Version	Text	Length = 50
	Description	Memo	

Languages Table

The field specifications for the Languages table are displayed in Table 5-8.

The primary key in this table is the LanguageID field. The other fields store data about the programming languages used for the code blocks.

Table 5-8	Field Name	Field Type	Notes
Languages Table Field Specifications	LanguageID	AutoNumber	Primary Key
	Language	Text	Length = 50
	Version	Text	Length = 50
	TheNote	Memo	

CodeBlocks Table

The field specifications for the CodeBlocks table are displayed in Table 5-9.

Table 5-9	Field Name	Field Type	Notes
CodeBlocks Table Field Specifications	CodeBlockID	AutoNumber	Primary Key
	FriendlyName	Text	Length = 50
	LanguageID	Number	Type = Long, Foreign Key
	DateCreated	Date/Time	
	LastModifed	Date/Time	
	CodeBlock	Memo	

The CodeBlockID field is the primary key in this table. The LanguageID field is a foreign key that links this table to the Languages table. It is displayed to the user as a combo box because the Display Control property is set to combo box. It has the following value in the Row Source property:

```
SELECT [Languages].[LanguageID], [Language] & " - " & [Version]
AS Expr1 FROM Languages;
```

The user sees the name of the programming language, but the ID of the language is stored with this record.

The DateCreated field stores the date that the record was added to the table. It is set to the system date since it has this value in the Default Value property:

```
Date()
```

Both of the date fields are locked on the form so the user cannot change them.

CodeBlockApps Table

The field specifications for the CodeBlockApps table are displayed in Table 5-10.

Table 5-10

CodeBlockApps Table Field Specifications

Field Name	Field Type	Notes
CodeBlockAppID	AutoNumber	Primary Key
CodeBlockID	Number	Type = Long, Foreign Key
ApplicationID	Number	Type = Long, Foreign Key

The CodeBlockAppID field is the primary key in this linking table. The other two fields are foreign keys. The CodeBlockID field links the table to the CodeBlocks table. The ApplicationID field connects this table to the Applications table. The field is displayed to the user as a combo box on the Code Blocks form. The field has this value in the Row Source property:

```
SELECT [Applications].[ApplicationID],
[ApplicationName] & " - " & [Version] AS Expr1 FROM Applications;
```

The ID of the application is stored with the record, but the user sees the name of the application along with the version of the application.

CodeBlockApps Table

The field specifications for the CodeBlockApps table are displayed in Table 5-11.

The OldCodeBlockID field is the primary key in this table. The Code-BlockID field is a foreign key that links this table to the CodeBlocks table.

Table 5-11	Field Name	Field Type	Notes
CodeBlockApps Table Field Specifications	OldCodeBlockID	AutoNumber	Primary Key
	CodeBlockID	Number	Type = Long, Foreign Key
	WhenEntered	Date/Time	
	CodeBlock	Memo	

Forms

Switchboard Form

The Switchboard form is used to navigate through the forms and report in the Code Library database. It was created using the Switchboard wizard, which is accessible within Access through the Tools/Database Utilities/Switchboard Manager menu item. Only the look and design of the form produced with that wizard have been altered.

Code Blocks Form

The code on the code blocks form provides the functionality for the buttons on the form, as well as other tasks.

When the user clicks on the Add Block button, the first code block fires.

```
Private Sub CommandAdd_Click()
    DoCmd.GoToRecord , , acNewRec
    [FriendlyName].SetFocus
End Sub
```

First, move the record pointer onto a new blank record:

```
DoCmd.GoToRecord , , acNewRec
```

Then move the insertion point to the FriendlyName field so the user can start entering data:

```
[FriendlyName].SetFocus
```

The next code block fires when the Delete Block button is pressed.

```
Private Sub CommandDelete_Click()
    On Error GoTo HandleError
    DoCmd.DoMenuItem acFormBar, acEditMenu, 8, , acMenuVer70
    DoCmd.DoMenuItem acFormBar, acEditMenu, 6, , acMenuVer70
    [FriendlyName].SetFocus
    Exit Sub
HandleError:
    If Err.Number <> 2501 Then
        MsgBox Err.Number & " " & Err.Description
    End If
End Sub
```

You need to trap for a known error that can occur when a record is deleted, so an On Error statement is necessary:

```
On Error GoTo HandleError
```

Then attempt to delete the record:

```
DoCmd.DoMenuItem acFormBar, acEditMenu, 8, , acMenuVer70
DoCmd.DoMenuItem acFormBar, acEditMenu, 6, , acMenuVer70
```

If the record was deleted, move the focus back to the detail section:

```
[FriendlyName].SetFocus
```

and exit this procedure:

```
Exit Sub
```

If an error were to occur, the code flows here:

```
HandleError:
```

Then check to see if the error was due to the user canceling the record deletion:

```
If Err.Number <> 2501 Then
```

If it wasn't, the following error message is displayed:

```
MsgBox Err.Number & " " & Err.Description
```

When the user presses the Code button, he or she is taken to the first page of the form. This is done through the GoToPage method of the DoCmd object:

```
Private Sub Command33_Click()
    DoCmd.GoToPage 1
End Sub
```

If the user clicks on the Old button, he or she is taken to the Previous Versions page, which is the second page of the form:

```
Private Sub Command34_Click()
    DoCmd.GoToPage 2
End Sub
```

If the user presses the Apps button, the third page of the form appears through the GoToPage method:

```
Private Sub Command35_Click()
    DoCmd.GoToPage 3
End Sub
```

When the user presses the Search button, the next code block fires.

```
Private Sub CommandSearch_Click()
    Screen.PreviousControl.SetFocus
    DoCmd.DoMenuItem acFormBar, acEditMenu, 10, , acMenuVer70
End Sub
```

It uses the SetFocus method to move the focus back to the control that the user was on before pressing the Search button:

```
Screen.PreviousControl.SetFocus
```

Open the Access Search dialog:

```
DoCmd.DoMenuItem acFormBar, acEditMenu, 10, , acMenuVer70
```

When the user presses the Close button, the Close method of the DoCmd object is used to close this form:

```
Private Sub CommandClose_Click()
    DoCmd.Close
End Sub
```

One other button, Copy Code to Clipboard, is on this form. It copies the code block to the Windows Clipboard.

```
Private Sub Command40_Click()
    [CodeBlock].SetFocus
    [CodeBlock].SelStart = 0
    [CodeBlock].SelLength = Len([CodeBlock].Text)
    DoCmd.RunCommand acCmdCopy
    [CodeBlock].SelLength = 0
End Sub
```

Start by setting focus to the Code Block text box on the form, which contains the text to be copied:

```
[CodeBlock].SetFocus
```

Highlight all the text in that text box so that it can be placed on the clipboard. We start our highlighted text before the first character in the Text Box:

```
[CodeBlock].SelStart = 0
```

Then set the length of the characters highlighted to the total number of characters in this Text Box:

```
[CodeBlock].SelLength = Len([CodeBlock].Text)
```

Copy that highlighted text onto the Clipboard:

```
DoCmd.RunCommand acCmdCopy
```

and clear the highlighted text:

```
[CodeBlock].SelLength = 0
```

This form links to the Languages form when the user double-clicks on the Languages field.

```
Private Sub LanguageID_DblClick(Cancel As Integer)
    If IsNull([LanguageID]) Or [LanguageID] = 0 Then
        DoCmd.OpenForm "Languages", , , , acFormAdd, acDialog
        [LanguageID].Requery
    Else
        DoCmd.OpenForm "Languages", , , _
            "[LanguageID] = " & [LanguageID], , acDialog
        [LanguageID].Requery
    End If
End Sub
```

First, check to see if the field is blank:

```
If IsNull([LanguageID]) Or [LanguageID] = 0 Then
```

If it is, assume the user wants to add a new record. The Languages form is opened in Add mode, enabling the user to add a new record:

```
DoCmd.OpenForm "Languages", , , , acFormAdd, acDialog
```

Since it is opened as a Dialog, the next line of code, which repopulates the combo box, will not run until the user is done with the Languages form:

```
[LanguageID].Requery
```

If the field was not empty, the code flows here:

```
Else
```

Open the Languages form and have it display the contents of the selected language:

```
DoCmd.OpenForm "Languages", , , _
    "[LanguageID] = " & [LanguageID], , acDialog
```

Then repopulate the list portion of the LanguageID combo box:

```
[LanguageID].Requery
```

Whenever the user changes the code block, save the old version of the code into the OldCodeBlocks table. To do this, a variable that will store the contents of the old version of the code is necessary:

```
Private OriginalCodeBlock As String
```

Every time the record pointer moves, store the contents of the current code block into this variable:

```
Private Sub Form_Current()
    OriginalCodeBlock = IIf(IsNull([CodeBlock]), "", [CodeBlock])
End Sub
```

Then when the record is updated, check to see if the code block has changed, which means the old value must be stored.

```
Private Sub Form_BeforeUpdate(Cancel As Integer)
    Dim MyDB As DAO.Database
    If [CodeBlock] <> OriginalCodeBlock And OriginalCodeBlock <> "" Then
        Set MyDB = CurrentDb
        MyDB.Execute "Insert Into OldCodeBlocks (CodeBlockID, WhenEntered, " _
            & "CodeBlock) Values (" _
            & [CodeBlockID] & ", " _
            & "#" & [LastModified] & "#, " _
            & "'" & Replace([OriginalCodeBlock], "'", "''", , , vbTextCompare) & "')"
        Old_Code_Blocks_subform.Requery
    End If
    [LastModified] = Date
End Sub
```

Connect to the current database to insert a new record through code:

```
Dim MyDB As DAO.Database
```

Then check to see if the code block has changed and that the old code block was not blank:

```
If [CodeBlock] <> OriginalCodeBlock And OriginalCodeBlock <> "" Then
```

If both of those conditions are met, connect to the database:

```
Set MyDB = CurrentDb
```

and store the old code block into the OldCodeBlocks table:

```
MyDB.Execute "Insert Into OldCodeBlocks (CodeBlockID, WhenEntered, " _
    & "CodeBlock) Values (" _
    & [CodeBlockID] & ", " _
    & "#" & [LastModified] & "#, " _
    & "'" & Replace([OriginalCodeBlock], "'", "''", , , vbTextCompare) & "')"
```

Then repopulate the records in the Previous Versions page's sub-form:

```
Old_Code_Blocks_subform.Requery
```

Change the date in the last modified date so that it contains the current system date:

```
[LastModified] = Date
```

Languages and Applications Forms

The Languages and Applications forms have nearly identical code, so they are discussed in this section together. Both forms contain code blocks that fire when the footer buttons are pressed.

When the user presses the Add button, the first code block fires.

```
Private Sub CommandAdd_Click()
    DoCmd.GoToRecord , , acNewRec
    [Language].SetFocus
End Sub
```

Start by moving the record pointer to a new record:

```
DoCmd.GoToRecord , , acNewRec
```

and setting the focus to the first editable field in the detail section of the form:

```
[Language].SetFocus
```

When the user presses the Delete button, the next code block fires.

```
Private Sub CommandDelete_Click()
    On Error GoTo HandleError
    DoCmd.DoMenuItem acFormBar, acEditMenu, 8, , acMenuVer70
    DoCmd.DoMenuItem acFormBar, acEditMenu, 6, , acMenuVer70
    [Language].SetFocus
    Exit Sub
HandleError:
    If Err.Number <> 2501 Then
        MsgBox Err.Number & " " & Err.Description
    End If
End Sub
```

Start by telling the compiler that errors will be handled that occur in this procedure:

```
On Error GoTo HandleError
```

Then delete the current record:

```
DoCmd.DoMenuItem acFormBar, acEditMenu, 8, , acMenuVer70
DoCmd.DoMenuItem acFormBar, acEditMenu, 6, , acMenuVer70
```

If the deletion is successful, move the focus back to the detail section:

```
[Language].SetFocus
```

and exit this procedure:

```
Exit Sub
```

If an error were to occur, the code flows to this label:

```
HandleError:
```

Then check to see if the error was due to the cancellation of the record deletion:

```
If Err.Number <> 2501 Then
```

If it wasn't, display the current error to the user:

```
MsgBox Err.Number & " " & Err.Description
```

When the user presses the Search button, the next code block fires.

```
Private Sub CommandSearch_Click()
    Screen.PreviousControl.SetFocus
    DoCmd.DoMenuItem acFormBar, acEditMenu, 10, , acMenuVer70
End Sub
```

Start by moving the focus back to the control the user was on before pressing the Search button:

```
Screen.PreviousControl.SetFocus
```

Then open the built-in Access Search dialog:

```
DoCmd.DoMenuItem acFormBar, acEditMenu, 10, , acMenuVer70
```

The other procedure on this form closes the form when the Close button is pressed:

```
Private Sub CommandClose_Click()
    DoCmd.Close
End Sub
```

Report

Top Five Blocks Report

The Top Five Blocks report displays the five most popular code blocks based on the number of applications that use the code block. The report is based on the Top Five Blocks query, which has the following syntax:

```
SELECT TOP 5 CodeBlocks.FriendlyName, CodeBlocks.CodeBlock,
Count(CodeBlockApps.ApplicationID) AS [Count]
FROM CodeBlocks LEFT JOIN CodeBlockApps ON
CodeBlocks.CodeBlockID = CodeBlockApps.CodeBlockID
GROUP BY CodeBlocks.FriendlyName, CodeBlocks.CodeBlock
ORDER BY Count(CodeBlockApps.ApplicationID) DESC;
```

Note the Top 5 text, which tells the compiler that you only want the first five records, based on the sort indicated. Note that the number of applications that the code block is used in is counted. Also note that the data comes from two tables: the CodeBlocks table and the CodeBlockApps table.

Software - Hardware Profiles Database

Next, we will review the Software - Hardware Profiles database application. This database enables someone such as a network administrator to track the computers in their network, the software and hardware on those computers and other network devices.

Sample Walk-through

When the user first enters this application, they see the menu displayed in Figure 5-19.

This form was selected in the Startup dialog. Therefore, it is displayed when the database first opens. From here the user can select from the six forms and the two reports.

If the user selects the Computers button, he or she sees the form displayed in Figure 5-20.

Figure 5-19

Entry form into the Software - Hardware Profiles application

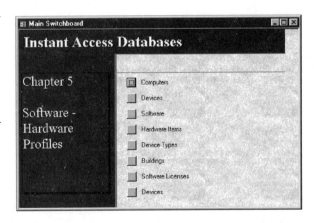

Figure 5-20

General page
from the
Computers form

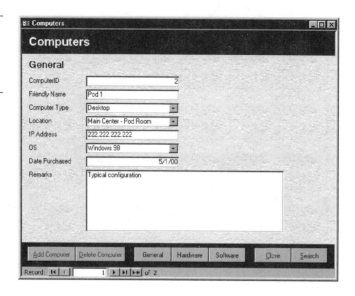

The Computers form has three pages. The first is the General page that
contains general, singular information about the computer. The OS field is
self-populating, so as the user enters a new value in that field, it will be
there for future records.

When the user presses the Hardware button, he or she is taken to the
Hardware page shown in Figure 5-21.

On the Hardware page, the user selects the specific configuration of
this computer. Each of the items listed here comes from the Hardware
Items form.

When the user clicks on the Software button, he or she sees the Software page shown in Figure 5-22.

The user would use this page to select all the software titles that are
installed on that computer. Each of the software titles has a maximum
number of licenses associated with it. If the user exceeds that allotment,
a warning message box is displayed.

The next form accessible through the menu is the Devices form, which
is displayed in Figure 5-23.

Devices are other pieces of equipment on the network that are not computers. The user would select the location for the device and the type. The
types listed come from another table.

Figure 5-21

Hardware page of
the Computers
form

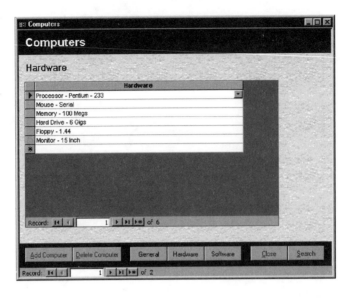

Figure 5-22

Software page
from the
Computers form

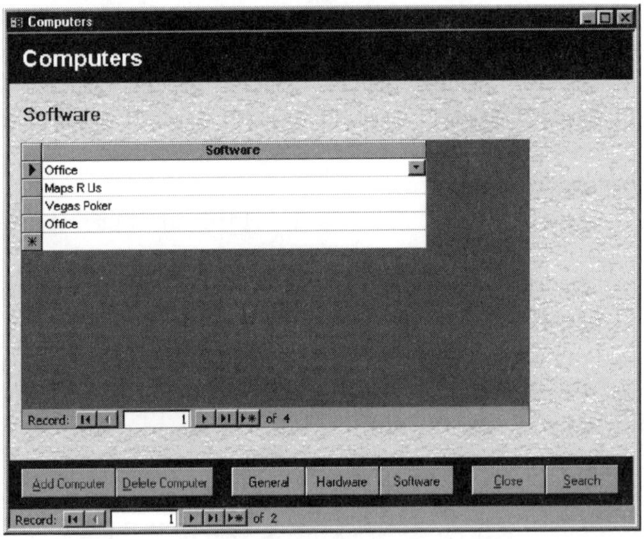

When the user clicks on the Software button on the menu, they see the
form displayed in Figure 5-24.

Here the user would enter the different software titles owned by the
company and the number of licenses of each that are held.

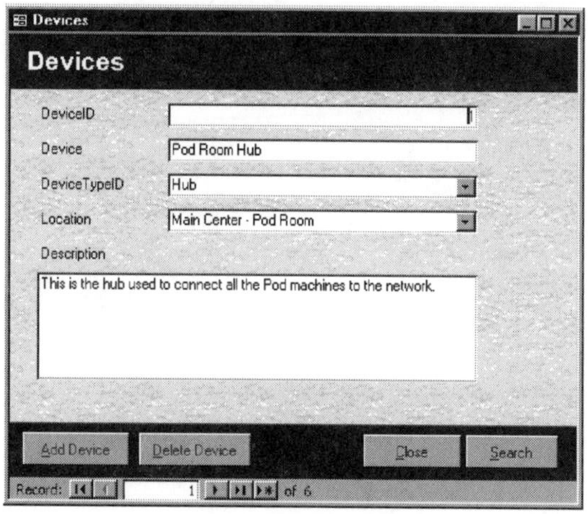

Figure 5-23

Devices form

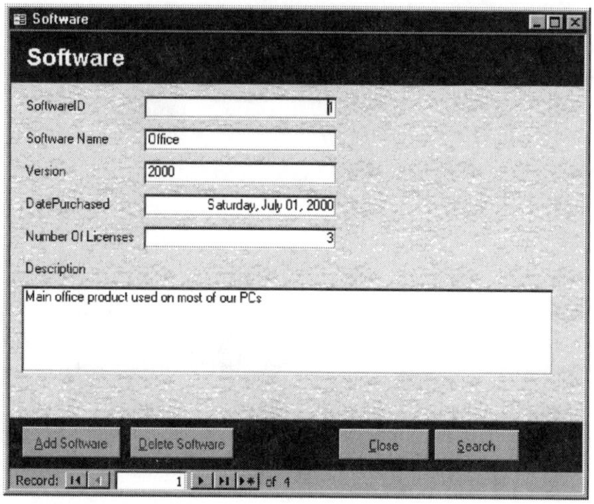

Figure 5-24

Software form

The next form accessible through the main menu is the Hardware Items form shown in Figure 5-25.

Here the user would enter all the possible hardware pieces that can be in a computer. The Category field self-populates. Whenever a new entry is added, it becomes part of the list portion of the combo box for other records.

The next form is the Device Types form displayed in Figure 5-26.

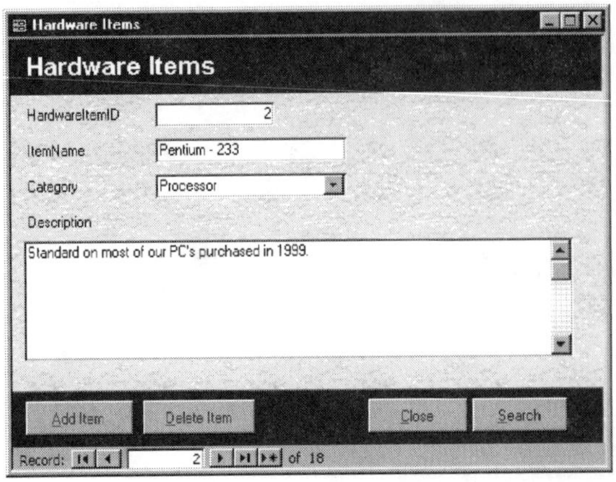

Figure 5-25

Hardware Items
form

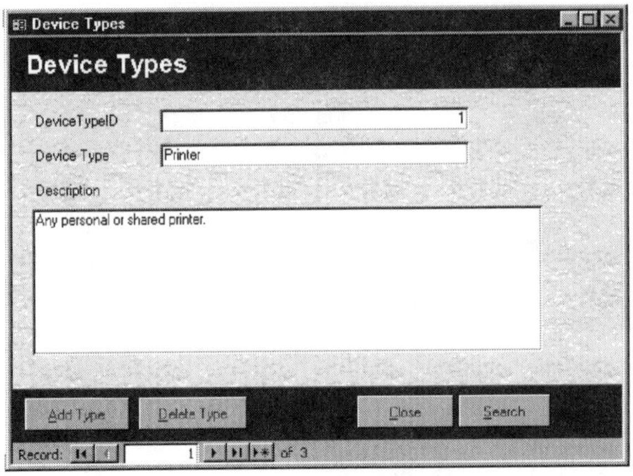

Figure 5-26

Device Types
form

Each of the devices entered on the Device form were of a specific type. The Device Types form is used to enter those types.

The other form available in this database is the Buildings form displayed in Figure 5-27.

Each of the computers and the devices are located in a particular room. Each of the rooms is in a particular building. The user would use the Buildings form to work with that information.

Two reports are part of this database application. The first one is called Software Licenses and is displayed in Figure 5-28.

Figure 5-27

Buildings form

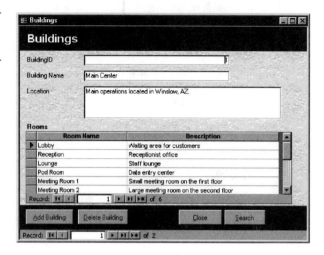

Figure 5-28

Software Licenses

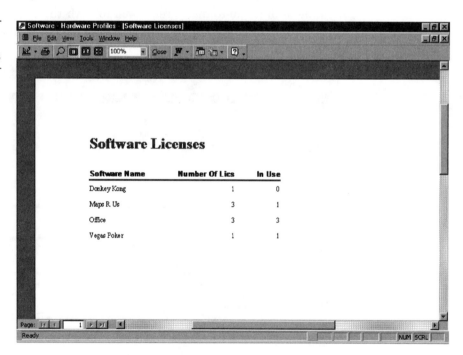

This report displays to the user all the software titles with the number of licenses available and the number in use.

The other report is called Devices and is displayed in Figure 5-29.

The Devices report groups information about the devices first by the location of the device and then by the type of device.

Table Definitions and Relationships

Buildings Table

The Buildings table stores information about the buildings. In this database, buildings contain rooms and computers, and devices are located in rooms.

Rooms Table

The Rooms table stores information about the rooms in the buildings. The table is in a one-to-many relationship with the Buildings table. Each of the rooms is located in a building, but each building can have more than one room.

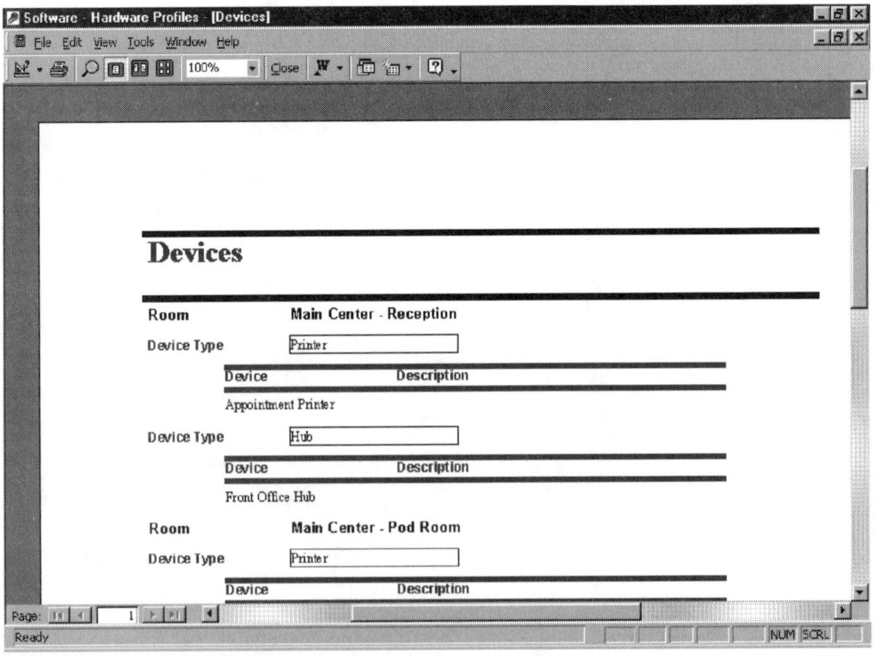

Figure 5-29

Devices report

DeviceTypes Table

Devices are pieces of equipment that are part of the network, but are not computers. The DeviceTypes table stores the different categories of these pieces of equipment, such as printers or hubs.

Devices Table

The Devices table stores information on the non-computer equipment on the network. The table is in a one-to-many relationship with the Device-Types table. Each device is of a specific type, but you can have many devices of the same type. The table is also in a one-to-many relationship with the Rooms table. Each Device is located in a room, but each room can hold many devices.

Software Table

The Software table stores data about the software that can be installed on the computers.

HardwareItems Table

The HardwareItems table stores the detailed components that make up a computer. This includes things like monitors, CPUs and drives.

Computers Table

The Computers table stores the top-level information about the computers on the network. The table is in a one-to-many relationship with the Rooms table. Each of the Computers is located in a room, but each room can have many computers.

ComputerSoftware Table

Each computer can have many software titles installed on it. And each software title can be installed on many computers. That means that the Computers table and the Software table are in a many-to-many relationship. The ComputerSoftware table satisfies that relationship by filling the role of the connecting table. It is in a one-to-many relationship with the Computers table and the Software table.

ComputerHardware Table

Similarly, the Computers table and the HardwareItems table are in a many-to-many relationship. Each computer has many pieces of hardware components in it. And each type of hardware can be used in more than one computer. The ComputerHardware table links these two tables together. It is in a one-to-many relationship with the Computers table and the HardwareItems table.

Field Specifications

Buildings Table

The field specifications for the Buildings table are displayed in Table 5-12.

The BuildingID field is the primary key of the table. It is automatically populated with a value when a new record is added since it is an Auto-Number field. The rest of the fields store information about the building.

Rooms Table

The field specifications for the Rooms table are displayed in Table 5-13.

The RoomID field is the primary key for this table. The BuildingID field is a foreign key. It links this table to the Buildings table.

Table 5-12

Buildings Table Field Specifications

Field Name	Field Type	Notes
BuildingID	AutoNumber	Primary Key
BuildingName	Text	Length = 50
Location	Memo	

Table 5-13

Rooms Table Field Specifications

Field Name	Field Type	Notes
RoomID	AutoNumber	Primary Key
BuildingID	Number	Type = Long, Foreign Key
RoomName	Text	Length = 50
Description	Memo	

DeviceTypes Table

The field specifications for the DeviceTypes table are displayed in Table 5-14.

The DeviceType field is the primary key in this table. The other fields store information about the device type.

Devices Table

The field specifications for the Devices table are displayed in Table 5-15.

The DeviceID field is the primary key. The DeviceTypeID field is a foreign key that links this table to the DeviceTypes table. The field is displayed to the user as a combo box since the Display Control property is set to combo box. It has the following value in the Row Source property:

```
SELECT [DeviceTypes].[DeviceTypeID], [DeviceTypes].[DeviceType]
FROM DeviceTypes;
```

The first column, DeviceTypeID, is the bound column. The type of device is what the user sees in the list portion of the combo box.

The RoomID field is another foreign key and it links this table to the Rooms table. It, too, is displayed as a combo box on the form to the user and has this value in its Row Source property:

Table 5-14

DeviceTypes Table Field Specifications

Field Name	Field Type	Notes
DeviceTypeID	AutoNumber	Primary Key
DeviceType	Text	Length = 50
Description	Memo	

Table 5-15

Devices Table Field Specifications

Field Name	Field Type	Notes
DeviceID	AutoNumber	Primary Key
Device	Text	Length = 50
DeviceTypeID	Number	Type = Long, Foreign Key
RoomID	Number	Type = Long, Foreign Key
Description	Memo	

```
SELECT [Rooms].[RoomID], [BuildingName] & " - " & [RoomName] AS
Expr1
FROM Buildings INNER JOIN Rooms
ON [Buildings].[BuildingID]=[Rooms].[BuildingID]
ORDER BY [BuildingName] & " - " & [RoomName];
```

The ID of the room is stored in the table, but the user sees the name of the building and room concatenated together. Since those names come from two different tables, the Rooms table and the Buildings table are joined together in this query.

Software Table

The field specifications for the Software table are displayed in Table 5-16.

Field Name	Field Type	Notes
SoftwareID	AutoNumber	Primary Key
SoftwareName	Text	Length = 50
Version	Text	Length = 50
DatePurchased	Date/Time	
NumberOfLics	Number	Type = Long
Description	Memo	

Table 5-16

Software Table Field Specifications

The SoftwareID field is the primary key in this table. The DatePurchase field stores the date that the software was purchased. It has the following text in the Input Mask property:

```
99/99/0000;0;_
```

This allows the user to enter a one or two-digit day and month, but they must enter a four-digit year.

The NumberOfLics field stores the number of licenses that are owned for this software title. The field has this Validation Rule property value:

```
>0
```

so the value entered must be a number greater than zero. If the rule is violated, the user sees this message:

```
This field must be a positive number.
```

HardwareItems Table

The field specifications for the HardwareItems table are displayed in Table 5-17.

	Field Name	Field Type	Notes
Table 5-17 HardwareItems Table Field Specifications	HardwareItemsID	AutoNumber	Primary Key
	ItemName	Text	Length = 50
	Category	Text	Length = 50
	Description	Memo	

The HardwareItemsID field is a primary key for this table. The Category field stores the type of hardware item this is. It is displayed as a combo box. The list portion contains all the previously entered values in this field, which means that it is self-populating. This is done by setting the Row Source property to the following value:

```
SELECT DISTINCT [HardwareItems].[Category] FROM HardwareItems;
```

Computers Table

The field specifications for the Computers table are displayed in Table 5-18.

	Field Name	Field Type	Notes
Table 5-18 Computers Table Field Specifications	ComputerID	AutoNumber	Primary Key
	FriendlyName	Text	Length = 50
	ComputerType	Text	Length = 50
	RoomID	Number	Type = Long, Foreign Key
	IPAddress	Text	Length = 50
	OS	Text	Length = 50
	DatePurchased	Date/Time	
	Remarks	Memo	

The ComputerID field is the primary key for this table. The Computer-Type field stores the type of computer such as Laptop or Desktop. It is displayed as a combo box that has the following fixed list entered into the Row Source property:

```
"Desktop";"Laptop";"Workstation";"Server"
```

The RoomID field is a foreign key that links this table to the Rooms table. It is displayed as a combo box to the user on the Computers form and has the following value in the Row Source property:

```
SELECT [Rooms].[RoomID], [BuildingName] & " - " &
[RoomName] AS Expr1 FROM Buildings INNER JOIN Rooms ON
Buildings].[BuildingID]=[Rooms].[BuildingID];
```

The ID of the room is the bound column but the user sees the name of the building with the name of the room in the list portion of the combo box. Since these names come from two different tables, the Rooms table and the Buildings table are joined together in this query.

The IPAddress stores the network IP Address of the computer. The following text was placed in the Input Mask property for this field:

```
999.999.999.999;0;_
```

This mask allows the user to enter the IP Address without putting in any of the periods. Each of the number sections are optional.

The OS field is meant to store the operating system of the computer. It is displayed as a self-populating combo box to the user since it has this value in the Row Source property:

```
SELECT [Computers].[OS] FROM Computers;
```

The DatePurchased field stores the date that the computer was purchased. The date entered cannot be a date in the future because of this validation rule:

```
<=Date()
```

Remember that the function Date() returns the current system date. If the rule is violated, the user sees this message, which was placed in the Validation Text property:

```
This field must have a date that is either today or in the past.
```

ComputerSoftware Table

The field specifications for the ComputerSoftware table are displayed in Table 5-19.

Table 5-19	Field Name	Field Type	Notes
ComputerSoftware Table Field Specifications	ComputerSoftwareID	AutoNumber	Primary Key
	ComputerD	Number	Type = Long, Foreign Key
	SoftwareID	Number	Type = Long, Foreign Key

The ComputerSoftwareID field is the primary key in this table. The other fields in this table are foreign keys. The ComputerID field links this table to the Computers table. The SoftwareID field links this table to the Software table. That field is displayed to the user as a combo box and has this value in the Row Source property:

```
SELECT [Software].[SoftwareID], [Software].[SoftwareName] FROM
Software;
```

The user sees the name of the software but the ID of the software is stored in the record since the Bound Column property is set to 1.

ComputerHardware Table

The field specifications for the ComputerHardware table are displayed in Table 5-20.

Table 5-20	Field Name	Field Type	Notes
Computer Hardware Table Field Specifications	ComputerHardwareID	AutoNumber	Primary Key
	ComputerD	Number	Type = Long, Foreign Key
	HardwareItemID	Number	Type = Long, Foreign Key

The ComputerHardwareID field is the primary key in this table. The ComputerID field is a foreign key that links this table to the Computers table. The HardwareItemsID field is also a foreign key that links this table to the HardwareItems table. The user sees this field as a combo box on the Computers form. The field has this value in the Row Source property:

```
SELECT [HardwareItems].[HardwareItemID],
[Category] & " - " & [ItemName] AS Expr1 FROM HardwareItems;
```

The user sees the category and name of the hardware item, but the ID of the hardware item is stored in the database.

Forms

Switchboard Form

The Switchboard form is used to navigate through the forms and reports in the Software - Hardware Profiles database application. It was created using the Switchboard wizard, which is accessible within Access through the Tools/Database Utilities/Switchboard Manager menu item. Only the look and design of the form produced with that wizard have been altered.

Computers Form

The code on the Computers form provides the functionality for the footer buttons. It also prompts the user if they use a software title more times than the number of licenses they own to that title.

The first code block fires when the Add Computer button is pressed.

```
Private Sub CommandAdd_Click()
    DoCmd.GoToRecord , , acNewRec
    [FriendlyName].SetFocus
End Sub
```

First, move the record pointer onto a new record using the GoToRecord method:

```
DoCmd.GoToRecord , , acNewRec
```

Then set the focus to the FriendlyName field, so the user can start entering data:

```
[FriendlyName].SetFocus
```

When the user presses the Delete Computer button, the next code block fires.

```
Private Sub CommandDelete_Click()
    On Error GoTo HandleError
    DoCmd.DoMenuItem acFormBar, acEditMenu, 8, , acMenuVer70
    DoCmd.DoMenuItem acFormBar, acEditMenu, 6, , acMenuVer70
    [FriendlyName].SetFocus
    Exit Sub
HandleError:
    If Err.Number <> 2501 Then
        MsgBox Err.Number & " " & Err.Description
    End If
End Sub
```

Tell the compiler that you will manage errors that occur in this procedure:

```
On Error GoTo HandleError
```

Then delete the current record:

```
DoCmd.DoMenuItem acFormBar, acEditMenu, 8, , acMenuVer70
DoCmd.DoMenuItem acFormBar, acEditMenu, 6, , acMenuVer70
```

Set the focus back to the detail section of the form:

```
[FriendlyName].SetFocus
```

and leave this procedure:

```
Exit Sub
```

If an error were to occur, the code flows here:

```
HandleError:
```

Check to see if the error was due to the user canceling the record deletion:

```
If Err.Number <> 2501 Then
```

If it wasn't, display the error message to the user:

```
MsgBox Err.Number & " " & Err.Description
```

The Computers form is divided into three pages. The General, Hardware and Software buttons provide the way for the user to view those different pages. When the user clicks on the General button, she sees the first page of the form:

```
Private Sub Command37_Click()
    DoCmd.GoToPage 1
End Sub
```

If the user clicks on the Hardware button, she needs to be taken to the second page of the form. This is done through the GoToPage method of the DoCmd object:

```
Private Sub Command38_Click()
    DoCmd.GoToPage 2
End Sub
```

If the user clicks on the Software button, she sees the third page of the form:

```
Private Sub Command39_Click()
    DoCmd.GoToPage 3
End Sub
```

When the user clicks on the Search button, the next code block runs.

```
Private Sub CommandSearch_Click()
    Screen.PreviousControl.SetFocus
    DoCmd.DoMenuItem acFormBar, acEditMenu, 10, , acMenuVer70
End Sub
```

First, move back to the field the user was on before clicking on the Search button:

```
Screen.PreviousControl.SetFocus
```

Then open the Access Search dialog so that field can be searched:

```
DoCmd.DoMenuItem acFormBar, acEditMenu, 10, , acMenuVer70
```

The other procedure on this form fires when the Close button is pressed. It closes the current form:

```
Private Sub CommandClose_Click()
    DoCmd.Close
End Sub
```

The Computers form also contains a sub-form called ComputerSoftware sub-form that contains a code block. This code block checks each time a software title is added or updated to a computer and makes sure the user has enough licenses for that title. The code is placed in the BeforeUpdate event of the sub-form, which fires whenever a record is added or updated.

```
Private Sub Form_BeforeUpdate(Cancel As Integer)
    Dim MyDB As DAO.Database
    Dim RSLics As DAO.Recordset
    Dim RSMaxLics As DAO.Recordset
    Set MyDB = CurrentDb
    Set RSLics = MyDB.OpenRecordset("Select Count(SoftwareID) as
TheCOunt " _
        & "from ComputerSoftware where SoftwareID = " &
[SoftwareID], dbOpenSnapshot)
    Set RSMaxLics = MyDB.OpenRecordset("Select NumberOfLics from
Software " _
        & "where SoftwareID = " & [SoftwareID], dbOpenSnapshot)
    If RSLics("TheCount") >= RSMaxLics("NumberOfLics") Then
        MsgBox "You have exceeded the maximum number of Licenses "
_
            & "for this software product."
    End If
End Sub
```

A connection to the database in the code is needed:

```
Dim MyDB As DAO.Database
```

as well as a recordset object that will retrieve the total number of licenses in use for this title:

```
Dim RSLics As DAO.Recordset
```

and the number of licenses owned for this title:

```
Dim RSMaxLics As DAO.Recordset
```

Then connect to the current database:

```
Set MyDB = CurrentDb
```

and retrieve the number of licenses for this title that are in use:

```
Set RSLics = MyDB.OpenRecordset("Select Count(SoftwareID) as
TheCOunt " _
        & "from ComputerSoftware where SoftwareID = " &
[SoftwareID], dbOpenSnapshot)
```

and the maximum number allowed for the software title:

```
Set RSMaxLics = MyDB.OpenRecordset("Select NumberOfLics from
Software " _
        & "where SoftwareID = " & [SoftwareID], dbOpenSnapshot)
```

Then compare the two to see if there are more in use than allowed:

```
If RSLics("TheCount") >= RSMaxLics("NumberOfLics") Then
```

If so, inform the user of the problem through a message box:

```
MsgBox "You have exceeded the maximum number of Licenses " _
        & "for this software product."
```

Devices, Software, Hardware Items, Device Types and Buildings Forms

The remaining forms have nearly identical code and are discussed in this section collectively.

Each of these forms has code that fires when the buttons in the footer of the form are pressed. When the Add button is pressed, the first code block fires.

```
Private Sub CommandAdd_Click()
    DoCmd.GoToRecord , , acNewRec
    [DeviceType].SetFocus
End Sub
```

Start by moving the record pointer to a new blank record:

```
DoCmd.GoToRecord , , acNewRec
```

and then set focus to the first editable field in the detail section:

```
[DeviceType].SetFocus
```

The next code block fires when the delete button is pressed.

```
Private Sub CommandDelete_Click()
    On Error GoTo HandleError
    DoCmd.DoMenuItem acFormBar, acEditMenu, 8, , acMenuVer70
    DoCmd.DoMenuItem acFormBar, acEditMenu, 6, , acMenuVer70
    [DeviceType].SetFocus
    Exit Sub
HandleError:
    If Err.Number <> 2501 Then
        MsgBox Err.Number & " " & Err.Description
    End If
End Sub
```

An On Error statement tells the compiler what action to take if an error occurs. Here, tell it to go to a label called HandleError:

```
On Error GoTo HandleError
```

Then delete the current record:

```
DoCmd.DoMenuItem acFormBar, acEditMenu, 8, , acMenuVer70
DoCmd.DoMenuItem acFormBar, acEditMenu, 6, , acMenuVer70
```

and then set the focus back to the detail section:

```
[DeviceType].SetFocus
Exit Sub
```

If an error were to occur, the code would flow here as indicated in the On Error statement:

```
HandleError:
```

Check to see if the error that occurred is the one that means the user canceled the record deletion:

```
If Err.Number <> 2501 Then
```

If it was, take no action. Otherwise, display the error to the user:

```
MsgBox Err.Number & " " & Err.Description
```

When the user presses the Search button on any of these forms, the next code block fires.

```
Private Sub CommandSearch_Click()
    Screen.PreviousControl.SetFocus
    DoCmd.DoMenuItem acFormBar, acEditMenu, 10, , acMenuVer70
End Sub
```

Start by moving the focus back to the control the user was on before they clicked on the Search button:

```
Screen.PreviousControl.SetFocus
```

Then open the Access Search dialog:

```
DoCmd.DoMenuItem acFormBar, acEditMenu, 10, , acMenuVer70
```

The other button on these forms closes the form when the Close button is pressed, by using the Close method of the DoCmd object:

```
Private Sub CommandClose_Click()
    DoCmd.Close
End Sub
```

Reports

Software Licenses Report

The Software Licenses report displays the current number and maximum number of licenses allowed for each of the software titles. The report is based on two queries. The first is called Software Use Count and has the following SQL Syntax:

```
SELECT ComputerSoftware.SoftwareID,
Count(ComputerSoftware.ComputerID) AS [Count] FROM ComputerSoftware
GROUP BY ComputerSoftware.SoftwareID;
```

The query groups each of the software title and counts the number of times each is in use.

The second query is called Software Licenses, and it combines the results of the previous query with data in the Software table:

```
SELECT Software.SoftwareName, Software.NumberOfLics AS [Max
Lincenses], IIf(IsNumeric([Count]),[Count],0) AS [In Use]
FROM Software LEFT JOIN [Software Use Count]
ON Software.SoftwareID = [Software Use Count].SoftwareID
ORDER BY Software.SoftwareName;
```

First note that the join is a left join. This means that the query will output all the records in the Software table, even if no one is using that software title.

The query outputs three fields. The first is the name of the software. The second is the number of licenses available for this title. The other field is the number of times the software is in use based on the results of our last query.

Devices Report

The Devices report displays information on all the devices grouped first by their location and then by their type. The report is based directly on the Devices table.

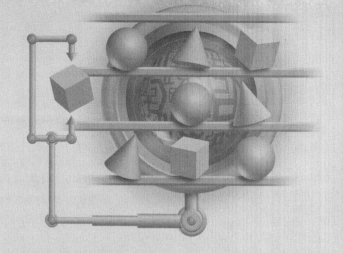

CHAPTER 6

Events

ON THE CD:

Events.mdb

Working with a Venue and Its Events

In this chapter, we will look at a database application called Events that
enables a user to host events at a venue, set the prices for seats, and then
reserve those seats. The database application is presented with a single
venue for hosting events, but you could easily add a form to add additional
venues to the system.

Events Database

Sample Walk-through

When the visitor first enters the Events database, he or she is presented with the navigational form shown in Figure 6-1. The menu enables the visitor to enter the various parts of the database application. When the visitor selects the Settings button, the form shown in Figure 6-2 appears.

The Settings form would most likely not be used by an end-user. It would most likely be used by a developer to define additional settings or venues that are supported in the database application. In fact, this part of the application is somewhat like a database within a database.

A setting, or venue, is a place where events occur. Each of the settings has its own form that contains the seating information for that venue. Thus, the developer creates a form for the setting, places labels on the

Figure 6-1

The Events database Navigational menu

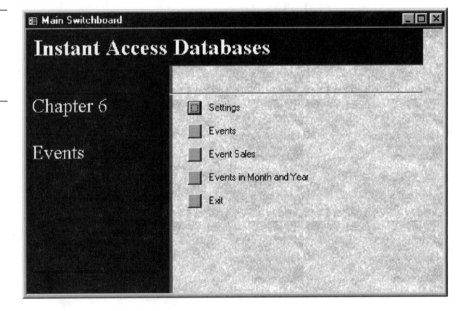

Figure 6-2

The Settings form

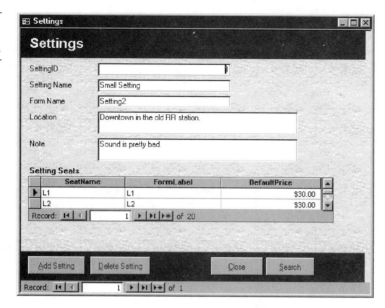

seating chart, and saves that form. He or she then comes to this form and indicates the basic information about the venue. Finally, the developer provides information about the seats on the venue.

This information is then used to host an event at a setting. The user does this through the Events form, which is displayed in Figure 6-3.

When the user wants to host a new event, he or she starts by providing the event information and selecting a venue. Notice that the user can't directly add seats to the event. This is done instead by pressing the "Add Seats for this Event" button. When the user does this, the Seats subform is populated as shown in Figure 6-4.

When the user adds the seats, the code uses the information supplied for this venue in the Settings form to add a new record for each of the seats in the venue. The user can't, however, add any new seats through this form; that has to be done through the Settings form. The user can change the price for any of the seats for this event.

Notice the summary information about the seating of this event located in the top-left corner of the form. Since the seating was just added, all the seats are available.

Figure 6-3

The Events form

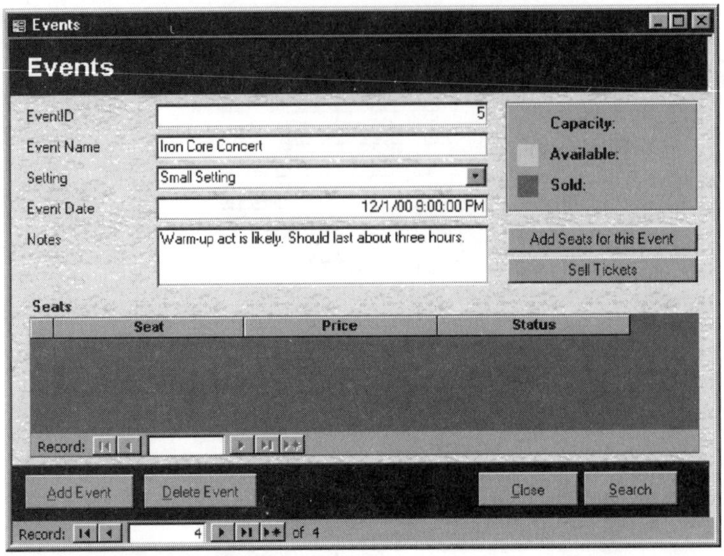

Figure 6-4

Adding seats to an event

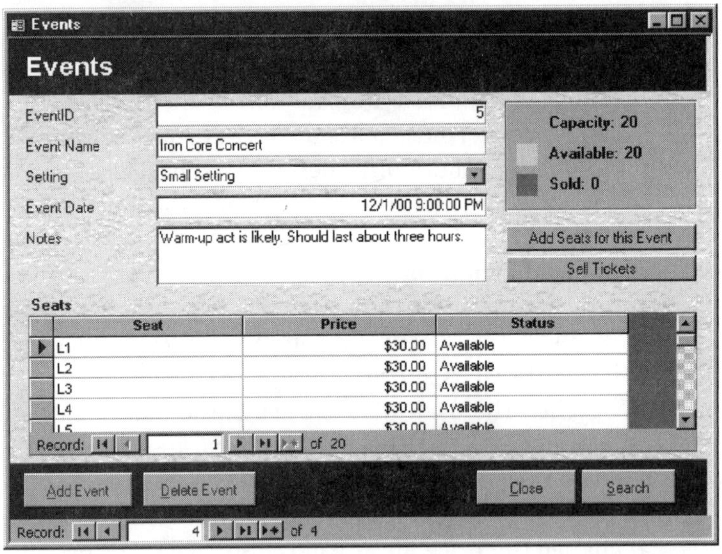

When the user is ready to reserve seats for this event, he or she will press the "Sell Tickets" button. When the user presses this button, a seating chart for this venue is displayed like the one shown in Figure 6-5.

The code goes to this form because it is the name provided for this setting on the Settings form. The seating chart shows which seats are available, held, or sold. When the user enters this form, he or she reserves seats by clicking on any available seat. After this is done, the seat color changes to blue and the summary fields on the form are updated. The user can then toggle a seat off by clicking on it. When the user is done with this order, he or she presses the Reserve Seats button and the seats are then marked as sold, as shown in Figure 6-6.

Now the seats that the user has just reserved are marked as sold in the Seats subform, and the summary information about the event reflects the change. The user can then reserve more seats for this event or other events at other venues.

Figure 6-5

The venue seating chart

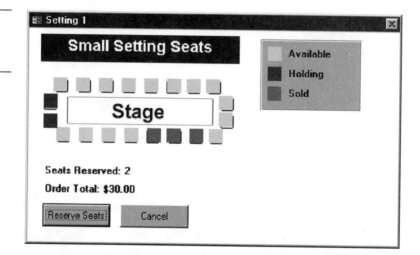

Figure 6-6

The Events form after the seats have been reserved

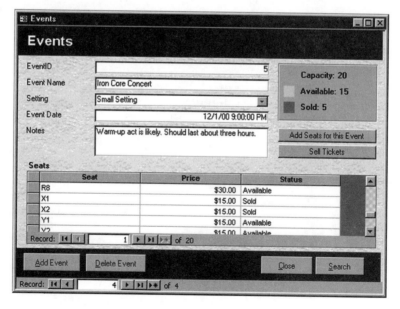

The Events database application has two reports. The first is the Events Sales report, which is displayed in Figure 6-7.

When the user first selects this report, he or she is asked to supply a date range for the report. The code then uses that date range to filter the records displayed and shows those dates in the report header. The report shows ticket sales information for each of the events in that date range.

The other report is displayed in Figure 6-8. This report groups the events by month and year and reports the total number of events in that time period.

Table Definitions and Relationships

Settings Table

The Settings table stores the information about the settings or venues. This information is then used to link some of the other tables.

Figure 6-7

The Event Sales report

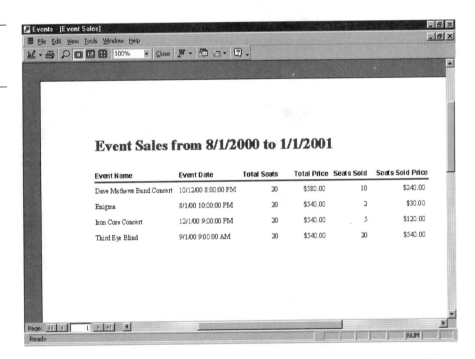

Event Sales from 8/1/2000 to 1/1/2001

Event Name	Event Date	Total Seats	Total Price	Seats Sold	Seats Sold Price
Dave Mathews Band Concert	10/12/00 8:00:00 PM	20	$580.00	10	$240.00
Enigma	8/1/00 10:00:00 PM	20	$540.00	2	$30.00
Iron Core Concert	12/1/00 9:00:00 PM	20	$540.00	5	$120.00
Third Eye Blind	9/1/00 9:00:00 AM	20	$540.00	20	$540.00

Figure 6-8

Events in Month
and Year report

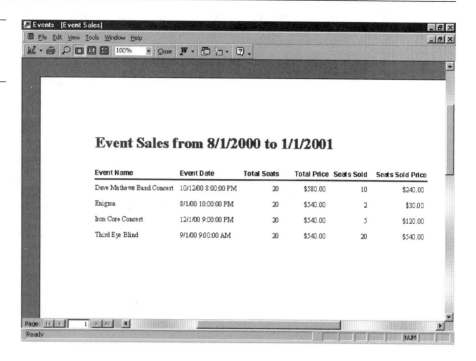

SettingSeats Table

The SettingSeats table stores information on the seats at a setting. The table is in a one-to-many relationship with the Settings table. Each setting has many seats, but each seat is located at a single setting. The data in this table is then used in code to add seats to an event when one is created.

Events Table

The Events table stores the top-level information about an event. The table links to the Settings table in a one-to-many relationship. Each of the events occurs at a specific setting, but each setting can have many events help it.

EventSeats Table

The EventSeats table stores the seating status and other information for each of the seats at an event. If the application is used as intended, the records in this table are added through the default values for the venue's seats stored in the SettingSeats table. The table is in a one-to-many relationship with the Events table. Each event can have numerous seats, but each seat goes with a specific event.

Field Specifications

Settings Table

The field specifications for the Settings table are displayed in Table 6-1. The SettingID field is the primary key for this table. It uniquely identifies each of the records. The SettingName field is a friendly name for the setting. The FormName field stores the name of the form within Access that contains the seating chart for this setting.

Table 6-1	Field Name	Field Type	Notes
	SettingID	AutoNumber	Primary Key
The Settings	SettingName	Text	Length = 50
Table Field	FormName	Text	Length = 70
Specifications	Location	Memo	
	Note	Memo	

SettingSeats Table

The field specifications for the SettingSeats table are displayed in Table 6-2. The SettingSeatID field is the primary key for this table, while the SettingID field is a foreign key that links this table with the Setting table. The SeatName field stores the name used for this seat as it is displayed on the seating chart and on the Seating subform. The FormLabel field stores the name of the label that represents this seat on the seating chart. The DefaultPrice field stores the initial value that a seat costs when a new event is added.

Table 6-2	Field Name	Field Type	Notes
The SettingSeats Table Field Specifications	SettingSeatID	AutoNumber	Primary Key
	SettingID	Number	Type = Long, Foreign Key
	SeatName	Text	Length = 50
	FormLabel	Text	Length = 50
	DefaultPrice	Currency	

Events Table

The field specifications for the Events table are displayed in Table 6-3. The EventID is the primary key for the table, while the SettingID field links the table to the Settings table. The field is displayed to the user as a combo box since the Display Control property is set to that type. The Row Source property is set to this query:

```
SELECT [Settings].[SettingID], [Settings].[SettingName] FROM Settings;
```

Table 6-3	Field Name	Field Type	Notes
The Events Table Field Specifications	EventID	AutoNumber	Primary Key
	EventName	Text	Length = 50
	SettingID	Number	Type = Long, Foreign Key
	EventDate	Date/Time	
	Notes	Memo	

The ID of the setting is stored in this table, but the user sees the name of the setting. The user must choose from a value in the combo box since the Limit to List property is set to Yes.

Events in this sample scenario cannot be entered if the event date is more than a year in the future. To satisfy this rule, the Validation Rule property for the EventDate field is set to this value:

```
<= DateAdd("yyyy",1,Date())
```

The DateAdd function is used to add one year to the current date. The date entered in this field must be less than or equal to that value. If the rule is violated, the user sees this text:

```
The event date cannot be more than a year in the future.
```

EventSeats Table

The field specifications for the EventSeats table are displayed in Table 6-4. The EventSeatID is the primary key for this table and the EventID field links this table to the Events table. The Status field stores the availability of the seat. The field can either have the values Available or Sold.

Table 6-4

The EventSeats Table Field Specifications

Field Name	Field Type	Notes
EventSeatID	AutoNumber	Primary Key
EventID	Number	Type = Long, Foreign Key
Seat	Text	Length = 50
Price	Currency	
Status	Text	Length = 50

Forms

Switchboard Form

The Switchboard form is used to navigate through the forms and reports in the Events database application. It was created using the Switchboard Wizard, which is accessible within Access through the Tools/Database Utilities/Switchboard Manager menu item. Only the look and layout of the form produced with that wizard have been altered.

Settings Form

The code on the Settings form provides the functionality needed for the buttons in the footer of the form. The first code block fires when the user clicks on the Add Setting button:

```
Private Sub CommandAdd_Click()
    DoCmd.GoToRecord , , acNewRec
    [SettingName].SetFocus
End Sub
```

First, move the record pointer to a new record using the GoToRecord method:

```
DoCmd.GoToRecord , , acNewRec
```

Then set the focus to the first data entry field on the form:

```
[SettingName].SetFocus
```

The next code block fires when the user clicks on the Delete button in the footer of the form:

```
Private Sub CommandDelete_Click()
    On Error GoTo HandleError
    DoCmd.DoMenuItem acFormBar, acEditMenu, 8, , acMenuVer70
    DoCmd.DoMenuItem acFormBar, acEditMenu, 6, , acMenuVer70
    [SettingName].SetFocus
    Exit Sub
HandleError:
    If Err.Number <> 2501 Then
        MsgBox Err.Number & " " & Err.Description
    End If
End Sub
```

Start by telling Access that you will manage errors in the code:

```
On Error GoTo HandleError
```

Then delete the current record:

```
DoCmd.DoMenuItem acFormBar, acEditMenu, 8, , acMenuVer70
DoCmd.DoMenuItem acFormBar, acEditMenu, 6, , acMenuVer70
```

If the deletion is successful, move the focus back to the detail section of the form:

```
[SettingName].SetFocus
```

and leave this procedure:

```
Exit Sub
```

If an error occurs, the code flows to this label:

```
HandleError:
```

One error that can occur is if the user clicks on the No button when prompted to confirm the record deletion. If that error occurs, skip it:

```
If Err.Number <> 2501 Then
```

Any other error is displayed in a message box:

```
MsgBox Err.Number & " " & Err.Description
```

When the user clicks on the Search button, the next code block fires:

```
Private Sub CommandSearch_Click()
    Screen.PreviousControl.SetFocus
    DoCmd.DoMenuItem acFormBar, acEditMenu, 10, , acMenuVer70
End Sub
```

You can assume that the user wants to search the field that he or she was at before clicking on the Search button, so return the focus to that field:

```
Screen.PreviousControl.SetFocus
```

Then open the Access Search dialog:

```
DoCmd.DoMenuItem acFormBar, acEditMenu, 10, , acMenuVer70
```

The last code block fires when the user presses the Close button. The code block uses the Close method of the DoCmd object to close the current form:

```
Private Sub CommandClose_Click()
    DoCmd.Close
End Sub
```

Events Form

The code on the Events form populates the initial seat records for an event, opens the Seat Chart form, displays the summary information about the event, and provides the functionality for the buttons in the footer of the form.

Once the user provides the basic information about an event, he or she is ready to add the seats for the event. The seat records come from the default information that was entered on the Settings form for the venue selected. This code block adds those records when the user clicks on the Add Seats for this Event button:

```
Private Sub Command28_Click()
    Dim MyDB As DAO.Database
    Dim rs As DAO.Recordset
    Dim TotalSeats As Long
    If IsNumeric([EventID]) And IsNumeric([SettingID]) Then
        Set MyDB = CurrentDb
        Set rs = MyDB.OpenRecordset("Select Count(EventSeatID) as TheSeats " _
            & "From EventSeats Where EventID = " & [EventID], dbOpenSnapshot)
        TotalSeats = rs("TheSeats")
        If TotalSeats > 0 Then
            MsgBox "Seats have already been added for this event!"
        Else
            Set rs = MyDB.OpenRecordset("Select SeatName, DefaultPrice from " _
                & "SettingSeats where SettingID = " & [SettingID], dbOpenSnapshot)
            Do Until rs.EOF
                MyDB.Execute "Insert Into EventSeats (EventID, Seat, Price, " _
                    & "Status) values (" _
                    & [EventID] & ", " _
                    & """" & rs("SeatName") & """, " _
                    & rs("DefaultPrice") & ", " _
                    & """Available"")"
                rs.MoveNext
            Loop
                Form_Current
            [EventSeats_subform].Requery
        End If
    Else
        MsgBox "You must enter the event and venue information before adding seats."
    End If
End Sub
```

You need to connect to the current database in code:

```
Dim MyDB As DAO.Database
```

You also need to retrieve records:

```
Dim rs As DAO.Recordset
```

One other variable that stores the total number of seats in the selected venue is declared:

```
Dim TotalSeats As Long
```

Before adding the seats, make sure that the user has supplied the needed information about the event:

```
If IsNumeric([EventID]) And IsNumeric([SettingID]) Then
```

If the user has done so, connect to the database:

```
Set MyDB = CurrentDb
```

Then check to see if seats have already been added for this event:

```
Set rs = MyDB.OpenRecordset("Select Count(EventSeatID) as TheSeats " _
    & "From EventSeats Where EventID = " & [EventID], dbOpenSnapshot)
```

Now place that value in a variable:

```
TotalSeats = rs("TheSeats")
```

If seats have already been assigned for this event, the total value will be more than zero:

```
If TotalSeats > 0 Then
```

In this case, don't add the seat records since they have already been added:

```
MsgBox "Seats have already been added for this event!"
```

Otherwise, you can retrieve the template seat records for the setting selected from the SettingSeats table:

```
Set rs = MyDB.OpenRecordset("Select SeatName, DefaultPrice from " _
    & "SettingSeats where SettingID = " & [SettingID], dbOpenSnapshot)
```

Then start a loop that takes you through all the seats:

```
Do Until rs.EOF
```

Each of the seats at the venue needs to be added for this event. The name of the seat is used, as is the default price for the seat, which is marked as available:

```
MyDB.Execute "Insert Into EventSeats (EventID, Seat, Price, " _
    & "Status) values (" _
    & [EventID] & ", " _
    & """" & rs("SeatName") & """, " _
    & rs("DefaultPrice") & ", " _
    & """Available""")"
```

Now move to the next seat record,

```
rs.MoveNext
```

and loop so it can be processed:

```
Loop
```

Then call the Current event of the form, which will populate the summary information about the event:

```
Form_Current
```

and repopulate the child seats form:

```
[EventSeats_subform].Requery
```

If the user hasn't entered the event information, the code flows here:

```
MsgBox "You must enter the event and venue information before adding seats."
    End If
```

When the user presses the Sell Tickets button, you need to show the seating chart for the setting selected displaying the seats available for this event:

```
Private Sub Command33_Click()
    Dim MyDB As DAO.Database
    Dim rs As DAO.Recordset
    If IsNumeric([EventID]) And IsNumeric([SettingID]) Then
        Set MyDB = CurrentDb
        Set rs = MyDB.OpenRecordset("Select Count(EventSeatID) as TheSeats "  _
            & "From EventSeats Where EventID = " & [EventID], dbOpenSnapshot)
        If rs("TheSeats") = 0 Then
            MsgBox "You need to add seats before selling tickets!"
        Else
            Set rs = MyDB.OpenRecordset("Select FormName from Settings "  _
                & "Where SettingID = " & [SettingID], dbOpenSnapshot)
            DoCmd.OpenForm rs("FormName"), , , , , acDialog, [EventID]
            [EventSeats_subform].Requery
            Form_Current
        End If
    Else
        MsgBox "You must enter the event and venue information before adding seats."
    End If
End Sub
```

You now need to connect to the database:

```
Dim MyDB As DAO.Database
```

and retrieve data:

```
Dim rs As DAO.Recordset
```

Before you do, however, verify that the event information has been entered:

```
If IsNumeric([EventID]) And IsNumeric([SettingID]) Then
```

If so, you can connect to the database:

```
Set MyDB = CurrentDb
```

and check to see if seating information has been established for this event:

```
Set rs = MyDB.OpenRecordset("Select Count(EventSeatID) as TheSeats " _
    & "From EventSeats Where EventID = " & [EventID], dbOpenSnapshot)
```

If it hasn't, you won't find any seats:

```
If rs("TheSeats") = 0 Then
```

In that case, inform the user of the problem:

```
MsgBox "You need to add seats before selling tickets!"
```

Otherwise, retrieve the name of the form that has the seating chart for the selected setting from the database:

```
Set rs = MyDB.OpenRecordset("Select FormName from Settings " _
    & "Where SettingID = " & [SettingID], dbOpenSnapshot)
```

Then open that form as a dialog, passing it the current event number through its OpenArgs property:

```
DoCmd.OpenForm rs("FormName"), , , , , acDialog, [EventID]
```

After the user is done with that form, you must repopulate the child form:

```
[EventSeats_subform].Requery
```

and reset the summary information for this event:

```
Form_Current
```

If the user hasn't entered the event information, he or she is shown this message:

```
MsgBox "You must enter the event and venue information before
adding seats."
```

Each time the record pointer moves to a different record, you need to update the labels that display the number of tickets sold, available, and in total for this event. The code that does this is in the Current event of the form:

```
Private Sub Form_Current()
    Dim MyDB As DAO.Database
    Dim rs As DAO.Recordset
    Dim TotalSeats As Long
    If IsNumeric([EventID]) Then
        Set MyDB = CurrentDb
        Set rs = MyDB.OpenRecordset("Select Count(EventSeatID) as TheSeats " _
            & "From EventSeats Where EventID = " & [EventID], dbOpenSnapshot)
        TotalSeats = rs("TheSeats")
        Label51.Caption = "Capacity: " & Format(TotalSeats, "General Number")
        Set rs = MyDB.OpenRecordset("Select Count(EventSeatID) as TheSeats " _
            & "From EventSeats Where EventID = " & [EventID] _
            & " and Status = ""Available""", dbOpenSnapshot)
        Label53.Caption = "Available: " & Format(rs("TheSeats"), "General Number")
        Label55.Caption = "Sold: " & _
            Format(TotalSeats - rs("TheSeats"), "General Number")
    Else
        Label51.Caption = "Capacity:"
        Label53.Caption = "Available:"
        Label55.Caption = "Sold:"
    End If
End Sub
```

You now need to connect to the database:

```
Dim MyDB As DAO.Database
```

and retrieve information:

```
Dim rs As DAO.Recordset
```

Another variable is used to store the total number of seats at the event:

```
Dim TotalSeats As Long
```

But first make sure that the event information has been entered:

```
If IsNumeric([EventID]) Then
```

If it has, connect to the current database:

```
Set MyDB = CurrentDb
```

The first thing you need to retrieve from the database is the total number of seats for this event:

```
Set rs = MyDB.OpenRecordset("Select Count(EventSeatID) as TheSeats " _
    & "From EventSeats Where EventID = " & [EventID], dbOpenSnapshot)
```

You should place that value in a temporary variable:

```
TotalSeats = rs("TheSeats")
```

and in a label on the form:

```
Label51.Caption = "Capacity: " & Format(TotalSeats, "General
Number")
```

Next, retrieve the total number of seats at this event that are marked as available:

```
Set rs = MyDB.OpenRecordset("Select Count(EventSeatID) as TheSeats " _
    & "From EventSeats Where EventID = " & [EventID] _
    & " and Status = ""Available""", dbOpenSnapshot)
```

That value is placed in the Available label:

```
Label53.Caption = "Available: " & Format(rs("TheSeats"), "General Number")
```

Then calculate the total number of seats that have been sold and place that value in the third summary label. Note the use of the Format function, which will display the number appropriately:

```
Label55.Caption = "Sold: " & _
    Format(TotalSeats - rs("TheSeats"), "General Number")
```

If an event has not been entered for this record, clear the summary labels:

```
Label51.Caption = "Capacity:"
Label53.Caption = "Available:"
Label55.Caption = "Sold:"
```

The next code block fires when the Add Event button is pressed:

```
Private Sub CommandAdd_Click()
    DoCmd.GoToRecord , , acNewRec
    [EventName].SetFocus
End Sub
```

The code block moves the record pointer to a new record:

```
DoCmd.GoToRecord , , acNewRec
```

and moves the insertion point to the first data entry field on the form:

```
[EventName].SetFocus
```

When the user presses the Delete Event button, the next code block runs:

```
Private Sub CommandDelete_Click()
    On Error GoTo HandleError
    DoCmd.DoMenuItem acFormBar, acEditMenu, 8, , acMenuVer70
    DoCmd.DoMenuItem acFormBar, acEditMenu, 6, , acMenuVer70
    [EventName].SetFocus
    Exit Sub
HandleError:
    If Err.Number <> 2501 Then
        MsgBox Err.Number & " " & Err.Description
    End If
End Sub
```

Start with an error handler:

```
On Error GoTo HandleError
```

and then you can delete the current record:

```
DoCmd.DoMenuItem acFormBar, acEditMenu, 8, , acMenuVer70
DoCmd.DoMenuItem acFormBar, acEditMenu, 6, , acMenuVer70
```

Now shift the focus back to the detail section of the form:

```
[EventName].SetFocus
```

and leave this procedure:

```
Exit Sub
```

If an error occurs, the code flows here:

```
HandleError:
```

Skip over the known error that occurs when the user cancels a record deletion:

```
If Err.Number <> 2501 Then
```

But display any other error message:

```
MsgBox Err.Number & " " & Err.Description
```

The next code block fires when the Search button is pressed:

```
Private Sub CommandSearch_Click()
    Screen.PreviousControl.SetFocus
    DoCmd.DoMenuItem acFormBar, acEditMenu, 10, , acMenuVer70
End Sub
```

Start by returning the focus back to the field the user was at before clicking on this button:

```
Screen.PreviousControl.SetFocus
```

Then open the Access Search dialog:

```
DoCmd.DoMenuItem acFormBar, acEditMenu, 10, , acMenuVer70
```

The last code block uses the Close method to close this form when the user clicks the Close button:

```
Private Sub CommandClose_Click()
    DoCmd.Close
End Sub
```

Setting2 Form

Each of the settings needs to have its own seating chart form that enables the user to select seats that they want to reserve. In this sample implementation, a single venue is created and the Setting2 form contains the seating chart for that venue. The code on that form displays the correct color for each seat based on its availability and reserves the desired seats. The General Declaration section of the form contains two variables that are used in some of the procedures of this form:

```
Private TotalSeats As Long
Private OrderTotal As Currency
```

The TotalSeats variable stores the total number of seats that have been selected so far for this order:

```
Private TotalSeats As Long
```

The OrderTotal variable stores the dollar amount total for the seats selected:

```
Private OrderTotal As Currency
```

When the form first loads, you need to set the color of the labels for each seat based on its availability:

```
Private Sub Form_Load()
    Dim MyDB As DAO.Database
    Dim rs As DAO.Recordset
    Set MyDB = CurrentDb
    Set rs = MyDB.OpenRecordset("SELECT EventSeats.Seat, " _
```

```
        & "EventSeats.Price, EventSeats.Status, SettingSeats.FormLabel " _
        & "FROM EventSeats INNER JOIN SettingSeats ON " _
        & " EventSeats.Seat = SettingSeats.SeatName " _
        & "Where EventSeats.EventID = " & Me.OpenArgs, dbOpenSnapshot)
    Do Until rs.EOF
        If rs("Status") = "Sold" Then
            Me.Controls(rs("FormLabel")).BackColor = 255
        End If
        Me.Controls(rs("FormLabel")).ControlTipText = "Seat Name: " _
            & rs("Seat") & ", Price: " & Format(rs("Price"), "Currency") _
            & ", Status: " & rs("Status")
        rs.MoveNext
    Loop
End Sub
```

You now need to connect to the database:

```
Dim MyDB As DAO.Database
```

and retrieve information:

```
Dim rs As DAO.Recordset
```

Then open a connection to the current database you are working with:

```
Set MyDB = CurrentDb
```

You must also retrieve information about the seat at the current event as well as the name of the label that represents the seat. This information comes from the EventSeats table and the SettingSeats table. Note that the Where clause limits the records returned so that they are just for the event number passed in through the OpenArgs property to this form:

```
Set rs = MyDB.OpenRecordset("SELECT EventSeats.Seat, " _
        & "EventSeats.Price, EventSeats.Status, SettingSeats.FormLabel " _
        & "FROM EventSeats INNER JOIN SettingSeats ON " _
        & " EventSeats.Seat = SettingSeats.SeatName " _
& "Where EventSeats.EventID = " & Me.OpenArgs, dbOpenSnapshot)
```

Then start a loop that takes you through each of the seats for this event:

```
Do Until rs.EOF
```

When the form opens, all the seats are colored green, which means they are available. But if the Status field is set to sold, such as

```
If rs("Status") = "Sold" Then
```

the color of this label needs to be set to red:

```
Me.Controls(rs("FormLabel")).BackColor = 255
```

Then set the ControlTipText property of the label. This is the text that appears if the user moves their cursor over the label, which contains the name of the seat, the price, and the status:

```
Me.Controls(rs("FormLabel")).ControlTipText = "Seat Name: " _
    & rs("Seat") & ", Price: " & Format(rs("Price"), "Currency") _
    & ", Status: " & rs("Status")
```

Now move on to process the next record:

```
rs.MoveNext
Loop
```

When the user clicks on a label, you need to mark that seat as held, if it is available. Each of the labels has a click event like this one that calls a procedure called HoldSeat and passes the name of the seat that was clicked to it:

```
Private Sub L1_Click()
    HoldSeat "L1"
End Sub
```

The HoldSeat procedure then toggles the color of the label and maintains the summary information:

```
Public Sub HoldSeat(LabelName As String)
    Dim MyDB As DAO.Database
    Dim rs As DAO.Recordset
    Set MyDB = CurrentDb
    Set rs = MyDB.OpenRecordset("SELECT EventSeats.Price " _
        & "FROM EventSeats Where EventID = " _
        & Me.OpenArgs & " and Seat = """ & LabelName & """", dbOpenSnapshot)

    If Me.Controls(LabelName).BackColor = 4259584 Then
        Me.Controls(LabelName).BackColor = 16711680
        Me.Controls(LabelName).ControlTipText = _
            Replace(Me.Controls(LabelName).ControlTipText, _
                "Available", "Holding", 1, -1, vbTextCompare)
        TotalSeats = TotalSeats + 1
        OrderTotal = OrderTotal + rs("Price")
    ElseIf Me.Controls(LabelName).BackColor = 16711680 Then
        Me.Controls(LabelName).BackColor = 4259584
        Me.Controls(LabelName).ControlTipText = _
            Replace(Me.Controls(LabelName).ControlTipText, _
                "Holding", "Available", 1, -1, vbTextCompare)
        TotalSeats = TotalSeats - 1
        OrderTotal = OrderTotal - rs("Price")
    End If
```

```
      Label59.Caption = "Seats Reserved: " & Format(TotalSeats, "General Number")
      Label60.Caption = "Order Total: " & Format(OrderTotal, "Currency")
End Sub
```

You now need a Database object:

```
Dim MyDB As DAO.Database
```

and a Recordset object:

```
Dim rs As DAO.Recordset
```

Then connect to the current database:

```
Set MyDB = CurrentDb
```

and retrieve the price for the seat selected by the user:

```
Set rs = MyDB.OpenRecordset("SELECT EventSeats.Price " _
    & "FROM EventSeats Where EventID = " _
    & Me.OpenArgs & " and Seat = """ & LabelName & """", dbOpenSnapshot)
```

If the color of the seat is currently green, such as:

```
If Me.Controls(LabelName).BackColor = 4259584 Then
```

then set the color of it to blue, so that it is marked as held:

```
Me.Controls(LabelName).BackColor = 16711680
```

Now change the ControlTipText property so that the text also indicates that the seat is held:

```
Me.Controls(LabelName).ControlTipText = _
    Replace(Me.Controls(LabelName).ControlTipText, _
    "Available", "Holding", 1, -1, vbTextCompare)
```

Then increment the total number of seats in this order:

```
TotalSeats = TotalSeats + 1
```

and add the price of this seat to the total dollar amount of the order:

```
OrderTotal = OrderTotal + rs("Price")
```

If the color of the seat is blue, the user wants to unselect it from this order:

```
ElseIf Me.Controls(LabelName).BackColor = 16711680 Then
```

So, change the color back to green for this seat:

```
Me.Controls(LabelName).BackColor = 4259584
```

and modify the ControlTipText property:

```
Me.Controls(LabelName).ControlTipText = _
    Replace(Me.Controls(LabelName).ControlTipText, _
    "Holding", "Available", 1, -1, vbTextCompare)
```

Then decrement the number of seats in this order:

```
TotalSeats = TotalSeats - 1
```

and subtract the dollar amount for this seat from the order total:

```
OrderTotal = OrderTotal - rs("Price")
```

Then update the summary labels:

```
Label59.Caption = "Seats Reserved: " & Format(TotalSeats, "General Number")
Label60.Caption = "Order Total: " & Format(OrderTotal, "Currency")
```

When the user clicks on the Reserve Seats button, all the seats marked as held need to be marked as sold:

```
Private Sub Command61_Click()
    Dim MyDB As DAO.Database
    Dim rs As DAO.Recordset
    Set MyDB = CurrentDb
    Set rs = MyDB.OpenRecordset("SELECT EventSeats.EventSeatID, " _
        & "SettingSeats.FormLabel " _
        & "FROM EventSeats INNER JOIN SettingSeats ON " _
        & " EventSeats.Seat = SettingSeats.SeatName " _
        & "Where EventSeats.EventID = " & Me.OpenArgs, dbOpenSnapshot)
    Do Until rs.EOF
        If Me.Controls(rs("FormLabel")).BackColor = 16711680 Then
            MyDB.Execute "Update EventSeats set Status = ""Sold"" " _
                & "Where EventSeatID = " & rs("EventSeatID")
        End If
        rs.MoveNext
    Loop
    DoCmd.Close
End Sub
```

Now you need a Database object:

```
Dim MyDB As DAO.Database
```

and a Recordset object:

```
Dim rs As DAO.Recordset
```

Then connect to the current database:

```
Set MyDB = CurrentDb
```

and retrieve information for each of the seats:

```
Set rs = MyDB.OpenRecordset("SELECT EventSeats.EventSeatID, " _
    & "SettingSeats.FormLabel " _
    & "FROM EventSeats INNER JOIN SettingSeats ON " _
    & " EventSeats.Seat = SettingSeats.SeatName " _
    & "Where EventSeats.EventID = " & Me.OpenArgs, dbOpenSnapshot)
```

Then start a loop so each of the seats can be processed:

```
Do Until rs.EOF
```

Next, check to see if the color of the current seat is blue, which means it is being held:

```
If Me.Controls(rs("FormLabel")).BackColor = 16711680 Then
```

If it is, update that seat and mark it as Sold:

```
MyDB.Execute "Update EventSeats set Status = ""Sold"" " _
    & "Where EventSeatID = " & rs("EventSeatID")
```

Now move on to process the next record:

```
rs.MoveNext
Loop
```

and close this form:

```
DoCmd.Close
```

If the user presses the Cancel button, you just need to close the form:

```
Private Sub Command62_Click()
    DoCmd.Close
End Sub
```

Reports

Event Sales Report

The Event Sales report combines three queries to display summary information about each of the events in a specified date range. The first query is called *Event Seats* and has the following syntax:

```
SELECT EventSeats.EventID, Count(EventSeats.EventSeatID) AS [Total
Seats], Sum(EventSeats.Price) AS [Total Price] FROM EventSeats
GROUP BY EventSeats.EventID;
```

The query returns the total number of seats and the total price for all the seats grouped by the event. The next query is called *Event Seats Sold:*

```
SELECT EventSeats.EventID, Count(EventSeats.EventSeatID) AS [Seats
Sold], Sum(EventSeats.Price) AS [Seats Sold Price] FROM EventSeats
WHERE (((EventSeats.Status)="Sold")) GROUP BY EventSeats.EventID;
```

It also returns the total number of seats and the total price for all the seats grouped by the event, but this is just for the seats that are marked as sold.

The third query combines the first two queries with information about the event. It is called *Event Sales* and has the following syntax:

```
SELECT Events.EventName, Events.EventDate, [Event Seats].[Total Seats],
[Event Seats].[Total Price], [Event Seats Sold].[Seats Sold],
[Event Seats Sold].[Seats Sold Price] FROM (Events
INNER JOIN [Event Seats] ON Events.EventID = [Event Seats].EventID)
INNER JOIN [Event Seats Sold] ON Events.EventID = [Event Seats
Sold].EventID;
```

When the user opens the report, he or she is prompted for a date range. This is used to limit the events reported and is displayed in the label on the report header. The code that does this is located in the Open event of the report:

```
Private Sub Report_Open(Cancel As Integer)
    Dim StartDate As String
    Dim EndDate As String
    StartDate = InputBox("Enter the start date for the report:", "Start Date")
    If Not IsDate(StartDate) Then
        Cancel = True
        Exit Sub
    End If
    EndDate = InputBox("Enter the end date for the report:", "End Date")
    If Not IsDate(EndDate) Then
        Cancel = True
        Exit Sub
```

```
        End If
        Me.Filter = "[EventDate] >= #" & StartDate & "# and [EventDate] <= #" _
            & EndDate & "#"
        Me.FilterOn = True
        Label12.Caption = "Event Sales from " & StartDate _
            & " to " & EndDate
    End Sub
```

Variables are needed to store the start and end dates. Note that they are not declared as dates, but as strings. This is because the user may not enter a valid date:

```
Dim StartDate As String
Dim EndDate As String
```

Now retrieve the start date from the user through an InputBox:

```
StartDate = InputBox("Enter the start date for the report:", "Start
Date")
```

Then check to see if what he or she entered was a date:

```
If Not IsDate(StartDate) Then
```

If it wasn't, exit this report:

```
Cancel = True
Exit Sub
```

Now prompt the user for the end date used on the report:

```
EndDate = InputBox("Enter the end date for the report:", "End
Date")
```

Again, check to see if he or she actually entered a date:

```
If Not IsDate(EndDate) Then
```

If the user didn't, close the report:

```
Cancel = True
Exit Sub
```

If the dates are good, they are used to filter the form:

```
Me.Filter = "[EventDate] >= #" & StartDate & "# and [EventDate] <= #" _
    & EndDate & "#"
Me.FilterOn = True
```

Then set the Header label so it displays the dates entered:

```
Label12.Caption = "Event Sales from " & StartDate _
    & " to " & EndDate
```

Events in Month and Year Report

The Events in Month and Year report displays the count of events in each month and year that has events. The report is based on the Events in Month and Year query, which has the following SQL syntax:

```
SELECT Year([EventDate]) AS [Year], Month([EventDate]) AS [Month],
Count(Events.EventID) AS [Event Count] FROM Events
GROUP BY Year([EventDate]), Month([EventDate]);
```

The Year and Month functions are used to parse the year and month out of the EventDate field. The records are then grouped by the year and month of the event.

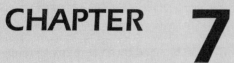

CHAPTER 7

Working with Customers

ON THE CD:

Customers.mdb

Contact Manager.mdb

Managing Customers, Orders, and Contacts

In this chapter, we will review two database applications. The first is called the *Customers* database. This database enables you to manage customers, their orders, and the products that you make available to them.

The other database application reviewed in this chapter is called *Contact Manager*. This database provides a way for users to manage their own leads and the leads of a company. *Contact Manager* also provides reports relating to when contact needs to be remade.

Customers Database

The Customers database application could be used by a company to manage orders placed by customers or customer service representatives, and the products offered to customers. As you review this database, pay particular attention to the code used on the Orders form that calculates the customer's order based on the prices of shipping and tax. Also look closely at the summary queries that group information together to produce the reports.

Sample Walk-through

When a user first enters the Customers database application, he or she sees the menu shown in Figure 7-1.

The menu has a total of three screens. The first enables the user to select a submenu or to exit this database. The second menu, which is accessible by pressing the Forms button, contains a list of all the forms that can be viewed directly. The Reports button displays the third menu, which displays a list of the reports in this application.

Figure 7-1

The Customers database menu

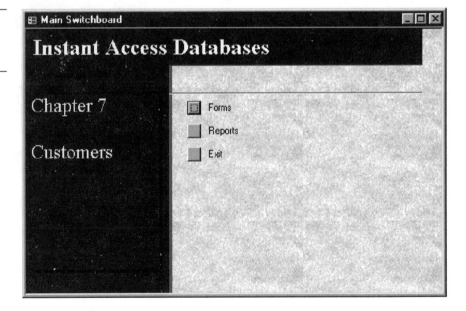

If the user selects the Forms menu and then presses the Customers button, he or she sees the form shown in Figure 7-2.

The Customers form is the heart of this database application. In the header of the page, the name of the customer is always displayed so the user can be reminded of whom they are working with. The first page of this form is the General page and enables the user to view basic information about the customer. Each customer is assigned a specific customer representative. The user can view more information about the representative by double-clicking on that field.

Besides the basic buttons located in the footer of the form, the user also can view the different pages of the form. By selecting the Contact Info button, the user will see the page shown in Figure 7-3.

The Contact Info page contains two subforms. The first shows a list of contact phone numbers for the customer. Here the user can view and store different phone contact information for the customer, along with notes describing what the phone numbers are for.

The second subform contains the different addresses used to bill and ship to this customer. These addresses are then used on orders and provide the needed information to accurately calculate shipping and tax information. An address can be a billing address, a shipping address, or both.

Figure 7-2

The General page of the Customers form

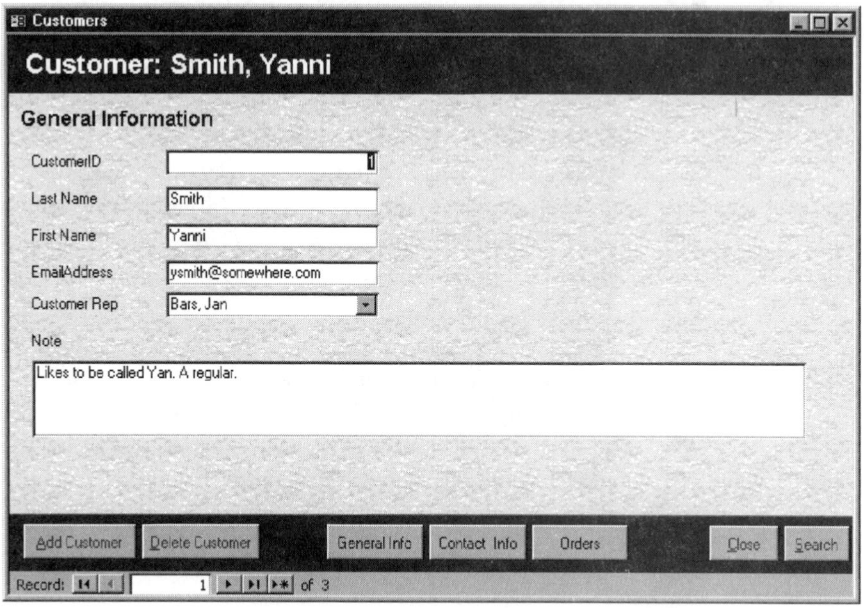

Figure 7-3

The Contact Info
page of the
Customers form

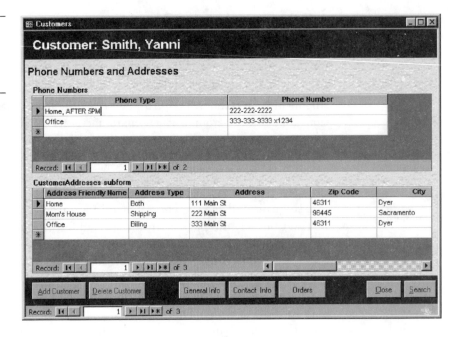

The tax and shipping values are tied to the zip code of the address, so the zip code must be selected from the list provided. When the zip code is selected, the city, state, and country fields are automatically populated.

When the user presses the Orders button, he or she sees the Orders page shown in Figure 7-4.

The Orders page contains a subform that contains information about the customers' orders. This subform also contains its own subform, which details all the items in this order. When the user selects an item to be ordered, the Price field is automatically populated with the current price. Only those products that are available for order are shown in the Products field. Once the user leaves the Order Items subform and returns to the Orders subform, or presses the Recalculate button, the order totals are automatically calculated.

The shipping value is based on the total weight of the products ordered, the location of the destination for the order, and the shipping method used. The tax is calculated based on the order total and the shipping location.

If the user double-clicks on any of the products, the Products form, shown in Figure 7-5, is displayed.

Figure 7-4

The Orders page of the Customers form

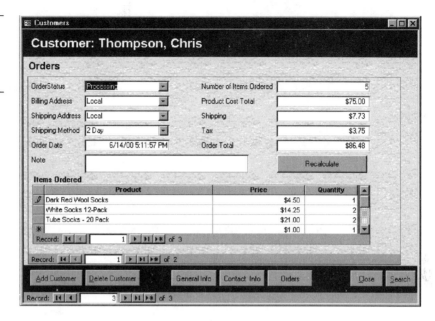

Figure 7-5

The Products form

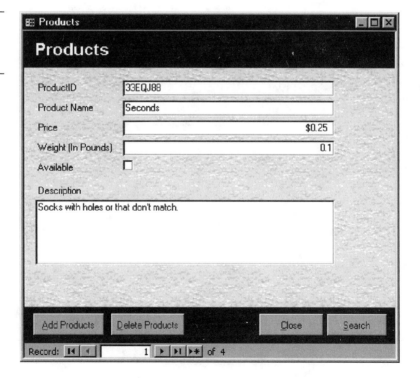

The Products form is also accessible to the user from the Forms submenu. From this form, the user can search, add, edit, and delete the products in the product catalog. The Available field is used to determine whether the product is listed when customer orders are being made.

The next form accessible through the Forms submenu is the Customer Reps form, displayed in Figure 7-6.

Each customer has his or her own customer rep who manages all the orders and information for the customer. From this form, the user can manage the information about those customers.

The next form accessible from the Forms submenu is the Shipping Methods form, which is shown in Figure 7-7.

The Shipping Methods form enables the user to manage the different shipping methods available for an order. These values are then used when calculating the shipping charge for an order. For example, here a Shipping Method called "2 Day" adds an additional 20 percent to the total cost of shipping.

The last form accessible through the Forms submenu is the Zip Codes form. This form is displayed in Figure 7-8.

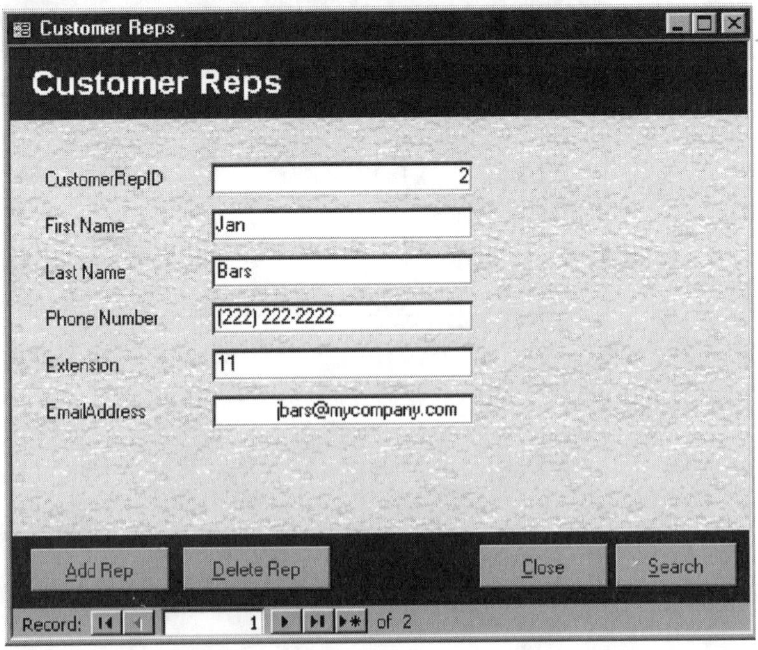

Figure 7-6

The Customer Reps form

Figure 7-7

The Shipping
Methods form

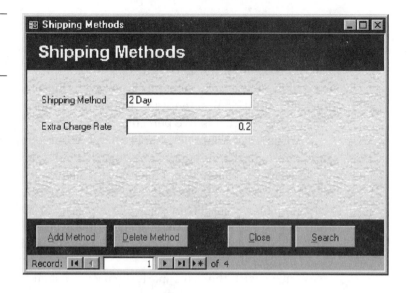

Figure 7-8

The Zip Codes
form

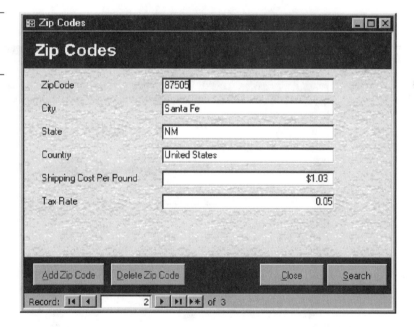

The Zip Codes form enables users to manage the zip codes offered for the customer addresses on the Customer Address subform of the Customers form. These zip codes are used to calculate the shipping and taxes used. For example, in the record shown in Figure 7-8, each pound of product costs $1.03 to ship. Remember, however, that the shipping method can then add additional amounts to the shipping cost. The tax rate used to ship to this location is five percent.

The Customers database application has three reports that are accessible through the Reports submenu. The first is called Order Totals Grouped by Customer Rep. This report is displayed in Figure 7-9.

When this report first opens, the user is asked to supply start and end dates to be used for retrieving the orders used in this report. The report then displays the total amount of sales made by each customer representative in that date range. Figure 7-10 shows the next report, Quantity Sold Grouped by Product.

Again, as with the last report, the user is asked to supply a date range for the record selection, so that he or she can view the products sold during the past month, the last week, today, the last year, or whatever range is needed. The report then shows all the products sold in that time frame.

Figure 7-9

The Order Totals Grouped by Customer Rep report

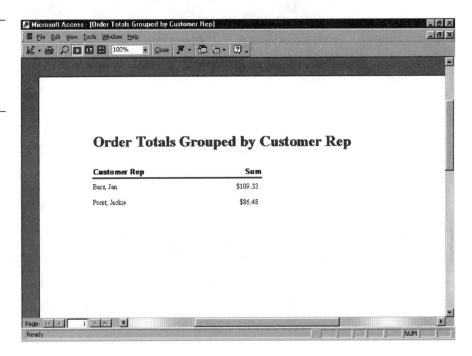

Figure 7-10

The Quantity
Sold Grouped by
Product report

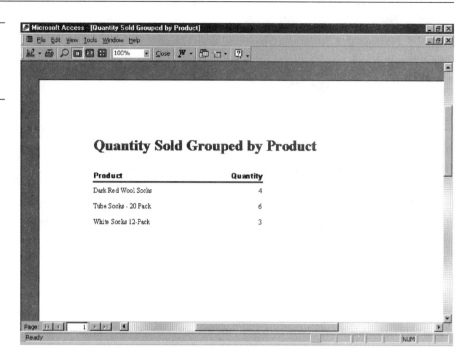

The last report is called Orders by Month and is shown in Figure 7-11. This report groups the orders first by year and then by month. Thus, the user sees how many orders were placed in each month and year that had orders.

Table Definitions and Relationships

Customers Table

The Customers table is the top-level table among the tables that store information about the customer. The table is related directly or indirectly to all the other tables in the database.

CustomerAddresses Table

The CustomerAddresses table stores all the addresses associated with a customer. These can be billing and/or shipping addresses. The table relates to the Customers table in a one-to-many relationship. Each of the

Figure 7-11

The Orders By
Month report

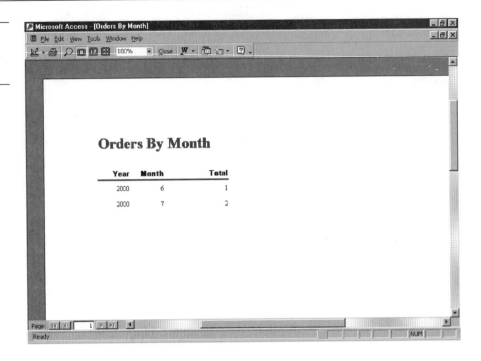

addresses belongs to a single customer, but each customer can have numerous addresses.

CustomerPhoneNumbers Table

The CustomerPhoneNumbers table stores all the phone numbers for a specific customer. The table is in a one-to-many relationship with the Customers table. Each customer can have many phone numbers, but each phone number belongs to a single customer.

Orders Table

The Orders table stores the middle-level information about an order. The table relates to the Customers table in a one-to-many relationship. Each customer can have many orders, but each order goes with a single customer.

OrderItems Table

Each order can have many products placed in it. The OrderItems table contains a list of all the products that were ordered, so the table is in a one-to-many relationship with the Orders table. The OrderItems table is also in a one-to-many relationship with the Products table. Each item belongs to a single product, but a single product can be ordered many times. Thus, the Orders table is actually in a many-to-many relationship with the Products table, and the OrderItems table satisfies that relationship by being in a one-to-many relationship with both tables.

Products Table

The Products table contains the information for all the products available for order. The table, as mentioned previously, is in a one-to-many relationship with the OrderItems table and a many-to-many relationship with the Orders table.

CustomerReps Table

The CustomerReps table stores the names and contact information for employees who fill the role of customer representatives. The table is in a one-to-many relationship with the Customers table. Each customer has a single customer representative, but each customer representative can represent many customers.

ShippingMethods Table

The ShippingMethods table stores the different methods that are available for shipping orders placed by customers. The table is in a one-to-many relationship with the Orders table. Each order must be of a specific shipping type.

ZipCodes Table

The ZipCodes table stores all the zip codes used for customer addresses. The table is in a one-to-many relationship with the CustomerAddresses table. Each address has a single zip code, but each zip code can be used by many addresses.

Field Specifications

Customers Table

The field specifications for the Customers table are displayed in Table 7-1.

The CustomerID field is the primary key for the table. Since it is defined as an AutoNumber field, it is automatically populated with a unique value when a new record is added. The CustomerRepID field is a foreign key that links this table to the CustomerReps table. The field is also displayed as a combo box and has the following text in the Row Source property:

```
SELECT [CustomerReps].[CustomerRepID], [LastName] & ", " & [FirstName] AS Expr1
FROM CustomerReps ORDER BY [LastName] & ", " & [FirstName];
```

	Field Name	Field Type	Notes
Table 7-1	CustomerID	AutoNumber	Primary Key
The Customers Table Field Specifications	LastName	Text	Length = 50
	FirstName	Text	Length = 50
	EmailAddress	Text	Length = 50
	CustomerRepID	Number	Type = Long Integer, Foreign Key
	Note	Memo	

Two fields are output by this query. The first is the ID of the rep. This is what is stored in the Customers table. The other field is the concatenation of the first and last name of the rep. This is what is displayed to the user in the combo box.

CustomerAddresses Table

The field specifications for the CustomerAddresses table are displayed in Table 7-2.

The CustomerAddressID field is the primary key for the table, while the CustomerID field is a foreign key and links the table to the Customers table. The AddressFriendlyName field stores an identifying name for this

Table 7-2

The CustomerAddress es Table Field Specifications

Field Name	Field Type	Notes
CustomerAddressID	AutoNumber	Primary Key
CustomerID	Number	Type = Long Integer, Foreign Key
AddressFriendlyName	Text	Length = 50
AddressType	Text	Length = 50
Address	Text	Length = 100
ZipCode	Text	Length = 50
City	Text	Length = 50
State	Text	Length = 50
Country	Text	Length = 50

address to make it easier for the customer to convey which address an order should be billed or shipped to.

The AddressType field stores whether the address is a shipping address, billing address, or both. The field is displayed as a combo box. The Row Source Type property is set to Value List and the Row Source property has the following value:

```
"Billing";"Shipping";"Both"
```

The Limit to List property is set to Yes, so the user must select from one of these values.

CustomerPhoneNumbers Table

The field specifications for the CustomerPhoneNumbers table are displayed in Table 7-3.

Table 7-3

The Customer PhoneNumbers Table Field Specifications

Field Name	Field Type	Notes
CustomerPhoneNumberID	AutoNumber	Primary Key
CustomerID	Number	Type = Long Integer, Foreign Key
PhoneType	Text	Length = 100
PhoneNumber	Text	Length = 50

The CustomerPhoneNumberID field is the primary key for this table. The CustomerID field is a foreign key that links this table to the Customers table.

Orders Table

The field specifications for the Orders table are displayed in Table 7-4.

	Field Name	Field Type	Notes
Table 7-4	OrderID	AutoNumber	Primary Key
The Orders Table Field Specifications	CustomerID	Number	Type = Long Integer, Foreign Key
	OrderStatus	Text	Length = 50
	BillingAddress	Number	Type = Long Integer, Foreign Key
	ShippingAddress	Number	Type = Long Integer, Foreign Key
	OrderDate	Date/Time	
	NumberOfItemsOrdered	Number	Type = Long Integer
	ProductCostTotal	Currency	
	Shipping	Currency	
	Tax	Currency	
	OrderTotal	Currency	
	OrderNote	Memo	

The OrderID field is the primary key for this table, while the CustomerID field is a foreign key that links this table to the Customers table. The OrderStatus field stores the status of the order. The field is displayed as a combo box since the Display Control property is set to combo box. The Rows Source Type property is set to Value List. The Row Source property is set to the following value:

```
"Processing";"On Hold";"Ready to Go";"Shipping";"Received"
```

The Limit to List property is set to Yes, so the user must select one of the values specified in the Row Source property.

The BillingAddress and ShippingAddress fields are both foreign keys that link this table to the CustomerAddresses table. Both fields are displayed as combo boxes and have the following query in the Row Source property:

```
SELECT [CustomerAddresses].[CustomerAddressID],
[CustomerAddresses].[AddressFriendlyName] FROM CustomerAddresses;
```

The ID of the address is stored with the record in this table, but the user sees the friendly name of the address in the combo box. The ShippingMethod field is also a foreign key that links this table to the ShippingMethods table. The field is displayed as a combo box and has the following value in the Row Source property:

```
SELECT [ShippingMethods].[ShippingMethod] FROM ShippingMethods;
```

The user must select one of the values returned from this query because the Limit to List property is set to Yes. The OrderDate field defaults to the current system date because it has the following in its Default Value property:

```
Date()
```

OrderItems Table

The field specifications for the OrderItems table are displayed in Table 7-5.

The OrderItemID field is the primary key for this table, while the OrderID field is a foreign key that links this table with the Orders table. The ProductID field is also a foreign key and links this table with the

	Field Name	Field Type	Notes
Table 7-5 The OrderItems Table Field Specifications	OrderItemID	AutoNumber	Primary Key
	OrderID	Number	Type = Long Integer, Foreign Key
	ProductID	Number	Type = Long Integer, Foreign Key
	Price	Currency	
	Quantity	Number	Type = Long Integer

Products table. The field is displayed to the user as a combo box in which the user sees the name of the product, but the ID of the product is stored in this table. The Row Source property is set to this value:

```
SELECT [Products].[ProductID], [Products].[ProductName] FROM Products;
```

The Price field stores the price charged to the customer for this product on the order. The field has the following Validation Rule property value:

```
>=0.01 And <=10000
```

Thus, the price charged must be at least $0.01 and must not be greater than $10,000. If the rule is violated, the user sees the following message:

```
This field must be in the range of $0.01 and $10,000.
```

The Quantity field also has a validation rule:

```
>=1 And <=10000
```

The user must order at least one of the products selected, but the customer cannot order more than 10,000 items of the product. If that rule is violated, the user sees this message:

```
This field must be in the range of 1 and 10,000.
```

That value is placed in the Validation Text property.

Products Table

The field specifications for the Products table are displayed in Table 7-6.

Table 7-6	Field Name	Field Type	Notes
The Products Table Field Specifications	ProductID	AutoNumber	Primary Key
	ProductName	Text	Length = 50
	Price	Currency	
	Weight	Number	Type = Single
	Description	Memo	
	Available	Yes/No	

The ProductID field is the primary key for this table. The Price field stores the price of the product with the following limitation placed in the Validation Rule property:

```
>=0.25 And <=10000
```

If the rule is violated, the user sees this message:

```
This field must be in the range of $0.25 and $10,000.
```

The Weight field stores the weight of a single item of this product. This value is used when calculating the shipping charge to the customer. The field has the following value in the Validation Rule property:

```
>=0.01 And <=10000
```

The weight of the product must be at least 0.01 pounds, but not more than 10,000 pounds. If that rule is violated, the user sees this message:

```
This field must be in the range of 0.01 and 10,000.
```

CustomerReps Table

The field specifications for the CustomerReps table are displayed in Table 7-7.

Table 7-7

The CustomerReps Table Field Specifications

Field Name	Field Type	Notes
CustomerRepID	AutoNumber	Primary Key
LastName	Text	Length = 50
FirstName	Text	Length = 50
PhoneNumber	Text	Length = 50
Extension	Text	Length = 50
EmailAddress	Text	Length = 50

The CustomerRepID field is the primary key for the table. The rest of the fields store information about the customer representative. The EmailAddress field eases the data entry task by using the following input mask:

```
!??????????????????"
```

The first part of the mask enables the user to enter the first part of the user's email address. Appended to that is the domain name for the company. Then, after the first semicolon, you can indicate that you want to store the mask with the data. The "_" at the end of the property value indicates that the user sees the "_" character as he or she is typing in this field.

ShippingMethods Table

The field specifications for the ShippingMethods table are displayed in Table 7-8.

Table 7-8	Field Name	Field Type	Notes
The ShippingMethods Table Field Specifications	ShippingMethod	Text	Length = 50, Primary Key
	ExtraChargeRate	Number	Type = Single

The ShippingMethod field is the primary key for the table. The ExtraChargeRate field stores the additional percent charged for selecting this type of shipping. The field has the following range set using the Validation Rule property:

```
>=0 And <=5
```

Thus, the field must be at least 0, which would mean the standard shipping is used but could go up to five, which would increase the shipping charge by 500 percent. If the user violates that rule, he or she sees this message:

```
This field must have a value from 0 to 5.
```

ZipCodes Table

The field specifications for the ZipCodes table are displayed in Table 7-9.

Table 7-9

The ZipCodes
Table Field
Specifications

Field Name	Field Type	Notes
ZipCode	Text	Length = 50, Primary Key
City	Text	Length = 70
State	Text	Length = 50
Country	Text	Length = 50
ShippingCostPerPound	Currency	
TaxRate	Number	Type = Single

The ZipCode field is the primary key for the table. The ShippingCost-PerPound field stores the amount charged to ship to this zip code, per pound. This is the base shipping charge. Remember that an additional amount could be added based on the shipping method used. The field has a validation rule to limit the range of values:

```
>=0.01 And <=1000
```

The field must have a value of at least one penny, but it cannot be more than $1,000. If the rule is violated, the user sees this message:

```
This field must be in the range of $0.01 and $1,000.
```

The TaxRate field stores the percent tax that should be charged for items shipped to this location. The field can be in the following range as established in the Validation Rule property:

```
>=0 And <=0.3
```

The number must be at least 0, but not greater than 30 percent. If the rule were violated, the user would see this message:

```
This field must be in the range of 0 and 0.3.
```

Forms

Switchboard Form

The Switchboard form is used to navigate through the forms and reports in the Customers database application. It was created using the Switchboard Wizard, which is accessible within Access through the Tools/Database Utilities/Switchboard Manager menu item. Only the look and layout of the form produced with that wizard have been altered.

Customers Form

The code on the Customers form enables the user to add, delete, and search the data on this form. It also closes the form, enables the user to navigate through the different pages of the form, and links the form to the Customer Reps form.

When the user clicks on the General Info button, the first code block runs:

```
Private Sub Command33_Click()
    DoCmd.GoToPage 1
End Sub
```

The code uses the GoToPage method to send the user to the first page of this form, which is the one that contains the basic information about the customer.

When the user clicks on the Contact Info button, the GoToPage method of the DoCmd object is used to display the second page of the form, which contains the contact information for the customer:

```
Private Sub Command35_Click()
    DoCmd.GoToPage 2
End Sub
```

When the user clicks on the Orders button, he or she is taken to the third page of this form, which contains the Orders subform:

```
Private Sub Command37_Click()
    DoCmd.GoToPage 3
End Sub
```

The next code block fires when the user clicks on the Add button:

```
Private Sub CommandAdd_Click()
    DoCmd.GoToRecord , , acNewRec
    [LastName].SetFocus
End Sub
```

The GoToRecord method is used to move the record pointer to a new record:

```
DoCmd.GoToRecord , , acNewRec
```

Then set the focus to the LastName field so the user can start entering data:

```
[LastName].SetFocus
```

The next code block fires when the delete button is pressed:

```
Private Sub CommandDelete_Click()
    On Error GoTo HandleError
    DoCmd.DoMenuItem acFormBar, acEditMenu, 8, , acMenuVer70
    DoCmd.DoMenuItem acFormBar, acEditMenu, 6, , acMenuVer70
    [LastName].SetFocus
    Exit Sub
HandleError:
    If Err.Number <> 2501 Then
        MsgBox Err.Number & " " & Err.Description
    End If
End Sub
```

Start with your error-handling statement:

```
On Error GoTo HandleError
```

Then delete the current record:

```
DoCmd.DoMenuItem acFormBar, acEditMenu, 8, , acMenuVer70
DoCmd.DoMenuItem acFormBar, acEditMenu, 6, , acMenuVer70
```

and return to the LastName field:

```
[LastName].SetFocus
```

If no error occurred, exit this procedure:

```
Exit Sub
```

If an error did occur, then the code will flow here:

```
HandleError:
```

Then filter out an error that occurs when the user cancels out of the record deletion:

```
If Err.Number <> 2501 Then
```

If the error is some other error, you should display it to the user:

```
MsgBox Err.Number & " " & Err.Description
```

The next code block fires when the user clicks on the Search button.

```
Private Sub CommandSearch_Click()
    Screen.PreviousControl.SetFocus
    DoCmd.DoMenuItem acFormBar, acEditMenu, 10, , acMenuVer70
End Sub
```

Start by setting the focus back to the field the user was at before pressing the Search button:

```
Screen.PreviousControl.SetFocus
```

Now open the Access search dialog:

```
DoCmd.DoMenuItem acFormBar, acEditMenu, 10, , acMenuVer70
```

When the user presses the Close button, the Close method of the DoCmd object is used to close the form:

```
Private Sub CommandClose_Click()
    DoCmd.Close
End Sub
```

The next code block fires when the user double-clicks on the CustomerRepID field.

```
Private Sub CustomerRepID_DblClick(Cancel As Integer)
    If [CustomerRepID] = 0 Or IsNull([CustomerRepID]) Then
        DoCmd.OpenForm "Customer Reps", , , , acFormAdd, acDialog
        [CustomerRepID].Requery
    Else
        DoCmd.OpenForm "Customer Reps", , , "[CustomerRepID] = " _
            & [CustomerRepID], , acDialog
        [CustomerRepID].Requery
    End If
End Sub
```

First, check to see if the CustomerRepID field is empty:

```
If [CustomerRepID] = 0 Or IsNull([CustomerRepID]) Then
```

If it is, you can assume that the user wants to add a new customer rep, so open the Customer Reps form in the Add mode:

```
DoCmd.OpenForm "Customer Reps", , , , acFormAdd, acDialog
```

After the user is done with that form, repopulate the CustomerRepID combo box:

```
[CustomerRepID].Requery
```

If the field contains a value, assume the user wants to see the information on that customer rep. Open the Customer Reps form with a Where Condition parameter so that it displays the information for the selected customer rep:

```
DoCmd.OpenForm "Customer Reps", , , "[CustomerRepID] = " _
    & [CustomerRepID], , acDialog
```

Then repopulate the combo box after the user is done with the Customer Reps form:

```
[CustomerRepID].Requery
```

The Current event of the Form object fires whenever the record pointer moves to a different record. Use that event to display the name of the current customer in the label that is on the header of the form:

```
Private Sub Form_Current()
    Label16.Caption = "Customer: " & [LastName] & ", " & [FirstName]
End Sub
```

The Customers form also contains subforms that have code on them. The CustomerAddresses subform contains a code block that fires when the user leaves the ZipCode field:

```
Private Sub Zip_Code_Exit(Cancel As Integer)
    Dim MyDB As DAO.Database
    Dim RSZipCode As DAO.Recordset
    If [ZipCode] <> "" Then
        Set MyDB = CurrentDb
        Set RSZipCode = MyDB.OpenRecordset("Select City, State, Country " _
            & "From ZipCodes where ZipCode = """ & [ZipCode] & """", _
            dbOpenSnapshot)
        If Not RSZipCode.EOF Then
            [City] = RSZipCode("City")
            [State] = RSZipCode("state")
            [Country] = RSZipCode("Country")
        End If
    End If
End Sub
```

The procedure is used to populate the City, State, and Country fields based on the zip code selected. Thus, you will need a Database object:

```
Dim MyDB As DAO.Database
```

and a Recordset object:

```
Dim RSZipCode As DAO.Recordset
```

First, make sure that a zip code has been selected:

```
If [ZipCode] <> "" Then
```

If it has, connect through the code to the current database you are working with:

```
Set MyDB = CurrentDb
```

Now retrieve the City, State, and Country fields from the database, based on the zip code entered by the user:

```
Set RSZipCode = MyDB.OpenRecordset("Select City, State, Country " _
    & "From ZipCodes where ZipCode = """ & [ZipCode] & """", _
    dbOpenSnapshot)
```

Then make sure that you found a record based on that zip code:

```
If Not RSZipCode.EOF Then
```

If so, use the values returned to set the City field:

```
[City] = RSZipCode("City")
```

the State field:

```
[State] = RSZipCode("state")
```

and the Country field:

```
[Country] = RSZipCode("Country")
```

The CustomerOrders subform has two procedures that run in two separate locations. The BillingAddress and ShippingAddress combo boxes need to contain only those addresses for the current customer. So if the customer on an order is changed or the current record changes, you need to repopulate these address lists. Therefore, the following code runs in the Current event of the form and the Exit event of the CustomerID field:

```
Private Sub CustomerID_Exit(Cancel As Integer)
    [ShippingAddress].RowSource = "SELECT [CustomerAddresses].[CustomerAddressID], " _
        & "[CustomerAddresses].[AddressFriendlyName] FROM CustomerAddresses " _
        & "Where ([AddressType] = ""Both"" or [AddressType] = ""Shipping"") " _
        & "And [CustomerID] = " & [CustomerID]
```

```
    [ShippingAddress].Requery
    [BillingAddress].RowSource = "SELECT [CustomerAddresses].[CustomerAddressID], " _
        & "[CustomerAddresses].[AddressFriendlyName] FROM CustomerAddresses " _
        & "Where ([AddressType] = ""Both"" or [AddressType] = ""Billing"") " _
        & "And [CustomerID] = " & [CustomerID]
    [BillingAddress].Requery
End Sub
```

First, set the RowSource property of the ShippingAddress combo box so that it shows the Shipping and Both addresses for the current customer:

```
[ShippingAddress].RowSource = "SELECT
[CustomerAddresses].[CustomerAddressID], " _
    & "[CustomerAddresses].[AddressFriendlyName] FROM CustomerAddresses " _
    & "Where ([AddressType] = ""Both"" or [AddressType] = ""Shipping"") " _
    & "And [CustomerID] = " & [CustomerID]
```

Then repopulate the ShippingAddress combo box by calling the Requery method:

```
[ShippingAddress].Requery
```

Next, set the RowSource property of the BillingAddress combo box so only those addresses for the current customer that are marked as Billing or Both are displayed:

```
[BillingAddress].RowSource = "SELECT
[CustomerAddresses].[CustomerAddressID], " _
    & "[CustomerAddresses].[AddressFriendlyName] FROM CustomerAddresses " _
    & "Where ([AddressType] = ""Both"" or [AddressType] = ""Billing"") " _
    & "And [CustomerID] = " & [CustomerID]
```

Now repopulate that combo box by calling the Requery method:

```
[BillingAddress].Requery
```

The Amount fields on the CustomerOrders subform are calculated values based on the products that have been ordered. Whenever the user returns to the CustomerOrders subform after leaving the OrderItems sub-form, or he or she presses the Recalculate button, the next code block runs:

```
Private Sub OrderItems_subform_Exit(Cancel As Integer)
    Dim MyDB As DAO.Database
    Dim rs As DAO.Recordset
    Dim TotalWeight As Single
    If IsNumeric([CustomerID]) And [CustomerID] <> 0 Then
        Set MyDB = CurrentDb
        Set rs = MyDB.OpenRecordset("Select Sum(Quantity) as TheQuantity " _
            & "from OrderItems Where OrderID = " & [OrderID], dbOpenSnapshot)
```

```
        [NumberOfItemsOrdered] = rs("TheQuantity")
        Set rs = MyDB.OpenRecordset("Select Sum([Price] * [Quantity]) as TheSum " _
            & "from OrderItems Where OrderID = " & [OrderID], dbOpenSnapshot)
        [ProductCostTotal] = rs("TheSum")
        Set rs = MyDB.OpenRecordset("SELECT Sum([Quantity] * [Weight]) " _
            & "as TotalWeight From Products INNER JOIN OrderItems ON " _
            & "Products.ProductID = OrderItems.ProductID " _
            & "Where OrderID = " & [OrderID], dbOpenSnapshot)
        TotalWeight = rs("TotalWeight")
        Set rs = MyDB.OpenRecordset("SELECT ZipCodes.ShippingCostPerPound, " _
            & "ZipCodes.TaxRate, ShippingMethods.ExtraChargeRate " _
            & "From ShippingMethods INNER JOIN " _
            & "(Orders INNER JOIN (ZipCodes INNER JOIN " _
            & "CustomerAddresses ON ZipCodes.ZipCode = CustomerAddresses.ZipCode) " _
            & "ON Orders.ShippingAddress = CustomerAddresses.CustomerAddressID) " _
            & "ON ShippingMethods.ShippingMethod = Orders.ShippingMethod " _
            & "Where OrderID = " & [OrderID], dbOpenSnapshot)
        [Shipping] = (TotalWeight * rs("ShippingCostPerPound")) * _
            (1 + rs("ExtraChargeRate"))
        [Tax] = [ProductCostTotal] * rs("TaxRate")
        [OrderTotal] = [ProductCostTotal] + [Shipping] + [Tax]
    End If
End Sub
```

You now need a Database object:

```
Dim MyDB As DAO.Database
```

and a Recordset object:

```
Dim rs As DAO.Recordset
```

The following variable is used to store the total weight of all the products in the customer's order:

```
Dim TotalWeight As Single
```

First, make sure that a customer has been selected for this order:

```
If IsNumeric([CustomerID]) And [CustomerID] <> 0 Then
```

If one has, you can connect to the database:

```
Set MyDB = CurrentDb
```

Then retrieve the sum of all the products that are in this order:

```
Set rs = MyDB.OpenRecordset("Select Sum(Quantity) as TheQuantity " _
    & "from OrderItems Where OrderID = " & [OrderID], dbOpenSnapshot)
```

This value is placed into the NumberOfItemsOrdered field:

```
[NumberOfItemsOrdered] = rs("TheQuantity")
```

Next, calculate the total price of the products ordered by summing the price of each item and multiplying it by the quantity of products ordered:

```
Set rs = MyDB.OpenRecordset("Select Sum([Price] * [Quantity]) as TheSum " _
    & "from OrderItems Where OrderID = " & [OrderID], dbOpenSnapshot)
```

That value is placed into the ProductCostTotal field:

```
[ProductCostTotal] = rs("TheSum")
```

To calculate the shipping charge, you need to know the total weight of all the products. You can do that here by joining together the Products table, where you get the weight, with the OrderItems table, where you get the quantity of products ordered. These two values are multiplied and the sum of all these values is returned from the query:

```
Set rs = MyDB.OpenRecordset("SELECT Sum([Quantity] * [Weight]) " _
    & "as TotalWeight From Products INNER JOIN OrderItems ON " _
    & "Products.ProductID = OrderItems.ProductID " _
    & "Where OrderID = " & [OrderID], dbOpenSnapshot)
```

You can then store that total weight in a temporary variable:

```
TotalWeight = rs("TotalWeight")
```

Now that you know the weight of the order, you need to retrieve the cost of shipping this product per pound to its destination. You also need to know what the shipping method is so that you can add that extra value. Also use this query to return the tax rate for the shipping location. This is all retrieved in one query by combining the ShippingMethods table with the Orders table and the Customers table:

```
Set rs = MyDB.OpenRecordset("SELECT ZipCodes.ShippingCostPerPound, " _
    & "ZipCodes.TaxRate, ShippingMethods.ExtraChargeRate " _
    & "From ShippingMethods INNER JOIN " _
    & "(Orders INNER JOIN (ZipCodes INNER JOIN " _
    & "CustomerAddresses ON ZipCodes.ZipCode =
CustomerAddresses.ZipCode) " _
    & "ON Orders.ShippingAddress =
CustomerAddresses.CustomerAddressID) " _
    & "ON ShippingMethods.ShippingMethod = Orders.ShippingMethod " _
    & "Where OrderID = " & [OrderID], dbOpenSnapshot)
```

Then calculate the shipping charge by multiplying the shipping price per pound by the total weight of the order and then multiplying that by the extra shipping charge value:

```
[Shipping] = (TotalWeight * rs("ShippingCostPerPound")) * _
    (1 + rs("ExtraChargeRate"))
```

The tax on the order is simply the total cost of the order multiplied by the tax rate for the shipping location:

```
[Tax] = [ProductCostTotal] * rs("TaxRate")
```

The grand total for the order is then calculated by adding the product order total with the shipping and the tax:

```
[OrderTotal] = [ProductCostTotal] + [Shipping] + [Tax]
```

The CustomerOrders subform contains its own subform called OrderItems. That subform also has a couple of procedures. The first fires when the user double-clicks on the ProductID field:

```
Private Sub Product_DblClick(Cancel As Integer)
    If [ProductID] = "" Or IsNull([ProductID]) Then
        DoCmd.OpenForm "Products", , , , acFormAdd, acDialog
        [Product].Requery
    Else
        DoCmd.OpenForm "Products", , , "[ProductID] = """ _
            & [ProductID] & """", , acDialog
        [Product].Requery
    End If
End Sub
```

First, make sure the field has a value:

```
If [ProductID] = "" Or IsNull([ProductID]) Then
```

If it doesn't, you can assume that the user wants to add a new product, so open the Products form in Add mode:

```
DoCmd.OpenForm "Products", , , , acFormAdd, acDialog
```

Now repopulate the Product combo box:

```
[Product].Requery
```

If the ProductID field contains a value, open the Products form and filter it so that it displays the product selected:

```
DoCmd.OpenForm "Products", , , "[ProductID] = """ _
    & [ProductID] & """", , acDialog
```

Again, after the user is done with that form, repopulate the Product combo box:

```
[Product].Requery
```

The next code block fires when the user leaves the ProductID field on the OrderItems subform:

```
Private Sub Product_Exit(Cancel As Integer)
    Dim MyDB As DAO.Database
    Dim RSProduct As DAO.Recordset
    If [ProductID] <> 0 Then
        Set MyDB = CurrentDb
        Set RSProduct = MyDB.OpenRecordset("Select Price " _
            & "From Products where ProductID = """ & [ProductID] & """", _
            dbOpenSnapshot)
        If Not RSProduct.EOF Then
            [Price] = RSProduct("Price")
        End If
    End If
End Sub
```

When the user leaves the product field, you need to show the price of the product in the Price field. This needs to be done because at a later time the price of the product could change. Thus, you will need to connect to the current database:

```
Dim MyDB As DAO.Database
```

and retrieve data:

```
Dim RSProduct As DAO.Recordset
```

Then make sure a product has been selected:

```
If [ProductID] <> 0 Then
```

If one was, connect to the database:

```
Set MyDB = CurrentDb
```

and retrieve the price of the product selected:

```
Set RSProduct = MyDB.OpenRecordset("Select Price " _
    & "From Products where ProductID = """ & [ProductID] & """", _
    dbOpenSnapshot)
```

If you found the product in the Products table, the EOF flag is False:

```
If Not RSProduct.EOF Then
```

In this case, you can set the price of the product in the OrderItems table:

```
[Price] = RSProduct("Price")
```

Products, Customer Reps, Shipping Methods, and Zip Codes Forms

The Products, Customer Reps, Shipping Methods, and Zip Codes forms all contain the same code blocks, so they are discussed together in this section. Each of these forms has code that fires when the Add, Delete, Search, and Close buttons are pressed.

The first code block fires when the user clicks on the Add button:

```
Private Sub CommandAdd_Click()
    DoCmd.GoToRecord , , acNewRec
    [ZipCode].SetFocus
End Sub
```

Use the GoToRecord method and pass to it the constant acNewRec to move the record pointer to a new record:

```
DoCmd.GoToRecord , , acNewRec
```

Then move the focus to the first edited field in the Detail section so the user can start entering the data for this record:

```
[ZipCode].SetFocus
```

The next code block runs when the user clicks on the Delete button:

```
Private Sub CommandDelete_Click()
    On Error GoTo HandleError
    DoCmd.DoMenuItem acFormBar, acEditMenu, 8, , acMenuVer70
    DoCmd.DoMenuItem acFormBar, acEditMenu, 6, , acMenuVer70
    [ZipCode].SetFocus
    Exit Sub
HandleError:
    If Err.Number <> 2501 Then
        MsgBox Err.Number & " " & Err.Description
    End If
End Sub
```

You need to turn on error handling to trap for a known error:

```
On Error GoTo HandleError
```

Now delete the current record:

```
DoCmd.DoMenuItem acFormBar, acEditMenu, 8, , acMenuVer70
DoCmd.DoMenuItem acFormBar, acEditMenu, 6, , acMenuVer70
```

If the record deletion is successful, move the focus back to the detail section:

```
[ZipCode].SetFocus
```

and exit the procedure:

```
Exit Sub
```

If an error occurred, the code would flow to this label, as specified in the error statement at the top of this procedure:

```
HandleError:
```

When the record is being deleted, Access prompts the user and asks if he or she wants to delete the record. If the user clicks the No button in that message, Access does not delete the record but returns error number 2501 to your procedure. If that happens, it really isn't an error, so skip that error number here:

```
If Err.Number <> 2501 Then
```

However, you should display any other message to the user:

```
MsgBox Err.Number & " " & Err.Description
```

When the user clicks on the Search button, the next code block fires:

```
Private Sub CommandSearch_Click()
    Screen.PreviousControl.SetFocus
    DoCmd.DoMenuItem acFormBar, acEditMenu, 10, , acMenuVer70
End Sub
```

Assume that the field that the user wants to search is the field that he or she was at before clicking on the Search button. So use the SetFocus method of the PreviousControl object to return the focus back to the field that he or she wants to search:

```
Screen.PreviousControl.SetFocus
```

Then open the Access Search dialog:

```
DoCmd.DoMenuItem acFormBar, acEditMenu, 10, , acMenuVer70
```

The last procedure fires when the Close button is pressed. It uses the Close method of the DoCmd object to close the current form:

```
Private Sub CommandClose_Click()
    DoCmd.Close
End Sub
```

Reports

Order Totals Grouped by Customer Rep Report

The Order Totals Grouped by Customer Rep report shows, within a date range, the total number of orders processed by each customer rep that had any orders. The report is based on the Order Totals Grouped by Customer Rep query. That query has the following syntax:

```
SELECT Customers.CustomerRepID, Sum(Orders.OrderTotal) AS [Sum]
FROM (CustomerReps INNER JOIN Customers ON
CustomerReps.CustomerRepID = Customers.CustomerRepID)
INNER JOIN Orders ON Customers.CustomerID = Orders.CustomerID
WHERE (((Orders.OrderDate)>=[Start Date:] And
(Orders.OrderDate)<=[End Date]))
GROUP BY Customers.CustomerRepID;
```

The query joins three tables together. The CustomerReps table is joined with the Customers table, which is joined to the Orders table. Be sure to limit the records used in the query by supplying a date range that the records must fall within. The records are then grouped by the Customer-RepID field.

Quantity Sold Grouped by Product Report

The Quantity Sold Grouped by Product report shows the number of products sold within a date range that is specified by the user. The report is based on the Quantity Sold Grouped by Product query, which has the following syntax:

```
SELECT OrderItems.ProductID, Sum(OrderItems.Quantity) AS Quantity
FROM Orders INNER JOIN OrderItems ON Orders.OrderID =
OrderItems.OrderID
WHERE (((Orders.OrderDate)>=[Start Date:] And
(Orders.OrderDate)<=[End Date:]))
GROUP BY OrderItems.ProductID;
```

The query groups the Orders table with the OrderItems table. The records returned are limited by the date range specified by the user. The user is prompted for the start and end dates. The resulting records are then grouped by the ProductID field.

Orders by Month Report

The Orders by Month report shows how many orders have been placed in each month of every year that has orders. The report is based on the Orders by Month query, which has the following SQL syntax:

```
SELECT Year([OrderDate]) AS [Year], Month([OrderDate]),
Count(Orders.OrderID) AS CountOfOrderID
FROM Orders GROUP BY Year([OrderDate]), Month([OrderDate]);
```

The query returns the year of the order date using the Year function. The month of the order is also returned using the Month function. The Count of the orders is the other field returned. The records are grouped by year and then by month.

Contact Manager Database

The Contact Manager database application enables the user to track contacts or leads. Reports on the leads enable the user to see the age of the lead contact and to print out a To Do List of leads that need to be contacted. Most of the reports and forms also enable the user to see all the leads or only the leads being managed by a specific employee.

Sample Walk-through

When the user first enters the Contact Manager database application, the Start Up properties are set so that he or she sees the menu shown in Figure 7-12.

The menu enables the user to view any of the forms and reports used in this application. The user also can choose to see only the leads for a specific employee. If he or she does that, then the Contacts form shows just the leads for the name selected. The To Do List and the Days Since Last Contact reports also show just those leads that are for that person. If the user clicks on the Clear button, the filtering is cleared and he or she will see all the leads on all the forms and reports. When the user clicks on the Contacts button, the Contacts form is shown, as in Figure 7-13.

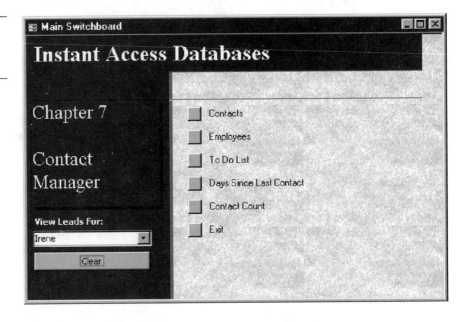

This form is the heart of the application. Here the user manages all of
his or her own leads. The top of the form shows the name of the contact
along with the person managing this lead. The subform on this form displays each of the contacts that have been made to this individual. The

form has a second page called Notes, which is shown in Figure 7-14. The user would use this page to store any notes and comments about the contact.

The other form in this application is the Employees form, which is shown in Figure 7-15. Each of the leads is managed by an employee. The Employees form is the place where the user would add, edit, and delete employees.

The user can view the To Do List report by clicking on that button on the menu. When he or she does, the report is shown, as in Figure 7-16.

Each of the leads has a field that indicates when the lead should be contacted next. The To Do List report displays all the leads that need to be contacted based on that date. This report can display all the leads that need to be contacted or just the leads of one employee.

When the user clicks on the Days Since Last Contact button, the report is shown, as in Figure 7-17. This report displays the number of days since the lead was last contacted. It can display all the leads or just the leads of a specific employee.

Figure 7-14

The Notes page of the Contact form

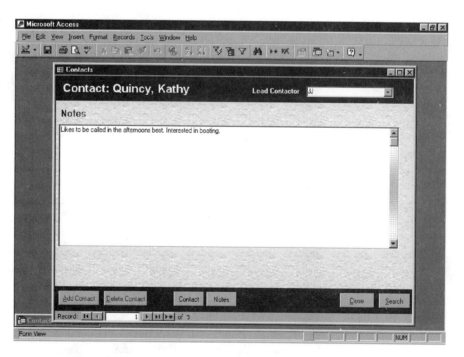

Figure 7-15

The Employees
form

Figure 7-16

The To Do List
report

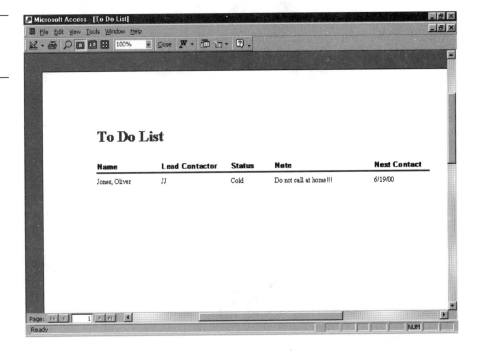

Figure 7-17

The Days Since
Last Contact
report

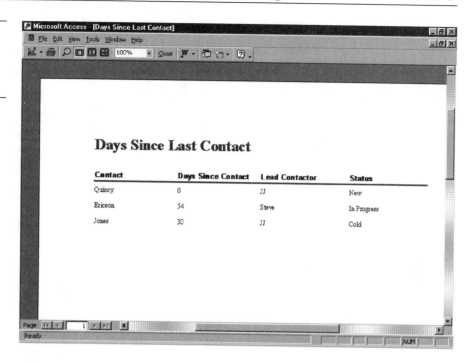

When the Contact Count button is pressed, the user sees the report displayed in Figure 7-18. The Contact Count report shows the number of contacts grouped by the employee and the status of the contact. This enables a manager to quickly review the caseload and the results of each of the employees.

Table Definitions and Relationships

Contacts Table

The Contacts table stores all the pertinent information for the contacts themselves. The table is in a one-to-many relationship with the Employees table. Each customer is managed by a single employee, but each employee can manage many customers.

ContactsMade Table

The ContactsMade table stores the individual contacts made to a particular lead and is in a one-to-many relationship with the Contacts table.

Figure 7-18

The Contact
Count report

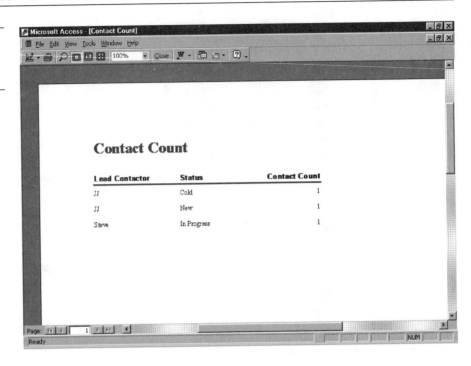

Each contact made goes with a particular lead, but each lead could have been contacted many times. The table is also in a one-to-many relationship with the Employees table. Each of the contacts made to a lead is made by one of the employees.

Employees Table

The Employees table stores information about individual employees. This information is then used on the forms and reports and is used to show just the records for individual employees.

Field Specifications

Contacts Table

The field specifications for the Contacts table are displayed in Table 7-10.
    The ContactID field is the primary key for this table. It uniquely identifies each of the records. The EmployeeID field is a foreign key that links

Table 7-10	Field Name	Field Type	Notes
The Contacts Table Field Specifications	ContactID	AutoNumber	Primary Key
	FirstName	Text	Length = 50
	LastName	Text	Length = 50
	Address	Text	Length = 100
	City	Text	Length = 50
	State	Text	Length = 50
	ZipCode	Text	Length = 50
	HomePhone	Text	Length = 50
	WorkPhone	Text	Length = 50
	OtherPhone	Text	Length = 50
	EmployeeID	Number	Type = Long, Foreign Key
	ReferredBy	Text	Length = 50
	FirstContact	Date/Time	
	NextContact	Date/Time	
	Status	Text	Length = 50
	Note	Memo	

this table to the Employees table. The field is displayed as a combo box and has the following SQL statement in the Row Source property:

```
SELECT [Employees].[EmployeeID], [Employees].[ShortName] FROM Employees;
```

The ID of the employee is stored with the record, but the user sees the ShortName field in the combo box.

The Status field also is displayed as a combo box. The Row Source Type property is set to Value List and the Row Source property is set to the following text:

```
"New";"In Progress";"Hot";"Success";"Cold";"Do Not Contact"
```

The Limit To List property is set to Yes, so the user must select one of the values in the Row Source property.

ContactsMade Table

The field specifications for the ContactsMade table are displayed in Table 7-11.

The ContactMadeID field is the primary key. The table has two foreign keys. The first is the ContactID field that links this table to the Contacts table in a one-to-many relationship. The other is the EmployeeID field that links this table to the Employees table. The EmployeeID field has the Display Control property set to combo box. The Row Source property is set to the following SQL statement:

```
SELECT [Employees].[EmployeeID], [Employees].[ShortName] FROM Employees;
```

	Field Name	Field Type	Notes
Table 7-11	ContactMadeID	AutoNumber	Primary Key
The ContactsMade Table Field Specifications	ContactID	Number	Type = Long, Foreign Key
	EmployeeID	Number	Type = Long, Foreign Key
	WhenMade	Date/Time	
	Note	Memo	

Employees Table

The field specifications for the Employees table are displayed in Table 7-12.

The EmployeeID field is the primary key for the table. The rest of the fields store the information about the employee.

	Field Name	Field Type	Notes
Table 7-12	EmployeeID	AutoNumber	Primary Key
The Employees Table Field Specifications	ShortName	Text	Length = 50
	FirstName	Text	Length = 50
	LastName	Text	Length = 50
	PhoneNumber	Text	Length = 50
	EmailAddress	Text	Length = 50

Modules

PublicProcs Module

The Contact Manager database application contains a single module called PublicProcs. That module has one variable declaration:

```
Public CurrentEmployee As Long
```

The variable is declared with a Public scope, so it is accessible to any procedure in any form or report. The variable also is used by some of the forms and reports to limit the leads displayed to just those of the person that was selected on the Menu form.

Forms

Switchboard Form

The Switchboard form is used to navigate through the forms and reports in the Contacts Manager database application. It was created using the Switchboard Wizard, which is accessible within Access through the Tools/Database Utilities/Switchboard Manager menu item. The look and layout of the form produced with that wizard have been altered. Also added to the form are a button and combo box. These controls are used for selecting the current employee whose leads the user wants to work with.

The combo box displays a list of all the employees in the Employees table. When the user selects a record, the following code block fires:

```
Private Sub Combo23_Change()
    Dim MyDB As DAO.Database
    Dim RS As DAO.Recordset
    If Combo23.Text <> "" Then
        Set MyDB = CurrentDb
        Set RS = MyDB.OpenRecordset("Select EmployeeID from Employees " _
            & "Where [ShortName] = """ & Combo23.Text & """", dbOpenSnapshot)
        If RS.EOF Then
            CurrentEmployee = 0
        Else
            CurrentEmployee = RS("EmployeeID")
        End If
    End If
End Sub
```

Now a Database object is needed:

```
Dim MyDB As DAO.Database
```

as well as a Recordset object:

```
Dim RS As DAO.Recordset
```

Now make sure that the user has selected an employee from the list:

```
If Combo23.Text <> "" Then
```

If the user has, you can connect to the database:

```
Set MyDB = CurrentDb
```

and retrieve the ID for the employee selected:

```
Set RS = MyDB.OpenRecordset("Select EmployeeID from Employees " _
        & "Where [ShortName] = """ & Combo23.Text & """",
dbOpenSnapshot)
```

Make sure an employee with that name was found:

```
If RS.EOF Then
```

If one wasn't, clear the current employee variable:

```
CurrentEmployee = 0
```

Otherwise, set the current employee variable to the employee selected by the user:

```
CurrentEmployee = RS("EmployeeID")
```

You will see that this value is used on one of the forms and two of the reports to determine which records are displayed. The other procedure on this form fires when the user clicks on the Clear button. This button resets the current employee variable to 0, so all leads are displayed:

```
Private Sub Command25_Click()
    CurrentEmployee = 0
End Sub
```

Contacts Form

When the Contacts form first opens, the Load event fires. This event enables you to modify which records are displayed before the form itself is displayed to the user:

```
Private Sub Form_Load()
    If CurrentEmployee <> 0 Then
```

```
        Me.Filter = "[EmployeeID] = " & CurrentEmployee
        Me.FilterOn = True
    End If
End Sub
```

First, check to see if the user has selected an employee whose leads he or she wants to see. If so, the CurrentEmployee variable will contain a value other than 0:

```
If CurrentEmployee <> 0 Then
```

If this is the case, filter the form so that only those leads that are managed by that employee are displayed:

```
Me.Filter = "[EmployeeID] = " & CurrentEmployee
```

Then turn the filter on:

```
Me.FilterOn = True
```

The label in the header of the form displays the name of the current lead. The code that does this is in the Current event, which fires every time the record pointer moves:

```
Private Sub Form_Current()
    Label16.Caption = "Contact: " & [LastName] & ", " & [FirstName]
End Sub
```

The footer of the form contains buttons that enable the user to navigate through the two pages of the form. When the user clicks on the Contact button, the GoToPage method is used to display the first page of the form:

```
Private Sub Command33_Click()
    DoCmd.GoToPage 1
End Sub
```

When the user clicks on the Notes button, the code displays the Notes page, which is page 2:

```
Private Sub Command34_Click()
    DoCmd.GoToPage 2
End Sub
```

The next code block fires when the user clicks on the Add button:

```
Private Sub CommandAdd_Click()
    DoCmd.GoToRecord , , acNewRec
    [FirstName].SetFocus
End Sub
```

The GoToRecord method is used to move the record pointer to a new record:

```
DoCmd.GoToRecord , , acNewRec
```

Now move the focus to the first name so the user can start entering data:

```
[FirstName].SetFocus
```

The next code block fires when the Delete button is pressed:

```
Private Sub CommandDelete_Click()
    On Error GoTo HandleError
    DoCmd.DoMenuItem acFormBar, acEditMenu, 8, , acMenuVer70
    DoCmd.DoMenuItem acFormBar, acEditMenu, 6, , acMenuVer70
    [FirstName].SetFocus
    Exit Sub
HandleError:
    If Err.Number <> 2501 Then
        MsgBox Err.Number & " " & Err.Description
    End If
End Sub
```

Now an error needs to be trapped:

```
On Error GoTo HandleError
```

Next, delete the current record:

```
DoCmd.DoMenuItem acFormBar, acEditMenu, 8, , acMenuVer70
DoCmd.DoMenuItem acFormBar, acEditMenu, 6, , acMenuVer70
```

If the record was successfully deleted, the code will flow here. Now the focus can be shifted back to the detail section of the form:

```
[FirstName].SetFocus
```

Then exit the procedure:

```
Exit Sub
```

If an error occurred, the code will flow here:

```
HandleError:
```

Now screen out the error that occurs if the user cancels the record deletion:

```
If Err.Number <> 2501 Then
```

and display any other error message:

```
MsgBox Err.Number & " " & Err.Description
```

The next code block fires when the Search button is pressed:

```
Private Sub CommandSearch_Click()
    Screen.PreviousControl.SetFocus
    DoCmd.DoMenuItem acFormBar, acEditMenu, 10, , acMenuVer70
End Sub
```

It uses the SetFocus method to return the focus to the last field, which you can assume is the field that the user wants to search:

```
Screen.PreviousControl.SetFocus
```

Now open the Search dialog:

```
DoCmd.DoMenuItem acFormBar, acEditMenu, 10, , acMenuVer70
```

The other procedure on this form fires when the Close button is pressed. It uses the Close method of the DoCmd object to close this form:

```
Private Sub CommandClose_Click()
    DoCmd.Close
End Sub
```

Employees Form

The code on the Employees form provides the functionality needed for the four buttons on the footer of the form. The first code block fires when the Add button is pressed:

```
Private Sub CommandAdd_Click()
    DoCmd.GoToRecord , , acNewRec
    [ShortName].SetFocus
End Sub
```

You can start by moving to a new record:

```
DoCmd.GoToRecord , , acNewRec
```

Then set the focus to the first edited field in the detail section of the form so the user can start entering data:

```
[ShortName].SetFocus
```

The next code block enables the user to delete a record by clicking the Delete button:

```
Private Sub CommandDelete_Click()
    On Error GoTo HandleError
    DoCmd.DoMenuItem acFormBar, acEditMenu, 8, , acMenuVer70
    DoCmd.DoMenuItem acFormBar, acEditMenu, 6, , acMenuVer70
    [ShortName].SetFocus
    Exit Sub
HandleError:
    If Err.Number <> 2501 Then
        MsgBox Err.Number & " " & Err.Description
    End If
End Sub
```

Start with an error handler:

```
On Error GoTo HandleError
```

and then delete the current record:

```
DoCmd.DoMenuItem acFormBar, acEditMenu, 8, , acMenuVer70
DoCmd.DoMenuItem acFormBar, acEditMenu, 6, , acMenuVer70
```

Then shift the focus to the detail section and exit this procedure:

```
[ShortName].SetFocus
Exit Sub
```

If an error occurred, the code will flow to this point:

```
HandleError:
```

Make sure the error isn't because the user canceled the record deletion:

```
If Err.Number <> 2501 Then
```

If it wasn't, display the error to the user:

```
MsgBox Err.Number & " " & Err.Description
```

The next procedure fires when the Search button is pressed:

```
Private Sub CommandSearch_Click()
    Screen.PreviousControl.SetFocus
    DoCmd.DoMenuItem acFormBar, acEditMenu, 10, , acMenuVer70
End Sub
```

The code starts by setting the focus to the control that the user had selected before clicking on the Search button:

```
Screen.PreviousControl.SetFocus
```

Then open the Search dialog:

```
DoCmd.DoMenuItem acFormBar, acEditMenu, 10, , acMenuVer70
```

The last code block on this form closes the form when the Close button is pressed by using the Close method of the DoCmd object:

```
Private Sub CommandClose_Click()
    DoCmd.Close
End Sub
```

Reports

To Do List Report

The To Do List report displays a list of all the leads that need to be contacted, as indicated by the NextContact field. The report can display all the Contacts that need to be contacted or just the leads of the employee selected on the Menu form. The code in the Open event fires when the report first opens to provide this distinction:

```
Private Sub Report_Open(Cancel As Integer)
    If CurrentEmployee <> 0 Then
        Me.Filter = "[EmployeeID] = " & CurrentEmployee
        Me.FilterOn = True
    End If
End Sub
```

Check to make sure that an employee has been selected:

```
If CurrentEmployee <> 0 Then
```

If so, filter the report based on the employee selected:

```
Me.Filter = "[EmployeeID] = " & CurrentEmployee
```

Then turn the filter on:

```
Me.FilterOn = True
```

The report is based on the To Do List query that has the following syntax:

```
SELECT [LastName] & ", " & [FirstName] AS Name,
Contacts.EmployeeID, Contacts.Status, Contacts.Note,
Contacts.NextContact
FROM Contacts WHERE (((Contacts.NextContact)<=Now()));
```

The query concatenates the first and last name of the lead into a single field called Name. The Where clause limits the records returned so that only those who have a next contact date that is today or any day in the past are reported.

Days Since Last Contact Report

The Days Since Last Contact report displays the number of days since a lead was last contacted. The report can show the leads for all the employees or just one employee. The code in the Open event of the report determines whether a filter is needed:

```
Private Sub Report_Open(Cancel As Integer)
    If CurrentEmployee <> 0 Then
        Me.Filter = "[EmployeeID] = " & CurrentEmployee
        Me.FilterOn = True
    End If
End Sub
```

Start by seeing if the user has selected an employee from the menu:

```
If CurrentEmployee <> 0 Then
```

If so, filter the report so that it shows just the leads for the employee selected:

```
Me.Filter = "[EmployeeID] = " & CurrentEmployee
Me.FilterOn = True
```

The underlying data in the report comes from two queries. The first query is called last contact and has the following SQL syntax:

```
SELECT ContactsMade.ContactID, Max(ContactsMade.WhenMade) AS
MaxOfWhenMade
FROM ContactsMade GROUP BY ContactsMade.ContactID;
```

This query retrieves the most recent date on which a lead was contacted and places it in a field called MaxOfWhenMade. The results of this query are then used by another query called Days Since Last Contact, which is used by this report. The query has the following SQL syntax:

```
SELECT [Last Contact].ContactID,
DateDiff("d",[MaxOfWhenMade],Date())
AS [Days Since Last Contact], Contacts.EmployeeID, Contacts.Status
FROM [Last Contact] INNER JOIN
Contacts ON [Last Contact].ContactID = Contacts.ContactID;
```

The query combines the results of the last query with the Contacts table. The query returns the number of days between the MaxOfWhen-Made and the current system date with this call to the DateDiff function:

```
DateDiff("d",[MaxOfWhenMade],Date())
```

The first parameter, "d", indicates that you want to know the difference in days. The next two parameters are the dates in which you want to know the difference.

Contact Count Report

The Contact Count report displays the number of leads for each of the employees grouped by the status of the lead. The report is based on the Contact Count query, which has the following syntax:

```
SELECT Contacts.EmployeeID, Contacts.Status,
Count(Contacts.ContactID) AS [Contact Count]
FROM Contacts GROUP BY Contacts.EmployeeID, Contacts.Status;
```

The query retrieves data from the Contacts table. The data is grouped first by employee and then by status.

CHAPTER 8

Products

ON THE CD:

Products.mdb

Managing Inventory and Warehouses

In this chapter, we will look at a single database application called Products.mdb. This application enables you to manage Warehouses, locations in a Warehouse, containers, which are in those locations, and products in the locations. The application also manages vendors of the products.

As you are reading through this chapter, pay particular attention to the Warehouse Map form. This form graphically displays the layout of a Warehouse enabling easy comprehension of the products and containers in a Warehouse. Think about how you could adapt the code on this form to your own needs. You could use it to display rooms in a conference or maybe tapes in a tape back-up system.

Products Database

Sample Walk-through

Figure 8-1 shows the form viewed when the user first launches this database application.

From this menu, the user can access most of the functionality of the application. The menu system has two sub-menus; one contains the forms in the application and the other contains the reports in the application.

If the user enters the Forms menu and selects the Warehouse option, the form in Figure 8-2 is shown.

The Warehouse is at the top-level of the information hierarchy in this database. The fields at the top of this form link to that table. Under the Warehouse is the Container Position data.

Each Warehouse in this sample company has places where containers can be placed called Container Positions. Each of the Warehouses has 100 of the Container Positions. Since the size of these spots may vary, each can hold their own defined number of containers. In the examples shown in

Figure 8-1

Products database Main Menu

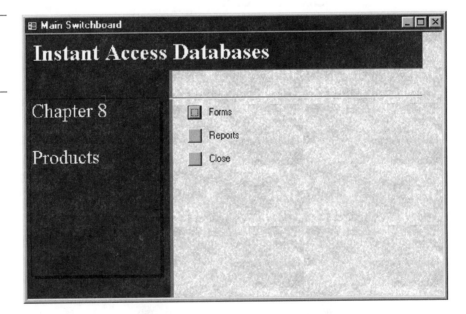

Figure 8-2

Warehouse form

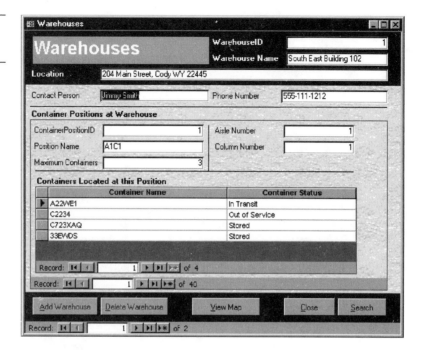

Figure 8-2, a maximum of three containers can be held. To manage a container, the user selects Containers from the Forms sub-menu which displays the form shown in Figure 8-3.

From this form, the user can assign the location of a form. The form status indicates whether a form is currently stored at the indicated location, is in transit, or is out of service. Code on this form prevents the user from placing a container in a spot that is already storing its maximum number of containers; but, since the size of products in a container could be vastly different, the container can have an unlimited number of products inside of it. Those products are assigned on this form.

If the user wishes to work with products, he or she can select that item from the Forms sub-menu or double-click on a Product on the Containers form. Then the form shown in Figure 8-4 appears.

From this form, the user can create new products, view his or her information, change the information or delete products. The location of those products across all the Warehouses can also be seen. The code on the form enables the user to return back to the Warehouse or Container when those fields on this form are double-clicked.

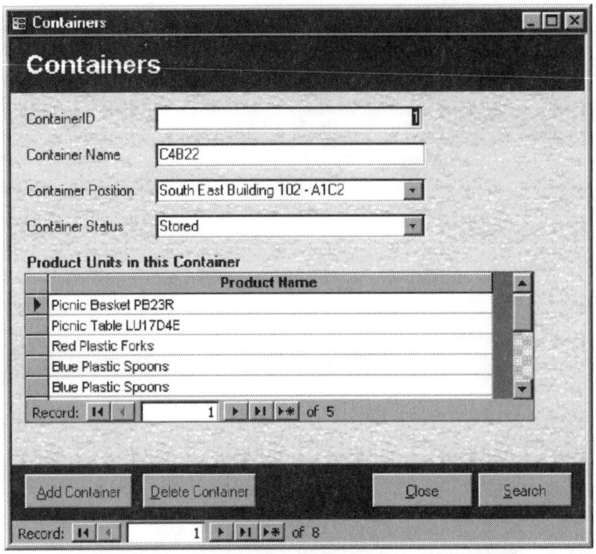

Figure 8-3

Containers form

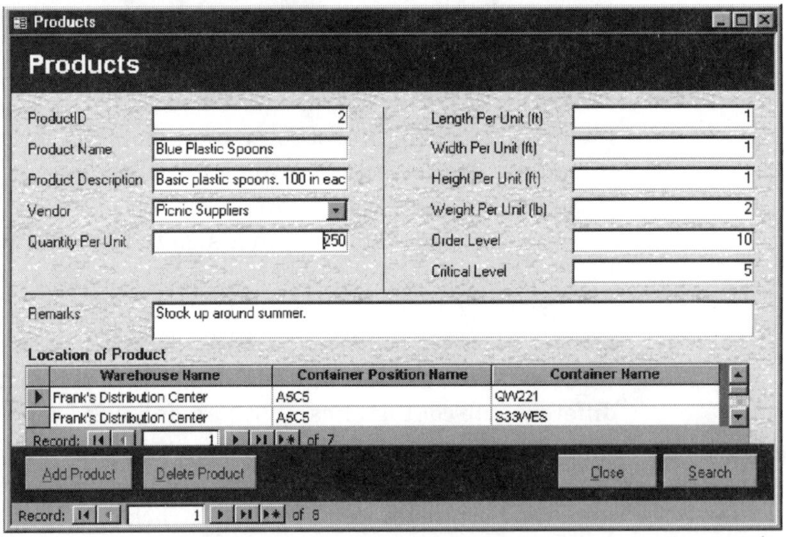

Figure 8-4

Products form

Each of the products comes from a specific Vendor. The Vendors form shown in Figure 8-5 enables the user to manage that portion of the data in the database. This form displays all the Vendor information, as well as any of the products that the Vendor offers. Double-clicking on a product returns the user to the Products form.

If you look back at the Warehouse form shown in Figure 8-2, notice a View Map button. This button brings up another form that graphically displays the layout of the products within a Warehouse. Figure 8-6 shows the map of the first Warehouse.

As noted before, each of the warehouses in this sample company has 100 spots or is 10 by 10. The map in this figure shows the user, through color-keying, exactly which of the spots in the Warehouse are unused, which are empty, which are full, and which are partly full.

This Warehouse layout is made up of even rows that would enable equipment to be easily brought in to manipulate the containers. However,

Figure 8-5

Vendors form

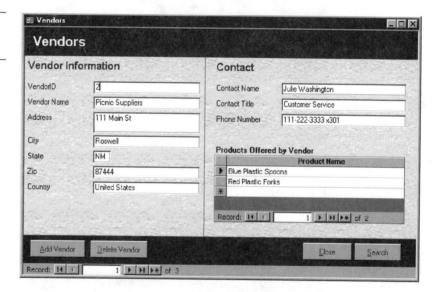

Figure 8-6

Map view of first Warehouse

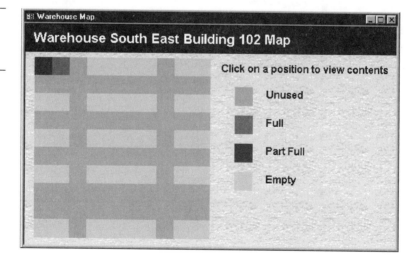

another Warehouse may look completely different, such as the one shown in Figure 8-7.

This Warehouse uses just a small portion of its space for containers. Regardless of the layout, the user can click on any of the user spots to see the details of what containers are located at those locations. This form is shown in Figure 8-8.

Figure 8-7

Map view of second Warehouse

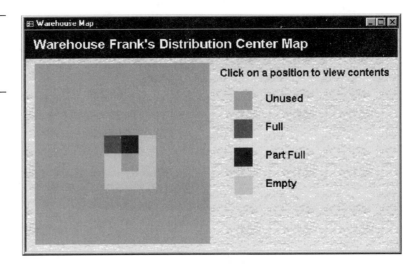

Figure 8-8

Container Position form

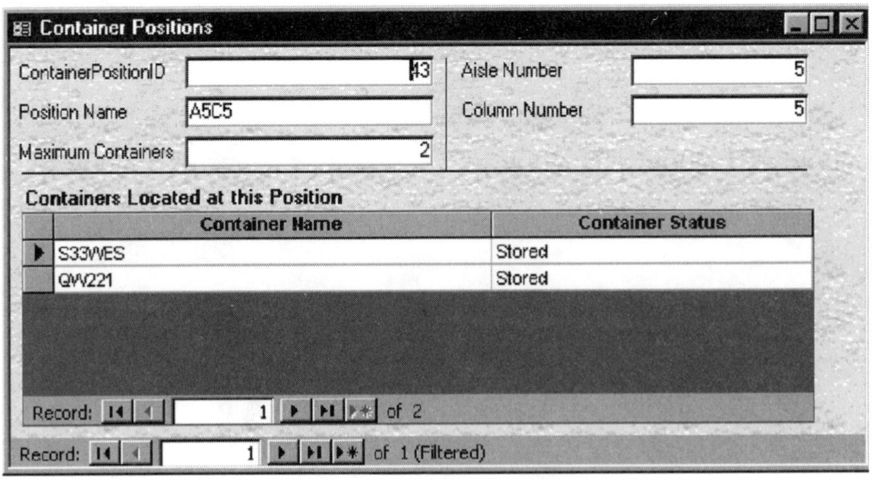

This form is actually the same sub-form that is displayed on the Warehouses form. From the other sub-menu, Reports, the user can select from three reports. The first is called Products Grouped by Container and is displayed in Figure 8-9.

This report displays a list of the products that are contained within each container. The next report available from the Reports sub-menu is the Containers Grouped by Status report shown in Figure 8-10.

This summary report provides the user with a quick look at statuses of all the containers throughout all of the Warehouses. The last report is the Containers in Warehouses report, shown in Figure 8-11.

This report groups the containers by the Warehouse in which they are located and displays them with their status.

Figure 8-9

Products Grouped by Container Report

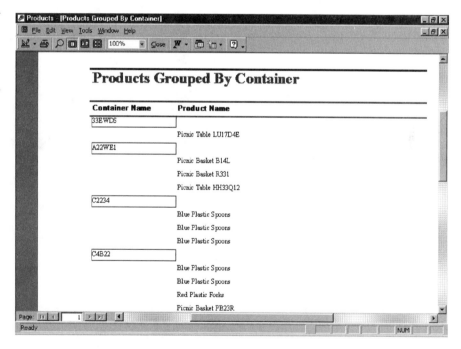

Figure 8-10

Containers
Grouped by
Status report

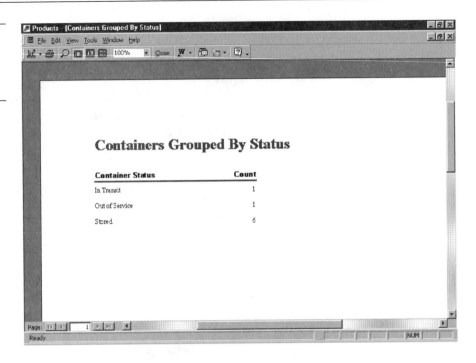

Figure 8-11

Containers in
Warehouses
report

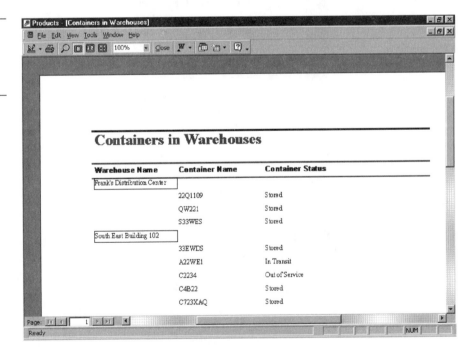

Table Definitions and Relationships

Warehouses Table

One of the top-level tables in this database is the Warehouses table. This table contains information about the Warehouse itself and contact information for the Warehouse.

ContainerPositions Table

Below the Warehouses table is the ContainerPositions table. Each of the Warehouses is divided up in grid fashion. Each of the spots on the grid is a container position. If that spot on the grid can contain a container, then it must have a record in this table. In this sample company each of the Warehouses is in the form of a 10 by 10 grid. The Warehouses table and the ContainerPositions table relate to each other in a one-to-many relationship. Each warehouse can have many positions, but each position is at a single warehouse.

Containers Table

The third table down in the warehouse hierarchy of data is the Containers table. At each of the defined positions at a warehouse, a container or containers can be placed. The ContainerPositions table and the Containers table are in a one-to-many relationship. Each of the positions can have many containers but each container is located at a single spot.

ProductsInContainers Table

Numerous products can be placed into each of the containers, and each of the products can be in numerous containers. So, a many-to-many relationship exists between the Containers table and the Products table which means a go-between table is needed to satisfy that relationship. The ProductsInContainers table fills that role because each product and each container can have many records in this table.

Products Table

The Products table, as stated above, is in a many-to-many relationship with the Containers table. The table stores detailed information about each of the products.

Vendors Table

Each of the products comes from a specific vendor. So, the Vendors table is in a one-to-many relationship with the Products table. The Vendors table stores contact information about a vendor.

Field Specifications

Warehouse Table

The field specifications for the Warehouse table are displayed in Table 8-1.

The WarehouseID field is the Primary Key for the table. Automatically populated, it uniquely identifies each record. The WarehouseName field is required and is indexed.

Field Name	Field Type	Notes
WarehouseID	AutoNumber	Primary Key
WarehouseName	Text	Length = 50
Location	Text	Length = 200
ContactPerson	Text	Length = 100
ContactPhoneNumber	Text	Length = 50

Table 8-1

Warehouse Table Field Specifications

ContainerPositions Table

The field specifications for the ContainerPositions table are displayed in Table 8-2.

The ContainerPositionID is the Primary Key for this table. The WarehouseID field is a Foreign Key linking this table to the Warehouse table. The Lookup properties are used with this field, so it will be displayed as a combo box. The Row Source property is set to this query:

```
SELECT [Warehouses].[WarehouseID], [Warehouses].[WarehouseName] FROM Warehouses;
```

Field Name	Field Type	Notes
ContainerPositionID	AutoNumber	Primary Key
WarehouseID	Number	Type = Long Integer, Foreign Key
ContainerPositionName	Text	Length = 50
AisleNumber	Number	Type = Integer
ColumnNumber	Number	Type = Integer
MaxContainers	Byte	Type = Byte

Table 8-2

ContainerPositions Table Field Specifications

The first column is bound so the user sees the ID of the warehouse is stored with the record, but the user sees the name of the warehouse. The ContainerPositionName field stores a friendly name for this specific position at a Warehouse. The AisleNumber field must be in the range of 1 to 100 in this example. So the Validation Rule property is set to this value:

```
>=1 And <=10
```

If the rule is violated, the user sees the text supplied in the Validation Text property:

```
The value in this field must be between 1 and 10
```

The same rule applies for the ColumnNumber field.

The MaxContainers field stores the maximum number of containers that are allowed at this position in the warehouse. Because that is assumed to be a small number, the Byte data type, which has a range from 0 to 255, is used. A Validation Rule is actually set up to limit the range of this value from 1 to 5:

```
>=1 And <=5
```

The following text is displayed if the rule is violated:

```
The value in this field must be between 1 and 5.
```

Containers Table

The field specifications for the Containers table are displayed in Table 8-3.

The ContainerID field is the Primary Key for this table. The ContainerPositionID field acts as a Foreign Key, linking this table with the ContainerPositions table. The Lookup properties are used, so it is displayed as a combo box. The Row Source property is set to this value:

```
SELECT [ContainerPositions].[ContainerPositionID],
[ContainerPositions].[ContainerPositionName] FROM
ContainerPositions;
```

Table 8-3	Field Name	Field Type	Notes
Containers Table Field Specifications	ContainerID	AutoNumber	Primary Key
	ContainerPositionID	Number	Type = Long Integer, Foreign Key
	ContainerName	Text	Length = 50
	ContainerStatus	Text	Length = 50

The ID is bound, but the name is displayed.

The ContainerStatus field stores the status of the container. This status can be one of three predefined values: Stored, In Transit, or Out of Service. The Row Source Type property for this field is set to the Value list with the following Row Source:

```
"Stored";"In Transit";"Out of Service"
```

The Limit to List property is set to Yes, so the user must select from one of these values.

ProductsInContainers Table

The field specifications for the ProductsInContainers table are displayed in Table 8-4.

The fields in this table simply satisfy the many-to-many relationship between the Products and Containers tables. All fields are required. The ProductInContainerID field is the primary key for the table. The ProductID field is a Foreign Key linking this table with the Products

Table 8-4	Field Name	Field Type	Notes
ProductsIn Containers Table Field Specifications	ProductInContainerID	AutoNumber	Primary Key
	ProductID	Number	Type = Long Integer, Foreign Key
	ContainerID	Number	Type = Long Integer, Foreign Key

table. The field uses the Lookup properties, so it is displayed as a combo box and has the following Row Source:

```
SELECT [Products].[ProductID], [Products].[ProductName] FROM Products;
```

The ID of the product is bound, so it is stored in the table, but the user sees the name of the product.

The ContainerID field is also a Foreign Key. It links this table to the Containers table. It also uses the lookup properties so it will be displayed as a combo box. The Row Source property is set to the following query:

```
SELECT [Containers].[ContainerID], [Containers].[ContainerName] FROM Containers;
```

Note that the Limit to List property is set to Yes for both of these Foreign Keys. So, the user must select from a value in the combo box.

Products Table

The field specifications for the ProductsInContainers table are displayed in Table 8-5.

The ProductID field is the Primary Key for this table. The ProductName and ProductDescription fields are used to provide identifying information about the product.

The VendorID field is a Foreign Key and links this table to the Vendors table. The Lookup properties are set in this field so it is displayed as a combo box. The Row Source property is set to the following query:

```
SELECT [Vendors].[VendorID], [Vendors].[VendorName] FROM Vendors;
```

The ID field is the bound field, which means that that value is stored in the record. The user sees the name of the vendor only because the Column Width property is set to this value:

```
0";1"
```

Table 8-5

ProductsIn Containers Table Field Specifications

Field Name	Field Type	Notes
ProductID	AutoNumber	Primary Key
ProductName	Text	Length = 50
ProductDescription	Text	Length = 255
VendorID	Number	Type = Long Integer, Foreign Key
QuantityPerUnit	Number	Type = Long Integer
LengthPerUnit	Number	Type = Single
WidthPerUnit	Number	Type = Single
HeightPerUnit	Number	Type = Single
WeightPerUnit	Number	Type = Single
OrderLevel	Number	Type = Long Integer
CriticalLevel	Number	Type = Long Integer
Remarks	Memo	

When the product is stored in a container, it probably would be in a box with numerous items of the product. The QuantityPerUnit field stores that number of items. A Validation Rule is used to set the range for this field:

```
>=0 And <=50000
```

If the rule is violated, the following text is displayed:

```
The value for this field must be between 0 and 50,000.
```

The LengthPerUnit, WidthPerUnit and HeightPerUnit fields store the dimensions of the box that contains the product. The Validation Rule property is set for these fields to limit the range of values:

```
>=0 And <=100
```

With the following value in the Validation Text:

```
This value must be between 0 and 100.
```

those fields and the WeightPerUnit field are set to the Single data type. This allows these fields to contain a fractional part of a number. The WeightPerUnit field stores the weight of the box that contains the product and has the following validation rule limiting its range from 0 to 20,000:

```
>=0 And <=20000
```

since the Validation Text property is set to this value:

```
This value must be between 0 and 20000.
```

the user will see that value in a Message Box if they violate the rule.

The OrderLevel and CriticalLevel fields store values at which the inventory should not fall below, otherwise it needs to be ordered. Both fields have the same Validation Rule:

```
>=0 And <=100000
```

which limits the number entered so that it is between 0 and 100,000. The following text is displayed if the user violates that rule:

```
This number must be between 0 and 100,000.
```

Vendors Table

The field specifications for the Vendors table are displayed in Table 8-6.

Table 8-6 Vendors Table Field Specifications	**Field Name**	**Field Type**	**Notes**
	VendorID	AutoNumber	Primary Key
	VendorName	Text	Length = 50
	Address	Text	Length = 100
	City	Text	Length = 50
	State	Text	Length = 2
	Zip	Text	Length = 50
	Country	Text	Length = 50
	ContactName	Text	Length = 100
	ContactTitle	Text	Length = 50
	ContactPhoneNumber	Text	Length = 50

The VendorID is the Primary Key for this table. The rest of the fields store descriptive information about the vendor.

Forms

Switchboard Form

The Switchboard form is used to navigate through the forms and reports in the Products application. It was created using the Switchboard wizard, which is accessible within Access through the Tools/Database Utilities/Switchboard Manager menu item. Only the look and layout of the form produced with that wizard have been altered.

Warehouses Form

The code on the Warehouses form allows the user to add records, delete records, search the data, close the form, and open the Warehouse Map form. The first code block below opens the Warehouse Map form:

```
Private Sub Command32_Click()
    CurrentWarehouseID = [WarehouseID]
    DoCmd.OpenForm "Warehouse Map"
End Sub
```

The database has a single module called PublicProcs that contains a single public variable called CurrentWarehouseID. A public variable provides a way to store temporary information that you want to use in different procedures of your code that are on different forms. Here, set the public variable so that it contains the value of the Warehouse currently being viewed:

```
CurrentWarehouseID = [WarehouseID]
```

Then, when you look at the code on the Warehouse Map form, see that you use the value that is stored here. The next line of code opens that form:

```
DoCmd.OpenForm "Warehouse Map"
```

The next code block fires when the user clicks on the Add Warehouse button:

```
Private Sub CommandAdd_Click()
    DoCmd.GoToRecord , , acNewRec
```

```
    [WarehouseName].SetFocus
End Sub
```

First, use the GoToRecord method of the DoCmd object to move the record pointer to a new record:

```
DoCmd.GoToRecord , , acNewRec
```

Then move the focus to the WarehouseName field so the user can start entering data:

```
[WarehouseName].SetFocus
```

The next code block enables the user to delete a record when he or she clicks on the Delete Warehouse button:

```
Private Sub CommandDelete_Click()
    On Error GoTo HandleError
    DoCmd.DoMenuItem acFormBar, acEditMenu, 8, , acMenuVer70
    DoCmd.DoMenuItem acFormBar, acEditMenu, 6, , acMenuVer70
    [WarehouseName].SetFocus
    Exit Sub
HandleError:
    If Err.Number <> 2501 Then
        MsgBox Err.Number & " " & Err.Description
    End If
End Sub
```

Start with an error statement in order to trap for a known error:

```
On Error GoTo HandleError
```

Then delete the current record:

```
DoCmd.DoMenuItem acFormBar, acEditMenu, 8, , acMenuVer70
DoCmd.DoMenuItem acFormBar, acEditMenu, 6, , acMenuVer70
```

Set the focus back to the WarehouseName field:

```
[WarehouseName].SetFocus
```

If no error has occurred, the code ends here:

```
Exit Sub
```

Otherwise, the code flows to this label:

```
HandleError:
```

Then check to see if the user canceled the deletion of the record. If so, skip that error:

```
If Err.Number <> 2501 Then
```

All other error messages are displayed to the user:

```
MsgBox Err.Number & " " & Err.Description
```

The next code block enables the user to search the data on this form:

```
Private Sub CommandSearch_Click()
    Screen.PreviousControl.SetFocus
    DoCmd.DoMenuItem acFormBar, acEditMenu, 10, , acMenuVer70
End Sub
```

Assume that the user wants to search the field that was being viewed before clicking on this button so the focus is returned to that control:

```
Screen.PreviousControl.SetFocus
```

Then open the Access search dialog so the user can perform his or her search:

```
DoCmd.DoMenuItem acFormBar, acEditMenu, 10, , acMenuVer70
```

The last code block on this form closes it when the Close button is clicked:

```
Private Sub CommandClose_Click()
    DoCmd.Close
End Sub
```

The Warehouses form contains a sub-form called Container Positions Subform. This form allows the entry of positions at a Warehouse. Because the coordinates of the aisle and column of a position should only occur once, code that checks for that needs to be provided. When the user leaves either the AisleNumber field or the ColumnNumber field, the following code block fires:

```
Private Sub AisleNumber_Exit(Cancel As Integer)
    Dim MyDB As DAO.Database
    Dim rs As DAO.Recordset
    If IsNumeric([AisleNumber]) And IsNumeric([ColumnNumber]) _
        And IsNumeric([ContainerPositionID]) Then
            Set MyDB = CurrentDb
```

```
Set rs = MyDB.OpenRecordset("Select ContainerPositionID " _
    & "from ContainerPositions where WarehouseID = " & [WarehouseID] _
    & " and AisleNumber = " & [AisleNumber] & " and ColumnNumber = " _
    & [ColumnNumber] & " and ContainerPositionID <> " _
    & [ContainerPositionID], dbOpenSnapshot)
If Not rs.EOF Then
    Cancel = True
    MsgBox "The Aisle Number and Column Number already " _
        & "exist at this Warehouse!", vbCritical, "Error!"
End If
End If
End Sub
```

To check for an existing record in the database at this position, a Database object is needed:

```
Dim MyDB As DAO.Database
```

and a Recordset object:

```
Dim rs As DAO.Recordset
```

Then make sure that the user has entered data into these fields and that the record is not blank:

```
If IsNumeric([AisleNumber]) And IsNumeric([ColumnNumber]) _
    And IsNumeric([ContainerPositionID]) Then
```

If those checks pass, connect to the current database:

```
Set MyDB = CurrentDb
```

Then look for another container position that occurs at this aisle and column in this warehouse that is not this record itself:

```
Set rs = MyDB.OpenRecordset("Select ContainerPositionID " _
    & "from ContainerPositions where WarehouseID = " & [WarehouseID] _
    & " and AisleNumber = " & [AisleNumber] & " and ColumnNumber = " _
    & [ColumnNumber] & " and ContainerPositionID <> " _
    & [ContainerPositionID], dbOpenSnapshot)
```

If a record is found, the EOF flag is true:

```
If Not rs.EOF Then
```

In that case, do not allow the user to leave this field:

```
Cancel = True
```

Let the user know what has gone wrong:

```
MsgBox "The Aisle Number and Column Number already " _
       & "exist at this Warehouse!", vbCritical, "Error!"
```

Containers Form

The code on the Containers form enables the user to add, delete, search the records and close the form. The form also has a procedure that makes sure the container is not placed in a position that is already filled with containers.

Before looking at the code, look at one of the properties. The ContainerPositionID combo box is, by default, set to display the name of the container. This is how it is defined on the table. But on this form, the user needs to see the warehouse name with the location name so that the container is placed in the right place. So, the Row Source property was changed to the following query:

```
SELECT [ContainerPositions].[ContainerPositionID], [WarehouseName]
& " - " &
[ContainerPositionName] AS Expr1 FROM Warehouses INNER JOIN
ContainerPositions ON
[Warehouses].[WarehouseID]=[ContainerPositions].[WarehouseID]
ORDER BY [WarehouseName] & " - " & [ContainerPositionName];
```

The query joins the Warehouses table with the ContainerPositions table so that the WarehouseName and the ContainerPositionName fields can be concatenated together. The first code block on the form enables the user to add a new record to this table:

```
Private Sub CommandAdd_Click()
    DoCmd.GoToRecord , , acNewRec
    [ContainerName].SetFocus
End Sub
```

This is done using the GoToRecord method:

```
DoCmd.GoToRecord , , acNewRec
```

Then move the focus to the ContainerName field:

```
    [ContainerName].SetFocus
```

The next code block fires when the user clicks on the Delete Container button:

```
Private Sub CommandDelete_Click()
    On Error GoTo HandleError
    DoCmd.DoMenuItem acFormBar, acEditMenu, 8, , acMenuVer70
    DoCmd.DoMenuItem acFormBar, acEditMenu, 6, , acMenuVer70
    [ContainerName].SetFocus
    Exit Sub
HandleError:
    If Err.Number <> 2501 Then
        MsgBox Err.Number & " " & Err.Description
    End If
End Sub
```

Start with an error statement to trap an error. With this statement, any error that occurs sends the code to the HandleError label:

```
On Error GoTo HandleError
```

Then attempt to delete the record:

```
DoCmd.DoMenuItem acFormBar, acEditMenu, 8, , acMenuVer70
DoCmd.DoMenuItem acFormBar, acEditMenu, 6, , acMenuVer70
```

Then set the focus back to the ContainerName field:

```
[ContainerName].SetFocus
```

Before exiting the procedure:

```
Exit Sub
```

If an error occurs, the code flows here:

```
HandleError:
```

One error that can occur is the user canceling the record deletion when prompted to confirm the record deletion. The error number for such an error is 2501. Skip that error with this line of code:

```
If Err.Number <> 2501 Then
```

Otherwise, display the error message:

```
MsgBox Err.Number & " " & Err.Description
```

The next code block enables the user to search the data on this form using the built-in Access search dialog:

```
Private Sub CommandSearch_Click()
    Screen.PreviousControl.SetFocus
    DoCmd.DoMenuItem acFormBar, acEditMenu, 10, , acMenuVer70
End Sub
```

First, move the focus back to the field that the user wants to search:

```
Screen.PreviousControl.SetFocus
```

Then use the DoMenuItem method to open the Search dialog:

```
DoCmd.DoMenuItem acFormBar, acEditMenu, 10, , acMenuVer70
```

If the user clicks on the Close button, the following code runs to close the form:

```
Private Sub CommandClose_Click()
    DoCmd.Close
End Sub
```

Each container position can hold a maximum number of containers as defined in the ContainerPositions table. So when a container is placed in a position, make sure that that position has the space for another container:

```
Private Sub Form_BeforeUpdate(Cancel As Integer)
    Dim MyDB As DAO.Database
    Dim RSCount As DAO.Recordset
    Dim RSMaxAllowed As DAO.Recordset
    If [ContainerStatus] = "Stored" And
IsNumeric([ContainerPositionID]) Then
        Set MyDB = CurrentDb
        Set RSCount = MyDB.OpenRecordset("Select Count(ContainerID)
" _
            & "As TheCount from Containers where ContainerStatus "
_
            & " = ""Stored"" and ContainerPositionID = " _
            & [ContainerPositionID], dbOpenSnapshot)
        Set RSMaxAllowed = MyDB.OpenRecordset("Select
MaximumContainers " _
            & "From ContainerPositions where ContainerPositionID =
" _
            & [ContainerPositionID], dbOpenSnapshot)
        If RSCount("TheCount") >= RSMaxAllowed("MaximumContainers")
Then
            Cancel = True
            MsgBox "The container position you have selected for
this " _
                & "container is already full. Please select a
different " _
                & "location!", vbCritical, "Position Full"
        End If
    End If
End Sub
```

To perform the check, a Database object is needed:

```
Dim MyDB As DAO.Database
```

One recordset object is also needed to count the number of containers at this position:

```
Dim RSCount As DAO.Recordset
```

and another to retrieve the maximum allowed at this position:

```
Dim RSMaxAllowed As DAO.Recordset
```

Only do this check if the container is being stored at a position:

```
If [ContainerStatus] = "Stored" And
IsNumeric([ContainerPositionID]) Then
```

If that is the case, point our Database object to the current database:

```
Set MyDB = CurrentDb
```

Then run a query that returns the total number of containers already stored at this position:

```
Set RSCount = MyDB.OpenRecordset("Select Count(ContainerID) " _
             & "As TheCount from Containers where ContainerStatus " _
             & " = ""Stored"" and ContainerPositionID = " _
             & [ContainerPositionID], dbOpenSnapshot)
```

Next, retrieve the maximum number of containers allowed in this position:

```
Set RSMaxAllowed = MyDB.OpenRecordset("Select MaximumContainers " _
             & "From ContainerPositions where ContainerPositionID = " _
             & [ContainerPositionID], dbOpenSnapshot)
```

Check to see if the current count meets or exceeds the maximum allowed for this position in the Warehouse:

```
If RSCount("TheCount") >= RSMaxAllowed("MaximumContainers") Then
```

If so, prevent the user from leaving this field:

```
Cancel = True
```

Explain to them the problem that has occurred:

```
MsgBox "The container position you have selected for this " _
       & "container is already full. Please select a different " _
       & "location!", vbCritical, "Position Full"
```

The Containers form contains a sub-form called ProductsInContainers Subform. The sub-form contains a single procedure that loads the Products form when the Product Name field is double-clicked:

```
Private Sub Product_Name_DblClick(Cancel As Integer)
    If [ProductID] = 0 Or IsNull([ProductID]) Then
        DoCmd.OpenForm "Products", , , , acFormAdd, acDialog
        [ProductID].Requery
    Else
        DoCmd.OpenForm "Products", , , "[ProductID] = " &
[ProductID], , acDialog
    End If
End Sub
```

First, check to see if the ProductID field is 0 or empty:

```
If [ProductID] = 0 Or IsNull([ProductID]) Then
```

If it is, assume the user wants to add a new record. Open the Products form in Add mode, displayed as a dialog, so that it retains the focus:

```
DoCmd.OpenForm "Products", , , , acFormAdd, acDialog
```

Once the user is finished with that form, the code flows back here and the ProductID combo box is repopulated to reflect the new record added by the user:

```
[ProductID].Requery
```

If a product is listed in the ProductID field, open the Products form so that it displays the information for that product:

```
DoCmd.OpenForm "Products", , , "[ProductID] = " & [ProductID], ,
acDialog
```

Products Form

The code on the Products form provides the functionality for the four buttons in the footer off the form. The form also has code that launches the Vendors form when the VendorID field is double-clicked.

The first procedure adds a record to the table when the user clicks on the Add Product button:

```
Private Sub CommandAdd_Click()
    DoCmd.GoToRecord , , acNewRec
    [ProductName].SetFocus
End Sub
```

This is done using the GoToRecord method:

```
DoCmd.GoToRecord , , acNewRec
```

Then move the insertion point to the ProductName field, giving it the focus:

```
[ProductName].SetFocus
```

The next code block deletes the current record from the table when the Delete Product button is clicked:

```
Private Sub CommandDelete_Click()
    On Error GoTo HandleError
    DoCmd.DoMenuItem acFormBar, acEditMenu, 8, , acMenuVer70
    DoCmd.DoMenuItem acFormBar, acEditMenu, 6, , acMenuVer70
    [ProductName].SetFocus
    Exit Sub
HandleError:
    If Err.Number <> 2501 Then
        MsgBox Err.Number & " " & Err.Description
    End If
End Sub
```

Start with our error trap:

```
On Error GoTo HandleError
```

Then delete the record:

```
DoCmd.DoMenuItem acFormBar, acEditMenu, 8, , acMenuVer70
DoCmd.DoMenuItem acFormBar, acEditMenu, 6, , acMenuVer70
```

Then return the focus back to the detail part of the form:

```
[ProductName].SetFocus
```

If no error occurred, flow out of the procedure here:

```
Exit Sub
```

Otherwise, the code flows to this label:

```
HandleError:
```

Then check for the known error that the user canceled the record deletion:

```
If Err.Number <> 2501 Then
```

If the error was some other error, it is displayed to the user:

```
MsgBox Err.Number & " " & Err.Description
```

The next code block searches the fields on the form:

```
Private Sub CommandSearch_Click()
    Screen.PreviousControl.SetFocus
    DoCmd.DoMenuItem acFormBar, acEditMenu, 10, , acMenuVer70
End Sub
```

Assume that the user wants to search the field he or she was viewing:

```
Screen.PreviousControl.SetFocus
```

Then open the Search dialog:

```
DoCmd.DoMenuItem acFormBar, acEditMenu, 10, , acMenuVer70
```

The next code block closes the form when the Close button is clicked. It uses the Close method of the DoCmd object, which closes the current form:

```
Private Sub CommandClose_Click()
    DoCmd.Close
End Sub
```

The last code block on this form fires when the VendorID field is double-clicked, linking this form to the Vendors form:

```
Private Sub VendorID_DblClick(Cancel As Integer)
    If [VendorID] = 0 Or IsNull([VendorID]) Then
        DoCmd.OpenForm "Vendors", , , , acFormAdd, acDialog
        [VendorID].Requery
    Else
        DoCmd.OpenForm "Vendors", , , "[VendorID] = " & [VendorID],
, acDialog
    End If
End Sub
```

The first line of code checks to see if the VendorID field has been left blank:

```
If [VendorID] = 0 Or IsNull([VendorID]) Then
```

If it has, assume that the user wants to add a new Vendor record:

```
DoCmd.OpenForm "Vendors", , , , acFormAdd, acDialog
```

After adding the new record, repopulate the VendorID combo box so the new record is displayed:

```
[VendorID].Requery
```

If the VendorID field already contains a value, the code flows here. In that case, open the Vendors form displaying the information on the selected vendor:

```
DoCmd.OpenForm "Vendors", , , "[VendorID] = " & [VendorID], ,
    acDialog
```

The Products form contains a sub-form called Warehouse to Product Subform that contains two procedures. The first fires when the ContainerName field is double-clicked and links this form to the Containers form:

```
Private Sub Container_Name_DblClick(Cancel As Integer)
    If [ContainerName] <> "" And Not IsNull([ContainerName]) Then
        DoCmd.OpenForm "Containers", , , "[ContainerName] = """ _
            & [ContainerName] & """", , acDialog
    End If
End Sub
```

Before linking to that form, make sure that a value is entered in the ContainerName field:

```
If [ContainerName] <> "" And Not IsNull([ContainerName]) Then
```

If so, open the Containers form and filter it so it contains the information for the selected container:

```
DoCmd.OpenForm "Containers", , , "[ContainerName] = """ _
    & [ContainerName] & """", , acDialog
```

The other procedure runs when the WarehouseName field is double-clicked and links to the Warehouses form:

```
Private Sub Warehouse_Name_DblClick(Cancel As Integer)
    If [WarehouseName] <> "" And Not IsNull([WarehouseName]) Then
        DoCmd.OpenForm "Warehouses", , , "[WarehouseName] = """ _
            & [WarehouseName] & """", , acDialog
    End If
End Sub
```

First, verify that the WarehouseName field contains a value:

```
If [WarehouseName] <> "" And Not IsNull([WarehouseName]) Then
```

If it does, open the Warehouses form so that it displays information for the Warehouse based on the WarehouseName of the current record:

```
DoCmd.OpenForm "Warehouses", , , "[WarehouseName] = """ _
        & [WarehouseName] & """", , acDialog
```

Vendors Form

The code on the Vendors form provides the functionality for the footer buttons to run when the buttons are clicked. The first procedure allows the user to add a new record to this table:

```
Private Sub CommandAdd_Click()
    DoCmd.GoToRecord , , acNewRec
    [VendorName].SetFocus
End Sub
```

The GoToRecord method allows us to add a new record from code:

```
DoCmd.GoToRecord , , acNewRec
```

Then set the focus to the VendorName field so the user can start entering data:

```
[VendorName].SetFocus
```

When the user clicks on the Delete Vendor button, the following code block runs:

```
Private Sub CommandDelete_Click()
    On Error GoTo HandleError
    DoCmd.DoMenuItem acFormBar, acEditMenu, 8, , acMenuVer70
    DoCmd.DoMenuItem acFormBar, acEditMenu, 6, , acMenuVer70
    [VendorName].SetFocus
    Exit Sub
HandleError:
    If Err.Number <> 2501 Then
        MsgBox Err.Number & " " & Err.Description
    End If
End Sub
```

Start by turning on error handling, pointing any errors to the HandleError label:

```
On Error GoTo HandleError
```

Next, delete the record from the table:

```
DoCmd.DoMenuItem acFormBar, acEditMenu, 8, , acMenuVer70
DoCmd.DoMenuItem acFormBar, acEditMenu, 6, , acMenuVer70
```

After the record is deleted, set focus back to the VendorName field:

```
[VendorName].SetFocus
```

Leave this procedure:

```
Exit Sub
```

If an error did occur, the code would flow to this label. Note that a label itself is not running code; it is just a reference point that indicates where the code should flow:

```
HandleError:
```

Then check for the known problem of the user canceling the record deletion:

```
If Err.Number <> 2501 Then
```

Any other error would be displayed to the user:

```
MsgBox Err.Number & " " & Err.Description
```

The next code block runs when the user clicks on the Search button:

```
Private Sub CommandSearch_Click()
    Screen.PreviousControl.SetFocus
    DoCmd.DoMenuItem acFormBar, acEditMenu, 10, , acMenuVer70
End Sub
```

For the Search dialog to work correctly, it needs to point back to the field that the user wants to search:

```
Screen.PreviousControl.SetFocus
```

Then open the Search dialog:

```
DoCmd.DoMenuItem acFormBar, acEditMenu, 10, , acMenuVer70
```

The last code block on this form closes the form when the Close button is clicked:

```
Private Sub CommandClose_Click()
    DoCmd.Close
End Sub
```

The Vendors form contains a single sub-form called Products Offered by Vendor Subform. That sub-form contains a single procedure that fires when the ProductName field is double-clicked, linking this form to the Products form:

```
Private Sub Product_Name_DblClick(Cancel As Integer)
    If [ProductName] = "" Or IsNull([ProductName]) Then
        DoCmd.OpenForm "Products", , , , acFormAdd, acDialog
        [Product Name].Requery
    Else
        DoCmd.OpenForm "Products", , , "[ProductName] = """ &
[ProductName] & """", , acDialog
    End If
End Sub
```

First, check to see if the ProductName field is empty:

```
If [ProductName] = "" Or IsNull([ProductName]) Then
```

If it is, open the Products form in Add mode:

```
DoCmd.OpenForm "Products", , , , acFormAdd, acDialog
```

Then repopulate the ProductName field:

```
[Product Name].Requery
```

Otherwise, open the Products form and have it display the selected product:

```
DoCmd.OpenForm "Products", , , "[ProductName] = """ &
[ProductName] & """", , acDialog
```

Warehouse Map Form

The Warehouse Map form is the form of 101 procedures, but one of the procedures is repeated 99 times for each of the grid positions on the map. The grid on the form is made up of 100 labels. These labels have their background colors set based on the containers located at that position. The code that draws the map is located in the Form_Open event and fires whenever the form is opened:

```
Private Sub Form_Open(Cancel As Integer)
    Dim MyDB As DAO.Database
    Dim RSWareHouse As DAO.Recordset
    Dim RSCount As DAO.Recordset
    Dim RSMaxAllowed As DAO.Recordset
    Dim I As Integer
    Dim J As Integer
    Dim BGGrey As String
    Dim BGRed As String
    Dim BGGreen As String
    Dim BGBlue As String
    BGGrey = "12632256"
    BGRed = "255"
    BGGreen = "65280"
    BGBlue = "16711680"
    Set MyDB = CurrentDb
    Set RSWareHouse = MyDB.OpenRecordset("Select WarehouseName " _
        & "From Warehouses Where WarehouseID = " _
        & CurrentWarehouseID, dbOpenSnapshot)
    Label16.Caption = "Warehouse " & RSWareHouse("WarehouseName") _
        & " Map"
    For I = 1 To 10
        For J = 1 To 10
            Set RSMaxAllowed = MyDB.OpenRecordset("Select
MaximumContainers, " _
                & "ContainerPositionID From ContainerPositions " _
                & "where WarehouseID = " & CurrentWarehouseID _
                & " and AisleNumber = " & I _
                & " and ColumnNumber = " & J, dbOpenSnapshot)
            If RSMaxAllowed.EOF Then
                Me.Controls("Grid" & I & J).BackColor = BGGrey
            ElseIf RSMaxAllowed("MaximumContainers") = 0 Then
                Me.Controls("Grid" & I & J).BackColor = BGGrey
            Else
                Set RSCount = MyDB.OpenRecordset("Select
Count(ContainerID) " _
                    & "As TheCount from Containers where
ContainerStatus " _
                    & " = ""Stored"" and ContainerPositionID = " _
                    & RSMaxAllowed("ContainerPositionID"),
dbOpenSnapshot)
                If RSCount("TheCount") = 0 Then
                    Me.Controls("Grid" & I & J).BackColor = BGGreen
                ElseIf RSCount("TheCount") <
RSMaxAllowed("MaximumContainers") Then
                    Me.Controls("Grid" & I & J).BackColor = BGBlue
                Else
                    Me.Controls("Grid" & I & J).BackColor = BGRed
                End If
            End If
        Next
    Next
End Sub
```

The procedure starts with the variable declaration section. You need to connect in code to this database:

```
Dim MyDB As DAO.Database
```

One Recordset is used to retrieve information about the desired Warehouse:

```
Dim RSWareHouse As DAO.Recordset
```

The next Recordset object stores the count of containers at a spot:

```
Dim RSCount As DAO.Recordset
```

This one retrieves the maximum containers allowed at a spot:

```
Dim RSMaxAllowed As DAO.Recordset
```

Then you have two variables that will be used in For/Next blocks:

```
Dim I As Integer
Dim J As Integer
```

To make our code a little more readable, store the background colors used for the labels in the grid in variables:

```
Dim BGGrey As String
Dim BGRed As String
Dim BGGreen As String
Dim BGBlue As String
```

Next, set those variables to their respective colors:

```
BGGrey = "12632256"
BGRed = "255"
BGGreen = "65280"
BGBlue = "16711680"
```

Then connect the Database object to the current database:

```
Set MyDB = CurrentDb
```

Retrieve the name of the desired Warehouse. Note that the desired Warehouse is based on the public variable that was set when opening this form from the View Map button located back on the Vendors form:

```
Set RSWareHouse = MyDB.OpenRecordset("Select WarehouseName " _
        & "From Warehouses Where WarehouseID = " _
        & CurrentWarehouseID, dbOpenSnapshot)
```

The name of the Warehouse is used in building the title caption for the form:

```
Label16.Caption = "Warehouse " & RSWareHouse("WarehouseName") _
        & " Map"
```

Then enter our first For/Next block that takes you through the 10 aisles of the grid:

```
For I = 1 To 10
```

The inner For/Next block loops you through each of the columns in each of the rows:

```
For J = 1 To 10
```

Then look for a position record at this Warehouse for this aisle and column number:

```
Set RSMaxAllowed = MyDB.OpenRecordset("Select MaximumContainers, " _
        & "ContainerPositionID From ContainerPositions " _
        & "where WarehouseID = " & CurrentWarehouseID _
        & " and AisleNumber = " & I _
        & " and ColumnNumber = " & J, dbOpenSnapshot)
```

Check to see if a position record was found:

```
If RSMaxAllowed.EOF Then
```

If it wasn't, the position is unused, and you set the color for this spot on the grid to grey:

```
Me.Controls("Grid" & I & J).BackColor = BGGrey
```

Next, check to see if the maximum number of containers allowed is 0:

```
ElseIf RSMaxAllowed("MaximumContainers") = 0 Then
```

If it is, that means the spot is unused and you mark it as grey:

```
Me.Controls("Grid" & I & J).BackColor = BGGrey
```

Otherwise, check to see how many containers are located at this spot:

```
Set RSCount = MyDB.OpenRecordset("Select Count(ContainerID) " _
        & "As TheCount from Containers where ContainerStatus " _
        & " = ""Stored"" and ContainerPositionID = " _
        & RSMaxAllowed("ContainerPositionID"), dbOpenSnapshot)
```

Then check to see if the number of containers at this spot is 0:

```
If RSCount("TheCount") = 0 Then
```

If that is the case, set the background color for this label on the grid to green:

```
Me.Controls("Grid" & I & J).BackColor = BGGreen
```

Then check to see if some containers are located at this spot, but the spot is not yet full of containers:

```
ElseIf RSCount("TheCount") < RSMaxAllowed("MaximumContainers") Then
```

In that case, indicate a partially full spot with the color blue:

```
Me.Controls("Grid" & I & J).BackColor = BGBlue
```

The Else condition means that the spot is full:

```
Else
```

Color that place on the grid Red:

```
Me.Controls("Grid" & I & J).BackColor = BGRed
```

Then move on to the next column in this aisle:

```
Next
```

and then move on to the next aisle:

```
Next
```

When the user clicks on any of the used spots on the grid, show them the information for that Container through the Containers Positions Sub-form form. This means you have 100 procedures, one for each label on the grid that fires when the label is clicked. Each procedure is nearly identical. Only the grid coordinate is different. The code block for the first label is as follows:

```
Private Sub Grid11_Click()
    Dim MyDB As DAO.Database
    Dim rs As DAO.Recordset
    If Grid11.BackColor <> "12632256" Then
        Set MyDB = CurrentDb
        Set rs = MyDB.OpenRecordset("Select " _
            & "ContainerPositionID From ContainerPositions " _
            & "where WarehouseID = " & CurrentWarehouseID _
            & " and AisleNumber = " & 1 _
            & " and ColumnNumber = " & 1, dbOpenSnapshot)
        DoCmd.OpenForm "Container Positions Subform", , ,
```

```
" [ContainerPositionID] = " _
            & rs("ContainerPositionID")
    End If
End Sub
```

Connect back to this database:

```
Dim MyDB As DAO.Database
```

and retrieve information:

```
Dim rs As DAO.Recordset
```

Only link to the Containers Positions Subform form if the grid spot is in use so it cannot be grey:

```
If Grid11.BackColor <> "12632256" Then
```

If it is not, connect to the database:

```
Set MyDB = CurrentDb
```

Retrieve the ID for this spot based on the coordinates of the spot clicked on and on the current Warehouse:

```
Set rs = MyDB.OpenRecordset("Select " _
    & "ContainerPositionID From ContainerPositions " _
    & "where WarehouseID = " & CurrentWarehouseID _
    & " and AisleNumber = " & 1 _
    & " and ColumnNumber = " & 1, dbOpenSnapshot)
```

Then open the Containers Positions Subform form and have it display the information for this position:

```
DoCmd.OpenForm "Container Positions Subform", , ,
" [ContainerPositionID] = " _
    & rs("ContainerPositionID")
```

Reports

Products Grouped by Container Report

The Products Grouped by Container report enables the user to see in detail the contents of each of the containers. The report shows the information grouped by the name of the container. The report is based on the Products in Containers query, which has the following syntax:

```
SELECT Containers.ContainerName, ProductsInContainers.ProductID
FROM Containers INNER JOIN ProductsInContainers ON
Containers.ContainerID = ProductsInContainers.ContainerID;
```

The query joins together the two tables Containers with ProductsIn-Containers. Note that this is an Inner Join, which means that only records existing in both tables are displayed. So an empty container is not in this report, as well as a product that is not in a container.

Containers Grouped by Status Report

The Containers Grouped by Status report shows in summary the count of all the containers based on their current status. The report is based on the Containers Grouped by Status query, which has the following syntax:

```
SELECT Containers.ContainerStatus, Count(Containers.ContainerID)
AS CountOfContainerID FROM Containers
GROUP BY Containers.ContainerStatus;
```

The query uses the Count function to count the occurrence of each record in each status group. Note the use of the As keyword, which outputs that count into a temporary field called CountOfContainerID.

Containers in Warehouses Report

The Containers in Warehouses report enables the user to see what containers are in the different Warehouses and the status of those containers. The report is based on the Containers in Warehouses query, which has the following syntax:

```
SELECT Warehouses.WarehouseName, Containers.ContainerName,
Containers.ContainerStatus FROM
(Warehouses INNER JOIN ContainerPositions ON
Warehouses.WarehouseID = ContainerPositions.WarehouseID)
INNER JOIN Containers ON
ContainerPositions.ContainerPositionID =
Containers.ContainerPositionID;
```

The query needs to display information from the Warehouses and Containers tables. Those tables do not directly relate to each other. The ContainerPositions table needs to link these two tables together. So, the query joins three tables together; the Warehouse table is joined with the ContainerPositions table, which is joined with the Containers table.

CHAPTER 9

Help Desk

ON THE CD:

Help Desk.mdb

Managing Customer Problems and Resolutions

In this chapter, a single database called Help Desk is presented. The database enables an organization to manage customer problems with products. The database tracks the progress of resolving those issues, contains a library for tracking problems, allows for the management of Managers and Investigators, and provides reports summarizing the customer cases.

Help Desk Database

Sample Walk-through

In this sample walk-through of the database, the data presented is for a company that sells computer software. Note, though, that the database could easily apply to any company that tracked customer problems and resolutions. For example, the products listed could be kitchen appliances or furniture instead of software titles. When the user first enters the database application, the menu shown in Figure 9-1 is displayed.

From the Main Menu, the user can enter a submenu. The first submenu is the Main Data Entry form. From here, the user can go to the Customers, Investigators, Managers, and Library Notes forms. The Supplemental Forms menu options allow the user to enter forms that are not the core of the application. These include the Countries, Phone Types, Products, Statuses, and Zip Codes forms. The third submenu is called Reports and contains the reports for this application. Here the user can view the Cases by Status in Date Range, Open Cases Grouped by Investigator, and the Total Cases by Product Reports.

Figure 9-1

Help Desk menu

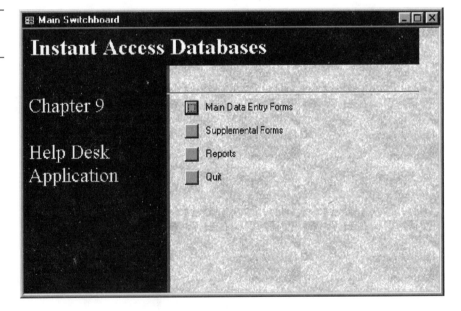

Back on the Main Data Entry forms submenu, the user can select to see the Customers form. The first page of this form is shown in Figure 9-2. The Customers form is the main part of the application. From here, the user manages customer cases. At the top of the form, the name of the customer is listed, and a button labeled View Library is displayed. If this button is pressed, the user is taken to the Library Notes form.

In the detail part of the first page, the customer's contact information appears. The zip code field displays a list of all the zip codes found in the ZipCode table. When the user selects a Zip Code that appears in the list, the City and State are automatically filled in based on that Zip Code. If the user double-clicks on the Zip Code field, they are taken to the Zip Code form. Zip codes can be added or edited on this form.

A sub-form on this detail page allows the entry of unlimited phone numbers for the customer. If the user double-clicks on the Phone Type field, the Phone Type form appears. A new Phone Type can be added or the existing one can be edited here.

At the bottom of this form are the standard buttons for adding and deleting customers, as well as Close and Search buttons. This form also contains buttons for toggling between the two pages of this form. The cur-

Figure 9-2

Customers form

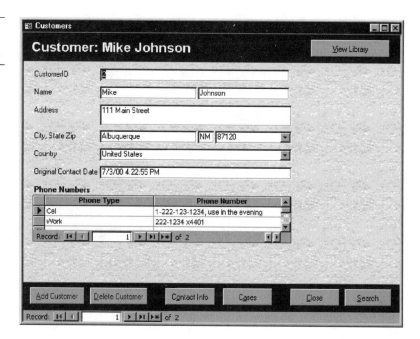

rent page shown in Figure 9-2 is the Contact Info page. If the user selects the Cases page, the view of the form shown in Figure 9-3 is displayed.

The Cases page in the detail section of the Customers form is completely made up of a sub-form. This sub-form lists all the cases, or problems, made by this customer. The Case sub-form enables the user to track the progress and information on each of the cases. If the user clicks on the Status field, the Statuses form appears and Status values can be added and edited. The same is true for the Product and Investigator fields.

The Cases sub-form contains its own sub-form called CustomerContacts. From here the user enters in each contact made about this case for this specific customer. As with the Investigator field in the Cases sub-form, double-clicking on the Investigator field in this sub-form brings up the Investigators form so Investigator information can be added, edited, and viewed.

From the Main Data Entry forms menu, if the user clicks on the Investigator button, the form shown in Figure 9-4 is displayed. The Investigators form enables the user to add, delete, and view Investigator information. In this database, an Investigator is a person who works with a customer to help resolve a problem.

Figure 9-3

Cases page of the Customers form

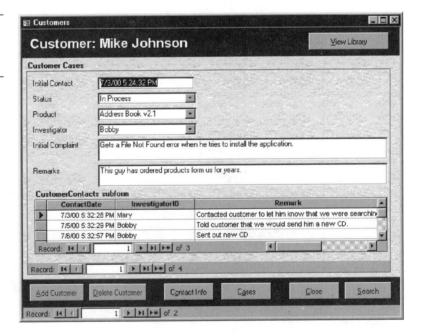

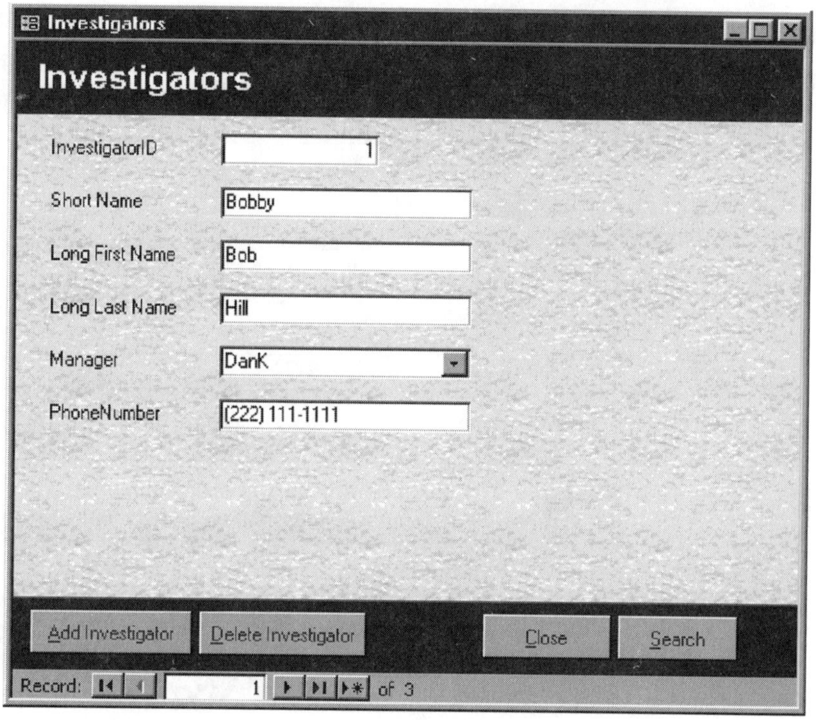

Figure 9-4

Investigators
form

To prevent confusion, when the user enters the Short Name field, the code checks to make sure that the value entered is unique in the Investigator table. The Manager field contains a list of all the Managers in the Manager table. If the user double-clicks on this field, the Managers form appears.

The Managers form is also accessible from the Main Data Entry forms menu, which is shown in Figure 9-5.

The Managers form enables the user to add, edit, delete, and view Managers. As with the Investigator form, the Short Name field needs to be unique. Therefore, code on this form prevents the user from entering a value that already exists. A sub-form at the bottom of the detail section enables the user to see all the Investigators that are managed by this Manager. If the user double-clicks on the name of an Investigator, the Investigators form is displayed. The next form accessible through the Main Data Entry Forms menu is the Library Notes form, shown in Figure 9-6.

This form is also accessible by clicking on the View Library button on the Customers form. Known problems and ideas that the user may want

Figure 9-5

Managers form

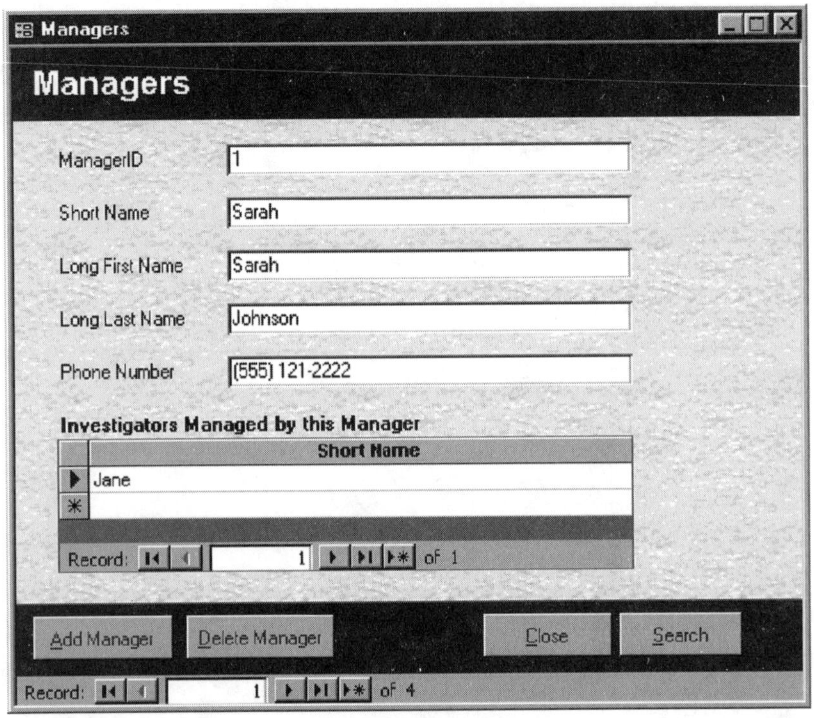

Figure 9-6

Library Notes form

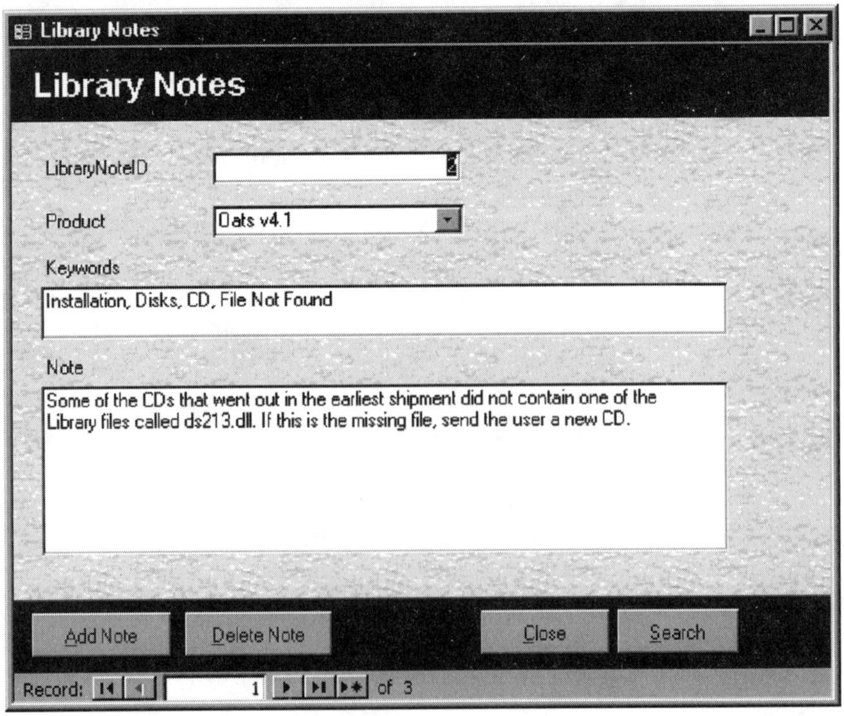

to try to resolve his or her current problem are stored in the Library Notes. The user could then uses the search button to search the Product, Keyword, and Note fields. If the user double-clicks on the Product field, the Products form appears, showing additional fields for this Product or allowing the user to enter a new Product. From the Supplemental Forms sub-menu, the user can select the Countries form, which is shown in Figure 9-7.

The Countries form would probably only be used by the person administering the database. The form enables you to add, edit, and delete Countries that are used to populate the Country field on the Customers table. The next form accessible from the Supplemental Forms sub-menu is the Phone Types form shown in Figure 9-8.

This single-field form is also accessible from the Phone Numbers sub-form of the Customers form. The form is used to add, edit, and delete values that appear in the Phone Types list on the Phone Numbers sub-form. The next form listed on the Supplemental Forms sub-menu is the Products form, shown in Figure 9-9.

The Products form is also accessible from the Customer Cases sub-form, as well as the Library Notes form, by double-clicking on the Product field. The form enables the user to add, edit, delete, and view extended

Figure 9-7

Countries form

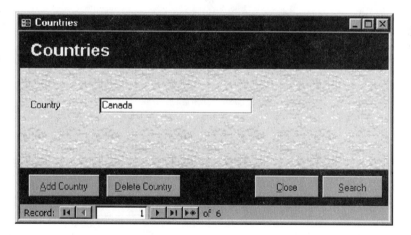

Figure 9-8

Phone Types form

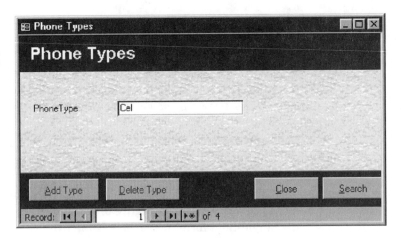

Figure 9-9

Products form

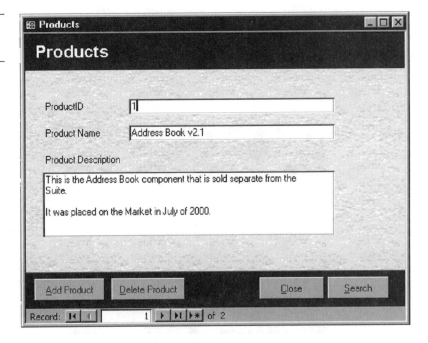

information about the products. On the Supplemental Forms sub-menu, that form is followed by the Statuses form shown in Figure 9-10.

Statuses are used on the Customer Cases sub-form to track what stage of the resolution process the Case is in. This important field is also used on some of the reports to track the overall view of Customer Cases.

One more form, the Zip Code form as shown in Figure 9-11, is available through the Supplemental Forms sub-menu. This form enables the user to add, edit and delete Zip Codes. The information is used on the Customer form to automatically populate the City and State fields.

Three reports are listed on the Reports sub-menu. The first report is the Cases by Status in Date Range and is shown in Figure 9-12. Before the Report appears, the user is prompted for the start and end dates to be used by the report. The query then summarizes the number of Cases with each of the Statuses that have at least one Case in that date range.

The next report is the Open Cases Grouped by Investigator, which is shown in Figure 9-13. This reports shows some of the basic information for cases grouped by the Investigator's short name that are currently open. Any case with the status Pending, In Progress, or New is considered an Open Case.

Figure 9-10

Statuses form

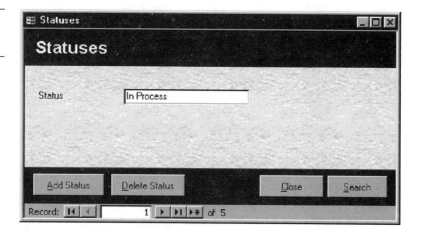

Figure 9-11

Zip Codes form

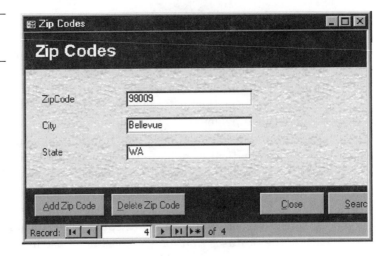

Figure 9-12

Cases by Status
in Date Range
Report

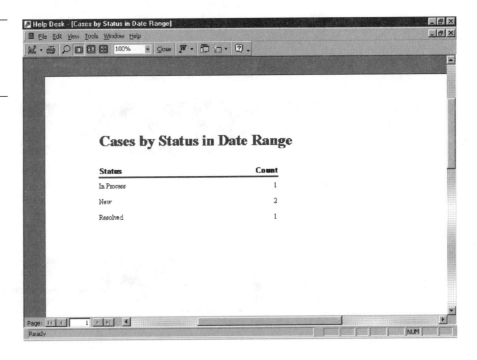

Figure 9-13

Open Cases
Grouped by
Investigator

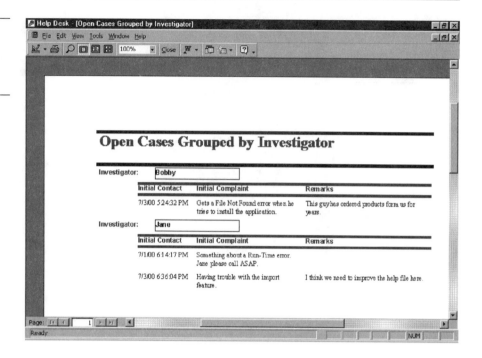

The third report listed on the Reports sub-menu is the Total Cases by Product Report, which is shown in Figure 9-14. This report shows the user the total number of cases that have been reported for each of the products that has had any cases made against it.

Table Definitions and Relationships

Customers Table

The Customers table is the top-level table in the Customer's hierarchy of information. The table contains basic information about the customer. The table is in relationship with numerous tables that are described below.

CustomerPhoneNumbers Table

The CustomerPhoneNumbers table contains all the phone numbers for each customer. This table is needed because the customer can have an unknown number of possible contacts. The table is in a one-to-many relationship with the Customer's table. Each customer can have zero or more

Figure 9-14

The Total Cases
by Product report

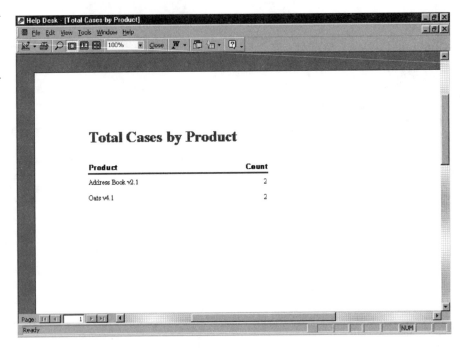

records in this table, but each record in this table belongs to a single customer. The table is used in the Customer Phone Numbers sub-form of the Customers form.

CustomerCases Table

The CustomerCases table contains the high-level information about each of the problems registered by a customer. This table is below the Customers table and is in a one-to-many relationship with the Customers table. Each customer can have numerous cases.

CustomersContacts Table

Once the customer has brought forth a problem that needs resolution, he or she could be contacted numerous times by different people to resolve that problem. The CustomersContacts table stores those contacts. It is in a one-to-many relationship with the CustomerCases table. Each case can have numerous contacts. So at the top of the customer data is the Customer table; below that is the CustomerCases table, and below that, the CustomerContacts table.

Investigators Table

The Investigators table contains personal information about each Investigator. Remember that an investigator in this scenario is the person who works with a customer to find a solution to a problem.

Managers Table

The Managers table contains information about each manager. The table is in a one-to-many relationship with the Investigators table. Each Manager can have many Investigators beneath them, but each Investigator is managed by a single manager.

LibraryNotes Table

The LibraryNotes table contains documentation about the products. The data would be used by the Investigator to find resolutions to problems. The table is in a one-to-many relationship with the Products table. Each record goes with a single product, but each product can have numerous notes relating to it.

Products Table

The Products table stores information about each product. In addition to being in a relationship with the LibraryNotes table, it is also in a relationship with the CustomerCases table. Each customer case is based on a single product, but a single product can have many customer cases.

Countries Table

The Countries table contains a list of countries that is used to populate the combo box for the Country field on the Customers form.

PhoneTypes Table

The PhoneTypes table contains a list of possible phone types that are used in the CustomerContacts table. The PhoneTypes table is used to populate the combo box in the PhoneTypes field.

Statuses Table

The Statuses table contains a list of possible statuses at which a case can be. The table is used to populate the Status field in the CustomerCases table.

ZipCodes Table

The ZipCodes table contains all the zip codes that need to be made available on the Zip Code field on the Customers form. The data is also used to populate the City and State fields in the Customer table.

Field Specifications

Customers Table

The field specifications for the Customers table are displayed in Table 9-1.

The CustomerID field is the primary key for this table. The field is automatically populated because it is set up as an AutoNumber field. The LastName field is indexed because it would be used as a search field when the database becomes large. That field is also required.

The Lookup properties are used in the ZipCode and Country fields so that a combo box is displayed with the available zip codes from the Zip-Codes table and the countries from the Country table.

The OriginalContactDate field has a default value of the current system date and time. This is done by placing the following code in the Default Value property for this field:

```
Now()
```

Now is a Visual Basic function that returns the current system date and time.

Table 9-1	Field Name	Field Type	Notes
Customers Table Field Specifications	CustomerID	AutoNumber	Primary Key
	FirstName	Text	Length = 50
	LastName	Text	Length = 50
	Address	Text	Length = 100
	City	Text	Length = 50
	State	Text	Length = 2
	ZipCode	Text	Length = 12
	Country	Text	Length = 50
	OriginalContactDate	Date/Time	

CustomerPhoneNumbers Table

The field specifications for the CustomerPhoneNumbers table are displayed in Table 9-2.

The CustomerPhoneNumberID field is the primary key for the table. The CustomerID field is a Foreign Key, linking this table with the Customers table in a one-to-many relationship. The Lookup properties are used for this field so that the field is displayed as a combo box with the customers' names from the Customers table. The query placed in the Row Source property that accomplishes this is below:

```
SELECT [Customers].[CustomerID], [Customers].[LastName], [Customers].[FirstName]
FROM Customers ORDER BY [Customers].[LastName], [Customers].[FirstName];
```

The bound column is set to the first field, CustomerID, but the user sees the customer's name instead. The Limit to List property is set to Yes, which forces the user to select a name from the list.

The Lookup properties are also put to use on the PhoneType field. This one is set to combo box and uses the following query to populate the drop-down portion of the box:

```
SELECT [PhoneTypes].[PhoneType] FROM PhoneTypes;
```

The Limit to List property is also set to Yes for this field.

CustomerCases Table

The field specifications for the CustomerCases table are displayed in Table 9-3.

The CustomerCaseID field is an automatically populated primary key. So as a new record is added, this field is set to a unique value.

The CustomerID field is a foreign key and links this table to the Customers table. The field is required with each record and displayed as a

	Field Name	Field Type	Notes
Table 9-2	CustomerPhoneNumberID		AutoNumber Primary Key
CustomerPhone-Numbers Table Field Specifications	CustomerID	Number	Type = Long Integer, Foreign Key
	PhoneType	Text	Length = 50
	PhoneNumber	Text	Length = 50

	Field Name	Field Type	Notes
Table 9-3	CustomerCaseID	AutoNumber	Primary Key
CustomerCases	CustomerID	Number	Type = Long Integer, Foreign Key
Table Field	Status	Text	Length = 50
Specifications	InitialContact	Date/Time	
	ProductID	Number	Type = Long Integer, Foreign Key
	InvestigatorID	Number	Type = Long Integer, Foreign Key
	InitialComplaint	Memo	
	Remarks	Memo	

combo box so the Lookup properties are utilized. The Row Source property is set to the query below:

```
SELECT [Customers].[CustomerID], [Customers].[LastName], [Customers].[FirstName]
FROM Customers ORDER BY [Customers].[LastName], [Customers].[FirstName];
```

The CustomerID field is the bound column. The ID of the customer is stored in this table but the user sees the Last Name and first names fields. These fields are also used to sort the records that are displayed. The Limit to List property is set to Yes, which forces the user to select an item from the list.

The Status field is also displayed as a combo box. This one shows all the Statuses from the Statuses table using this query in the Row Source property:

```
SELECT [Statuses].[Status] FROM Statuses;
```

The Limit to List property is set to Yes.

The InitialContact field has a default value set to the current date and time by placing this code in the Default Value property for that field:

```
Now()
```

The ProductID field is a foreign key connecting this table to the Products table. The Lookup properties are also used with this ID field. The query in the Row Source property pulls data from the Products table to populate the combo box:

```
SELECT [Products].[ProductID], [Products].[ProductName] FROM Products;
```

The ProductID field is the Bound column; so it is stored in the CustomerCases table, but the user sees the names of the products instead of the product number. This table is also linked to the Investigators table through the foreign key field InvestigatorID. The field is also displayed as a combo box in the data sheet view and on the form. The Row Source property pulls the values in the combo box from the Investigators table:

```
SELECT [Investigators].[InvestigatorID], [Investigators].[ShortName]
FROM Investigators ORDER BY [ShortName];
```

The first field, the InvestigatorID field, is bound.

CustomerContacts Table

The field specifications for the CustomerContacts table are displayed in Table 9-4.

The CustomerContactID field is the primary key, uniquely identifying each record. The CustomerCaseID field is a foreign key field that links this table to the CustomerCases table.

The ContactDate field defaults to the current system date and time by setting the Default Value property to the value below:

```
Now()
```

Table 9-4

CustomerContacts Table Field Specifications

Field Name	Field Type	Notes
CustomerContactID	AutoNumber	Primary Key
CustomerCaseID	Number	Type = Long Integer, Foreign Key
ContactDate	Date/Time	
InvestigatorID	Number	Type = Long Integer, Foreign Key
Remark	Memo	

The InvestigatorID field is another foreign key and links this table to the Investigators table. The field is displayed as a combo box by using the Lookup properties. The Row Source property is set to the following query:

```
SELECT [Investigators].[InvestigatorID], [Investigators].[ShortName]
FROM Investigators;
```

The ID of the investigator is stored with the record, but the short name of the Investigator is what is displayed to the user.

Investigators Table

The field specifications for the Investigators table are displayed in Table 9-5.

The InvestigatorID field is the Primary Key for this table. The Required property is set to Yes for the ShortName field since that is the field used in combo boxes on some of the forms.

The ManagerID field is a foreign key linking this table to the Managers table. The Lookup properties are used for this field, so it is displayed as a combo box. The values listed in the combo box come from the Managers table through the following query, which is placed in the Row Source property:

```
SELECT [Managers].[ManagerID], [Managers].[ShortName]
FROM Managers ORDER BY [ShortName];
```

The ManagerID field is the bound column, but the ShortName is what the user sees. The Limit to List property is set to Yes, so the user must select one of the managers in the list.

	Field Name	Field Type	Notes
Table 9-5	InvestigatorID	AutoNumber	Primary Key
Investigators Table Field Specifications	ShortName	Text	Length = 50
	LongFirstName	Text	Length = 50
	LongLastName	Text	Length = 50
	ManagerID	Number	Type = Long Integer, Foreign Key
	PhoneNumber	Text	Length = 50

Managers Table

The field specifications for the Managers table are displayed in Table 9-6.

The ManagerID field is the primary key for this table. As such, it is Indexed. Since the ShortName field is displayed in combo boxes for other tables, it is a required field.

LibraryNotes Table

The field specifications for the LibraryNotes table are displayed in Table 9-7.

The LibraryNoteID field is the primary key for this table. The Product-ID field is a foreign key, linking this table with the Products table. For data entry purposes, it is displayed as a combo box. The combo box shows all the products from the Products table because the Row Source property of this field is set to this value:

```
SELECT [Products].[ProductID], [Products].[ProductName]
FROM Products ORDER BY [ProductName];
```

Note that the ProductID field is the bound field, but the name of the product is displayed to the user. Also note that the records are sorted by the name of the product.

Table 9-6

Managers Table Field Specifications

Field Name	Field Type	Notes
ManagerID	AutoNumber	Primary Key
ShortName	Text	Length = 50
LongFirstName	Text	Length = 50
LongLastName	Text	Length = 50
PhoneNumber	Text	Length = 50

Table 9-7

LibraryNotes Table Field Specifications

Field Name	Field Type	Notes
LibraryNoteID	AutoNumber	Primary Key
ProductID	Number	Type = Long Integer, Foreign Key
Keywords	Text	Length = 255
Note	Memo	

Products Table

The field specifications for the Products table are displayed in Table 9-8.

The ProductID field is the primary key for this table. The ProductName field is required because it is used in combo boxes on other tables. The field is also indexed because it is likely that the field would be searched heavily.

Countries Table

The field specification for the Countries table is displayed in Table 9-9.

The Countries table contains a single field Country. The field is the primary key for the table and is used to populate the Country combo box in the Customers table and form.

PhoneTypes Table

The field specification for the PhoneTypes table is displayed in Table 9-10.

The PhoneTypes table also contains a single field, the PhoneType field. This field is the primary key. It is displayed in the combo box for the PhoneType field in the CustomerPhoneNumbers table and form.

Table 9-8

Products Table Field Specifications

Field Name	Field Type	Notes
ProductID	AutoNumber	Primary Key
ProductName	Text	Length = 50
ProductDescription	Memo	

Table 9-9

Countries Table Field Specifications

Field Name	Field Type	Notes
Country	Text	Length = 50, Primary Key

Table 9-10

PhoneTypes Table Field Specifications

Field Name	Field Type	Notes
PhoneType	Text	Length = 50, Primary Key

Statuses Table

The field specification for the Statuses table is displayed in Table 9-11.

The Status field is the primary key for this table, so the field is required and must be unique. The field is used in the combo box for the Status field in the CustomerCases table and form.

ZipCodes Table

The field specifications for the ZipCodes table are displayed in Table 9-12.

The ZipCode field is the primary key for the table. All three fields are used for the customer's City, State, and Zip. When the user selects a zip code for the customer, the City and State, are automatically filled in.

Table 9-11

Statuses Table Field Specifications

Field Name	Field Type	Notes
Statuses	Text	Length = 50, Primary Key

Table 9-12

ZipCodes Table Field Specifications

Field Name	Field Type	Notes
ZipCode	Text	Length = 50, Primary Key
City	Text	Length = 50
State	Text	Length = 50

Forms

Switchboard Form

The Switchboard form is used to navigate through the forms and reports in the Help Desk application. It was created using the Switchboard wizard, which is accessible within Access through the Tools/Database Utilities/Switchboard Manager menu item. Only the look and layout of the form produced with that wizard have been altered.

Customers Form

The code on the Customers form is responsible for a variety of tasks, such as displaying other forms and adding and deleting records, to name a few. The first code block runs in the Current event of the form itself. The Current event fires every time a different record in the table is displayed. The code block is below:

```
Private Sub Form_Current()
    Label16.Caption = "Customer: " & [FirstName] & " " & [LastName]
End Sub
```

The code in this event displays the name of the Customer on the Label that is at the header of the form:

```
Label16.Caption = "Customer: " & [FirstName] & " " & [LastName]
```

The next six blocks of code are for the buttons in the footer. The first code block is for the Add Customer button:

```
Private Sub Command17_Click()
    DoCmd.GoToRecord , , acNewRec
    [FirstName].SetFocus
End Sub
```

First, use the DoCmd object to add a record to the table:

```
DoCmd.GoToRecord , , acNewRec
```

Then, return the focus to the first data entry field on the form, the FirstName field:

```
[FirstName].SetFocus
```

The next code block allows for the deletion of a record:

```
Private Sub Command18_Click()
    On Error GoTo HandleError
    DoCmd.DoMenuItem acFormBar, acEditMenu, 8, , acMenuVer70
    DoCmd.DoMenuItem acFormBar, acEditMenu, 6, , acMenuVer70
    [FirstName].SetFocus
    Exit Sub
HandleError:
    If Err.Number <> 2501 Then
        MsgBox Err.Number & " " & Err.Description
    End If
End Sub
```

Start with an On Error statement that directs the code to a label in the code block if an error occurs:

```
On Error GoTo HandleError
```

Then, use the DoCmd object to delete the current record:

```
DoCmd.DoMenuItem acFormBar, acEditMenu, 8, , acMenuVer70
DoCmd.DoMenuItem acFormBar, acEditMenu, 6, , acMenuVer70
And set focus back to the FirstName field:
[FirstName].SetFocus
```

If an error occurs while you are trying to delete, the code flows to this label:

```
HandleError:
```

Check to see if the error number is 2501. If it is, the user pressed the No button when he or she was asked by Access to confirm the record deletion. If that is the case, there is no error to process even though Access throws one:

```
If Err.Number <> 2501 Then
```

Otherwise, display the error to the user:

```
MsgBox Err.Number & " " & Err.Description
```

The next code block fires when the user clicks on the Search button:

```
Private Sub Command19_Click()
    Screen.PreviousControl.SetFocus
    DoCmd.DoMenuItem acFormBar, acEditMenu, 10, , acMenuVer70
End Sub
```

Because the Search button was just clicked, you need to return to the field the user was previously viewing so it will be searched:

```
Screen.PreviousControl.SetFocus
```

Then, open the Access search dialog:

```
DoCmd.DoMenuItem acFormBar, acEditMenu, 10, , acMenuVer70
```

One line of code runs when the visitor clicks on the Close button. This line uses the DoCmd object to close the current form:

```
Private Sub Command20_Click()
    DoCmd.Close
End Sub
```

The next code block fires when the user clicks on the Contact Info button. This button uses the DoCmd object to take the user to the first page of the form:

```
Private Sub Command28_Click()
    DoCmd.GoToPage 1
End Sub
```

The other button in the footer, labeled Cases, takes the user to the second page of the form:

```
Private Sub Command30_Click()
    DoCmd.GoToPage 2
End Sub
```

One more button appears on the form. This one is on the header of the form and uses the DoCmd object to load the Library Notes form:

```
Private Sub Command40_Click()
    DoCmd.OpenForm "Library Notes"
End Sub
```

When the user double-clicks on the Country combo box, the Country form loads. This code block accomplishes that task:

```
Private Sub Country_DblClick(Cancel As Integer)
    If [Country] = "" Or IsNull([Country]) Then
        DoCmd.OpenForm "Countries", , , , acFormAdd, acDialog
        [Country].Requery
    Else
        DoCmd.OpenForm "Countries", , , "[Country] = """ & [Country] & """", , acDialog
    End If
End Sub
```

First, check to see if the Country field is empty:

```
If [Country] = "" Or IsNull([Country]) Then
```

If it is, the user wants to add a new record. In that case, load the Countries form in Add mode:

```
DoCmd.OpenForm "Countries", , , , acFormAdd, acDialog
```

Note that it is loaded as a dialog, which means that the user will have to finish with that form completely before returning to this form. Once the user is finished, repopulate the Country combo box because a new country may have been added:

```
[Country].Requery
```

Otherwise, open the Countries form filtered so that it shows the country that has currently been selected by the user:

```
DoCmd.OpenForm "Countries", , , "[Country] = """ & [Country] & """", , acDialog
```

If the user double-clicks on the Zip Code combo box, show them the Zip Code form:

```
Private Sub ZipCode_DblClick(Cancel As Integer)
    If [ZipCode] = "" Or IsNull([ZipCode]) Then
        DoCmd.OpenForm "Zip Codes", , , , acFormAdd, acDialog
        [ZipCode].Requery
    Else
        DoCmd.OpenForm "Zip Codes", , , "[ZipCode] = """ & [ZipCode] & """", , acDialog
    End If
End Sub
```

First, check to see if the current Zip Code is empty:

```
If [ZipCode] = "" Or IsNull([ZipCode]) Then
```

If it is, assume that the user wants to add a new Zip Code:

```
DoCmd.OpenForm "Zip Codes", , , , acFormAdd, acDialog
```

After the addition is made, reload the Zip Code combo box:

```
[ZipCode].Requery
```

If the combo box contained a value when the user double-clicked on it, assume that the user wants to see the values for that record on the Zip Code form:

```
DoCmd.OpenForm "Zip Codes", , , "[ZipCode] = """ & [ZipCode] & """", , acDialog
```

The last code block on this form fires when the user leaves the Zip Code combo box. This code block populates the City and State based on the Zip Code selected:

```
Private Sub ZipCode_Exit(Cancel As Integer)
    Dim MyDB As DAO.Database
```

```
    Dim rs As DAO.Recordset
    Set MyDB = CurrentDb
    Set rs = MyDB.OpenRecordset("select City, State from ZipCodes " _
        & "Where ZipCode = """ & [ZipCode] & """", dbOpenSnapshot)
    If rs.EOF = False Then
        [State] = rs("State")
        [City] = rs("City")
    End If
End Sub
```

A Database object is needed:

```
Dim MyDB As DAO.Database
```

and a Recordset object also is needed:

```
Dim rs As DAO.Recordset
```

Then connect to the current database with which you are working:

```
Set MyDB = CurrentDb
```

and retrieve the City and State that go with the Zip Code selected by the user:

```
Set rs = MyDB.OpenRecordset("select City, State from ZipCodes " _
    & "Where ZipCode = """ & [ZipCode] & """", dbOpenSnapshot)
```

If the EOF flag is False, a matching record has been found:

```
If rs.EOF = False Then
```

Use the values in that record to populate the State field:

```
[State] = rs("State")
```

and the City field:

```
[City] = rs("City")
```

The CustomerPhoneNumbers sub-form contains a single code block. This code block loads the Phone Type form when the Phone Type combo box is double-clicked:

```
Private Sub Phone_Type_DblClick(Cancel As Integer)
    If [PhoneType] = "" Or IsNull([PhoneType]) Then
        DoCmd.OpenForm "Phone Types", , , , acFormAdd, acDialog
        [Phone Type].Requery
```

```
    Else
        DoCmd.OpenForm "Phone Types", , , "[PhoneType] = """ & [PhoneType] & """", ,
acDialog
    End If
End Sub
```

First, check to see if the PhoneType field is empty:

```
If [PhoneType] = "" Or IsNull([PhoneType]) Then
```

If it is, open the Phone Types form in Add mode:

```
DoCmd.OpenForm "Phone Types", , , , acFormAdd, acDialog
```

Reload the Phone Type combo box:

```
[Phone Type].Requery
```

Otherwise, open the Phone Types form based on the value of the current record:

```
DoCmd.OpenForm "Phone Types", , , "[PhoneType] = """ & [PhoneType] & """", , acDialog
```

The Customer Cases sub-form of the Customers form has four code blocks. The first displays the Investigators form when the InvestigatorID combo box is double-clicked:

```
Private Sub InvestigatorID_DblClick(Cancel As Integer)
    If [InvestigatorID] = 0 Or IsNull([InvestigatorID]) Then
        DoCmd.OpenForm "Investigators", , , , acFormAdd, acDialog
        [InvestigatorID].Requery
    Else
        DoCmd.OpenForm "Investigators", , , "[InvestigatorID] = " _
                                & [InvestigatorID], , acDialog
    End If
End Sub
```

First, check to see if the InvestigatorID field is empty:

```
If [InvestigatorID] = 0 Or IsNull([InvestigatorID]) Then
```

If it is, open the Investigator form in Add mode before repopulating the InvestigatorID combo box:

```
DoCmd.OpenForm "Investigators", , , , acFormAdd, acDialog
[InvestigatorID].Requery
```

Otherwise, show the information for the investigator that is currently selected in the Customer Cases sub-form:

```
DoCmd.OpenForm "Investigators", , , "[InvestigatorID] = " _
          & [InvestigatorID], , acDialog
```

The next code block similarly shows the Products form based on the Product that is currently selected:

```
Private Sub ProductID_DblClick(Cancel As Integer)
    If [ProductID] = 0 Or IsNull([ProductID]) Then
        DoCmd.OpenForm "Products", , , , acFormAdd, acDialog
        [ProductID].Requery
    Else
        DoCmd.OpenForm "Products", , , "[ProductID] = " & [ProductID], , acDialog
    End If
End Sub
```

If the ProductID field is blank, assume a new record is to be added:

```
If [ProductID] = 0 Or IsNull([ProductID]) Then
        DoCmd.OpenForm "Products", , , , acFormAdd, acDialog
        [ProductID].Requery
```

Otherwise, assume information on the current product needs to be shown:

```
Else
    DoCmd.OpenForm "Products", , , "[ProductID] = " & [ProductID], , acDialog
```

The other code block on this sub-form fires when the Status combo box is double-clicked:

```
Private Sub Status_DblClick(Cancel As Integer)
    If [Status] = "" Or IsNull([Status]) Then
        DoCmd.OpenForm "Statuses", , , , acFormAdd, acDialog
        [Status].Requery
    Else
        DoCmd.OpenForm "Statuses", , , "[Status] = """ & [Status] & """", , acDialog
    End If
End Sub
```

If the Status field is empty, display the Statuses form in Add mode and repopulate the Status combo box:

```
If [Status] = "" Or IsNull([Status]) Then
        DoCmd.OpenForm "Statuses", , , , acFormAdd, acDialog
        [Status].Requery
```

Otherwise, show the Statuses form for the current selected status to allow for addition:

```
Else
    DoCmd.OpenForm "Statuses", , , "[Status] = """ & [Status] & """", ,
acDialog
```

Investigators Form

The code on the Investigators form provides the functionality for the buttons and links to the Managers form. It also makes sure that the Short-Name entered is unique. The first code block allows the user to add a new record:

```
Private Sub Command17_Click()
    DoCmd.GoToRecord , , acNewRec
    [ShortName].SetFocus
End Sub
```

First, the GoToRecord of the DoCmd object is used to add a new record to this table:

```
DoCmd.GoToRecord , , acNewRec
```

Then set the focus to the first data entry field so the user can start entering data:

```
[ShortName].SetFocus
```

The next code block enables the user to delete a record:

```
Private Sub Command18_Click()
    On Error GoTo HandleError
    DoCmd.DoMenuItem acFormBar, acEditMenu, 8, , acMenuVer70
    DoCmd.DoMenuItem acFormBar, acEditMenu, 6, , acMenuVer70
    [ShortName].SetFocus
    Exit Sub
HandleError:
    If Err.Number <> 2501 Then
        MsgBox Err.Number & " " & Err.Description
    End If
End Sub
```

Check for errors in this procedure:

```
On Error GoTo HandleError
```

and then use the DoMenuItem method to delete the record:

```
DoCmd.DoMenuItem acFormBar, acEditMenu, 8, , acMenuVer70
DoCmd.DoMenuItem acFormBar, acEditMenu, 6, , acMenuVer70
```

After that, return the focus to the ShortName field:

```
[ShortName].SetFocus
```

If an error occurs, the code flows to this point:

```
HandleError:
```

One error that should be skipped over occurs if the user cancels a deletion. Check for that here:

```
If Err.Number <> 2501 Then
```

If that was not the error that occurred, report the error to the user:

```
MsgBox Err.Number & " " & Err.Description
```

The next code block fires when the user clicks on the Search button:

```
Private Sub Command19_Click()
    Screen.PreviousControl.SetFocus
    DoCmd.DoMenuItem acFormBar, acEditMenu, 10, , acMenuVer70
End Sub
```

Assume that the field wanting to be searched is the field the user was viewing before entering this field:

```
Screen.PreviousControl.SetFocus
```

The DoCmd object is then used to display the Search dialog:

```
DoCmd.DoMenuItem acFormBar, acEditMenu, 10, , acMenuVer70
```

The other button on the form uses the DoCmd object to close this form:

```
Private Sub Command20_Click()
    DoCmd.Close
End Sub
```

If the user double-clicks on the Manager combo box, the following code is fired:

```
Private Sub ManagerID_DblClick(Cancel As Integer)
    If [ManagerID] = 0 Or IsNull([ManagerID]) Then
```

```
        DoCmd.OpenForm "Managers", , , , acFormAdd, acDialog
        [ManagerID].Requery
    Else
        DoCmd.OpenForm "Managers", , , "[ManagerID] = " & [ManagerID], , acDialog
    End If
End Sub
```

First, check and see if the Manager field is empty:

```
If [ManagerID] = 0 Or IsNull([ManagerID]) Then
```

If it is, use the OpenForm method to open the Managers form in Add mode:

```
DoCmd.OpenForm "Managers", , , , acFormAdd, acDialog
```

and then repopulate the Manager combo box:

```
[ManagerID].Requery
```

If the Manager combo box was not empty, open the Managers form and display the information for the current manager selected:

```
DoCmd.OpenForm "Managers", , , "[ManagerID] = " & [ManagerID], , acDialog
```

The last code block on this form fires when the user leaves the Short Name Text Box. The code checks to make sure that the value entered in the field is unique:

```
Private Sub ShortName_Exit(Cancel As Integer)
    Dim MyDB As DAO.Database
    Dim rs As DAO.Recordset
    If Not IsNull([InvestigatorID]) Then
        Set MyDB = CurrentDb
        Set rs = MyDB.OpenRecordset("select InvestigatorID from " _
            & "Investigators where " _
            & "ShortName = """ & [ShortName] _
            & """ and InvestigatorID <> " & [InvestigatorID], dbOpenSnapshot)
        If rs.EOF = False Then
            Cancel = True
            MsgBox "You need to supply a unique short name for the investigator."
            ShortName.SelStart = 0
            ShortName.SelLength = Len([ShortName])
        End If
    End If
End Sub
```

To check for a unique value, a Database object is needed:

```
Dim MyDB As DAO.Database
```

and a Recordset object also is needed:

```
Dim rs As DAO.Recordset
```

Then make sure that the user has actually selected a Manager:

```
If Not IsNull([InvestigatorID]) Then
```

If the user has, connect to the current open database:

```
Set MyDB = CurrentDb
```

Then look for the value entered in this field in a record in the database other than this record:

```
Set rs = MyDB.OpenRecordset("select InvestigatorID from " _
    & "Investigators where " _
    & "ShortName = """ & [ShortName] _
    & """ and InvestigatorID <> " & [InvestigatorID], dbOpenSnapshot)
```

If a record is found, EOF is False because the record pointer is pointing to the existing record:

```
If rs.EOF = False Then
```

Then cancel the visitor leaving this field:

```
Cancel = True
```

Report to the user that the value entered was not unique:

```
MsgBox "You need to supply a unique short name for the investigator."
```

and highlight the value that was just entered:

```
ShortName.SelStart = 0
ShortName.SelLength = Len([ShortName])
```

Managers Form

The code on the Managers form enables the user to add, delete, and search records. It also verifies that the ShortName field is unique. The code block below enables the user to add a new record to the Managers table:

```
Private Sub Command17_Click()
    DoCmd.GoToRecord , , acNewRec
    [ShortName].SetFocus
End Sub
```

The GoToRecord method of the DoCmd object accomplishes this task:

```
DoCmd.GoToRecord , , acNewRec
```

Then set the focus back to the ShortName field so the user can start entering data for this new record:

```
[ShortName].SetFocus
```

The next code block allows for the deletion of a Managers record:

```
Private Sub Command18_Click()
    On Error GoTo HandleError
    DoCmd.DoMenuItem acFormBar, acEditMenu, 8, , acMenuVer70
    DoCmd.DoMenuItem acFormBar, acEditMenu, 6, , acMenuVer70
    [ShortName].SetFocus
    Exit Sub
HandleError:
    If Err.Number <> 2501 Then
        MsgBox Err.Number & " " & Err.Description
    End If
End Sub
```

Check for errors in this procedure:

```
On Error GoTo HandleError
```

The DoCmd object is used to delete the current record:

```
DoCmd.DoMenuItem acFormBar, acEditMenu, 8, , acMenuVer70
DoCmd.DoMenuItem acFormBar, acEditMenu, 6, , acMenuVer70
```

Then return the focus to the ShortName field:

```
[ShortName].SetFocus
```

If an error occurs during deletion, the code flows here:

```
HandleError:
```

The error is displayed unless it occurred because the user canceled the record deletion:

```
If Err.Number <> 2501 Then
    MsgBox Err.Number & " " & Err.Description
End If
```

The next code block fires when the user clicks on the Search button:

```
Private Sub Command19_Click()
    Screen.PreviousControl.SetFocus
    DoCmd.DoMenuItem acFormBar, acEditMenu, 10, , acMenuVer70
End Sub
```

In that case, set the focus back to the control the user was at last:

```
Screen.PreviousControl.SetFocus
```

Then open the Search dialog, enabling the user to search that field:

```
DoCmd.DoMenuItem acFormBar, acEditMenu, 10, , acMenuVer70
```

The other button on the form is the close button. When pressed, the code uses the DoCmd object to close this form:

```
Private Sub Command20_Click()
    DoCmd.Close
End Sub
```

The other code block on this form verifies that the ShortName entered into the Short Name text box is unique:

```
Private Sub ShortName_Exit(Cancel As Integer)
    Dim MyDB As DAO.Database
    Dim rs As DAO.Recordset
    If Not IsNull([ManagerID]) Then
        Set MyDB = CurrentDb
        Set rs = MyDB.OpenRecordset("select ManagerID from Managers where " _
            & "ShortName = """ & [ShortName] _
            & """ and ManagerID <> " & [ManagerID], dbOpenSnapshot)
        If rs.EOF = False Then
            Cancel = True
            MsgBox "You need to supply a unique short name for the manager."
            ShortName.SelStart = 0
            ShortName.SelLength = Len([ShortName])
        End If
    End If
End Sub
```

To perform this check, programmatically connect to this database:

```
Dim MyDB As DAO.Database
```

and retrieve data from a table:

```
Dim rs As DAO.Recordset
```

Before you check the uniqueness of this field, make sure that the visitor has entered a value:

```
If Not IsNull([ManagerID]) Then
```

If a value has been entered, connect to this database:

```
Set MyDB = CurrentDb
```

and look for another record that has the same ShortName entered by the user:

```
Set rs = MyDB.OpenRecordset("select ManagerID from Managers where " _
    & "ShortName = """ & [ShortName] _
    & """ and ManagerID <> " & [ManagerID], dbOpenSnapshot)
```

If one was found, the end of file flag is off:

```
If rs.EOF = False Then
```

In that case, prevent the user from leaving this field:

```
Cancel = True
```

and inform him of the problem:

```
MsgBox "You need to supply a unique short name for the manager."
```

Then highlight the value entered into the ShortName field by first placing the insertion point at the beginning of the field:

```
ShortName.SelStart = 06
```

and highlighting the length of the field:

```
ShortName.SelLength = Len([ShortName])
```

Library Notes Form

The code on the Library Notes form enables the user to add and delete records. It also closes the form, enables the user to search the underlying table, and links to the Products table. The first code block below enables the user to add a new record to this table:

```
Private Sub Command17_Click()
    DoCmd.GoToRecord , , acNewRec
    [ProductID].SetFocus
End Sub
```

The GoToRecord is used to add a new record to the table and to move to that record:

```
DoCmd.GoToRecord , , acNewRec
```

Then move the focus to the first data entry field on the form so the user can start entering the new record:

```
[ProductID].SetFocus
```

The code that fires when the user clicks on the Delete Note button is below.

```
Private Sub Command18_Click()
    On Error GoTo HandleError
    DoCmd.DoMenuItem acFormBar, acEditMenu, 8, , acMenuVer70
    DoCmd.DoMenuItem acFormBar, acEditMenu, 6, , acMenuVer70
    [ProductID].SetFocus
    Exit Sub
HandleError:
    If Err.Number <> 2501 Then
        MsgBox Err.Number & " " & Err.Description
    End If
End Sub
```

Watch for a specific error thrown by Access in this procedure:

```
On Error GoTo HandleError
```

Then delete the current record:

```
DoCmd.DoMenuItem acFormBar, acEditMenu, 8, , acMenuVer70
DoCmd.DoMenuItem acFormBar, acEditMenu, 6, , acMenuVer70
```

and move the focus to the ProductID field:

```
[ProductID].SetFocus
```

If an error occurs, the code flows here:

```
HandleError:
```

If the user cancels the record deletion, an error occurs that you don't want to display to the user. The error displayed to the user is as follows:

```
If Err.Number <> 2501 Then
        MsgBox Err.Number & " " & Err.Description
End If
```

The next code block enables the user to search the fields on this page:

```
Private Sub Command19_Click()
    Screen.PreviousControl.SetFocus
    DoCmd.DoMenuItem acFormBar, acEditMenu, 10, , acMenuVer70
End Sub
```

Assume that the user wants to search the field he or she was on before clicking on the Search button so the focus is returned to that field:

```
Screen.PreviousControl.SetFocus
```

Then display the Search dialog:

```
DoCmd.DoMenuItem acFormBar, acEditMenu, 10, , acMenuVer70
```

The DoCmd object is also used to close this form when the user clicks on the Close button:

```
Private Sub Command20_Click()
    DoCmd.Close
End Sub
```

The other code block on this form displays the Products form when the user double-clicks on the ProductID field:

```
Private Sub ProductID_DblClick(Cancel As Integer)
    If [ProductID] = 0 Or IsNull([ProductID]) Then
        DoCmd.OpenForm "Products", , , , acFormAdd, acDialog
        [ProductID].Requery
    Else
        DoCmd.OpenForm "Products", , , "[ProductID] = " & _
        [ProductID], , acDialog
    End If
End Sub
```

First, check to see if the ProductID field is empty:

```
If [ProductID] = 0 Or IsNull([ProductID]) Then
```

If it is, open the Products form in add mode:

```
DoCmd.OpenForm "Products", , , , acFormAdd, acDialog
```

Then, repopulate the ProductID combo box so the new value entered is part of the list:

```
[ProductID].Requery
```

Otherwise, show the information for the product that is currently selected in the Product ID field:

```
DoCmd.OpenForm "Products", , , "[ProductID] = " & [ProductID], , acDialog
```

Countries, Phone Types, Products, Statuses and Zip Codes Forms

The code on these forms is almost identical, so it is presented in this section collectively. The code on these forms enables the visitor to add, delete, and search records, as well as close the form.

The first code block below is used to add a record to the underlying table:

```
Private Sub Command17_Click()
    DoCmd.GoToRecord , , acNewRec
    [Country].SetFocus
End Sub
```

To add a record, use the GoToRecord method of the DoCmd object to pass the constant acNewRec to the object. This method can be used for other navigational purposes:

```
DoCmd.GoToRecord , , acNewRec
```

After a new record is added, shift the focus to the first data entry field on that form:

```
[Country].SetFocus
```

The next code block is for the deletion of a record:

```
Private Sub Command18_Click()
    On Error GoTo HandleError
    DoCmd.DoMenuItem acFormBar, acEditMenu, 8, , acMenuVer70
    DoCmd.DoMenuItem acFormBar, acEditMenu, 6, , acMenuVer70
    [Country].SetFocus
    Exit Sub
HandleError:
    If Err.Number <> 2501 Then
        MsgBox Err.Number & " " & Err.Description
    End If
End Sub
```

Skip a specific error if it occurs, which requires an error handler:

```
On Error GoTo HandleError
```

Then delete the current record:

```
DoCmd.DoMenuItem acFormBar, acEditMenu, 8, , acMenuVer70
DoCmd.DoMenuItem acFormBar, acEditMenu, 6, , acMenuVer70
```

and set the focus back to the first data entry field on this form:

```
[Country].SetFocus
```

If an error occurs while deleting a record, the code flows here:

```
HandleError:
```

In that case, show the error message, unless it was caused by the user canceling the record deletion. If so, the error number is 2501:

```
If Err.Number <> 2501 Then
        MsgBox Err.Number & " " & Err.Description
End If
```

The next code block fires when the Search button is pressed:

```
Private Sub Command19_Click()
    Screen.PreviousControl.SetFocus
    DoCmd.DoMenuItem acFormBar, acEditMenu, 10, , acMenuVer70
End Sub
```

The search feature uses the built-in Access Search dialog, which enables the visitor to search any of the fields on the form. Assume that the user wants to search the field being viewed before clicking on the Search button by setting the focus back to that field:

```
Screen.PreviousControl.SetFocus
```

Then use the DoMenuItem to display the Search dialog:

```
DoCmd.DoMenuItem acFormBar, acEditMenu, 10, , acMenuVer70
```

The other code block on these forms uses the DoCmd object to close the current form:

```
Private Sub Command20_Click()
    DoCmd.Close
End Sub
```

Reports

Cases by Status in Date Range Report

The Cases by Status in Date Range report enables the users to see the number of cases that have occurred in a date range grouped by the status. The user enters a start and end date within which the cases must have occurred. The Report is based on the Cases by Status in Date Range query. The SQL for that query is below:

```
SELECT CustomerCases.Status, Count(CustomerCases.CustomerCaseID)
AS CountOfCustomerCaseID FROM CustomerCases
WHERE (((CustomerCases.InitialContact)>=[Enter the Start Date for this report]
And (CustomerCases.InitialContact)<=[Enter the End Date for this report]))
GROUP BY CustomerCases.Status;
```

First notice that the Count function is used on the CustomerCaseID field to count the number of records in each of the Grouped field Statuses. Also, notice in the Where clause that the date must be between the text for the start and end date. Because the start and end date text is not a field in the table, the user is prompted to supply a value for that field.

Open Cases Grouped by Investigator Report

The Open Cases Grouped by Investigator report displays each of the cases that are currently open and sorted by the ShortName of the Investigator. The report is based on the Open Cases Grouped by Investigator query. The syntax for that query is below:

```
SELECT Investigators.ShortName, CustomerCases.InitialContact,
CustomerCases.InitialComplaint, CustomerCases.Remarks
FROM Investigators INNER JOIN CustomerCases ON
Investigators.InvestigatorID = CustomerCases.InvestigatorID
WHERE (((CustomerCases.Status)="Pending" Or (CustomerCases.Status)="In Process"
Or (CustomerCases.Status)="New")) ORDER BY Investigators.ShortName;
```

Two tables, the Investigators table and the CustomerCases table, have to be combined in this query. The CustomerCases table contains the information about the cases, but the Investigators table needs to grab the name of the investigator. The two tables are linked together by the InvestigatorID field.

Notice in the Where clause that the Status of the case must be either Pending, In Process, or New for the record to be included. Also note that the records are sorted by the ShortName field:

Total Cases by Project Report

The Total Cases by Project report shows the count of all the cases grouped by the name of the product. The report is based on the Total Cases by Project query, which is shown below.

```
SELECT CustomerCases.ProductID,
       Count(CustomerCases.CustomerCaseID) AS CountOfCustomerCaseID
       FROM CustomerCases GROUP BY CustomerCases.ProductID;
```

Note in the query that the CustomerCaseID field is counted and the ProductID field is grouped.

CHAPTER 10

Project Management

ON THE CD:

Project Management.mdb

Working with Projects, Milestones, and Steps

In this chapter, we will look at a database application that is used to manage projects. The person using the database will be able to create projects and then add milestones to those projects, which are major levels of completion in a project. Each of the milestones has steps that are needed to occur before the milestone is considered complete.

Reports that enable the user to view the project as well as summary information about the project are available. Support tables enable the user to track project managers and other employees that are involved in the project.

Project Management Database

Sample Walk-through

When the user first enters the application, he or she will see the menu shown in Figure 10-1.

The menu enables the user to access all the functionality of the application and contains two submenus. One provides access to the forms of the application and the other enables access to the reports.

The first menu item listed under the Forms submenu is the Projects form. This form is shown in Figure 10-2.

The Projects form is the center of this application. This is the form that the user uses to manage his or her projects. The form is made up of three pages of information. The first page contains the top-level general information about the project. This page is viewed by pressing the General button in the footer of the form.

If the user presses the Participants button, the form shown in Figure 10-3 will be displayed.

Figure 10-1

The Menu system from the Project Management database

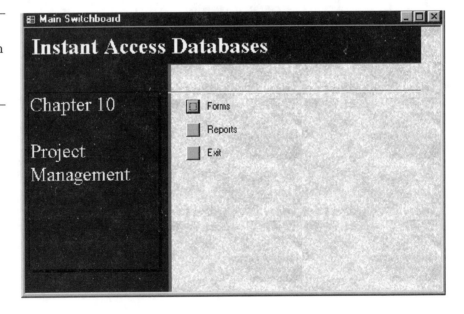

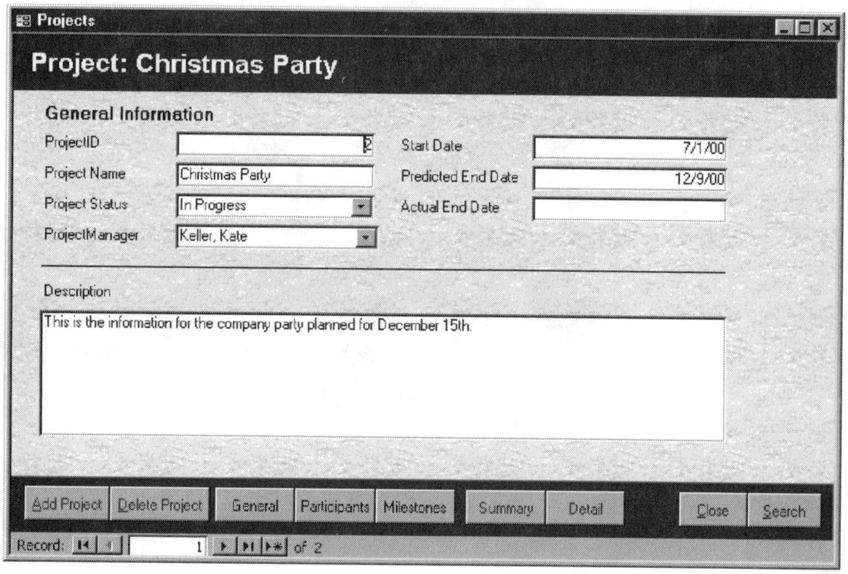

Figure 10-2

The General Information page from the Projects form

Participants, other than the project manager, are those that are involved in a project. The user selects an employee and then specifies the employee's role in this project. Each employee can be listed more than once since he or she could have multiple roles.

The other page of this form is the Milestones page, which is shown in Figure 10-4. The Milestones page is used to track and define the major points of completion for the project and the steps that have to be taken for that point to be met.

The user also can choose to see the project as a report in two different versions that are available just from this form. The first is accessible to the user by clicking on the Summary button. This report is displayed in Figure 10-5.

The Project Summary report enables the user to see quickly how the project is coming along toward its conclusion. The user sees summary information about the project, the milestones, and the steps.

The Detail report shows all the information about the project in report format. This report is accessible by pressing the Detail button on the Projects form and is displayed in Figure 10-6.

Figure 10-3

The Participants page of the Projects form

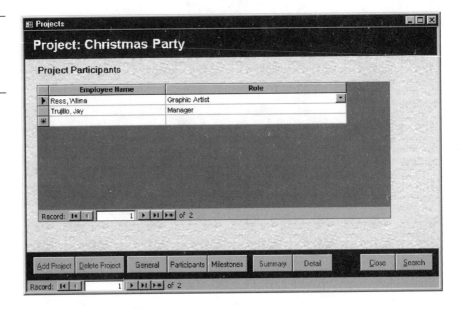

Figure 10-4

The Milestones page of the Projects form.

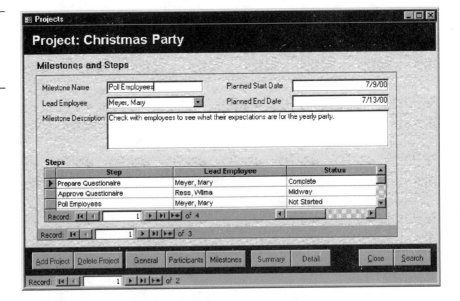

Figure 10-5

The Project
Summary report

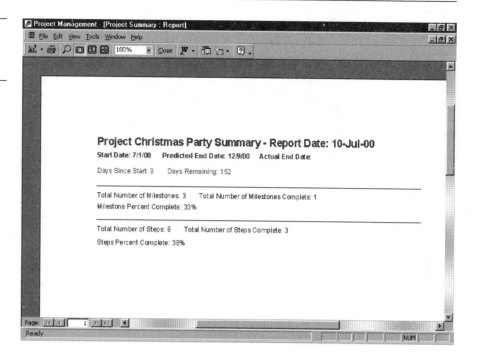

Figure 10-6

The Project
Detail report

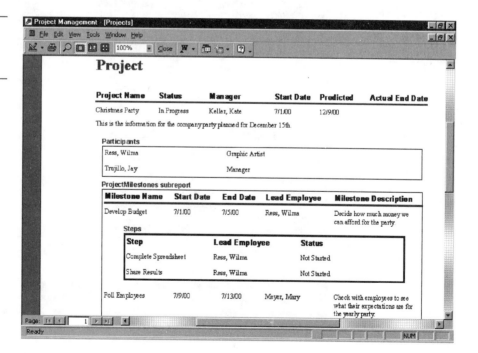

Note that the report contains subreports as well as a subreport within a subreport in order to be able to display the top-level project information with the bottom-level step information.

The next form available on the Forms submenu is the Project Managers form. This form is shown in Figure 10-7. In this database application, a project manager is the person who is in charge of a project. Each project can have one project manager. This form enables the user to enter contact information about the project manager.

Note the department field, which links to the Department form. Since the Departments table has only a single field in it, you must allow the user to enter new values in this list and ask the user if he or she wants that department added to the database. The dialog that does this is shown in Figure 10-8.

As you will see when you look at the code, if the user selects Yes, then the value the users entered is added to the database as a new record and the combo box is updated to show this new value.

The next form available from the Form submenu is the Departments form. This form is displayed in Figure 10-9.

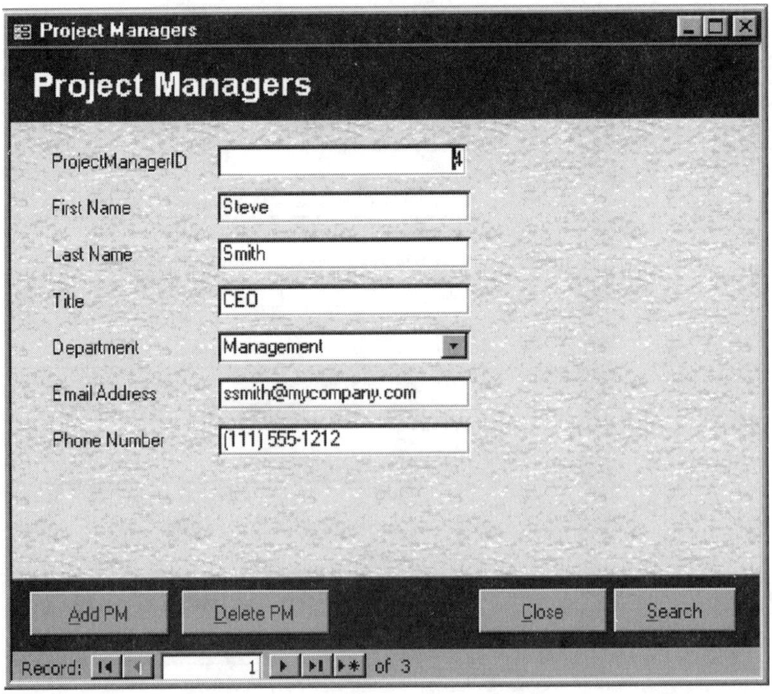

Figure 10-7

The Project Managers form

Figure 10-8

The Add
Department
dialog

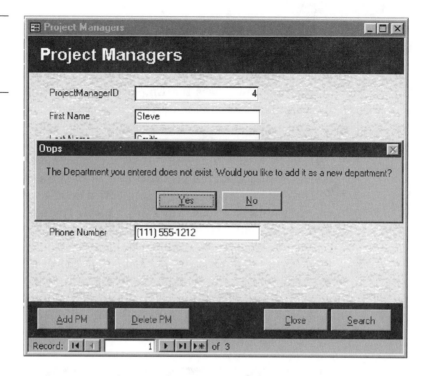

Figure 10-9

The Departments
form

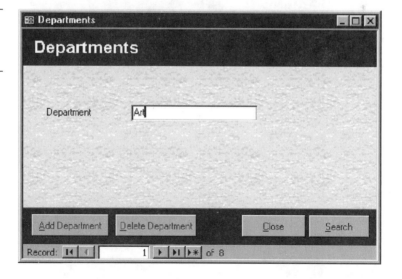

The Departments form enables the user to manage the departments that are displayed in the Departments combo box on the Project Manager form and the Employees form. From here, the user can add, edit, delete, and view the Departments.

The user can access the Employees form by selecting the next menu item on the Forms submenu. This form is shown in Figure 10-10.

Employees, as opposed to project managers, are individuals who provide a different role in the project. Each project can have many employees associated with it, but only a single project manager. The role that an employee plays in a project is defined on the Projects form.

The other form used in this application enables the management of the roles. This form is shown in Figure 10-11. The single field Roles form is used to add, edit, delete, and view roles.

The Reports menu contains two reports that are different from the two reports that you have already looked at. The first is called Project with Project Manager and is displayed in Figure 10-12.

The Project with Project Manager report shows information about a project with information about the person in charge of the project. The

Figure 10-10

The Employees form

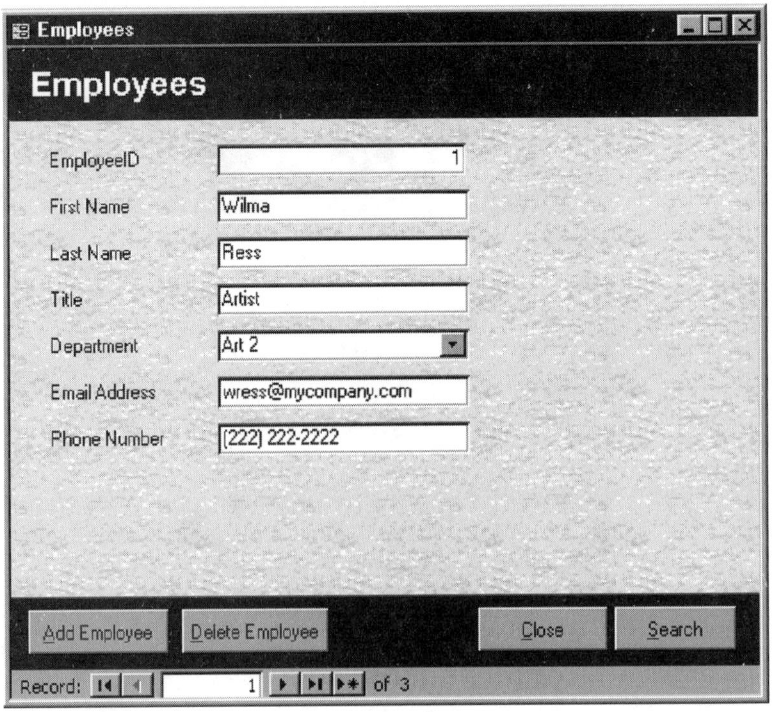

Figure 10-11

The Roles form

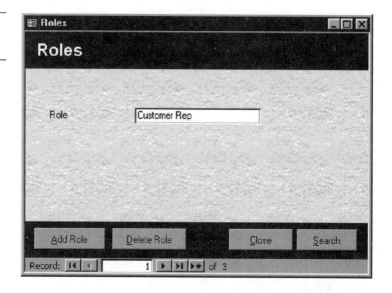

Figure 10-12

The Project with Project Manager report

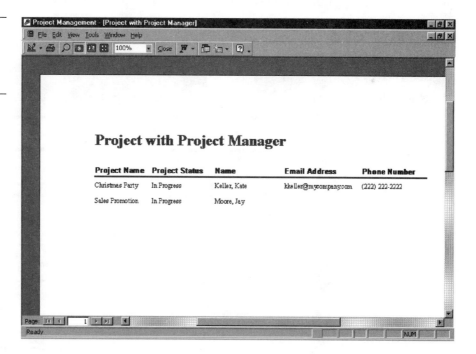

report could be used as a contact list to quickly locate the person in charge of a project.

The other report is called Steps Not Complete and is shown in Figure 10-13. This report groups information first at the project level and then at the milestone level. It then shows each of the steps for that milestone that are not yet complete.

Table Definitions and Relationships

Projects Table

The top-level table in the database is the Projects table. Most of the other tables in the database relate to this table directly or indirectly. The table contains information about the project itself.

ProjectParticipants Table

Under the Projects table is the ProjectParticipants table, which actually links three tables in a many-to-many relationship. Each project can have

Figure 10-13

The Steps Not Complete report

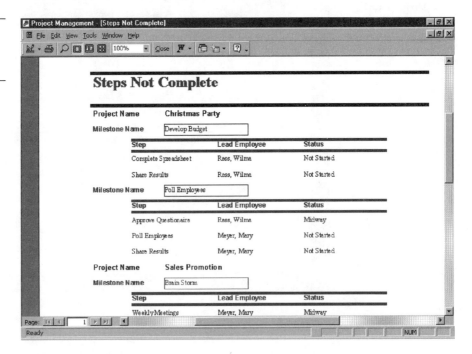

many employees participating in it, and each employee can be involved in many projects. That's a many-to-many relationship.

The other involves the Roles table. Each of the employees participating in a project has a role, and each employee can have numerous roles in each project. Also, each role can be filled by more than one employee, so you have another many-to-many relationship. The ProjectParticipants table satisfies these relationships by linking to the Projects, Employees, and Roles tables in a one-to-many relationship.

ProjectMilestones Table

Another table that relates to the Projects table is the ProjectMilestones table. In the scenario used in this database application, milestones are major points of completion within a project. A project can have many milestones, but each milestone belongs to a single project. Thus, the two tables are in a one-to-many relationship.

ProjectMilestoneSteps Table

Under the ProjectMilestones table is the ProjectMilestoneSteps table. These two tables relate to each other in a one-to-many relationship. Steps are small points of completion that are a subcomponent of a milestone. For a milestone to be complete, all the steps in that milestone must be complete. Also, each of the milestones can have many steps, but each step goes with a single milestone.

ProjectManagers Table

The ProjectManagers table stores information on individuals who can be in charge of projects. This table relates to the Projects table in a one-to-many relationship. Each of the projects has a single project manager, but a single project manager can be in charge of many projects.

Employees Table

The Employees table stores contact information about people who can be involved in a project. The table is in a many-to-many relationship with the Projects table. Each employee can be involved in many projects and each project can have many employees. The ProjectParticipants table also satisfies the many-to-many middle table role.

Departments Table

The Departments table stores the names of the departments that are listed in the Project Manager and Employees tables. This table is thus in a one-to-many relationship with those two tables. Each employee or project manager works in a single department, but each department can have numerous project managers and employees.

Roles Table

The last table in this database is the Roles table. This table stores the roles that employees can play in a project. The table relates to the Projects table in a many-to-many relationship. Each of the projects can have numerous roles associated with them and each of the roles can be used by numerous projects. The ProjectParticipants table satisfies the many-to-many middle table role.

Field Specifications

Projects Table

The field specifications for the Projects table are displayed in Table 10-1.
The ProjectID field is the primary key field for this table. Because it is an AutoNumber field, it is automatically populated with a unique value when a new record is added.

Table 10-1

The Projects Table Field Specifications

Field Name	Field Type	Notes
ProjectID	AutoNumber	Primary Key
ProjectName	Text	Length = 50
ProjectStatus	Text	Length = 50
ProjectManagerID	Number	Type = Long Integer, Foreign Key
StartDate	Date/Time	
PredictedEndDate	Date/Time	
ActualEndDate	Date/Time	
Description	Memo	

The ProjectStatus field stores the status of the project. The Lookup properties are used, so this field is displayed as a combo box. The Limit to List property is set to Yes, which means the user must select a value from the list. The Row Source Type property is set to Value List with the following Row Source:

```
"Planned";"In Progress";"Completed";"Canceled"
```

The ProjectManagerID field is a foreign key that links this table with the ProjectManagers table. The Lookup properties are used also with this field so it is displayed as a combo box. It has the following Row Source value:

```
SELECT [ProjectManagers].[ProjectManagerID], [LastName] & ", " &
[FirstName] AS FullName FROM ProjectManagers ORDER BY [LastName] & ", " & [FirstName];
```

In the combo box, the user sees the first name and last name listed together, but the value in the ProjectManagerID is stored in the field.

The StartDate field stores the date when the project started or is going to start. It has the following default value:

```
Date()
```

which means that whenever a new record is added, this field will default to the current system date.

The PredictedEndDate field stores the estimated date when the project will conclude. This field defaults to two months from the current system date using this code:

```
DateAdd("m",2,Date())
```

The DateAdd function adds values to dates. The first parameter, "m," indicates that what you want to add are months. The second parameter, 2, indicates that you want to add two months. The third parameter is the date that you want to add to. In this case, it is the current system date. Thus, you have a function call within a function call.

ProjectParticipants Table

The field specifications for the ProjectParticipants table are displayed in Table 10-2.

Table 10-2	Field Name	Field Type	Notes
The ProjectParticipants Table Field Specifications	ProjectParticipiantID	AutoNumber	Primary Key
	ProjectID	Number	Type = Long Integer, Foreign Key
	EmployeeID	Number	Type = Long Integer, Foreign Key
	Role	Text	Length = 50, Foreign Key

The ProjectParticipantID field is the primary key for the table, uniquely identifying each record. The ProjectID field is a foreign key that links this table to the Projects table. It uses the Lookup properties to display it as a combo box. The Row Source property is set to the following value:

```
SELECT [Projects].[ProjectID], [Projects].[ProjectName] FROM Projects;
```

The bound column is set to the first part of the value, so the ID of the project is stored, but the name of the project is displayed in the combo box.

The EmployeeID field is also a foreign key. It links this table to the Employees table. The field has the following value in its Row Source property:

```
SELECT [Employees].[EmployeeID], [LastName] & ", " & [FirstName] AS FullName
FROM Employees ORDER BY [LastName] & ", " & [FirstName];
```

Two fields are output in this query. The first is the ID of the employee, which is the bound field. The other is a temporary concatenated field that is made up of the employee's last name followed by his or her first name. This is also how the query results are sorted.

The other field in this table, Role, is also a primary key. The field links this table to the Roles table. The Row Source property for this field is set to the following value:

```
SELECT [Roles].[Role] FROM Roles;
```

In this case, only one field is output from the query, so the bound column and the displayed column are the same as the Role field.

ProjectMilestones Table

The field specifications for the ProjectMilestones table are displayed in Table 10-3.

Table 10-3	Field Name	Field Type	Notes
The ProjectMilestones Table Field Specifications	ProjectMilestoneID	AutoNumber	Primary Key
	ProjectID	Number	Type = Long Integer, Foreign Key
	MilestoneName	Text	Length = 50
	PlannedStartDate	Date/Time	
	PlannedEndDate	Date/Time	
	LeadEmployee	Number	Type = Long Integer, Foreign Key
	MilestoneDescription	Memo	

The ProjectMilestoneID field is the primary key for this table. The ProjectID field is a foreign key that links this table to the Projects table. The field uses the Lookup properties, so it is displayed as a combo box. The Row Source property is set to this value:

```
SELECT [Projects].[ProjectID], [Projects].[ProjectName] FROM Projects;
```

The ID of the project is stored in the table since the Bound Column property is set to 1, but the name of the project is what the user sees. The Limit to List property is set to Yes.

The LeadEmployee field is also a foreign key. This field links this table to the Employees table. The field stores the person who is in charge of this particular milestone. The field is also displayed as a combo box and has the following value in the Row Source property:

```
SELECT [Employees].[EmployeeID], [LastName] & ", " & [FirstName] AS FullName
FROM Employees ORDER BY [LastName] & ", " & [FirstName];
```

So here the ID of the employee is stored in the table, but the concatenation of the first and last name of the employee is displayed to the user.

ProjectMilestoneSteps Table

The field specifications for the ProjectMilestoneSteps table are displayed in Table 10-4.

Table 10-4	Field Name	Field Type	Notes
The ProjectMilestone Steps Table Field Specifications	ProjectMilestoneStepID	AutoNumber	Primary Key
	ProjectMilestoneID	Number	Type = Long Integer, Foreign Key
	Step	Text	Length = 50
	LeadEmployee	Number	Type = Long Integer, Foreign Key
	Status	Number	Type = Byte

The ProjectMilestoneStepID field is the primary key in the Project-MilestoneSteps table, while the ProjectMilestoneID field is a foreign key that links this table with the ProjectMilestones table. The ProjectMilestoneID field is displayed as a combo box since the Lookup properties are used. The Row Source property is set to this value:

```
SELECT [ProjectMilestones].[ProjectMilestoneID],
[ProjectMilestones].[MilestoneName] FROM ProjectMilestones;
```

Therefore, the name of the milestone is displayed in the combo box, but the ID of the milestone is stored in this field.

The LeadEmployee stores the employee who is responsible for completing this step. The field is a foreign key that links to the Employees table. The user sees a combo box for this field because it uses the Lookup properties. The Row Source property has this value:

```
SELECT [Employees].[EmployeeID], [LastName] & ", " & [FirstName] AS FullName
FROM Employees ORDER BY [LastName] & ", " & [FirstName];
```

The Status field stores how close the step is to completion. This field is stored as a number so you can do calculations on the level of completeness of each step, but the user sees text that describes the level of completion. You can accomplish this by setting the Row Source Type property to Value List with the following Row Source:

```
0;"Not Started";50;"Midway";100;"Complete"
```

Byte is used as the field type since the values for this field stay below 255 and all values are whole numbers.

ProjectManagers Table

The field specifications for the ProjectManagers table are displayed in Table 10-5.

Table 10-5

The ProjectManagers Table Field Specifications

Field Name	Field Type	Notes
ProjectManagerID	AutoNumber	Primary Key
FirstName	Text	Length = 50
LastName	Text	Length = 50
Title	Text	Length = 50
Department	Text	Length = 50, Foreign Key
EmailAddress	Text	Length = 50
PhoneNumber	Text	Length = 50

The ProjectManagerID field is the primary key for the ProjectManagers table. The Department field is a foreign key and links the table to the Departments table. This field is displayed as a combo box and has the following value in the Row Source property:

```
SELECT [Departments].[Department] FROM Departments;
```

Just the name of the department is output by this query. The department field is used as the bound field and the field that is displayed in the combo box

Each of the project managers is assumed to be working for this example company. So, to make data entry easier, the EmailAddress field has the following input mask:

```
??????????????"@mycompany.com";0;_
```

This mask enables the user to enter just the name part of the email address without the domain name. An input mask is made up of three parts, each separated by semicolons. The first part is the mask itself, which in this example is the following:

```
??????????????"@mycompany.com"
```

The question marks mean that an optional character can be placed here. The text in quotes is a literal, so after the user enters the option part, the domain part is appended.

The second parameter of an input mask enables you to specify whether you want the mask stored with the record or just the data entered. A 0 means you want the mask stored also.

The third parameter indicates which character you want to use as the placeholder as the user is typing in the field. In this case, an underscore is used.

The PhoneNumber field also uses an input mask:

```
!\(999") "000\-0000;0;_
```

The exclamation point says that you want the mask to fill from right to left. A "\" is an escape character that indicates that the following character should be treated as a literal instead of its special value. The 9 stands for an optional number, while the 0 stands for a required number.

Employees Table

The field specifications for the Employees table are displayed in Table 10-6.

The EmployeeID field is the primary key for this table. It uniquely identifies each of the records. The Department field is a foreign key linking the Employees table to the Departments table. The Department field is also displayed to the user as a combo box by using the Lookup properties. The Row Source property is set to the following value:

```
SELECT [Departments].[Department] FROM Departments;
```

Table 10-6

The Employees Table Field Specifications

Field Name	Field Type	Notes
EmployeeID	AutoNumber	Primary Key
FirstName	Text	Length = 50
LastName	Text	Length = 50
Title	Text	Length = 50
Department	Text	Length = 50, Foreign Key
EmailAddress	Text	Length = 50
PhoneNumber	Text	Length = 50

The EmailAddress and PhoneNumber fields use the same input mask discussed in the ProjectManagers table.

Departments Table

The field specifications for the Departments table are displayed in Table 10-7.

The Department field is the primary key in this one-field table. The table is used to populate the Department combo boxes on the Project Manager and Employees forms.

Table 10-7

The Departments Table Field Specifications

Field Name	Field Type	Notes
Department	Text	Length = 50, Primary Key

Roles Table

The field specifications for the Roles table are displayed in Table 10-8.

The other one-field table in this database application is the Roles table. The primary key for this table is the Role field. This field is used to define the role of an employee for a project on the Projects form.

Table 10-8

The Roles Table Field Specifications

Field Name	Field Type	Notes
Role	Text	Length = 50, Primary Key

Forms

Switchboard Form

The Switchboard form is used to navigate through the forms and reports in the Project Management database application. It was created using the Switchboard Wizard, which is accessible within Access through the Tools/Database Utilities/Switchboard Manager menu item. Only the look and layout of the form produced with that wizard have been altered.

Projects Form

The Projects form is where the user is likely to spend most of his or her time, using it to manage the projects. The code on the form enables the user to navigate to the different pages on the form. The code also enables the user to open reports; add, delete, and search records; and perform a few other procedures.

The first code block fires when the user clicks on the General button in the footer:

```
Private Sub Command28_Click()
    DoCmd.GoToPage 1
End Sub
```

Using the Page Break control, the detail part of the form is made up of three pages. The GoToPage method with a parameter of one is used to send the user to the first page of the form:

```
DoCmd.GoToPage 1
```

This next procedure fires when the user clicks on the Participants button.

```
Private Sub Command29_Click()
    DoCmd.GoToPage 2
End Sub
```

The GoToPage method of the DoCmd object is used to change the focus of the detail section of the form to the second page, which contains the Project Participants subform:

```
DoCmd.GoToPage 2
```

If the user clicks on the Milestones button, the following code runs:

```
Private Sub Command30_Click()
    DoCmd.GoToPage 3
End Sub
```

Here the GoToPage method is used to change the view to the third page of the detail section, which contains the information on the milestones and steps for this project.

The next code block runs when the user clicks on the Summary button:

```
Private Sub Command31_Click()
    CurrentProjectID = [ProjectID]
    DoCmd.OpenReport "Project Summary", acViewPreview
End Sub
```

The Project Management database application contains a single-code module called PublicProcs. In that module, one public variable that is available to any of the procedures from anywhere within this application is declared. The variable is called CurrentProjectID and is used to pass the ID of the current project to the Project Summary report where it is used in code.

The first line of code in this procedure sets that value:

```
CurrentProjectID = [ProjectID]
```

You then open the Project Summary report in Preview mode where the variable you just set is used:

```
DoCmd.OpenReport "Project Summary", acViewPreview
```

The next procedure runs when the user clicks on the Detail button:

```
Private Sub Command42_Click()
    DoCmd.OpenReport "Projects", acViewPreview, , _
        "[ProjectID] = " & [ProjectID]
End Sub
```

The code uses the OpenReport method to open the Project report. The report is filtered so that only the current project is displayed:

```
DoCmd.OpenReport "Projects", acViewPreview, , _
    "[ProjectID] = " & [ProjectID]
```

The next code block fires when the Add button on the footer of the form is clicked:

```
Private Sub CommandAdd_Click()
    DoCmd.GoToRecord , , acNewRec
    [ProjectName].SetFocus
End Sub
```

The method uses the DoCmd object to move the record pointer onto a new record:

```
DoCmd.GoToRecord , , acNewRec
```

Now set the focus to the ProjectName field so that the user can start his or her data entry:

```
[ProjectName].SetFocus
```

The code that runs when the user clicks on the Delete button is shown here:

```
Private Sub CommandDelete_Click()
    On Error GoTo HandleError
    DoCmd.DoMenuItem acFormBar, acEditMenu, 8, , acMenuVer70
    DoCmd.DoMenuItem acFormBar, acEditMenu, 6, , acMenuVer70
    [ProjectName].SetFocus
    Exit Sub
HandleError:
    If Err.Number <> 2501 Then
        MsgBox Err.Number & " " & Err.Description
    End If
End Sub
```

You also need an error handler to trap for a known error:

```
On Error GoTo HandleError
```

Now delete the record:

```
DoCmd.DoMenuItem acFormBar, acEditMenu, 8, , acMenuVer70
DoCmd.DoMenuItem acFormBar, acEditMenu, 6, , acMenuVer70
```

and set the focus back to the ProjectName field:

```
[ProjectName].SetFocus
```

Exit the procedure if no errors have occurred:

```
Exit Sub
```

If an error occurs, then the code flows here:

```
HandleError:
```

The known error you want to trap for occurs when the user clicks No when asked to confirm the record deletion. You can check for that error number here:

```
If Err.Number <> 2501 Then
```

If that error is not the problem, report the error to the user through a Message Box dialog:

```
MsgBox Err.Number & " " & Err.Description
```

The next procedure runs when the Search button is clicked:

```
Private Sub CommandSearch_Click()
    Screen.PreviousControl.SetFocus
    DoCmd.DoMenuItem acFormBar, acEditMenu, 10, , acMenuVer70
End Sub
```

You can assume that the user wants to search the field that he or she was last at:

```
Screen.PreviousControl.SetFocus
```

Then open the Access Search dialog:

```
DoCmd.DoMenuItem acFormBar, acEditMenu, 10, , acMenuVer70
```

The last button on the footer is the Close button. The code behind it uses the DoCmd object to close the form:

```
Private Sub CommandClose_Click()
    DoCmd.Close
End Sub
```

Whenever the user moves to a different record or through code, you can move to a different record, and the Current event fires after the move is complete. On this form, you can use the Current event to display the name of the current project in the label at the header of the form:

```
Private Sub Form_Current()
    Label16.Caption = "Project: " & [ProjectName]
End Sub
```

Notice the concatenation that occurs between the first literal part of the text and the second field value part of the text:

```
Label16.Caption = "Project: " & [ProjectName]
```

You also have the same code in the Change event of the ProjectName field. This event fires every time the user changes the value in that field. The effect is that the user sees the text he or she is typing in the Project-Name field in the header as he or she is typing it:

```
Private Sub ProjectName_Change()
    Label16.Caption = "Project: " & ProjectName.Text
End Sub
```

The other procedure on this form occurs when the user double-clicks on the ProjectManagerID field:

```
Private Sub ProjectManagerID_DblClick(Cancel As Integer)
    If [ProjectManagerID] = 0 Or IsNull([ProjectManagerID]) Then
        DoCmd.OpenForm "Project Managers", , , , acFormAdd, acDialog
        [ProjectManagerID].Requery
    Else
        DoCmd.OpenForm "Project Managers", , , "[ProjectManagerID] = " _
            & [ProjectManagerID], , acDialog
    End If
End Sub
```

First, check to see if the ProjectManagerID field is empty:

```
If [ProjectManagerID] = 0 Or IsNull([ProjectManagerID]) Then
```

If it is, you can assume that the user wants to add a new project manager. The Project Manager form is opened in Add mode:

```
DoCmd.OpenForm "Project Managers", , , , acFormAdd, acDialog
```

Note that the Project Manager form is opened as a dialog. This means that the next line of code does not run until the user is completely done with the Project Manager form. Once he or she is done, you must repopulate the ProjectManagerID combo box:

```
[ProjectManagerID].Requery
```

If the ProjectManagerID field is not blank, the code flows to this point:

```
Else
```

In this case, open the Project Manager form and show the information for the project manager currently selected:

```
DoCmd.OpenForm "Project Managers", , , "[ProjectManagerID] = " _
        & [ProjectManagerID], , acDialog
```

The Projects menu also includes a few subforms. The first is the Project Participants subform that includes procedures that link this subform to other forms. The first fires when the user double-clicks on the Employee Name combo box.

```
Private Sub Employee_Name_DblClick(Cancel As Integer)
    If [EmployeeID] = 0 Or IsNull([EmployeeID]) Then
        DoCmd.OpenForm "Employees", , , , acFormAdd, acDialog
        [Employee_Name].Requery
    Else
        DoCmd.OpenForm "Employees", , , "[EmployeeID] = " _
            & [EmployeeID], , acDialog
    End If
End Sub
```

First check to see if the field is currently empty:

```
If [EmployeeID] = 0 Or IsNull([EmployeeID]) Then
```

If it is empty, you need to open the Employees form in Add mode:

```
DoCmd.OpenForm "Employees", , , , acFormAdd, acDialog
```

After the user is done with that form, repopulate the Employee Name combo box:

```
[Employee_Name].Requery
```

If the user selected a value in the Employee Name field, the code flows to this point. In this case, you would open the Employees form and have it display the information on the currently selected employee:

```
DoCmd.OpenForm "Employees", , , "[EmployeeID] = " _
        & [EmployeeID], , acDialog
```

The other code block on this subform fires when the user double-clicks on the Role field:

```
Private Sub Role_DblClick(Cancel As Integer)
    If [Role] = "" Or IsNull([Role]) Then
        DoCmd.OpenForm "Roles", , , , acFormAdd, acDialog
        [Role].Requery
```

```
      Else
          DoCmd.OpenForm "Roles", , , "[role] = """ _
              & [Role] & """", , acDialog
      End If
End Sub
```

First check to see if the user has left the field blank:

```
If [Role] = "" Or IsNull([Role]) Then
```

If the user has, you can assume that he or she wants to add a new record to the Roles table. Thus, the OpenForm method of the DoCmd object is used to open the Roles form, in Add mode, displayed as a dialog:

```
DoCmd.OpenForm "Roles", , , , acFormAdd, acDialog
```

After the user is done with that form, the Role combo box is repopulated:

```
[Role].Requery
```

If the Role field contains a value, you need to open the Roles form so that it displays that role:

```
DoCmd.OpenForm "Roles", , , "[role] = """ _
& [Role] & """", , acDialog
```

The other subform on the Projects form that contains any code is the ProjectMilestoneSteps subform. The form contains a single procedure that fires when the Lead Employee combo box is double-clicked. The procedure links this form to the Employees form:

```
Private Sub Lead_Employee_DblClick(Cancel As Integer)
    If [LeadEmployee] = 0 Or IsNull([LeadEmployee]) Then
        DoCmd.OpenForm "Employees", , , , acFormAdd, acDialog
        [Lead_Employee].Requery
    Else
        DoCmd.OpenForm "Employees", , , "[EmployeeID] = " _
            & [LeadEmployee], , acDialog
    End If
End Sub
```

The first line of code checks to see if the LeadEmployee field contains a value:

```
If [LeadEmployee] = 0 Or IsNull([LeadEmployee]) Then
```

If it doesn't, the user is indicating that he or she wants to add a new employee:

```
DoCmd.OpenForm "Employees", , , , acFormAdd, acDialog
```

After the user adds the new employee, repopulate the combo box so the value the user just entered will be found:

```
[Lead_Employee].Requery
```

If the field contains a value, then open the Employees form and have it show just the information for the selected employee:

```
DoCmd.OpenForm "Employees", , , "[EmployeeID] = " _
        & [LeadEmployee], , acDialog
```

Program Managers and Employees Forms

The Program Managers form and the Employees form contain the same procedures, so they are discussed in this section together. Both of these forms have procedures that enable the user to add, delete, and search the records. The procedures also close the form, link to the Departments table, and enable a new department to be added on the fly. The first procedure fires when the Add button is clicked:

```
Private Sub CommandAdd_Click()
    DoCmd.GoToRecord , , acNewRec
    [FirstName].SetFocus
End Sub
```

The DoCmd object provides us with much of the basic functionality available to the user through the Access menus, but you should always consider adding basic buttons to your forms because many users will never learn to find these items on the menus. Here the DoCmd object is used to add a record to the table:

```
DoCmd.GoToRecord , , acNewRec
```

Then set the focus to the FirstName field to ease the data entry task for the user:

```
[FirstName].SetFocus
```

The next procedure enables the user to delete a record.

```
Private Sub CommandDelete_Click()
    On Error GoTo HandleError
    DoCmd.DoMenuItem acFormBar, acEditMenu, 8, , acMenuVer70
    DoCmd.DoMenuItem acFormBar, acEditMenu, 6, , acMenuVer70
    [FirstName].SetFocus
    Exit Sub
HandleError:
    If Err.Number <> 2501 Then
        MsgBox Err.Number & " " & Err.Description
    End If
End Sub
```

Now start with an error handler:

```
On Error GoTo HandleError
```

and then delete the record:

```
DoCmd.DoMenuItem acFormBar, acEditMenu, 8, , acMenuVer70
DoCmd.DoMenuItem acFormBar, acEditMenu, 6, , acMenuVer70
```

After the record is deleted, move the focus back to the detail section so the user can continue with his or her work:

```
[FirstName].SetFocus
```

Then exit the procedure if an error did not occur:

```
Exit Sub
```

If one did occur, the code will flow to this label:

```
HandleError:
```

Now check to see if the user clicked No when prompted to confirm the record deletion:

```
If Err.Number <> 2501 Then
```

If that isn't the error, concatenate the number of the error with its message and display that to the user:

```
MsgBox Err.Number & " " & Err.Description
```

The next procedure fires when the Search button is pressed:

```
Private Sub CommandSearch_Click()
    Screen.PreviousControl.SetFocus
```

```
        DoCmd.DoMenuItem acFormBar, acEditMenu, 10, , acMenuVer70
End Sub
```

When the user clicks on the Search button, the focus moves to the Search button. However, the Search button itself is not what the user wants to search. He or she wants to search the field he or she was at before clicking on the Search button. The PreviousControl object is used to send the focus back to where the user was:

```
Screen.PreviousControl.SetFocus
```

Then open the built-in Search dialog:

```
DoCmd.DoMenuItem acFormBar, acEditMenu, 10, , acMenuVer70
```

The other button on the footer of these forms closes the form when it is pressed:

```
Private Sub CommandClose_Click()
    DoCmd.Close
End Sub
```

The next procedure fires when the user double-clicks on the Department combo box:

```
Private Sub Department_DblClick(Cancel As Integer)
    If [Department] = "" Or IsNull([Department]) Then
        DoCmd.OpenForm "Departments", , , , acFormAdd, acDialog
        [Department].Requery
    Else
        DoCmd.OpenForm "Departments", , _
        , "[Department] = """ & [Department] & """", , acDialog
    End If
End Sub
```

First, check to see whether the Department field is blank:

```
If [Department] = "" Or IsNull([Department]) Then
```

If it is, assume the user wants to add a new record:

```
DoCmd.OpenForm "Departments", , , , acFormAdd, acDialog
```

After the new record is added, the Department field is repopulated:

```
[Department].Requery
```

If the Department field contains a value, open the Departments form displaying that value:

```
DoCmd.OpenForm "Departments", , _
, "[Department] = """ & [Department] & """", , acDialog
```

One other procedure on the Departments form is in conjunction with the Department field: the NotInList event. If the LimitToList property is set to True for the combo box and the user enters a value that is not one of the items in the combo box, the NotInList event fires.

The event also gives you the opportunity to take your own action when the user types in a value that is not found, instead of just displaying the default Access message. The event receives two parameters. The first is the value entered by the user that was not found in the list. The second is the action you want to take, such as displaying the default message or not displaying any Access message.

Because the Department field is the only field in the Departments table, use this event to add the new value to the Departments table if the user desires. This keeps the user from having to go to a separate form to add a new value. The code for this procedure is as follows:

```
Private Sub Department_NotInList(NewData As String, Response As Integer)
    Dim MyDB As DAO.Database
    If MsgBox("The Department you entered does not exist. " _
        & "Would you like to add it as a new department?", vbYesNo, "Oops") _
        = vbYes Then
            Set MyDB = CurrentDb
            MyDB.Execute "insert into Departments (Department) " _
                & "values (""" & NewData & """)"
            Response = acDataErrContinue
            [Department].LimitToList = False
            DoCmd.DoMenuItem acFormBar, acRecordsMenu, acSaveRecord, , acMenuVer70
            [Department].Requery
            [Department].LimitToList = True
            [EmailAddress].SetFocus
    Else
        Response = acDataErrContinue
        [Department].Undo
    End If
End Sub
```

You also need a connection to the database because you are adding a new record to the Departments table:

```
Dim MyDB As DAO.Database
```

Then ask the user, through a message box, if he or she wants to add the new department. Note the parameters in this message box call. The first is the message itself, the second says to display Yes and No buttons in the message box, and the third parameter is the title for the message box. Note that in the If statement, you are checking to see if the user selected the Yes button:

```
If MsgBox("The Department you entered does not exist. " _
    & "Would you like to add it as a new department?", vbYesNo, "Oops") _
    = vbYes Then
```

If the user did select the Yes button, this means he or she wants to add a new record, and you need to connect to the database:

```
Set MyDB = CurrentDb
```

Use the Execute method of the Database object to insert a new record into the Departments table. Note that the value for the new department comes from the NewData parameter, which contains the value entered by the user in this field:

```
MyDB.Execute "insert into Departments (Department) " _
    & "values ("" & NewData & "")"
```

Then set the response so that Access doesn't display the default Not In List message:

```
Response = acDataErrContinue
```

You also need to temporarily turn off the LimitToList property:

```
[Department].LimitToList = False
```

so that you can save the current record:

```
DoCmd.DoMenuItem acFormBar, acRecordsMenu, acSaveRecord, , acMenuVer70
```

and repopulate the Department combo box:

```
[Department].Requery
```

After which, you can turn the LimitToList back on:

```
[Department].LimitToList = True
```

and set the focus to the next field:

```
[EmailAddress].SetFocus
```

If the user says that he or she doesn't want to add the new value, the code flows here:

```
Else
```

In this case, tell Access not to display the default Not In List message:

```
Response = acDataErrContinue
```

Also, clear out the entry made in this field by the user:

```
[Department].Undo
```

Departments and Roles Forms

The Departments and Roles forms contain the same code, so they are discussed together in this section. Both of these forms contain procedures that enable the user to add, delete, and search records, as well as to close the form. The first procedure is used to add a new record to the underlying table:

```
Private Sub CommandAdd_Click()
    DoCmd.GoToRecord , , acNewRec
    [Department].SetFocus
End Sub
```

The DoCmd object is used to move the record pointer to a new record:

```
DoCmd.GoToRecord , , acNewRec
```

Then set the focus to the first field on the form so the user can start adding information for this record:

```
[Department].SetFocus
```

The next procedure fires when the user clicks on the Delete button:

```
Private Sub CommandDelete_Click()
    On Error GoTo HandleError
    DoCmd.DoMenuItem acFormBar, acEditMenu, 8, , acMenuVer70
    DoCmd.DoMenuItem acFormBar, acEditMenu, 6, , acMenuVer70
    [Department].SetFocus
    Exit Sub
HandleError:
    If Err.Number <> 2501 Then
        MsgBox Err.Number & " " & Err.Description
    End If
End Sub
```

You will also need an error handler in this procedure:

```
On Error GoTo HandleError
```

Then use the DoCmd to delete the current record:

```
DoCmd.DoMenuItem acFormBar, acEditMenu, 8, , acMenuVer70
DoCmd.DoMenuItem acFormBar, acEditMenu, 6, , acMenuVer70
```

Also set the focus back to the field in the Detail section of the form:

```
[Department].SetFocus
```

If no error occurred during the deletion, exit the procedure:

```
Exit Sub
```

Otherwise, the code flows here:

```
HandleError:
```

Check for the user that canceled the record deletion:

```
If Err.Number <> 2501 Then
```

You can skip that error but show any other:

```
MsgBox Err.Number & " " & Err.Description
```

The next procedure fires when the Search button is pressed:

```
Private Sub CommandSearch_Click()
    Screen.PreviousControl.SetFocus
    DoCmd.DoMenuItem acFormBar, acEditMenu, 10, , acMenuVer70
End Sub
```

Start by moving the focus back to the previous field:

```
Screen.PreviousControl.SetFocus
```

and then let Access take over with its Search dialog:

```
DoCmd.DoMenuItem acFormBar, acEditMenu, 10, , acMenuVer70
```

The last procedure on these forms closes them when the user clicks on the Close button:

```
Private Sub CommandClose_Click()
    DoCmd.Close
End Sub
```

Reports

Summary Report

The Summary report is viewed by clicking on the Summary button located on the Projects form. It shows summary information about the current project, but the report does not have any underlying recordset. All the information displayed is set through code in the Open event, which fires when the report is first opened:

```
Private Sub Report_Open(Cancel As Integer)
    Dim MyDB As DAO.Database
    Dim RSProject As DAO.Recordset
    Dim RSMS As DAO.Recordset
    Dim RSSteps As DAO.Recordset
    Dim TotalDays As Long
    Dim DaysLeft As Long
    Dim TotalMS As Long
    Dim MSComplete As Long
    Dim TotalSteps As Long
    Dim StepsComplete As Long
    Set MyDB = CurrentDb
    Set RSProject = MyDB.OpenRecordset("Select ProjectName, StartDate, " _
        & "PredictedEndDate, ActualEndDate From Projects Where " _
        & "ProjectID = " & CurrentProjectID, dbOpenSnapshot)
    Label0.Caption = "Project " & RSProject("ProjectName") _
        & " Summary - Report Date: " & Format(Date, "Medium Date")
    Label1.Caption = "Start Date: " & RSProject("StartDate") _
        & "      Predicted End Date: " & RSProject("PredictedEndDate") _
        & "      Actual End Date: " & RSProject("ActualEndDate")
    TotalDays = DateDiff("d", RSProject("StartDate"), Date)
    DaysLeft = DateDiff("d", RSProject("PredictedEndDate"), Date)
    If DaysLeft <= 0 Then
        Label2.Caption = "Days Since Start: " & TotalDays _
            & "        Days Remaining: " & Abs(DaysLeft)
    Else
        Label2.Caption = "Days Since Start: " & TotalDays _
            & "        Days Over: " & DaysLeft
    End If
    Set RSMS = MyDB.OpenRecordset("Select Count(ProjectMilestoneID) as TheCount " _
        & "from ProjectMilestones Where ProjectID = " & CurrentProjectID, dbOpenSnapshot)
    TotalMS = RSMS("TheCount")
    Set RSMS = MyDB.OpenRecordset("Select Count(ProjectMilestoneID) as TheCount " _
        & "from [Milestone Summary with Project] Where CountOfStatus = SumOfStatus " _
        & "and ProjectID = " & CurrentProjectID, dbOpenSnapshot)
    MSComplete = RSMS("TheCount")
    Label4.Caption = "Total Number of Milestones: " & TotalMS _
        & "        Total Number of Milestones Complete: " & MSComplete
    Label5.Caption = "Milestone Percent Complete: " _
        & CInt((MSComplete / TotalMS) * 100) & "%"
    Set RSSteps = MyDB.OpenRecordset("Select Count(Step) as TheCount " _
        & "from [Project with Steps] Where " _
        & "ProjectID = " & CurrentProjectID, dbOpenSnapshot)
    TotalSteps = RSSteps("TheCount")
```

```
Set RSSteps = MyDB.OpenRecordset("Select Count(Step) as TheCount " _
    & "from [Project with Steps] Where " _
    & "Status = 100 and ProjectID = " & CurrentProjectID, dbOpenSnapshot)
StepsComplete = RSSteps("TheCount")
Label7.Caption = "Total Number of Steps: " & TotalSteps _
    & "        Total Number of Steps Complete: " & StepsComplete
Label8.Caption = "Steps Percent Complete: " _
    & CInt((StepsComplete / TotalSteps) * 100) & "%"
End Sub
```

The procedure starts with a variable declaration section. You need a database object:

```
Dim MyDB As DAO.Database
```

and a Recordset object that retrieves information about the current project:

```
Dim RSProject As DAO.Recordset
```

and one that retrieves information about the milestones in this project:

```
Dim RSMS As DAO.Recordset
```

and one that will retrieve information about the steps in the milestones in this project:

```
Dim RSSteps As DAO.Recordset
```

Then you have some numeric variables that will store values retrieved from the database:

```
Dim TotalDays As Long
Dim DaysLeft As Long
Dim TotalMS As Long
Dim MSComplete As Long
Dim TotalSteps As Long
Dim StepsComplete As Long
```

Now open your connection to the database:

```
Set MyDB = CurrentDb
```

Then retrieve data on the current project based on the CurrentProject-ID public variable. Remember that you set this variable before this report was called back on the Projects form:

```
Set RSProject = MyDB.OpenRecordset("Select ProjectName, StartDate, " _
    & "PredictedEndDate, ActualEndDate From Projects Where " _
    & "ProjectID = " & CurrentProjectID, dbOpenSnapshot)
```

The first label on the form needs to be set to the name of the project with today's date. Note that the Format function is used to format the date in the medium format:

```
Label0.Caption = "Project " & RSProject("ProjectName") _
        & " Summary - Report Date: " & Format(Date, "Medium Date")
```

The next label needs to have the dates that the project started, the end prediction, and the actual end:

```
Label1.Caption = "Start Date: " & RSProject("StartDate") _
    & "       Predicted End Date: " & RSProject("PredictedEndDate") _
    & "       Actual End Date: " & RSProject("ActualEndDate")
```

You need then to calculate the number of days that have passed since the project first started. The DateDiff function is used for this calculation. The first parameter in this function refers to the unit to use in coming up with the difference. You'll want the difference in days, so "d" is used. The second parameter is the date to subtract, and the third parameter is the date to be subtracted from. The function in this case returns the number of days that have passed from the start date of the project to the current system date:

```
TotalDays = DateDiff("d", RSProject("StartDate"), Date)
```

Now similarly calculate the number of days before the project ends:

```
DaysLeft = DateDiff("d", RSProject("PredictedEndDate"), Date)
```

If that value is 0 or less, that represents the number of days remaining before the project is scheduled to end:

```
If DaysLeft <= 0 Then
```

In this case, display the days since the start and the number of days until the end of the project. Note that the Abs function returns the absolute value of a number:

```
Label2.Caption = "Days Since Start: " & TotalDays _
        & "       Days Remaining: " & Abs(DaysLeft)
```

If the days left are greater than zero, the project is past its due date, so display slightly different text:

```
Label2.Caption = "Days Since Start: " & TotalDays _
        & "        Days Over: " & DaysLeft
```

Next, you need to retrieve the number of milestones in the project. This is done by using the Count function in a query based on the current project ID:

```
Set RSMS = MyDB.OpenRecordset("Select Count(ProjectMilestoneID) as TheCount " _
    & "from ProjectMilestones Where ProjectID = " & CurrentProjectID, dbOpenSnapshot)
```

Then store that count in a variable:

```
TotalMS = RSMS("TheCount")
```

Next, you need to retrieve the number of milestones that are complete. A milestone is complete if all the steps in the milestone are complete. To do this, you need a couple of queries. The first is called Milestone Summary and has the following *Structured Query Language* (SQL):

```
SELECT ProjectMilstoneSteps.ProjectMilestoneID,
Count(ProjectMilstoneSteps.Status)
AS CountOfStatus, Sum([ProjectMilstoneSteps].[Status])/100 AS SumOfStatus
FROM ProjectMilstoneSteps GROUP BY
ProjectMilstoneSteps.ProjectMilestoneID;
```

This query groups together the steps based on the milestone they go with. It then outputs the count of those steps and the sum of those steps divided by 100. Remember that a completed step is given the value of 100. Thus, if you divide that completed step by 100, you get the amount completed. If the count of steps is equal to this sum, you have a completed milestone. This query is then used by the Milestone Summary with the Project query:

```
SELECT ProjectMilestones.ProjectID,
[Milstone Summary].ProjectMilestoneID, [Milstone Summary].CountOfStatus,
[Milstone Summary].SumOfStatus FROM [Milstone Summary]
INNER JOIN ProjectMilestones
ON [Milstone Summary].ProjectMilestoneID =
ProjectMilestones.ProjectMilestoneID;
```

This query takes the results of the last query and adds to it the ID of the project that the milestone is from. Therefore, this query, based on a query, is then used in the following line of code. Here you count the number of milestones that have the current project ID and that show all steps as being complete:

```
Set RSMS = MyDB.OpenRecordset("Select Count(ProjectMilestoneID) as TheCount " _
    & "from [Milestone Summary with Project] Where CountOfStatus = SumOfStatus " _
    & "and ProjectID = " & CurrentProjectID, dbOpenSnapshot)
```

Then store that value in a variable:

```
MSComplete = RSMS("TheCount")
```

and use it as well as the total number of milestones in the next caption:

```
Label4.Caption = "Total Number of Milestones: " & TotalMS _
        & "        Total Number of Milestones Complete: " & MSComplete
```

Next, calculate and display the percent of the steps that are complete. Note the use of the CInt function, which chops the fraction of the number off:

```
Label5.Caption = "Milestone Percent Complete: " _
        & CInt((MSComplete / TotalMS) * 100) & "%"
```

Now you need to retrieve information about the steps in this project. Also retrieve the count of all the steps for the project based on the query discussed earlier:

```
Set RSSteps = MyDB.OpenRecordset("Select Count(Step) as TheCount " _
    & "from [Project with Steps] Where " _
    & "ProjectID = " & CurrentProjectID, dbOpenSnapshot)
```

and set the value retrieved into a variable:

```
TotalSteps = RSSteps("TheCount")
```

Next, retrieve the count of the steps from the same query based on the same project, but this time only those that are marked as complete. A step is complete if the status is set to 100:

```
Set RSSteps = MyDB.OpenRecordset("Select Count(Step) as TheCount " _
    & "from [Project with Steps] Where " _
    & "Status = 100 and ProjectID = " & CurrentProjectID, dbOpenSnapshot)
```

Then store that in another variable:

```
StepsComplete = RSSteps("TheCount")
```

Those values are placed in the next label:

```
Label7.Caption = "Total Number of Steps: " & TotalSteps _
    & "          Total Number of Steps Complete: " & StepsComplete
```

The last label is set to the percent of steps that are marked as complete.

```
Label8.Caption = "Steps Percent Complete: " _
    & CInt((StepsComplete / TotalSteps) * 100) & "%"
```

Projects Report

The Projects report displays all the information about the project. The report is accessed through the Detail button on the footer of the Products form. The main report is based directly on the Products table. The report also contains subreports that display the ProjectParticipants table through the ProjectParticipants subreport, the ProjectMilestones table though the ProjectMilestones subreport, and the ProjectMilestoneSteps table through the ProjectMilestoneSteps subreport.

The Project with Project Managers Report

The Project with Project Managers report displays the names of each of the Project Managers with information about the project. The report is based on the Project with Project Managers query, which has the following syntax:

```
SELECT Projects.ProjectName, Projects.ProjectStatus,
[LastName] & ", " & [FirstName] AS Name, ProjectManagers.EmailAddress,
ProjectManagers.PhoneNumber FROM ProjectManagers
INNER JOIN Projects ON
ProjectManagers.ProjectManagerID = Projects.ProjectManagerID;
```

The query concatenates the project manager's name into a single field. It also joins together the Project table with the ProjectManagers table. Note that an Inner Join is used, so only records that are in both tables will appear. In other words, if a project doesn't have a Project Manager, it won't be part of this report. If the Project Manager isn't managing any projects, they won't appear on this report.

The Steps Not Complete Report

The Steps Not Complete report groups information by project and then by milestone. It also shows any steps that are not yet complete, along with the person who is to complete that step. The Steps Not Complete report is based on the Steps Not Complete query, which has the following syntax:

```
SELECT Projects.ProjectName, ProjectMilestones.MilestoneName,
ProjectMilstoneSteps.Step, ProjectMilstoneSteps.LeadEmployee,
ProjectMilstoneSteps.Status FROM Projects
INNER JOIN (ProjectMilestones INNER JOIN
ProjectMilstoneSteps ON
ProjectMilestones.ProjectMilestoneID =
ProjectMilstoneSteps.ProjectMilestoneID)
ON Projects.ProjectID = ProjectMilestones.ProjectID
WHERE (((ProjectMilstoneSteps.Status)<>100));
```

Note that the query joins three tables together. The Projects table is joined with the ProjectMilestones table, which is then joined with the ProjectMilestoneSteps table. The Where clauses then just returns steps that aren't complete, as indicated by the Status field not containing the value 100.

CHAPTER 11

Students, Teachers, and Courses

ON THE CD:

Students, Teachers and Courses.mdb

Managing the Functionality of an Educational Institution

In this chapter, we will examine the Students, Teachers, and Courses database application. This database provides some of the functionality needed to run a school. The database enables the user to create students and enroll the students in programs. The student then takes courses and receives grades in a program. The user can manage courses, including where and when they are held. The user can also manage instructors and the courses that they teach. As you review this database application, pay particular attention to the code used to calculate the grade point average and the code that reports the courses the student needs to complete a program.

Students, Teachers and Courses Database

Sample Walk-through

When the user first enters the application, the menu system displayed in Figure 11-1 is seen. The main menu contains three submenus where the user selects the form or report to open. The first submenu is called Main Forms. This submenu contains the primary data entry forms in the application, such as Students and Instructors. The second submenu is called Support Forms. It contains buttons that link to the forms that are not the primary components of this application, such as Buildings and Rooms. The third submenu enables the user to access the four reports available in this application.

The first item on the Main Forms submenu is the Students button. Clicking on this button shows the user the Students form in Figure 11-2. The name of the student is in the header, no matter which page of the form the user is working on. Toward the top of the detail section of this page is the student's GPA, that is, the grade point average across all the courses he or she has taken at the school.

Figure 11-1

The menu from the Students, Teachers and Courses database application

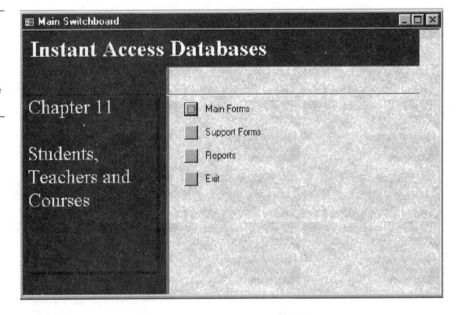

The form has three pages, accessible through the buttons in the middle of the footer. This is the General page. Clicking on the Programs button takes the user to the Programs page, shown in Figure 11-3.

The student can enter into many programs, so this page contains a sub-form that displays information about the program in which the student is involved. The subform also displays the Core GPA. This is the grade point average across required courses in this program.

Each of the programs also can require elective credit hours. The sub-form shows how many elective hours the student has remaining. Finally, the subform lists the core or required courses the student still needs to take to complete this program. By clicking on the Courses button, the user sees the Courses page shown in Figure 11-4.

The Courses page displays all the courses that the student has taken or is going to take at this school. Back on the Main Forms submenu, the user can click on the Programs button to see the form displayed in Figure 11-5.

As you saw on the Students form, students can enter programs which are groups of courses that, when taken, result in some degree or certification. On the General page of this form, the user supplies the basic information about the program. By clicking on the Core button, the user sees the Core page shown in Figure 11-6.

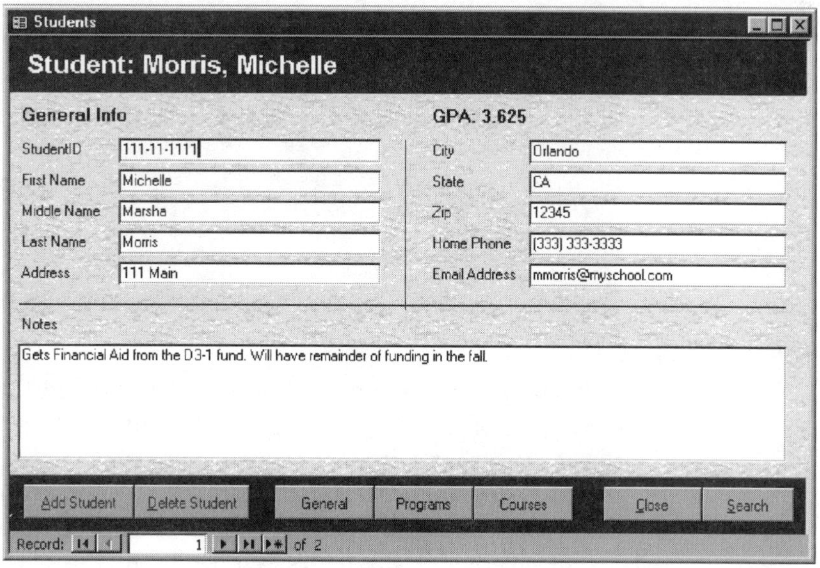

Figure 11-2

The General page of the Students form

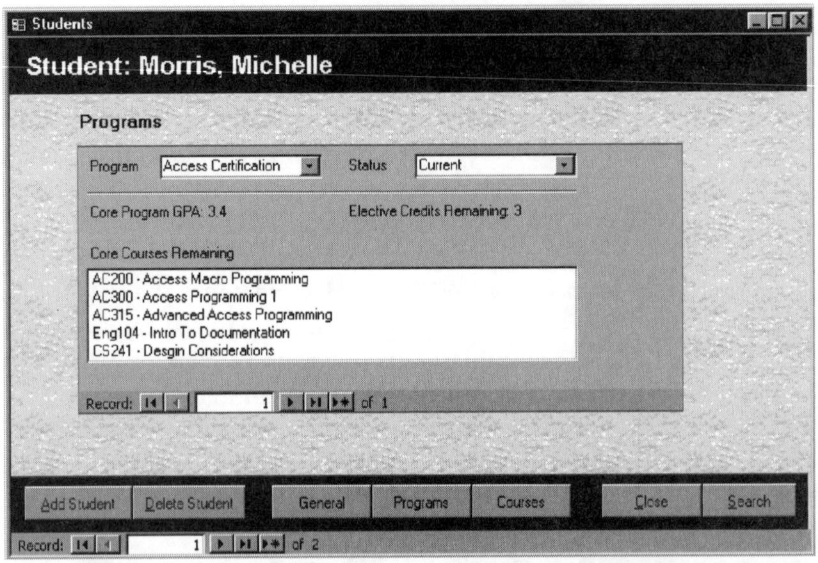

Figure 11-3

The Programs
page of the
Students form

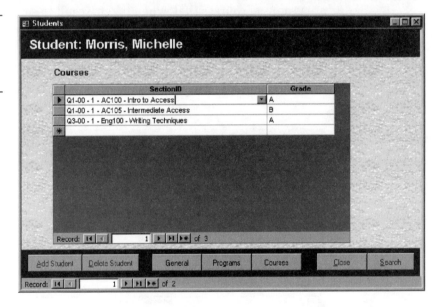

Figure 11-4

The Courses page
of the Students
form

Each program can have required courses, and these are shown on the Core page of the Programs form. This information is used to display all the courses that a student still needs to take to complete a program. Figure 11-7 shows the Electives page of the Programs form.

As you saw on the General page of this form, the user enters the number of elective credit hours required. On the Electives page, the user

Figure 11-5

The General page
of the Programs
form

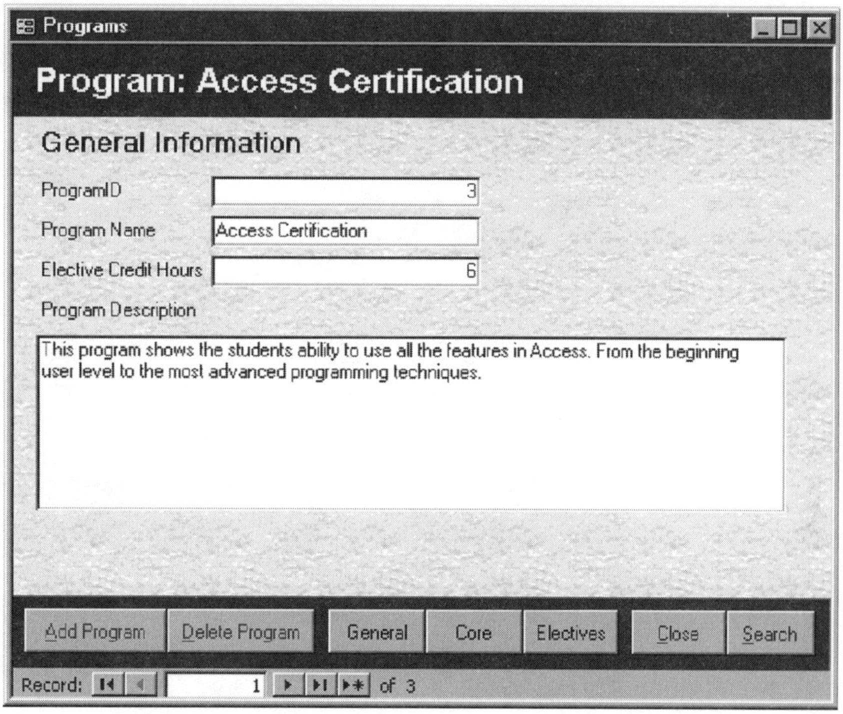

defines which courses the student can choose from to satisfy an elective requirement. The user can double-click on any of the courses listed here or on the Core page to link to the Courses form, which is displayed in Figure 11-8.

The Courses form is also accessible through the Main Forms submenu. Through this form, the user enters in all the information for all the courses offered at the school. Particular classes of a course are offered during a Term. This is done through the Terms form shown in Figure 11-9.

A term is a period of time during which courses are offered. At the top of the form, the user defines the information about the term. They then select all the courses that are being offered in that term. These offerings are what the student signs up for to take a course. When the user double-clicks on the Course, Instructor, or Room fields they are taken to the corresponding form. The Instructor form, which is also accessible through the Main Forms menu, is shown in Figure 11-10.

Figure 11-6

The Core page of
the Programs
form

Figure 11-6

The Core page of
the Programs
form

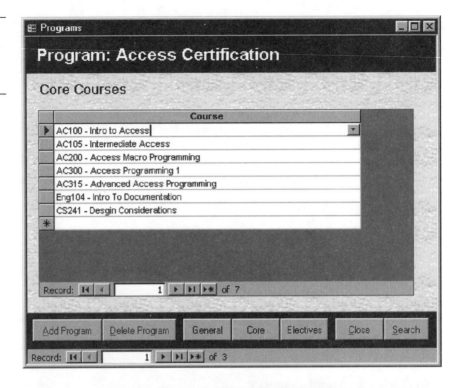

Figure 11-7

The Electives
page of the
Programs form

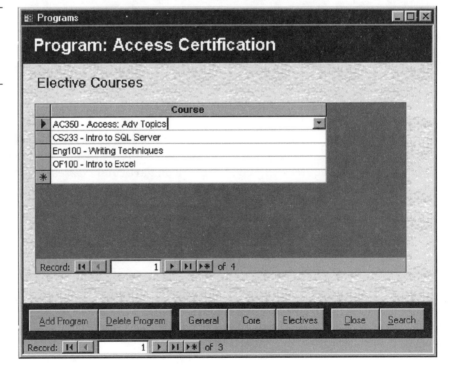

Figure 11-8

The Courses form

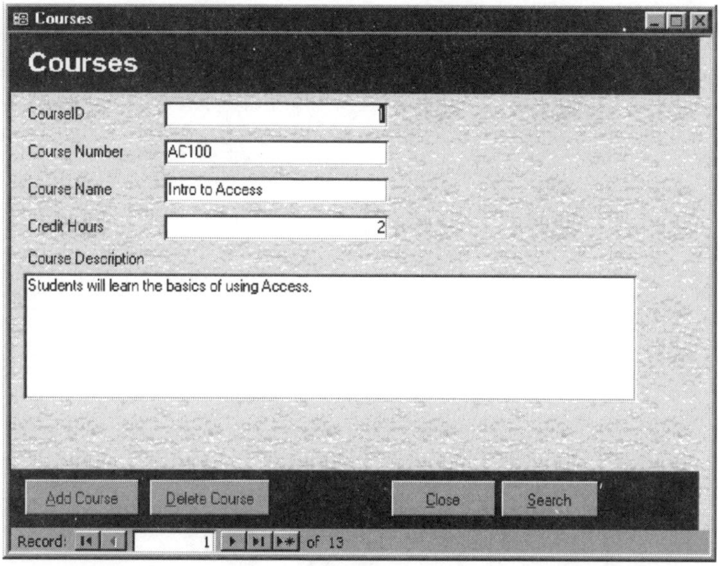

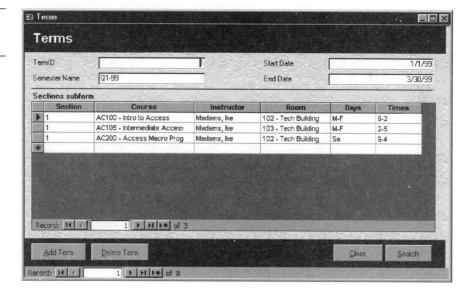

Figure 11-9

The Term form

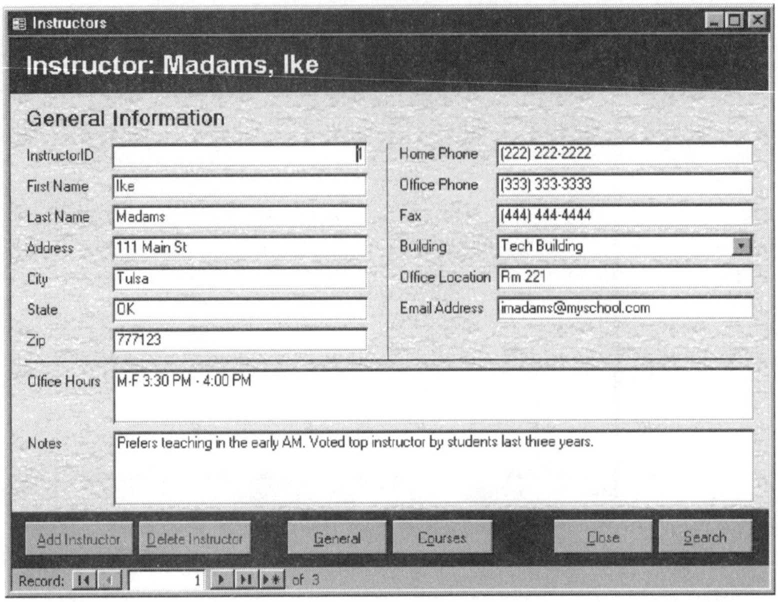

Figure 11-10

The General page
of the Instructors
form

The Instructor form has two pages. The first is the General page, which
enables the user to enter the basic information about the instructor. The
second page is accessible to the user by clicking on the Courses button.
This page is displayed in Figure 11-11.

Each of the instructors can teach many classes, so the Courses page
contains a subform that enables the user to select from all the courses
available that the instructor teaches. This listing also links to the Courses
form. Three more forms are available to the user through the Support
Forms submenu. The first is the Buildings form shown in Figure 11-12.

Each of the classes is held in a room that is located in a building. This
form enables the user to enter the building information. This data also is
used on the Instructors form to indicate the location of the instructor's
office.

The next form accessible through the Support Forms submenu is the
Rooms form. This form is displayed in Figure 11-13.

This form is where the user enters room information, which is used
when adding a class to a term. The form links to the Buildings form by a
double-click action on the Building combo box.

The last form in this database application is the Grades form shown in
Figure 11-14. When the student completes a class, a grade is received.
When the GPA is calculated, that grade is converted into its point value.
The user uses this form to enter the point value for each of the grades.

Figure 11-11

The Courses page of the Instructors form

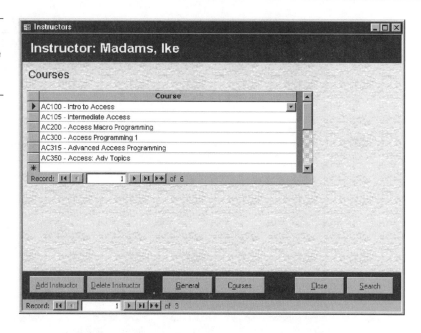

Figure 11-12

The Buildings form

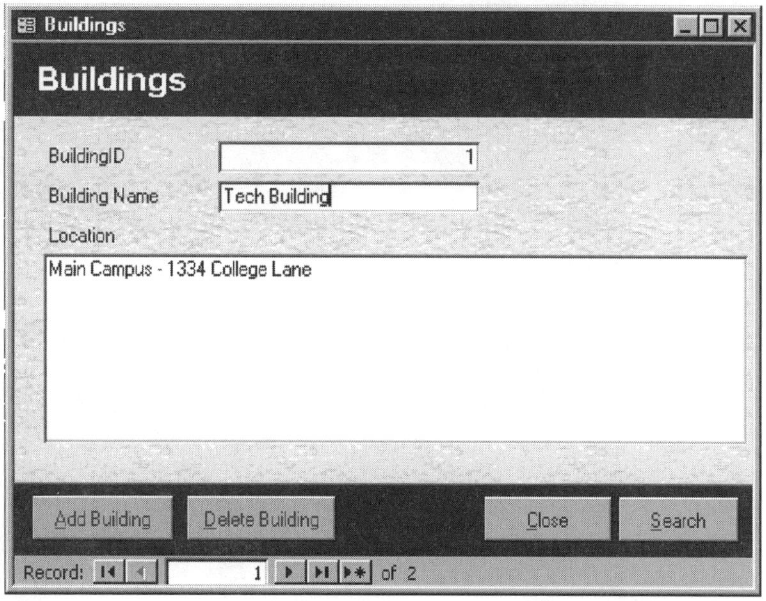

Figure 11-13
The Rooms form

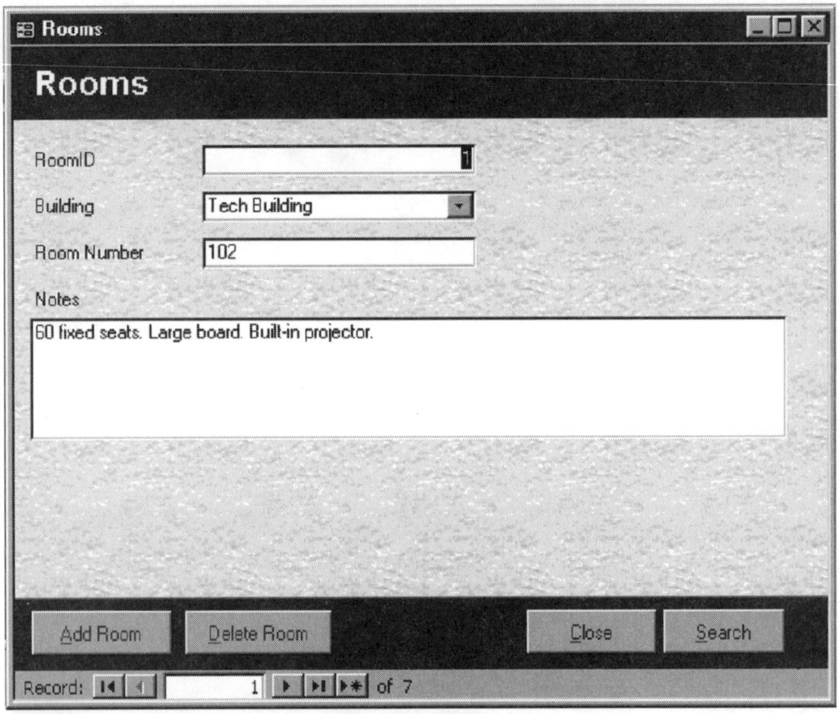

Figure 11-14
The Grades form

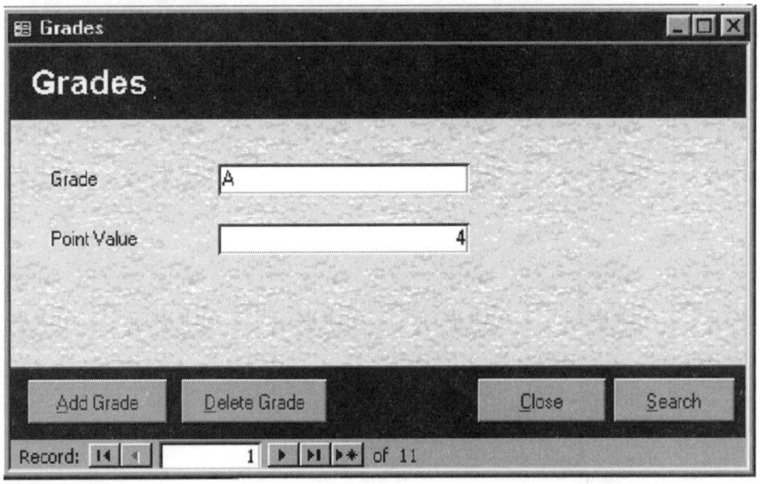

The last submenu is called Reports and enables the user to select from one of the four reports available in this database application. The first is shown in Figure 11-15.

The Program report enables the user to print out a list of all the programs. Each program contains two subreports. The first shows the required courses for the program and the second shows the elective courses in this program. The second report is called Term Information and is displayed in Figure 11-16. When the user selects this report, a specific term to report on must be supplied. The report then shows the information for that term as well as all the class offerings.

The third report is called Course Catalog and is displayed in Figure 11-17. The Course Catalog report enables the user to print out information on all the courses. This report then can be distributed as a Course Catalog.

The final report is displayed in Figure 11-18. The Instructor Courses report combines information about the instructors and the courses they teach.

Figure 11-15

The Programs report

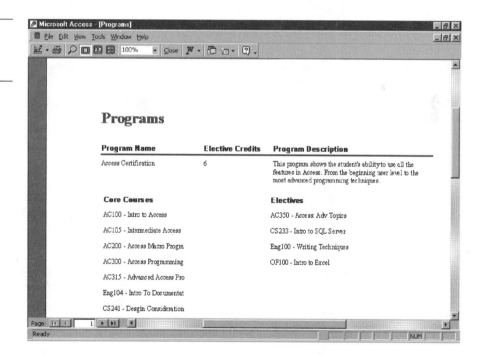

Figure 11-16

The Term
Information
report

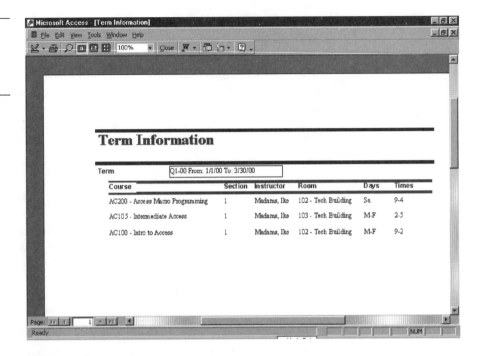

Figure 11-17

The Course
Catalog report

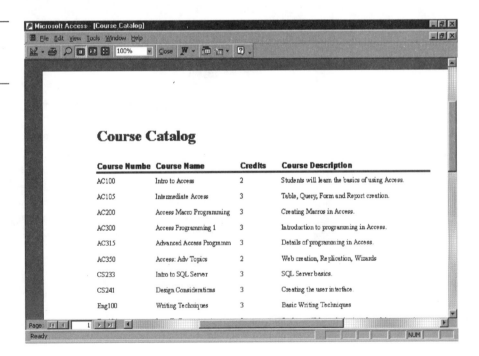

Figure 11-18

The Instructor
Courses report

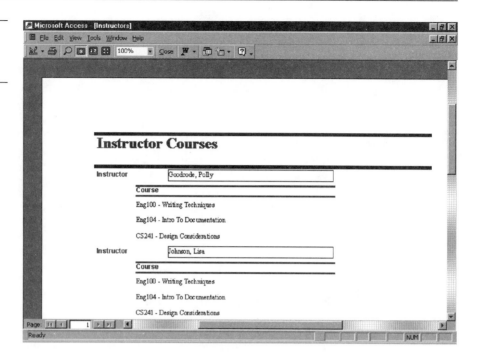

Table Definitions and Relationships

Students Table

One of the top-level tables in this database is the Students table. This table stores the general information about the student. The table is linked to, directly or indirectly, by many of the other tables in this database.

StudentPrograms Table

The StudentPrograms table stores information about which programs the students are in. The table is in a one-to-many relationship with the Students table. Each student can be in many programs. The table is also in a one-to-many relationship with the Programs table. Each program can have many students. Therefore, the Students table and the Programs table are in a many-to-many relationship with the StudentPrograms table connecting the two.

StudentCourses Table

The StudentCourses table tracks the classes that the student has taken and the grades they have earned. The table is in a one-to-many relationship with the Students table. Each student can take many classes. The table is also in a one-to-many relationship with the Sections table. A section is a course offering, so many students can participate in a class. That means that the StudentCourses table and the Sections table are in a many-to-many relationship. Each student can be in many sections and each section can have many students.

Programs Table

Programs are groups of courses that, when all are taken, satisfy a requirement for degree or certification. The Programs table stores the top-level information about the programs.

ProgramRequiredCourses Table

Each of the programs can have many courses that are required. The ProgramRequiredCourses table stores that information. The table is in a one-to-many relationship with the Programs table because each program can require many courses. The table is also in a one-to-many relationship with the Courses table since each course can be offered in many programs. Therefoer, the Programs table and the Courses table are in a many-to-many relationship with this table satisfying the connecting table role.

ProgramElectiveCourses Table

Each of the programs also can have a list of options, elective courses that the student can take. That information is stored in the ProgramElectiveCourses table. The table is in a one-to-many relationship with the Programs table because each program can have many electives. And the table is also in a one-to-many relationship with the Courses table because many programs can have the same course as an elective. So for a second time, the Programs and Courses tables are in a many-to-many relationship.

Courses Table

The Courses table stores the general information about a course at the school. This table is used then in many other relationships in the database.

Terms Table

Courses are offered to students through a section, which occurs during a term. A term is like a semester. It is a period of time during which the classes are offered. The Terms table stores that information.

Sections Table

The Sections table displays the specific information about when a course is offered. The table is in a one-to-many relationship with the Courses table because each course can be in many sections. The table is also in a one-to-many relationship with the Terms table because many sections can be offered during a term. So once again, the Courses table is a many-to-many relationship, this time with the Terms table through the Sections table. The table also relates to the Instructors table and the Rooms table in a one-to-many relationship.

Instructors Table

The Instructors table contains the top-level information about the instructors. The table is in a one-to-many relationship with the Rooms table. Each instructor has an office in a single room, but each room can house more than one instructor.

InstructorCourses Table

Each of the instructors can teach many courses. The InstructorCourses table stores the information about what instructors teach. The table is in a one-to-many relationship with the Instructors and Courses tables. So the Instructors table and the Courses table are in a many-to-many relationship with each other.

Buildings Table

Each class is held in a room that is in a building. Each instructor has an office that is in a building. The Buildings table stores information about those buildings.

Rooms Table

Each of the buildings can have numerous rooms. The Rooms table stores information about those rooms. The table is in a one-to-many relationship with the Buildings table.

Grades Table

The final table in this database is the Grades table. The Grades table stores the letter grade and its corresponding point value for calculating the GPA of a student.

Field Specifications

Students Table

The field specifications for the Students table are displayed in Table 11-1.

The StudentID field is the primary key for the table. It could have been set up as an AutoNumber field, but instead was created as a text field to give the user the capability to use some other numbering system such as the student's Social Security Number for the identifying identification. The rest of the fields store information about the student.

StudentPrograms Table

The field specifications for the StudentPrograms table are displayed in Table 11-2. The StudentProgramID field is the primary key for the table.

	Field Name	Field Type	Notes
Table 11-1	StudentID	Text	Length = 50, Primary Key
Students Table	FirstName	Text	Length = 50
Field	MiddleName	Text	Length = 50
Specifications	LastName	Text	Length = 50
	Address	Text	Length = 100
	City	Text	Length = 50
	State	Text	Length = 50
	Zip	Text	Length = 50
	Phone	Text	Length = 50
	EmailAddress	Text	Length = 50
	Notes	Memo	

	Field Name	Field Type	Notes
Table 11-2	StudentProgramID	AutoNumber	Primary Key
StudentPrograms Table Field Specifications	StudentID	Text	Length = 50, Foreign Key
	ProgramID	Number	Type = Long, Foreign Key
	Status	Text	Length = 50

It is an AutoNumber field so it is automatically populated when a new record is added to the table. The StudentID field is a foreign key that links this table to the Students table.

The ProgramID field is also a foreign key that links this table to the Programs table. The field is displayed as a combo box and has the following SQL in the Row Source property:

```
SELECT [Programs].[ProgramID], [Programs].[ProgramName] FROM Programs;
```

The first field is the bound column, so the table will store the ID of the program but the user will see the name of the program. The Status field is also set to be displayed as a combo box. The Row Source Type property is set to Value List. The Row Source property is set to this value:

```
"Current";"Dropped";"Suspended";"On Hold";"Graduated"
```

The Limit To List property is set to Yes so the user must select one of these values in the combo box list.

StudentCourses Table

The field specifications for the StudentCourses table are displayed in Table 11-3. The StudentCourseID field is the primary key for the table. The StudentID field links this table to the Students table, so it is a foreign key.

The SectionID field is also a foreign key. It links this table to the Sections table. The field is set to be displayed as a combo box with the following value in the Row Source property:

```
SELECT [Sections].[SectionID], [TermName] & " - " & [SectionName]
& " - " & [CourseNumber] & " - " & [CourseName] AS Expr1
FROM Courses INNER JOIN (Terms INNER JOIN Sections ON
[Terms].[TermID]=[Sections].[TermID]) ON
```

Table 11-3	Field Name	Field Type	Notes
StudentCourses Table Field Specifications	StudentCourseID	AutoNumber	Primary Key
	StudentID	Text	Length = 50, Foreign Key
	SectionID	Number	Type = Long, Foreign Key
	Grade	Text	Length = 50

```
[Courses].[CourseID]=[Sections].[CourseID] ORDER BY
[TermName] & " - " & [SectionName] & " - " & [CourseNumber] & " - " & [CourseName];
```

The property needs to have a fairly complex query because you need to display extended information to the user in this combo box, but the query outputs just two fields. The first is the ID for the section, which is stored in this table. The second is a concatenation of the term that the section is being offered along with the name of the section, the number of the course, and the name of the course. The user will know exactly for what the student is being signed up. The join is needed because the data required comes from three tables.

Programs Table

The field specifications for the Programs table are displayed in Table 11-4. The ProgramID field is the primary key for the table. The ElectiveCreditHours field stores the number of elective credit hours that are required to complete this program.

Table 11-4	Field Name	Field Type	Notes
Programs Table Field Specifications	ProgramID	AutoNumber	Primary Key
	ProgramName	Text	Length = 50
	ElectiveCreditHours	Number	Type = Integer
	ProgramDescription	Memo	

ProgramRequiredCourses Table

The field specifications for the ProgramRequiredCourses table are displayed in Table 11-5. The ProgramRequiredCourseID field is the primary key for the table. The ProgramID is a foreign key that links this table to the Programs table in a one-to-many relationship.

The CourseID field is also a foreign key that links this table to the Courses table. The field is displayed as a combo box. It has the following value in the Row Source property:

```
SELECT [Courses].[CourseID], [CourseNumber] & " - " & [CourseName]
AS Expr1 FROM Courses ORDER BY [CourseNumber] & " - " & [CourseName];
```

The ID of the course is stored with the table. The user sees a concatenation of the number of the course with the name of the course. The list is sorted by this concatenated value.

	Field Name	Field Type	Notes
Table 11-5 ProgramRequired Courses Table Field Specifications	ProgramRequiredCourseID		AutoNumber Primary Key
	ProgramID	Number	Type = Long, Foreign Key
	CourseID	Number	Type = Long, Foreign Key

ProgramElectiveCourses Table

The field specifications for the ProgramElectiveCourses table are displayed in Table 11-6. The ProgramElectiveCourseID field is the primary key for the table. The ProgramID is a foreign key that links this table to the Programs table.

	Field Name	Field Type	Notes
Table 11-6 ProgramElective Courses Table Field Specifications	ProgramElectiveCourseID		AutoNumber Primary Key
	ProgramID	Number	Type = Long, Foreign Key
	CourseID	Number	Type = Long, Foreign Key

The CourseID field is another foreign key that links this table to the Courses table. The CourseID field is displayed as a combo box with the following value in the Row Source property:

```
SELECT [Courses].[CourseID], [CourseNumber] & " - " & [CourseName]
AS Expr1 FROM Courses ORDER BY [CourseNumber] & " - " & [CourseName];
```

The ID of the course is stored with the table. The user sees a concatenation of the number of the course with the name of the course. The list is sorted by this concatenated value.

Courses Table

The field specifications for the Courses table are displayed in Table 11-7. The CourseID field is the primary key for this table.

The CreditHours field stores the number of credit hours that this course counts for. This value then is used with the grade value when calculating the GPA.

	Field Name	Field Type	Notes
Table 11-7 Courses Table Field Specifications	CourseID	AutoNumber	Primary Key
	CourseNumber	Text	Length = 15
	CourseName	Text	Length = 50
	CreditHours	Number	Type = Integer
	CourseDescription	Memo	

Terms Table

The field specifications for the Terms table are displayed in Table 11-8. The TermID field is the primary key for this table. The rest of the fields store information about the term.

Table 11-8	Field Name	Field Type	Notes
Terms Table Field Specifications	TermID	AutoNumber	Primary Key
	TermName	Text	Length = 50
	StartDate	Date/Time	
	CourseDescription	Date/Time	

Sections Table

The field specifications for the Sections table are displayed in Table 11-9. The SectionID is the primary key for this table. The table also contains four foreign keys that link this table with many other tables in this database.

Table 11-9	Field Name	Field Type	Notes
Sections Table Field Specifications	SectionID	AutoNumber	Primary Key
	SectionName	Text	Length = 50
	TermID	Number	Type = Long, Foreign Key
	CourseID	Number	Type = Long, Foreign Key
	InstructorID	Number	Type = Long, Foreign Key
	RoomID	Number	Type = Long, Foreign Key
	Days	Text	Length = 50
	Times	Text	Length = 50

Remember that a section is actually an offering of a course. That offering is made during a specific term. So the TermID field links this table to the Terms table. The field is displayed as a combo box with the following Row Source value:

```
SELECT [Terms].[TermID], [Terms].[TermName] FROM Terms;
```

So the ID of the term is stored while the name of the term is displayed to the user. Each section is based on a specific course. The CourseID field is a foreign key that links this table to the Courses table. Its Row Source property is set to this value:

```
SELECT [Courses].[CourseID], [CourseNumber] & " - " & [CourseName] AS Expr1
FROM Courses ORDER BY [CourseNumber] & " - " & [CourseName];
```

The ID of the course is stored, but the user sees the number and name of the course. Each of the sections is taught by a single instructor, so the InstructorID field links this table to the Instructors table. It has this value in the Row Source property:

```
SELECT [Instructors].[InstructorID], [LastName] & ", " & [FirstName] AS Expr1
FROM Instructors ORDER BY [LastName] & ", " & [FirstName];
```

The user sees the name of the instructor while the ID of the instructor is stored in the database. Finally, the section is held at a particular location. The RoomID field provides that information, thus linking this table to the Rooms table. It is also displayed as a combo box with the following Row Source property value:

```
SELECT [Rooms].[RoomID], [RoomNumber] & " - " & [BuildingName] AS Expr1
FROM Buildings INNER JOIN Rooms ON
[Buildings].[BuildingID]=[Rooms].[BuildingID];
```

Note that the query displays the room number with its building name. The user will pick the correct room in case a room is repeated in two buildings.

Instructors Table

The field specifications for the Instructors table are displayed in Table 11-10. The InstructorID is the primary key for this table.

The BuildingID is a foreign key that links this table to the Buildings table. The field is displayed to the user as a combo box. The Row Source property is set to this SQL statement:

```
SELECT [Buildings].[BuildingID], [Buildings].[BuildingName] FROM Buildings;
```

The ID of the building is stored in the database, but the name of the building is displayed to the user. The rest of the fields in this table store general information about the instructor.

Table 11-10

Instructors Table Field Specifications

Field Name	Field Type	Notes
InstructorID	AutoNumber	Primary Key
FirstName	Text	Length = 50
LastName	Text	Length = 50
Address	Text	Length = 100
City	Text	Length = 50
State	Text	Length = 50
Zip	Text	Length = 50
HomePhone	Text	Length = 50
OfficePhone	Text	Length = 50
Fax	Text	Length = 50
BuildingID	Number	Type = Long, Foreign Key
OfficeLocation	Text	Length = 50
OfficeHours	Memo	
EmailAddress	Text	Length = 50
Notes	Memo	

InstructorCourses Table

The field specifications for the InstructorCourses table are displayed in Table 11-11. The InstructorCourses field is the primary key for this table.

Table 11-11

InstructorCourses Table Field Specifications

Field Name	Field Type	Notes
InstructorCourses	AutoNumber	Primary Key
InstructorID	Number	Type = Long, Foreign Key
CourseID	Number	Type = Long, Foreign Key

The InstructorID field is a foreign key that links this table to the Instructors table.

The CourseID field is also a foreign key. It links this table to the Courses table. The field is displayed to the user as a combo box. The Row Source property is set to this value:

```
SELECT [Courses].[CourseID], [CourseNumber] & " - " & [CourseName] AS Expr1 FROM Courses;
```

The ID of the course is stored in the database, but the user sees the number and name of the course.

Buildings Table

The field specifications for the Buildings table are displayed in Table 11-12. The BuildingID is set as the primary key for this table. The rest of the fields store descriptive information about the building.

Table 11-12	Field Name	Field Type	Notes
Buildings Table Field Specifications	BuildingID	AutoNumber	Primary Key
	BuildingName	Text	Length = 50
	Location	Memo	

Rooms Table

The field specifications for the Rooms table are displayed in Table 11-13. The RoomID is the primary key for this table. The BuildingID field is a foreign key. It links this table to the Buildings table.

Table 11-13	Field Name	Field Type	Notes
Rooms Table Field Specifications	RoomID	AutoNumber	Primary Key
	BuildingID	Number	Type = Long, Foreign Key
	RoomNumber	Text	Length = 50
	Notes	Memo	

Grades Table

The field specifications for the Rooms table are displayed in Table 11-14. The Grade field, which stores the letter grade, is the primary key for the table. The other field, PointValue, stores the points used for this grade when calculating the GPA.

Table 11-14	Field Name	Field Type	Notes
Grades Table Field Specifications	Grade	Text	Length = 50, Primary Key
	PointValue	Number	Type = Single

Forms

Switchboard Form

The Switchboard form is used to navigate through the forms and reports in the Students, Teachers and Courses database application. It was created using the Switchboard wizard, which is accessible within Access through the Tools/Database Utilities/Switchboard Manager menu item. Only the look and feel of the form produced with that wizard have been altered.

Students Form

The code on the main part of the Students form provides the functionality for the footer buttons. It also calculates the GPA of the student when a new record is displayed and places the name of the student in the header of the page. When the user clicks on the Add button, the following code block fires:

```
Private Sub CommandAdd_Click()
    DoCmd.GoToRecord , , acNewRec
    [StudentID].SetFocus
End Sub
```

Start by moving the record pointer to a new blank record:

```
DoCmd.GoToRecord , , acNewRec
```

Then, set the focus to the StudentID field:

```
[StudentID].SetFocus
```

The next button in the footer is the Delete button:

```
Private Sub CommandDelete_Click()
    On Error GoTo HandleError
    DoCmd.DoMenuItem acFormBar, acEditMenu, 8, , acMenuVer70
    DoCmd.DoMenuItem acFormBar, acEditMenu, 6, , acMenuVer70
    [StudentID].SetFocus
    Exit Sub
HandleError:
    If Err.Number <> 2501 Then
        MsgBox Err.Number & " " & Err.Description
    End If
End Sub
```

Watch for errors in this procedure:

```
On Error GoTo HandleError
```

Then, delete the current record:

```
DoCmd.DoMenuItem acFormBar, acEditMenu, 8, , acMenuVer70
DoCmd.DoMenuItem acFormBar, acEditMenu, 6, , acMenuVer70
```

If the record deleted successfully, set focus to the StudentID field:

```
[StudentID].SetFocus
```

and exit the procedure:

```
Exit Sub
```

If an error did occur, the code flows here:

```
HandleError:
```

Check to see if the error has to do with the user canceling the record deletion:

```
If Err.Number <> 2501 Then
```

If that is the case, do nothing. Otherwise, display the error message to the user:

```
MsgBox Err.Number & " " & Err.Description
```

The next button on the form is the General button. The user clicks on that button to go to the General page of the form, which is the first page. The DoCmd object is used to send the user to that page:

```
Private Sub Command35_Click()
    DoCmd.GoToPage 1
End Sub
```

The user clicks on the Programs button to go to the second page of the form. Again, the DoCmd object passes the GoToPage method to the page number the user wants:

```
Private Sub Command36_Click()
    DoCmd.GoToPage 2
End Sub
```

The next button uses the GoToPage method to take the user to the third page, which contains the course information:

```
Private Sub Command37_Click()
    DoCmd.GoToPage 3
End Sub
```

The next code block fires when the Search button is pressed:

```
Private Sub CommandSearch_Click()
    Screen.PreviousControl.SetFocus
    DoCmd.DoMenuItem acFormBar, acEditMenu, 10, , acMenuVer70
End Sub
```

Assuming that the user wants to search the field viewed before pressing the Search button, set the focus back to that field:

```
Screen.PreviousControl.SetFocus
```

and open the Access Search dialog:

```
DoCmd.DoMenuItem acFormBar, acEditMenu, 10, , acMenuVer70
```

The last button on the footer of the Student form uses the Close method of the DoCmd object to close the form when the Close button is pressed:

```
Private Sub CommandClose_Click()
    DoCmd.Close
End Sub
```

Every time the record pointer moves, display the name of the student in the header of the form and calculate the student's GPA. The Current event is used to take this action because it fires whenever the record pointer moves.

```
Private Sub Form_Current()
    Dim MyDB As DAO.Database
    Dim rs As DAO.Recordset
    Label16.Caption = "Student: " & [LastName] & ", " & [FirstName]
    If [StudentID] <> "" Then
        Set MyDB = CurrentDb
        Set rs = MyDB.OpenRecordset("SELECT Round(Round(Sum([PointValue]*" _
            & "[CreditHours]),2)/Sum([CreditHours]),4) AS TheGPA " _
            & "FROM Courses INNER JOIN (Sections INNER JOIN " _
            & "(Grades INNER JOIN StudentCourses ON Grades.Grade = " _
            & "StudentCourses.Grade) ON Sections.SectionID = " _
            & "StudentCourses.SectionID) ON Courses.CourseID = Sections.CourseID " _
            & "WHERE StudentCourses.StudentID=""" & [StudentID] & """", dbOpenSnapshot)
        Label40.Caption = "GPA: " & rs("TheGPA")
    Else
        Label40.Caption = "GPA: "
    End If
End Sub
```

To calculate the GPA, connect to the database:

```
Dim MyDB As DAO.Database
```

and retrieve information:

```
Dim rs As DAO.Recordset
```

Then, set the header label so it contains the name of the current student:

```
Label16.Caption = "Student: " & [LastName] & ", " & [FirstName]
```

Before taking database action, make sure the record is valid:

```
If [StudentID] <> "" Then
```

If so, connect to the current database:

```
Set MyDB = CurrentDb
```

Then, through a query, calculate the student's GPA across all the courses taken. This complex query first sums the point value for each grade, multiplied by the number of credit hours for each course. That result is then divided by the total number of credit hours taken by the student.

Note the use of the Round function to round the result. Also note that the data needed comes from four different tables being joined together:

```
Set rs = MyDB.OpenRecordset("SELECT Round(Round(Sum([PointValue]*" _
    & "[CreditHours]),2)/Sum([CreditHours]),4) AS TheGPA " _
    & "FROM Courses INNER JOIN (Sections INNER JOIN " _
    & "(Grades INNER JOIN StudentCourses ON Grades.Grade = " _
    & "StudentCourses.Grade) ON Sections.SectionID = " _
    & "StudentCourses.SectionID) ON Courses.CourseID = Sections.CourseID " _
    & "WHERE StudentCourses.StudentID=""" & [StudentID] & """", dbOpenSnapshot)
```

Then, set a label so it contains the GPA:

```
Label40.Caption = "GPA: " & rs("TheGPA")
```

If the current student record is not valid, simply display no GPA:

```
Label40.Caption = "GPA: "
```

The Students form has a subform called StudentPrograms. That subform also contains code that fires whenever the record pointer in that table moves. The code displays the student's core GPA, the number of elective credit hours and the core courses remaining for that program:

```
Private Sub Form_Current()
    Dim MyDB As DAO.Database
    Dim RSProgram As DAO.Recordset
    Dim RSStuCourses As DAO.Recordset
    Dim RSElectives As DAO.Recordset
    Dim RSCore As DAO.Recordset
    Dim GradeTotal As Single
    Dim CreditHourTotal As Long
    If [StudentID] <> "" And IsNumeric([ProgramID]) Then
        Set MyDB = CurrentDb
        Set RSProgram = MyDB.OpenRecordset("SELECT Courses.CourseID, " _
            & "Courses.CreditHours FROM Courses INNER JOIN " _
            & "ProgramRequiredCourses ON Courses.CourseID = " _
            & "ProgramRequiredCourses.CourseID Where ProgramID = " _
            & [ProgramID], dbOpenSnapshot)
        Set RSStuCourses = MyDB.OpenRecordset("SELECT Sections.CourseID, " _
            & "Grades.PointValue FROM Sections INNER JOIN " _
            & "(Grades INNER JOIN StudentCourses ON Grades.Grade = " _
            & "StudentCourses.Grade) ON Sections.SectionID = " _
            & "StudentCourses.SectionID WHERE StudentCourses.StudentID = """ _
            & [StudentID] & """", dbOpenSnapshot)
        Do Until RSStuCourses.EOF
            RSProgram.FindFirst "[CourseID] = " & RSStuCourses("CourseID")
            If RSProgram.NoMatch = False Then
                GradeTotal = GradeTotal + (RSProgram("CreditHours") _
                    * RSStuCourses("PointValue"))
                CreditHourTotal = CreditHourTotal + RSProgram("CreditHours")
            End If
            RSStuCourses.MoveNext
        Loop
        If CreditHourTotal > 0 Then
            Label8.Caption = "Core Program GPA: " & _
                Round(GradeTotal / CreditHourTotal, 4)
        Else
```

```
            Label8.Caption = "Core Program GPA: "
        End If
        Set RSElectives = MyDB.OpenRecordset("SELECT Sum([CreditHours]) AS EH " _
            & "FROM ((Sections INNER JOIN StudentCourses ON " _
            & "Sections.SectionID = StudentCourses.SectionID) " _
            & "INNER JOIN ProgramElectiveCourses ON Sections.CourseID = " _
            & "ProgramElectiveCourses.CourseID) INNER JOIN Courses ON " _
            & "ProgramElectiveCourses.CourseID = Courses.CourseID " _
            & "WHERE StudentCourses.StudentID = """ _
            & [StudentID] & """ AND ProgramElectiveCourses.ProgramID = " _
            & [ProgramID], dbOpenSnapshot)
        Label9.Caption = "Elective Credits Taken: " & RSElectives("EH")
        Set RSCore = MyDB.OpenRecordset("SELECT Courses.CourseID, " _
            & "Courses.CourseNumber, Courses.CourseName FROM Courses " _
            & "INNER JOIN ProgramRequiredCourses ON Courses.CourseID = " _
            & "ProgramRequiredCourses.CourseID " _
            & "WHERE ProgramRequiredCourses.ProgramID = " & [ProgramID], dbOpenSnapshot)
        List10.RowSource = ""
        Do Until RSCore.EOF
            RSStuCourses.FindFirst "[PointValue] > 0 and [CourseID] = " _
                & RSCore("CourseID")
            If RSStuCourses.NoMatch Then
                List10.RowSource = List10.RowSource & RSCore("CourseNumber") _
                    & " - " & RSCore("CourseName") & ";"
            End If
            RSCore.MoveNext
        Loop
        List10.Requery
    Else
        Label8.Caption = "Core Program GPA: "
        Label9.Caption = "Elective Credits Remaining: "
        List10.RowSource = ""
        List10.Requery
    End If
End Sub
```

A Database object is needed:

```
Dim MyDB As DAO.Database
```

Create a Recordset object that grabs program information:

```
Dim RSProgram As DAO.Recordset
```

and another that retrieves the courses taken by the student:

```
Dim RSStuCourses As DAO.Recordset
```

and one that retrieves the elective courses for the program:

```
Dim RSElectives As DAO.Recordset
```

as well as one that retrieves the core courses for the program:

```
Dim RSCore As DAO.Recordset
```

This variable stores the sum of the grade points as they are added:

```
Dim GradeTotal As Single
```

and this stores the credit hour total as it is being added:

```
Dim CreditHourTotal As Long
```

Then, make sure that the record has a valid StudentID and ProgramID:

```
If [StudentID] <> "" And IsNumeric([ProgramID]) Then
```

If so, connect to the database:

```
Set MyDB = CurrentDb
```

and retrieve all the courses that are part of the core courses for this program:

```
Set RSProgram = MyDB.OpenRecordset("SELECT Courses.CourseID, " _
            & "Courses.CreditHours FROM Courses INNER JOIN " _
            & "ProgramRequiredCourses ON Courses.CourseID = " _
            & "ProgramRequiredCourses.CourseID Where ProgramID = " _
            & [ProgramID], dbOpenSnapshot)
```

Then retrieve all the courses with the point value for the grade in each course taken by the student:

```
Set RSStuCourses = MyDB.OpenRecordset("SELECT Sections.CourseID, " _
        & "Grades.PointValue FROM Sections INNER JOIN " _
        & "(Grades INNER JOIN StudentCourses ON Grades.Grade = " _
        & "StudentCourses.Grade) ON Sections.SectionID = " _
        & "StudentCourses.SectionID WHERE StudentCourses.StudentID = """ _
        & [StudentID] & """", dbOpenSnapshot)
```

Next, start a loop that takes you through each of the courses that the student has taken:

```
Do Until RSStuCourses.EOF
```

Check to see if this course is one of the core courses for this program:

```
RSProgram.FindFirst "[CourseID] = " & RSStuCourses("CourseID")
```

If it is, the NoMatch flag will be off:

```
If RSProgram.NoMatch = False Then
```

In that case, this course counts in the core GPA, so add the point value to the total:

```
GradeTotal = GradeTotal + (RSProgram("CreditHours") _
        * RSStuCourses("PointValue"))
```

and the credit hour total:

```
CreditHourTotal = CreditHourTotal + RSProgram("CreditHours")
```

Then, move on to process the next record:

```
        RSStuCourses.MoveNext
Loop
```

Next, make sure at least one course that is part of this core is found:

```
If CreditHourTotal > 0 Then
```

If so, display the GPA:

```
Label8.Caption = "Core Program GPA: " & _
        Round(GradeTotal / CreditHourTotal, 4)
```

Otherwise, display an empty core GPA:

```
Label8.Caption = "Core Program GPA: "
```

Next, retrieve the total number of elective credit hours the student has completed that are part of this program:

```
Set RSElectives = MyDB.OpenRecordset("SELECT Sum([CreditHours]) AS
EH " _
    & "FROM ((Sections INNER JOIN StudentCourses ON " _
    & "Sections.SectionID = StudentCourses.SectionID) " _
    & "INNER JOIN ProgramElectiveCourses ON Sections.CourseID = " _
    & "ProgramElectiveCourses.CourseID) INNER JOIN Courses ON " _
    & "ProgramElectiveCourses.CourseID = Courses.CourseID " _
    & "WHERE StudentCourses.StudentID = """ _
    & [StudentID] & """ AND ProgramElectiveCourses.ProgramID = " _
    & [ProgramID], dbOpenSnapshot)
```

That value is placed in the next label:

```
Label9.Caption = "Elective Credits Taken: " & RSElectives("EH")
```

The next recordset retrieves all the required courses in this program:

```
Set RSCore = MyDB.OpenRecordset("SELECT Courses.CourseID, " _
    & "Courses.CourseNumber, Courses.CourseName FROM Courses " _
```

```
& "INNER JOIN ProgramRequiredCourses ON Courses.CourseID = " _
& "ProgramRequiredCourses.CourseID " _
& "WHERE ProgramRequiredCourses.ProgramID = " & [ProgramID], dbOpenSnapshot)
```

Clear the list that contains the core courses that the student still needs to take:

```
List10.RowSource = ""
```

and start a loop through each of the core courses:

```
Do Until RSCore.EOF
```

Check to see if the student has taken this course and received a passing grade:

```
RSStuCourses.FindFirst "[PointValue] > 0 and [CourseID] = " _
        & RSCore("CourseID")
```

If not, the NoMatch flag will be set:

```
If RSStuCourses.NoMatch Then
```

So, add this courses to the list that displays the courses remaining for the student in this program:

```
List10.RowSource = List10.RowSource & RSCore("CourseNumber") _
        & " - " & RSCore("CourseName") & ";"
```

Then, move on to process the next course:

```
RSCore.MoveNext
Loop
```

Repopulate the list so that it shows all the core courses the student still needs to take:

```
List10.Requery
```

If the StudentID field or the ProgramID field is empty, the code flows here. In that case, clear the labels and the list box:

```
Label8.Caption = "Core Program GPA: "
```

```
Label9.Caption = "Elective Credits Remaining: "
```

```
List10.RowSource = ""
List10.Requery
```

Programs Form

The code on the Programs form enables the user to navigate through the pages on the form and provides the functionality for the buttons on the form. It also displays the name of the program in the header of the form. When the user clicks on the Add button, the Click event of that button fires:

```
Private Sub CommandAdd_Click()
    DoCmd.GoToRecord , , acNewRec
    [ProgramName].SetFocus
End Sub
```

The code in that event first moves the focus to a new record:

```
DoCmd.GoToRecord , , acNewRec
```

It then sets the focus to the ProgramName field so the user can start entering data:

```
[ProgramName].SetFocus
```

The next button on the Programs form footer is the Delete button:

```
Private Sub CommandDelete_Click()
    On Error GoTo HandleError
    DoCmd.DoMenuItem acFormBar, acEditMenu, 8, , acMenuVer70
    DoCmd.DoMenuItem acFormBar, acEditMenu, 6, , acMenuVer70
    [ProgramName].SetFocus
    Exit Sub
HandleError:
    If Err.Number <> 2501 Then
        MsgBox Err.Number & " " & Err.Description
    End If
End Sub
```

Start with an error statement:

```
On Error GoTo HandleError
```

and then delete the current record:

```
DoCmd.DoMenuItem acFormBar, acEditMenu, 8, , acMenuVer70
DoCmd.DoMenuItem acFormBar, acEditMenu, 6, , acMenuVer70
```

Next, set the focus back to the detail section of the form:

```
[ProgramName].SetFocus
```

and exit the procedure:

```
Exit Sub
```

The error statement above tells the compiler to go here if an error occurs:

```
HandleError:
```

If one did, check to see whether the error was due to the user canceling the record deletion:

```
If Err.Number <> 2501 Then
```

If it wasn't, show the information on the error:

```
MsgBox Err.Number & " " & Err.Description
```

The user clicks on the General button to view the General page of the form. This is done using the GoToPage method:

```
Private Sub Command28_Click()
      DoCmd.GoToPage 1
End Sub
```

The next procedure fires when the user clicks on the Core button to go to the second page of the form, where the core course information is displayed:

```
Private Sub Command29_Click()
    DoCmd.GoToPage 2
End Sub
```

The user is taken to the third page of the form by clicking on the Electives button:

```
Private Sub Command30_Click()
    DoCmd.GoToPage 3
End Sub
```

The next code block fires when the user clicks on the Search button:

```
Private Sub CommandSearch_Click()
    Screen.PreviousControl.SetFocus
    DoCmd.DoMenuItem acFormBar, acEditMenu, 10, , acMenuVer70
End Sub
```

It sends the focus of the form back to the previous control. This is assumed to be the one the user wants to search:

```
Screen.PreviousControl.SetFocus
```

Then open the Access Search dialog:

```
DoCmd.DoMenuItem acFormBar, acEditMenu, 10, , acMenuVer70
```

The last button on this form is the Close button. It uses the Close method of the DoCmd object to close the current form:

```
Private Sub CommandClose_Click()
    DoCmd.Close
End Sub
```

The header of the form displays the name of the current program regardless of the page the user is working on. The code that sets the caption of the label is in the current event of the Form.:

```
Private Sub Form_Current()
    Label16.Caption = "Program: " & [ProgramName]
End Sub
```

The KeyUp event of a control fires when the user types in a keystroke, but after it appears on the screen. Use that event here to update the caption in the header label when the user modifies the name of the program:

```
Private Sub ProgramName_KeyUp(KeyCode As Integer, Shift As Integer)
    Label16.Caption = "Program: " & [ProgramName].Text
End Sub
```

Both of the subforms on this form have a single code block that loads the Courses form when the user double-clicks on the Course combo box.

```
Private Sub Course_DblClick(Cancel As Integer)
    If [CourseID] = 0 Or IsNull([CourseID]) Then
        DoCmd.OpenForm "Courses", , , , acFormAdd, acDialog
        [Course].Requery
    Else
        DoCmd.OpenForm "Courses", , , "[CourseID] = " & [CourseID], , acDialog
        [Course].Requery
    End If
End Sub
```

First check to see if the value in the field is empty:

```
If [CourseID] = 0 Or IsNull([CourseID]) Then
```

If it is, assume that the user wants to add a new course record, so show the Courses form in add mode:

```
DoCmd.OpenForm "Courses", , , , acFormAdd, acDialog
```

and then repopulate the combo box:

```
[Course].Requery
```

If the field was not blank, assume the user wants to see the contents of that field. Show the Courses form and filter it, so only the current course is displayed:

```
DoCmd.OpenForm "Courses", , , "[CourseID] = " & [CourseID], , acDialog
```

Then, repopulate the Course combo box:

```
[Course].Requery
```

Instructors Form

The code on the Instructors form provides the functionality for the Footer buttons, links to the Buildings form and displays the name of the instructor in the header of the form. The first code block fires when the user selects the Add button:

```
Private Sub CommandAdd_Click()
    DoCmd.GoToRecord , , acNewRec
    [FirstName].SetFocus
End Sub
```

The GoToRecord method is used to move the record pointer on to a new record:

```
DoCmd.GoToRecord , , acNewRec
```

Then, set the focus to the FirstName field so the user can start entering data:

```
[FirstName].SetFocus
```

The next code block fires when the Delete button is pressed:

```
Private Sub CommandDelete_Click()
```

Start with an Error Handler:

```
On Error GoTo HandleError
```

and then delete the current record:

```
DoCmd.DoMenuItem acFormBar, acEditMenu, 8, , acMenuVer70
DoCmd.DoMenuItem acFormBar, acEditMenu, 6, , acMenuVer70
```

If no error occurred, the code flows here and the focus is set back to the detail section:

```
[FirstName].SetFocus
```

Leave this procedure:

```
Exit Sub
```

If an error occurs, the code flows here:

```
HandleError:
```

Then make sure the error wasn't due to the user canceling the record deletion:

```
If Err.Number <> 2501 Then
```

and display any other error message:

```
MsgBox Err.Number & " " & Err.Description
```

By pressing the General button, the user is taken to the first page on the form:

```
Private Sub Command33_Click()
    DoCmd.GoToPage 1
End Sub
```

The user presses the Courses button to be taken to the second page of the form, which contains the courses taught by this instructor:

```
Private Sub Command34_Click()
    DoCmd.GoToPage 2
End Sub
```

The next code block fires when the Search button is selected:

```
Private Sub CommandSearch_Click()
    Screen.PreviousControl.SetFocus
    DoCmd.DoMenuItem acFormBar, acEditMenu, 10, , acMenuVer70
End Sub
```

Assume that the user wants to search the last field viewed before selecting this button:

```
Screen.PreviousControl.SetFocus
```

Open the Access Search dialog:

```
DoCmd.DoMenuItem acFormBar, acEditMenu, 10, , acMenuVer70
```

When the user presses the Close button, the form closes, using the Close method of the DoCmd object:

```
Private Sub CommandClose_Click()
    DoCmd.Close
End Sub
```

When the record changes, the header of the form needs to be updated so that it displays the name of the instructor. This is done through the Current event of the Form object, which fires whenever the record pointer moves:

```
Private Sub Form_Current()
    Label16.Caption = "Instructor: " & [LastName] & ", " & [FirstName]
End Sub
```

This form links to the Building form when the user double-clicks on the BuildingID combo box.

```
Private Sub BuildingID_DblClick(Cancel As Integer)
    If [BuildingID] = 0 Or IsNull([BuildingID]) Then
        DoCmd.OpenForm "Buildings", , , , acFormAdd, acDialog
        [BuildingID].Requery
    Else
        DoCmd.OpenForm "Buildings", , , "[BuildingID] = " & [BuildingID], , acDialog
        [BuildingID].Requery
    End If
End Sub
```

The form can be loaded in two ways. If the BuildingID field is empty:

```
If [BuildingID] = 0 Or IsNull([BuildingID]) Then
```

If the user wants to add a new building record:

```
DoCmd.OpenForm "Buildings", , , , acFormAdd, acDialog
```

The form is loaded as a dialog, so this line of code only runs after the user finishes with the Buildings form:

```
[BuildingID].Requery
```

The other way the form is loaded is if the user has already selected a building. In that case, assume that the user wants to see the information for that specific building:

```
DoCmd.OpenForm "Buildings", , , "[BuildingID] = " & [BuildingID], , acDialog
```

Then repopulate the combo box:

```
[BuildingID].Requery
```

Courses, Terms, Buildings, Rooms and Grades Forms

The Courses, Terms, Buildings, Rooms, and Grades forms all have similar code. Each of them contains code that fires when the user clicks on the buttons in the footer of the form. This first code block fires when the user clicks on the Add button:

```
Private Sub CommandAdd_Click()
    DoCmd.GoToRecord , , acNewRec
    [BuildingID].SetFocus
End Sub
```

The DoCmd object is used to move the record pointer to a new record:

```
DoCmd.GoToRecord , , acNewRec
```

Set the focus to the first control in the detail section of the form that is used for data entry:

```
[BuildingID].SetFocus
```

The next code block fires when the Delete button is pressed:

```
Private Sub CommandDelete_Click()
    On Error GoTo HandleError
    DoCmd.DoMenuItem acFormBar, acEditMenu, 8, , acMenuVer70
    DoCmd.DoMenuItem acFormBar, acEditMenu, 6, , acMenuVer70
    [BuildingID].SetFocus
    Exit Sub
HandleError:
    If Err.Number <> 2501 Then
        MsgBox Err.Number & " " & Err.Description
    End If
End Sub
```

Start with an error statement that tells the compiler that errors are handled, and to break the code to a label called HandleError if an error does occur:

```
On Error GoTo HandleError
```

Then, delete the current record:

```
DoCmd.DoMenuItem acFormBar, acEditMenu, 8, , acMenuVer70
DoCmd.DoMenuItem acFormBar, acEditMenu, 6, , acMenuVer70
```

If no error occurred, set the focus back to the detail section of the form:

```
[BuildingID].SetFocus
```

Before leaving this procedure:

```
Exit Sub
```

Without the line of code above, the code flows down to the error handler even if no error were to occur:

```
HandleError:
```

Make sure the error wasn't due to the user canceling the record deletion:

```
If Err.Number <> 2501 Then
```

Display any other error message:

```
MsgBox Err.Number & " " & Err.Description
```

The next code block fires when the Search button is pressed:

```
Private Sub CommandSearch_Click()
    Screen.PreviousControl.SetFocus     DoCmd.DoMenuItem acFormBar,
acEditMenu, 10, , acMenuVer70
End Sub
```

Start by moving focus back to the control that had the focus before the user selected the Search button:

```
Screen.PreviousControl.SetFocus
```

Open the Access Search dialog:

```
DoCmd.DoMenuItem acFormBar, acEditMenu, 10, , acMenuVer70
```

The last code block uses the Close method to close the current form when the user selects the Close button:

```
Private Sub CommandClose_Click()
    DoCmd.Close
End Sub
```

Reports

Programs Report

The Programs report displays all the information about programs and the courses in a program. The main part of the report is based directly on the Programs table.

The report also contains two subreports. The first is the ProgramRequiredCourses subreport. It is based directly on the ProgramRequiredCourses table. The other subreport is called ProgramElectiveCourses. It is based on the ProgramElectiveCourses table.

Term Information Report

The Term Information report displays all the information about a term and the courses offered during it. The report is based on the Term Information query, which has the following SQL syntax:

```
SELECT [TermName] & " From: " & [StartDate] & " To: " & [EndDate] AS Term,
Sections.CourseID, Sections.SectionName, Sections.InstructorID,
Sections.RoomID AS Room, Sections.Days, Sections.Times
FROM Terms INNER JOIN Sections ON Terms.TermID = Sections.TermID
WHERE (((Terms.TermName)=[Enter the Name of the Term]))
ORDER BY Sections.CourseID;
```

The query grabs data from the Sections table and the Terms table. The output is limited in the Where clause by the name of the term that the user enters through the text:

```
[Enter the Name of the Term]
```

Note that the first field outputted in this query is a concatenation of the name of the term and the dates of the term into a single output field called Term:

```
[TermName] & " From: " & [StartDate] & " To: " & [EndDate] AS Term
```

Instructor Courses Report

The Instructor Courses report displays information about an instructor and what they teach. The report is based on the Instructor Courses query. That query has the following syntax:

```
SELECT [LastName] & ", " & [FirstName] AS Instructor,
InstructorCourses.CourseID FROM Instructors INNER JOIN
InstructorCourses ON Instructors.InstructorID =
InstructorCourses.InstructorID;
```

The query combines data from the Instructors table with data from the InstructorCourses table.

Course Catalog Report

The Course Catalog report displays information about all the courses that are listed in the Courses table. The report is based directly on that table and does not require a query to run.

CHAPTER 12

Company Specific

ON THE CD:

Room Reservations.mdb

Property Manager.mdb

Databases That Meet the Needs of Specific Companies

In this chapter, we will look at a pair of databases that perform some functionality meant for a certain type of company. But as you review these databases, even if your company doesn't manage the types of data presented, think about how the code could be helpful to the needs of your company.

First, we will look at the Room Reservations database. This database would be used by something like a bed and breakfast to manage their room reservations. The other database covered in this chapter is the Property Manager database. This database would be used by property managers to manage their properties and the tenants within.

Room Reservations Database

The Room Reservations database allows a small hotel, motel, or bed and breakfast to manage rooms, customers, and the reservations made by the customers. As you review this database application, pay close attention to the code that manipulates the database to check for room availability and to make a room reservation.

Sample Walk-through

The menu displayed in Figure 12-1 is shown when the visitor first enters this database.

The menu automatically opens when the database is opened, because it is set as the startup form through the Startup Properties dialog. The menu enables the user to enter any of the forms and reports in the database. The Rooms form displayed in Figure 12-2 is shown when the user clicks on the Rooms button.

The Rooms form has three pages. The first page is the General page. On this page, the user enters the specific configuration and what is allowed in the room. On the footer of the form, the user can choose to go to one of the

Figure 12-1

The menu from the Room Reservations database application

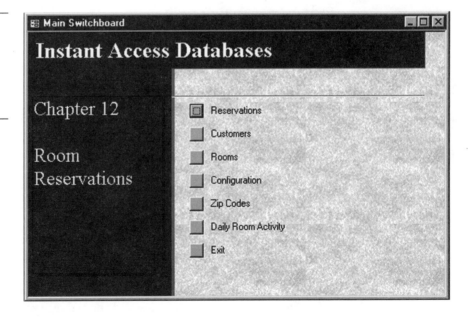

Figure 12-2

The General page
of the Rooms
form

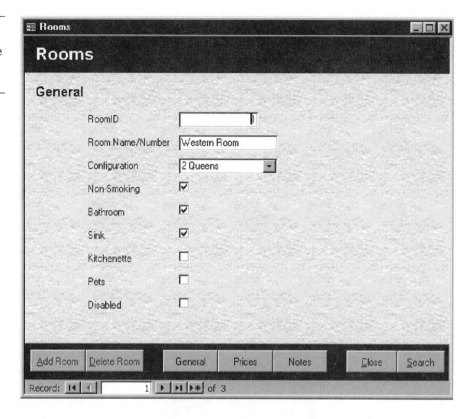

Figure 12-2

The General page
of the Rooms
form

other pages of the form. Pressing on the Prices button shows the page displayed in Figure 12-3.

The Prices and Occupancy page enables the user to enter default prices charged for the room each day of the week. These values then are used when a reservation is made to determine the price of the customer's stay at a room. The page displayed in Figure 12-4 appears when the user presses the Notes button.

The Notes page enables the user to enter any comments or special instructions for the room. Back on the menu form, the user can press the Zip Codes button to see the Zip Codes form displayed in Figure 12-5.

Data on Zip Codes is used on the Customers form to automatically populate the City and State of the customer based on the zip code. So here, the user would enter in zip codes that he wanted automatically populated for the customer. A list of all zip codes can be purchased from a third-party vendor. Another form accessible through the main menu is the Configuration form shown in Figure 12-6.

Figure 12-3

The Prices and
Occupancy page
of the Rooms
form

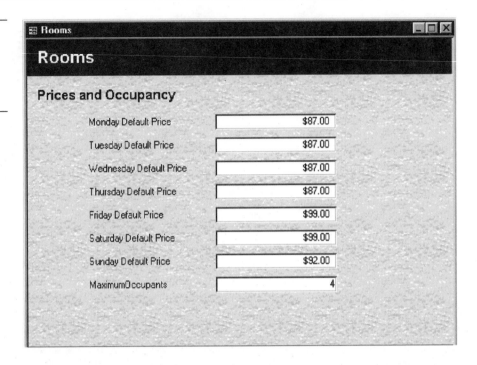

Figure 12-4

The Notes page of
the Rooms form

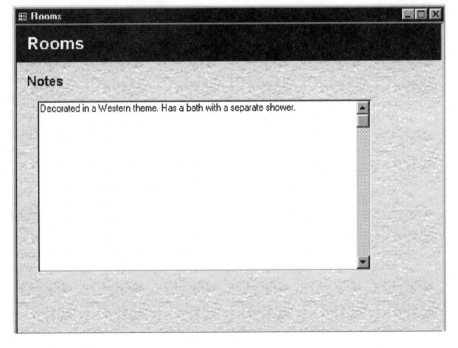

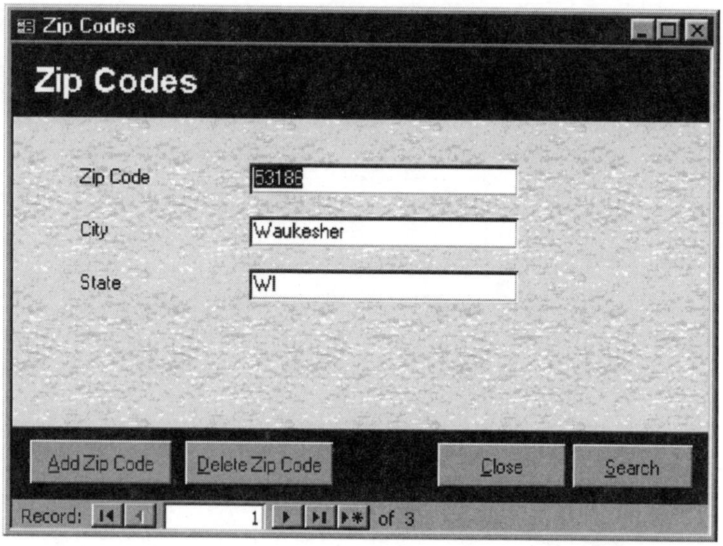

Figure 12-5

The Zip Codes form

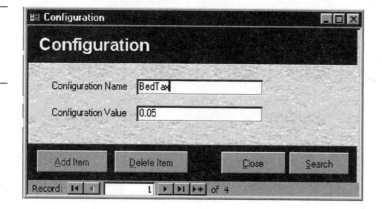

Figure 12-6

The Configuration form

The Configuration form is a special form that enables the user to enter values with a specific name that are used in code to calculate the customer's reservation total. For this database to work correctly, you must enter values for a BedTax, CityTax, and StateTax with those exact names. This kind of configuration information can also be used to store things such as company names and user settings. Another form accessible through the menu is the Customers form displayed in Figure 12-7.

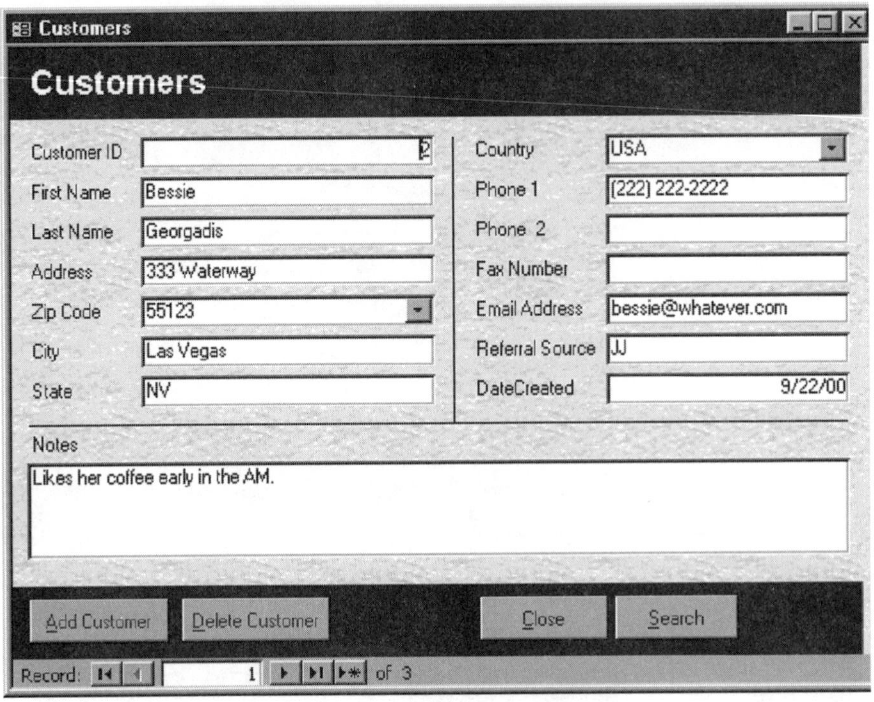

Figure 12-7

The Customers
form

In the Customers form, the user can store personal information about
the customers who stay at their hotel. When the user leaves the Zip Code
field, the City and State fields are populated automatically if the zip code
was entered on the Zip Codes form. The Country field is displayed as a
combo box that self-populates, so when the user enters a new value, it is
available in the list for future additions. The user is ready to start using
the Reservations form, displayed in Figure 12-8, once the information is
entered on the other form.

The Room page is divided into two pages. The first page is the Room
page. It displays the top-level information about the customer's stay. Here,
the user sees the room the customer is staying in, the name of the customer, the reservation dates, and the charges. The user then can view the
prices for the individual days shown in Figure 12-9 by clicking the Days
button.

From this page of the form, the user can change the value of any of the
charges for each of the days. Then back on the Room page, the Update
Totals button can be pressed to update all the price fields.

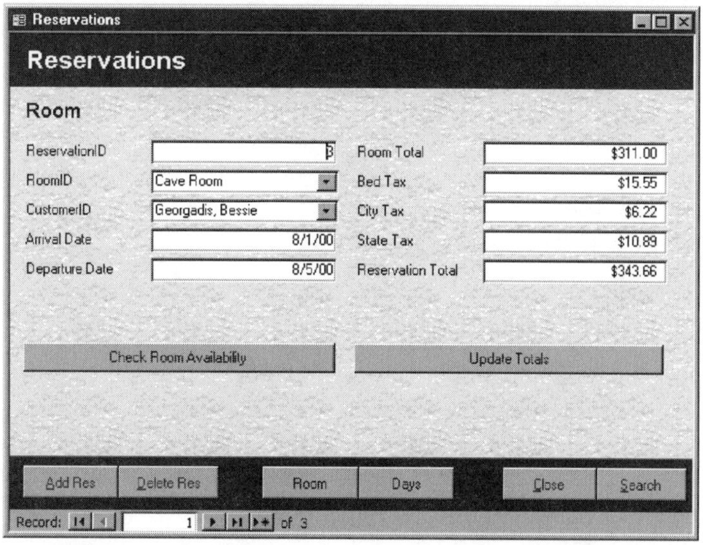

Figure 12-8

The Room page of the Reservations form

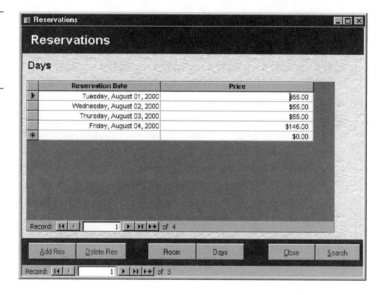

Figure 12-9

The Days page of the Reservations form

When making a new reservation, the user presses the Check Room Availability button displayed on the Room page, and the first page of the wizard is displayed in Figure 12-10.

The user is first asked to enter the dates that the customer will be staying. The code then makes sure what the user enters are dates and that the end date comes after the start date. The code also makes sure rooms are available during the range selected. If any of the problems occur, the user

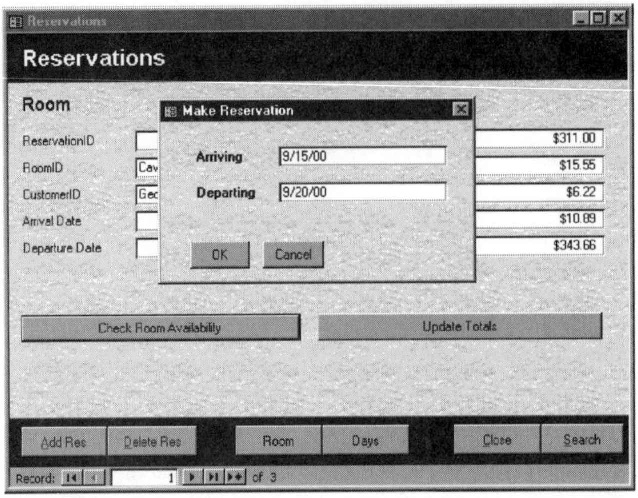

Figure 12-10

The Make
Reservation
part 1

sees a message box with the problem. Otherwise, the second part of the reservation wizard appears, as shown in Figure 12-11.

On the second part of the wizard, the user sees a list of all the rooms that are available during the specified dates. The user then selects from the list. Once this is done, the reservation is created. All the price amounts and days for the reservation are entered. Then, the Reservation form is shown with the new record added, as in Figure 12-12. The user then can modify the prices and enter the information for the customer staying in the room.

One report is included in the database and accessible through the menu, the Daily Room Activity report, which is displayed in Figure 12-13.

When the report first opens, the user is asked to enter a date. All the rooms occupied for that date and the range of reserved dates are shown.

Table Definitions and Relationships

Configuration Table

The Configuration table stores special values that must be present for calculations on the room price to work correctly. The table must have a record for BedTax, CityTax, and StateTax. The value entered for those records is the tax percentage for the type.

Figure 12-11

The Make
Reservation
part 2

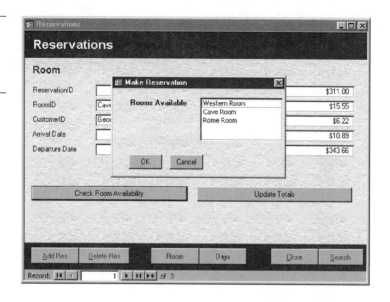

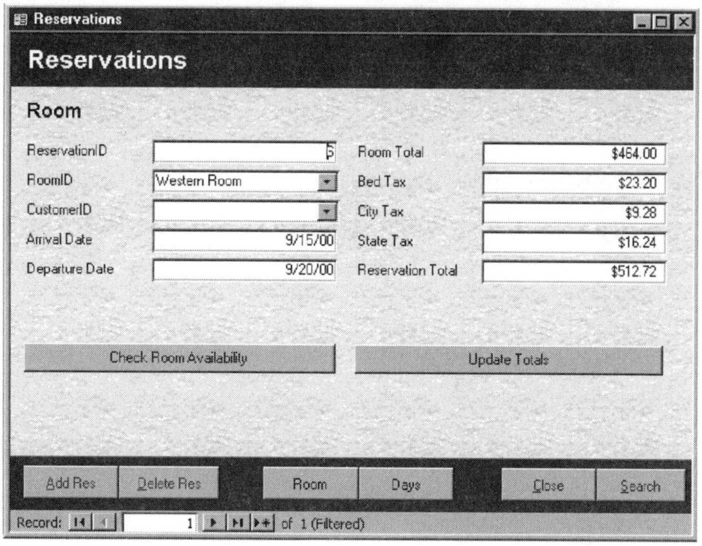

Figure 12-12

The Reservations
form after a new
reservation is
added

ZipCodes Table

The ZipCodes table stores all possible customer zip codes. These values
then are used on the customer's form to elect a value for the city and state
of the customer based on the zip code.

Figure 12-13

The Daily Room
Activity report

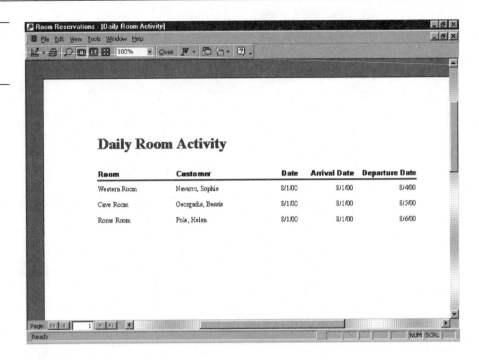

Rooms Table

The Rooms table stores information about the hotel rooms. Some values in
this table are used to calculate the amount that the user is charged for a
reservation.

Customers Table

The Customers table stores data on the customers who stay at the hotel.
This information then is used when a reservation is made.

Reservations Table

Each customer can stay in many rooms. Each room can be used by many
customers. Therefore, the Customers table and the Rooms table are in a
many-to-many relationship. The Reservations table provides the linkage
table between these two tables. It is in a one-to-many relationship with
both tables. The table also stores top-level information about the reservation.

ReservationDays Table

The ReservationDays table stores information on each day that occurs during the visitor's stay. The table is in a one-to-many relationship with the Reservations table. Each reservation can extend over many days, but each day record goes with a single reservation.

Field Specifications

Configuration Table

The field specifications for the Configuration table are displayed in Table 12-1. The Configuration table is made up of name/value pair records such as you would see in an INI file. The ConfigurationName field stores the name of the setting. The ConfigurationValue field stores the value for the setting.

Table 12-1

Configuration Table Field Specifications

Field Name	Field Type	Notes
ConfigurationName	Text	Length = 50, Primary Key
ConfigurationValue	Text	Length = 50

ZipCodes Table

The field specifications for the ZipCodes table are displayed in Table 12-2. The ZipCode field is the primary key in this table. The other fields store information about the zip code entered.

Table 12-2

ZipCodes Table Field Specifications

Field Name	Field Type	Notes
ZipCode	Text	Length = 10, Primary Key
City	Text	Length = 50
State	Text	Length = 50

Rooms Table

The field specifications for the Rooms table are displayed in Table 12-3. The RoomID field is the primary key for this table. Because it is an AutoNumber field, it is populated automatically when a new record is added to the table.

The Configuration field stores the bed configuration for the room. It is displayed as a combo box since the Display Control property is set to combo box. The user must select from one of the items entered into the Row Source property which has a Row Source type set to Value List:

```
"1 King";"2 Kings";"1 Queen";"2 Queens";"2 Doubles"
```

Table 12-3	Field Name	Field Type	Notes
Rooms Table Field Specifications	RoomID	AutoNumber	Primary Key
	RoomNameNumber	Text	Length = 50
	Configuration	Text	Length = 20
	Non-Smoking	Yes/No	
	Bathroom	Yes/No	
	Sink	Yes/No	
	Kitchenette	Yes/No	
	Pets	Yes/No	
	Disabled	Yes/No	
	MondayDefaultPrice	Currency	
	TuesdayDefaultPrice	Currency	
	WednesdayDefaultPrice	Currency	
	ThursdayDefaultPrice	Currency	
	FridayDefaultPrice	Currency	
	SaturdayDefaultPrice	Currency	
	SundayDefaultPrice	Currency	
	MaximumOccupants	Number	Type = Byte
	Description	Memo	

The default price fields, MondayDefaultPrice through FridayDefault-Price, store the initial value entered for each day's stay, based on the day of the week on which the stay will occur. The fields have the following in their Default Value property:

```
99
```

Each of these fields has a validation rule that makes sure the amount entered is between $20 and $1,000:

```
>=20 And <=1000
```

If the rule is violated, the user sees this message:

```
This field must be in the range of $20 and $1,000.
```

The MaximumOccupants field stores the maximum number of people allowed in the room. It has this in its Default Value property:

```
2
```

The value entered must be from one to 10 because it has this validation rule:

```
>0 And <11
```

If the rule is violated the user sees the message in the Validation Text property:

```
This field must be in the range of 1 to 10.
```

Customers Table

The field specifications for the Customers table are displayed in Table 12-4. The CustomerID field is the primary key for this table, uniquely identifying each of the customers.

The ZipCode field is displayed as a combo box. It has the following value in the Row Source property:

```
SELECT [ZipCodes].[ZipCode] FROM ZipCodes;
```

So, the user sees a list of the zip codes.

The Country field also is displayed as a combo box. It is self-populating, which means that as new countries are added in new records, they become part of the list:

```
SELECT [Customers].[Country] FROM Customers;
```

	Field Name	Field Type	Notes
Table 12-4	**Field Name**	**Field Type**	**Notes**
	CustomerID	AutoNumber	Primary Key
Customers Table	FirstName	Text	Length = 50
Field	LastName	Text	Length = 50
Specification	Address	Text	Length = 255
	ZipCode	Text	Length = 10
	City	Text	Length = 50
	State	Text	Length = 50
	Country	Text	Length = 50
	PhoneNumber1	Text	Length = 30
	PhoneNumber2	Text	Length = 30
	FaxNumber	Text	Length = 30
	EmailAddress	Text	Length = 50
	RefSource	Text	Length = 50
	DateCreated	Date/Time	
	Notes	Memo	

The DateCreated field has a default value of the current system date, because this function is in the Default Value property:

```
Date()
```

Reservations Table

The field specifications for the Reservations table are displayed in Table 12-5. The ReservationID field is the primary key in this table.

The RoomID field is a foreign key that links this table to the Rooms table. The field is displayed to the user as a combo box with this value in the Row Source property:

```
SELECT [Rooms].[RoomID], [Rooms].[RoomNameNumber] FROM Rooms;
```

Field Name	Field Type	Notes
ReservationID	AutoNumber	Primary Key
RoomID	Number	Type = Long, Foreign Key
CustomerID	Number	Type = Long, Foreign Key
ArrivalDate	Date/Time	
DepartureDate	Date/Time	
RoomTotal	Currency	
BedTax	Currency	
CityTax	Currency	
StateTax	Currency	
ReservationTotal	Currency	

Table 12-5

Reservations
Table Field
Specifications

The ID field is bound; therefore, it is stored in the Rooms table. But the user sees the name of the room in the combo box.

The CustomerID field is also a foreign key. It links this table to the Customers table. The field is displayed to the user as a combo box because the Display Control property is set to combo box. The Row Source property is set to:

```
SELECT [Customers].[CustomerID], [LastName] & ", " & [FirstName]
AS Expr1 FROM Customers;
```

The user sees the name of the customer, but the ID of the customer is stored with the record.

ReservationDays Table

The field specifications for the ReservationDays table are displayed in Table 12-6. The ReservationDayID field is the primary key for this table. The ReservationID field is a foreign key and links this table to the Reservations table.

Table 12-6	Field Name	Field Type	Notes
ReservationDays Table Field Specifications	ReservationDaysID	AutoNumber	Primary Key
	ReservationID	Number	Type = Long, Foreign Key
	DateOfReservation	Date/Time	
	DayPrice	Currency	

Forms

Switchboard Form

The Switchboard form is used to navigate through the forms and report in the Room Reservations database application. It was created using the Switchboard wizard, which is accessible within Access through the Tools/Database Utilities/Switchboard Manager menu item. Only the look and design of the form produced with that wizard have been altered.

Reservations Form

The code on the Reservations form provides the functionality for the buttons in the footer of the form and in the detail section of the form. This first code block fires when the Add Res button is pressed:

```
Private Sub CommandAdd_Click()
    DoCmd.GoToRecord , , acNewRec
    [RoomID].SetFocus
End Sub
```

First, use the GoToRecord method of the DoCmd object to move to a new record:

```
DoCmd.GoToRecord , , acNewRec
```

Then, set the focus to the RoomID field of the form, which is the first field into which the user can enter data:

```
[RoomID].SetFocus
```

When the user presses the Delete button, the next code block fires:

```
Private Sub CommandDelete_Click()
    On Error GoTo HandleError
    DoCmd.DoMenuItem acFormBar, acEditMenu, 8, , acMenuVer70
    DoCmd.DoMenuItem acFormBar, acEditMenu, 6, , acMenuVer70
    [RoomID].SetFocus
    Exit Sub
HandleError:
    If Err.Number <> 2501 Then
        MsgBox Err.Number & " " & Err.Description
    End If
End Sub
```

Check for an error that occurs when the user cancels the record deletion:

```
On Error GoTo HandleError
```

Then, delete the current record using the DoCmd object:

```
DoCmd.DoMenuItem acFormBar, acEditMenu, 8, , acMenuVer70
DoCmd.DoMenuItem acFormBar, acEditMenu, 6, , acMenuVer70
```

Set the focus back to the detail section:

```
[RoomID].SetFocus
```

and exit the procedure:

```
Exit Sub
```

If an error does occur, the code flows to this label:

```
HandleError:
```

Then, check to see if the error was due to the user canceling the record deletion:

```
If Err.Number <> 2501 Then
```

If it wasn't, display the error to the user:

```
MsgBox Err.Number & " " & Err.Description
```

If the Room button is pressed, the user needs to go to the Room page. This is done using the GoToPage method of the DoCmd object:

```
Private Sub Command33_Click()
    DoCmd.GoToPage 1
End Sub
```

The Days button takes the user to the second page of the form through the GoToPage method, passing to it the parameter of 2 for the second page of the form:

```
Private Sub Command34_Click()
    DoCmd.GoToPage 2
End Sub
```

When the Search button is pressed, the code below fires:

```
Private Sub CommandSearch_Click()
    Screen.PreviousControl.SetFocus
    DoCmd.DoMenuItem acFormBar, acEditMenu, 10, , acMenuVer70
End Sub
```

Assume the user wants to search the field he or she was on before clicking the Search button, and therefore return the focus back to that field:

```
Screen.PreviousControl.SetFocus
```

Then, open the Search dialog:

```
DoCmd.DoMenuItem acFormBar, acEditMenu, 10, , acMenuVer70
```

When the user presses the close button, the Close method is used to close this form:

```
Private Sub CommandClose_Click()
    DoCmd.Close
End Sub
```

When the user makes a reservation, the ID of the reservation that was added to the database must be passed back from the Make Reservation form. This is done through a Public variable that is declared in the General Declaration section of a Module called PublicProcs:

```
Public CurrentReservation As Long
```

Because it is declared as Public, it is visible to any procedure on any form in this database application. You will see it used on the Make Reservation form as well as on this form.

When the user presses the Check Room Availability button, use that variable to call the Make Reservation form and to show the new reservation added, if any.

```
Private Sub Command29_Click()
    CurrentReservation = 0
```

```
DoCmd.OpenForm "Make Reservation", , , , , acDialog
If CurrentReservation <> 0 Then
    Me.Requery
    Me.Filter = "[ReservationID] = " & CurrentReservation
    Me.FilterOn = True
End If
End Sub
```

Start by clearing the Public variable:

```
CurrentReservation = 0
```

Then, open the Make Reservation form as a Dialog. Therefore, the rest of this code does not run until the user is done with that form:

```
DoCmd.OpenForm "Make Reservation", , , , , acDialog
```

After the user is finished with that form, check to see if the reservation was completed:

```
If CurrentReservation <> 0 Then
```

If so, refresh the data on this form:

```
Me.Requery
```

and set a filter so that the reservation that was just added by the user is the current record:

```
Me.Filter = "[ReservationID] = " & CurrentReservation
```

Then turn on this filter:

```
Me.FilterOn = True
```

When the User presses the Update Totals button, update all the dollar totals for this reservation.

```
Private Sub Command37_Click()
    Dim MyDB As DAO.Database
    Dim RSConfig As DAO.Recordset
    Dim RSRoomTotal As DAO.Recordset
    Set MyDB = CurrentDb
    Set RSConfig = MyDB.OpenRecordset("Select * from Configuration", _
        dbOpenSnapshot)
    Set RSRoomTotal = MyDB.OpenRecordset("Select Sum(DayPrice) " _
        & "As TheTotal From ReservationDays Where " _
        & "ReservationID = " & ReservationID, dbOpenSnapshot)
    [RoomTotal] = RSRoomTotal("TheTotal")
    RSConfig.FindFirst "[ConfigurationName] = ""BedTax"""
    [BedTax] = RSRoomTotal("TheTotal") * RSConfig("ConfigurationValue")
```

```
        RSConfig.FindFirst "[ConfigurationName] = ""CityTax"""
        [CityTax] = RSRoomTotal("TheTotal") * RSConfig("ConfigurationValue")
        RSConfig.FindFirst "[ConfigurationName] = ""StateTax"""
        [StateTax] = RSRoomTotal("TheTotal") * RSConfig("ConfigurationValue")
        [ReservationTotal] = [BedTax] + [CityTax] + [StateTax] _
            + RSRoomTotal("TheTotal")
End Sub
```

To do this, connect to the database:

```
Dim MyDB As DAO.Database
```

and retrieve data from the Configuration table:

```
Dim RSConfig As DAO.Recordset
```

Also retrieve the total amount of days the user is staying at the hotel:

```
Dim RSRoomTotal As DAO.Recordset
```

Then, connect to the current database:

```
Set MyDB = CurrentDb
```

Next, retrieve the configuration information. Remember that the Configuration table contains the value for the different taxes used on the total owed:

```
Set RSConfig = MyDB.OpenRecordset("Select * from Configuration", _
        dbOpenSnapshot)
```

Then, retrieve from the database the total amount due for all the days just for the room:

```
Set RSRoomTotal = MyDB.OpenRecordset("Select Sum(DayPrice) " _
        & "As TheTotal From ReservationDays Where " _
        & "ReservationID = " & ReservationID, dbOpenSnapshot)
```

Then set the room total of this reservation to that value:

```
[RoomTotal] = RSRoomTotal("TheTotal")
```

Find the value for the bed tax:

```
RSConfig.FindFirst "[ConfigurationName] = ""BedTax"""
```

and set the bed tax amount for this reservation based on that value:

```
[BedTax] = RSRoomTotal("TheTotal") * RSConfig("ConfigurationValue")
```

Next, do the same for the city tax:

```
RSConfig.FindFirst "[ConfigurationName] = ""CityTax"""
[CityTax] = RSRoomTotal("TheTotal") *
RSConfig("ConfigurationValue")
```

and the state tax:

```
RSConfig.FindFirst "[ConfigurationName] = ""StateTax"""
[StateTax] = RSRoomTotal("TheTotal") *
RSConfig("ConfigurationValue")
```

Then, set the grand total to the sum of all these values:

```
[ReservationTotal] = [BedTax] + [CityTax] + [StateTax] _
        + RSRoomTotal("TheTotal")
```

Make Reservation Form

As you saw in Figure 12-11 and Figure 12-12, the Make Reservation form has two views to it. Both views are the same form. The code merely makes certain controls visible and invisible based on where the user is in the wizard. The code that manages the main functionality of the form is on the OK button. However, code also fires when the User presses the Cancel button. That code simply closes this form:

```
Private Sub cmdCancel_Click()
    DoCmd.Close
End Sub
```

For the code in the OK button to work, pass the dates entered by the user between presses of the OK button. These variables are declared in the General Declaration section of the form:

```
Private StartDate As Date
Private EndDate As Date
```

Because the dates are declared as Private, they are available to any procedure on this form but not to other forms. The code that fires when the OK button is pressed has two states. The first state runs when the user presses on the OK button the first time. This means that the dates of the reservation have been entered. The second state is when the user presses the OK button a second time. This happens after a room has been selected for the reservation.

```
Private Sub cmdOK_Click()
    Dim MyDB As DAO.Database
```

```
Dim RSDays As DAO.Recordset
Dim RSRooms As DAO.Recordset
Dim RSCurrentReservation As DAO.Recordset
Dim RSConfig As DAO.Recordset
Dim RSRoomTotal As DAO.Recordset
Dim RoomFound As Boolean
Dim CurrentPrice As Currency
Dim BedTax As Currency
Dim CityTax As Currency
Dim StateTax As Currency
If txtArr.Visible = True Then
    txtArr.SetFocus
    If Not IsDate(txtArr.Text) Then
        MsgBox "The Arrival Date must be a date!"
        Exit Sub
    End If
    StartDate = txtArr.Text
    txtDep.SetFocus
    If Not IsDate(txtDep.Text) Then
        MsgBox "The Departure Date must be a date!"
        Exit Sub
    End If
    EndDate = txtDep.Text
    EndDate = DateAdd("d", -1, EndDate)
    If EndDate < StartDate Then
        MsgBox "The Departure Date must be after the Arrival Date."
        Exit Sub
    End If
    Set MyDB = CurrentDb
    Set RSDays = MyDB.OpenRecordset("SELECT Reservations.RoomID, " _
        & "ReservationDays.DateOfReservation FROM Reservations " _
        & "INNER JOIN ReservationDays ON Reservations.ReservationID " _
        & "= ReservationDays.ReservationID WHERE " _
        & "ReservationDays.DateOfReservation >= #" & StartDate _
        & "# And ReservationDays.DateOfReservation <= #" _
        & EndDate & "#", dbOpenSnapshot)
    Set RSRooms = MyDB.OpenRecordset("Select RoomID, RoomNameNumber " _
        & "From Rooms", dbOpenSnapshot)
    Do Until RSRooms.EOF
        RSDays.FindFirst "[RoomID] = " & RSRooms("RoomID")
        If RSDays.NoMatch Then
            lstRooms.RowSource = lstRooms.RowSource _
                & RSRooms("RoomNameNumber") & ";"
            RoomFound = True
        End If
        RSRooms.MoveNext
    Loop
    If RoomFound Then
        lstRooms.Visible = True
        Label35.Visible = True
        lstRooms.SetFocus
        Label29.Visible = False
        Label31.Visible = False
        txtArr.Visible = False
        txtDep.Visible = False
        lstRooms.Visible = True
        Label35.Visible = True
    Else
```

```
                MsgBox "No rooms are avialble during the dates selected."
            End If
    Else
        If IsNull(lstRooms.Value) Then
            MsgBox "Please select a room for the reservation!"
            Exit Sub
        End If
        Set MyDB = CurrentDb
        Set RSRooms = MyDB.OpenRecordset("Select RoomID, MondayDefaultPrice, " _
            & "TuesdayDefaultPrice, WednesdayDefaultPrice, ThursdayDefaultPrice, " _
            & "FridayDefaultPrice, SaturdayDefaultPrice, SundayDefaultPrice " _
            & "From Rooms Where RoomNameNumber = """ & lstRooms.Value & """", _
            dbOpenSnapshot)
        MyDB.Execute "Insert Into Reservations (RoomID, ArrivalDate, " _
            & "DepartureDate) values (" _
            & RSRooms("RoomID") & ", " _
            & "'" & StartDate & "', " _
            & "'" & DateAdd("d", 1, EndDate) & "')"
        Set RSCurrentReservation = MyDB.OpenRecordset("Select Max(ReservationID) " _
            & "As TheID From Reservations", dbOpenSnapshot)
        CurrentReservation = RSCurrentReservation("TheID")
        Do Until StartDate > EndDate
            If Weekday(StartDate) = 1 Then
                CurrentPrice = RSRooms("SundayDefaultPrice")
            ElseIf Weekday(StartDate) = 2 Then
                CurrentPrice = RSRooms("MondayDefaultPrice")
            ElseIf Weekday(StartDate) = 3 Then
                CurrentPrice = RSRooms("TuesdayDefaultPrice")
            ElseIf Weekday(StartDate) = 4 Then
                CurrentPrice = RSRooms("WednesdayDefaultPrice")
            ElseIf Weekday(StartDate) = 5 Then
                CurrentPrice = RSRooms("ThursdayDefaultPrice")
            ElseIf Weekday(StartDate) = 6 Then
                CurrentPrice = RSRooms("FridayDefaultPrice")
            Else
                CurrentPrice = RSRooms("SaturdayDefaultPrice")
            End If
            MyDB.Execute "Insert Into ReservationDays (ReservationID, " _
                & "DateOfReservation, DayPrice) Values (" _
                & CurrentReservation & ", " _
                & "'" & StartDate & "', " _
                & CurrentPrice & ")"
            StartDate = DateAdd("d", 1, StartDate)
        Loop
        Set RSConfig = MyDB.OpenRecordset("Select * from Configuration", _
            dbOpenSnapshot)
        Set RSRoomTotal = MyDB.OpenRecordset("Select Sum(DayPrice) " _
            & "As TheTotal From ReservationDays Where " _
            & "ReservationID = " & CurrentReservation, dbOpenSnapshot)
        RSConfig.FindFirst "[ConfigurationName] = ""BedTax"""
        BedTax = RSRoomTotal("TheTotal") * RSConfig("ConfigurationValue")
        RSConfig.FindFirst "[ConfigurationName] = ""CityTax"""
        CityTax = RSRoomTotal("TheTotal") * RSConfig("ConfigurationValue")
        RSConfig.FindFirst "[ConfigurationName] = ""StateTax"""
        StateTax = RSRoomTotal("TheTotal") * RSConfig("ConfigurationValue")
        MyDB.Execute "Update Reservations Set RoomTotal = " & _
            RSRoomTotal("TheTotal") _
            & ", BedTax = " & BedTax _
```

```
              & ", CityTax = " & CityTax _
              & ", StateTax = " & StateTax _
              & ", ReservationTotal = " _
              & (BedTax + CityTax + StateTax + RSRoomTotal("TheTotal")) _
              & " Where ReservationID = " & CurrentReservation
          DoCmd.Close
      End If
End Sub
```

Here, a database object is needed:

```
Dim MyDB As DAO.Database
```

This recordset is used to look for reservations that overlap this reservation:

```
Dim RSDays As DAO.Recordset
```

This one retrieves room information:

```
Dim RSRooms As DAO.Recordset
```

Another recordset is used to retrieve the ID of the reservation just added:

```
Dim RSCurrentReservation As DAO.Recordset
```

Another grabs data from the Configuration table:

```
Dim RSConfig As DAO.Recordset
```

and the total dollar amount of the stay for the room:

```
Dim RSRoomTotal As DAO.Recordset
```

This flag is used to see if a room is available during the dates specified:

```
Dim RoomFound As Boolean
```

This variable stores the price for the room on a given day:

```
Dim CurrentPrice As Currency
```

Another stores the total amount due for bed tax:

```
Dim BedTax As Currency
```

city tax:

```
Dim CityTax As Currency
```

and state tax:

```
Dim StateTax As Currency
```

If the Arrival text box is visible, this indicates the first state of the form, meaning that the user has just entered the dates for the stay:

```
If txtArr.Visible = True Then
```

Set the focus to the Arrival text box:

```
txtArr.SetFocus
```

and check to see if the user entered a date:

```
If Not IsDate(txtArr.Text) Then
```

If not, use a message box to inform the user of the problem:

```
MsgBox "The Arrival Date must be a date!"
```

and leave this procedure:

```
Exit Sub
```

Otherwise, store the arrival date in a Private variable:

```
StartDate = txtArr.Text
```

and set the focus to the Departure date:

```
txtDep.SetFocus
```

Then check to see if that also is a date:

```
If Not IsDate(txtDep.Text) Then
```

If it isn't, inform the user of the problem:

```
MsgBox "The Departure Date must be a date!"
```

and leave this procedure:

```
Exit Sub
```

Otherwise, place the date entered into a Private form-wide variable:

```
EndDate = txtDep.Text
```

Because the departure date isn't a date when the customer will be spending the night, but is the date of departure, subtract one day from that date:

```
EndDate = DateAdd("d", -1, EndDate)
```

Next, check to see if the departure date is before the date of arrival:

```
If EndDate < StartDate Then
```

If not, let the user know the problem:

```
MsgBox "The Departure Date must be after the Arrival Date."
```

and leave the procedure:

```
Exit Sub
```

Otherwise, the data is good and you can connect to the database:

```
Set MyDB = CurrentDb
```

The first things retrieved are reservation day records that overlap the requested date range:

```
Set RSDays = MyDB.OpenRecordset("SELECT Reservations.RoomID, " _
    & "ReservationDays.DateOfReservation FROM Reservations " _
    & "INNER JOIN ReservationDays ON Reservations.ReservationID " _
    & "= ReservationDays.ReservationID WHERE " _
    & "ReservationDays.DateOfReservation >= #" & StartDate _
    & "# And ReservationDays.DateOfReservation <= #" _
    & EndDate & "#", dbOpenSnapshot)
```

Retrieve information on the Rooms themselves:

```
Set RSRooms = MyDB.OpenRecordset("Select RoomID, RoomNameNumber " _
    & "From Rooms", dbOpenSnapshot)
```

Then, start a loop that goes through all the records in the Rooms table:

```
Do Until RSRooms.EOF
```

Look for a reservation day in this room within the dates specified in the reservation:

```
RSDays.FindFirst "[RoomID] = " & RSRooms("RoomID")
```

If none are found, the NoMatch flag is set:

```
If RSDays.NoMatch Then
```

In that case, the room is available during the requested dates, so it can be added to the Rooms list box:

```
lstRooms.RowSource = lstRooms.RowSource _
        & RSRooms("RoomNameNumber") & ";"
```

Then, set your flag to show that a room is found after this loop:

```
RoomFound = True
```

Move on to process the next room:

```
RSRooms.MoveNext
Loop
```

If the flag is set, at least one room is available:

```
If RoomFound Then
```

so you must switch states. Make visible the Rooms list box and its label:

```
lstRooms.Visible = True
Label35.Visible = True
```

Set the focus to that list box:

```
lstRooms.SetFocus
```

and make the date fields and their labels invisible:

```
Label29.Visible = False
Label31.Visible = False
txtArr.Visible = False
txtDep.Visible = False
lstRooms.Visible = True
Label35.Visible = True
```

If no rooms were available, the code flows here:

```
Else
```

Inform the user of the problem, so he or she can enter new dates:

```
MsgBox "No rooms are avialble during the dates selected."
```

Now, you are at the point of the second state. This state occurs when the user presses the OK button a second time after selecting a room for the reservation:

```
Else
```

First, make sure a room was actually selected:

```
If IsNull(lstRooms.Value) Then
```

If not, tell them the problem:

```
MsgBox "Please select a room for the reservation!"
```

and exit this procedure:

```
Exit Sub
```

Otherwise, connect to the current database:

```
Set MyDB = CurrentDb
```

and retrieve price information for the selected room :

```
Set RSRooms = MyDB.OpenRecordset("Select RoomID, MondayDefaultPrice, " _
     & "TuesdayDefaultPrice, WednesdayDefaultPrice, ThursdayDefaultPrice, " _
     & "FridayDefaultPrice, SaturdayDefaultPrice, SundayDefaultPrice " _
     & "From Rooms Where RoomNameNumber = """ & lstRooms.Value & """", _
     dbOpenSnapshot)
```

Then, create a new reservation by entering just the basic information known so far about the reservation. Note that this excludes the price information:

```
MyDB.Execute "Insert Into Reservations (RoomID, ArrivalDate, " _
          & "DepartureDate) values (" _
          & RSRooms("RoomID") & ", " _
          & "'" & StartDate & "', " _
          & "'" & DateAdd("d", 1, EndDate) & "')"
```

Retrieve the ID of the reservation that was just added:

```
Set RSCurrentReservation = MyDB.OpenRecordset("Select
Max(ReservationID) " _
          & "As TheID From Reservations", dbOpenSnapshot)
```

and set the Public variable to that value. Remember that after the user is finished with this form, this value will be used back on the Reservation form to show the proper reservation:

```
CurrentReservation = RSCurrentReservation("TheID")
```

Then enter a loop to add a record for each of the days that the customer will be staying at the hotel:

```
Do Until StartDate > EndDate
```

Next, determine the price to charge for each of the days. Do this by using the WeekDay function to derive the day of the week of the date being added. Here, check to see if the day of the week is Sunday:

```
If Weekday(StartDate) = 1 Then
```

If so, use Sunday's price for this room:

```
CurrentPrice = RSRooms("SundayDefaultPrice")
```

Then, check to see if the day of the week is Monday through Friday:

```
ElseIf Weekday(StartDate) = 2 Then
        CurrentPrice = RSRooms("MondayDefaultPrice")
ElseIf Weekday(StartDate) = 3 Then
        CurrentPrice = RSRooms("TuesdayDefaultPrice")
ElseIf Weekday(StartDate) = 4 Then
        CurrentPrice = RSRooms("WednesdayDefaultPrice")
ElseIf Weekday(StartDate) = 5 Then
        CurrentPrice = RSRooms("ThursdayDefaultPrice")
ElseIf Weekday(StartDate) = 6 Then
        CurrentPrice = RSRooms("FridayDefaultPrice")
```

The else means that the day of the week is Saturday:

```
Else
```

So use Saturday's price:

```
CurrentPrice = RSRooms("SaturdayDefaultPrice")
```

Now that the price for this day in the room and the date are known, add a record to the ReservationDays table:

```
MyDB.Execute "Insert Into ReservationDays (ReservationID, " _
        & "DateOfReservation, DayPrice) Values (" _
        & CurrentReservation & ", " _
        & "'" & StartDate & "', " _
        & CurrentPrice & ")"
```

Then, move on to process the next day of the customer's stay:

```
        StartDate = DateAdd("d", 1, StartDate)
Loop
```

Once all the days of the customer's stay have been added, retrieve the tax configuration information:

```
Set RSConfig = MyDB.OpenRecordset("Select * from Configuration", _
        dbOpenSnapshot)
```

Also retrieve the total dollar amount for the days in the room just added:

```
Set RSRoomTotal = MyDB.OpenRecordset("Select Sum(DayPrice) " _
        & "As TheTotal From ReservationDays Where " _
        & "ReservationID = " & CurrentReservation, dbOpenSnapshot)
```

Then retrieve the bed tax percentage:

```
RSConfig.FindFirst "[ConfigurationName] = ""BedTax"""
```

and calculate the bed tax amount on this reservation:

```
BedTax = RSRoomTotal("TheTotal") * RSConfig("ConfigurationValue")
```

Do the same for the city tax:

```
RSConfig.FindFirst "[ConfigurationName] = ""CityTax"""
CityTax = RSRoomTotal("TheTotal") * RSConfig("ConfigurationValue")
```

and the state tax:

```
RSConfig.FindFirst "[ConfigurationName] = ""StateTax"""
StateTax = RSRoomTotal("TheTotal") * RSConfig("ConfigurationValue")
```

Now, add the price fields to update the reservation that was added earlier in this procedure:

```
MyDB.Execute "Update Reservations Set RoomTotal = " & _
        RSRoomTotal("TheTotal") _
        & ", BedTax = " & BedTax _
        & ", CityTax = " & CityTax _
        & ", StateTax = " & StateTax _
```

```
            & ", ReservationTotal = " _
            & (BedTax + CityTax + StateTax + RSRoomTotal("TheTotal")) _
            & " Where ReservationID = " & CurrentReservation
```

Then close this form:

```
DoCmd.Close
```

Customers Form

The code on the Customers form provides the functionality for the footer buttons. It also populates the City and State fields based on the Zip Code entered. The first code block fires when the Add Customer button is pressed:

```
Private Sub CommandAdd_Click()
    DoCmd.GoToRecord , , acNewRec
    [FirstName].SetFocus
End Sub
```

Start by moving the record pointer to a new record:

```
DoCmd.GoToRecord , , acNewRec
```

Then, set the Focus to the FirstName field:

```
[FirstName].SetFocus
```

If the Delete button is pressed, the next code block fires:

```
Private Sub CommandDelete_Click()
    On Error GoTo HandleError
    DoCmd.DoMenuItem acFormBar, acEditMenu, 8, , acMenuVer70
    DoCmd.DoMenuItem acFormBar, acEditMenu, 6, , acMenuVer70
    [FirstName].SetFocus
    Exit Sub
HandleError:
    If Err.Number <> 2501 Then
        MsgBox Err.Number & " " & Err.Description
    End If
End Sub
```

Start by telling the compiler that any errors that occur will:

```
On Error GoTo HandleError
```

Next, delete the current record:

```
DoCmd.DoMenuItem acFormBar, acEditMenu, 8, , acMenuVer70
DoCmd.DoMenuItem acFormBar, acEditMenu, 6, , acMenuVer70
```

and set the focus to the first field in the detail section of the form:

```
[FirstName].SetFocus
```

Then leave this procedure:

```
Exit Sub
```

Errors are routed by the compiler to this label:

```
HandleError:
```

Filter out an error that occurs when the record deletion is canceled:

```
If Err.Number <> 2501 Then
```

but display any other error message to the user:

```
MsgBox Err.Number & " " & Err.Description
```

If the user presses the Search button, the code block fires:

```
Private Sub CommandSearch_Click()
    Screen.PreviousControl.SetFocus
    DoCmd.DoMenuItem acFormBar, acEditMenu, 10, , acMenuVer70
End Sub
```

Start by moving the focus to the control the user was at prior to clicking on the Search button:

```
Screen.PreviousControl.SetFocus
```

Then, display the Access Search dialog:

```
DoCmd.DoMenuItem acFormBar, acEditMenu, 10, , acMenuVer70
```

When the user presses the Close button, the Close method of the DoCmd object is used to close this form:

```
Private Sub CommandClose_Click()
    DoCmd.Close
End Sub
```

When the user exits the ZipCode field, populate the City and State based on the zip code entered. Do this through the LostFocus event.

```
Private Sub ZipCode_LostFocus()
    Dim MyDB As DAO.Database
```

```
      Dim RSZip As DAO.Recordset
      Set MyDB = CurrentDb
      Set RSZip = MyDB.OpenRecordset("Select City, State from
ZipCodes " _
          & "Where ZipCode = """ & [ZipCode] & """", dbOpenSnapshot)
      If Not RSZip.EOF Then
          [City] = RSZip("City")
          [State] = RSZip("State")
      End If
  End Sub
```

Connect to the database:

```
Dim MyDB As DAO.Database
```

and retrieve data from the ZipCodes table:

```
Dim RSZip As DAO.Recordset
```

Then, connect to this database:

```
Set MyDB = CurrentDb
```

and look for the zip code entered:

```
Set RSZip = MyDB.OpenRecordset("Select City, State from ZipCodes " _
    & "Where ZipCode = """ & [ZipCode] & """", dbOpenSnapshot)
```

Check to see if a matching record was found:

```
If Not RSZip.EOF Then
```

If so, use the data found for the City and the State fields:

```
[City] = RSZip("City")
[State] = RSZip("State")
```

Rooms, Zip Codes, and Configuration Forms

The Rooms, Zip Codes, and Configuration forms have almost identical code so are discussed here collectively. All have code blocks that fire when the footer buttons are pressed. The first code fires behind the Add button:

```
Private Sub CommandAdd_Click()
    DoCmd.GoToRecord , , acNewRec
    [ZipCode].SetFocus
End Sub
```

It uses the GoToRecord method to move the record pointer to a new record:

```
DoCmd.GoToRecord , , acNewRec
```

Move the focus to the first data entry field on the detail section of the form:

```
[ZipCode].SetFocus
```

The next code block goes with the Delete button:

```
Private Sub CommandDelete_Click()
    On Error GoTo HandleError
    DoCmd.DoMenuItem acFormBar, acEditMenu, 8, , acMenuVer70
    DoCmd.DoMenuItem acFormBar, acEditMenu, 6, , acMenuVer70
    [ZipCode].SetFocus
    Exit Sub
HandleError:
    If Err.Number <> 2501 Then
        MsgBox Err.Number & " " & Err.Description
    End If
End Sub
```

Start by instructing the compiler to handle errors that may occur:

```
On Error GoTo HandleError
```

Then, attempt to delete the current record:

```
DoCmd.DoMenuItem acFormBar, acEditMenu, 8, , acMenuVer70
DoCmd.DoMenuItem acFormBar, acEditMenu, 6, , acMenuVer70
```

If the record was deleted, the code flows here and the focus moves back to the detail section:

```
[ZipCode].SetFocus
```

Exit this procedure:

```
Exit Sub
```

If an error were to occur, the code would flow here:

```
HandleError:
```

Check to see if the error was due to the user canceling the record deletion:

```
If Err.Number <> 2501 Then
```

If not, display that error message through a message box:

```
MsgBox Err.Number & " " & Err.Description
```

If the user presses the Search button, the next code block fires:

```
Private Sub CommandSearch_Click()
    Screen.PreviousControl.SetFocus
    DoCmd.DoMenuItem acFormBar, acEditMenu, 10, , acMenuVer70
End Sub
```

Start by moving the focus back to the field the user wants to search, which is the one he or she was on before clicking on the Search button:

```
Screen.PreviousControl.SetFocus
```

Then, open the Access Search dialog:

```
DoCmd.DoMenuItem acFormBar, acEditMenu, 10, , acMenuVer70
```

The other code block fires when the Close button is pressed. It uses the Close method to close the current form:

```
Private Sub CommandClose_Click()
    DoCmd.Close
End Sub
```

Report

Daily Room Activity Report

The Daily Room Activity report prompts the user for a date, and then displays the activity for any room that has a customer staying on that date. The report is based on the Daily Room Activity query, which has the following syntax:

```
SELECT Reservations.RoomID AS Room, Reservations.CustomerID AS
Customer, ReservationDays.DateOfReservation, Reservations.ArrivalDate,
Reservations.DepartureDate FROM Reservations INNER JOIN
ReservationDays ON Reservations.ReservationID =
ReservationDays.ReservationID
WHERE ReservationDays.DateOfReservation=[Enter Date for Report]
```

The query combines the data in the Reservations table with data in the ReservationDays table. Note that the query contains this parameter in the Where clause:

```
[Enter Date for Report]
```

This is not a field in the tables, so the user is prompted for the value.

Property Manager Database

Next you will review the Property Manager database. This database enables the user to manage tenants, properties, and financial transactions between those two entities.

Sample Walk-through

The menu in Figure 12-14 is displayed when the user first enters this database application. From this menu the user can view any of the forms and reports of the database application.

Figure 12-14

The Property Manager database menu

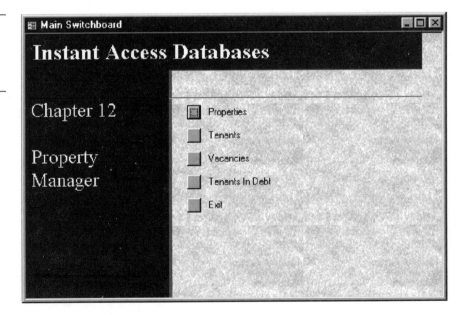

If the user presses the Properties button, the first page of the Properties form is displayed, as shown in Figure 12-15.

The General page of the Properties form enables the user to enter basic information on the property. Note the Status and Becomes Vacant fields. These fields are used to generate the Vacancy report reviewed in a later section.

If the user clicks on the Specific button, the page of the form displayed in Figure 12-16 is shown.

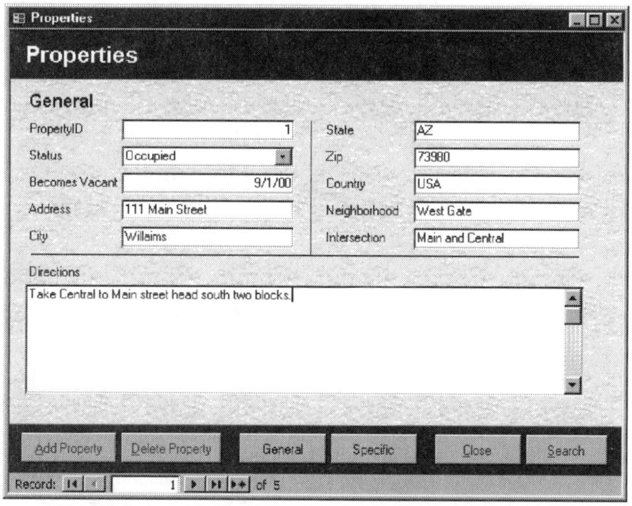

Figure 12-15

The General page of the Properties form

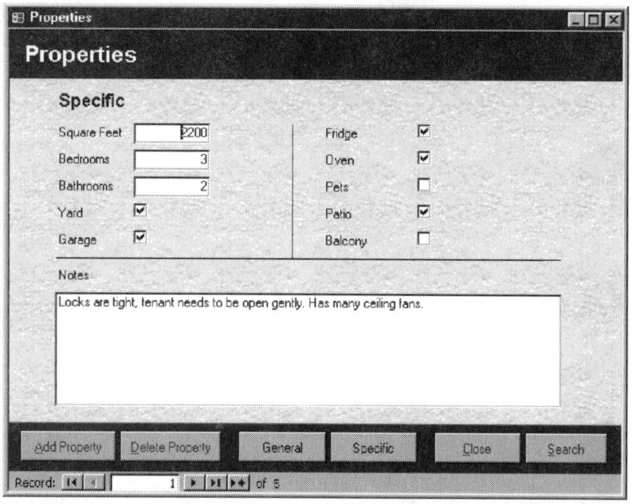

Figure 12-16

The Specific page from the Properties form

The second page of the Properties form enables the user to enter low-level information about the property, including a series of check boxes. The other form in this database is the Tenants form, which is displayed in Figure 12-17.

The Tenants form is divided into two pages. The first page is called Tenant and stores information about the tenant themselves. If the user presses the Bill Rent button and enters an amount in the Rent field, an entry is made on the Account page for that rent amount, as displayed in Figure 12-18.

The Account Activity page of the Tenants form displays all the debits and credits entered into this tenant's account. At the bottom of the form is a summary field that displays the current overall balance of the account.

The database application includes two reports that are accessible from the menu. The first is the Vacancies report displayed in Figure 12-19.

The Vacancies report displays information on any property that is currently vacant, or that will become vacant within the next 30 days. The other report that is accessible through the menu is the Tenants in Debt report, which is displayed in Figure 12-20. The Tenants in Debt report displays a list of all tenants who currently have a balance due.

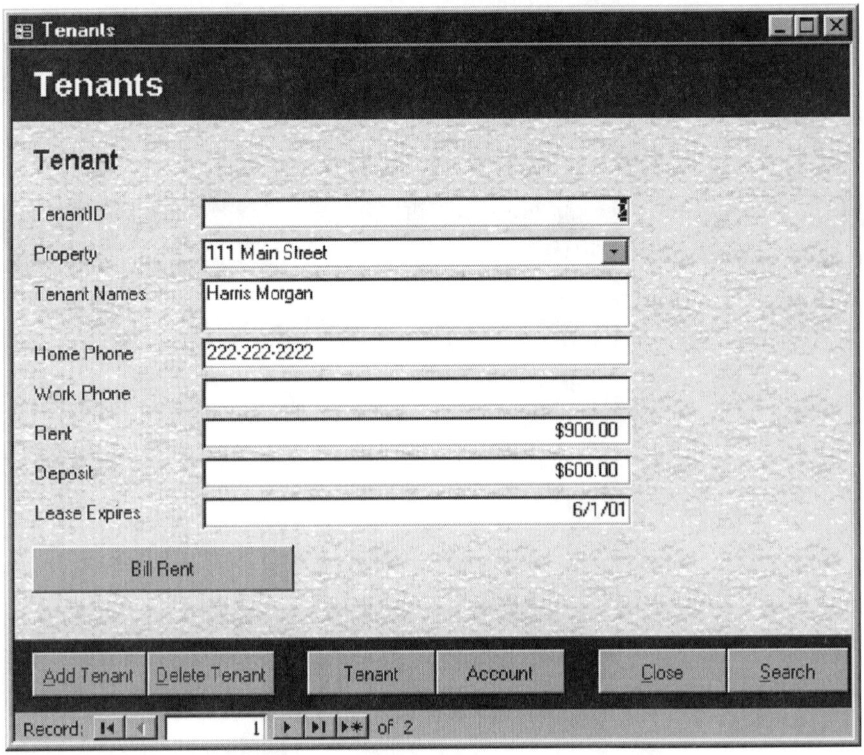

Figure 12-17

The Tenant page of the Tenants form

Figure 12-18

The Account
Activity page of
the Tenants form

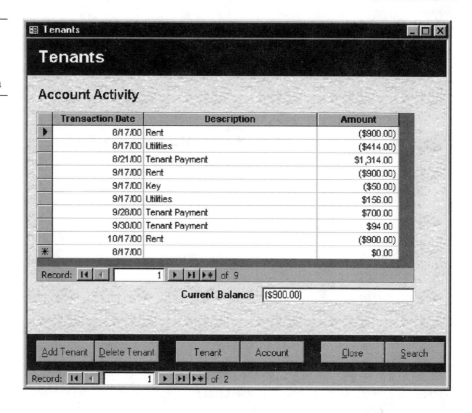

Figure 12-19

The Vacancies
Report

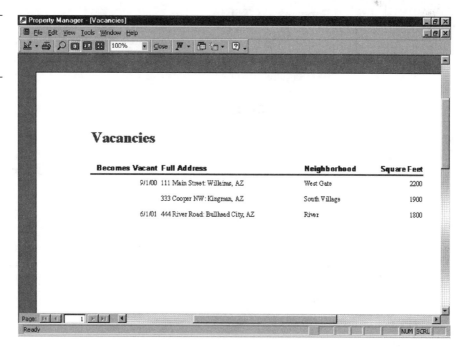

Figure 12-20

The Tenants in
Debt report

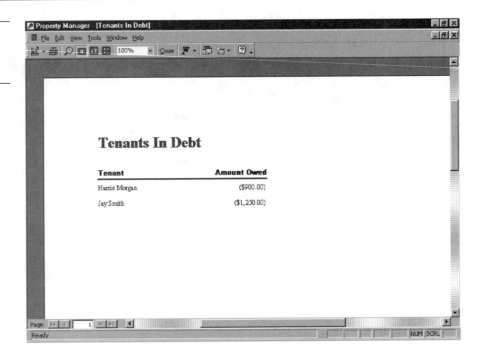

Table Definitions and Relationships

Properties Table

The Properties table stores all the information on each property included
in the database. The table is a top-level table related directly or indirectly
to the other tables in the database.

Tenants Table

The Tenants table stores data on the tenants. The table is in a one-to-
many relationship with the Properties table. Each tenant stays at one
property at a time. But over time, a property can have more than one tenant.

AccountActivity Table

The AccountActivity table stores each of the credits and debits for a tenant's account. The table is in a one-to-many relationship with the Tenants
table. Each tenant can have many debits and credits, but each of these
debits and credits go with a single tenant's account.

Field Specifications

Properties Table

The field specifications for the Properties table are displayed in Table 12-7. The PropertyID field is the primary key for this table. It is populated automatically as a new record is added, because it is an AutoNumber field.

Table 12-7

Properties Table Field Specifications

Field Name	Field Type	Notes
PropertyID	AutoNumber	Primary Key
Status	Text	Length = 50
BecomesVacant	Date/Time	
Address	Text	Length = 100
City	Text	Length = 50
State	Text	Length = 2
Zip	Text	Length = 10
Country	Text	Length = 50
Neighborhood	Text	Length = 50
MajorIntersection	Text	Length = 50
Directions	Memo	
SquareFeet	Number	Type = Long
Bedrooms	Number	Type = Byte
Bathrooms	Number	Type = Byte
Yard	Yes/No	
Garage	Yes/No	
Fridge	Yes/No	
Oven	Yes/No	
Pets	Yes/No	
Patio	Yes/No	
Balcony	Yes/No	
Notes	Memo	

The Status field is displayed as a combo box, since the Display Control property is set to combo box. The user must select from one of the values entered into the Row Source property:

```
"Occupied";"Vacant";"Not in Use"
```

The SquareFeet field stores the number of square feet in the property. The field has a default value of 100 and has the following Validation Rule property, which requires that the value entered is from 100 to 50,000:

```
>=100 And <=50000
```

This message is shown when the user violates this rule:

```
This field must be from 100 to 50,000.
```

The Bedrooms and Bathrooms fields have a default value of one and the following text in their Validation Rule property:

```
>=1 And <=20
```

The following text appears in a message box if that rule is violated:

```
This field must be from 1 to 20.
```

Tenants Table

The field specifications for the Tenants table are displayed in Table 12-8. The TenantID field is the primary key for this table.

Table 12-8	Field Name	Field Type	Notes
Tenants Table Field Specifications	TenantID	AutoNumber	Primary Key
	PropertyID	Number	Type = Long, Foreign Key
	TenantNames	Text	Length = 100
	HomePhone	Text	Length = 50
	WorkPhone	Text	Length = 50
	Rent	Currency	
	Deposit	Currency	
	LeaseExpires	Date/Time	

The PropertyID field is a foreign key that links this table to the Properties table. The field is displayed to the user as a combo box and has the following value in the Row Source property:

```
SELECT [Properties].[PropertyID], [Properties].[Address] FROM Properties;
```

The ID of the property is the bound column, so it is stored with the record. The user sees the address of the property in the list portion of the combo box.

AccountActivity Table

The field specifications for the AccountActivity table are displayed in Table 12-9. The AccountActivityID field is the primary key in this table.

Table 12-9	Field Name	Field Type	Notes
AccountActivity Table Field Specifications	AccountActivityID	AutoNumber	Primary Key
	TenantID	Number	Type = Long, Foreign Key
	TransactionDate	Date/Time	
	Description	Text	Length = 50
	Amount	Currency	

The TenantID field is a foreign key that links this table to the Tenants table. The TrasactionDate field stores the date that the entry was made. It has this value in its Default Value property:

```
Date()
```

which means that when a new record is added the current system date is inserted into this field.

Forms

Switchboard Form

The Switchboard form is used to navigate through the forms and reports in the Property Manager database. It was created using the Switchboard wizard, which is accessible within Access through the Tools/Database Utilities/Switchboard Manager menu item. Only the look and design of the form produced with that wizard have been altered.

Properties Form

The code on the Properties form provides the functionality for the buttons in the footer of the form. The first code block fires when the user clicks on the Add Property button.

```
Private Sub CommandAdd_Click()
    DoCmd.GoToRecord , , acNewRec
    [Status].SetFocus
End Sub
```

Start by moving the record pointer to a new, blank record:

```
DoCmd.GoToRecord , , acNewRec
```

Then, set the focus to the Status field so the user can start entering data:

```
[Status].SetFocus
```

When the user clicks on the Delete button, the next code block fires:

```
Private Sub CommandDelete_Click()
    On Error GoTo HandleError
    DoCmd.DoMenuItem acFormBar, acEditMenu, 8, , acMenuVer70
    DoCmd.DoMenuItem acFormBar, acEditMenu, 6, , acMenuVer70
    [Status].SetFocus
    Exit Sub
HandleError:
    If Err.Number <> 2501 Then
        MsgBox Err.Number & " " & Err.Description
    End If
End Sub
```

Start by telling the compiler that errors that occur will be processed:

```
On Error GoTo HandleError
```

Then, delete the current record:

```
DoCmd.DoMenuItem acFormBar, acEditMenu, 8, , acMenuVer70
DoCmd.DoMenuItem acFormBar, acEditMenu, 6, , acMenuVer70
```

Return the focus to the detail section of the form:

```
[Status].SetFocus
```

and then leave this procedure:

```
Exit Sub
```

If an error were to occur, the code would flow here:

```
HandleError:
```

Check to see if the error was due to the user canceling the record deletion:

```
If Err.Number <> 2501 Then
```

If it wasn't, display the error message to the user in a message box:

```
MsgBox Err.Number & " " & Err.Description
```

The user needs to be taken to the first page of the form when the General button is pressed. This is done using the GoToPage method of the DoCmd object:

```
Private Sub Command28_Click()
    DoCmd.GoToPage 1
End Sub
```

The GoToPage method is also used when the user presses the Specific button. The second page of the form appears:

```
Private Sub Command29_Click()
    DoCmd.GoToPage 2
End Sub
```

When the user presses the Search button, the next code block fires:

```
Private Sub CommandSearch_Click()
    Screen.PreviousControl.SetFocus
    DoCmd.DoMenuItem acFormBar, acEditMenu, 10, , acMenuVer70
End Sub
```

Assume the user wants to search the field he or she was on before entering this form. Therefore, start by moving the focus to that field:

```
Screen.PreviousControl.SetFocus
```

Then, open the Access Search dialog.

```
DoCmd.DoMenuItem acFormBar, acEditMenu, 10, , acMenuVer70
```

When the user presses the Close button, the Close method is used to close the current form:

```
Private Sub CommandClose_Click()
    DoCmd.Close
End Sub
```

Tenants Form

The code on the Tenants form provides the functionality for the buttons on the form. It also links the form to the Properties form and displays the balance of the tenant's account. A text box displays that balance with the following value in its Control Source property:

```
=[Forms]![Tenants]![AccountActivity subform].[Form]![txtSum]
```

The value refers to a field on the activity sub-form called txtSum. That text box has this Control Source:

```
=Sum([Amount])
```

So, what the user sees on the Tenants form is the sum of all the values in the Amount field on the sub-form. When the user clicks on the Bill Rent button, add a debit to the tenant's account for the rent amount.

```
Private Sub Command40_Click()
    Dim MyDB As DAO.Database
    If IsNumeric([Rent]) And IsNumeric([TenantID]) Then
        Set MyDB = CurrentDb
        MyDB.Execute "Insert Into AccountActivity (TenantID, " _
            & "TransactionDate, Description, Amount) Values (" _
            & [TenantID] & ", " _
            & "'" & Date & "', " _
            & "'Rent', " _
            & (Rent * -1) & ")"
        [accountactivity subform].Requery
    End If
End Sub
```

Connect to the current database:

```
Dim MyDB As DAO.Database
```

but before that, make sure that this is a valid record to which you can add rent:

```
If IsNumeric([Rent]) And IsNumeric([TenantID]) Then
```

If so, connect to the database:

```
Set MyDB = CurrentDb
```

and insert a record in the AccountActivity table:

```
MyDB.Execute "Insert Into AccountActivity (TenantID, " _
        & "TransactionDate, Description, Amount) Values (" _
```

that is for the current tenant:

```
& [TenantID] & ", " _
```

that was entered on this date:

```
& "'" & Date & "', " _
```

with a description of rent:

```
& "'Rent', " _
```

for the rent amount as a debit:

```
& (Rent * -1) & ")"
```

Then, repopulate the sub-form so that it will include the new record just added:

```
[accountactivity subform].Requery
```

When the user double-clicks on the PropertyID field, send him or her to the Properties form:

```
Private Sub PropertyID_DblClick(Cancel As Integer)
    If [PropertyID] = 0 Or IsNull([PropertyID]) Then
        DoCmd.OpenForm "Properties", , , , acFormAdd, acDialog
        PropertyID.Requery
    Else
        DoCmd.OpenForm "Properties", , , "[PropertyID] = " & [PropertyID], , acDialog
        PropertyID.Requery
    End If
End Sub
```

Check to see if the field is blank:

```
If [PropertyID] = 0 Or IsNull([PropertyID]) Then
```

If it is, assume that the user wants to add a new record:

```
DoCmd.OpenForm "Properties", , , , acFormAdd, acDialog
```

Then, repopulate the combo box:

```
PropertyID.Requery
```

If the field has a value, assume that the user wants to see the information for that property:

```
DoCmd.OpenForm "Properties", , , "[PropertyID] = " & [PropertyID], , acDialog
```

When that form is completed, refresh the combo box so that it will display any changes made by the user:

```
PropertyID.Requery
```

The next code block fires when the Add Tenant button is pressed:

```
Private Sub CommandAdd_Click()
    DoCmd.GoToRecord , , acNewRec
    [PropertyID].SetFocus
End Sub
```

Mmove to a new record:

```
DoCmd.GoToRecord , , acNewRec
```

and send the focus to the first data entry field on the form:

```
[PropertyID].SetFocus
```

When the Delete Tenant button is pressed, this code block fires:

```
Private Sub CommandDelete_Click()
    On Error GoTo HandleError
    DoCmd.DoMenuItem acFormBar, acEditMenu, 8, , acMenuVer70
    DoCmd.DoMenuItem acFormBar, acEditMenu, 6, , acMenuVer70
    [PropertyID].SetFocus
    Exit Sub
HandleError:
    If Err.Number <> 2501 Then
        MsgBox Err.Number & " " & Err.Description
    End If
End Sub
```

Start by telling the compiler that any errors that occur will be handled:

```
On Error GoTo HandleError
```

then, delete the current record:

```
DoCmd.DoMenuItem acFormBar, acEditMenu, 8, , acMenuVer70
DoCmd.DoMenuItem acFormBar, acEditMenu, 6, , acMenuVer70
```

Move the focus back to the detail section:

```
[PropertyID].SetFocus
```

before leaving the procedure:

```
Exit Sub
```

If an error was to occur, your error statement indicates that the code should flow here:

```
HandleError:
```

Then, check to see if the error that occurred was due to the user canceling the record deletion:

```
If Err.Number <> 2501 Then
```

If not, display the error message:

```
MsgBox Err.Number & " " & Err.Description
```

When the user presses the Tenant button, the first page of the form, through the GoToPage method of the DoCmd object, appears:

```
Private Sub Command28_Click()
    DoCmd.GoToPage 1
End Sub
```

The Account button opens the second page of the form:

```
Private Sub Command29_Click()
    DoCmd.GoToPage 2
End Sub
```

If the user presses the Search button, the next code block fires:

```
Private Sub CommandSearch_Click()
    Screen.PreviousControl.SetFocus
    DoCmd.DoMenuItem acFormBar, acEditMenu, 10, , acMenuVer70
End Sub
```

Start by moving the focus to the field the user was on before pressing the Search button:

```
Screen.PreviousControl.SetFocus
```

Then open the built-in Search dialog:

```
DoCmd.DoMenuItem acFormBar, acEditMenu, 10, , acMenuVer70
```

The other code on the form fires when the user presses the Close button and closes this form:

```
Private Sub CommandClose_Click()
    DoCmd.Close
End Sub
```

Reports

Vacancies Report

The Vacancies report displays information on any property that is currently vacant or is set to become vacant within the next 30 days. The report is based on the Vacancies query, which has the following SQL syntax:

```
SELECT Properties.BecomesVacant,
[Address] & ": " & [City] & ", " & [State] AS [Full Address],
Properties.Neighborhood, Properties.SquareFeet FROM Properties
WHERE Properties.Status = "Vacant" OR DateDiff("d",Date(),[BecomesVacant]) <=30
ORDER BY [Address] & ": " & [City] & ", " & [State];
```

First note that one of the fields outputted, Full Address, is a concatenation of the Address, City, and State fields:

```
[Address] & ": " & [City] & ", " & [State]
```

Then look at the Where clause. Note the use of the DateDiff function to see if the property will become vacant within the next 30 days:

```
DateDiff("d",Date(),[BecomesVacant]) <=30
```

Tenants in Debt Report

The Tenants in Debt report displays a list of all the tenants who currently owe money, along with the amounts they owe. It is based on the Tenants in Debt query, which has this syntax:

```
SELECT AccountActivity.TenantID AS Tenant,
Sum(AccountActivity.Amount) AS [Amount Owed] FROM AccountActivity
GROUP BY AccountActivity.TenantID HAVING
(((Sum(AccountActivity.Amount))<0));
```

Note that the records are grouped by the TenantID, so the sum for each tenant is shown. Then note that a Having clause instead of a Where clause limits the records outputted based on a grouped value instead of an initial value in the original records.

CHAPTER 13

PIM

ON THE CD:

PIM.mdb

Personal Information Manager

In this chapter, we will look at a Personal Information Manager database application. The application enables the user to manage items on a calendar, and record contacts and daily notes. The user can also print out a daily schedule. As you review this database application, take particular note of the Calendar form. This form does not have any bound controls. It uses code to populate all aspects of it. Also note the use of the Timer event on that form to notify the user when a calendar item is about to occur.

PIM Database

Sample Walk-through

When the user first enters the PIM Access database application, the navigational form is displayed, as shown in Figure 13-1.

The menu form enables the user to access any of the forms and reports used in this application. If the user clicks on the Calendar button, the form displayed in Figure 13-2 appears.

When the Calendar form first opens, the user sees his or her schedule for the current day. Items are displayed in 1/2 hour increments across the entire day. Note the use of color in the text boxes that indicate the time an event is scheduled. The buttons in the header of the form enable the user to quickly navigate between days, weeks, or months in forward and backward directions.

The user can quickly see additional information without leaving this form by clicking on any item. Then the full caption for the event with its start and end times can be seen. This is shown in Figure 13-3.

Figure 13-1

PIM menu form

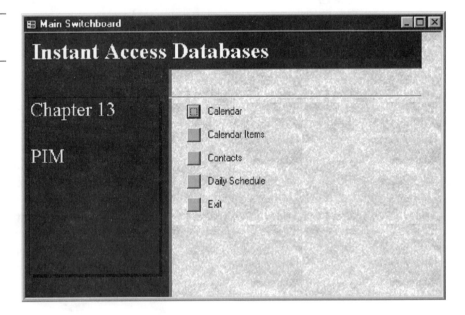

Figure 13-2

Calendar form

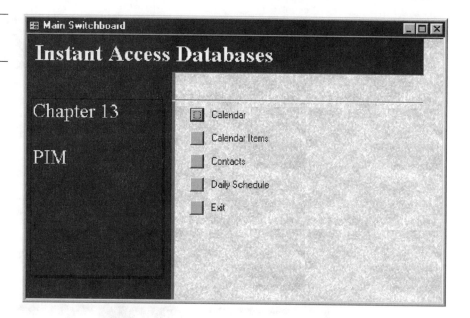

Figure 13-3

The status bar is used to show additional information for an item

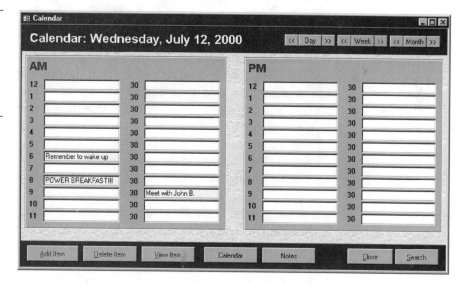

The user can also view the entire entry for an item. This is done by clicking on the item and then clicking on the View Item button. The form that opens is shown in Figure 13-4.

Figure 13-4

Calendar Items form

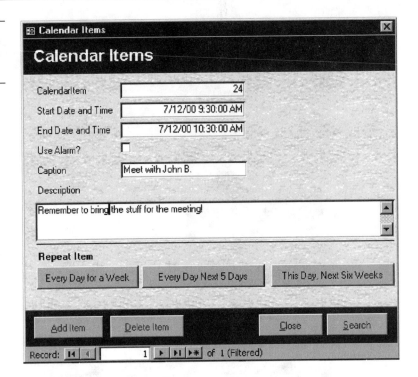

The Calendar Items form displays all the information about the Calendar Item. The form is also accessible from the Main Menu. From this form, the user can edit this item, add new items, and delete items. The buttons on the form can also be used to make this item repeat over the next week or over the next six weeks. When the user is finished with this form, the changes made are reflected back in their schedule.

Notice the Alarm field on the Calendar Items form, which enables the user to be notified when an item is about to occur. If this box is checked and the Calendar form is opened, the user is notified 15 minutes before the event occurs. Such a message is displayed in Figure 13-5.

Alarms run every five minutes. Any item that is within 15 minutes of occurring, or has started and has the alarm turned on, is reported to the user. The user can then elect to turn off the alarm or can leave it on to have it fire again in five minutes. Notice the other buttons on the footer of the Calendar form. The user can also use this form to add and delete items.

The form has another page, in addition to the Calendar page. If the user presses the Notes button, the Notes page is displayed, as shown in Figure 13-6.

Figure 13-5

Alarm dialog

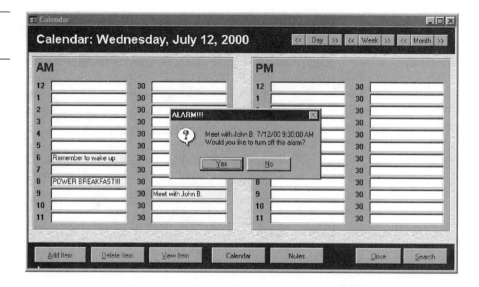

Figure 13-6

Notes page of the
Calendar form

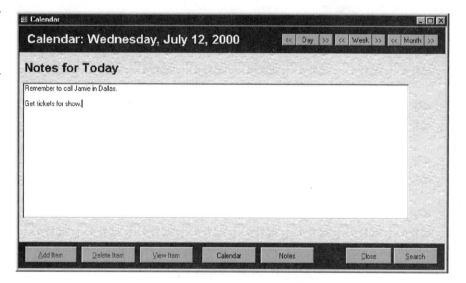

The Notes page enables the user to have text that he or she wants associated with a given day. Therefore, each day has its own note, and as the user navigates between days, the note for that day is seen. The other form in this application is the Contacts form. This form is accessible from the Main Menu and is displayed in Figure 13-7. This basic form enables the user to manage his or her contacts. The user can add, edit, view, delete, and search contacts from this form.

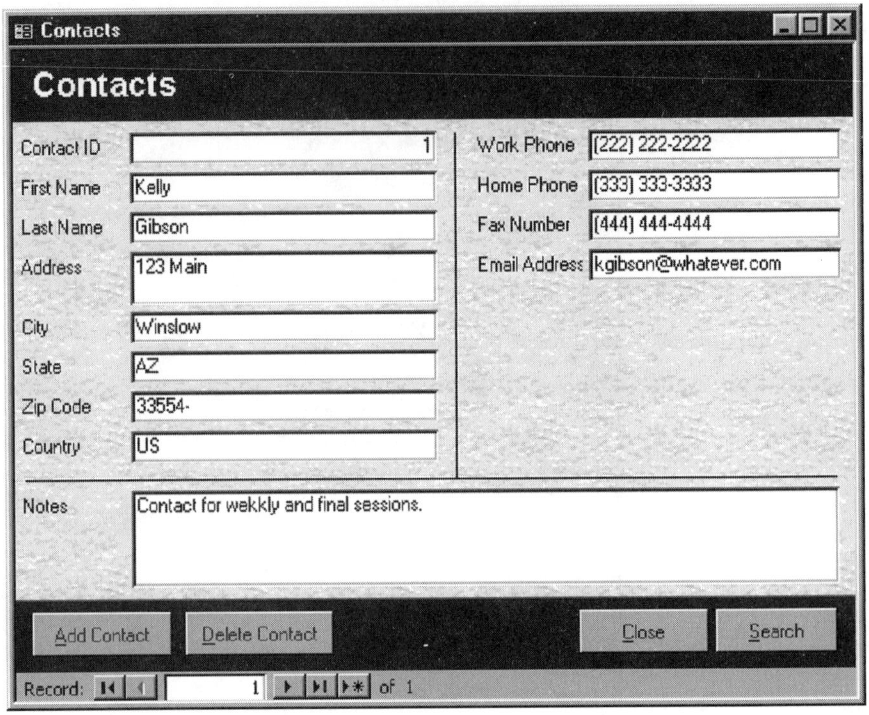

Figure 13-7

Contacts form

The PIM database application has one report called Daily Schedule which is accessible from the Main Menu. When the Daily Schedule button is clicked, the user is prompted for the date of the schedule and sees a report like the one shown in Figure 13-8.

Table Definitions and Relationships

CalendarItems Table

When the user looks at his or her calendar, the events seen in the schedule come from the CalendarItems table. The CalendarItems table stores all the information about the scheduled events.

TheNotes Table

As you saw in Figure 13-6, each of the days in the user's schedule can have notes associated with it. The TheNotes table stores that information.

Figure 13-8

Daily Schedule
report

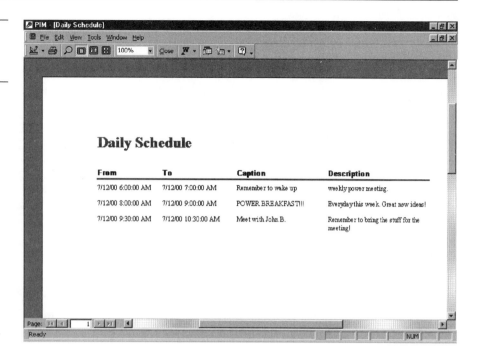

Contacts Table

The other table used in this database is the Contacts table. This table stores the user's contact list, which is displayed on the Contacts form.

Field Specifications

CalendarItems Table

The field specifications for the CalendarItems table are displayed in Table 13-1. The CalendarItemID field is the primary key for this table. It is automatically populated when a new record is added and uniquely identifies each record.

The WhenStarts and WhenEnds fields store the beginning and ending points of the calendar item. The Caption field stores a brief name for the record. This field is what is used on the Calendar form. The Alarm field is a Boolean field that indicates whether the user wants to see a reminder as the start time for this event approaches.

Field Name	Field Type	Notes
CalendarItemID	AutoNumber	Primary Key
WhenStarts	Date/Time	
WhenEnds	Date/Time	
Caption	Text	Length = 50
Alarm	Yes/No	
Description	Memo	

TheNotes Table

The field specifications for the TheNotes table are displayed in Table 13-2. The NoteID field is the primary key for this table. The NoteDate field stores the date that goes with this note, and the TheNote field stores the text of the note that is displayed on the Calendar form.

Field Name	Field Type	Notes
NoteID	AutoNumber	Primary Key
NoteDate	Date/Time	
TheNote	Memo	

Contacts Table

The field specifications for the Contacts table are displayed in Table 13-3. The ContactID field is the primary key for this table.

The rest of the fields, except the Notes field, are used to store basic information about the contact. Remember that the maximum length for a Text field is 255, so the Notes field was made a Memo field enabling the user to go beyond the Text field limitation.

Table 13-3

Contacts Table
Field
Specifications

Field Name	Field Type	Notes
ContactID	AutoNumber	Primary Key
FirstName	Text	Length = 50
LastName	Text	Length = 50
Address	Text	Length = 100
City	Text	Length = 50
State	Text	Length = 2
ZipCode	Text	Length = 20
Country	Text	Length = 50
WorkPhone	Text	Length = 30
HomePhone	Text	Length = 30
FaxNumber	Text	Length = 30
EmailAddress	Text	Length = 50
Notes	Memo	

Forms

Switchboard Form

The Switchboard form is used to navigate through the forms and report in
the PIM database. It was created using the Switchboard Wizard, which is
accessible within Access through the Tools/Database Utilities/Switch-
board Manager menu item. Only the appearance and layout of the form
produced with that wizard have been altered.

Calendar Form

The Calendar form is the heart of this application. It is not bound to any
table; instead, it uses code to completely control how and what data is displayed. Before looking at the code, one of the properties of the form needs
to be discussed.

As you saw when looking at the application, the Calendar has alarms that fire when an event is approaching. If you are familiar with Visual Basic, the Timer Control may also be familiar. In Visual Basic, this control is used to fire your code at timed intervals. Access has no such control. Instead, each form has its own timer event and property.

The property for a form is called TimerInterval. The property stores the number of milliseconds between calls to your timer event. So in this example, the alarm for upcoming events fires every five minutes, that is, 300 seconds or 300,000 milliseconds. This property on the Calendar form was set to 300,000.

The code that you want to run at the timer's interval is placed in the Form_Timer event. In this case, you want your code to look for any items that are within 15 minutes or are in the past and have their alarm set. Then, inform the user about these events. The code block below accomplishes this task:

```
Private Sub Form_Timer()
    Dim MyDB As DAO.Database
    Dim RS As DAO.Recordset
    Set MyDB = CurrentDb
    Set RS = MyDB.OpenRecordset("Select CalendarItemID, Caption, WhenStarts " _
        & "From CalendarItems where CDate(DateAdd(""n"",-15,WhenStarts)) " _
        & "<= #" & Now & "# and Alarm = True Order By WhenStarts", dbOpenSnapshot)
    Do Until RS.EOF
        If MsgBox(RS("Caption") & " " & RS("WhenStarts") & vbNewLine _
            & "Would you like to turn off this alarm?", _
            vbQuestion + vbYesNo, "ALARM!!!") = vbYes Then
            MyDB.Execute "Update CalendarItems set Alarm = False " _
                & "Where CalendarItemID = " & RS("CalendarItemID")
        End If
        RS.MoveNext
    Loop
End Sub
```

Connect through code to this database:

```
Dim MyDB As DAO.Database
```

and retrieve data:

```
Dim RS As DAO.Recordset
```

Then, connect your Database object to the current database with which you are working:

```
Set MyDB = CurrentDb
```

Next, retrieve from the CalendarItems table any records that have a start date that is less than 15 minutes from now and have alarms which are activated. Note the use of the DateAdd function in the query. The first parameter indicates that we want to add minutes, the "n." The second parameter indicates that we want to add -15 minutes. The date to add to is named in the third parameter. Also note the use of the Now function, which returns the current system date and time:

```
Set RS = MyDB.OpenRecordset("Select CalendarItemID, Caption, WhenStarts " _
    & "From CalendarItems where CDate(DateAdd(""n"",-15,WhenStarts)) " _
    & "<= #" & Now & "# and Alarm = True Order By WhenStarts", dbOpenSnapshot)
```

Then start a loop that goes through each of the records that have just been retrieved from the database:

```
Do Until RS.EOF
```

Display information on each of these records in a message box. Note that the message box displays the Yes and No buttons. Also notice whether the user presses the Yes button:

```
If MsgBox(RS("Caption") & " " & RS("WhenStarts") & vbNewLine _
        & "Would you like to turn off this alarm?", _
        vbQuestion + vbYesNo, "ALARM!!!") = vbYes Then
```

If the Yes button is pressed, the user wants to turn off this item's alarm, which is done with an SQL Update statement:

```
MyDB.Execute "Update CalendarItems set Alarm = False " _
        & "Where CalendarItemID = " & RS("CalendarItemID")
```

Then, move on to the next record before looping:

```
        RS.MoveNext
Loop
```

In the General Declaration section, note a few lines of code:

```
Option Explicit
Private CurrentDate As Date
Private IsOnLoad As Boolean
```

As with all forms, start by indicating that you will declare your variables:

```
Option Explicit
```

Also declare a Private variable that stores the current date with which you are working. A Private variable is available to any procedure on this form but not to other forms:

```
Private CurrentDate As Date
```

The other Private variable is used to indicate that the form is currently loading:

```
Private IsOnLoad As Boolean
```

When the form first opens, the Open event fires. At that point, the Calendar, the notes page, and the current date need to be set. The following code does that:

```
Private Sub Form_Open(Cancel As Integer)
    IsOnLoad = True
    CurrentDate = Date
    DateHasChanged
    Form_Timer
    IsOnLoad = False
End Sub
```

Start by indicating that the form is currently loading. This variable is used in another procedure:

```
IsOnLoad = True
```

Then set the CurrentDate variable to the current system date:

```
CurrentDate = Date
```

Many of the procedures on this form need to have the Calendar redrawn. For example, when the user switches the day, the Calendar needs to be redisplayed. Because this needs to occur in many locations, a procedure called DateHasChanged was created. This procedure is called here and will be discussed next:

```
DateHasChanged
```

Then, fire your Timer event so the user is made aware of any past or impending events right when the form first opens:

```
Form_Timer
```

You are now finished loading the form, so toggle the IsOnLoad variable to indicate that fact:

```
IsOnLoad = False
```

As recently mentioned, the DateHasChanged method is called by numerous other procedures and is responsible for populating the controls on the form:

```
Public Sub DateHasChanged()
    Dim MyDB As DAO.Database
    Dim RS As DAO.Recordset
    Dim RSNotes As DAO.Recordset
    Dim TheControl As Control
    lblTitle.Caption = "Calendar: " & Format(CurrentDate, "Long Date")
    For Each TheControl In Me.Controls
        If TypeOf TheControl Is TextBox Then
            If InStr(TheControl.Name, "lblTime") Then
                TheControl.SetFocus
                TheControl.Locked = False
                TheControl.Text = ""
                TheControl.Locked = True
                TheControl.StatusBarText = ""
                TheControl.BackColor = "16777215"
            End If
        End If
    Next
    lblTime00.SetFocus
    Set MyDB = CurrentDb
    Set RS = MyDB.OpenRecordset("Select WhenStarts, WhenEnds, Caption " _
        & "From CalendarItems where
CDate(format(WhenStarts,""MM/DD/YY"")) " _
        & " = #" & CurrentDate & "#", dbOpenSnapshot)
    Do Until RS.EOF
        If Hour(RS("WhenStarts")) > 11 Then
            Me.Controls("lbltimep" & Hour(RS("whenstarts")) _
                & Minute(RS("whenstarts"))) = RS("caption")
            Me.Controls("lbltimep" & Hour(RS("whenstarts")) _
                & Minute(RS("whenstarts"))).StatusBarText _
                    = RS("caption") & " " & RS("WhenStarts") _
                    & " - " & RS("WhenEnds")
            Me.Controls("lbltimep" & Hour(RS("whenstarts")) _
                & Minute(RS("whenstarts"))).BackColor _
                = "8454143"
        Else
            Me.Controls("lbltime" & Hour(RS("whenstarts")) _
                & Minute(RS("whenstarts"))) = RS("caption")
            Me.Controls("lbltime" & Hour(RS("whenstarts")) _
                & Minute(RS("whenstarts"))).StatusBarText _
                    = RS("caption") & " " & RS("WhenStarts") _
                    & " - " & RS("WhenEnds")
            Me.Controls("lbltime" & Hour(RS("whenstarts")) _
                & Minute(RS("whenstarts"))).BackColor _
                = "8454143"
```

```
            End If
            RS.MoveNext
    Loop
    txtNotes = ""
    Set RSNotes = MyDB.OpenRecordset("Select TheNote from TheNotes " _
        & "Where Format(NoteDate, ""mm/dd/yy"") = '" _
        & Format(CurrentDate, "mm/dd/yy") & "'", dbOpenSnapshot)
    If RSNotes.EOF Then
        MyDB.Execute "Insert Into TheNotes (NoteDate) values (""" _
            & CurrentDate & """)"
    Else
        txtNotes = RSNotes("TheNote")
    End If
    DoCmd.GoToPage 1
End Sub
```

Start by declaring the necessary variables. Then, connect to the database:

```
Dim MyDB As DAO.Database
```

and retrieve calendar data:

```
Dim RS As DAO.Recordset
```

as well as note data:

```
Dim RSNotes As DAO.Recordset
```

The Calendar part of the form has 48 text boxes that can contain events for a given day. Instead of working with these controls one at a time, iterate through the collection of all the controls and work on them together:

```
Dim TheControl As Control
```

Next, set the label in the header so it displays the current date with which you are working:

```
lblTitle.Caption = "Calendar: " & Format(CurrentDate, "Long Date")
```

Then, start a loop that iterates through all the controls on this form, enabling you to reset the calendar:

```
For Each TheControl In Me.Controls
```

Check to see if the control that has been iterated to is a text box:

```
If TypeOf TheControl Is TextBox Then
```

If it is, check to see if it is one of the 48 text boxes used to display item information. Do this by looking at its name. Each of the 48 text boxes at issue has a name that starts with lblTime. Look for that name here:

```
If InStr(TheControl.Name, "lblTime") Then
```

If it is that name, set focus to that text box:

```
TheControl.SetFocus
```

and unlock it so its value can be cleared:

```
TheControl.Locked = False
TheControl.Text = ""
```

Then lock the control back up so the user can't change its data here:

```
TheControl.Locked = True
```

Also clear the text displayed for this text box in the status bar:

```
TheControl.StatusBarText = ""
```

and reset the background color to white:

```
TheControl.BackColor = "16777215"
```

Then move on to the next control:

```
            End If
        End If
Next
```

Set the focus back to the first calendar text box:

```
lblTime00.SetFocus
```

Next, connect to the database:

```
Set MyDB = CurrentDb
```

and retrieve all the calendar items that are for the current date with which you are working:

```
Set RS = MyDB.OpenRecordset("Select WhenStarts, WhenEnds, Caption " _
    & "From CalendarItems where CDate(format(WhenStarts,""MM/DD/YY"")) " _
    & " = #" & CurrentDate & "#", dbOpenSnapshot)
```

Start a loop so each of the items for this date can be processed:

```
Do Until RS.EOF
```

If the hour for the event is noon or later, the controls are named slightly differently. Check for that here:

```
If Hour(RS("WhenStarts")) > 11 Then
```

Then, place the caption for this calendar item in the correct text box by extracting the hour and minute that the events start. Because they must start on either the hour or 1/2 hour, the text boxes have been named to match those 48 intervals of the day. For example, the text box for 10:30 PM is named lblTimeP2230:

```
Me.Controls("lbltimep" & Hour(RS("whenstarts")) _
        & Minute(RS("whenstarts"))) = RS("caption")
```

After setting the text for the text box, set the status bar text so it also contains the beginning and ending times of the event:

```
Me.Controls("lbltimep" & Hour(RS("whenstarts")) _
        & Minute(RS("whenstarts"))).StatusBarText _
        = RS("caption") & " " & RS("WhenStarts") _
        & " - " & RS("WhenEnds")
```

Also set the background color of the text box to yellow:

```
Me.Controls("lbltimep" & Hour(RS("whenstarts")) _
        & Minute(RS("whenstarts"))).BackColor _
        = "8454143"
```

The Else portion of the If statement does the same code, except for the AM times, because they have a slightly different name:

```
Else
        Me.Controls("lbltime" & Hour(RS("whenstarts")) _
                & Minute(RS("whenstarts"))) = RS("caption")
        Me.Controls("lbltime" & Hour(RS("whenstarts")) _
                & Minute(RS("whenstarts"))).StatusBarText _
                = RS("caption") & " " & RS("WhenStarts") _
                & " - " & RS("WhenEnds")
        Me.Controls("lbltime" & Hour(RS("whenstarts")) _
                & Minute.(RS("whenstarts"))).BackColor _
        = "8454143"
End If
```

Move on to the next record:

```
RS.MoveNext
```

and loop:

```
Loop
```

Also display the notes for this date. First, clear the existing text in that text box:

```
txtNotes = ""
```

Then, retrieve the text for this date from the database:

```
Set RSNotes = MyDB.OpenRecordset("Select TheNote from TheNotes "  _
        & "Where Format(NoteDate, ""mm/dd/yy"")  = '"  _
        & Format(CurrentDate, "mm/dd/yy") & "'", dbOpenSnapshot)
```

If no record is found, the EOF flag is set:

```
If RSNotes.EOF Then
```

This is the first item for which the user is displaying this date. In that case, create a note record:

```
MyDB.Execute "Insert Into TheNotes (NoteDate) values ("""  _
        & CurrentDate & """)"
```

Otherwise, find a record and place it in the notes text box:

```
txtNotes = RSNotes("TheNote")
```

At the end of this procedure, return the user to the Calendar page of this form:

```
DoCmd.GoToPage 1
```

After the user leaves the notes text box, assume that he or she has changed it and needs to save the new information. This is done in the Exit event of the notes text box.

```
Private Sub txtNotes_Exit(Cancel As Integer)
    Dim MyDB As DAO.Database
    If Not IsOnLoad Then
        Set MyDB = CurrentDb
        MyDB.Execute "Update TheNotes set TheNote = """  _
            & txtNotes.Text & """ Where NoteDate = #"  _
            & CurrentDate & "#"
    End If
End Sub
```

A connection to the database is needed:

```
Dim MyDB As DAO.Database
```

Now you see where the IsOnLoad variable is used. When the form first loads, the control receives the focus before the field has any data in it. So you don't want the event to fire at that time:

```
If Not IsOnLoad Then
```

At any other time, connect to the database:

```
Set MyDB = CurrentDb
```

and update the TheNotes record for the current date:

```
MyDB.Execute "Update TheNotes set TheNote = """ _
        & txtNotes.Text & """ Where NoteDate = #" _
& CurrentDate & "#"
```

In the header of the Calendar form, the user can press one of six buttons that change the date. The first one subtracts a day from the current date.

```
Private Sub cmdLessDay_Click()
    CurrentDate = DateAdd("d", -1, CurrentDate)
    DateHasChanged
End Sub
```

The Date Add function is used to subtract one day from the current date:

```
CurrentDate = DateAdd("d", -1, CurrentDate)
```

Then, reload the calendar:

```
DateHasChanged
```

The next button uses the DateAdd function to add one day to the current date. Remember that the DateHasChanged function is your own procedure that repopulates the Calendar and Notes text box:

```
Private Sub cmdMoreDay_Click()
    CurrentDate = DateAdd("d", 1, CurrentDate)
    DateHasChanged
End Sub
```

The user can also press a button to go back one week. Again the DateAdd function is used, but this time seven days are subtracted from the current date:

```
Private Sub cmdLessWeek_Click()
    CurrentDate = DateAdd("d", -7, CurrentDate)
    DateHasChanged
End Sub
```

The button after that adds seven days to the current date:

```
Private Sub cmdMoreWeek_Click()
    CurrentDate = DateAdd("d", 7, CurrentDate)
    DateHasChanged
End Sub
```

The user can also move back a month. Notice that the first parameter is now an "m," indicating that you want to manipulate the date in months:

```
Private Sub cmdLessMonth_Click()
    CurrentDate = DateAdd("m", -1, CurrentDate)
    DateHasChanged
End Sub
```

The user can also elect to go forward a month:

```
Private Sub cmdMoreMonth_Click()
    CurrentDate = DateAdd("m", 1, CurrentDate)
    DateHasChanged
End Sub
```

The footer of the form contains a variety of buttons that provide specific functionality. The first button is the Add Item button:

```
Private Sub CommandAdd_Click()
    DoCmd.OpenForm "Calendar Items", , , , acFormAdd, acDialog, CurrentDate
    DateHasChanged
End Sub
```

Use the OpenForm method to open the Calendar Items form. Note that the CurrentDate is being passed to the form in the last parameter. This data used on the Calendar Items form is also seen later in this chapter:

```
DoCmd.OpenForm "Calendar Items", , , , acFormAdd, acDialog,
CurrentDate
```

After the user is finished with that form, redisplay your Calendar:

```
DateHasChanged
```

The next button on the footer is the Delete button:

```
Private Sub CommandDelete_Click()
    Dim MyDB As DAO.Database
    Screen.PreviousControl.SetFocus
    If TypeOf Screen.ActiveControl Is TextBox Then
        If InStr(Screen.ActiveControl.Name, "lblTime") Then
            If Screen.ActiveControl.Text <> "" Then
                Set MyDB = CurrentDb
                MyDB.Execute "Delete From CalendarItems Where " _
                    & "CDate(format(WhenStarts,""MM/DD/YY"")) " _
                    & " = #" & CurrentDate & "# and Caption = """ _
                    & Screen.ActiveControl.Text & """"
                DateHasChanged
            End If
        End If
    End If
End Sub
```

When the user presses the Delete button, delete the current calendar item. Then, a Database object is needed:

```
Dim MyDB As DAO.Database
```

Assume that the event the user wants to delete was the one being viewed before clicking on the Delete button. Move the focus back to that control:

```
Screen.PreviousControl.SetFocus
```

Then, make sure that it is actually a text box:

```
If TypeOf Screen.ActiveControl Is TextBox Then
```

and that it is one of the 48 time slot text boxes:

```
If InStr(Screen.ActiveControl.Name, "lblTime") Then
```

and that it contains an appointment:

```
If Screen.ActiveControl.Text <> "" Then
```

If all those conditions are met, connect to the database:

```
Set MyDB = CurrentDb
```

and delete the record based on the current date and the caption of the item being deleted:

```
MyDB.Execute "Delete From CalendarItems Where " _
    & "CDate(format(WhenStarts,""MM/DD/YY"")) " _
    & " = #" & CurrentDate & "# and Caption = """ _
    & Screen.ActiveControl.Text & """"
```

Then, repopulate the calendar:

```
DateHasChanged
```

The next code block fires when the user clicks on the View Item button:

```
Private Sub Command173_Click()
    Screen.PreviousControl.SetFocus
    If TypeOf Screen.ActiveControl Is TextBox Then
        If InStr(Screen.ActiveControl.Name, "lblTime") Then
            If Screen.ActiveControl.Text <> "" Then
                DoCmd.OpenForm "Calendar Items", , , _
                    "CDate(format(WhenStarts,""MM/DD/YY"")) " _
                    & " = #" & CurrentDate & "# and Caption = """ _
                    & Screen.ActiveControl.Text & """", , acDialog
                DateHasChanged
            End If
        End If
    End If
End Sub
```

The item that the user wants to view was the one that last had the focus:

```
Screen.PreviousControl.SetFocus
```

Confirm that that control is actually a text box:

```
If TypeOf Screen.ActiveControl Is TextBox Then
```

is one of your 48 labels:

```
If InStr(Screen.ActiveControl.Name, "lblTime") Then
```

and has a value:

```
If Screen.ActiveControl.Text <> "" Then
```

If those conditions are met, open the Calendar Items and have it display the currently selected record:

```
DoCmd.OpenForm "Calendar Items", , , _
    "CDate(format(WhenStarts,""MM/DD/YY"")) " _
    & " = #" & CurrentDate & "# and Caption = """ _
    & Screen.ActiveControl.Text & """", , acDialog
```

Since the user could have made changes to the item, refresh your calendar by calling the DateHasChanged procedure:

```
DateHasChanged
```

The Calendar form has two pages. The first is the Calendar itself; the other is the Notes page. When the user clicks on the Calendar button, he or she returns to the Calendar page:

```
Private Sub Command176_Click()
    DoCmd.GoToPage 1
End Sub
```

If the user clicks on the Notes button, he or she is sent to the second page using the GoToPage method of the DoCmd object:

```
Private Sub Command177_Click()
    DoCmd.GoToPage 2
End Sub
```

The last code block on the form fires when the user clicks on the Close button. The procedure closes the form:

```
Private Sub CommandClose_Click()
    DoCmd.Close
End Sub
```

Calendar Items Form

The code on the Calendar Items form enables the user to add, delete, and repeat items. It also makes sure no conflicting records are entered. When the form is first opened the Activate event fires:

```
Private Sub Form_Activate()
    If IsDate(Me.OpenArgs) Then
        [WhenStarts] = Me.OpenArgs
    End If
End Sub
```

Remember that on the Calendar form, when the user clicked on the Add Item button, this form was called, passing to it the date that was in use. That date is now available on this form through the OpenArgs property of the form. Check here to see if it is a date:

```
If IsDate(Me.OpenArgs) Then
```

If it is, use that value for the WhenStarts field:

```
[WhenStarts] = Me.OpenArgs
```

When the user leaves the WhenStarts field, check the value entered:

```
Private Sub WhenStarts_Exit(Cancel As Integer)
    Dim MyDB As DAO.Database
    Dim RS As DAO.Recordset
    If Not IsDate([WhenStarts]) Then
        MsgBox "This field is required. Please enter a date!"
        Cancel = True
    Else
        If Minute([WhenStarts]) < 30 Then
            [WhenStarts] = DateAdd("n", Minute([WhenStarts]) * -1, [WhenStarts])
        Else
            [WhenStarts] = DateAdd("n", (Minute([WhenStarts]) - 30) * -1, [WhenStarts])
        End If
        Set MyDB = CurrentDb
        Set RS = MyDB.OpenRecordset("Select CalendarItemID from CalendarItems " _
            & "Where WhenStarts = #" & [WhenStarts] & "# and " _
            & "CalendarItemID <> " & [CalendarItemID], dbOpenSnapshot)
        If Not RS.EOF Then
            MsgBox "An item already starts at this date and time. " _
                & "Please enter a different start time."
            Cancel = True
        End If
    End If
End Sub
```

One of the checks is made to see if any other records conflict with this time. So, connect to the database:

```
Dim MyDB As DAO.Database
```

and retrieve information:

```
Dim RS As DAO.Recordset
```

But first, make sure the value entered is a date:

```
If Not IsDate([WhenStarts]) Then
```

If it isn't, prompt the user to enter a date:

```
MsgBox "This field is required. Please enter a date!"
```

and prevent them from leaving this field:

```
Cancel = True
```

Otherwise, round the time entered to either on the hour or at the half-hour. Check to see if the minutes entered is less than 30:

```
If Minute([WhenStarts]) < 30 Then
```

If so, subtract out the number of minutes:

```
[WhenStarts] = DateAdd("n", Minute([WhenStarts]) * -1, [WhenStarts])
```

Otherwise, round to the half-hour:

```
[WhenStarts] = DateAdd("n", (Minute([WhenStarts]) - 30) * -1, [WhenStarts])
```

Next, connect to the database:

```
Set MyDB = CurrentDb
```

and look for a conflicting record:

```
Set RS = MyDB.OpenRecordset("Select CalendarItemID from
CalendarItems " _
        & "Where WhenStarts = #" & [WhenStarts] & "# and " _
        & "CalendarItemID <> " & [CalendarItemID], dbOpenSnapshot)
```

If one is found, EOF is turned off:

```
If Not RS.EOF Then
```

Then inform the user of the problem:

```
MsgBox "An item already starts at this date and time. " _
& "Please enter a different start time."
```

and prevent them from leaving this field:

```
Cancel = True
```

Make similar checks when the user leaves the WhenEnds field:

```
Private Sub WhenEnds_Exit(Cancel As Integer)
    If Not IsDate([WhenEnds]) Then
        MsgBox "This field is required. Please enter a date!"
        Cancel = True
    Else
        If Minute([WhenEnds]) < 30 Then
            [WhenEnds] = DateAdd("n", Minute([WhenEnds]) * -1, [WhenEnds])
        Else
            [WhenEnds] = DateAdd("n", (Minute([WhenEnds]) - 30) * -1,
```

```
[WhenEnds])
            End If
        End If
End Sub
```

Start by making sure the value entered is a date:

```
If Not IsDate([WhenEnds]) Then
```

If it isn't, inform the user of the problem:

```
MsgBox "This field is required. Please enter a date!"
```

and prevent them from leaving the field:

```
Cancel = True
```

Otherwise, round the minutes to the nearest half-hour:

```
If Minute([WhenEnds]) < 30 Then
```

First, round down to 0 any minutes below 30:

```
[WhenEnds] = DateAdd("n", Minute([WhenEnds]) * -1, [WhenEnds])
```

If the number of minutes is above 30, round to 30:

```
[WhenEnds] = DateAdd("n", (Minute([WhenEnds]) - 30) * -1, [WhenEnds])
```

Three buttons in the detail section of this form enable the user to repeat this calendar item. The first code block fires when the user clicks on the Every Day for a Week button.

```
Private Sub Command30_Click()
    Dim MyDB As DAO.Database
    Dim RS As DAO.Recordset
    Dim I As Integer
    Dim CurrentStartDate As Date
    Dim CurrentEndDate As Date
    If IsDate([WhenStarts]) And IsDate([WhenEnds]) _
        And [Caption] <> "" Then
        Set MyDB = CurrentDb
        CurrentStartDate = [WhenStarts]
        CurrentEndDate = [WhenEnds]
        For I = 1 To 7
            CurrentStartDate = DateAdd("d", 1, CurrentStartDate)
            CurrentEndDate = DateAdd("d", 1, CurrentEndDate)
            Set RS = MyDB.OpenRecordset("Select CalendarItemID from CalendarItems " _
                & "Where WhenStarts = #" & CurrentStartDate & "#", dbOpenSnapshot)
```

```
            If RS.EOF Then
                MyDB.Execute "Insert Into CalendarItems (Caption, WhenStarts, " _
                    & "WhenEnds, Description, Alarm) values (" _
                    & """" & Me.Detail.Controls("Caption") & """, " _
                    & """" & CurrentStartDate & """, " _
                    & """" & CurrentEndDate & """, " _
                    & """" & [Description] & """, " _
                    & [Alarm] & ")"
            End If
        Next
        Me.Requery
    Else
        MsgBox "Please complete this item before repeating it."
    End If
End Sub
```

Connect to the database:

```
Dim MyDB As DAO.Database
```

and retrieve information:

```
Dim RS As DAO.Recordset
```

This variable is used in a For block:

```
Dim I As Integer
```

This one stores the start date as you loop through the code block:

```
Dim CurrentStartDate As Date
```

This one stores the end date:

```
Dim CurrentEndDate As Date
```

Before any changes are made, make sure that the record is valid:

```
If IsDate([WhenStarts]) And IsDate([WhenEnds]) _
        And [Caption] <> "" Then
```

If it is, connect to your database:

```
Set MyDB = CurrentDb
```

Set the start date to the date of the current record:

```
CurrentStartDate = [WhenStarts]
```

and the end date to the end date of the current record:

```
CurrentEndDate = [WhenEnds]
```

Because records for a week need to be added, loop seven times:

```
For I = 1 To 7
```

Then, add one day to our start date:

```
CurrentStartDate = DateAdd("d", 1, CurrentStartDate)
```

and end date:

```
CurrentEndDate = DateAdd("d", 1, CurrentEndDate)
```

Make sure that a conflicting record does not exist:

```
Set RS = MyDB.OpenRecordset("Select CalendarItemID from CalendarItems " _
    & "Where WhenStarts = #" & CurrentStartDate & "#", dbOpenSnapshot)
```

If the spot is open, EOF is set:

```
If RS.EOF Then
```

In that case, add the new calendar item based on the values of the current record on this form:

```
MyDB.Execute "Insert Into CalendarItems (Caption, WhenStarts, " _
        & "WhenEnds, Description, Alarm) values (" _
        & """" & Me.Detail.Controls("Caption") & """, " _
        & """" & CurrentStartDate & """, " _
        & """" & CurrentEndDate & """, " _
        & """" & [Description] & """, " _
        & [Alarm] & ")"
```

Move on to process the item for the next day:

```
Next
```

After completing your loop, the form is refreshed so the new records can be seen:

```
Me.Requery
```

If the code flows here, the record did not have valid information:

```
Else
```

Inform the user of the problem:

```
MsgBox "Please complete this item before repeating it."
```

The next code block repeats the current record over the next five days:

```
Private Sub Command31_Click()
    Dim MyDB As DAO.Database
    Dim RS As DAO.Recordset
    Dim I As Integer
    Dim CurrentStartDate As Date
    Dim CurrentEndDate As Date
If IsDate([WhenStarts]) And IsDate([WhenEnds]) _
        And [Caption] <> "" Then
        Set MyDB = CurrentDb
        CurrentStartDate = [WhenStarts]
        CurrentEndDate = [WhenEnds]
        For I = 1 To 5
            CurrentStartDate = DateAdd("d", 1, CurrentStartDate)
            CurrentEndDate = DateAdd("d", 1, CurrentEndDate)
            Set RS = MyDB.OpenRecordset("Select CalendarItemID from CalendarItems " _
                & "Where WhenStarts = #" & CurrentStartDate & "#", dbOpenSnapshot)
            If RS.EOF Then
                MyDB.Execute "Insert Into CalendarItems (Caption, WhenStarts, " _
                    & "WhenEnds, Description, Alarm) values (" _
                    & """" & Me.Detail.Controls("Caption") & """, " _
                    & """" & CurrentStartDate & """, " _
                    & """" & CurrentEndDate & """, " _
                    & """" & [Description] & """, " _
                    & [Alarm] & ")"
            End If
        Next
        Me.Requery
    Else
        MsgBox "Please complete this item before repeating it."
    End If
End Sub
```

A connection to the database is needed:

```
Dim MyDB As DAO.Database
```

and a Recordset object:

```
Dim RS As DAO.Recordset
```

a variable for a loop:

```
Dim I As Integer
```

and variables to store the dates with which you are working:

```
Dim CurrentStartDate As Date
Dim CurrentEndDate As Date
```

Check the validity of the current record that the user wants to repeat:

```
If IsDate([WhenStarts]) And IsDate([WhenEnds]) _
        And [Caption] <> "" Then
```

If it is valid, connect to the database:

```
Set MyDB = CurrentDb
```

Set the start and end dates based on the current record that is to be repeated:

```
CurrentStartDate = [WhenStarts]
CurrentEndDate = [WhenEnds]
```

Your loop will iterate five times for the five days that the user indicated:

```
For I = 1 To 5
```

Then increment your start and end dates by one day:

```
CurrentStartDate = DateAdd("d", 1, CurrentStartDate)
CurrentEndDate = DateAdd("d", 1, CurrentEndDate)
```

and make sure the time slot is open for an appointment:

```
Set RS = MyDB.OpenRecordset("Select CalendarItemID from
CalendarItems " _
        & "Where WhenStarts = #" & CurrentStartDate & "#",
dbOpenSnapshot)
```

If it is available, EOF is set since no record was found:

```
If RS.EOF Then
```

Then add the record to the table:

```
MyDB.Execute "Insert Into CalendarItems (Caption, WhenStarts, " _
        & "WhenEnds, Description, Alarm) values (" _
        & """" & Me.Detail.Controls("Caption") & """, " _
        & """" & CurrentStartDate & """, " _
        & """" & CurrentEndDate & """, " _
        & """" & [Description] & """, " _
& [Alarm] & ")"
```

Move on to the next iteration:

```
Next
```

After the For block, refresh the form so the new records are visible:

```
Me.Requery
```

If the record to be repeated is not valid, inform the user of the problem:

```
MsgBox "Please complete this item before repeating it."
```

The other button in the detail section of the form enables the user to repeat the item once a week for the next six weeks:

```
Private Sub Command32_Click()
    Dim MyDB As DAO.Database
    Dim RS As DAO.Recordset
    Dim I As Integer
    Dim CurrentStartDate As Date
    Dim CurrentEndDate As Date
If IsDate([WhenStarts]) And IsDate([WhenEnds]) _
        And [Caption] <> "" Then
        Set MyDB = CurrentDb
        CurrentStartDate = [WhenStarts]
        CurrentEndDate = [WhenEnds]
        For I = 1 To 6
            CurrentStartDate = DateAdd("d", 7, CurrentStartDate)
            CurrentEndDate = DateAdd("d", 7, CurrentEndDate)
            Set RS = MyDB.OpenRecordset("Select CalendarItemID from CalendarItems " _
                & "Where WhenStarts = #" & CurrentStartDate & "#", dbOpenSnapshot)
            If RS.EOF Then
                MyDB.Execute "Insert Into CalendarItems (Caption, WhenStarts, " _
                    & "WhenEnds, Description, Alarm) values (" _
                    & """" & Me.Detail.Controls("Caption") & """, " _
                    & """" & CurrentStartDate & """, " _
                    & """" & CurrentEndDate & """, " _
                    & """" & [Description] & """, " _
                    & [Alarm] & ")"
            End If
        Next
        Me.Requery
    Else
        MsgBox "Please complete this item before repeating it."
    End If
End Sub
```

Start by declaring a Database object:

```
Dim MyDB As DAO.Database
```

and a DAO Recordset object:

```
Dim RS As DAO.Recordset
```

You need a variable for a loop:

```
Dim I As Integer
```

and two to hold the dates of the event:

```
Dim CurrentStartDate As Date
Dim CurrentEndDate As Date
```

Then check the validity of the record that the user wants to repeat:

```
If IsDate([WhenStarts]) And IsDate([WhenEnds]) _
        And [Caption] <> "" Then
```

If the record is valid, connect to the current database with which you are working:

```
Set MyDB = CurrentDb
```

and set the dates based on the current record on the form:

```
CurrentStartDate = [WhenStarts]
CurrentEndDate = [WhenEnds]
```

Repeat the record over the next six weeks:

```
For I = 1 To 6
```

so add one week to the start date:

```
CurrentStartDate = DateAdd("d", 7, CurrentStartDate)
```

and one week to the end date:

```
CurrentEndDate = DateAdd("d", 7, CurrentEndDate)
```

Then make sure the time-slot is open:

```
Set RS = MyDB.OpenRecordset("Select CalendarItemID from
CalendarItems " _
        & "Where WhenStarts = #" & CurrentStartDate & "#",
dbOpenSnapshot)
```

If the time-slot is open, no record should be found:

```
If RS.EOF Then
```

In that case, insert a new record at this week interval with the information coming from the calendar item that the user wants to repeat:

```
MyDB.Execute "Insert Into CalendarItems (Caption, WhenStarts, " _
    & "WhenEnds, Description, Alarm) values (" _
    & """" & Me.Detail.Controls("Caption") & """, " _
    & """" & CurrentStartDate & """, " _
    & """ & CurrentEndDate & """, " _
    & """" & [Description] & """, " _
    & [Alarm] & ")"
```

Then move on to the next iteration of the loop:

```
Next
```

After looping, refresh the form so the new records are visible:

```
Me.Requery
```

If the record that the user wants to repeat isn't valid, display a message box with that information:

```
MsgBox "Please complete this item before repeating it."
```

The footer of the form contains four other buttons. The first one fires when the user clicks on the Add button:

```
Private Sub CommandAdd_Click()
    DoCmd.GoToRecord , , acNewRec
    [WhenStarts].SetFocus
End Sub
```

The GoToRecord method is used to move the record pointer on to a new record:

```
DoCmd.GoToRecord , , acNewRec
```

Then, set the focus to the first field on the form so the user can start entering data:

```
[WhenStarts].SetFocus
```

The next code block fires when the user clicks on the Delete button:

```
Private Sub CommandDelete_Click()
    On Error GoTo HandleError
    DoCmd.DoMenuItem acFormBar, acEditMenu, 8, , acMenuVer70
    DoCmd.DoMenuItem acFormBar, acEditMenu, 6, , acMenuVer70
    [WhenStarts].SetFocus
    Exit Sub
```

```
HandleError:
    If Err.Number <> 2501 Then
        MsgBox Err.Number & " " & Err.Description
    End If
End Sub
```

Trap an error:

```
On Error GoTo HandleError
```

Then attempt to delete the record:

```
DoCmd.DoMenuItem acFormBar, acEditMenu, 8, , acMenuVer70
DoCmd.DoMenuItem acFormBar, acEditMenu, 6, , acMenuVer70
```

If possible, move the focus back to the detail section:

```
[WhenStarts].SetFocus
```

and leave this procedure:

```
Exit Sub
```

If an error occurred, the code flows to this line:

```
HandleError:
```

show all error messages unless it is 2501, which means that the user pressed No when asked to confirm the record deletion:

```
If Err.Number <> 2501 Then
```

If that isn't the error, the error is displayed in a message box:

```
MsgBox Err.Number & " " & Err.Description
```

The next code block fires when the user clicks on the Search button:

```
Private Sub CommandSearch_Click()
    Screen.PreviousControl.SetFocus
    DoCmd.DoMenuItem acFormBar, acEditMenu, 10, , acMenuVer70
End Sub
```

Assume that the user wants to search the field that was viewed last:

```
Screen.PreviousControl.SetFocus
```

Open the Search dialog:

```
DoCmd.DoMenuItem acFormBar, acEditMenu, 10, , acMenuVer70
```

The last code block fires when the user clicks on the Close button. The code uses the Close method of the DoCmd object to close the current form:

```
Private Sub CommandClose_Click()
    DoCmd.Close
End Sub
```

Contacts Form

The code on the Contact form enables the user to add a new contact, delete a contact, search the table, and close the form. The first code block fires when the Add button is pressed:

```
Private Sub CommandAdd_Click()
    DoCmd.GoToRecord , , acNewRec
    [FirstName].SetFocus
End Sub
```

The GoToRecord method is used to add a new record because the third parameter contains the new record constant:

```
DoCmd.GoToRecord , , acNewRec
```

Set the focus to the first field on the form:

```
[FirstName].SetFocus
```

The next code block fires when the Delete button is pressed:

```
Private Sub CommandDelete_Click()
    On Error GoTo HandleError
    DoCmd.DoMenuItem acFormBar, acEditMenu, 8, , acMenuVer70
    DoCmd.DoMenuItem acFormBar, acEditMenu, 6, , acMenuVer70
    [FirstName].SetFocus
    Exit Sub
HandleError:
    If Err.Number <> 2501 Then
        MsgBox Err.Number & " " & Err.Description
    End If
End Sub
```

Start by telling the compiler that any errors are processed here in our procedure:

```
On Error GoTo HandleError
```

Then, delete the current record:

```
DoCmd.DoMenuItem acFormBar, acEditMenu, 8, , acMenuVer70
DoCmd.DoMenuItem acFormBar, acEditMenu, 6, , acMenuVer70
```

If deletion was successful, return the focus to the FirstName field:

```
[FirstName].SetFocus
```

Exit this procedure:

```
Exit Sub
```

If an error did occur, the code flows here to this label:

```
HandleError:
```

Filter out the error thrown if the user cancels the record deletion:

```
If Err.Number <> 2501 Then
```

All other errors are displayed to the user:

```
MsgBox Err.Number & " " & Err.Description
```

The next code block fires when the user clicks on the Search button:

```
Private Sub CommandSearch_Click()
    Screen.PreviousControl.SetFocus
    DoCmd.DoMenuItem acFormBar, acEditMenu, 10, , acMenuVer70
End Sub
```

Assume that the user wants to search the field that he or she was viewing before clicking on the Search button. So, use the SetFocus method of the PreviousControl object to return to that control:

```
Screen.PreviousControl.SetFocus
```

Then, we open the built-in Access Search dialog:

```
DoCmd.DoMenuItem acFormBar, acEditMenu, 10, , acMenuVer70
```

The last procedure closes the form when the Close button is clicked:

```
Private Sub CommandClose_Click()
    DoCmd.Close
End Sub
```

Report

Daily Schedule Report

The Daily Schedule report displays all the calendar items in a specified date. The report is based on a query called Calendar Items on Date that has the following syntax:

```
SELECT CalendarItems.*, CDate(Format([WhenStarts],"mm/dd/yy"))
AS Exp1 FROM CalendarItems
WHERE (((CDate(Format([WhenStarts],"mm/dd/yy")))=
CDate([Enter the date for the schedule])));
```

Note the use of the fake field:

```
[Enter the date for the schedule]
```

Since this isn't a field in the table, the user sees an Input box where the value for the field is entered. The text seen is the text placed between the brackets.

14

Working with MS Office

ON THE CD:

Word Form Letters.mdb

Word Table.mdb

Using Excel.mdb

Using PowerPoint.mdb

Using Word, Excel, and PowerPoint to Enhance your Database Applications

In this chapter, we will review databases and tools that enable you to encapsulate the functionality of Word, Excel, and PowerPoint within your database applications. To take advantage of this functionality, your users must have the Office product for the library you were using on their machine. However, if he or she is already running your Access database, the chances are pretty good that the user has the full suite of office products.

First, we will look at using Word as a tool to create form letters. In this database, the user will be able to generate form letters that combine customer data with a Word document. Then we will look at a form that could be used with just about any database. The form enables the user to select from most tables or queries in that database. It then generates a table in Word based on the data in the database table or query that he or she selected. After that, we will look at a database that uses the functionality of Excel. It outputs data from a database into different Excel spreadsheets. Finally, we will review a database that dynamically builds a PowerPoint presentation based on database information.

But before we start looking at these solutions, we need to answer a question. How do we know which code takes which action in the libraries for the Office products? Almost everything that you want to be able to do in code, based on the Office libraries, you can do manually. You just need to automate that manual process. An easy way to learn which code is needed is to create a macro, take the action you want to code, stop the macro, and then view the code that is contained in the macro you just created.

For example, let's say that you need to send text in code to a Word document that is in Arial, size 12, bold, and italicized. To figure out the code that is needed to take this action, start Word. Go to Tools/Macro/Record New Macro, as is displayed in Figure 14-1.

When you select that menu item, you can see the Record Macro dialog displayed, as in Figure 14-2.

Enter the name that you want to give the macro. Note that this name will be what you are looking for when you look at the code. You can also select the location where the macro is stored and supply the location with a description. Then press the OK button and you are now recording a macro.

Next, take the action that contains the code you want to examine. For example, you could change the font, size, bold, and italic options. Then stop your macro by pressing the small square Stop button on the screen. Now from the menu, select Tools/Macro/Visual Basic Editor, as displayed in Figure 14-3.

When you select this item, Word opens a Visual Basic editor such as you would find in Access. In the right drop-down list, find the name of the macro you just recorded and select it. Figure 14-4 shows the macro called TestMacro that takes the action described earlier. You can now, with minor modifications, paste this code into your Access database to accomplish the same functionality.

Figure 14-1

Selecting a new
macro from the
menu in Word

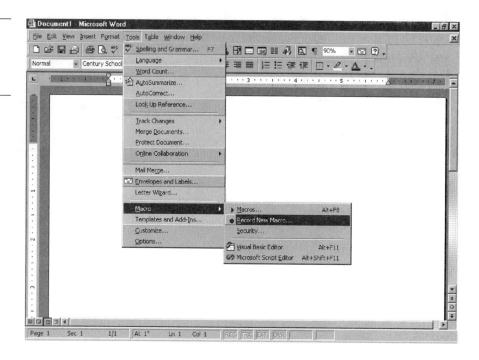

Figure 14-2

The Record
Macro dialog

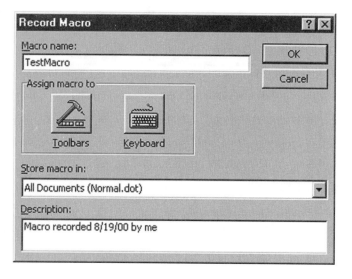

Figure 14-3

Selecting the VB
Editor

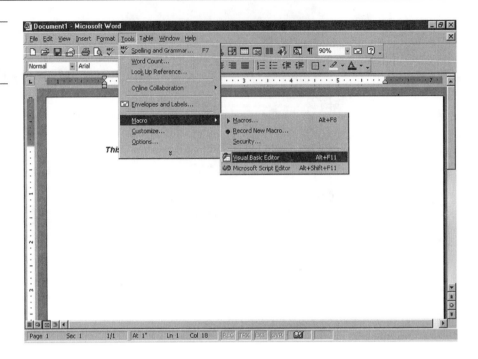

Figure 14-4

Visual Basic
Editor

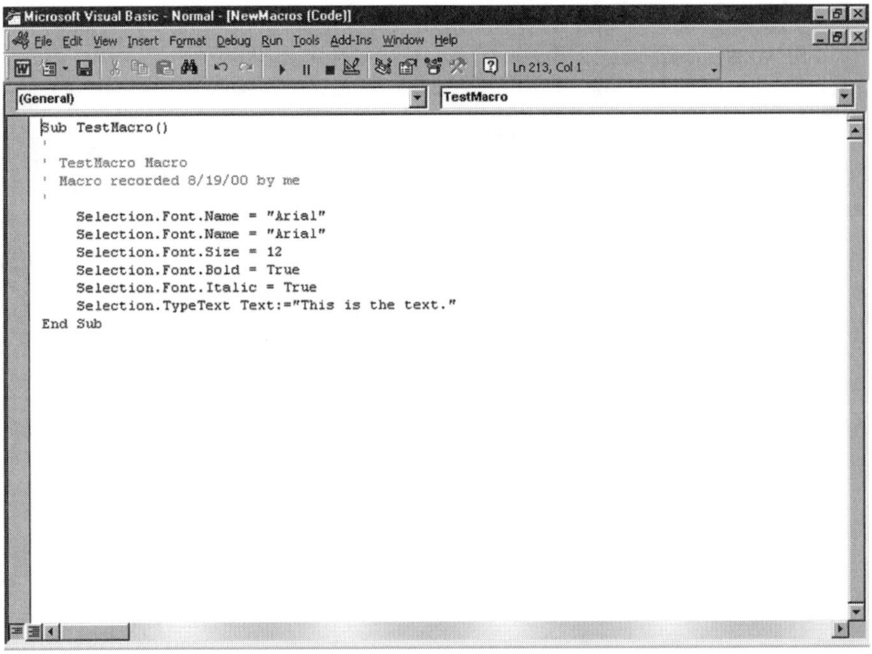

Word Form Letters Database

The Word Form Letters database demonstrates how you can use the functionality of Word in code to act as your report engine in order to generate form letters. The technique of doing this involves creating a document that looks like the form letter you want to produce. You then substitute all the variable pieces of information with bookmarks. Then in code you place data in those bookmarks.

The first thing you need to do to use this technique is to turn Bookmarks on. You can do this by selecting Tools/Options from within Word. When you do so, you will see the Options dialog displayed in Figure 14-5.

Towards the top of the View tab is a check box labeled Bookmarks, which should be checked. Next, create a word document that contains a complete version of the form letter you want to create, such as the one displayed in Figure 14-6.

Figure 14-5

The Options dialog

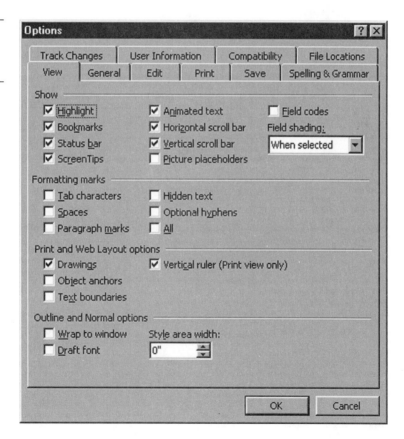

Figure 14-6

The sample
template
document

Notice that in this sample document, placeholder text is used in place of actual data. Next, you need to substitute each of those placeholders with a bookmark. For example, wipe out the NameGoesHere text. Then from the Insert menu, select Bookmarks. You then see the Bookmarks dialog displayed in Figure 14-7.

Supply a name for the bookmark and press OK. Continue this process by replacing each of the areas where you have a placeholder with a bookmark. Be sure to note the names of these bookmarks. Later, you will see how these names are used to insert text in our code.

Sample Walk-through

The Word Form Letters database contains just a single form that displays customer information. The form is displayed in Figure 14-8.

The real focus of the form is on the buttons that are in the footer. Using these buttons, the user generates the form letters. When the user presses the Account Overdue button, he or she is prompted for a couple of values and then he or she sees the form letter displayed in Figure 14-9.

Figure 14-7

The Bookmarks
dialog

Figure 14-8

The Customers
form

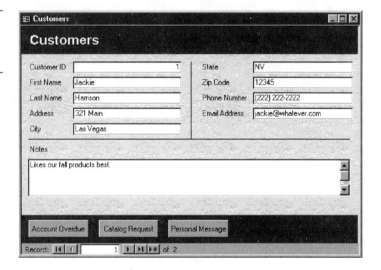

Notice that the Word document contains data from the record displayed on the Customers form. What happens is that the code combines the data on the Customers form with the text stored in the Word document to produce a document that contains data from both. When the user clicks on the Catalog Request button, the form letter displayed in Figure 14-10 is generated.

Figure 14-9

The Account
Overdue form
letter

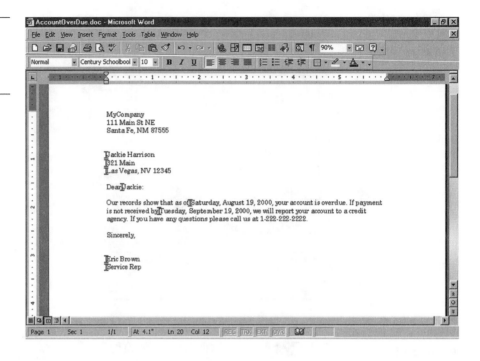

As you will see when you look at the code, the user is asked to enter the names of the catalogs enclosed along with their names and titles. That information and the data on the Customer form are used to generate this document. Notice the bookmarks in this Word document. At each of those points, data is placed.

When the user presses the Personal Message button, he or she sees the form letter displayed in Figure 14-11.

This time the user is asked to supply a message for the body of the document. Often, the customer's information is used to build the Word document.

Customers Table

The Word Form Letters database contains just one table called Customers. This table is used to generate the form letters discussed in the last section. The field specifications for this table are displayed in Table 14-1.

Figure 14-10

Catalog Request
form letter

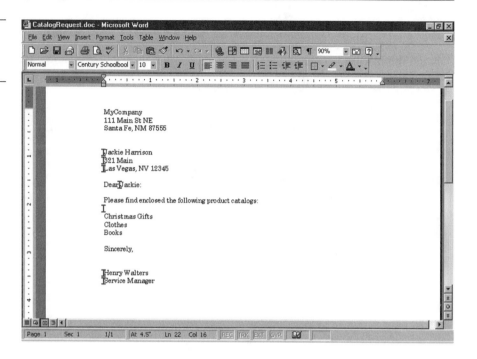

Figure 14-11

The Personal
Message form
letter

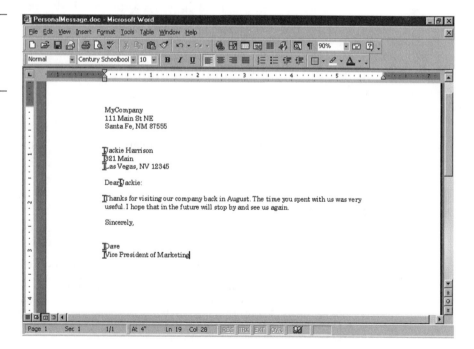

	Field Name	Field Type	Notes
Table 14-1 The Customers Table Field Specifications	CustomerID	Autonumber	Primary Key
	FirstName	Text	Length = 50
	LastName	Text	Length = 50
	Address	Text	Length = 255
	City	Text	Length = 50
	State	Text	Length = 20
	Zip Code	Text	Length = 50
	PhoneNumber	Text	Length = 30
	EmailAddress	Text	Length = 50
	Notes	Memo	

The CustomerID field is the primary key for this table. It is set as an AutoNumber field, so it will be automatically populated when a new record is added. The rest of the fields store general information about the customer.

Customers Form

The code on the Customers form creates the three form letters when the buttons in the footer of the form are clicked. The first code block fires when the Account Overdue button is clicked:

```
Private Sub cmdAccOverdue_Click()
    Dim MyWord As New Word.Application
    Dim ThePath As String
    ThePath = Left(Application.CurrentDb.Name, Len(Application.CurrentDb.Name) - 21)
    MyWord.Application.Documents.Open FileName:=ThePath & "AccountOverDue.doc", _
        ConfirmConversions:=False, _
        ReadOnly:=False, AddToRecentFiles:=False, PasswordDocument:="", _
        PasswordTemplate:="", Revert:=False, WritePasswordDocument:="", _
        WritePasswordTemplate:="", Format:=wdOpenFormatAuto
    MyWord.ActiveWindow.Selection.GoTo What:=wdGoToBookmark, Name:="FullName"
    MyWord.ActiveWindow.Selection.TypeText [FirstName] & " " & [LastName]
    MyWord.ActiveWindow.Selection.GoTo What:=wdGoToBookmark, Name:="Address"
    MyWord.ActiveWindow.Selection.TypeText [Address]
```

```
MyWord.ActiveWindow.Selection.GoTo What:=wdGoToBookmark, Name:="CityStateZip"
MyWord.ActiveWindow.Selection.TypeText [City] & ", " & [State] _
    & " " & [Zip Code]
MyWord.ActiveWindow.Selection.GoTo What:=wdGoToBookmark, Name:="FirstName"
MyWord.ActiveWindow.Selection.TypeText [FirstName]
MyWord.ActiveWindow.Selection.GoTo What:=wdGoToBookmark, Name:="CurrentDate"
MyWord.ActiveWindow.Selection.TypeText Format(Date, "Long Date")
MyWord.ActiveWindow.Selection.GoTo What:=wdGoToBookmark, Name:="OneMonthAhead"
MyWord.ActiveWindow.Selection.TypeText Format(DateAdd("m", 1, Date), "Long Date")
MyWord.ActiveWindow.Selection.GoTo What:=wdGoToBookmark, Name:="SendersName"
MyWord.ActiveWindow.Selection.TypeText _
    InputBox("Enter your name as you would like it to appear in the letter:")
MyWord.ActiveWindow.Selection.GoTo What:=wdGoToBookmark, Name:="SendersTitle"
MyWord.ActiveWindow.Selection.TypeText _
    InputBox("Enter your title as you would like it to appear in the letter:")
MyWord.Application.Visible = True
End Sub
```

Because you are using the Word library in these procedures, you need to reference them. Thus, the Microsoft Word 9.0 Object Library is checked in the References dialog listed under Tools in the Visual Basic editor of Access. Without that, you would not be able to declare this variable:

```
Dim MyWord As New Word.Application
```

This variable stores our connection to the Word application. You also need a variable to store the path to our template form letter:

```
Dim ThePath As String
```

Next, you need to determine the path to your template document. For this to work, it must be placed in the same directory as the database itself. The method Application.CurrentDb.Name returns the path to the current database, including the file name of the database. So if you chop off the name of the database, you have the folder that the database and the template document are located in:

```
ThePath = Left(Application.CurrentDb.Name, Len(Application.CurrentDb.Name) - 21)
```

Then use that path, along with the name of the document, to open the document within your instance of the Word application:

```
MyWord.Application.Documents.Open _
    FileName:=ThePath & "AccountOverDue.doc", ConfirmConversions:=False, _
    ReadOnly:=False, AddToRecentFiles:=False, PasswordDocument:="", _
    PasswordTemplate:="", Revert:=False, WritePasswordDocument:="", _
    WritePasswordTemplate:="", Format:=wdOpenFormatAuto
```

Next, you need to place data about the customer into each of the places where you have a bookmark. First, move to the FullName bookmark:

```
MyWord.ActiveWindow.Selection.GoTo What:=wdGoToBookmark, Name:="FullName"
```

and insert the customer's name from the Customer's form:

```
MyWord.ActiveWindow.Selection.TypeText [FirstName] & " " & [LastName]
```

Now move to the Address bookmark:

```
MyWord.ActiveWindow.Selection.GoTo What:=wdGoToBookmark, Name:="Address"
```

and insert the customer's address:

```
MyWord.ActiveWindow.Selection.TypeText [Address]
```

Do the same for the customer's city, state, and zip:

```
MyWord.ActiveWindow.Selection.GoTo What:=wdGoToBookmark, Name:="CityStateZip"
MyWord.ActiveWindow.Selection.TypeText [City] & ", " & [State] _
    & " " & [Zip Code]
```

This bookmark and data are entered in the salutation of the form letter:

```
MyWord.ActiveWindow.Selection.GoTo What:=wdGoToBookmark, Name:="FirstName"
MyWord.ActiveWindow.Selection.TypeText [FirstName]
```

Within the message of the form letter, enter the current date:

```
MyWord.ActiveWindow.Selection.GoTo What:=wdGoToBookmark, Name:="CurrentDate"
MyWord.ActiveWindow.Selection.TypeText Format(Date, "Long Date")
```

and one month past the current date for when payment must be made:

```
MyWord.ActiveWindow.Selection.GoTo What:=wdGoToBookmark, Name:="OneMonthAhead"
MyWord.ActiveWindow.Selection.TypeText Format(DateAdd("m", 1, Date), "Long Date")
```

Next, enter whom the letter is from:

```
MyWord.ActiveWindow.Selection.GoTo What:=wdGoToBookmark, Name:="SendersName"
```

So, use an Input box to prompt the user for his or her name:

```
MyWord.ActiveWindow.Selection.TypeText _
    InputBox("Enter your name as you would like it to appear in the letter:")
```

Then use the GoTo method of the Selection object to move to the bookmark called SendersTitle:

```
MyWord.ActiveWindow.Selection.GoTo What:=wdGoToBookmark, Name:="SendersTitle"
```

Now prompt the user for his or her title and enter it into the form letter:

```
MyWord.ActiveWindow.Selection.TypeText _
    InputBox("Enter your title as you would like it to appear in the letter:")
```

Then make the Word document visible to the user, enabling he or she to modify, print, or save the document:

```
MyWord.Application.Visible = True
```

When the user presses the Catalog Request button, the next code block fires:

```
Private Sub cmdCatalog_Click()
    Dim MyWord As New Word.Application
    Dim ThePath As String
    Dim CatalogList As String
    Dim NextCatalog As String
    NextCatalog = InputBox("Enter the name of one of the catalogs. " _
        & "Press Cancel when you have entered all the catalogs:")
    Do Until NextCatalog = ""
        CatalogList = CatalogList & vbNewLine & NextCatalog
        NextCatalog = InputBox("Enter the name of one of the catalogs. " _
            & "Press Cancel when you have entered all the catalogs:")
    Loop
    ThePath = Left(Application.CurrentDb.Name, Len(Application.CurrentDb.Name) - 21)
    MyWord.Application.Documents.Open FileName:=ThePath & "CatalogRequest.doc", _
    ConfirmConversions:=False, _
        ReadOnly:=False, AddToRecentFiles:=False, PasswordDocument:="", _
        PasswordTemplate:="", Revert:=False, WritePasswordDocument:="", _
        WritePasswordTemplate:="", Format:=wdOpenFormatAuto
    MyWord.ActiveWindow.Selection.GoTo What:=wdGoToBookmark, Name:="FullName"
    MyWord.ActiveWindow.Selection.TypeText [FirstName] & " " & [LastName]
    MyWord.ActiveWindow.Selection.GoTo What:=wdGoToBookmark, Name:="Address"
    MyWord.ActiveWindow.Selection.TypeText [Address]
    MyWord.ActiveWindow.Selection.GoTo What:=wdGoToBookmark, Name:="CityStateZip"
    MyWord.ActiveWindow.Selection.TypeText [City] & ", " & [State] _
        & " " & [Zip Code]
    MyWord.ActiveWindow.Selection.GoTo What:=wdGoToBookmark, Name:="FirstName"
    MyWord.ActiveWindow.Selection.TypeText [FirstName]
    MyWord.ActiveWindow.Selection.GoTo What:=wdGoToBookmark, Name:="Cataloglist"
    MyWord.ActiveWindow.Selection.TypeText CatalogList
    MyWord.ActiveWindow.Selection.GoTo What:=wdGoToBookmark, Name:="SendersName"
    MyWord.ActiveWindow.Selection.TypeText _
        InputBox("Enter your name as you would like it to appear in the letter:")
    MyWord.ActiveWindow.Selection.GoTo What:=wdGoToBookmark, Name:="SendersTitle"
```

```
    MyWord.ActiveWindow.Selection.TypeText _
        InputBox("Enter your title as you would like it to appear in the letter:")
    MyWord.Application.Visible = True
End Sub
```

You now need an instance of the Word Application class:

```
Dim MyWord As New Word.Application
```

a variable to store the path to the form letter:

```
Dim ThePath As String
```

one to store the catalog list:

```
Dim CatalogList As String
```

and one to store the name of the catalog entered by the user:

```
Dim NextCatalog As String
```

Then ask the user to enter the name of the first catalog that is being sent out:

```
NextCatalog = InputBox("Enter the name of one of the catalogs. " _
        & "Press Cancel when you have entered all the catalogs:")
```

Now enter a loop that enables the user to enter as many catalogs as he or she wants. The loop stops when the user leaves the Input box blank or he or she presses the Cancel button:

```
Do Until NextCatalog = ""
```

Each catalog entered is appended to the catalog list:

```
CatalogList = CatalogList & vbNewLine & NextCatalog
```

Then you prompt the user for the name of the next catalog:

```
NextCatalog = InputBox("Enter the name of one of the catalogs. " _
        & "Press Cancel when you have entered all the catalogs:")
```

and loop to process that next item:

```
Loop
```

Now determine the path to the form letter, which must be placed in the same folder as the database:

```
ThePath = Left(Application.CurrentDb.Name, Len(Application.CurrentDb.Name) - 21)
```

and use our Word object to open that template:

```
MyWord.Application.Documents.Open _
    FileName:=ThePath & "CatalogRequest.doc", ConfirmConversions:=False, _
    ReadOnly:=False, AddToRecentFiles:=False, PasswordDocument:="", _
    PasswordTemplate:="", Revert:=False, WritePasswordDocument:="", _
    WritePasswordTemplate:="", Format:=wdOpenFormatAuto
```

Then use the GoTo method to move the insertion point within the Word document to the bookmark called FullName:

```
MyWord.ActiveWindow.Selection.GoTo What:=wdGoToBookmark, Name:="FullName"
```

At this insertion point, place the customer's name based on the data for the current customer on the Customers form:

```
MyWord.ActiveWindow.Selection.TypeText [FirstName] & " " & [LastName]
```

Then do the same for the customer's address:

```
MyWord.ActiveWindow.Selection.GoTo What:=wdGoToBookmark, Name:="Address"
MyWord.ActiveWindow.Selection.TypeText [Address]
```

as well as his city, state, and zip:

```
MyWord.ActiveWindow.Selection.GoTo What:=wdGoToBookmark, Name:="CityStateZip"
MyWord.ActiveWindow.Selection.TypeText [City] & ", " & [State] _
    & " " & [Zip Code]
```

Next, insert the customer's name into the salutation:

```
MyWord.ActiveWindow.Selection.GoTo What:=wdGoToBookmark, Name:="FirstName"
MyWord.ActiveWindow.Selection.TypeText [FirstName]
```

Then insert the catalog list entered by the user:

```
MyWord.ActiveWindow.Selection.GoTo What:=wdGoToBookmark, Name:="Cataloglist"
MyWord.ActiveWindow.Selection.TypeText CatalogList
```

Now prompt the user for his name:

```
MyWord.ActiveWindow.Selection.GoTo What:=wdGoToBookmark, Name:="SendersName"
MyWord.ActiveWindow.Selection.TypeText _
    InputBox("Enter your name as you would like it to appear in the letter:")
```

as well as his title:

```
MyWord.ActiveWindow.Selection.GoTo What:=wdGoToBookmark, Name:="SendersTitle;"
MyWord.ActiveWindow.Selection.TypeText _
    InputBox("Enter your title as you would like it to appear in the letter:")
```

You are now done inserting data into the document, so you can show it to the user:

```
MyWord.Application.Visible = True
```

When the user presses the Personal Message button, the other code block on this form fires:

```
Private Sub cmdPersonalMessage_Click()
    Dim MyWord As New Word.Application
    Dim ThePath As String
    ThePath = Left(Application.CurrentDb.Name, Len(Application.CurrentDb.Name) - 21)
    MyWord.Application.Documents.Open FileName:=ThePath & "PersonalMessage.doc",
    ConfirmConversions:=False, _
        ReadOnly:=False, AddToRecentFiles:=False, PasswordDocument:="", _
        PasswordTemplate:="", Revert:=False, WritePasswordDocument:="", _
        WritePasswordTemplate:="", Format:=wdOpenFormatAuto
    MyWord.ActiveWindow.Selection.GoTo What:=wdGoToBookmark, Name:="FullName"
    MyWord.ActiveWindow.Selection.TypeText [FirstName] & " " & [LastName]
    MyWord.ActiveWindow.Selection.GoTo What:=wdGoToBookmark, Name:="Address"
    MyWord.ActiveWindow.Selection.TypeText [Address]
    MyWord.ActiveWindow.Selection.GoTo What:=wdGoToBookmark, Name:="CityStateZip"
    MyWord.ActiveWindow.Selection.TypeText [City] & ", " & [State] _
        & " " & [Zip Code]
    MyWord.ActiveWindow.Selection.GoTo What:=wdGoToBookmark, Name:="FirstName"
    MyWord.ActiveWindow.Selection.TypeText [FirstName]
    MyWord.ActiveWindow.Selection.GoTo What:=wdGoToBookmark, Name:="TheMessage"
    MyWord.ActiveWindow.Selection.TypeText _
        InputBox("Please enter your personal message here:")
    MyWord.ActiveWindow.Selection.GoTo What:=wdGoToBookmark, Name:="SendersName"
    MyWord.ActiveWindow.Selection.TypeText _
        InputBox("Enter your name as you would like it to appear in the letter:")
    MyWord.ActiveWindow.Selection.GoTo What:=wdGoToBookmark, Name:="SendersTitle"
    MyWord.ActiveWindow.Selection.TypeText _
        InputBox("Enter your title as you would like it to appear in the letter:")
    MyWord.Application.Visible = True
End Sub
```

Start by creating an instance of the Application object of the Word library:

```
Dim MyWord As New Word.Application
```

and declare a variable that will store the path to your template form letter:

```
Dim ThePath As String
```

Then determine the folder that the database and form letters are located in:

```
ThePath = Left(Application.CurrentDb.Name, Len(Application.CurrentDb.Name) - 21)
```

and open your template form letter in Word:

```
MyWord.Application.Documents.Open
  FileName:=ThePath & "PersonalMessage.doc", ConfirmConversions:=False, _
  ReadOnly:=False, AddToRecentFiles:=False, PasswordDocument:="", _
  PasswordTemplate:="", Revert:=False, WritePasswordDocument:="", _
  WritePasswordTemplate:="", Format:=wdOpenFormatAuto
```

Next, start inserting data for this customer into the form letter. First, move the insertion point within Word to the FullName bookmark:

```
MyWord.ActiveWindow.Selection.GoTo What:=wdGoToBookmark, Name:="FullName"
```

Also insert the customer's name at this point:

```
MyWord.ActiveWindow.Selection.TypeText [FirstName] & " " & [LastName]
```

Do the same for the customer's full address:

```
MyWord.ActiveWindow.Selection.GoTo What:=wdGoToBookmark, Name:="Address"
MyWord.ActiveWindow.Selection.TypeText [Address]
MyWord.ActiveWindow.Selection.GoTo What:=wdGoToBookmark, Name:="CityStateZip"
MyWord.ActiveWindow.Selection.TypeText [City] & ", " & [State] _
    & " " & [Zip Code]
```

Insert his or her salutation as well:

```
MyWord.ActiveWindow.Selection.GoTo What:=wdGoToBookmark, Name:="FirstName"
MyWord.ActiveWindow.Selection.TypeText [FirstName]
```

Then in the body of the Word document, insert the text entered by the user:

```
MyWord.ActiveWindow.Selection.GoTo What:=wdGoToBookmark, Name:="TheMessage"
MyWord.ActiveWindow.Selection.TypeText _
    InputBox("Please enter your personal message here:")
```

as well as his or her name and title:

```
MyWord.ActiveWindow.Selection.GoTo What:=wdGoToBookmark, Name:="SendersName"
MyWord.ActiveWindow.Selection.TypeText _
    InputBox("Enter your name as you would like it to appear in the letter:")
MyWord.ActiveWindow.Selection.GoTo What:=wdGoToBookmark, Name:="SendersTitle"
MyWord.ActiveWindow.Selection.TypeText _
    InputBox("Enter your title as you would like it to appear in the letter:")
```

With all the data in place, you can show the Word document to the user:

```
MyWord.Application.Visible = True
```

Word Table Database

Next, take a look at a form in a database that enables the user to turn just about any table or query into a table within a Word document. Note that the database that is used in this sample is the Student, Teachers, and Courses database from Chapter 11, "Students, Teachers, and Courses." Only the one form discussed in this section is added to that database.

Sample Walk-through

The new form added to the database is called the Word Table and is displayed in Figure 14-12. Listed on this form are the names of all the tables and queries that are part of this database. The user selects one of those items in the list and enters a title for their report.

Once the user is through, he or she presses the Create Document button. The user then sees something like the document displayed in Figure 14-13.

In this first instance, the table named Courses is selected. Note that the Word table shows the field name in the first row of the table followed by

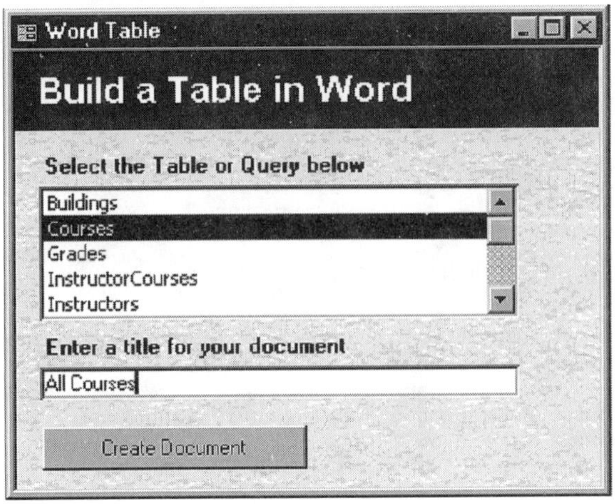

Figure 14-12

The Word Table form

Figure 14-13

The All Courses table

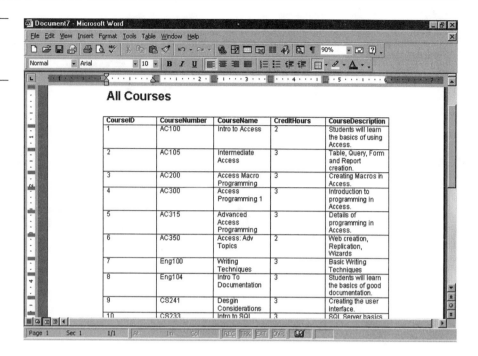

all the records in that table. Also note that the title entered by the user is at the top of the document.

The user can also select one of the queries that is in the database. Figure 14-14 shows one of the queries output into a Word document.

Again, all the fields and records are included in the output of this Word document.

Word Table Form

The code on the Word Table form first populates the List box with all the tables and queries in the database. The code also must generate the Word document when the user presses the button. The first code block fires when the form is loaded:

```
Private Sub Form_Load()
    Dim MyDB As DAO.Database
    Dim MyTableDef As DAO.TableDef
    Dim MyQueryDef As DAO.QueryDef
    Set MyDB = CurrentDb
    For Each MyTableDef In MyDB.TableDefs
        lstTable.RowSource = lstTable.RowSource _
```

Figure 14-14

The Instructor
Courses query

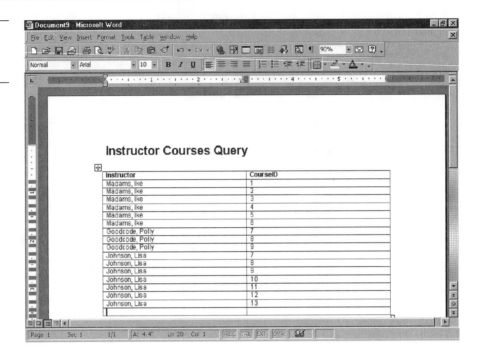

```
                    & MyTableDef.Name & ";"
        Next
        For Each MyQueryDef In MyDB.QueryDefs
            lstTable.RowSource = lstTable.RowSource _
                & MyQueryDef.Name & ";"
        Next
    End Sub
```

You now need to connect to your database:

```
Dim MyDB As DAO.Database
```

and retrieve the names of the tables:

```
Dim MyTableDef As DAO.TableDef
```

as well as the names of the queries:

```
Dim MyQueryDef As DAO.QueryDef
```

Start by connecting to your current database:

```
Set MyDB = CurrentDb
```

and start a loop that will take you through each of the tables:

```
For Each MyTableDef In MyDB.TableDefs
```

The name of the table is appended to the List box:

```
lstTable.RowSource = lstTable.RowSource _
        & MyTableDef.Name & ";"
```

Move on to process the next table:

```
Next
```

Then start a loop so you can process each of the queries in the database:

```
For Each MyQueryDef In MyDB.QueryDefs
```

The name of each query is added to our list:

```
lstTable.RowSource = lstTable.RowSource _
        & MyQueryDef.Name & ";"
```

Now move on to process the next query:

```
Next
```

The other code block on the form fires when the Create Document button is pressed:

```
Private Sub cmdGo_Click()
    Dim MyWord As New Word.Application
    Dim MyDB As DAO.Database
    Dim RS As DAO.Recordset
    Dim TheField As DAO.Field
    Dim TotalRecords As Long
    If IsNull(lstTable.Value) Then
        MsgBox "Please select a table or query first."
        Exit Sub
    End If
    txtTitle.SetFocus
    If txtTitle.Text = "" Then
        MsgBox "Please enter a title name for the document."
        Exit Sub
    End If
    Set MyDB = CurrentDb
    Set RS = MyDB.OpenRecordset("Select * from [" & lstTable.Value & "]", _
        dbOpenSnapshot)
    If RS.EOF Then
```

```
         MsgBox "No records found!"
         Exit Sub
     End If
     RS.MoveLast
     TotalRecords = RS.RecordCount
     RS.MoveFirst
     MyWord.Documents.Add DocumentType:=wdNewBlankDocument
     MyWord.Selection.Font.Name = "Arial"
     MyWord.Selection.Font.Size = 18
     MyWord.Selection.Font.Bold = True
     MyWord.Selection.TypeText Text:=txtTitle.Text
     MyWord.Selection.TypeParagraph
     MyWord.Selection.TypeParagraph
     MyWord.Selection.Font.Size = 10
     MyWord.Selection.Font.Bold = False
     MyWord.ActiveDocument.Tables.Add Range:=Selection.Range, _
         NumRows:=TotalRecords + 1, NumColumns:= _
         RS.Fields.Count, DefaultTableBehavior:=wdWord9TableBehavior, AutoFitBehavior:= _
         wdAutoFitFixed
     For Each TheField In RS.Fields
         MyWord.Selection.Font.Bold = True
         Selection.TypeText Text:=TheField.Name
         Selection.MoveRight Unit:=wdCell
     Next
     Do Until RS.EOF
         For Each TheField In RS.Fields
             Selection.TypeText Text:=TheField.Value
             Selection.MoveRight Unit:=wdCell
         Next
         RS.MoveNext
     Loop
     MyWord.Application.Visible = True
 End Sub
```

You will need a Word object:

```
Dim MyWord As New Word.Application
```

a Database object:

```
Dim MyDB As DAO.Database
```

a Recordset object to retrieve data from this database:

```
Dim RS As DAO.Recordset
```

and a Field object so you can create the column headers in the Word table:

```
Dim TheField As DAO.Field
```

This variable stores the total number of records in the table:

```
Dim TotalRecords As Long
```

But before you create the Word table, you need to make sure the user selected a table or query name from the list:

```
If IsNull(lstTable.Value) Then
```

If the users didn't select a table or query name, inform them of the problem:

```
MsgBox "Please select a table or query first."
```

and leave this procedure:

```
Exit Sub
```

Then move the focus to the Title text box:

```
txtTitle.SetFocus
```

and make sure the user entered a title:

```
If txtTitle.Text = "" Then
```

If the user didn't, inform them of the problem:

```
MsgBox "Please enter a title name for the document."
```

and leave this procedure:

```
Exit Sub
```

If both of those values have been selected, you can connect to your database:

```
Set MyDB = CurrentDb
```

and retrieve data from the table or query selected by the user:

```
Set RS = MyDB.OpenRecordset("Select * from [" & lstTable.Value & "]", _
    dbOpenSnapshot)
```

Then make sure the table or query selected the returned records:

```
If RS.EOF Then
```

If it didn't, inform the user of the problem:

```
MsgBox "No records found!"
```

and leave this procedure:

```
Exit Sub
```

If you have data, move to the last record:

```
RS.MoveLast
```

so you have an accurate record count:

```
TotalRecords = RS.RecordCount
```

Then move back to the beginning of the recordset:

```
RS.MoveFirst
```

Next, add a document to your Word object:

```
MyWord.Documents.Add DocumentType:=wdNewBlankDocument
```

Then set the font and style for the title text:

```
MyWord.Selection.Font.Name = "Arial"
MyWord.Selection.Font.Size = 18
MyWord.Selection.Font.Bold = True
```

which is then inserted based on the title entered by the user in the text box:

```
MyWord.Selection.TypeText Text:=txtTitle.Text
```

along with a couple of new lines:

```
MyWord.Selection.TypeParagraph
MyWord.Selection.TypeParagraph
```

Now set the font style for the table:

```
MyWord.Selection.Font.Size = 10
MyWord.Selection.Font.Bold = False
```

Create the table with the number of rows based on the record count, plus one for the column headers and the number of columns based on the number of fields in the recordset:

```
MyWord.ActiveDocument.Tables.Add Range:=Selection.Range, _
    NumRows:=TotalRecords + 1, NumColumns:= _
```

```
RS.Fields.Count, DefaultTableBehavior:=wdWord9TableBehavior, AutoFitBehavior:= _
wdAutoFitFixed
```

Now enter a loop so you can process each of the column headers:

```
For Each TheField In RS.Fields
```

Each one is displayed in a bold type:

```
MyWord.Selection.Font.Bold = True
```

Then insert the name of the field:

```
Selection.TypeText Text:=TheField.Name
```

and move on to the next column in the table:

```
Selection.MoveRight Unit:=wdCell
Next
```

Now that you are done with the column headers, you need to process each record in the recordset:

```
Do Until RS.EOF
```

For each of the records in the recordset, you need to process each field:

```
For Each TheField In RS.Fields
```

The value for that field in the current record is inserted into the table:

```
Selection.TypeText Text:=TheField.Value
```

Now move on to the next cell of the document table:

```
Selection.MoveRight Unit:=wdCell
Next
```

After processing all the fields in the current record, move on to the next record:

```
RS.MoveNext
```

and loop:

```
Loop
```

Finally, display the Word document to the user:

```
MyWord.Application.Visible = True
```

Using Excel Database

One of the things you will hear from your users as you work with Access is that they often don't feel comfortable creating their own queries or analyzing data within Access. However, they are often very comfortable working with data in Excel and as an added plus, when a user works with data in Excel, he or she shouldn't be able to mess up the original data in the Access database. This section will look at an Access database that calls on the functionality of Excel to export data into an Excel spreadsheet from the database.

Sample Walk-through

The Using Excel database uses the Students, Teachers, and Courses database that was created and discussed in Chapter 11. Only one form has been added to that database and is displayed in Figure 14-15.

The Using Excel form provides the functionality to export data from the database into three different spreadsheets. When the user clicks on the Average Grade Per Course button, the spreadsheet displayed in Figure 14-16 opens.

The user sees each of the courses that students have taken. The average grade received is also displayed with that course. When the user clicks on the Courses Taught by Instructor button, he or she sees the spreadsheet displayed in Figure 14-17.

Figure 14-15

The Using Excel form

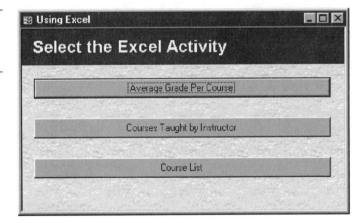

Figure 14-16

The Average GPA
per Course
spreadsheet

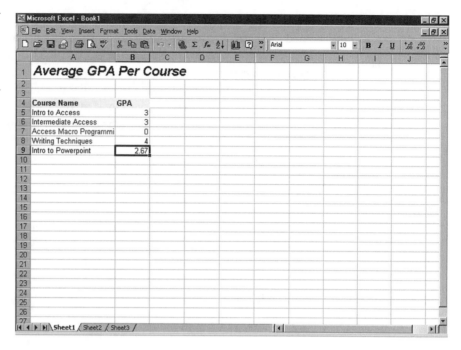

Figure 14-17

The Courses
Taught by
Instructor
spreadsheet

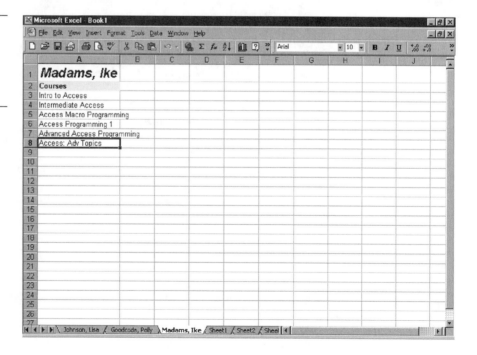

This spreadsheet displays all the courses taught by each teacher. Notice the tabs at the bottom of the spreadsheet. Each instructor has his or her own tab. The other spreadsheet produced by this database is displayed in Figure 14-18.

The Course List spreadsheet shows a list of all the courses in the course catalog. As you will see when you look at the code, you can easily modify this procedure so that it works with just about any other table and most queries.

Using Excel Form

The Using Excel form contains all the code that generates the spreadsheets discussed in the last section. The code fires when the different buttons on the form are pressed.

When the user clicks on the Average Grade Per Course button, the following code block fires:

Figure 14-18

The Course List spreadsheet

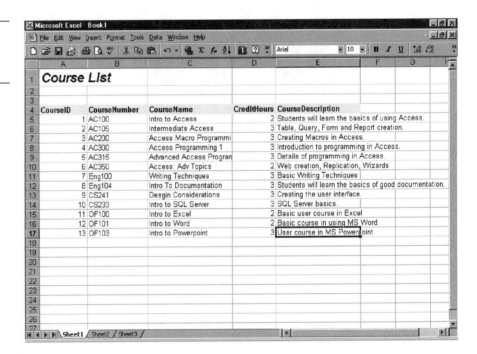

```
Private Sub cmdAverageGradePerCourse_Click()
    Dim MyDB As DAO.Database
    Dim RS As DAO.Recordset
    Dim MyExcel As New Excel.Application
    Set MyDB = CurrentDb
    Dim CurrentRow As Long
    Set RS = MyDB.OpenRecordset("SELECT Courses.CourseID, Courses.CourseName, " _
        & "Avg(Grades.PointValue) AS AvgGPA FROM Grades INNER JOIN " _
        & "(Courses INNER JOIN (Sections INNER JOIN StudentCourses ON " _
        & "Sections.SectionID = StudentCourses.SectionID) ON " _
        & "Courses.CourseID = Sections.CourseID) ON " _
        & "Grades.Grade = StudentCourses.Grade GROUP BY " _
        & "Courses.CourseID, Courses.CourseName;", dbOpenSnapshot)
    MyExcel.Workbooks.Add
    MyExcel.Selection.Font.Name = "Arial"
    MyExcel.Selection.Font.Size = 18
    MyExcel.Selection.Font.Bold = True
    MyExcel.Selection.Font.Italic = True
    MyExcel.ActiveCell.FormulaR1C1 = "Average GPA Per Course"
    MyExcel.Cells(4, 1).Select
    MyExcel.Selection.Interior.ColorIndex = 34
    MyExcel.Selection.Interior.Pattern = xlSolid
    MyExcel.Selection.Interior.PatternColorIndex = xlAutomatic
    MyExcel.Selection.Font.Bold = True
    MyExcel.ActiveCell.FormulaR1C1 = "Course Name"
    MyExcel.Columns("A:A").ColumnWidth = 21.43
    MyExcel.Cells(4, 2).Select
    MyExcel.Selection.Interior.ColorIndex = 34
    MyExcel.Selection.Interior.Pattern = xlSolid
    MyExcel.Selection.Interior.PatternColorIndex = xlAutomatic
    MyExcel.Selection.Font.Bold = True
    MyExcel.ActiveCell.FormulaR1C1 = "GPA"
    CurrentRow = 5
    Do Until RS.EOF
        MyExcel.Cells(CurrentRow, 1).Select
        MyExcel.ActiveCell.FormulaR1C1 = RS("CourseName")
        MyExcel.Cells(CurrentRow, 2).Select
        MyExcel.ActiveCell.FormulaR1C1 = RS("AvgGPA")
        CurrentRow = CurrentRow + 1
        RS.MoveNext
    Loop
    MyExcel.Visible = True
End Sub
```

You now need to connect to the database:

```
Dim MyDB As DAO.Database
```

and retrieve data from the database:

```
Dim RS As DAO.Recordset
```

You also need an instance of the Application class of Excel. Note that for this to be available, you need to select the Excel library in the References dialog, which is accessible through the Tools/References menu item:

```
Dim MyExcel As New Excel.Application
```

You also need a variable that stores the current row number:

```
Dim CurrentRow As Long
```

Start by connecting to the current database:

```
Set MyDB = CurrentDb
```

Then retrieve the average grade per course:

```
Set RS = MyDB.OpenRecordset("SELECT Courses.CourseID, Courses.CourseName, " _
    & "Avg(Grades.PointValue) AS AvgGPA FROM Grades INNER JOIN " _
    & "(Courses INNER JOIN (Sections INNER JOIN StudentCourses ON " _
    & "Sections.SectionID = StudentCourses.SectionID) ON " _
    & "Courses.CourseID = Sections.CourseID) ON " _
    & "Grades.Grade = StudentCourses.Grade GROUP BY " _
    & "Courses.CourseID, Courses.CourseName;", dbOpenSnapshot)
```

Now you can start modifying your spreadsheet. First, you need to add a workbook to your Application object:

```
MyExcel.Workbooks.Add
```

The current cell at this point in the worksheet would be A1, the top left. This is where you want the title of the worksheet placed. You'll need to format that cell and make the font type Arial:

```
MyExcel.Selection.Font.Name = "Arial"
```

Size the font to 18:

```
MyExcel.Selection.Font.Size = 18
```

Turn on Bold:

```
MyExcel.Selection.Font.Bold = True
```

and Italic:

```
MyExcel.Selection.Font.Italic = True
```

Then place the title text into that cell:

```
MyExcel.ActiveCell.FormulaR1C1 = "Average GPA Per Course"
```

Now you need to set up the column headers for your output. You will place the name of the course in the first column and the column headers are placed in the fourth row:

```
MyExcel.Cells(4, 1).Select
```

The background color of this cell is set to light blue:

```
MyExcel.Selection.Interior.ColorIndex = 34
```

and the background is a solid pattern:

```
MyExcel.Selection.Interior.Pattern = xlSolid
MyExcel.Selection.Interior.PatternColorIndex = xlAutomatic
```

You'll want the text to be bold in this cell:

```
MyExcel.Selection.Font.Bold = True
```

and you must set the column header for the cell to the text, Course Name:

```
MyExcel.ActiveCell.FormulaR1C1 = "Course Name"
```

You also need to widen this column so that it will display most of the course names:

```
MyExcel.Columns("A:A").ColumnWidth = 21.43
```

Next, move on to process the next column header:

```
MyExcel.Cells(4, 2).Select
```

It is also set to a solid light blue:

```
MyExcel.Selection.Interior.ColorIndex = 34
MyExcel.Selection.Interior.Pattern = xlSolid
MyExcel.Selection.Interior.PatternColorIndex = xlAutomatic
```

and the text will be bold in this cell:

```
MyExcel.Selection.Font.Bold = True
```

This column contains the average GPA, so the text in the cell is set to "GPA:"

```
MyExcel.ActiveCell.FormulaR1C1 = "GPA"
```

The first row of data is placed in the fifth row of the Excel spreadsheet:

```
CurrentRow = 5
```

Now you can process the Course-GPA records. Start a loop that will run through each of the records:

```
Do Until RS.EOF
```

Move to the first column of the current row:

```
MyExcel.Cells(CurrentRow, 1).Select
```

and place the name of the course in that cell:

```
MyExcel.ActiveCell.FormulaR1C1 = RS("CourseName")
```

Then move to the second column in the current row:

```
MyExcel.Cells(CurrentRow, 2).Select
```

and place the average GPA in that cell:

```
MyExcel.ActiveCell.FormulaR1C1 = RS("AvgGPA")
```

Then add one to the current row:

```
CurrentRow = CurrentRow + 1
```

and move on to process the next record:

```
RS.MoveNext
Loop
```

Finally, show the spreadsheet to the user:

```
MyExcel.Visible = True
```

The code behind the Courses Taught by Instructor produces the Courses Taught by Instructor spreadsheet. The code block contains two main loops. The outer loop processes each instructor and the inner loop processes each course taught by each instructor:

```
Private Sub cmdCoursesTaughtByInstructor_Click()
    Dim MyDB As DAO.Database
    Dim RSCourses As DAO.Recordset
    Dim RSInstructors As DAO.Recordset
    Dim MyExcel As New Excel.Application
    Dim CurrentSheet As Long
    Set MyDB = CurrentDb
    Dim CurrentRow As Long
    Set RSInstructors = MyDB.OpenRecordset("Select InstructorID, FirstName, " _
        & "LastName from Instructors", dbOpenSnapshot)
    MyExcel.Workbooks.Add
    CurrentSheet = 4
    Do Until RSInstructors.EOF
        Set RSCourses = MyDB.OpenRecordset("SELECT InstructorCourses.InstructorID, " _
            & "Courses.CourseName FROM Courses INNER JOIN InstructorCourses " _
            & "ON Courses.CourseID = InstructorCourses.CourseID " _
            & "WHERE InstructorCourses.InstructorID = " _
            & RSInstructors("InstructorID"), dbOpenSnapshot)
        MyExcel.Sheets.Add
        MyExcel.Sheets("Sheet" & CurrentSheet).Select
        MyExcel.Sheets("Sheet" & CurrentSheet).Name = RSInstructors("LastName") _
            & ", " & RSInstructors("FirstName")
        MyExcel.Range("A1").Select
        MyExcel.Selection.Font.Name = "Arial"
        MyExcel.Selection.Font.Size = 18
        MyExcel.Selection.Font.Bold = True
        MyExcel.Selection.Font.Italic = True
        MyExcel.ActiveCell.FormulaR1C1 = RSInstructors("LastName") _
            & ", " & RSInstructors("FirstName")
        MyExcel.Columns("A:A").ColumnWidth = 20.86
        MyExcel.Range("A2").Select
        MyExcel.Selection.Interior.ColorIndex = 34
        MyExcel.Selection.Interior.Pattern = xlSolid
        MyExcel.Selection.Interior.PatternColorIndex = xlAutomatic
        MyExcel.Selection.Font.Name = "Arial"
        MyExcel.Selection.Font.Size = 10
        MyExcel.Selection.Font.Bold = True
        MyExcel.ActiveCell.FormulaR1C1 = "Courses"
        CurrentRow = 3
        Do Until RSCourses.EOF
            MyExcel.Range("A" & CurrentRow).Select
            MyExcel.ActiveCell.FormulaR1C1 = RSCourses("CourseName")
            CurrentRow = CurrentRow + 1
            RSCourses.MoveNext
        Loop
        CurrentSheet = CurrentSheet + 1
        RSInstructors.MoveNext
    Loop
    MyExcel.Visible = True
End Sub
```

You now need a Database object:

```
Dim MyDB As DAO.Database
```

one recordset that will retrieve course information taught by an instructor:

```
Dim RSCourses As DAO.Recordset
```

and one that will retrieve instructor information:

```
Dim RSInstructors As DAO.Recordset
```

You will also need an instance of Excel in our code:

```
Dim MyExcel As New Excel.Application
```

This variable stores the current worksheet you are working with:

```
Dim CurrentSheet As Long
```

and the current row number you are working with:

```
Dim CurrentRow As Long
```

You can then connect to the current database:

```
Set MyDB = CurrentDb
```

and retrieve information about the instructors:

```
Set RSInstructors = MyDB.OpenRecordset("Select InstructorID, FirstName, " _
    & "LastName from Instructors", dbOpenSnapshot)
```

Then add a workbook into your Excel object:

```
MyExcel.Workbooks.Add
```

and set the current worksheet to four since three already exist with a new workbook:

```
CurrentSheet = 4
```

Then start your outer loop, which will process each of the instructor records:

```
Do Until RSInstructors.EOF
```

For each instructor, you need to retrieve the names of the courses that he or she teaches:

```
Set RSCourses = MyDB.OpenRecordset("SELECT InstructorCourses.InstructorID, " _
    & "Courses.CourseName FROM Courses INNER JOIN InstructorCourses " _
    & "ON Courses.CourseID = InstructorCourses.CourseID " _
    & "WHERE InstructorCourses.InstructorID = " _
    & RSInstructors("InstructorID"), dbOpenSnapshot)
```

Each instructor is placed on his or her own worksheet within the workbook, so you need to add a new worksheet:

```
MyExcel.Sheets.Add
```

Then make that worksheet the active worksheet:

```
MyExcel.Sheets("Sheet" & CurrentSheet).Select
```

and give the tab for it a name based on the name of the instructor:

```
MyExcel.Sheets("Sheet" & CurrentSheet).Name = RSInstructors("LastName") _
    & ", " & RSInstructors("FirstName")
```

Also put that name into the top left cell, which is selected here:

```
MyExcel.Range("A1").Select
```

and format it so that it is in Arial:

```
MyExcel.Selection.Font.Name = "Arial"
```

and is sized to 18:

```
MyExcel.Selection.Font.Size = 18
```

It should also be bold:

```
MyExcel.Selection.Font.Bold = True
```

and italicized:

```
MyExcel.Selection.Font.Italic = True
```

Then place the name of the instructor in that cell:

```
MyExcel.ActiveCell.FormulaR1C1 = RSInstructors("LastName") _
    & ", " & RSInstructors("FirstName")
```

Widen the first column, which is where the name of the courses taught will be placed:

```
MyExcel.Columns("A:A").ColumnWidth = 20.86
```

The cell under the title should contain a column header:

```
MyExcel.Range("A2").Select
```

The background for that cell is set to a solid light blue:

```
MyExcel.Selection.Interior.ColorIndex = 34
MyExcel.Selection.Interior.Pattern = xlSolid
MyExcel.Selection.Interior.PatternColorIndex = xlAutomatic
```

The font for that cell is also set to Arial, size 10:

```
MyExcel.Selection.Font.Name = "Arial"
MyExcel.Selection.Font.Size = 10
```

with the text in bold:

```
MyExcel.Selection.Font.Bold = True
```

Then place the text "Courses" into this column header:

```
MyExcel.ActiveCell.FormulaR1C1 = "Courses"
```

The courses taught by the instructor need to be placed in the third row:

```
CurrentRow = 3
```

Then start a loop to process each of those course records:

```
Do Until RSCourses.EOF
```

The name of the course will be placed in the first column of the current row:

```
MyExcel.Range("A" & CurrentRow).Select
MyExcel.ActiveCell.FormulaR1C1 = RSCourses("CourseName")
```

Then move on to the next row in the Excel worksheet:

```
CurrentRow = CurrentRow + 1
```

and the next record in the Course Recordset:

```
RSCourses.MoveNext
Loop
```

After the inner loop is complete, you are ready to move on to the next worksheet:

```
CurrentSheet = CurrentSheet + 1
```

and the next instructor record:

```
RSInstructors.MoveNext
Loop
```

When you are done manipulating the workbook, display it to the user:

```
MyExcel.Visible = True
```

When the user presses the Course List button, a spreadsheet that contains all the information from the course table appears. As you look at this code block, note that you could easily use this code block to generate a spreadsheet for almost any table or query just by changing the name of the table in the SQL statement and the spreadsheet title:

```
Private Sub cmdCourseList_Click()
    Dim MyDB As DAO.Database
    Dim RS As DAO.Recordset
    Dim MyExcel As New Excel.Application
    Dim MyField As DAO.Field
    Dim CurrentRow As Long
    Dim CurrentColumn
    Set MyDB = CurrentDb
    Set RS = MyDB.OpenRecordset("SELECT * From Courses", dbOpenSnapshot)
    MyExcel.Workbooks.Add
    MyExcel.Selection.Font.Name = "Arial"
    MyExcel.Selection.Font.Size = 18
    MyExcel.Selection.Font.Bold = True
    MyExcel.Selection.Font.Italic = True
    MyExcel.ActiveCell.FormulaR1C1 = "Course List"
    CurrentColumn = 1
    For Each MyField In RS.Fields
        MyExcel.Cells(4, CurrentColumn).Select
        MyExcel.Selection.Interior.ColorIndex = 34
        MyExcel.Selection.Interior.Pattern = xlSolid
        MyExcel.Selection.Interior.PatternColorIndex = xlAutomatic
        MyExcel.Selection.Font.Bold = True
        MyExcel.ActiveCell.FormulaR1C1 = MyField.Name
        MyExcel.Columns(CurrentColumn).ColumnWidth = 21.43
        CurrentColumn = CurrentColumn + 1
```

```
            Next
        CurrentRow = 5
        Do Until RS.EOF
            CurrentColumn = 1
            For Each MyField In RS.Fields
                MyExcel.Cells(CurrentRow, CurrentColumn).Select
                MyExcel.ActiveCell.FormulaR1C1 = MyField.Value
                CurrentColumn = CurrentColumn + 1
            Next
            CurrentRow = CurrentRow + 1
            RS.MoveNext
        Loop
        MyExcel.Visible = True
    End Sub
```

You will need three things: a Database object:

```
Dim MyDB As DAO.Database
```

a Recordset object:

```
Dim RS As DAO.Recordset
```

and an instance of Excel in our code:

```
Dim MyExcel As New Excel.Application
```

You will also need a Field object so you can loop through each field in the database table:

```
Dim MyField As DAO.Field
```

You'll also need variables to store the current row number:

```
Dim CurrentRow As Long
```

and the current column number:

```
Dim CurrentColumn
```

Then connect to the current database:

```
Set MyDB = CurrentDb
```

and retrieve all the data from the Courses table:

```
Set RS = MyDB.OpenRecordset("SELECT * From Courses", dbOpenSnapshot)
```

Then add a workbook to your Excel object:

```
MyExcel.Workbooks.Add
```

The current cell is the top left cell, which is where you want to place the title of the spreadsheet. The title will be displayed in an Arial, size-18 font:

```
MyExcel.Selection.Font.Name = "Arial"
MyExcel.Selection.Font.Size = 18
```

which is in bold:

```
MyExcel.Selection.Font.Bold = True
```

and Italic:

```
MyExcel.Selection.Font.Italic = True
```

Then place the title text into this formatted cell:

```
MyExcel.ActiveCell.FormulaR1C1 = "Course List"
```

and set the current column to the first:

```
CurrentColumn = 1
```

Now start a loop that will enable you to process each of the field names in this table that will serve as column headers:

```
For Each MyField In RS.Fields
```

The column headers are placed in the fourth row:

```
MyExcel.Cells(4, CurrentColumn).Select
```

and will have a solid light blue background:

```
MyExcel.Selection.Interior.ColorIndex = 34
MyExcel.Selection.Interior.Pattern = xlSolid
MyExcel.Selection.Interior.PatternColorIndex = xlAutomatic
```

with a bold typeface:

```
MyExcel.Selection.Font.Bold = True
```

Place the name of the current field into that cell:

```
MyExcel.ActiveCell.FormulaR1C1 = MyField.Name
```

and set the width for it:

```
MyExcel.Columns(CurrentColumn).ColumnWidth = 21.43
```

Then move on to process the next column:

```
CurrentColumn = CurrentColumn + 1
Next
```

The data on the courses themselves begins in the fifth row:

```
CurrentRow = 5
```

Then start a loop that will enable you to process each of the courses:

```
Do Until RS.EOF
```

Each course listing starts in the first column:

```
CurrentColumn = 1
```

Now start a loop that will enable you to process each of the fields in the current record:

```
For Each MyField In RS.Fields
```

Move to the current row for the record and the current cell for the field within the spreadsheet:

```
MyExcel.Cells(CurrentRow, CurrentColumn).Select
```

Place the value of that field for the current record within the recordset:

```
MyExcel.ActiveCell.FormulaR1C1 = MyField.Value
```

Then move on to process the next field in this record:

```
    CurrentColumn = CurrentColumn + 1
Next
```

and the next record in the recordset:

```
    CurrentRow = CurrentRow + 1
    RS.MoveNext
Loop
```

Once you are done with these loops, you can show the completed spreadsheet to the user:

```
MyExcel.Visible = True
```

Using PowerPoint Database

Last in this chapter, you will review a database that creates a PowerPoint presentation in code. The code uses the PowerPoint library to dynamically generate a presentation based on data in a database table.

Sample Walk-through

The Using PowerPoint database is based on the Students, Teachers, and Courses database that was reviewed in Chapter 11. Only one form was added, which is displayed in Figure 14-19.

The form enables the user to create a PowerPoint presentation based on the different programs that the school offers. The user would enter a title for the first slide in the presentation and then press the button. After this is done, the PowerPoint presentation is created for the user. The first slide of that presentation is displayed in Figure 14-20.

Figure 14-19

The Using
PowerPoint form

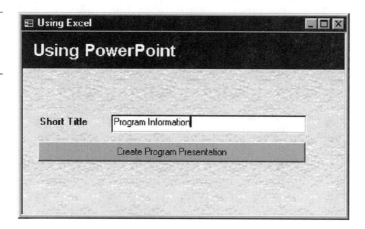

Figure 14-20

The first slide of
the presentation

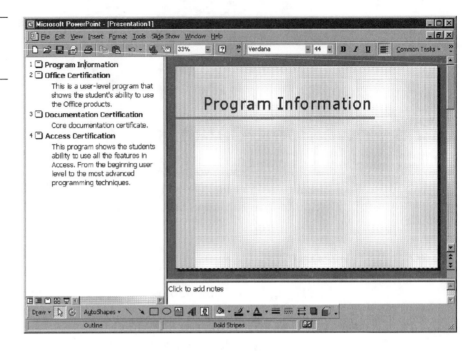

Notice the text in this first slide. It is the text that was entered on the
form by the user. The presentation also contains a slide for each of the programs the school offers. Such a slide is displayed in Figure 14-21.

Notice that the slide contains the name and description of a program.
This information is displayed for each program on its own slide.

Using PowerPoint Form

The only code on the Using PowerPoint form runs when the button on the
form is pressed. It generates the PowerPoint presentation based on data
in the Programs table:

```
Private Sub cmdCreateProgramPresentation_Click()
    Dim MyDB As DAO.Database
    Dim RSPrograms As DAO.Recordset
    Dim MyPowerPoint As New PowerPoint.Application
    txtTitle.SetFocus
    If txtTitle.Text = "" Then
        MsgBox "Please enter a title for your presentation."
        Exit Sub
    End If
```

Figure 14-21

The program
slide

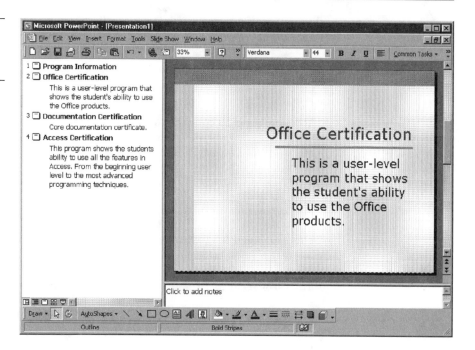

```
    Set MyDB = CurrentDb
    Set RSPrograms = MyDB.OpenRecordset("Select ProgramName, ProgramDescription " _
        & "From Programs Order By ProgramName", dbOpenSnapshot)
    MyPowerPoint.Presentations.Add
    MyPowerPoint.Presentations(1).ApplyTemplate FileName:="C:\Program Files\Microsoft
Office2000\Templates\Presentation Designs\Bold Stripes.pot"
    MyPowerPoint.Activate
    MyPowerPoint.Presentations(1).NewWindow
    MyPowerPoint.ActiveWindow.View.GotoSlide
Index:=MyPowerPoint.ActivePresentation.Slides.Add(Index:=1, _
Layout:=ppLayoutTitleOnly).SlideIndex
    MyPowerPoint.ActiveWindow.Selection.SlideRange.Shapes("Rectangle 2").Select
    MyPowerPoint.ActiveWindow.Selection.ShapeRange.TextFrame.TextRange.Select
MyPowerPoint.ActiveWindow.Selection.ShapeRange.TextFrame.TextRange.Characters
(Start:=1, Length:=0).Select
    MyPowerPoint.ActiveWindow.Selection.TextRange.Text = txtTitle.Text
    Do Until RSPrograms.EOF
        MyPowerPoint.ActiveWindow.View.GotoSlide
Index:=MyPowerPoint.ActivePresentation.Slides.Add(Index:=2,
Layout:=ppLayoutTitle).SlideIndex
        MyPowerPoint.ActiveWindow.Selection.SlideRange.Shapes("Rectangle 2").Select
        MyPowerPoint.ActiveWindow.Selection.ShapeRange.TextFrame.TextRange.Select

MyPowerPoint.ActiveWindow.Selection.ShapeRange.TextFrame.TextRange.Characters
(Start:=1, Length:=0).Select
        MyPowerPoint.ActiveWindow.Selection.TextRange.Text = RSPrograms("ProgramName")
        MyPowerPoint.ActiveWindow.Selection.SlideRange.Shapes("Rectangle 3").Select
        MyPowerPoint.ActiveWindow.Selection.ShapeRange.TextFrame.TextRange.Select
```

```
        MyPowerPoint.ActiveWindow.Selection.ShapeRange.TextFrame.TextRange.Characters _
        & (Start:=1, Length:=0).Select
        MyPowerPoint.ActiveWindow.Selection.TextRange.Text = RSPrograms _
        & ("ProgramDescription")
        RSPrograms.MoveNext
    Loop
End Sub
```

You now need to connect to the database:

```
Dim MyDB As DAO.Database
```

and retrieve data:

```
Dim RSPrograms As DAO.Recordset
```

You also need an instance of the PowerPoint application, which is referenced through the References dialog:

```
Dim MyPowerPoint As New PowerPoint.Application
```

Start by moving the focus to the text box on the form:

```
txtTitle.SetFocus
```

and make sure a title was entered:

```
If txtTitle.Text = "" Then
```

If one wasn't, inform the user of the problem:

```
MsgBox "Please enter a title for your presentation."
```

and leave this procedure:

```
Exit Sub
```

Otherwise, you can connect to your database:

```
Set MyDB = CurrentDb
```

and retrieve the program records:

```
Set RSPrograms = MyDB.OpenRecordset("Select ProgramName, ProgramDescription " _
    & "From Programs Order By ProgramName", dbOpenSnapshot)
```

Then add a presentation to your PowerPoint Application object:

```
MyPowerPoint.Presentations.Add
```

Then set the style for your presentation. Note that this is a hard-coded path. If PowerPoint is located in a different location on your machine, you will need to modify this line of code:

```
MyPowerPoint.Presentations(1).ApplyTemplate
FileName:="C:\Program Files\Microsoft Office2000\Templates\Presentation Designs\Bold
Stripes.pot"
```

Then activate the PowerPoint:

```
MyPowerPoint.Activate
```

and place your presentation into a window:

```
MyPowerPoint.Presentations(1).NewWindow
```

Next, add the Title slide:

```
MyPowerPoint.ActiveWindow.View.GotoSlide
        Index:=MyPowerPoint.ActivePresentation.Slides.Add(Index:=1,
        Layout:=ppLayoutTitleOnly).SlideIndex
```

Now select all the text in the title text box on the Title slide:

```
MyPowerPoint.ActiveWindow.Selection.SlideRange.Shapes("Rectangle 2").Select
MyPowerPoint.ActiveWindow.Selection.ShapeRange.TextFrame.TextRange.Select
MyPowerPoint.ActiveWindow.Selection.ShapeRange.
        TextFrame.TextRange.Characters(Start:=1, Length:=0).Select
```

Insert the text that the user entered for the title:

```
MyPowerPoint.ActiveWindow.Selection.TextRange.Text = txtTitle.Text
```

Then start a loop so you can process each of the program records:

```
Do Until RSPrograms.EOF
```

Each one goes on its own slide in the presentation:

```
MyPowerPoint.ActiveWindow.View.GotoSlide
        Index:=MyPowerPoint.ActivePresentation.Slides.
        Add(Index:=2, Layout:=ppLayoutTitle).SlideIndex
```

Then select all the text in the title text box for the program slide:

```
MyPowerPoint.ActiveWindow.Selection.SlideRange.Shapes("Rectangle 2").Select
MyPowerPoint.ActiveWindow.Selection.ShapeRange.TextFrame.TextRange.Select
MyPowerPoint.ActiveWindow.Selection.ShapeRange.TextFrame.
        TextRange.Characters(Start:=1, Length:=0).Select
```

Enter the name of the program into that text box:

```
MyPowerPoint.ActiveWindow.Selection.TextRange.Text = RSPrograms("ProgramName")
```

The other text box on the slide contains the description of the program. That text box and the text contained within are selected here:

```
MyPowerPoint.ActiveWindow.Selection.SlideRange.Shapes("Rectangle 3").Select
MyPowerPoint.ActiveWindow.Selection.ShapeRange.TextFrame.TextRange.Select
MyPowerPoint.ActiveWindow.Selection.ShapeRange.TextFrame.
    TextRange.Characters(Start:=1, Length:=0).Select
```

Insert the program description into that text box:

```
MyPowerPoint.ActiveWindow.Selection.TextRange.Text = RSPrograms("ProgramDescription")
```

Finally, move on to process the next program record:

```
RSPrograms.MoveNext
Loop
```

SECTION 3

Advanced Topics

15

Creating Add-Ins and Wizards

ON THE CD:

DBInfo.mda

fmDialog.mda

MyTW.mdb

Extending the Functionality of Access with Your Own Tools

If you work at a large organization, you may have different levels of Access programmers and users. Some may only know how to enter data, others may be able to create their own complex queries and reports, and still others may specialize in certain aspects of working with Access, such as security or ODBC. You may find in such an organization the need to provide a specific capability that Access doesn't offer, but that must be available to other users and developers. Maybe you have figured out a great way to increase the productivity of developing reports in Access by using a certain step-by step-technique, and now you would like to sell your technique or Wizard to other Access developers. Or possibly you work on your own, developing numerous databases in Access and are tired of repeating the same steps. Instead, you want to automate some of the processes you perform. Add-Ins and Wizards can provide resolutions to the problems.

In Access you can create a special kind of database called an Add-In that ends with an extension of .mda. These databases contain code that can run in other databases that perform such tasks as creating a table, up-sizing a database to SQL Server, writing code, and creating reports. Once the Add-In is registered within Access, the code is run just as if it were part of Access. In fact, if you have ever used the Form Wizard or the Report Wizard to create a form or report, you have used such an Add-In.

In this chapter, we will look at creating these Add-Ins and Wizards. First, we will walk through a very simple Add-In that displays information about the current database and we will examine the creation and use of that database step by step. Then we will look at the Form Dialog Wizard. This tool enables the user to generate a dialog form that contains the specific number of Text Boxes, Combo Boxes and Command Buttons entered by the user. After that, we will review the My Table Wizard database Add-In. This Add-In provides an interface for the user to create tables that have a common use across different database applications.

DBInfo Database

First, we will review a very simple Add-In called DBInfo. This Add-In simply displays information about the database in a form. You will see how a special table called USysRegInfo provides an entry point into your Add-In and how your Add-In looks internally. But first, let's see what it does.

Sample Walk-through

To use any of the Add-Ins discussed in this chapter, or any Add-Ins you create, they need to be installed within Access on the machine on which they are being used. The first step is to place the Add-In database, the .mda file, in the same directory as Access. This is usually at this location:

```
C:\Program Files\Microsoft Office\Office\
```

Then start Access and open any database. In this sample walk-through, I opened the Students, Instructors, and Courses database form Chapter 11, "Students, Teachers, and Courses." Then from the Access menu, select Tools\Add-Ins\Add-In Manager. You should then see the dialog displayed in Figure 15-1.

Press the Add New button and browse to the location where you placed the Add-In file and select it. The Add-In dialog should now look like the one displayed in Figure 15-2.

Figure 15-1

The Add-In Manager dialog

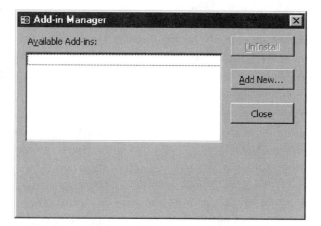

Figure 15-2

The Add-In Manager dialog with new Add-In present

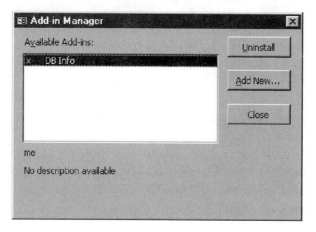

Notice that the new Add-In has an X to the left of its name. That means it has been installed, which means that entries have been made to the registry so that it will appear within the menus in Access.

Close the Add-In Manager dialog. From the menu, select Tools\Add-Ins and a new Add-In called DBInfo should be listed. Select that item to see what this Add-In does, as displayed in Figure 15-3.

The Add-In simply displays the number of tables and queries in the database, the user's name, and the path to the current database.

Creating the Add-In Database

To create an Add-In database, start Access and select New from the file menu. Save the database in the same directory as the Access executable, which is typically here:

```
C:\Program Files\Microsoft Office\Office\
```

Make sure to give the database a name that ends with .mda as is shown in Figure 15-4.

Figure 15-3

The DBInfo form

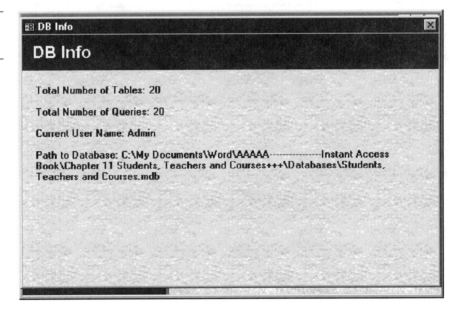

DB Info

DB Info

Total Number of Tables: 20

Total Number of Queries: 20

Current User Name: Admin

Path to Database: C:\My Documents\Word\AAAAA----------------Instant Access Book\Chapter 11 Students, Teachers and Courses+++\Databases\Students, Teachers and Courses.mdb

Figure 15-4

Creating an Add-In database

UsysRegInfo Table

The DBInfo database and any Add-In database must contain a table called USysRegInfo. But if you were to look at the DBInfo database, you may not see the USysRegInfo table listed. That is because the table is a system table, which by default is not visible. To make it visible, select Options from the Tools menu to see the dialog displayed in Figure 15-5.

Figure 15-5

The Options dialog

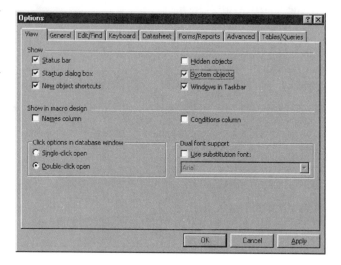

Go to the View tab and check the System objects check box. The USys-RegInfo table in the DBInfo database is now in view.

The USysRegInfo is used when your Add-In is first installed by the Add-In Manger. The Add-In Manager uses the values in the table to create entries in the system registry. These entries tell Access what kind of Add-In is being installed and what function within the Add-In to call when the user runs the Add-In. The field specifications for the USys-RegInfo table are displayed in Table 15-1.

	Field Name	Field Type	Notes
Table 15-1 The USysRegInfo Table Field Specifications	Subkey	Text	Length = 255
	Type	Number	Type = Long
	ValName	Text	Length = 255
	Value	Text	Length = 255

The first field, Subkey, stores the location in the registry where the entry should be made. The Type field stores the type of registry entry for which this record is to be used. The ValName stores the name of the key in the registry for this record, and the Value field stores the value placed in that key. Table 15-2 shows the records placed in the USysRegInfo table for the DBInfo database.

	Subkey	Type	ValName	Value
Table 15-2 The USysRegInfo Table Field Specifications	HKEY_LOCAL_MACHINE\ SOFTWARE\Microsoft\Office\9.0\ Access\Menu Add-Ins\DB Info	0		
	HKEY_LOCAL_MACHINE\ SOFTWARE\Microsoft\Office\9.0\ Access\Menu Add-Ins\DB Info	1	Expression	=LaunchAddIn()
	HKEY_LOCAL_MACHINE\ SOFTWARE\Microsoft\Office\9.0\ Access\Menu Add-Ins\DB Info	1	Library	|ACCDIR\ DBInfo.mda

The first record tells Access to add a new node to the Menu Add-Ins registry section and to give it the name DB Info. The second record tells Access to add a new key in the node just added, called Expression, and place this value in it:

```
=LaunchAddIn()
```

This function is the entry point in our Add-In. Somewhere in a module within our Add-In, you must create a function called LaunchAddIn. The third record indicates the physical location where the Add-In resides on the user's computer. The first part of that entry:

```
|ACCDIR
```

refers to the location of Access itself. So, look for this Add-In in the same folder as Access itself.

GeneralProcs Module

When someone runs your Add-In, Access launches whatever function you list in the Expression record in the USysRegInfo table. Therefore, somewhere in your Add-In, you must have a module that contains a function with the exact name listed in that USysRegInfo record.

The DBInfo Add-In has a module called GeneralProcs. That module has a function called LaunchAddIn. Note that this must be a function, not a procedure, even though it does not have a return value.

```
Public Function LaunchAddIn()
    DoCmd.OpenForm "DB Info", , , , , acDialog
End Function
```

This function simply displays the form called DB Info as a dialog so it retains the focus until it is closed.

DB Info Form

The code on the DB Info form displays summary information about the database to the user when the Add-In is invoked. This code is placed in the Load event of the Form object:

```
Private Sub Form_Load()
    Dim MyDB As DAO.Database
    Set MyDB = CurrentDb
    Label29.Caption = "Total Number of Tables: " _
        & MyDB.TableDefs.Count
    Label29.Caption = Label29.Caption & vbNewLine & vbNewLine _
        & "Total Number of Queries: " & MyDB.TableDefs.Count
    Label29.Caption = Label29.Caption & vbNewLine & vbNewLine _
        & "Current User Name: " & Application.CurrentUser
    Label29.Caption = Label29.Caption & vbNewLine & vbNewLine _
        & "Path to Database: " & CurrentDb.Name
End Sub
```

You will need to retrieve information from the user's database:

```
Dim MyDB As DAO.Database
```

Then connect to the database:

```
Set MyDB = CurrentDb
```

and place in the label in the detail section of the form, the number of tables in the database:

```
Label29.Caption = "Total Number of Tables: " _
    & MyDB.TableDefs.Count
```

Also display the number of queries in the database:

```
Label29.Caption = Label29.Caption & vbNewLine & vbNewLine _
    & "Total Number of Queries: " & MyDB.TableDefs.Count
```

the name of the user who is logged into the database:

```
Label29.Caption = Label29.Caption & vbNewLine & vbNewLine _
    & "Current User Name: " & Application.CurrentUser
```

and the path to the current database:

```
Label29.Caption = Label29.Caption & vbNewLine & vbNewLine _
    & "Path to Database: " & CurrentDb.Name
```

Form Dialog Wizard

The Form Dialog Wizard enables the user to add a Dialog form to their database application. The Wizard uses code to create a new form and to add controls to that form.

Sample Walk-through

As was discussed in the last section, the Add-In needs to be installed before it can be used by another database application. Once it is installed, it will be displayed in the Add-In Manager as shown in Figure 15-6.

Once the Wizard is installed, the user can access it from any of his or her database applications. In this example, the Students, Teachers and Courses database from Chapter 11 is used. When the user selects this Wizard from the Add-In menu, the form displayed in Figure 15-7 is shown.

Figure 15-6

The Add-In Manager

Figure 15-7

Create a Dialog form

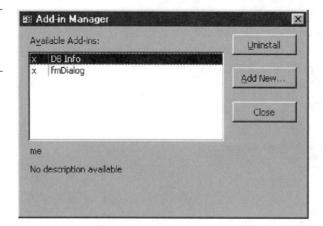

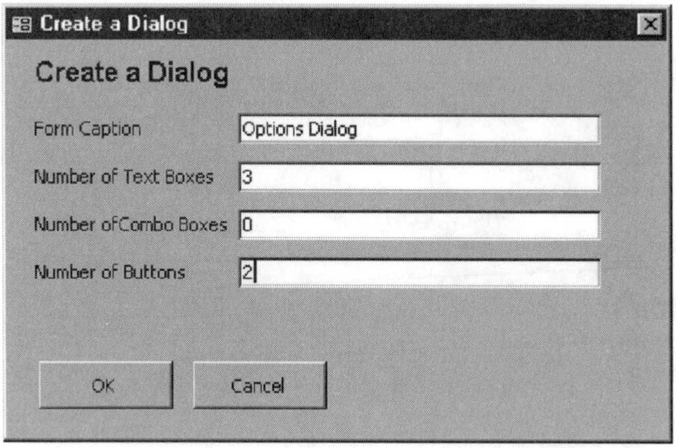

The user enters on this form the caption that he or she would like to appear on the new form and the number of text boxes, combo boxes and command buttons that he or she wants. When the OK button is pressed, the code makes sure that a value has been entered in each text box and that the number fields are within a specified range. Then the user is prompted for a caption for each of the new controls through an input box, such as the one displayed in Figure 15-8.

Once captions have been entered for each of the controls, the user sees a form like the one displayed in Figure 15-9.

Notice the caption on the form. It is the same as was entered in the Wizard. In fact, all the captions are entered through the Wizard. The form is created without scroll bars, navigation buttons, and record selectors because it is to be a dialog. The Wizard can also create a form that includes text boxes such as the one in Figure 15-10.

This form contains two of each of the controls. The Wizard enables up to nine text boxes and combo boxes. It also enables one or two command buttons.

Figure 15-8

Gathering captions through the Dialog Form Wizard

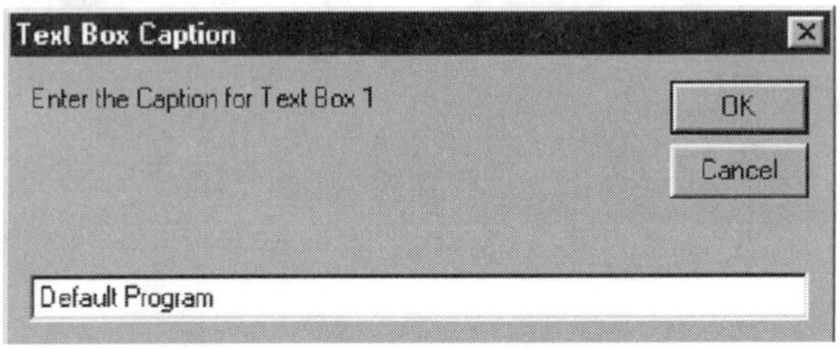

Figure 15-9

The Options dialog created using the Dialog Form Wizard

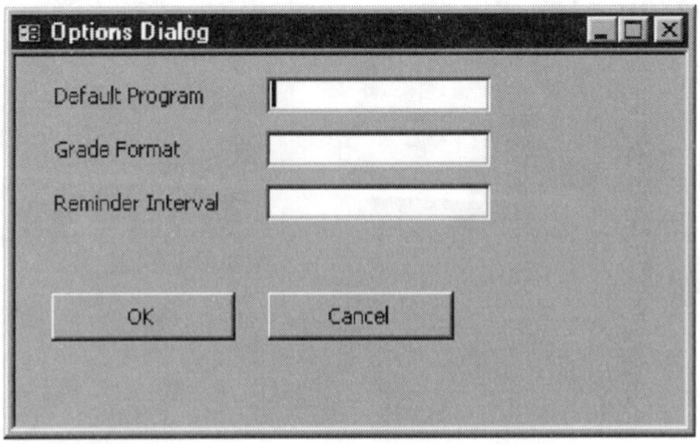

Figure 15-10

Course Report form created with the Dialog Form Wizard

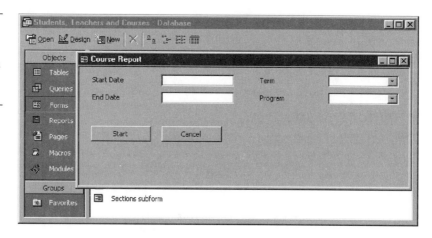

USysRegInfo Table

Because this database is an Add-In, it needs to have the USysRegInfo table as it was designed in the last section. The records in this table are shown in Table 15-3.

The first record in this table tells Access to create a node in the Registry called Dialog Form that is an Add-In for Access. The second record indicates that when the Wizard is invoked, the function:

```
AddInEntry()
```

Table 15-3

USysRegInfo Table Field Specifications

Subkey	Type	ValName	Value
HKEY_LOCAL_MACHINE\ SOFTWARE\Microsoft\Office\9.0\ Access\Menu Add-Ins\Dialog Form	0		
HKEY_LOCAL_MACHINE\ SOFTWARE\Microsoft\Office\9.0\ Access\Menu Add-Ins\Dialog Form	1	Expression	=AddInEntry()
HKEY_LOCAL_MACHINE\ SOFTWARE\Microsoft\Office\9.0\ Access\Menu Add-Ins\Dialog Form	1	Library	|ACCDIR\ fmDialog.mda

should run. The third record indicates that the Add-In is located in the Access directory and is called:

```
fmDialog.mda
```

GeneralProcs Module

When the user launches the Wizard, the entry point function runs. That function is located in a code module called GeneralProcs. The function has the following code:

```
Public Function AddInEntry()
    DoCmd.OpenForm "Create A Dialog", , , , , acDialog
End Function
```

The code simply uses the OpenForm method of the DoCmd object to open a form called Create a Dialog. The form is displayed as a dialog itself so the user will have to complete it using the Wizard before returning to the application.

Create a Dialog Form

The code guts of this Wizard are located on the Create a Dialog form. The form has two procedures. The first is the code behind the Cancel button:

```
Private Sub Command4_Click()
    DoCmd.Close
End Sub
```

It uses the Close method of the DoCmd object to close the Wizard. The other procedure on this form fires when the OK button is pressed. It checks the user's entries and creates a form based on those entries:

```
Private Sub Command3_Click()
    Dim MyNewForm As Form
    Dim MyNewControl As Control
    Dim TheCaption As String
    Dim NumTB As Integer
    Dim NumCB As Integer
    Dim NumButtons As Integer
    Dim CurrentLeft As Long
    Dim CurrentTop As Long
    Dim I As Integer
    Dim MaxTop As Long
    txtCaption.SetFocus
```

```
If txtCaption.Text = "" Then
    MsgBox "Please enter a caption for the new form."
    Exit Sub
End If
TheCaption = txtCaption.Text
txtTextBox.SetFocus
If Not IsNumeric(txtTextBox.Text) Then
    MsgBox "The Text Box field must be a number."
    Exit Sub
End If
NumTB = txtTextBox.Text
If NumTB < 0 Or NumTB > 10 Then
    MsgBox "The number of Text Boxes on the dialog must be from 0 to 10."
    Exit Sub
End If
txtComboBox.SetFocus
If Not IsNumeric(txtComboBox.Text) Then
    MsgBox "The Combo Box field must be a number."
    Exit Sub
End If
NumCB = txtComboBox.Text
If NumCB < 0 Or NumCB > 10 Then
    MsgBox "The number of Combo Boxes on the dialog must be from 0 to 10."
    Exit Sub
End If
txtButtons.SetFocus
If Not IsNumeric(txtButtons.Text) Then
    MsgBox "The Buttons field must be a number."
    Exit Sub
End If
NumButtons = txtButtons.Text
If NumButtons < 1 Or NumButtons > 2 Then
    MsgBox "The number of Buttons on the dialog must 1 or 2."
    Exit Sub
End If
Set MyNewForm = CreateForm()
MyNewForm.Caption = TheCaption
MyNewForm.ScrollBars = 0
MyNewForm.RecordSelectors = False
MyNewForm.NavigationButtons = False
MyNewForm.DividingLines = False
CurrentTop = 200
For I = 1 To NumTB
    CurrentLeft = 300
    Set MyNewControl = CreateControl(MyNewForm.Name, _
        acLabel, acDetail, , , CurrentLeft, CurrentTop, 1700, 220)
    MyNewControl.Caption = InputBox("Enter the Caption for Text Box " & I, _
        "Text Box Caption", "Text Box Caption")
    CurrentLeft = 2000
    Set MyNewControl = CreateControl(MyNewForm.Name, _
        acTextBox, acDetail, , , CurrentLeft, CurrentTop, 1700)
    CurrentTop = CurrentTop + 400
Next
MaxTop = CurrentTop
CurrentTop = 200
For I = 1 To NumCB
    CurrentLeft = 4300
    Set MyNewControl = CreateControl(MyNewForm.Name, _
```

```
            acLabel, acDetail, , , CurrentLeft, CurrentTop, 1700, 220)
        MyNewControl.Caption = InputBox("Enter the Caption for Combo Box " & I, _
            "Combo Box Caption", "Combo Box Caption")
        CurrentLeft = 6000
        Set MyNewControl = CreateControl(MyNewForm.Name, _
            acComboBox, acDetail, , , CurrentLeft, CurrentTop, 1700)
        CurrentTop = CurrentTop + 400
    Next
    If CurrentTop < MaxTop Then
        CurrentTop = MaxTop
    End If
    CurrentTop = CurrentTop + 400
    CurrentLeft = 300
    Set MyNewControl = CreateControl(MyNewForm.Name, _
        acCommandButton, acDetail, , , CurrentLeft, CurrentTop)
    MyNewControl.Caption = InputBox("Enter the Caption for first button.", _
        "Button 1 Caption", "Button 1 Caption")
    If NumButtons = 2 Then
        CurrentLeft = 2000
        Set MyNewControl = CreateControl(MyNewForm.Name, _
            acCommandButton, acDetail, , , CurrentLeft, CurrentTop)
        MyNewControl.Caption = InputBox("Enter the Caption for second button.", _
            "Button 2 Caption", "Button 2 Caption")
    End If
End Sub
```

A Form object is needed to store the new form that is going to create in code:

```
Dim MyNewForm As Form
```

A Control object is also needed. The controls can be placed and manipulated on the form:

```
Dim MyNewControl As Control
```

This variable stores the caption to be placed on the new form:

```
Dim TheCaption As String
```

This variable stores the number of text boxes the user wants on the form:

```
Dim NumTB As Integer
```

The number of combo boxes on the form:

```
Dim NumCB As Integer
```

and the number of buttons on the form:

```
Dim NumButtons As Integer
```

Another variable that stores the left position of the control being placed on the form is declared:

```
Dim CurrentLeft As Long
```

and this one stores the top position:

```
Dim CurrentTop As Long
```

Another variable is used in a For Next code block:

```
Dim I As Integer
```

and one more variable stores the position in which the command buttons are placed:

```
Dim MaxTop As Long
```

Then move focus to the caption text box:

```
txtCaption.SetFocus
```

and check to see if the user entered a caption:

```
If txtCaption.Text = "" Then
```

If the user didn't, inform him or her of the problem:

```
MsgBox "Please enter a caption for the new form."
```

and leave this procedure:

```
Exit Sub
```

Otherwise, store the caption entered into a local variable:

```
TheCaption = txtCaption.Text
```

Then set focus to the text box that stores the number of text boxes the user wants on their dialog:

```
txtTextBox.SetFocus
```

Check to see if it is a number:

```
If Not IsNumeric(txtTextBox.Text) Then
```

If it isn't, use a message box to tell the user:

```
MsgBox "The Text Box field must be a number."
```

and leave this procedure:

```
Exit Sub
```

Otherwise, store that value in a local variable:

```
NumTB = txtTextBox.Text
```

and check to see if the number entered is in the range of 0 to 9, which is the number of text boxes allowed:

```
If NumTB < 0 Or NumTB > 10 Then
```

If it isn't, tell the user the problem:

```
MsgBox "The number of Text Boxes on the dialog must be from 0 to 10."
```

and leave the procedure:

```
Exit Sub
```

Now, focus on the text box that stores the number of combo boxes the user wants on his or her form:

```
txtComboBox.SetFocus
```

Then make sure the value entered is a number:

```
If Not IsNumeric(txtComboBox.Text) Then
```

If it isn't, display an error message in a message box:

```
MsgBox "The Combo Box field must be a number."
```

and exit out of this procedure:

```
Exit Sub
```

Otherwise, store the number of combo boxes desired in a local variable:

```
NumCB = txtComboBox.Text
```

and make sure it is in the allowable range of 0 to 9:

```
If NumCB < 0 Or NumCB > 10 Then
```

If the number entered falls outside the range, tell the user:

```
MsgBox "The number of Combo Boxes on the dialog must be from 0 to 10."
```

and exit out:

```
Exit Sub
```

Next, move on to the text box that stores the number of command buttons the user wants:

```
txtButtons.SetFocus
```

and make sure that value is a number:

```
If Not IsNumeric(txtButtons.Text) Then
```

If it isn't, report an error to the user:

```
MsgBox "The Buttons field must be a number."
```

and exit:

```
Exit Sub
```

Otherwise, store the number desired:

```
NumButtons = txtButtons.Text
```

and verify that the number of command buttons is either one or two:

```
If NumButtons < 1 Or NumButtons > 2 Then
```

If it isn't, report the problem to the user:

```
MsgBox "The number of Buttons on the dialog must be 1 or 2."
```

and opt out of the rest of this procedure:

```
Exit Sub
```

If all the validation passes, your new form is ready to be created. This is done using the CreateForm method, which returns a reference to the new form into your object variable, MyNewForm:

```
Set MyNewForm = CreateForm()
```

Then place the caption entered by the user onto the new form:

```
MyNewForm.Caption = TheCaption
```

Because this is a dialog, remove the scroll bars:

```
MyNewForm.ScrollBars = 0
```

the record selectors:

```
MyNewForm.RecordSelectors = False
```

the navigation buttons:

```
MyNewForm.NavigationButtons = False
```

and the dividing lines:

```
MyNewForm.DividingLines = False
```

Now controls are ready to be added to your new form. The first control is placed 200 pixels from the top of the form:

```
CurrentTop = 200
```

Enter a loop so all of the text boxes desired can be processed:

```
For I = 1 To NumTB
```

The labels for the text boxes are placed 300 pixels from the left edge of the form:

```
CurrentLeft = 300
```

Use the CreateControl method to create a new control. The first parameter indicates the name of the form to which a control is being added. The second parameter is the type of control being added. The third parameter is the location on the form in which you want to place the control, such as Header, Footer, or Detail section. The sixth parameter stores the number of pixels from the left where the control on the form is placed. The seventh parameter stores the number of pixels down from the top where the control should be placed. The eighth parameter stores the width of the control, and the last parameter stores the height of the control:

```
Set MyNewControl = CreateControl(MyNewForm.Name, _
        acLabel, acDetail, , , CurrentLeft, CurrentTop, 1700, 220)
```

Then prompt the user for a caption for this label:

```
MyNewControl.Caption = InputBox("Enter the Caption for Text Box " & I, _
    "Text Box Caption", "Text Box Caption")
```

The text box needs to go to the left of the label just added:

```
CurrentLeft = 2000
```

Use the CreateControl method to create a text box on our new form:

```
Set MyNewControl = CreateControl(MyNewForm.Name, _
        acTextBox, acDetail, , , CurrentLeft, CurrentTop, 1700)
```

Then add 400 pixels to the top position so that the next text box is placed beneath the current text box:

```
CurrentTop = CurrentTop + 400
```

and loop to process the next text box:

```
Next
```

Then store how far down from the top of the form these controls were. The value is used to correctly place the command buttons at the bottom of the form:

```
MaxTop = CurrentTop
```

Reset the top position in order to process the combo boxes:

```
CurrentTop = 200
```

The next For Next block processes those combo boxes:

```
For I = 1 To NumCB
```

These are placed to the left of the labels and text boxes added on the last For Next block:

```
CurrentLeft = 4300
```

Then add a label for the combo box:

```
Set MyNewControl = CreateControl(MyNewForm.Name, _
        acLabel, acDetail, , , CurrentLeft, CurrentTop, 1700, 220)
```

and set the caption for the label based on the text entered by the user:

```
MyNewControl.Caption = InputBox("Enter the Caption for Combo Box " & I, _
        "Combo Box Caption", "Combo Box Caption")
```

The combo box appears to the left of its label:

```
CurrentLeft = 6000
```

Then create that combo box:

```
Set MyNewControl = CreateControl(MyNewForm.Name, _
        acComboBox, acDetail, , , CurrentLeft, CurrentTop, 1700)
```

and get the top position set for the next combo box:

```
CurrentTop = CurrentTop + 400
Next
```

The command buttons are placed beneath the other controls. Here determine which is lower, the position of the last text box or combo box:

```
If CurrentTop < MaxTop Then
```

If it was the text box, the value is stored here:

```
CurrentTop = MaxTop
```

Then add some additional space beneath the lowest text box or combo box:

```
CurrentTop = CurrentTop + 400
```

and set the position of the first command button so it is even with the labels used with the text boxes:

```
CurrentLeft = 300
```

Then create a new command button and place it on your form:

```
Set MyNewControl = CreateControl(MyNewForm.Name, _
        acCommandButton, acDetail, , , CurrentLeft, CurrentTop)
```

The caption that is placed on that command button comes from the user's entry into an Input box:

```
MyNewControl.Caption = InputBox("Enter the Caption for first button.", _
    "Button 1 Caption", "Button 1 Caption")
```

Next, check to see if the user wanted a second command button:

```
If NumButtons = 2 Then
```

If so, it is placed even with the text box position:

```
CurrentLeft = 2000
```

The CreateControl method is used to add the additional command button:

```
Set MyNewControl = CreateControl(MyNewForm.Name, _
        acCommandButton, acDetail, , , CurrentLeft, CurrentTop)
```

and a caption is placed on that control:

```
MyNewControl.Caption = InputBox("Enter the Caption for second button.", _
    "Button 2 Caption", "Button 2 Caption")
```

My Table Wizard Database Add-In

The My Table Wizard database Add-In enables the user to create new tables that are made up of commonly used field and table types. The code in this Wizard dynamically generates tables and fields in those tables.

Sample Walk-through

Before looking at the code that makes this Wizard run, let's look at what the user sees when the Wizard is used. Once installed, the Wizard is accessible, like the other Wizards in this chapter, through the Add-Ins menu item under the Tools menu. When the user first selects the Wizard, the form in Figure 15-11 is displayed.

Figure 15-11

The Table
Information page
from the Table
Builder Wizard

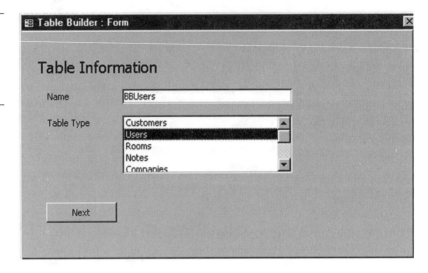

On this page, the name that the user would like to give the table is entered, along with the type of table that the user wants to create. The code makes sure a table with the name entered does not already exist and that the user has selected a table type.

Based on the table type, the user sees a different list. For example, if he or she selects the Users table type, the user will see the field list displayed in Figure 15-12.

This field list contains fields that go along with a Users table, but if the user selected Companies from the first page of the form, he or she would see the field list displayed in Figure 15-13.

Figure 15-12

Select Field page
for Users table
type

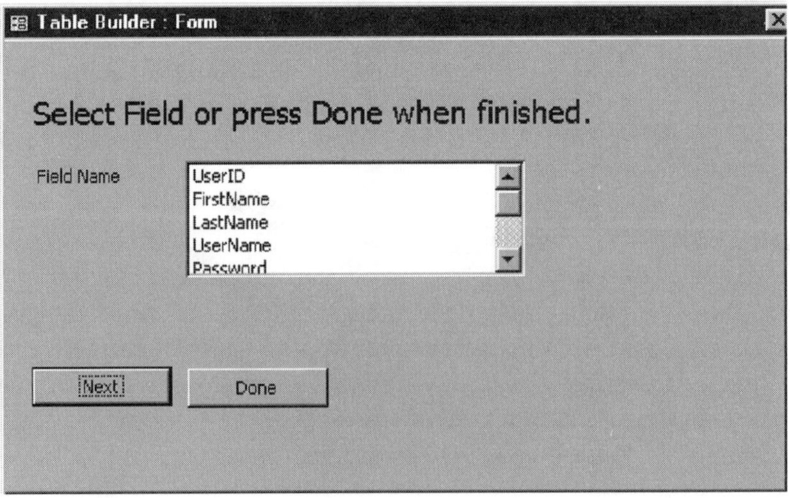

Now the field list contains fields pertinent to a Company table. Regardless of the table type, the user would select a field to add to the table. If the user tries to press Done at this point, he or she would see a message that says at least one field. Also, as the user selects a field and loops back to this page, the field he or she selected is no longer part of the list. This prevents the user from adding the same field more than once. Once the user has selected a field, he or she sees the third page of the Wizard displayed in Figure 15-14.

Figure 15-13

The Select Field page for Company table type

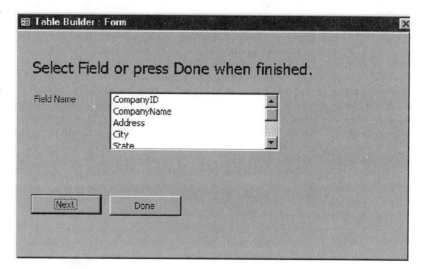

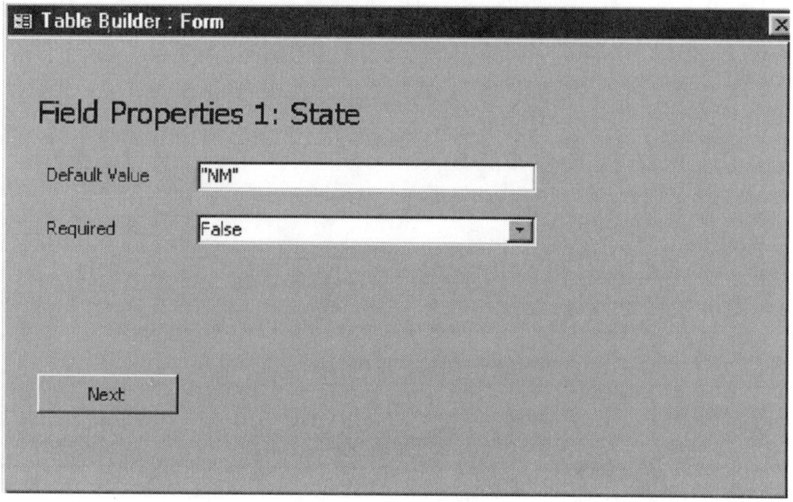

Figure 15-14

The Field Properties 1 page from the Table Builder Wizard

Notice first that the top label on the Wizard displays the name of the field so the user knows the field with which he or she is working. The user can then provide a default value for the field and whether the field is required or not. When the user presses the Next button, he or she sees the fourth page of the Wizard displayed in Figure 15-15.

From this page of the Wizard, the user can enter the validation rule and validation text that the field should contain. When the user presses the Next button, the code adds this field to the new table and sends the user back to the Select Field page that you looked at in Figure 15-13.

The user continues to loop through these pages of the Wizard until the Done button is pressed. When the user does so, the table is added to the database. The table produced in this sample walk-through is displayed in Figure 15-16.

Notice that the State field includes the default value, validation rule and validation text entered by the user. The same holds true for the other fields and the table is named based on the name entered by the user.

USysRegInfo Table

Because this database is an add-in, it needs to have the USysRegInfo table, as it was designed in the first section of this chapter. The records in this table are shown in Table 15-4.

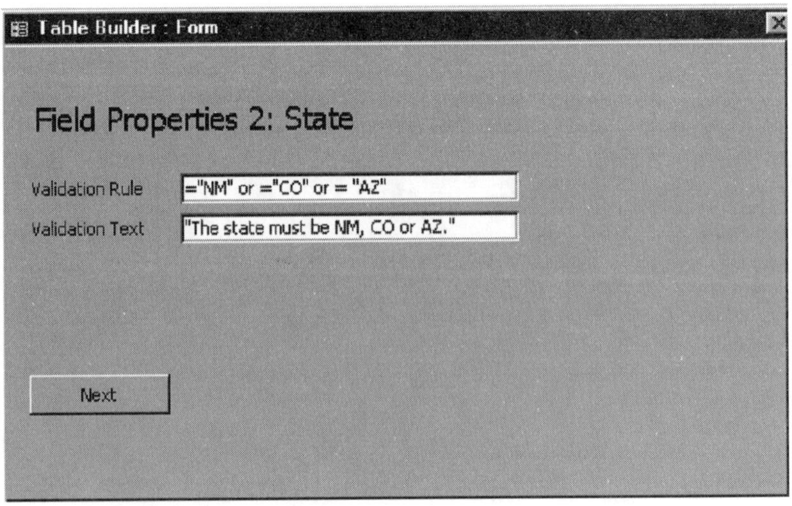

Figure 15-15

The Field Properties 2 page from the Table Builder Wizard

Figure 15-16

The table produced by the Build Table Wizard

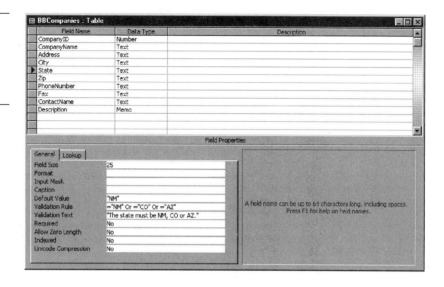

Table 15-4

The USysRegInfo Table Field Specifications

Subkey	Type	ValName	Value
HKEY_LOCAL_MACHINE\ SOFTWARE\Microsoft\Office\ 9.0\Access\Menu Add-Ins\ My Table Wizard	0		
HKEY_LOCAL_MACHINE\ SOFTWARE\Microsoft\Office\ 9.0\Access\Menu Add-Ins\ My Table Wizard	1	Expression	=EntryPoint()
HKEY_LOCAL_MACHINE\ SOFTWARE\Microsoft\Office\ 9.0\Access\Menu Add-Ins\ My Table Wizard	1	Library	|ACCDIR\ MyTW.mda

When the Wizard is installed, Access uses these records to add entries for the Wizard into the System Registry. The first record tells Access to add a new node in the registry for this Wizard. The second record tells Access that when the user launches the Wizard, it should run the function called EntryPoint. The last record tells Access where the Wizard is located.

GeneralProcs Module

Because this is an add-in, it must have a function defined as the entry point and that function must be defined in a code module. In this case, the code module is called GeneralProcs and the function within that module is called EntryPoint.

```
Public Function EntryPoint()
    DoCmd.OpenForm "Table Builder", , , , , acDialog
End Function
```

The function simply uses the OpenForm method of the DoCmd object to open the form called Table Builder. That form is displayed as a dialog, which means that the user must close the form before returning to the rest of the application.

Table Builder Form

The Table Builder form contains the code that creates the tables and the fields within those tables. The form is implemented as four pages of a Tab control that are made visible and invisible based on where the user is in the Wizard.

Most of the code is located behind the four Next buttons and the Done button, but the code requires some variables that store information from page to page. These variables are declared in the General Declaration section:

```
Private MyDB As DAO.Database
Private MyTB As New DAO.TableDef
Private MyField As DAO.Field
Private TheTableName As String
Private TheTableType As String
Private TheFieldName As String
```

The first variable is used to connect to the current database:

```
Private MyDB As DAO.Database
```

The next object variable stores your new table:

```
Private MyTB As New DAO.TableDef
```

The following one stores each field as you add them to the table:

```
Private MyField As DAO.Field
```

This variable stores the name of the table:

```
Private TheTableName As String
```

This one stores the type of table selected:

```
Private TheTableType As String
```

and this variable stores the name of the field currently being added to the table:

```
Private TheFieldName As String
```

When the user presses the Next button on the Table Information page, the following code block fires:

```
Private Sub cmdTableInformation_Click()
    Dim TempTableDef As DAO.TableDef
    lstTableType.SetFocus
    If IsNull(lstTableType.Value) Then
        MsgBox "Please select a table type!"
        Exit Sub
    End If
    TheTableType = lstTableType.Value
    txtTableName.SetFocus
    If txtTableName.Text = "" Then
        MsgBox "Please enter a name for the table"
        Exit Sub
    End If
    TheTableName = txtTableName.Text
    Set MyDB = CurrentDb
    For Each TempTableDef In MyDB.TableDefs
        If TempTableDef.Name = TheTableName Then
            MsgBox "A table witht he name you entered already exists!"
            Exit Sub
        End If
    Next
    MyTB.Name = TheTableName
    Page2.Visible = True
    Page2.SetFocus
    Page1.Visible = False
    If TheTableType = "Customers" Then
        lstFieldName.RowSource = "CustomerID;FirstName;LastName;Address;City;State;" _
            & "Zip;PhoneNumber;OfficeNumber;Fax;EmailAddress;"
    ElseIf TheTableType = "Users" Then
        lstFieldName.RowSource = "UserID;FirstName;LastName;UserName;Password;" _
            & "OfficeNumber;Extension;Fax;EmailAddress;"
    ElseIf TheTableType = "Rooms" Then
        lstFieldName.RowSource = "RoomID;RoomName;BuildingID;" _
```

```
            & "Location;Description;"
    ElseIf TheTableType = "Notes" Then
        lstFieldName.RowSource = "NoteID;NoteName;NoteText;"
    Else 'Companies
        lstFieldName.RowSource = "CompanyID;CompanyName;Address;City;State;" _
            & "Zip;PhoneNumber;Fax;ContactName;Description;"
    End If
    lstFieldName.Requery
End Sub
```

An additional table definition is needed in this procedure:

```
Dim TempTableDef As DAO.TableDef
```

Start by moving the focus to the table type list box:

```
lstTableType.SetFocus
```

Then make sure the user has selected a table type:

```
If IsNull(lstTableType.Value) Then
```

If the user hasn't, inform him or her of the problem:

```
MsgBox "Please select a table type!"
```

and exit this procedure:

```
Exit Sub
```

Otherwise, store the table type in a variable:

```
TheTableType = lstTableType.Value
```

Next, set focus to the table name text box:

```
txtTableName.SetFocus
```

and make sure the user has entered a name for the table:

```
If txtTableName.Text = "" Then
```

If he or she hasn't, display a message to them:

```
MsgBox "Please enter a name for the table"
```

and exit out of this procedure:

```
Exit Sub
```

Otherwise, store the name of the table in a variable:

```
TheTableName = txtTableName.Text
```

and connect to the database that the user has open:

```
Set MyDB = CurrentDb
```

You also need to make sure that the table name the user entered does not already exist. Therefore, you need to loop through all the tables in the database:

```
For Each TempTableDef In MyDB.TableDefs
```

and check to see if the name of the table is the same as the name of the table that the user is trying to create:

```
If TempTableDef.Name = TheTableName Then
```

If the table does exist, tell the user:

```
MsgBox "A table witht he name you entered already exists!"
```

and leave this procedure:

```
Exit Sub
```

Otherwise, move on to check the name of the next table in this database:

```
Next
```

If the code flows to this point, a table with the name entered by the user does not exist, so use that name in our table definition object:

```
MyTB.Name = TheTableName
```

Then make the next page visible, which is the Field Name page:

```
Page2.Visible = True
```

Set focus to that page:

```
Page2.SetFocus
```

and make the current page invisible:

```
Page1.Visible = False
```

If the table type selected by the user was Customers:

```
If TheTableType = "Customers" Then
```

enter these fields into the field name list box:

```
lstFieldName.RowSource = "CustomerID;FirstName;LastName;Address;City;State;" _
    & "Zip;PhoneNumber;OfficeNumber;Fax;EmailAddress;"
```

Next, check to see if the user selected the Users table type:

```
ElseIf TheTableType = "Users" Then
```

If so, these fields are used:

```
lstFieldName.RowSource = "UserID;FirstName;LastName;UserName;Password;" _
    & "OfficeNumber;Extension;Fax;EmailAddress;"
```

The next table type to check for is Rooms:

```
ElseIf TheTableType = "Rooms" Then
```

If the user selected that table type, the field name list box is populated with these values:

```
lstFieldName.RowSource = "RoomID;RoomName;BuildingID;" _
    & "Location;Description;"
```

The next table type to check for is Notes:

```
ElseIf TheTableType = "Notes" Then
```

If the user selected that type, use these fields:

```
lstFieldName.RowSource = "NoteID;NoteName;NoteText;"
```

The Else portion means that the user selected the Company table type:

```
Else 'Companies
```

and these fields are used:

```
lstFieldName.RowSource = "CompanyID;CompanyName;Address;City;State;" _
    & "ip;PhoneNumber;Fax;ContactName;Description;"
```

Then repopulate the field name list box.

```
lstFieldName.Requery
```

The next code block fires when the user presses the Next button on the Field Name page:

```
Private Sub CmdField_Click()
    lstFieldName.SetFocus
    If IsNull(lstFieldName.Value) Then
        MsgBox "Please select a field name!"
        Exit Sub
    End If
    TheFieldName = lstFieldName.Value
    If TheFieldName = "CustomerID" Or TheFieldName = "UserID" _
        Or TheFieldName = "RoomID" Or TheFieldName = "NoteID" _
        Or TheFieldName = "CompanyID" Or TheFieldName = "BuildingID" Then
            Set MyField = MyTB.CreateField(TheFieldName, dbLong)
    ElseIf TheFieldName = "Description" Or TheFieldName = "NoteText" _
        Or TheFieldName = "Location" Then
            Set MyField = MyTB.CreateField(TheFieldName, dbMemo)
    ElseIf TheFieldName = "FirstName" Or TheFieldName = "LastName" _
        Or TheFieldName = "City" Or TheFieldName = "EmailAddress" _
        Or TheFieldName = "RoomName" Or TheFieldName = "NoteName" _
        Or TheFieldName = "CompanyName" Or TheFieldName = "ContactName" Then
            Set MyField = MyTB.CreateField(TheFieldName, dbText, 50)
    ElseIf TheFieldName = "Address" _
        Or TheFieldName = "City" Or TheFieldName = "EmailAddress" Then
            Set MyField = MyTB.CreateField(TheFieldName, dbText, 255)
    Else
            Set MyField = MyTB.CreateField(TheFieldName, dbText, 25)
    End If
    lstFieldName.RowSource = Replace(lstFieldName.RowSource, _
        TheFieldName & ";", "", , , vbTextCompare)
    lstFieldName.Requery
    Page3.Visible = True
    Page3.SetFocus
    Label10.Caption = "Field Properties 1: " & TheFieldName
    Page2.Visible = False
End Sub
```

At this point, you have created the new table. Now the user has selected a field and that field needs to be added to the table. Start by setting the focus to the field name text box:

```
lstFieldName.SetFocus
```

and make sure the user has selected a field:

```
If IsNull(lstFieldName.Value) Then
```

If he or she hasn't, tell them to:

```
MsgBox "Please select a field name!"
```

and leave this procedure:

```
Exit Sub
```

Otherwise, store the name of the field in a variable:

```
TheFieldName = lstFieldName.Value
```

Then check to see if the field selected by the user is one of the ID fields:

```
If TheFieldName = "CustomerID" Or TheFieldName = "UserID" _
    Or TheFieldName = "RoomID" Or TheFieldName = "NoteID" _
    Or TheFieldName = "CompanyID" Or TheFieldName = "BuildingID" Then
```

If so, use the CreateField method to create a Field object. The first parameter is the name of the field. The second parameter is the data type for the field. In this case, use a long number:

```
Set MyField = MyTB.CreateField(TheFieldName, dbLong)
```

Next, check to see if the field selected is one of the Memo fields:

```
ElseIf TheFieldName = "Description" Or TheFieldName = "NoteText" _
    Or TheFieldName = "Location" Then
```

If so, the CreateField method of the TableDef object is used to create a Memo-type field:

```
Set MyField = MyTB.CreateField(TheFieldName, dbMemo)
```

Then check to see if the field selected is one of these text fields:

```
ElseIf TheFieldName = "FirstName" Or TheFieldName = "LastName" _
    Or TheFieldName = "City" Or TheFieldName = "EmailAddress" _
    Or TheFieldName = "RoomName" Or TheFieldName = "NoteName" _
    Or TheFieldName = "CompanyName" Or TheFieldName = "ContactName" Then
```

If so, create a text field. Note that the third parameter of the Create-Field method indicates the length of the field. In this case, the length is 50:

```
Set MyField = MyTB.CreateField(TheFieldName, dbText, 50)
```

Next, check to see if the field selected is one of the long text fields:

```
ElseIf TheFieldName = "Address" _
     Or TheFieldName = "City" Or TheFieldName = "EmailAddress" Then
```

If so, create a text field with a length of 255:

```
Set MyField = MyTB.CreateField(TheFieldName, dbText, 255)
```

Otherwise, the field selected is to be one of the short text fields:

```
Else
```

which is set as a text field with a length of 25:

```
Set MyField = MyTB.CreateField(TheFieldName, dbText, 25)
```

Next, you need to remove the field the user selected from the field list so that when the user comes back to this page, he or she can't select the same field again. This can be done by replacing the name of the field in the list with an empty string:

```
lstFieldName.RowSource = Replace(lstFieldName.RowSource, _
     TheFieldName & ";", "", , , vbTextCompare)
```

Then repopulate the field name list box:

```
    lstFieldName.Requery
```

Now you are ready to move on to the Field Properties 1 page:

```
Page3.Visible = True
```

that you set focus to

```
Page3.SetFocus
```

Set the caption of that page so that it displays the name of the field selected by the user:

```
Label10.Caption = "Field Properties 1: " & TheFieldName
```

Then make the current page invisible:

```
Page2.Visible = False
```

The next code block fires when the user presses the Next button on the Field Properties 1 page.

```
Private Sub cmdFP1_Click()
    txtDefaultValue.SetFocus
    MyField.DefaultValue = txtDefaultValue.Text
    cmbRequired.SetFocus
    If cmbRequired.Value = "True" Then
        MyField.Required = True
    Else
        MyField.Required = False
    End If
    Page4.Visible = True
    Page4.SetFocus
    Label11.Caption = "Field Properties 2: " & TheFieldName
    Page3.Visible = False
End Sub
```

Start by setting focus to the default value text box:

```
txtDefaultValue.SetFocus
```

Then set the DefaultValue property of our Field object to the value entered by the user:

```
MyField.DefaultValue = txtDefaultValue.Text
```

Next, move the focus to the required combo box:

```
cmbRequired.SetFocus
```

If the value selected in that combo box is True:

```
If cmbRequired.Value = "True" Then
```

the field is a required field:

```
MyField.Required = True
```

Otherwise, it is not a required field:

```
Else
        MyField.Required = False
```

Next, you need to display the fourth page of the Wizard, the Field Properties 2 page. Make that page visible:

```
Page4.Visible = True
```

and set focus to it:

```
Page4.SetFocus
```

Then set the label at the top of that form so that it contains the name of the current field:

```
Label11.Caption = "Field Properties 2: " & TheFieldName
```

and make the current page invisible:

```
Page3.Visible = False
```

The next code block fires when the Next button on the Field Properties 2 page is pressed:

```
Private Sub cmdFP2_Click()
    txtVR.SetFocus
    MyField.ValidationRule = txtVR.Text
    txtVT.SetFocus
    MyField.ValidationText = txtVT.Text
    MyTB.Fields.Append MyField
    Page2.Visible = True
    Page2.SetFocus
    Page4.Visible = False
End Sub
```

Start by moving the focus to the validation rule text box:

```
txtVR.SetFocus
```

and use that value for the ValidationRule property of our Field object:

```
MyField.ValidationRule = txtVR.Text
```

The same is done for the ValidationText property:

```
txtVT.SetFocus
MyField.ValidationText = txtVT.Text
```

Your field is now complete. Append it to the Fields collection of your TableDef object using the Append method of the Fields collection:

```
MyTB.Fields.Append MyField
```

Then loop the user back to the second page of the Wizard, the Field Name page:

```
Page2.Visible = True
```

Set focus to that page:

```
Page2.SetFocus
```

and make this page invisible:

```
Page4.Visible = False
```

The user keeps looping through the second, third, and fourth pages until he or she presses the Done button on the Field Name page. When he or she does, the last code block fires:

```
Private Sub cmdD0ne_Click()
    If MyTB.Fields.Count = 0 Then
        MsgBox "You must add at least one field before exiting!"
        Exit Sub
    End If
    MyDB.TableDefs.Append MyTB
    DoCmd.Close
End Sub
```

First make sure that he or she added at least one field to the table:

```
If MyTB.Fields.Count = 0 Then
```

If the user hasn't, tell them he or she needs to:

```
MsgBox "You must add at least one field before exiting!"
```

and exit this procedure:

```
Exit Sub
```

Otherwise, add the table you just created to the current database by using the Append method of the TableDefs collection, which is a collection of the Database objects:

```
MyDB.TableDefs.Append MyTB
```

Finally, close the Wizard:

```
DoCmd.Close
```

16

Creating Static Web Pages from Access

ON THE CD:

Students, Teachers and Courses.mdb

template.html

Building Simple Web Pages Based on Your Access Database

If it hasn't happened to you already, the request can't be too far away. The request is to port the data in your Access database into Web pages for your intranet and/or Internet Web sites. In this chapter, and the two that follow, we will look at using the data in your database as the basis for both static and dynamic Web pages.

Static Web pages are what you may be most familiar with. Those usually end in the file extension .htm or .html. Static Web pages only change when you create a new version of the page. As a visitor comes and goes to the page, he or she sees the same thing.

Dynamic Web pages often end with the file extension .asp, which stands for *Active Server pages*. Dynamic pages can and often do change each time the visitor opens the page. These pages frequently are based on data in a database and automatically reflect the current state of that data.

Chapter 17, "Creating Dynamic Web Content," and Chapter 18, "Using ASP," will focus on Dynamic Web pages. In this chapter, we will look at Static Web pages. First, we will look at using the built-in menu options to export data as a Web page. Then we will look at creating templates to shape the look and feel of those exported pages. After that, we will look at the special Hyperlink data type. Finally, we will use code to create our own custom static Web pages.

Exporting to HTML

Access really does make it simple to save much of your data into HTML pages that you can then place on your Internet or intranet server. The simplest thing to do is to export the contents of a table into a Web page. To do this, open the database that contains the table you want to export. Open that table and, from the menu, select File/Export. You should then see the Export Table dialog displayed in Figure 16-1.

Figure 16-1

Exporting a table to a Web page.

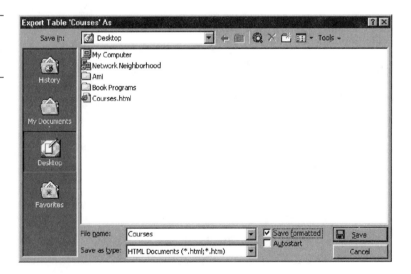

Change the "Save as type" combo box so that it displays HTML documents. Then check the Save Formatted box, enter a name for your Web page, and a folder to save that file. You will then be asked to supply a template. Leave that blank for now. Templates will be discussed in the next section.

Access then converts the table to an HTML page. Figure 16-2 shows the result of exporting the Courses table from the Students, Teachers, and Courses database discussed in Chapter 11, "Students, Teachers and Courses."

Once your database grows, it is likely that you will not want to export the entire contents of a table. Instead, you will want to export just some of the data through a query, or maybe you want to display the combined contents of more than one table. You can do that too. Just open the query and, as before, select File/Export from the Access menu. Select the file options as you did before and the records in your query will be exported to a Web page.

Figure 16-3 shows the Web page that resulted from exporting the Instructor Courses query in the Students, Teachers, and Courses database. The query combines the results of two of the tables in the database

Figure 16-2

Courses table converted to HTML

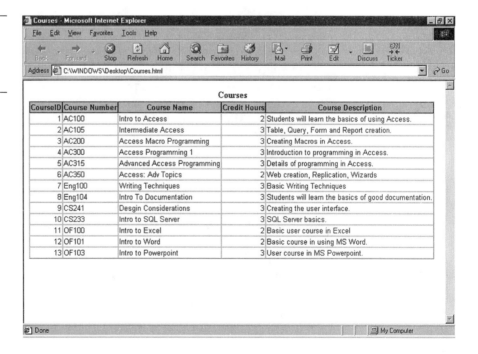

CourseID	Course Number	Course Name	Credit Hours	Course Description
1	AC100	Intro to Access	2	Students will learn the basics of using Access.
2	AC105	Intermediate Access	3	Table, Query, Form and Report creation.
3	AC200	Access Macro Programming	3	Creating Macros in Access.
4	AC300	Access Programming 1	3	Introduction to programming in Access.
5	AC315	Advanced Access Programming	3	Details of programming in Access.
6	AC350	Access: Adv Topics	2	Web creation, Replication, Wizards
7	Eng100	Writing Techniques	3	Basic Writing Techniques
8	Eng104	Intro To Documentation	3	Students will learn the basics of good documentation.
9	CS241	Desgin Considerations	3	Creating the user interface.
10	CS233	Intro to SQL Server	3	SQL Server basics.
11	OF100	Intro to Excel	2	Basic user course in Excel
12	OF101	Intro to Word	2	Basic course in using MS Word.
13	OF103	Intro to Powerpoint	3	User course in MS Powerpoint.

Figure 16-3

The Instructor
Courses query
exported into a
Web page

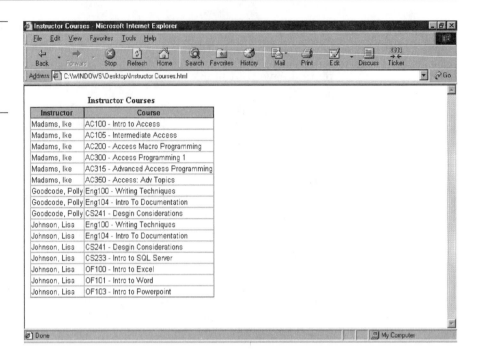

and the Web page reflects that join, with the page ready to be placed on just about any Web server without a connection to the database.

Even more powerful is how reports in an Access database are exported. When a report is exported, it is exported with the grouping and formatting that were in place in the report. So things like spacing, color, and fonts are exported with the report. Even your page breaks are retained, which means that if your report contains three paper pages, three HTML pages are exported from Access.

Let's take a look at an example of this. The Students, Teachers, and Courses database from Chapter 11 contains a report called Instructor Courses. That report displays the names of all the instructors that teach courses at the school, along with the courses that they teach. For this example, the report was modified so that the Report Header is now the Page Header. The Report Header appears only at the beginning of the report, but the Page Header appears on all the pages. Because you are exporting this data to Web pages, you want the report title at the top of each page.

The report was also changed so that a new page is generated for each instructor. This is done by setting the Force New Page property of the Instructor Footer section to After Section.

You now can run our report and export it using the File/Export method. Once you do that, a separate Web page is generated for each of the instructor records that are part of the report. Figure 16-4 shows the first Web page exported through this report.

Notice that Access exported nine Web pages. Each page lists just the courses for a particular instructor. Also notice the First, Previous, Next, and Last links at the bottom of the page. These are also generated by Access and provide the visitor with the navigation needed to move on to another Web page in this report. So if the visitor clicked on the Next link, he or she would be taken to the next page of the report displayed in Figure 16-5.

The nice part of all this is that you can change the look of the report and even create a whole different layout as far as font sizes and spacing, especially for your Web version of the report, and Access will use those settings.

Figure 16-4

The first page of the Instructor Courses Web pages

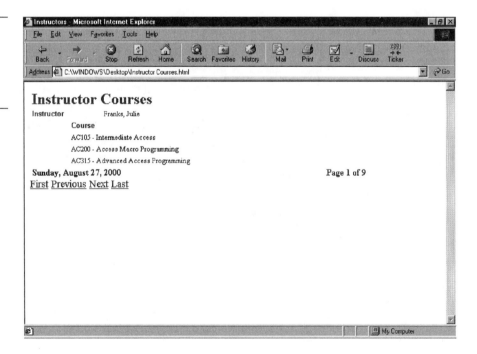

Figure 16-5

The second page from Instructor Courses Web pages

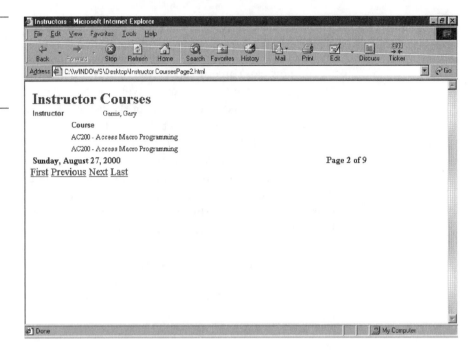

HTML Templates

When you export data from a report, you are asked for the name of an HTML template file. So far, that step has been skipped. This section will look at what a template file is and how to create one.

When Access exports your report into a series of Web pages, it uses a specific structure for placing the data on the page. For example, the title of the report is used in the title of the page and the links to the other pages are displayed as the text links First, Previous, Next, and Last. This may work some of the time, but you may find that you need to extend these pages so that the layout of the page fits in with the rest of your site or that the page contains other text components such as standard information about your company.

An HTML template provides the means to create a custom look to your exported Web pages. For example, take a look at Figure 16-6.

First, notice the title of the page. It contains the name and number of the page. Then note that the page has a background texture and that a

Figure 16-6

Page 1 of a report exported from Access using a custom template

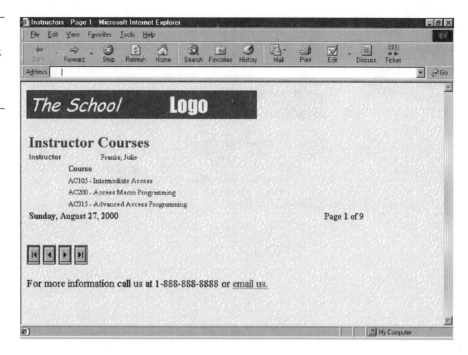

logo is at the top of the page. Also notice that instead of the text links, you now have a graphical navigation. Also notice the additional More information text added to the bottom of the page. Figure 16-7 shows the second Web page of the report.

Notice that the report still breaks the pages up by the instructor and that the same data is displayed. But now the page is formatted based on the HTML template that will be reviewed later.

But the template is not just for reports. You can use the same template when you export a table. Figure 16-8 shows the result of exporting the Courses table from the Students, Teachers, and Courses database.

When Access exports a report, table, or query to a Web page, it combines the data in the database with an HTML page that contains special tags. These special tags indicate where elements go, such as the title of the report or the link to the last page of the report. Table 16-1 summarizes these special tags.

What follows is the HTML template used to generate the table and report in this section:

Figure 16-7

The second page from the report using the custom template

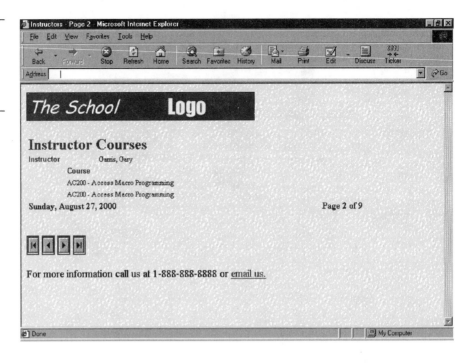

Figure 16-8

Using the HTML template to export a table

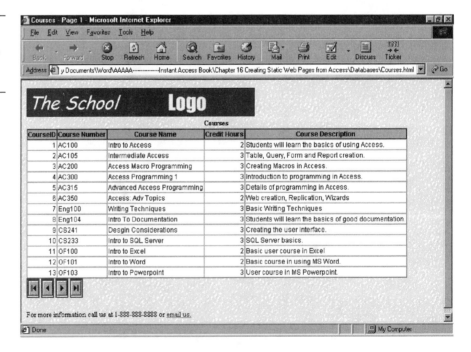

Table 16-1	Tag	Description
HTML Template Tags	<!--AccessTemplate_Title-->	Returns the name of the report being exported from Access.
	<!--AccessTemplate_PageNumber-->	Returns the current page number for this page in the report.
	<!--AcessTemplate_Body-->	Instructs Access to insert the data of the report at this position.
	<!--AccessTemplate_FirstPage-->	Returns the file name of the first page of the report for use in a link.
	<!--AccessTemplate_PreviousPage-->	Returns the file name of the previous page of the report for use in a link.
	<!--AccessTemplate_NextPage-->	Returns the file name of the next page of the report for use in a link.
	<!--AccessTemplate_LastPage-->	Returns the file name of the last page of the report for use in a link.

```
<HTML>
<HEAD>
<TITLE><!--AccessTemplate_Title--> - Page <!--AccessTemplate_PageNumber--></TITLE>
</HEAD>
<BODY BACKGROUND = "bg.gif">
<IMG SRC="logo.gif" ALT="School Logo" BORDER="1">
<BR><BR>
<!--AccessTemplate_Body-->
<BR><BR>
<A HREF="<!--AccessTemplate_FirstPage-->"><IMG SRC="first.gif" ALT="Move
First"></A>
<A HREF="<!--AccessTemplate_PreviousPage-->"><IMG SRC="prev.gif" ALT="Move
Previous"></A>
<A HREF="<!--AccessTemplate_NextPage-->"><IMG SRC="next.gif" ALT="Move Next"></A>
<A HREF="<!--AccessTemplate_LastPage-->"><IMG SRC="last.gif" ALT="Move Last"></A>
<P>For more information call us at 1-888-888-8888 or <A
HREF="mailto:watever@whatever.com">email us.</A></P>
</BODY>
</HTML>
```

Start with an opening HTML tag:

```
<HTML>
```

and a header tag:

```
<HEAD>
```

Then use the tag in the title. Tell Access to place the name of the table or report in this tag, along with the page number for this current page:

```
<TITLE><!--AccessTemplate_Title--> - Page <!--AccessTemplate_PageNumber--></TITLE>
```

Then close the header section:

```
</HEAD>
```

and start the body section so that it contains a textured background:

```
<BODY BACKGROUND = "bg.gif">
```

Place the school logo at the top of the body of the page:

```
<IMG SRC="logo.gif" ALT="School Logo" BORDER="1">
```

and provide two lines of blank space:

```
<BR><BR>
```

Then instruct Access to place the data for this page here:

```
<!--AccessTemplate_Body-->
```

After the data, provide a couple more lines of blank space:

```
<BR><BR>
```

Then place the navigation button for the first page of the report, which contains a link to that page:

```
<A HREF="<!--AccessTemplate_FirstPage-->"><IMG SRC="first.gif" ALT="Move First"></A>
```

That is followed by the button and link to the previous page:

```
<A HREF="<!--AccessTemplate_PreviousPage-->"><IMG SRC="prev.gif" ALT="Move Previous"></A>
```

one for the next page:

```
<A HREF="<!--AccessTemplate_NextPage-->"><IMG SRC="next.gif" ALT="Move Next"></A>
```

and one for the last page of the report:

```
<A HREF="<!--AccessTemplate_LastPage-->"><IMG SRC="last.gif" ALT="Move Last"></A>
```

Then put more information text at the bottom of the page:

```
<P>For more information call us at 1-888-888-8888 or
<A HREF="mailto:watever@whatever.com">email us.</A></P>
```

Now close the Body tag:

```
</BODY>
```

and the HTML tag:

```
</HTML>
```

Hyperlink Data Type

As you start to work with Web pages and your Access databases, you find that the Hyperlink data type provides a nice way to place links and email addresses on a Web page. Say, for example, that you need to expand the Students, Teachers, and Courses database so that it contains a table of Web resources. Let's also say that you are going to use the data in that table with the template you created in the last page to produce a Resources Web page. The page would need to contain addresses to Web sites and email addresses. You could define those fields as text and just display the links as straight text, as you have seen in previous sections, or you could define the table as is displayed in Table 16-2.

The Web and EmailAddress fields are created as Hyperlink fields. Such a field is made up of two parts. The first part is the text displayed to the user looking at the data and the second part is the location to go to when

Table 16-2	Field Name	Field Type	Notes
The Resources Table Field Specifications	ResourceID	AutoNumber	Type = Long, Primary Key
	Web	Hyperlink	
	EmailAddress	Hyperlink	
	Description	Memo	

the user clicks on the text in the field. When the user is adding data to this table for the Hyperlink fields, he or she can right-click on the field and select Hyperlink, followed by Edit Hyperlink. When the user does this, he or she sees the Edit Hyperlink dialog displayed in Figure 16-9.

The user then supplies the text that he or she wants displayed in this field and enters the location to go to when the link is clicked. Note that the user can also press the Email Address button in the bottom-left corner of the Window to make the link open to a new email message.

The real benefit of this data type comes once the user enters the information for this table and exports it. Figure 16-10 shows the result of exporting this table based on the template discussed in the last section of this chapter.

Notice what Access does when exporting this table. The fields that are defined as Hyperlink fields are displayed on the page as links. Thus, the visitor to the page can click on those links to be taken to the location of the Web sites and email addresses.

Figure 16-9

Edit Hyperlink
dialog

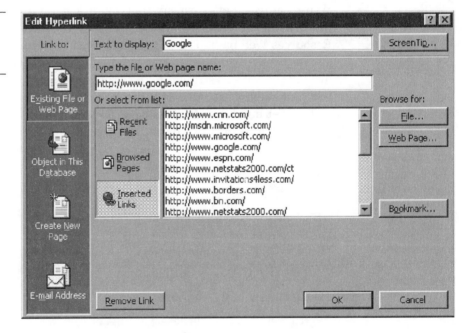

Figure 16-10

Exporting the
Resources table

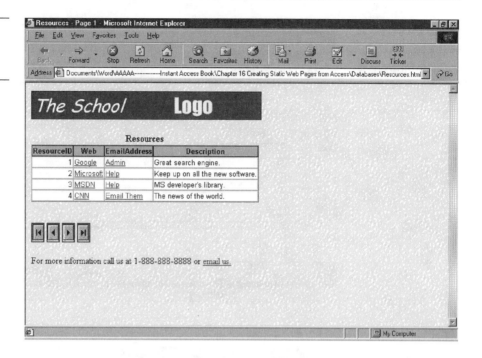

Creating Custom Static Pages Through Code

The procedures described so far enable you to create Web pages that follow a certain pattern, but sometimes you need more flexibility than that. Sometimes you need to have complete control of the placement of the data on a Web page. This section will look at generating Web pages from scratch through code.

The database in this section is based on the Students, Teachers, and Courses database discussed in Chapter 11. That database is enhanced to provide HTML output functionality. One of the enhancements to that database is on the Instructors form (see Figure 16-11).

The form is basically the same. The user would use this form to work with the instructor records, but the form contains a new button called Web Page. When the user presses the button, he or she is prompted for a file name to export this instructor record to as a Web page, as shown in Figure 16-12.

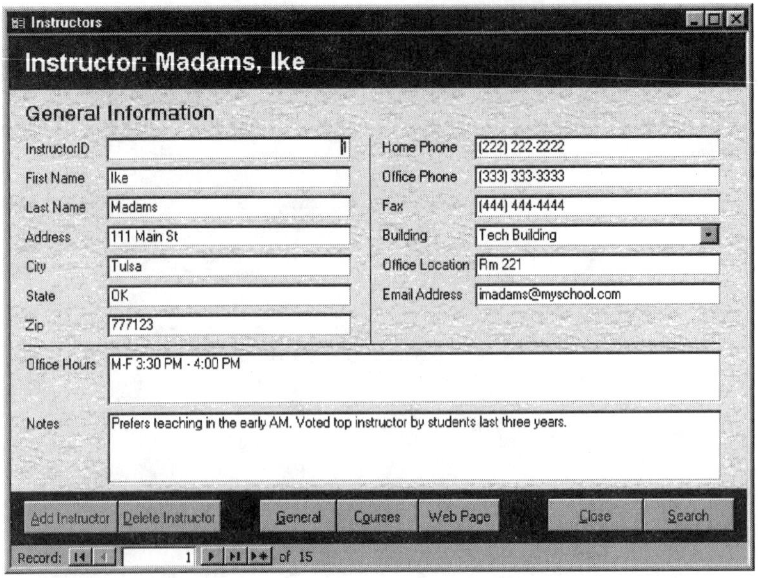

Figure 16-11

The Instructor form enhanced with Web page export

Figure 16-12

The Web Page Export dialog

By default, the name of the instructor is used to name the file, but the user can enter any name he or she wants. When the user presses the OK button, the code makes sure the file doesn't already exist. If it doesn't, a Web page is created based on the current instructor record saved to the file indicated by the user. The code then opens the file in a Browser window, as is displayed in Figure 16-13.

Note that this page is created from scratch within your code. The other change to this database is the addition of a new form called HTML Table. That form is displayed in Figure 16-14.

This form can be used with just about any database. When the form is first opened, the user sees a list of all the tables and queries in this database. The user then selects a table or query and gives the page a title. He

Figure 16-13

The Instructor
Web page

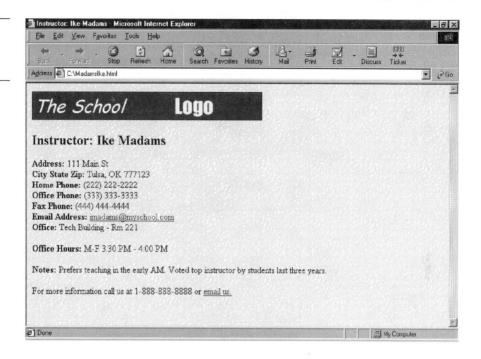

Figure 16-14

The HTML Table
form

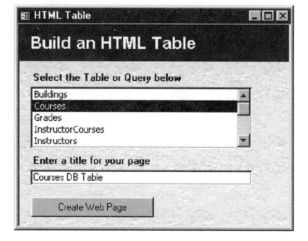

or she is then prompted for a file name. The code then takes the table and outputs it into a Web page like the one displayed in Figure 16-15.

Figure 16-15

The HTML Table output

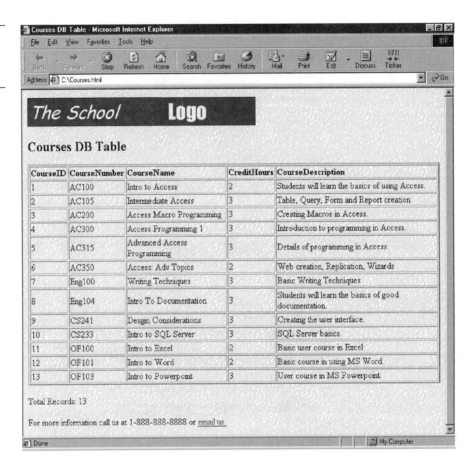

CourseID	CourseNumber	CourseName	CreditHours	CourseDescription
1	AC100	Intro to Access	2	Students will learn the basics of using Access.
2	AC105	Intermediate Access	3	Table, Query, Form and Report creation.
3	AC200	Access Macro Programming	3	Creating Macros in Access.
4	AC300	Access Programming 1	3	Introduction to programming in Access.
5	AC315	Advanced Access Programming	3	Details of programming in Access.
6	AC350	Access: Adv Topics	2	Web creation, Replication, Wizards
7	Eng100	Writing Techniques	3	Basic Writing Techniques
8	Eng104	Intro To Documentation	3	Students will learn the basics of good documentation.
9	CS241	Desgin Considerations	3	Creating the user interface.
10	CS233	Intro to SQL Server	3	SQL Server basics.
11	OF100	Intro to Excel	2	Basic user course in Excel
12	OF101	Intro to Word	2	Basic course in using MS Word.
13	OF103	Intro to Powerpoint	3	User course in MS Powerpoint.

Total Records: 13

For more information call us at 1-888-888-8888 or email us.

Instructors Form

The code added to the Instructors form generates the Web page based on the instructor data. That page is then displayed to the user. To display the Web page, a system command called ShellExecute is used. This command is defined in the General Declarations section of that form along with a constant:

```
Private Declare Function ShellExecute Lib "SHELL32.DLL" Alias
        "ShellExecuteA" (ByVal hWnd As Long, ByVal lpOperation As String,
        ByVal lpFile As String, ByVal lpParameters As String,
        ByVal lpDirectory As String, ByVal nShowCmd As Long) As Long
Const SW_SHOW = 5
```

The System function provides a method of opening a file that has a program association based on the file extension. The function is defined as Private, so it is only available to the procedures on this form:

```
Private Declare Function ShellExecute Lib "SHELL32.DLL" Alias
        "ShellExecuteA" (ByVal hWnd As Long, ByVal lpOperation As String,
        ByVal lpFile As String, ByVal lpParameters As String,
        ByVal lpDirectory As String, ByVal nShowCmd As Long) As Long
```

The function also relies on this constant that you will see used with this command in code:

```
Const SW_SHOW = 5
```

The code that uses this function and first creates the Web page is behind the Web Page button:

```
Private Sub cmdWebPage_Click()
    Dim MyDB As DAO.Database
    Dim RSBuilding As DAO.Recordset
    Dim TheFileName As String
    Dim TempPage As String
    TheFileName = InputBox("Enter the path and name of the Web page to export " _
        & "this instructor record to.", "File Name", "c:\" _
        & [LastName] & [FirstName] & ".html")
    If TheFileName = "" Then
        Exit Sub
    End If
    If Dir(TheFileName) <> "" Then
        MsgBox "A file with that name at that location already exists!"
        Exit Sub
    End If
    Set MyDB = CurrentDb
    Set RSBuilding = MyDB.OpenRecordset("Select BuildingName from Buildings " _
        & "Where BuildingID = " & [BuildingID], dbOpenSnapshot)
    TempPage = "<HTML>"
```

```
TempPage = TempPage & vbNewLine & "<HEAD>"
TempPage = TempPage & vbNewLine & "<TITLE>Instructor: " _
    & [FirstName] & " " & [LastName] & "</TITLE>"
TempPage = TempPage & vbNewLine & "</HEAD>"
TempPage = TempPage & vbNewLine & "<BODY BACKGROUND = ""bg.gif"">"
TempPage = TempPage & vbNewLine _
    & "<IMG SRC=""logo.gif"" ALT=""School Logo"" BORDER=""1"">"
TempPage = TempPage & vbNewLine & "<H2>Instructor: " _
    & [FirstName] & " " & [LastName] & "</H2>"
TempPage = TempPage & vbNewLine & "<P><B>Address:</B> " _
    & [Address] & "<BR>"
TempPage = TempPage & vbNewLine & "<B>City State Zip:</B> " _
    & [City] & ", " & [State] & " " & [Zip] & "<BR>"
TempPage = TempPage & vbNewLine & "<B>Home Phone:</B> " _
    & [HomePhone] & "<BR>"
TempPage = TempPage & vbNewLine & "<B>Office Phone:</B> " _
    & [OfficePhone] & "<BR>"
TempPage = TempPage & vbNewLine & "<B>Fax Phone:</B> " _
    & [Fax] & "<BR>"
TempPage = TempPage & vbNewLine & "<B>Email Address:</B> " _
    & "<A HREF=""mailto:" & [EmailAddress] & """>" _
    & [EmailAddress] & "</A><BR>"
If RSBuilding.EOF Then
    TempPage = TempPage & vbNewLine & "<B>Office:</B> " _
        & [OfficeLocation]
Else
    TempPage = TempPage & vbNewLine & "<B>Office:</B> " _
        & RSBuilding("BuildingName") & " - " & [OfficeLocation]
End If
TempPage = TempPage & vbNewLine & "<P><B>Office Hours:</B> " _
    & [OfficeHours]
TempPage = TempPage & vbNewLine & "<P><B>Notes:</B> " _
    & [Notes]
TempPage = TempPage & vbNewLine & "<P>For more information call us " _
    & "at 1-888-888-8888 or <A HREF=""mailto:watever@whatever.com"">" _
    & "email us.</A></P>"
TempPage = TempPage & vbNewLine & "</BODY></HTML>"
Open TheFileName For Append As #1
Print #1, TempPage
Close #1
Call ShellExecute(0&, vbNullString, TheFileName, vbNullString, vbNullString, SW_SHOW)
End Sub
```

In code, you need a connection to the database:

```
Dim MyDB As DAO.Database
```

where you will retrieve data:

```
Dim RSBuilding As DAO.Recordset
```

This variable stores the name of the file that will be used when generating the Web page:

```
Dim TheFileName As String
```

This variable also stores the contents of the page:

```
Dim TempPage As String
```

Then prompt the user for a file name for the Web page. Note that the default name for the page is based on the name of the instructor:

```
TheFileName = InputBox("Enter the path and name of the Web page to export " _
    & "this instructor record to.", "File Name", "c:\" _
    & [LastName] & [FirstName] & ".html")
```

If the user pressed the Cancel button in the Input box, or he or she wiped out the value in the Input box, the file name will be set to an empty string:

```
If TheFileName = "" Then
```

If this is the case, assume that the user does not want to generate the page:

```
Exit Sub
```

Otherwise, use the Dir function to see if the file exists. If it does, the Dir function will return the name of the file:

```
If Dir(TheFileName) <> "" Then
```

In this case, inform the user of the problem:

```
MsgBox " file with that name at that location already exists!"
```

and exit this procedure:

```
Exit Sub
```

Otherwise, open a connection to the database:

```
Set MyDB = CurrentDb
```

and retrieve the name of the building that the instructor's office resides in:

```
Set RSBuilding = MyDB.OpenRecordset("Select BuildingName from Buildings " _
    & "Where BuildingID = " & [BuildingID], dbOpenSnapshot)
```

Now you can start to generate your Web page that will be stored in the TempPage variable. Start with the opening HTML tag:

```
TempPage = "<HTML>"
```

and the Header tag:

```
TempPage = TempPage & vbNewLine & "<HEAD>"
```

Give the page a title based on the name of the instructor:

```
TempPage = TempPage & vbNewLine & "<TITLE>Instructor: " _
    & [FirstName] & " " & [LastName] & "</TITLE>"
```

Then close the Header tag:

```
TempPage = TempPage & vbNewLine & "</HEAD>"
```

Open the body of the Web page:

```
TempPage = TempPage & vbNewLine & "<BODY BACKGROUND = ""bg.gif"">"
```

At the top of the Body section, display the school logo graphic:

```
TempPage = TempPage & vbNewLine _
    & "<IMG SRC=""logo.gif"" ALT=""School Logo"" BORDER=""1"">"
```

Then, as a heading to the page, display the instructor's name:

```
TempPage = TempPage & vbNewLine & "<H2>Instructor: " _
    & [FirstName] & " " & [LastName] & "</H2>"
```

followed by their address:

```
TempPage = TempPage & vbNewLine & "<P><B>Address:</B> " _
    & [Address] & "<BR>"
TempPage = TempPage & vbNewLine & "<B>City State Zip:</B> " _
    & [City] & ", " & [State] & " " & [Zip] & "<BR>"
```

After that, their phone numbers are displayed:

```
TempPage = TempPage & vbNewLine & "<B>Home Phone:</B> " _
    & [HomePhone] & "<BR>"
TempPage = TempPage & vbNewLine & "<B>Office Phone:</B> " _
    & [OfficePhone] & "<BR>"
TempPage = TempPage & vbNewLine & "<B>Fax Phone:</B> " _
    & [Fax] & "<BR>"
```

Next, display their email addresses on the Web page. Note that they are displayed as text and as a link that opens a new email message addressed to them:

```
TempPage = TempPage & vbNewLine & "<B>Email Address:</B> " _
    & "<A HREF=""mailto:" & [EmailAddress] & """>" _
    & [EmailAddress] & "</A><BR>"
```

Now check to see if you found a Building record based on the instructor's location:

```
If RSBuilding.EOF Then
```

If you didn't, display just the office location information:

```
TempPage = TempPage & vbNewLine & "<B>Office:</B> " _
    & [OfficeLocation]
```

Otherwise, display the building and office location information:

```
TempPage = TempPage & vbNewLine & "<B>Office:</B> " _
    & RSBuilding("BuildingName") & " - " & [OfficeLocation]
```

Next, display the office hour text in a new HTML paragraph tag:

```
TempPage = TempPage & vbNewLine & "<P><B>Office Hours:</B> " _
    & [OfficeHours]
```

and one for the instructor notes:

```
TempPage = TempPage & vbNewLine & "<P><B>Notes:</B> " _
& [Notes]
```

Then append our footer test to the bottom of the page:

```
TempPage = TempPage & vbNewLine & "<P>For more information call us " _
    & "at 1-888-888-8888 or <A HREF=""mailto:watever@whatever.com"">"
    & "email us.</A></P>"
```

and close the Body and HTML tags:

```
TempPage = TempPage & vbNewLine & "</BODY></HTML>"
```

Then open a file stream to the file where the user wants to save this page:

```
Open TheFileName For Append As #1
```

Write the text of the page to that stream:

```
Print #1, TempPage
```

and close the file:

```
Close #1
```

Next, use the ShellExecute system command to open the page just created in a Browser window:

```
Call ShellExecute(0&, vbNullString, TheFileName, vbNullString, vbNullString, SW_SHOW)
```

HTML Table Form

The HTML Table form converts a table or query into a Web page. Like the last form, it displays the Web page to the user in a Browser window. Therefore, it also includes the ShellExecute system command declared in the General Declaration section of the form:

```
Private Declare Function ShellExecute Lib "SHELL32.DLL" Alias
    "ShellExecuteA" (ByVal hWnd As Long, ByVal lpOperation As String,
    ByVal lpFile As String, ByVal lpParameters As String,
    ByVal lpDirectory As String, ByVal nShowCmd As Long) As Long
Const SW_SHOW = 5
```

When the form first opens, the List box needs to contain the names of all the tables and queries in the database. The code that does this is in the Load event of the Form object.

```
Private Sub Form_Load()
    Dim MyDB As DAO.Database
    Dim MyTableDef As DAO.TableDef
    Dim MyQueryDef As DAO.QueryDef
    Set MyDB = CurrentDb
    For Each MyTableDef In MyDB.TableDefs
        lstTable.RowSource = lstTable.RowSource _
            & MyTableDef.Name & ";"
    Next
    For Each MyQueryDef In MyDB.QueryDefs
        lstTable.RowSource = lstTable.RowSource _
            & MyQueryDef.Name & ";"
    Next
End Sub
```

You also need a Database object:

```
Dim MyDB As DAO.Database
```

a TableDef object:

```
Dim MyTableDef As DAO.TableDef
```

and a QueryDef object:

```
Dim MyQueryDef As DAO.QueryDef
```

Then connect in code to the current database:

```
Set MyDB = CurrentDb
```

and start a loop that will take you through each of the tables in the database:

```
For Each MyTableDef In MyDB.TableDefs
```

The name of each table is added to the List box:

```
lstTable.RowSource = lstTable.RowSource _
    & MyTableDef.Name & ";"
```

before moving on to the next table:

```
Next
```

One more loop is needed to process each of the QueryDef objects:

```
For Each MyQueryDef In MyDB.QueryDefs
```

These objects are also added to the List box:

```
lstTable.RowSource = lstTable.RowSource _
    & MyQueryDef.Name & ";"
```

When the user presses the Create Web Page button, the code creates a Web page based on the data in the table or query selected:

```
Private Sub cmdGo_Click()
    Dim MyDB As DAO.Database
    Dim RS As DAO.Recordset
    Dim TheField As DAO.Field
    Dim TotalRecords As Long
    Dim TheFileName As String
    Dim TempPage As String
    If IsNull(lstTable.Value) Then
        MsgBox "Please select a table or query first."
        Exit Sub
    End If
    txtTitle.SetFocus
```

```
If txtTitle.Text = "" Then
    MsgBox "Please enter a title name for the Web page."
    Exit Sub
End If
TheFileName = InputBox("Enter the path and name of the Web page to export " _
    & "to.", "File Name", "c:\" _
    & lstTable.Value & ".html")
If TheFileName = "" Then
    Exit Sub
End If
If Dir(TheFileName) <> "" Then
    MsgBox "A file with that name at that location already exists!"
    Exit Sub
End If
Set MyDB = CurrentDb
Set RS = MyDB.OpenRecordset("Select * from [" & lstTable.Value & "]", _
    dbOpenSnapshot)
If RS.EOF Then
    MsgBox "No records found!"
    Exit Sub
End If
RS.MoveLast
TotalRecords = RS.RecordCount
RS.MoveFirst
TempPage = "<HTML>"
TempPage = TempPage & vbNewLine & "<HEAD>"
TempPage = TempPage & vbNewLine & "<TITLE>" _
    & txtTitle.Text & "</TITLE>"
TempPage = TempPage & vbNewLine & "</HEAD>"
TempPage = TempPage & vbNewLine & "<BODY BACKGROUND = ""bg.gif"">"
TempPage = TempPage & vbNewLine & "<IMG SRC=""logo.gif"" " _
    & "ALT=""School Logo"" BORDER=""1"">"
TempPage = TempPage & vbNewLine & "<H2>" _
    & txtTitle.Text & "</H2>"
TempPage = TempPage & vbNewLine & "<Table BORDER=2>"
TempPage = TempPage & vbNewLine & "<TR>"
For Each TheField In RS.Fields
    TempPage = TempPage & vbNewLine & "<TD><B>" _
        & TheField.Name & "</B></TD>"
Next
TempPage = TempPage & vbNewLine & "</TR>"
Do Until RS.EOF
    TempPage = TempPage & vbNewLine & "<TR>"
    For Each TheField In RS.Fields
        TempPage = TempPage & vbNewLine & "<TD>" _
            & TheField.Value & "</TD>"
    Next
    RS.MoveNext
    TempPage = TempPage & vbNewLine & "</TR>"
Loop
TempPage = TempPage & vbNewLine & "</Table>"
TempPage = TempPage & vbNewLine & "<P>Total Records: " _
    & TotalRecords
TempPage = TempPage & vbNewLine & "<P>For more information call us " _
    & "at 1-888-888-8888 or <A HREF=""mailto:watever@whatever.com"">" _
    & "email us.</A></P>"
TempPage = TempPage & vbNewLine & "</BODY></HTML>"
Open TheFileName For Append As #1
```

```
    Print #1, TempPage
    Close #1
    Call ShellExecute(0&, vbNullString, TheFileName, vbNullString, vbNullString, SW_SHOW)
End Sub
```

Now connect to this database:

```
Dim MyDB As DAO.Database
```

and retrieve data from the table or query selected:

```
Dim RS As DAO.Recordset
```

You also need to display the names of the fields in the table or query:

```
Dim TheField As DAO.Field
```

The following variable stores the number of records in the table:

```
Dim TotalRecords As Long
```

This variable stores the file name of the Web page:

```
Dim TheFileName As String
```

The following variable stores the text of the page as you build it:

```
Dim TempPage As String
```

Then make sure the user selected a table or query:

```
If IsNull(lstTable.Value) Then
```

If he or she didn't, inform them of the problem:

```
MsgBox "Please select a table or query first."
```

and exit this procedure:

```
Exit Sub
```

Then move the focus to the title Text box:

```
txtTitle.SetFocus
```

and make sure the user entered a title for the Web page:

```
If txtTitle.Text = "" Then
```

If the user didn't, tell them he or she needs to:

```
MsgBox "Please enter a title name for the Web page."
```

and leave the procedure:

```
Exit Sub
```

Otherwise, prompt the user for the file name of the Web page. Note the default used is the name of the table or query:

```
TheFileName = InputBox("Enter the path and name of the Web page to export " _
    & "to.", "File Name", "c:\" _
```

Then check to see if he or she pressed the Cancel button:

```
If TheFileName = "" Then
```

If so, exit this procedure:

```
Exit Sub
```

Otherwise, check to make sure the file doesn't already exist:

```
If Dir(TheFileName) <> "" Then
```

If it does, tell the user:

```
MsgBox "A file with that name at that location already exists!"
```

and exit out of this procedure:

```
Exit Sub
```

Otherwise, connect to the database:

```
Set MyDB = CurrentDb
```

and retrieve the data from the table or query selected by the user:

```
Set RS = MyDB.OpenRecordset("Select * from [" & lstTable.Value & "]", _
    dbOpenSnapshot)
```

Next, check to see if any data was found:

```
If RS.EOF Then
```

If none was found, tell the user:

```
MsgBox "No records found!"
```

and leave the procedure:

```
Exit Sub
```

If the code flows here, all the checks have passed. Now move to the last record:

```
RS.MoveLast
```

so you can retrieve an accurate count of the records in this table:

```
TotalRecords = RS.RecordCount
```

Then move back to the first record:

```
RS.MoveFirst
```

and store the opening tags of the Web page in your temporary string variable:

```
TempPage = "<HTML>"
TempPage = TempPage & vbNewLine & "<HEAD>"
```

Place the title entered by the user on the form in the title tag:

```
TempPage = TempPage & vbNewLine & "<TITLE>" _
    & txtTitle.Text & "</TITLE>"
TempPage = TempPage & vbNewLine & "</HEAD>"
```

and open the Body tag:

```
TempPage = TempPage & vbNewLine & "<BODY BACKGROUND = ""bg.gif"">"
```

At the top of the Body section will be the school logo:

```
TempPage = TempPage & vbNewLine & "<IMG SRC=""logo.gif"" " _
    & "ALT=""School Logo"" BORDER=""1"">"
```

Under that, place the title of the table or query entered by the user:

```
TempPage = TempPage & vbNewLine & "<H2>" _
    & txtTitle.Text & "</H2>"
```

Then start your HTML table:

```
TempPage = TempPage & vbNewLine & "<Table BORDER=2>"
```

The first row of the table contains the field names:

```
TempPage = TempPage & vbNewLine & "<TR>"
```

So, start a loop that will iterate you through each of the fields in this Recordset object:

```
For Each TheField In RS.Fields
```

Each field is placed in its own cell in this first row of the table:

```
TempPage = TempPage & vbNewLine & "<TD><B>" _
      & TheField.Name & "</B></TD>"
```

Then move on to process the next field in the table:

```
Next
```

After the loop, close the field row:

```
TempPage = TempPage & vbNewLine & "</TR>"
```

Then start another loop that will take you through each record in the recordset:

```
Do Until RS.EOF
```

Each record will be placed in its own row in the HTML table:

```
TempPage = TempPage & vbNewLine & "<TR>"
```

Now process each field in the record:

```
For Each TheField In RS.Fields
```

That value is placed in its own cell in the table:

```
TempPage = TempPage & vbNewLine & "<TD>" _
      & TheField.Value & "</TD>"
Next
```

After processing each field, move on to the next record:

```
RS.MoveNext
```

and end this row in the HTML table:

```
TempPage = TempPage & vbNewLine & "</TR>"
```

Also do so before looping:

```
Loop
```

After processing each record, close the Table tag:

```
TempPage = TempPage & vbNewLine & "</Table>"
```

Then the page contains the number of records in the table or query:

```
TempPage = TempPage & vbNewLine & "<P>Total Records: " _
    & TotalRecords
```

Display your footer text:

```
TempPage = TempPage & vbNewLine & "<P>For more information call us " _
    & "at 1-888-888-8888 or <A HREF=""mailto:watever
    & "email us.</A></P>"
```

before closing the tags on the page:

```
TempPage = TempPage & vbNewLine & "</BODY></HTML>"
```

Next, open a text stream to the file name entered by the user:

```
Open TheFileName For Append As #1
```

Write the Web page out to that stream:

```
Print #1, TempPage
```
and close the file:

```
Close #1
```

Then display the newly created Web page to the user:

```
Call ShellExecute(0&, vbNullString, TheFileName, vbNullString, vbNullString, SW_SHOW)
```

CHAPTER 17

Creating Dynamic Web Content

ON THE CD:

Students, Teachers and Courses.mdb

Courses.htm

TSC.htm

SamplePage.htm

Tags.htm

Instructors.htm

Working with Data Access Pages

In this chapter and the next, we will look at creating dynamic Web pages. Remember from our discussion in the last chapter that dynamic Web pages can change each time they are viewed by a visitor to your site. They typically contain data from a database and reflect the current contents of that database. In the next chapter, we will look at creating dynamic Web-based solutions using *Active Server Pages* (ASPs), a technology that enables you to generate dynamic content that runs on the server and can be output to the visitor's browser as standard HTML.

In this chapter, we will review another way of creating dynamic Web pages based on your database content through a new feature of Access called *Data Access Pages*. First, in this chapter, we will discuss ways that you can post your Web pages to the Internet or your intranet. Then we will look at what Data Access Pages are and how to create them using Wizards. We will also look at using themes. After that, we will review controls used on Data Access Pages as well as important properties of these objects. These will include some custom Data Access Pages.

IIS and PWS

If you only want to share your Data Access Pages with others that are on your own shared network, all you need to do is put the files and the database in some shared folder that the other users can connect to. If, instead, you want them to be available through your Internet or intranet, you will probably post them on an *Internet Information Server* (IIS) or a *Personal Web Server* (PWS).

IIS is a robust Web server that comes with and runs on an NT or Windows 2000 server. You can place your Data Access Pages on an IIS-run Web site to make them available to others through their Internet browsers or an intranet. The Active Server Pages discussed in the next chapter use IIS.

Sometimes, however, people don't have access to an IIS server. It may be at a small company where they can't afford such a server, or maybe a developer wants to test some dynamic pages without posting them to the main IIS server. Or, as is the case with some people, a developer wants to learn about dynamic Web content without having the overhead of an IIS server. For such situations, PWS often can solve the problem.

PWS is not a robust Web server and it certainly doesn't have the full capabilities to do the application-wide things you can do with IIS, but it certainly is a great tool for those situations just described.

PWS comes with Windows 98. You can install it from the Windows 98 CD by running

```
D:\add-ons\pws\setup.exe
```

D indicates the drive letter of your CD. Once you install PWS, you should see a new folder in the Start/Program menu called Microsoft Personal Web Server. If you go to that folder and select the Personal Web Manager shortcut, you will see the Personal Web Manager main window displayed in Figure 17-1.

From this interface, you can learn more about PWS, but, most importantly, you learn to start the Web server. To do so, press the Start button and the text in this dialog will look something like what is displayed in Figure 17-2.

Note the two very important text links in this dialog. The first, in Figure 17-2 is

```
http://greg-buczek
```

That is the name of my computer and is what I can type in to the browser window to view the Web site. If you click on the link, you will see your Web site, as displayed in Figure 17-3. If you get the "Work Offline" error message, press the Try Again button.

Note that besides entering the name of the computer, you can also link to your site from that computer by entering this:

```
http://localhost
```

Figure 17-1

The main window
of the Personal
Web Manager

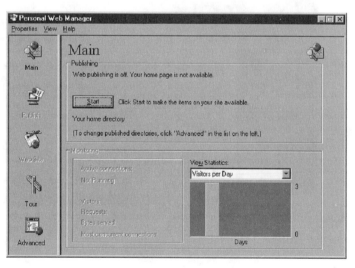

Figure 17-2

The Personal Web Manager with a service running

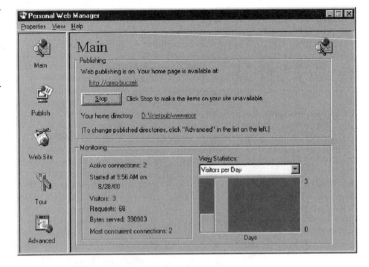

Figure 17-3

The home page for PWS site

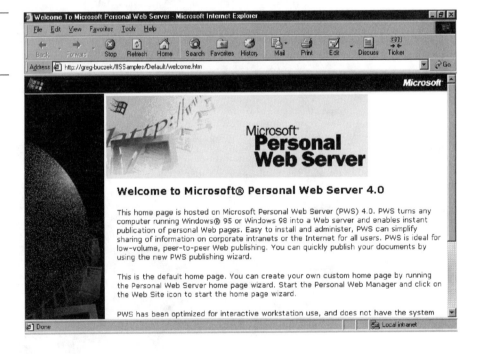

What you see on this Web page is the default home page for your server. You can modify these pages and post your own site, but note the other text link back on Figure 17-2. For me, it displays the following text:

```
d:\Inetpub\wwwroot
```

This is the physical location where my Web site resides. If I created a new folder in that folder with the location

```
d:\Inetpub\wwwroot\IAD
```

and I placed a page in that folder called

```
buildings.html
```

I could access that page in my browser through this link:

```
http://localhost/IAD/buildings.html
```

You will probably want to take this one step further and allow others to view your site through the Internet through an IP address. Many of you may connect to the Internet through an *Internet service provider* (ISP) that does not give you a fixed IP address. Instead, each time you connect, you are given a different IP address. Then when you disconnect, your IP address is passed on to another customer of your ISP.

To find out your IP address, first connect to your ISP. Then press the Start button and select Run. Enter winipcfg.exe, as is displayed in Figure 17-4.

Press the OK button to run the IP Configuration tool displayed in Figure 17-5.

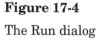

Figure 17-4

The Run dialog

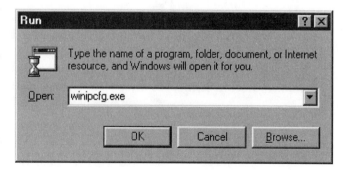

Figure 17-5

The IP
Configuration
tool

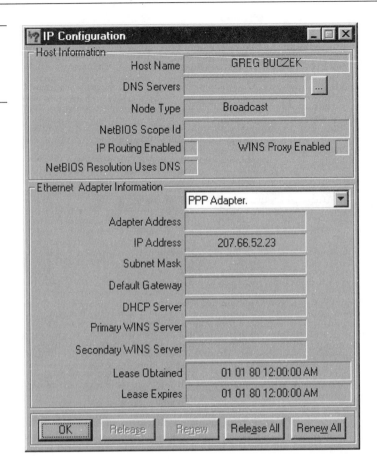

Notice the IP Address field that contains the number 207.66.52.23. That is my IP address that I am using to connect to the Internet through my ISP. If I reconnect and run this program again, I could see a different value, but for now, I can give that IP address out to someone on the Internet and they could connect to my Web site through PWS.

Data Access Pages

Defined

When you open a database in Access 2000, you see a new tab button in the Database window called Pages. That tab is displayed in Figure 17-6. This is where you create, edit, and delete Data Access Pages and you can even use your own pages here.

Data Access Pages are similar to forms and reports in your Access database. Like forms, they provide the user with the ability to add, edit, view, filter, or delete records. Like reports, they can be used to display information, but they are stored as HTML. In fact, when you create a Data Access Page, it doesn't even become part of the database. It is stored in an HTML file that is external to the database in a location that you indicate. The Page tab of the database Window then displays a link to that page.

The way a Data Access Page works is that it has special controls embedded in the HTML that link text boxes and navigation buttons to the database. These controls and the code placed within the page all run on the client side. This means that the browser the visitor is using must run the controls for the page to work.

This varies sharply from the Active Server Page approach presented in the next chapter. This approach processes all the code on the server. The significant difference is that with client-side code, the browser must support the code and objects that are contained in the HTML. With server-side code, the browser only needs to support standard HTML, because all the code runs on the server.

Figure 17-6

The Pages tab in the Access Database window

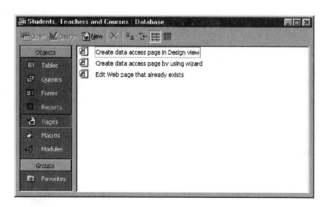

What this all means is that the person viewing your Data Access Pages must be using Internet Explorer 5+ and they must have Office 2000 installed on his or her computer. If the user doesn't, he or she won't see any of the special controls or data access capabilities you have placed on your page.

As restrictive as this sounds, circumstances may occur when this will be your solution. The Data Access Pages are pretty easy to create and provide a lot of built-in functionality. So if you have a database of contacts for your salespeople who travel across the country, you may know that they have the required software and can access your database through the Internet. If you need to reach a wider audience that has different browsers and operating systems, then Active Server Pages may be the better choice.

Creating Data Access Pages with Wizards

As with forms and reports, creating basic Data Access Pages can often be done just by using a Wizard. This section of the chapter will look at using the built-in Wizards to create two Data Access Pages. For these examples, the Students, Teachers, and Courses database discussed in Chapter 11, "Students, Teachers, and Courses," will be used.

To use the Wizard, select the "Create Data Access Page Using Wizard" item in the Pages tab of the Database window. You should then see the first page of the Wizard, as displayed in Figure 17-7.

The combo box on this page lists all the tables and queries in the database. The left list box lists the fields in the table and the right list box lists the fields that you are including on the page. Here all the fields have been selected to appear on this Data Access Page. As you add a field to the page, it will appear in the order in which it was added. Press the Next button to see the next page of the Wizard, displayed in Figure 17-8.

The second page of the Wizard enables you to group records. This allows you to display a one-to-many relationship in a hierarchical format. For example, later in this section, you will look at a page that contains courses offered in a semester. The data there is grouped by section and then semester. When you group data on a page, the visitor to the page can't update the data. For this first Data Access Page, you want the data to be editable, so no grouping is selected. Press the Next button to see the third page of the Wizard displayed in Figure 17-9.

Figure 17-7

The Data Access
Page Wizard,
page 1

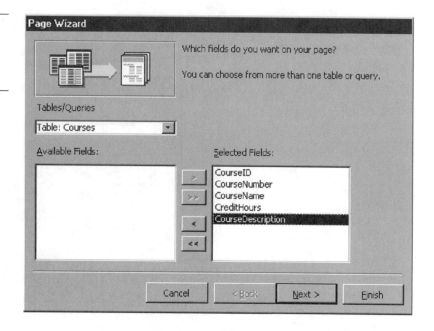

Figure 17-8

The Data Access
Page Wizard,
page 2

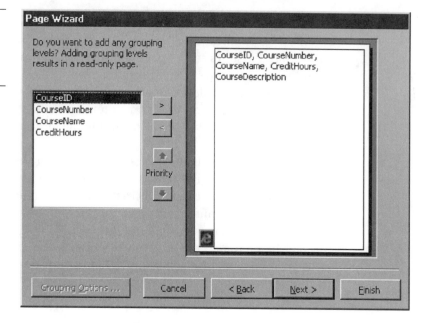

Figure 17-9

Page 3 of the
Data Access Page
Wizard

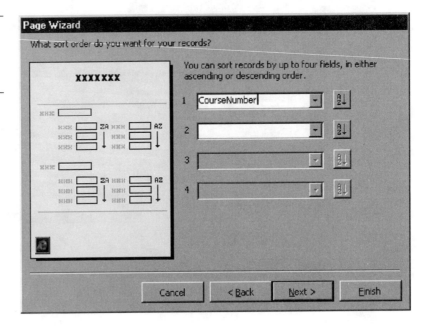

This page enables you to select up to four fields for sorting the records. Like a form, visitors to the page can sort the records by a different field than the one you select here. Press the Next button to see the final page of the Wizard, as displayed in Figure 17-10.

In the top text box on the form, enter the name that you want to give this page. That name will be the default name for this page when you save it.

Note the "Apply a Theme" check box. Themes in Data Access Pages provide an easy way to give your pages a unique look and feel. If you leave this box unchecked, Access will create the page using a default theme. If you check the box and then press the Finish button, Access opens the Theme dialog that is displayed in Figure 17-11.

The Theme dialog enables you to preview the different themes that come with Access. Once you select a theme, your page is formatted based on that style. If you decide that you want to change the theme, you can do so by selecting Format/Theme from the menu while in the design view of a page.

Now you can close the Data Access Page and provide a name and a location where you want to save the HTML file. Remember that Access does not save the page as part of the database. Instead, it creates an external

Figure 17-10

Page 4 of the
Data Access Page
Wizard

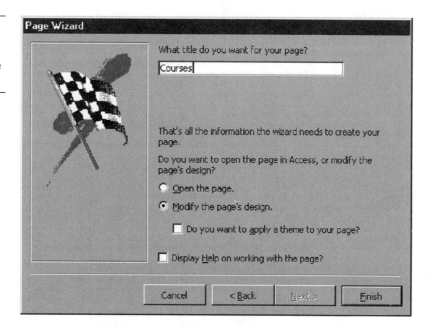

Figure 17-11

The Theme dialog
box

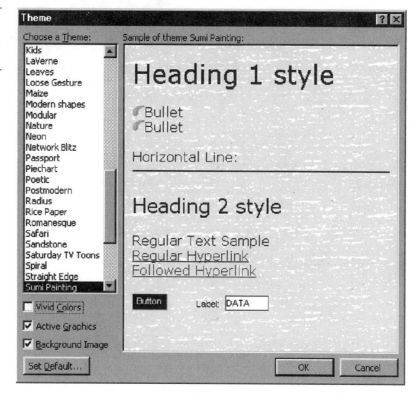

HTML file and creates a link to that page from the Pages tab in the Database dialog. Figure 17-12 shows the Data Access Page created through the Wizard.

Figure 17-12 shows the page as it would be seen through a browser. Remember that for the page to run correctly, the visitor must be viewing the page through Internet Explorer 5+, and he or she must have Office 2000 installed on his or her computer.

If the user does, he or she now has full access to the Courses table. He or she can use the navigation buttons on the bottom of the form to move through the records; add, delete, or save a record; and undo their changes. The user can even use the buttons to sort and filter the data. The last button on the navigation bar opens a help file. All of this can be created simply by using the Wizard.

Another nice way to use the Wizard is to display information in a one-to-many relationship. For example, let's say you wanted to display course information with the term and semester information for the course offered. On a form or report, you would use a subform or subreport.

Figure 17-12

The Courses Data Access Page

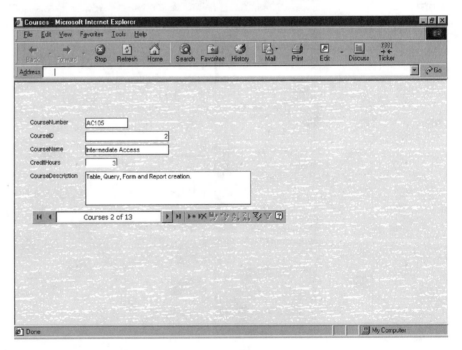

With a Data Access Page, you would create a query that combined the three tables with a *Structured Query Language* (SQL) statement like this:

```
SELECT Terms.TermName, Sections.SectionName, Courses.CourseNumber,
Courses.CourseName, Courses.CreditHours FROM Courses
INNER JOIN (Terms INNER JOIN Sections ON Terms.TermID = Sections.TermID)
ON Courses.CourseID = Sections.CourseID;
```

Then you would start the Data Access Page Wizard and select this query. On the second page of the Wizard, you would select Grouping, as is shown in Figure 17-13.

The resulting Web page that groups the data as described is displayed in Figure 17-14.

Notice the buttons with the "-" symbol on them. Those buttons enable the visitor to show and hide a section. So when the "-" button is pressed, that section is hidden and the button changes to a "+" symbol.

Figure 17-13

Grouping data using the Data Access Page Wizard

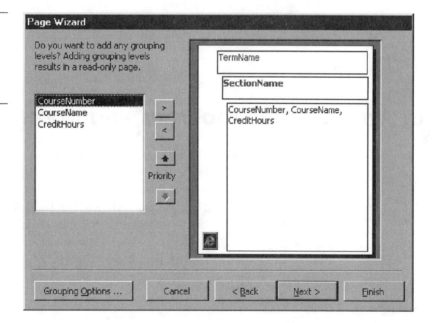

Figure 17-14

The Data Access Page that uses grouping

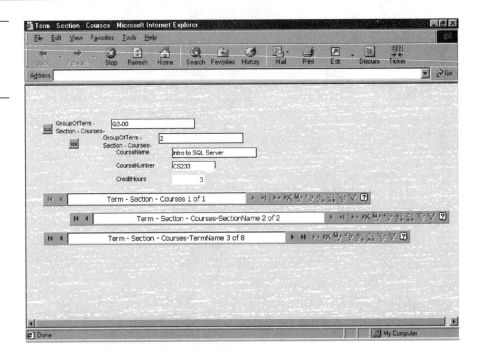

Data Access Page Properties and Controls

Sometimes the Wizards can't be used to build the exact Data Access Page you are looking for. Maybe they take you most of the way, but you need to refine the page to suit your needs. In this section of the chapter, you will look at important and unique properties of the Data Access Page and controls that can be placed on the page. You can create a new blank Data Access Page by selecting the "Create Data Access Page in Design View" item in the Pages tab of the Database window.

Data Access Page

When you work with a form, you can manipulate the properties of the form and can place bound controls on the form. When you create a report, similarly you can manipulate the look of a report with its properties and place bound controls on that report. For a Data Access Page, the Page object is the object you use to manipulate the look of the page through its properties and you can place special bound controls on that page. The properties of a Data Access Page can be viewed by clicking on the title bar of the Data Access Page window in Design view and selecting the Properties window.

DataEntry Property

Like a form or report, the Data Access Page has a DataEntry property. This property dictates the kind of data manipulation the Data Access Page will enable. If the value is set to True, the visitor to this page can only add new records and can only edit records that were just added in this section. If the property is set to False, the visitor has full control over the data in the underlying table of the Data Access Page. Unlike a Form, the Data Access Page does not have properties that let you further refine the specific data manipulation capabilities enabled through the Data Access Page.

DefaultControlType Property

When you add bound controls to a Data Access Page through the Field list, the type of control created is based on the value of this property. The property provides two choices. If Text Box is selected, a bound text box is added for the field to the Data Access Page. If Bound HTML is selected, then the Bound HTML control is added to the Data Access Page.

MaxRecords Property

The MaxRecords property returns and sets the maximum number of records that will be retrieved from the database and returned to the visitor's computer. Reducing this value will reduce the number of records that are brought out through the Recordset object.

RecordsetType Property

The RecordsetType property has different values than those used on a form or report. The property can be set to dscUpdatableSnapshot or dscSnapshot. The dscUpdatableSnapshot value for the property enables the records in the Recordset object to be changed. If you select dscSnapshot, the records in the Recordset are read-only.

LinkColor, AlinkColor, and VlinkColor Properties

The LinkColor, AlinkColor, and VlinkColor properties are special HTML properties for the Data Access Page and control the text color used with links. The LinkColor property stores the color of a link that has not yet been visited, the AlinkColor property stores the color of the text for a link that currently has the focus, and the VlinkColor property stores the color of a link that has been already selected or visited by the visitor.

Dir Property

When you look at the name of this property, you'll probably think it has something to do with a file directory. It doesn't. Instead, it stores the direction that the text in a field is to be displayed. You can set the property to ltr or rtl. Ltr displays text left to right, and rtl displays text right to left.

Sections, Sorting, and Grouping

This section examines sections, sorting, and grouping. When you create a Data Access Page, place the data-bound fields in a specific section. Other sections can hold a caption and the navigational buttons. You can also provide subforms through grouping information. You can also apply a sort to each of the grouping levels. Take a look at the Design view of a sample page displayed in Figure 17-15.

Notice that this Data Access Page has three sections. The top section is the Caption section, which equates to the Header section of a form. Here you can place a title for this area of the Web page. Note that you cannot place any bound controls in that section.

The next section is the Header section. This part of the Data Access Page is where you place your bound controls. It equates to the Detail section of a form.

At the bottom of the Data Access Page is the Navigation section. This is similar to the Footer section on a form, except that the record navigation bar is right in this section. Note that you cannot place bound controls in this section.

You can control which sections are viewed and how they are displayed through the Sorting and Grouping dialog. Select the Sorting and Grouping icon from the toolbar to see that dialog, as it is displayed in Figure 17-16.

The Caption Section property toggles whether or not the Caption Section is part of the Data Access Page. The same is true for the Group Header section, which is where you display your bound controls. The

Figure 17-15

The sections on a Data Access Page

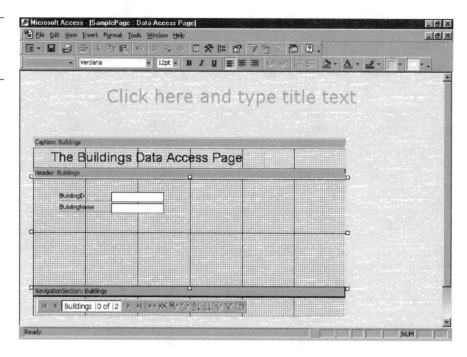

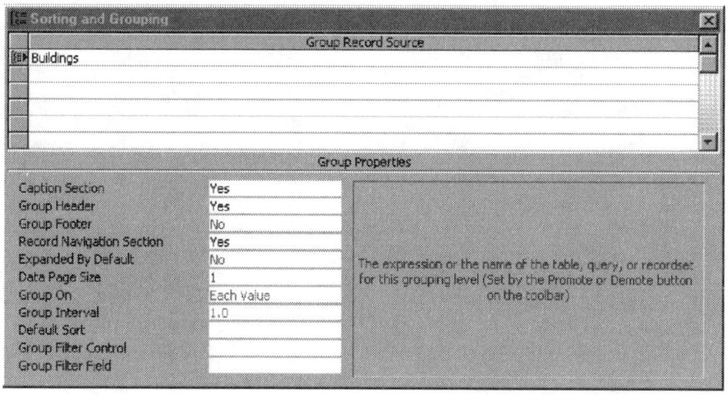

Figure 17-16

The Sorting and Grouping dialog

Group Footer property cannot be changed when you have just one table in the Data Access Page. The Record Navigation Section property toggles whether that section of the Data Access Page is visible. The Expanded by Default property is only used when you include a subtable within the Data Access Page. It dictates whether the subtable records are automatically displayed.

The Data Page Size controls the number of records you want to display at one time on the Data Access Page. With this table and just the two fields, you can easily fit more than one record on the Data Access Page. Take a look at the page in Figure 17-17.

Here the Data Page Size property is set to three. Therefore, the Data Access Page displays three records at a time. This is especially useful when you are just reporting data and you want to show a list of information.

The Default Sort property enables you to provide the name of the field or fields that you want to sort the records by. The other properties on the Sorting and Grouping dialog only apply when you are grouping data. So let's add another table to this sample report that shows the Rooms table, which relates to the Buildings table in a one-to-many relationship. Each of the buildings has many rooms, but each of the rooms goes with a single building. Take a look at Figure 17-18 and you will see the two tables now included on the Data Access Page.

To accomplish this task, first the Field List dialog is displayed by clicking on it on the toolbar. Then the fields from the Rooms table are added to the same section as the Buildings fields. Then one of the Buildings fields is selected and the Group By Table icon on the tool bar is selected. That

Figure 17-17

The Data Page Size property in use

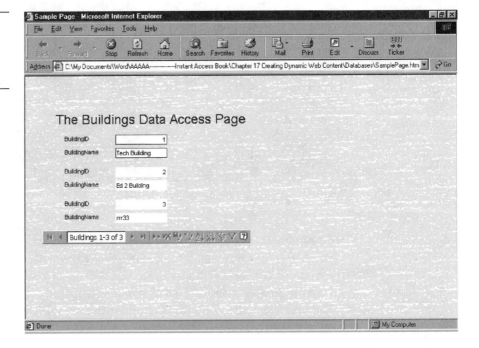

Figure 17-18

Two tables on the
Data Access Page

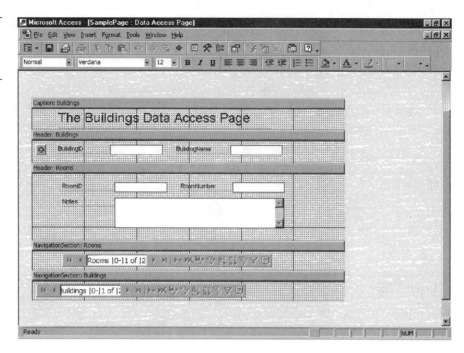

button moves the Building fields into their own sections at a higher level
in the Data Access Page and the "+" button is also automatically added to
that section. If you look again at the Sorting and Grouping dialog, you will
see two levels as displayed in Figure 17-19.

Now that you have a grouping level, you can change the values for the
Group Footer and Expand By Default properties. The Group Filter Control and Group Filter Field properties enable you to group the data
between the tables in a way that may not be part of the database relationships. The resulting page is displayed in Figure 17-20.

Notice again that you see all three building records because the Data
Page Size property is set to a value of at least three. Note too that initially
the Room data is hidden since you have the Expand By Default property
set to False. However, the user can press any of the "+" buttons to expand
the Building information and show the room data, as displayed in Figure
17-21.

Figure 17-19

Sorting and
Grouping
showing two
tables

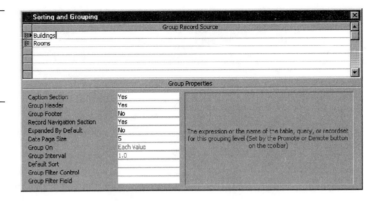

Figure 17-20

The initial view of
the grouped
sample page

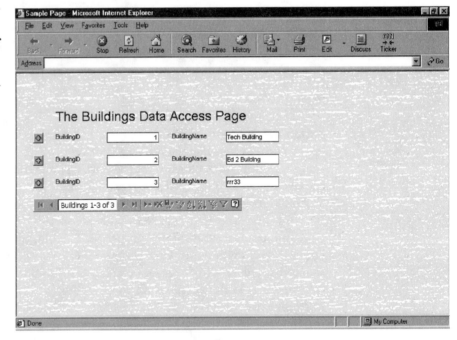

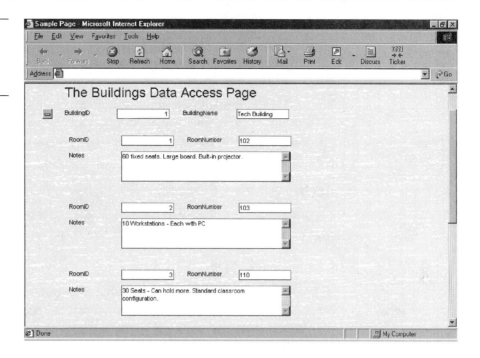

Figure 17-21

The expanded
view of the
grouped tables

RecordSource Property

Each of the grouped levels has a RecordSource property that can be set.
This value contains the name of the table or query that you want to display records for at that level.

Controls

When you create a Data Access Page, you have special controls available
to you that can be placed on the page, enabling you to navigate through
records and display bound fields, among other things. The controls are
available through the toolbox.

Record Navigation Control

The Record Navigation control is what you have seen in the Navigation
section of each of the Data Access Pages thus far. It enables the visitor to

navigate through the records, add, delete, save, and undo changes. It also enables the visitor to sort and filter records as well as display a Help page.

AltHTML Property

The AltHTML property contains the HTML you want to display if the object does not load. You could place text here that would work as an error message, letting the visitor know that the page could not be loaded and what the likely problems are.

RecordsetLabel Property

The RecordsetLabel stores which text to display in the Record Navigation control. By default, it is set to a value like this:

```
Rooms |0 of  |2;Rooms |0-|1 of |2
```

Rooms would be the name of the table. The first chunk, before the semicolon, is what is displayed if only one record is being displayed one page at a time. The second chunk is what is displayed if more than one record is being displayed at once. The special character combination "|0" refers to the current record in the recordset. The special character combination "|1" refers to the number of records on the page, if more than one is displayed, and the "|2" refers to the total number of records in the table.

If the visitor is looking at a page with one record at a time and he or she is on the fifth of 10 records, the visitor would see the following:

```
Rooms 5 of 10
```

If the records are grouped by two, he or she would see

```
Rooms 5-6 of 10
```

Show Properties

The Record Navigation control contains 14 properties that start with the word Show. These properties control which of the buttons you want to include on the Record Navigation control. By default, all are set to True.

Expand Control

The Expand Control is used to expand and collapse groups of records such as you saw when you looked at the Buildings and Rooms Data Access Page. The control displays either a "+" icon or a "−" icon.

Bound HTML Control

The Bound HTML control enables you to display the text in a field as HTML or as text. For example, let's say that you have a table that shows the visitor how to use the different HTML tags. Through a Data Access Page, you would want to show the visitor the structure of the tag and then an example that shows the syntax of the tag and the effect of that syntax, which could be done through Bound HTML control. It has a property called DataFormatAs that can be set to TEXT or HTML. If it is set to TEXT, then the tags are displayed as text. If you set the property to HTML, then the tags are processed and the effects of the tags are displayed.

Within this sample database, a table called Tags has been created for such a purpose. A Data Access Page has also been created based on this table, as shown in Figure 17-22.

Notice that a field called Sample is included twice. First, it is placed in a text box so that the visitor can see how to use the tag. It is then placed in a Bound HTML control so the user can see the effect of the tag. The page, as seen through a Browser, is displayed in Figure 17-23.

Figure 17-22

The Tags page in Design view

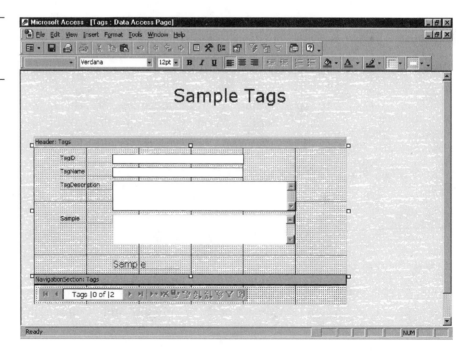

Figure 17-23

The Tags page
seen through a
browser

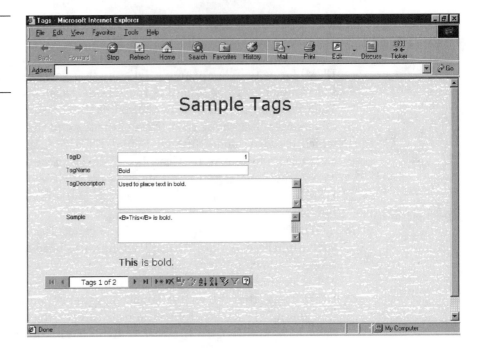

Figure 17-23

The Tags page
seen through a
browser

Scrolling Text Control

If you are familiar with a Marquee HTML element, then you will recognize the Scrolling Text control. It enables you to display text that scrolls across its space like a stock ticker or a news marquee.

ControlSource Property

As with all the bound controls, the control has a ControlSource property. This property is set to the name of the field that the control is bound to.

TotalType Property

The TotalType property enables you to use the field to display summary information. For example, if you were displaying order information, you could set the property to Sum and sum it on the price field.

Bound Hyperlink and Hyperlink Controls

The Bound Hyperlink and Hyperlink controls enable you to place a link on your Data Access Page. The difference between the two is that the bound displays text based on the value in a field, and the non-bound one is just a standard link that is fixed regardless of the record you are looking at. For example, take a look at Figure 17-24.

Here a new field is added to the Instructors table that stores the Web site of the instructor. That field is used here as the Control Source for the Bound Hyperlink control.

Figure 17-24

Using the Bound Hyperlink Control

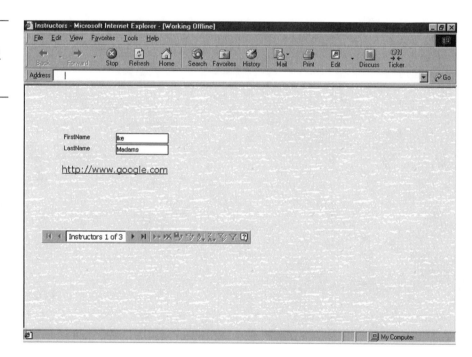

CHAPTER 18

Using Active Server Pages (ASP)

ON THE CD:

Students, Teachers and Courses.mdb

Index.asp

Add_Student.asp

Student_Info.asp

Course_Info.asp

Program_Info.asp

Creating Dynamic Server-Side Internet Solutions

In the last chapter, "Using Data Access Pages," you saw how you could create Web pages that enable the visitor to add, edit, delete and view information for your Access database. But you also saw that there were severe limitations to using Data Access Pages because they require that the visitor has Internet Explorer 5+ and Office 2000 on their computer.

This chapter looks at another approach to producing a Web site that provides current views of your database to the Internet visitor. The approach we will look at uses Active Server Pages, or ASP. As you will read in this chapter, ASP is processed on the server; therefore, you can return to the visitor a standard HTML page that contains the current data from your database.

First, the chapter will define ASP and how it works. To illustrate the functions of ASP, some very simple examples will be given. After that, the ASP Object Model will be reviewed. Then we will look at how to use an Access database as the back-end for some Active Server Pages that enable the visitor to access parts of the Students, Teachers, and Courses database that was reviewed in Chapter 11.

Note as you look at this code and these pages that they must be run through a Web server such as the Personal Web Server discussed in Chapter 17. Or, you could place them on your network's *Internet Information Server* (IIS), that comes with and runs on Windows NT or Windows 2000. For the samples in this chapter, IIS was used.

What Is ASP?

Static Pages, Web pages that have the same content each time we view them, are increasingly becoming a thing of the past. To encourage the development of your Web community, and to get visitors to revisit your site, you must provide them with a reason to come back. Probably the most compelling reason a person has for returning to your site is your offer of dynamic Web content.

Dynamic Web pages can change every time they are viewed. Examples of dynamic pages are pages that display the current weather, today's sales items or how stocks are doing right now. Each time the visitor revisits the pages, the site displays the most current information. Active Server Pages are the means for creating dynamic Web pages.

Active Server Pages enables us to combine standard HTML elements like tables, text, and titles with scripting language elements like database fields, date/time information, and personal customization to produce a Web page that is dynamically generated every time your page is requested from a browser. The browser requests the Active Server Page, which is then processed by IIS or PWS. IIS then runs your code, turning it into standard HTML tags and text. The resulting page contains none of your code and is viewable by virtually any browser such as Internet Explorer, Netscape Navigator, or AOL's browser. The visitors do not need to have Office 2000 on their machines as they did when we looked at Data Access Pages.

How ASP Works

Sending dynamic content to your visitor's browser involves your visitor requesting the page, IIS or PWS retrieving and interpreting the page and the resulting HTML is sent to the visitor's browser. Figure 18.1 shows this process.

First, your visitor types in a request to visit your site, http://www.whatever.com/sales.asp, for example, or clicks on a link that sends them to that page. Notice that the name of the page ends in .asp. This is referred to as a file extension. The request for the page, as shown in step two, routes its way to your Web server.

In step three, your Web server retrieves the requested file and notes that the request has the file extension of .asp, which tells the server that this is a dynamic page containing script that it must interpret. The Web server compiles the ASP code, which can require it to launch other components such as a data connection to Access, Browser Capabilities Component, Ad Rotator Component or your own shopping cart component.

Figure 18-1

The ASP Request and Response Process

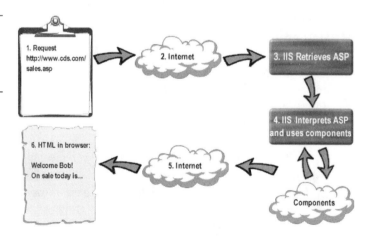

Launching these other components is where you really see the power of ASP. Components enable you to read the contents of a current order from a database , use a shipping calculator to figure shipping charges, or check to see if the person's browser supports frames.

All of this script and component code is converted into standard HTML that is sent back out through the Internet to the visitor's browser in step five. Then in our final step, the visitor's browser receives the HTML only and displays to the visitor all your Web site's dynamic content.

Advantages of Using ASP and Server-Side Scripting

Active Server Pages are a form of Server-Side Scripting. This means that the code is processed on your server by IIS or PWS as opposed to Client-Side Scripting, which relies on your customer's browser to process the code as we saw with the Data Access Pages.

Probably the most significant reason for using Server-Side Scripting is that you have control over which components are available. For example, if you needed to do some financial calculations, instead of writing a component yourself, you may wish to use the rich number-crunching capabilities of a program like Excel. If you are using Server-Side Scripting, you know that you have Excel on your server, so you can make these calculations. If you use client-side scripting instead, you take the risk that your code will fail if your visitor does not have Excel on his machine.

Or maybe you'd like to generate graphs on-the-fly that show sales reports to the managers of your company. If you use Server-Side Scripting, you can purchase a graph-engine component and all your visitors will see your graphs. If you used client-side scripting, you would have to require that the component be installed on all visitors' computers.

Even if you were able to require that your visitors had the component on their machines, you would still have problems because many browsers don't support client-side scripting. So another advantage of Server-Side Scripting is that the output to the visitor's browser is standard HTML, viewable by almost all browsers.

Most of the dynamic content on your Web site is based on some data in a database such as Access or SQL Server. One way that you could manage this data is by sending all the data to the customers and then letting the code on their side manage what records they can see. If you use Server-Side Scripting instead, you can rest with the knowledge that their browsers will be able to display the data because it is in standard HTML. Plus, because the browsers are always communicating with the data server, they are more likely to have the most up-to-date data.

One final advantage is bandwidth. When developing a Web site you must always be cognizant of file sizes. The number of bytes needed to be transmitted across the Internet to your visitors' computers can often determine how long they are viewing your site. If they have to wait more than half a minute to get the contents of the page, they are likely to move on to another page or leave your site. With Server-Side Scripting, you reduce the bandwidth by sending only the data that the person needs. For example, you may have complex rules regarding a customer order, like minimum purchase price, maximum quantities, certain states requiring tax, and so on. These rules could be implemented through your visitors' browsers, but that would mean that the rules would have to be retrieved with the page. Instead, using Server-Side Scripting enables you to keep your Business Rules, the rules that govern your data, in one place and reduce the bytes sent to the visitors' computers.

Simple ASP Samples

Now that you know what ASP is and how it works, let's look at some simple ASP samples. The objective here is to introduce you to what ASP looks like.

Simple Hello Web

Here is a very basic static HTML page that displays the message Hello Web:

```
<html>
<head>
<title>Sample Page</title>
</head>
<body>
<p>Hello Web!</p>
</body>
</html>
```

Now modify this simple Web page and make it dynamic by changing the name of the file so it ends with .asp. Then add VBScript code to the page as shown below. This code produces the page that is displayed in Figure 18-2.

```
<%@ Language=VBScript%>
<html>
<head>
<title>Sample Page for <% Response.Write Date() %></title>
</head>
<body>
<p>
<%
        'This is a Comment
        Response.write "<B>HELLO WEB FROM ASP!!!</B>"
%>
</p>
</body>
</html>
```

Take a closer look at the code:

```
<%@ Language=VBScript%>
```

This line tells IIS or PWS that the type of scripting language you use is VBScript. Also notice the "<%" and the "%>". The tags, without the quotes, denote the beginning and end of a code segment. So in the title line:

```
<title>Sample Page for <% Response.Write Date() %></title>
```

Figure 18-2

The ASP Hello
Web Sample

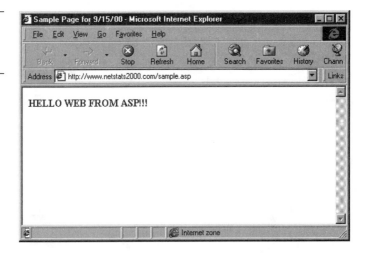

the "<%" says what follows is VBScript; it is not HTML. Then the "%>" indicates the end of your VBScript and what follows is HTML. This line of code shows how to send text back to the browser. In other words, after the text "Sample Page for," display the current system date on the server. Note in Figure 18-2 that the current date is displayed in the browser's title bar for this page.

The way the code is written in the title line is referred to as inline because it's in the same line as the HTML. In the next part of the code:

```
<%
        'This is a Comment
        Response.write "<B>HELLO WEB FROM ASP!!!</B>"
%>
```

we are using a code block. The block of code starts with the "<%" and ends with the "%>". Many lines of code can be included within a code block. The first line begins with a single quote character, often referred to as a tick which, as it does in Access, denotes a comment. Again, the response write method is used to send the "Hello Web From ASP!!!" text to the browser in bold. Note that HTML tags can be mixed in with our text in ASP to produce dynamic, formatted HTML. What you see in the browser window in Figure 18-2 is bold text.

An ASP That Tells Time

This next sample is a way to produce a Web page that is dynamic, based on the time of day. If it is daytime, bright colors will be displayed, and if it is night, the colors will be dark. The code is shown in the following section. Figures 18-3 and 18-4 show the output during different times of the day.

```
<%@ Language=VBScript%>
<%
if hour(now()) >= 6 and hour(now()) <= 18 then
%>
<html>
<head>
<title>Day Time Page</title>
</head>
<BODY BACKGROUND="#FFFFFF" TEXT="#000000">
<p><B>Good Day!</B></p>
</body>
</html>
<%
else
%>
```

Figure 18-3

The result of ASP
page during the
night

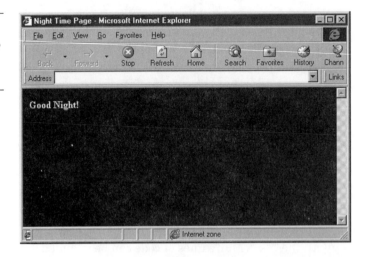

Figure 18-4

The page as it
appears during
the day

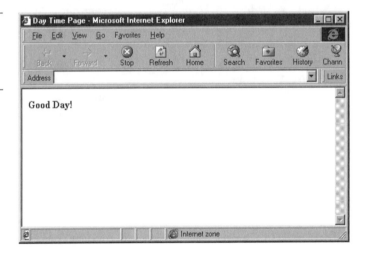

```
<html>
<head>
<title>Night Time Page</title>
</head>
<BODY BGCOLOR="#000000" TEXT="#FFFFFF">
<p><B>Good Night!</B></p>
</body>
</html>
<%
end if
%>
```

This ASP produces one page during the day and a different page during the night. Remember that only the processed HTML is sent to the visitor's browser. Visitors don't see your code nor do they receive the HTML for the day if they are visiting the night page. Also note the coding style here. If the condition is met, an entire HTML page is output and if it is not met, a different page is output. Let's take a closer look at the code. Here is the first code block:

```
<%
if hour(now()) >= 6 and hour(now()) <= 18 then
%>
```

Here, check the hour, in 24-hour format, of the system time as returned from the function Now. If the hour is between 6am and 6pm, display the day-time page. If it is not between those times, display the HTML after the else code block. Also note that you must include an "end if" at the end of your page.

ASP Object Model

The ASP Object Model defines five primary objects: the Request Object, the Response Object, the Application Object, the Server Object and the Session Object. These Objects are summarized in Table 18-1.

Through HTML, data can be sent to the server in the form of Post or Get methods. Retrieving this information is the responsibility of the Request Object. The request object supplies simple groupings of proper-

	Object	Purpose
Table 18-1 ASP Object Model Summary	Request Object	Supplies you with information from your visitor.
	Response Object	Methods and properties for building your response to the visitor.
	Application Object	Deals with properties that govern a grouping of Web pages referred to as an Application.
	Session Object	Methods and Properties pertaining to a particuliar visitor.
	Server Object	Deals with the creation of server components and server settings

ties called collections with which you can retrieve the submitted information. For example, an HTML form on the server with a text field called Login helps retrieve the value of the Login with the following code:

```
Response.Write "Hello and Welcome to: " & Request.Form("Login")
```

With the Request Object, information about the visitor's browser can also be retrieved, as shown in this code:

```
Request.ServerVariables("REMOTE_HOST")
```

This method would return the Internet Name or IP Address of the visitor's computer. The Response Object sends information back to the visitor's browser. For example, the user might be at a form-based page on a site that is a quiz. The user selects the answer to the question from a list of possible answers that are in a Select combo box. The name of the Select control is "Answer." Once an answer is selected, the visitor hits the Submit button. This action sends the selected answer to the Active Server Page, which will respond to the choice with this code:

```
If Request.Form("Answer") = "42" then
        Response.Write "You got the correct answer!"
Else
        Response.Write "WRONG! Try again..."
End If
```

Again, dynamic content is displayed based on the visitor's choice. Other browser properties that deal with how to display the response can also be set.

Grouping Active Server Pages into a collection that are related to each other creates an ASP Application. For example, if you have a set of pages that deal with adding, editing, deleting and viewing contacts for your company, you can group them together into an ASP Application. The Application Object contains properties at that level. ASP also has the ability to run a coded event procedure that runs the first time someone views one of the pages in our application, which would enable you to initialize variables. The code can be run when the Application ends.

Visitors at your site may visit more than one page. They may, for example, browse through your catalog, search for a specific item, look at the sales, order a few items and then check out. Stepping through each of these pages is called a session. The Session Object contains methods and properties to keep track of visitors.

Because Active Server Pages as files stand alone, a way to tie them together needs to be available. You wouldn't want your visitors to have to login to every page they visited at your site so you could maintain an order. Use the Session Object instead. For example, on an e-commerce store page, make sure the person has logged in before shopping around. This enables you to customize the pages visitors see to match the type of products that they are most often looking for. Therefore, place this code before any other content on pages from such a site.

```
If IsEmpty(Session("UserName") then
        Response.Redirect "http://www.whatever.com/login.asp"
Else
        'show normal page
End If
```

The first line of code checks to see if the person has logged in. If not, the UserName property of the Session object contains nothing or is empty. If that is the case, the visitor is sent to the Login page.

The main use of the Server Object is to enable connection to other components that you create or have installed on your system. For example, a component that comes with IIS but not with PWS, called *Collaborative Data Objects* (CDO), enables you to send an email from your ASP with just a few lines of code:

```
Set TheMail = Server@somewhere.com", _CreateObject("CDONTS.NewMail")
TheMail.Send "gbuczek
  "you@whoknows.com","What's Up", "The Text of the message..."
Set TheMail = Nothing
```

Here, use the CreateObject method of the Server Object to use the CDO component. Because CDO obeys the standard object model, use dot-syntax to call the "Send" method to send the email. Note that four parameters exist in the Send method. The first parameter is who the message is from, the second parameter is whom the message is to, the third parameter is the subject of the message and the fourth parameter is the body of the message.

Now that you have been introduced to some basic ASP samples, as well as the ASP Object model, we will take a closer look at the properties, methods, and events of the ASP Objects in the following sections.

The Request Object

Table 18-2 summarizes the properties, which are actually all collections or groupings of properties of the Request Object.

Table 18-2	Property/Collection	Purpose
Request Object Properties	Form	Enables you to retrieve the form field values from a form post.
	QueryString	Enables you to retrieve the form field values from a form get method.
	ServerVariables	A collection of properties that supply you with information about the visitor's browser
	Cookies	Supply you with a way to leave small configuration files on your visitor's computer.

With an HTML form, it is possible to see the information that was filled in on that form using the Post method or the Get method as shown here:

```
<FORM ACTION="http://www.whatever.com/checkout.asp" METHOD=POST>
<FORM ACTION="http://www.whatever.com/ShowProduct.asp" METHOD=GET>
```

Note that using the Get method limits all form parameters to 255 bytes. The parameters are visible in the URL with a question mark starting the parameter list and the ampersand used to separate the pairs of parameters and values as in:

```
http://www.whatever.com/ShowProduct.asp?id=24452&size=full&showprice=yes
```

This method is most often used when you want to make the call directly from the HTML without the user having to fill in the information. The Post method passes the parameters as a binary stream, so it doesn't have the same byte size limitations as the Get method and the values sent are not visible in the http:// request in their browser window.

When you use the Post method, the form field values are available in the Form collection of the Request Object. Note that a collection is a grouping of property values.

Most Web sites have a "Request for More Info" page. This page generally has a place for the visitor to supply a name, email address, comment/question and the subject of the message. When the person fills in the form and presses the submit button, a request is then routed through your ASP to the correct email address based on the subject of the message. The visitor then sees a message that the comment/question has been submitted. Figure 18-5 and the following code show the submitting page and the underlying HTML.

Figure 18-5

The Request for
More Info form

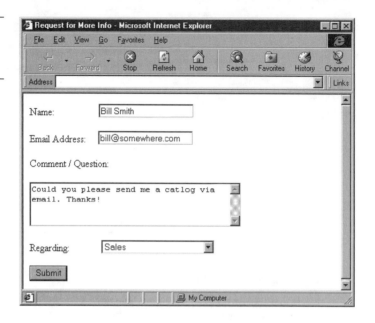

```
<html>
<head>
<title>Request for More Info</title>
</head>
<body>
<form method="POST" action=""http://www.netstats2000.com/sample.asp"">
<p>Name: <input type="text" name="Name" size="20"></p>
<p>Email Address:<input type="text" name="Email" size="20"></p>
<p>Comment / Question:</p>
<p><textarea rows="4" name="Comment" cols="40"></textarea></p>
<p>Regarding: <select name="Regarding" size="1">
    <option selected value="Sales">Sales</option>
    <option value="Support">Support</option>
    <option value="Employment Opportunities">Employment Opportunities
                    </option></select></p>
<p><input type="submit" value="Submit" name="Submit"></p>
</form>
</body>
</html>
```

Notice that the Form tag uses the Post method. Therefore, the ASP will retrieve the values for the form fields using the Form collection of the Request Object. Also note the name of each of the form fields. Those names also will be used in your ASP. Figure 18-6 shows the response that the visitor sees after submitting the request. The following code shows the ASP that produced this page.

Figure 18-6

The response
from the More
Info request

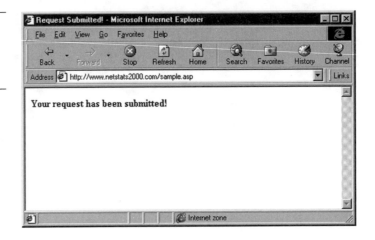

```
<%@ Language=VBScript%>
<%
Set TheMail = Server.CreateObject("CDONTS.NewMail")
TheMessage = "From: " & Request.Form("Name") _
 & vbnewline & Request.Form("Comment")
if Request.Form("Regarding") = "Sales" then
 TheMail.Send Request.Form("Email"),"sales@whatever.com", _
        Request.Form("Regarding"), TheMessage
elseif Request.Form("Regarding") = "Support" then
 TheMail.Send Request.Form("Email"), "support@ whatever.com", _
        Request.Form("Regarding"), TheMessage
else
 TheMail.Send Request.Form("Email"), "emps@ whatever.com", _
        Request.Form("Regarding"), TheMessage
end if
Set TheMail = Nothing
%>
<html>
<head>
<title>Request Submitted!</title>
</head>
<BODY>
<p><B>Your request has been submitted!</B></p>
</body>
</html>
```

Let's take a closer look at the code. First, as before we have:

```
<%@ Language=VBScript%>
```

This indicates that the default scripting language is VBScript. Then
"<%" indicates the beginning of a code block. Next you have:

```
Set TheMail = Server.CreateObject("CDONTS.NewMail")
```

which, as demonstrated earlier in this chapter, is using the CreateObject method of the Server Object to connect us to a component, in this case the Collaborative Data Objects or CDO, for sending email, which works with IIS but not PWS. Then you have:

```
TheMessage = "From: " & Request.Form("Name") & vbnewline & ⊕ Request.Form("Comment")
```

Here, the body for the message is created by concatenating the word "From:" with the name of the person who submitted the request. Retrieve the visitor's name from the Form collection's "Name" field of the request object. Remember that in the previous form in HTML, the name of the "Name" field was defined as "Name". Next, concatenate a new line and the "Comment" that the person submitted through the "Comment" field of the Form collection of the Request object. The body of the message is:

```
From: Bill Smith
Could you please send me a catalog via email? Thanks!
```

The next block of code sets up a condition based on the "Regarding" text for the subject of the email:

```
if Request.Form("Regarding") = "Sales" then
  TheMail.Send Request.Form("Email"), "sales@somewhere.com", _
       Request.Form("Regarding"), TheMessage
elseif Request.Form("Regarding") = "Support" then
  TheMail.Send Request.Form("Email"), "support@somewhere.com", _
       Request.Form("Regarding"), TheMessage
else
  TheMail.Send Request.Form("Email"),"emps@somewhere.com", _
       Request.Form("Regarding"), TheMessage
end if
```

Use the Regarding text to determine to whom the message is sent. In each of the conditions, the only difference is to whom the email is sent. The Send method of the NewMail object takes four parameters: whom the message is from, then whom the message is to, followed by the subject line, and finally the comment.

The QueryString collection of properties is used in the same way as the Form collection. Using the Get method for the form instead of the "Post" method, the line of code:

```
TheMessage = "From: " & Request.Form("Name") & vbnewline & Request.Form("Comment")
```

would now be:

```
TheMessage = "From: " & Request.QueryString("Name") & vbnewline & _
Request.QueryString("Comment")
```

Figure 18-7

The Server
Variables Partial
List

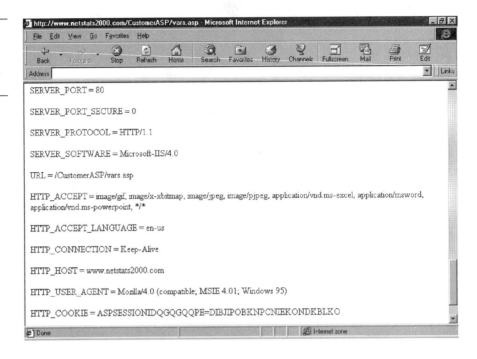

The ServerVariables collection is very helpful for generating statistics about the visitors to the site. For example, using the ServerVariable properties helps determine the visitor's IP Address, the browser type and what it supports, or information about the operating system. Figure 18-7 shows just a few of the variables and the following code is the complete code needed to generate this master list of server variables.

```
<% @ LANGUAGE="VBSCRIPT %>
<%
    For Each SV in Request.ServerVariables
        Response.Write "<p>" & SV & " = "  & Request.Servervariables(SV) &
"</p>" Next
%>
```

This example uses a For Each code block to display the entire Server-Variables collection. This indicates that something is to be done with each of the ServerVariables and that something is defined between the For and the Next statements. This code is very helpful because it can be used it to create a master list of all the ServerVariables.

The Cookies collection provides a way to store small amounts of data on the visitor's computer for later retrieval. For example, instead of requiring visitors to log-in to the Web site during each visit, who they are can be stored in a cookie on their machines and the cookie retrieved the next time they visit.

The Response Object

Tables 18-3 and 18-4, respectively, summarize the properties and methods of the Response Object. As already shown, the Response Object provides the methods and properties for communicating back to the browser.

Most browsers these days have what is referred to as a cache. A cache is a folder on the hard drive where Web pages, graphics, sound, and so on are stored from sites that the visitor has been to. If a person revisits a site, the page may not have to be downloaded again since it is already on his or her hard drive. This can be a problem for dynamic pages since the

Table 18-3	Property	Purpose
Response Object Properties	Buffer	Indicates whether the output to the browser is sent right away or stored until told to send.
	Expires	The number of minutes before the page expires in the visitor's cache.
	ExpiresAbsolute	The specific Date/Time that the returned output expires in the vistor's cache.
	ContentType	The type of output being sent to the browser.

Table 18-4	Methods	Purpose
Response Object Methods	Write	Returns text to the Browser.
	BinaryWrite	Returns non-textual output to the browser.
	Redirect	Returns result to browser from another file.
	Clear	Empties any buffered return information to the browser.
	Flush	Sends the data in the buffer immediately to the browser.
	End	Stops processing of ASP and returns any data in the buffer.

intent is for the data to change. Therefore, the data should not be cached. ASP provides two properties for dealing with this problem: Expires and ExpiresAbsolute. These properties enable you to decide how long the page should be cached, if at all. Expires takes as a value, the number of minutes until the page expires.

```
Response.Expires = 60
```

That line would cause the page to expire in one hour. It could be stated, for example, that the page would expire on a certain date, as in the following code:

```
Response.ExpiresAbsolute = "12/1/2001"
```

The Buffer property and the Clear, Flush and End methods deal with how we want our data returned to the browser. For example, an ASP page that calculates shipping and verifies credit card information may require several seconds for this code to complete. Choosing to buffer the output is an option that means waiting for all the code to complete before sending any HTML to the browser. Another option is choosing not to buffer the output that would send HTML to the browser as it becomes available. The following code is an example of buffering:

```
Response.Buffer = True
'code that calculates shipping goes here
Response.Write "Shipping charge = " & ShippingCharge
'code that verifies credit card information
Response.write "Credit Card is " & CCStatus
```

The code would not write the first line regarding shipping to the browser until the credit card processing was complete. Then both lines of text would be sent to the browser. The following is an example of not buffering:

```
Response.Buffer = False
'code that calculates shipping goes here
Response.Write "Shipping charge = " & ShippingCharge
'code that verifies credit card information
Response.write "Credit Card is " & CCStatus
```

The code would not write the first line about shipping to the browser until processing the credit card was complete. Both versions have advantages and disadvantages. Not buffering provides the benefit of the visitor receiving some feedback that the process has begun. But having the buffer activated provides more control over what is sent to the browser. If the credit card approval process fails, you may not want to provide shipping.

The Flush and Clear methods of the Response Object are used to control when the buffers is emptied and sent to the browser. Both of these methods can only be used if the Buffer is set to True. Using Flush, immediately sends the contents of the Buffer to the visitor's browser. Clearing the buffer, empties what is in the buffer and prepares new HTML to send to the browser, as in:

```
Response.Buffer = True
'code that calculates shipping goes here
Response.Write "Shipping charge = " & ShippingCharge
'code that verifies credit card information
If CCStatus = "Approved" then
        Response.write "Credit Card is Approved."
        Response.Flush
Else
        Response.Clear
        Response.Write "Not Approved!"
End If
```

If the credit card is approved, the Shipping Information and Credit Approved text are flushed or sent to the browser. If the credit card was not approved, the Buffer empties, which removes the line about shipping and only sends the Not Approved text to the browser. The End method of the Response Object ends all ASP processing and flushes the buffer to the visitor's browser.

Use the BinaryWrite method to write data that is not text to the browser when used in combination with the ContentType property. IIS and PWS, though, do not provide a method for reading non-text data from a file, so you would have to create your own component for this functionality. It is often easier to achieve this through Redirection.

The Redirect method of the Response Object provides the ability to route the visitor to a different page. This was mentioned earlier in the chapter, during the discussion of redirecting a person to a log-in page if he or she had not yet logged in.

```
If IsEmpty(Session("UserName") then
        Response.Redirect "http://www. whatever.com/login.asp"
Else
        'show normal page
End If
```

Redirect happens immediately and requires that no data has been sent to the browser at that point. Another great use of redirection is giving the visitor a list of possible places to go in the form of a drop-down list. When visitors select the pages they wish to see, redirect them to the selected pages. Figure 18-8 shows the selection Web page.

Figure 18-8

The Where Do
You Want To Go
Web page

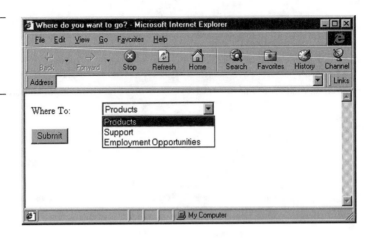

The two following listings show the HTML of the selection page:

```
<html>
<head>
<title>Where do you want to go?</title>
</head>
<body>
<form method="POST" action="http://www.whatever.com/sample.asp">
<select name="WhereTo" size="1">
<option selected value="http://www.whatever.com/products.html">Products</option>
<option value="http://www.whatever.com/Support.html">Support</option>
<option value="http://www.whatever.com/jobs.html">Employment Opportunities</option>
  </select></p>
  <p><input type="submit" value="Submit" name="Action"></p>
</form>
</body>
</html>
```

The next lines are the ASP code of the redirection page:

```
<%@ Language=VBScript%>
<%
response.redirect request.form("WhereTo")
%>
```

Notice in the HTML example that the drop-down list is called WhereTo. For each item in the list, text is visible to the visitor and a link that you read from the Form property.

GLOBAL.ASA and the Application and Session Objects

Grouping together Active Server Pages that are in the same directory structure creates an Active Server Page application. This is done from the Microsoft Management Console for IIS. Browse to the directory that contains your files and select the properties for that directory. In the Application Setting choose Create and give your application a name. At that point you have an application, but the real power of this comes into play with a special file called the global.asa file.

The global.asa is simply a text file with the name global.asa placed in the root directory of your Web application. In this text file, define the four events that are summarized in Table 18-5.

The purpose of these events is to enable you to run code or create variables that will persist across the life of your Application or during the stay of a visitor. Thus you can create log-in variables, constant information for use across your site or dedicated connections to a data source. The following code contains a sample global.asa file:

```
<SCRIPT LANGUAGE=VBScript RUNAT=Server>
Sub Application_OnStart
set Application("Gconn") = Gconn
Application("Gconn").open "DSN", "sa", "password"
        Application("Discount") = .1
End Sub

Sub Application_OnEnd
        'Insert script to be executed when the application ends
End Sub

Sub Session_OnStart
        Session("LoginEmpID") = " "
End Sub

Sub Session_OnEnd
```

Event	Purpose
Application_OnStart	Runs when the first .asp page is viewed with your application by any user.
Application_OnEnd	Runs when your application is shut down.
Session_OnStart	Runs when a visitor enters or returns to your application.
Session_OnEnd	Runs when the user leaves your Web site.

Table 18-5

Application Events

```
          'Insert script to be executed when a session ends
End Sub
</SCRIPT>
```

The first thing you notice with this listing is this code :

```
<SCRIPT LANGUAGE=VBScript RUNAT=Server>
</SCRIPT>
```

to denote the beginning and end of the code. Each of the events starts with the word sub, followed by the name of the event:

```
Sub Application_OnEnd
```

and ends with:

```
End Sub
```

The importance of the application and session variables is their Scope. Scope refers to the location where the variable can be seen and where its value can be retrieved. Creating an application variable as in:

```
Application("Discount") = .1
```

defines a variable for which the value is available anywhere within your ASP application. This is very powerful because instead of defining a discount on 10 different pages, it is defined in one place and the value is accessed in all of your pages. When it comes time to change the discount, the information has to be changed in only one place. Similarly, the scope of session variables can be defined only for a specific user's focus throughout the ASP application. This enables you to keep track of an order as a visitor selects more items throughout the e-commerce site or to keep track of security as a user goes from page to page.

A session begins when a visitor first enters your site and it ends when the session times out due to inactivity or you end the session in code. You can manage sessions with the TimeOut Property and the Abandon method of the Session object. The TimeOut property stores the number of minutes a session can be idle, during which the visitor makes no requests. So, if we coded:

```
Session.TimeOut = 30
```

a visitor's session is considered over when he or she goes through a period of 30 minutes without requesting a page. We can also explicitly end a session with the Abandon method:

```
Session.Abandon
```

You would use the Session.Abandon method when you want to give the user an End Session button or once the user has placed his or her order and all the processing for the order is complete. Once the session is abandoned or timed out, the code in the Session_OnEnd event runs.

The Server Object

The Server Object is used mostly to create instances or connect to external components. You saw an example of this earlier with the following code:

```
Set TheMail = Server.CreateObject("CDONTS.NewMail")
```

Use the CreateObject method of the Server object to create an instance of the object NewMail that you reference from the variable TheMail. Later in this chapter, you will be using the CreateObject method to create components that will enable you to work with your Access database.

A property of the Server object that is worth noting is the ScriptTime-Out property. This property defines the number of maximum seconds that your ASP page can take to complete. If your page takes longer to complete, the visitor will get a message that says the page has timed-out. So if you code

```
Server.ScriptTimeOut = 45
```

then your page must run in 45 seconds or it will be timed out.

Creating ASPs for the Students, Teachers, and Courses Database

Now that you know what ASP is and how it works, let's look at some sample ASPs that connect to an Access database to produce dynamic content. The database used in this section is the Students, Teachers, and Courses database from Chapter 11.

Sample Walk-through

The sample site enables the visitor to add new students, view student information, view course information, and view program information. When the visitor first enters the site, he or she sees the page displayed in Figure 18-9.

All the pages in this sample site are ASPs. These pages use code to connect to the database and populate the combo boxes, known as Select controls in HTML, with all the students, courses, and programs.

If the visitor were to click on the Add Student link, he or she would see the Add Student page displayed in Figure 18-10.

The visitor could use the Add Student page to add a new student to the database. Because the Student ID field is a primary key, the code must make sure that the visitor doesn't enter an ID for a student that already exists in the system. If the visitor does, he or she will see a different message at the top of the page, as shown in Figure 18-11.

The message tells the visitor that the ID is invalid and he or she is given another chance. Once the visitor supplies a valid entry, the record is added to the database and he or she is returned to the Menu page.

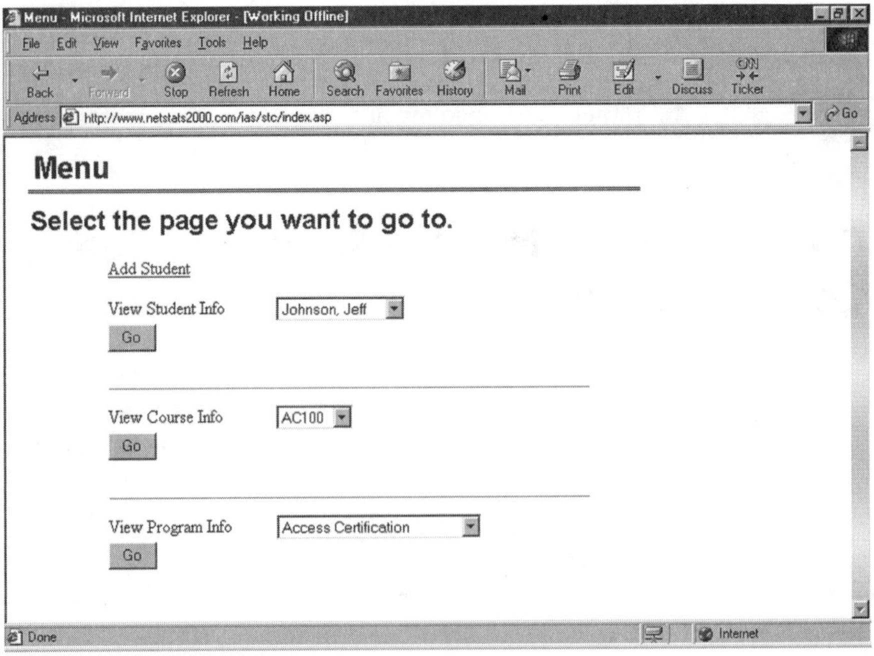

Figure 18-9

The Menu page

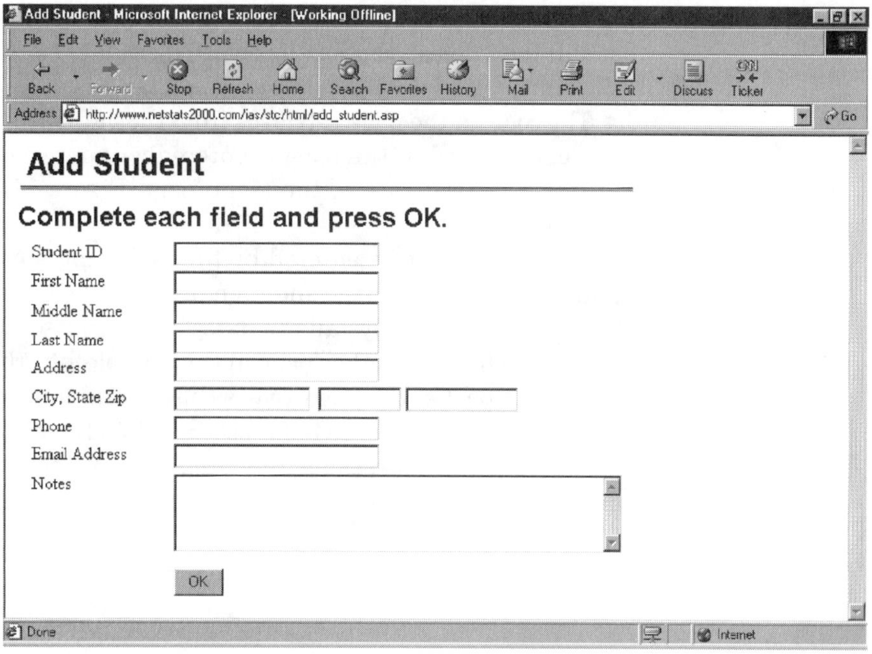

Figure 18-10

The Add Student page

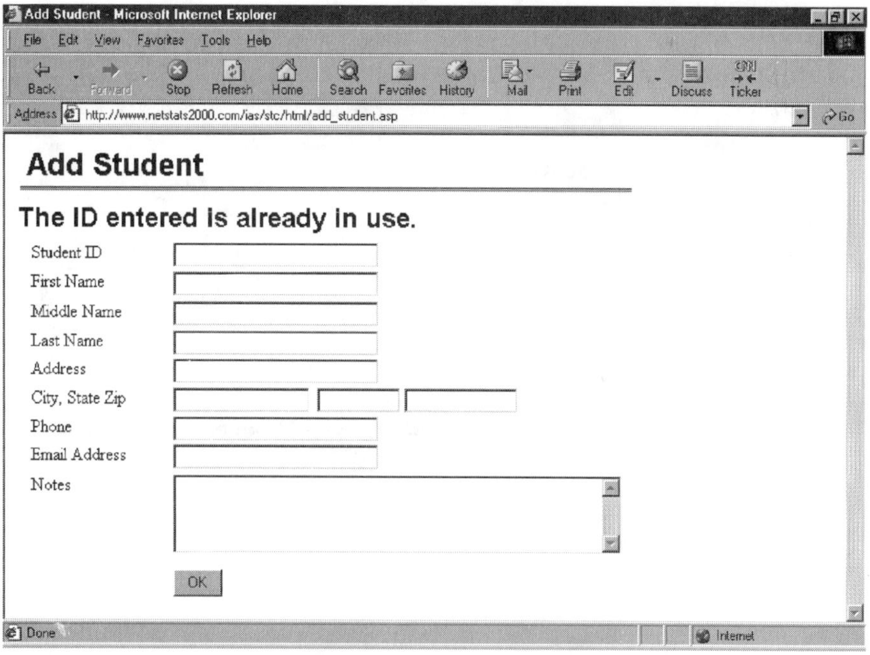

Figure 18-11

The Add Student page with an error message

If the user presses the Go button for the Student section, he or she will see all the information for the selected student selected, as in the sample shown in Figure 18-12.

The code on the page retrieves from the database the data based on the student selected. If the page is entered without selecting a student first, the visitor is returned to the Menu page. Figure 18-13 shows the Course Info page.

This page must be entered by first selecting a course from the Select control on the Menu page and then pressing the Go button in that section. The page then displays all the data for the course that was selected. Figure 18-14 shows the other page in this sample site, the Program Info page.

The top part of the page shows the general information about the program. Beneath that, the visitor sees an HMTL table that contains a list of all the required courses for this program. The bottom table on this page displays the elective courses for this program.

Figure 18-12

The Student Info page

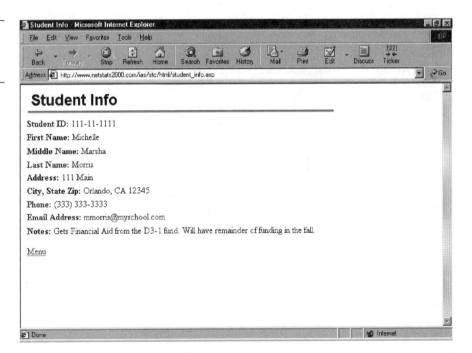

Figure 18-13

The Course Info page

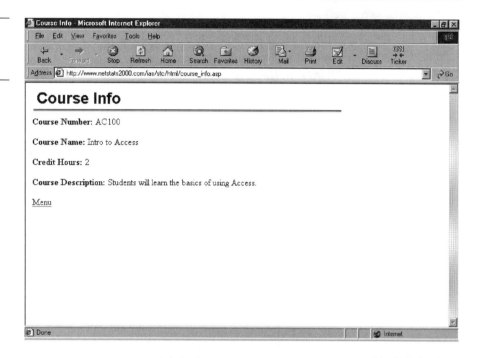

Figure 18-14

The Program Info page

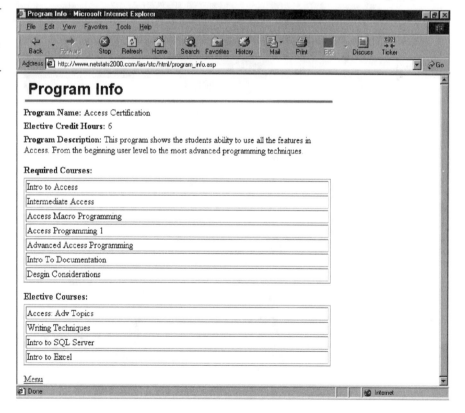

Creating a DSN

As you have seen throughout this book, we have used *Data Access Objects* (DAO) to connect to our database through code. This is done simply with this line of code:

```
Set MyDB = CurrentDb
```

The variable MyDB would now point to the current database.

When connecting to your database from ASPs, you will use a different object library, the *Active Data Object* (ADO). The approach that you will see in the code for this sample site uses ADO to connect to the database through a *Data Source Name* (DSN). A DSN contains information about which type a database is and where that database is located. Then, in code, point your database connection to a DSN.

To create a DSN, you need to select ODBC Data Sources through the control panel. Once you do, you will see a dialog like the one in Figure 18-15.

Figure 18-15

ODBC Data
Source
Administrator

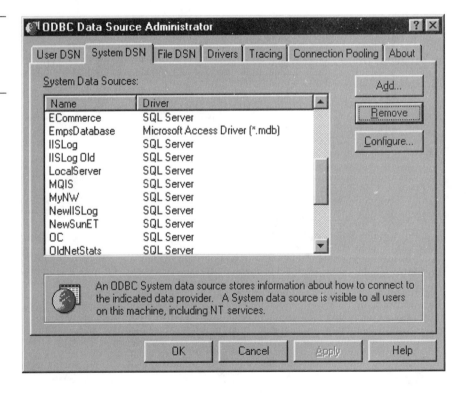

Notice that the System DSN has been selected. This enables us to create a DSN that will be available not just to us, but to all users. Press the Add button to see the dialog displayed in Figure 18-16.

Select the Microsoft Access Driver, because you are going to connect to your Access database. You will then see the configuration dialog similar to that displayed in Figure 18-17.

First, enter a name for this DSN in the Data Source Name text box. This name is very important, as this is what you will use in your code. For this sample site, the name STC is used. You can then enter a description for the DSN, which is just for your information. Then press the Select... button and browse to the location of the Access database that you want to connect to.

Notice the System Database section. Remember back in Chapter 4, "Company Management," using the Purchase Order database, you added security to it. When you did that, a special database was created that stored log-in information. If you secure a database and want to access the database through a DSN, this is where you specify the location of the special log-in database.

In fact, if you decide to use Access with an Internet application that is beyond learning purposes or for totally unsecured purposes, you must use security to encrypt and control access to the database. If you don't, your database in its entirety could easily be retrieved from a knowledgeable Internet visitor. Once you have completed filling in the information on this dialog, press the OK button and your DSN is now complete.

Active Server Page Application

Menu Page

The Menu page provides access to all the other pages in this sample site. The page contains a link to one page and three HTML forms that link to the other three pages.

The first link at the top of the page connects this page to the Add Student page:

```
<A HREF="./html/add_student.asp">Add Student</A>
```

From the link, you can see that the Add Student page is located in a subfolder of the current folder called HTML.

Figure 18-16

The Create New
Data Source
dialog

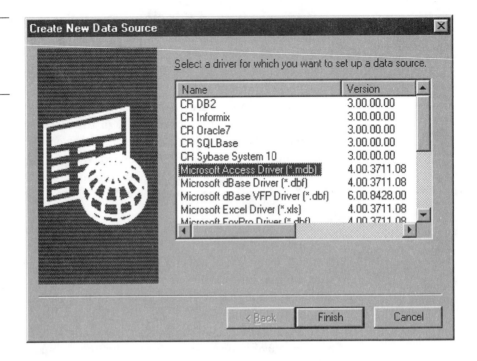

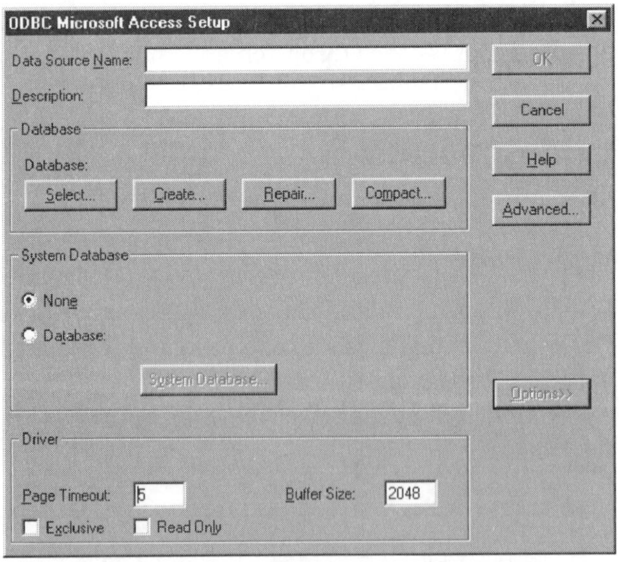

Figure 18-17

The ODBC
Microsoft Access
Setup dialog

As you saw earlier in this chapter, forms are used to submit data from one page to another or from a page back to itself. This page contains three forms. One is for the Student Info page, another is for the Course Info page, and the third is for the Program Info page.

The first form contains a Select control called Student and a button called Go. When the button is pressed, the Form HTML tag indicates where the data selected should be sent:

```
<FORM ACTION="./html/student_info.asp" METHOD=POST>
```

Notice the Action property. That means that when the visitor presses the OK button, he or she is taken to the page indicated in that property. Now notice the Method property. Because it is set to POST, the value the visitor selects in the Student Select control is available to you on the Student Info page through the Form fields collection.

The second HTML form on this page links the page to the Course Info page when the second Go button is pressed:

```
<FORM ACTION="./html/course_info.asp" METHOD=POST>
```

The page receives, through the Form fields collection, the Course selected by the visitor in the Course Select control.

The third HTML form on this page links this page to the Program Info page when the third Go button is pressed:

```
<FORM ACTION="./html/program_info.asp" METHOD=POST>
```

The value selected by the visitor in the Program Select control is posted to the Program Info page, so it will be available through the Form Fields collection.

At the top of this page, you will find the first code block. This code runs before any of the HTML on the page is output to the browser.

```
<%
Option Explicit
Dim MyConn
Dim RSStudents
Dim RSCourses
Dim RSPrograms
set MyConn = server.createobject ("adodb.connection")
MyConn.open "STC", "Admin", ""
set RSStudents = MyConn.Execute("Select StudentID, FirstName, LastName " _
      & "From Students Order By LastName, FirstName")
set RSCourses = MyConn.Execute("Select CourseID, CourseNumber " _
      & "From Courses Order By CourseNumber")
set RSPrograms = MyConn.Execute("Select ProgramID, ProgramName " _
      & "From Programs Order By ProgramName")
%>
```

Start with Option Explicit, which tells the compiler that all the variables that are used in this section are declared:

```
Option Explicit
```

This variable is used to connect to the database. Notice that a type is not indicated for a variable. This is because with VBScript, only one type is available, which is called variant. That type can be used to store any variable type:

```
Dim MyConn
```

This next variable is used to retrieve the student names for the Student Select control:

```
Dim RSStudents
```

one for the Course Select control:

```
Dim RSCourses
```

and one for the Program select control:

```
Dim RSPrograms
```

Now define the type of object that the MyConn variable will be. Set it to be a Connection object of the ADO library:

```
set MyConn = server.createobject ("adodb.connection")
```

Then open a connection to your database. The first parameter indicates the name of the DSN. Remember in the last section that it was called STC. The second parameter indicates the user name for logging into the database and the third parameter indicates the password:

```
MyConn.open "STC", "Admin", ""
```

Now that you are connected to the database, retrieve the names of all the students:

```
set RSStudents = MyConn.Execute("Select StudentID, FirstName, LastName " _
    & "From Students Order By LastName, FirstName")
```

the names of all the courses:

```
set RSCourses = MyConn.Execute("Select CourseID, CourseNumber " _
    & "From Courses Order By CourseNumber")
```

and the names of all the programs:

```
set RSPrograms = MyConn.Execute("Select ProgramID, ProgramName " _
                & "From Programs Order By ProgramName")
```

Then, within the HTML of your page, you need code blocks that go through each of the records retrieved from the database and add them to the appropriate select control.

This next code block populates the Student select control.

```
<SELECT NAME="Student">
<%
Do Until RSStudents.EOF
%>
        <OPTION VALUE="<% Response.Write RSStudents("StudentID") %>">
                <% Response.Write RSStudents("LastName") & ", " & RSStudents("FirstName") %>
        </OPTION>
<%
        RSStudents.MoveNext
Loop
%>
</SELECT>
```

The name of the Select control is Student. That name is what you will use to supply the student selected by the visitor:

```
<SELECT NAME="Student">
```

Then start a loop so each of the records in the Students Recordset object can be processed:

```
Do Until RSStudents.EOF
```

Each of the records in that recordset needs to be displayed as an option in the Select control. The value for the option is what is passed when the form on this page is submitted. The name of the student is what the visitor sees:

```
<OPTION VALUE="<% Response.Write RSStudents("StudentID") %>">
        <% Response.Write RSStudents("LastName") & ", " & RSStudents("FirstName") %>
</OPTION>
```

Then move on to process the next record:

```
RSStudents.MoveNext
```

and loop:

```
Loop
```

The next code block populates the options of the Course Select control:

```
<SELECT NAME="Course">
<%
Do Until RSCourses.EOF
%>
        <OPTION VALUE="<% Response.Write RSCourses("CourseID") %>">
                <% Response.Write RSCourses("CourseNumber") %>
        </OPTION>
<%
        RSCourses.MoveNext
Loop
%>
</SELECT>
```

The Select control is called Course:

```
<SELECT NAME="Course">
```

Then start a loop to process each of the course records:

```
Do Until RSCourses.EOF
```

Each of the courses is added as an option to the Select control. Note that the user sees the name of the course, but that the ID of the course is submitted with the HTML Form:

```
<OPTION VALUE="<% Response.Write RSCourses("CourseID") %>">
        <% Response.Write RSCourses("CourseNumber") %>
</OPTION>
```

Then move on to the next record:

```
RSCourses.MoveNext
```

and loop:

```
Loop
```

The other code block on this page processes the program records:

```
<SELECT NAME="Program">
<%
Do Until RSPrograms.EOF
%>
  <OPTION VALUE="<% Response.Write RSPrograms("ProgramID") %>">
        <% Response.Write RSPrograms("ProgramName") %>
  </OPTION>
<%
  RSPrograms.MoveNext
Loop
%>
</SELECT>
```

The name of the Select control is Program:

```
<SELECT NAME="Program">
```

Now start a loop that enables you to process each of the program records:

```
Do Until RSPrograms.EOF
```

Each record is added as an option to the Select control:

```
<OPTION VALUE="<% Response.Write RSPrograms("ProgramID") %>">
        <% Response.Write RSPrograms("ProgramName") %>
</OPTION>
```

Then move on to the next record:

```
RSPrograms.MoveNext
```

and loop:

```
Loop
```

Add Student Page

The code on the Add Student page enables the visitor to add a new student to the database. The page has two states. The first state of the page is when the visitor first views it and the form on the page is displayed. The second state is when the visitor presses the OK button. When this is done, the data entered is sent back to this page. The code then verifies the uniqueness of the Student ID. If the value is unique, a new student record is added and the visitor is sent back to the Menu page.

To submit the page back to itself and cause these two states, you have this HTML Form tag:

```
<FORM ACTION="./add_student.asp" METHOD=POST>
```

The Action property is set to the same name as this page, which causes it to be submitted back to itself. The main code block is at the top of the page:

```
<%
Option Explicit
Dim MyConn
Dim RSStudent
Dim TheMessage
If IsEmpty(Request.Form("OK")) Then
```

```
        TheMessage = "Complete each field and press OK."
Else
  Set MyConn = server.createobject ("adodb.connection")
  MyConn.open "STC", "Admin", ""
  set RSStudent = MyConn.Execute("Select StudentID from " _
          & "Students Where StudentID = '" & Request.Form("StudentID") _
          & "'")
If Not RSStudent.EOF Then
          TheMessage = "The ID entered is already in use."
  Else
          MyConn.Execute "Insert Into Students (StudentID, " _
                  & "FirstName, MiddleName, " _
                  & "LastName, Address, City, State, Zip, Phone, " _
                  & "EmailAddress, Notes) values (" _
                  & "'" & Replace(Request.Form("StudentID"), "'", "''") & "', " _
                  & "'" & Replace(Request.Form("FirstName"), "'", "''") & "', " _
                  & "'" & Replace(Request.Form("MiddleName"), "'", "''") & "', " _
                  & "'" & Replace(Request.Form("LastName"), "'", "''") & "', " _
                  & "'" & Replace(Request.Form("Address"), "'", "''") & "', " _
                  & "'" & Replace(Request.Form("City"), "'", "''") & "', " _
                  & "'" & Replace(Request.Form("State"), "'", "''") & "', " _
                  & "'" & Replace(Request.Form("Zip"), "'", "''") & "', " _
                  & "'" & Replace(Request.Form("Phone"), "'", "''") & "', " _
                  & "'" & Replace(Request.Form("EmailAddress"), "'", "''") & "', " _
                  & "'" & Replace(Request.Form("Notes"), "'", "''") & "')"
          Response.Redirect "../index.asp"
  End If
End If
%>
```

Start with Option Explicit, indicating that all variables will be declared:

```
Option Explicit
```

Then declare a variable for your Connection object:

```
Dim MyConn
```

one for a Recordset object:

```
Dim RSStudent
```

and one that will store the text of a message:

```
Dim TheMessage
```

To determine the state of this page, look to see if the OK button is present. If the button isn't, it won't be part of the Form fields collection:

```
If IsEmpty(Request.Form("OK")) Then
```

In that case, use the initial message for this page:

```
TheMessage = "Complete each field and press OK."
```

Otherwise, the visitor is trying to add a new student:

```
Else
```

In that case, you need to create your Connection object:

```
Set MyConn = server.createobject ("adodb.connection")
```

and connect to the database:

```
MyConn.open "STC", "Admin", ""
```

Then look for a student record that already uses the Student ID entered by the visitor:

```
set RSStudent = MyConn.Execute("Select StudentID from " _
    & "Students Where StudentID = '" & Request.Form("StudentID") _
    & "'")
```

If one is found, the EOF property will be set to false:

```
If Not RSStudent.EOF Then
```

In that case, show this page again and display a different message:

```
TheMessage = "The ID entered is already in use."
```

Otherwise, add a new student record to the Students table based on the data entered by the visitor:

```
MyConn.Execute "Insert Into Students (StudentID, " _
    & "FirstName, MiddleName, " _
    & "LastName, Address, City, State, Zip, Phone, " _
    & "EmailAddress, Notes) values (" _
    & "'" & Replace(Request.Form("StudentID"), "'", "''") & "', " _
    & "'" & Replace(Request.Form("FirstName"), "'", "''") & "', " _
    & "'" & Replace(Request.Form("MiddleName"), "'", "''") & "', " _
    & "'" & Replace(Request.Form("LastName"), "'", "''") & "', " _
    & "'" & Replace(Request.Form("Address"), "'", "''") & "', " _
    & "'" & Replace(Request.Form("City"), "'", "''") & "', " _
    & "'" & Replace(Request.Form("State"), "'", "''") & "', " _
    & "'" & Replace(Request.Form("Zip"), "'", "''") & "', " _
    & "'" & Replace(Request.Form("Phone"), "'", "''") & "', " _
    & "'" & Replace(Request.Form("EmailAddress"), "'", "''") & "', " _
    & "'" & Replace(Request.Form("Notes"), "'", "''") & "')"
```

Then send the visitor back to the Menu page:

```
Response.Redirect "../index.asp"
```

Then, within the HTML, display the text of the message:

```
<% Response.Write TheMessage %>
```

Student Info Page

The code on the Student Info page displays all the information for the student selected on the Menu page.

```
<%
Option Explicit
Dim MyConn
Dim RSStudent
If IsEmpty(Request.Form("Student")) Then
        Response.Redirect "../index.asp"
End If
Set MyConn = server.createobject ("adodb.connection")
MyConn.open "STC", "Admin", ""
Set RSStudent = MyConn.Execute("Select * from Students Where " _
        & "StudentID = '" & Request.Form("Student") & "'")
%>
```

Start with Option Explicit:

```
Option Explicit
```

and declare a variable for a Connection object:

```
Dim MyConn
```

and one for the Recordset object:

```
Dim RSStudent
```

This page should only be entered if the visitor came to it by selecting a student on the Menu page and pressing the Go button on that form. Check to see if that Form field is submitted to this page:

```
If IsEmpty(Request.Form("Student")) Then
```

If it isn't, send the visitor back to the Menu page:

```
Response.Redirect "../index.asp"
```

Otherwise, you can instantiate the Connection object:

```
Set MyConn = server.createobject ("adodb.connection")
```

connect to your database:

```
MyConn.open "STC", "Admin", ""
```

and retrieve all the data for the student selected in the Student Select control on the Menu page:

```
Set RSStudent = MyConn.Execute("Select * from Students Where " _
     & "StudentID = '" & Request.Form("Student") & "'")
```

Then, within the HML, display the ID of the student:

```
<P><B>Student ID:</B> <% Response.Write RSStudent("StudentID")
%></P>
```

his or her name:

```
<P><B>First Name:</B> <% Response.Write RSStudent("FirstName")
%></P>
<P><B>Middle Name:</B> <% Response.Write RSStudent("MiddleName")
%></P>
<P><B>Last Name:</B> <% Response.Write RSStudent("LastName") %></P>
```

address:

```
<P><B>Address: </B> <% Response.Write RSStudent("Address") %></P>
<P><B>City, State Zip:</B> <% Response.Write RSStudent("City") &
     ", " & RSStudent("State") & " " & RSStudent("Zip") %></P>
```

and other information:

```
<P><B>Phone:</B> <% Response.Write RSStudent("Phone") %></P>
<P><B>Email Address:</B> <% Response.Write
RSStudent("EmailAddress") %></P>
<P><B>Notes:</B> <% Response.Write RSStudent("Notes") %></P>
```

Course Info Page

The code on the Course Info page displays all the data for the course the visitor selects on the Menu page:

```
<%
Option Explicit
Dim MyConn
```

```
Dim RSCourse
If IsEmpty(Request.Form("Course")) Then
        Response.Redirect "../index.asp"
End If
Set MyConn = server.createobject ("adodb.connection")
MyConn.open "STC", "Admin", ""
Set RSCourse = MyConn.Execute("Select * from Courses Where " _
        & "CourseID = " & Request.Form("Course"))
%>
```

Start with Option Explicit, telling the compiler that all variables will be declared. If you neglect to declare a variable, an error will occur, which aids in debugging:

```
Option Explicit
```

Then declare a variable for a Connection object:

```
Dim MyConn
```

and a Recordset object:

```
Dim RSCourse
```

but the page should only be entered if a course is selected on the Menu page:

```
If IsEmpty(Request.Form("Course")) Then
```

If it isn't, send the visitor back to the Menu page:

```
Response.Redirect "../index.asp"
```

Otherwise, create the Connection object:

```
Set MyConn = server.createobject ("adodb.connection")
```

and use your DSN to connect to your database:

```
MyConn.open "STC", "Admin", ""
```

Then grab the information for the desired course from the database:

```
Set RSCourse = MyConn.Execute("Select * from Courses Where " _
        & "CourseID = " & Request.Form("Course"))
```

Then, within the HTML, display the information for this course:

```
<P><B>Course Number:</B> <% Response.Write RSCourse("CourseNumber")
%></P>
<P><B>Course Name:</B> <% Response.Write RSCourse("CourseName")
%></P>
<P><B>Credit Hours:</B> <% Response.Write RSCourse("CreditHours")
%></P>
<P><B>Course Description:</B> <% Response.Write
RSCourse("CourseDescription") %></P>
```

Program Info Page

The code on the Program Info page displays information on the selected program as well as the courses for that program. The first code block runs before any HTML is displayed:

```
<%
Option Explicit
Dim MyConn
Dim RSProgram
Dim RSReq
Dim RSElect
If IsEmpty(Request.Form("Program")) Then
   Response.Redirect "../index.asp"
End If
Set MyConn = server.createobject ("adodb.connection")
MyConn.open "STC", "Admin", ""
Set RSProgram = MyConn.Execute("Select * from Programs Where " _
   & "ProgramID = " & Request.Form("Program"))
Set RSReq = MyConn.Execute("Select " _
   & "Courses.CourseName from ProgramRequiredCourses Inner Join Courses " _
   & "on ProgramRequiredCourses.CourseID = Courses.CourseID where " _
   & "ProgramID = " & Request.Form("Program"))
Set RSElect = MyConn.Execute("Select " _
   & "Courses.CourseName from ProgramElectiveCourses Inner Join Courses " _
   & "on ProgramElectiveCourses.CourseID = Courses.CourseID where " _
   & "ProgramID = " & Request.Form("Program"))
%>
```

Start with Option Explicit:

```
Option Explicit
```

Then in your declaration section, declare a variable that will store your database connection:

```
Dim MyConn
```

one that will retrieve program information:

```
Dim RSProgram
```

one that will retrieve the required courses for this program:

```
Dim RSReq
```

and one that will retrieve elective courses for this program:

```
Dim RSElect
```

But before you start retrieving information, make sure the visitor entered the page by selecting a program from the Menu page:

```
If IsEmpty(Request.Form("Program")) Then
```

If the visitor didn't, send them back to the Menu page:

```
Response.Redirect "../index.asp"
```

Otherwise, you can create your connection object:

```
Set MyConn = server.createobject ("adodb.connection")
```

and connect to your Access database:

```
MyConn.open "STC", "Admin", ""
```

Then retrieve all the information for the selected program:

```
Set RSProgram = MyConn.Execute("Select * from Programs Where " _
        & "ProgramID = " & Request.Form("Program"))
```

a list of all the required courses for this program:

```
Set RSReq = MyConn.Execute("Select " _
    & "Courses.CourseName from ProgramRequiredCourses Inner Join Courses " _
    & "on ProgramRequiredCourses.CourseID = Courses.CourseID where " _
    & "ProgramID = " & Request.Form("Program"))
```

and a list of all elective courses:

```
Set RSElect = MyConn.Execute("Select " _
    & "Courses.CourseName from ProgramElectiveCourses Inner Join Courses " _
    & "on ProgramElectiveCourses.CourseID = Courses.CourseID where " _
    & "ProgramID = " & Request.Form("Program"))
```

Then, within the HTML, display the program information:

```
<P><B>Program Name:</B> <% Response.Write RSProgram("ProgramName") %></P>
<P><B>Elective Credit Hours:</B> <% Response.Write RSProgram("ElectiveCreditHours") %></P>
<P><B>Program Description:</B> <% Response.Write RSProgram("ProgramDescription") %></P>
```

The next code block adds each required course for the program into an HMTL table:

```
<%
Do Until RSReq.EOF
%>
                    <TR>
                        <TD WIDTH=552>
                            <P><% Response.Write RSReq("CourseName") %></P>
                        </TD>
                    </TR>
<%
        RSReq.MoveNext
Loop
%>
```

The block loops through all the records in the RSReq Recordset object:

```
Do Until RSReq.EOF
```

Each record is added as its own row in an HTML table:

```
<TR>
```

and the name of the course is placed in a cell for that row:

```
<TD WIDTH=552>
        <P><% Response.Write RSReq("CourseName") %></P>
</TD>
```

Then close the row:

```
</TR>
```

and move on to process the next record:

```
        RSReq.MoveNext
Loop
```

The other code block on this page adds all the elective courses to another HTML table.

```
<%
Do Until RSElect.EOF
%>
<TR>
        <TD WIDTH=552>
                <P><% Response.Write RSElect("CourseName") %></P>
        </TD>
</TR>
<%
        RSElect.MoveNext
Loop
%>
```

The code then loops through each of the elective course records:

```
Do Until RSElect.EOF
```

Each record is placed in its own row in the HTML table:

```
<TR>
```

The name of the course is placed in a cell in the row:

```
<TD WIDTH=552>
        <P><% Response.Write RSElect("CourseName") %></P>
</TD>
```

Then close the row:

```
</TR>
```

and move on to process the next record:

```
        RSElect.MoveNext
Loop
```

APPENDIX A

Upsizing to SQL Server

You will probably eventually come to the point, due to size constraints, multi-user issues, Internet flexibility, or security, that you need to upsize your Access database to a database server. A common path taken by Access developers is to upsize their database to a Microsoft SQL Server database.

Access 2000 comes with a Wizard that makes it pretty simple to migrate your Access database into an SQL Server database. Start the Wizard by selecting Upsizing Wizard from the Tools/Database Utilities menu. When you do so, the first dialog of the Wizard is displayed, as in Figure A-1.

You can choose to place your Access tables into an existing SQL Server database or you can use the Wizard to create a new database. In this example, you will create a new SQL Server database. So select that and press Next to see the second dialog of the Wizard displayed in Figure A-2.

In the first dialog box, select or type in the name of the SQL Server where you want to create the database. Then enter your user name and password for that SQL Server. Note that you need to have the privileges to create a database for this Wizard to work. In the last box on this dialog, enter a name for the new database. Then press the Next button to see the next dialog of the Wizard displayed in Figure A-3.

Figure A-1

Upsizing Wizard
step 1

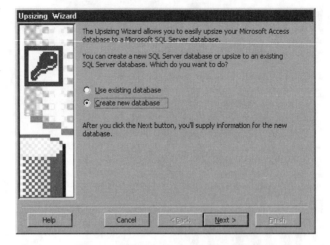

Figure A-2

Upsizing Wizard
step 2

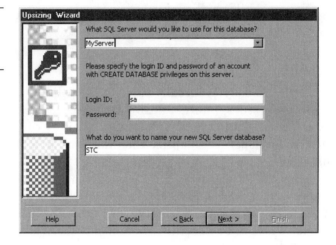

In this third step, select the tables that you want to export to SQL Server. You don't have to export them all. In fact, some would be more efficient to stay in the Access database. Any of the data that is shared by all should be upsized, but data that doesn't change, changes too infrequently, or that is just for a single user could stay in the Access database. You would then give each user his or her own front-end Access database that contains any data that he or she manages. That Access database would then link to the SQL Server database in which the shared data is located.

Press the Next button once you have selected the tables you want to export. You should then see the dialog displayed in Figure A-4.

Figure A-3

Upsizing Wizard
step 3

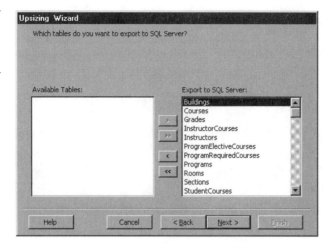

Figure A-4

Upsizing Wizard
step 4

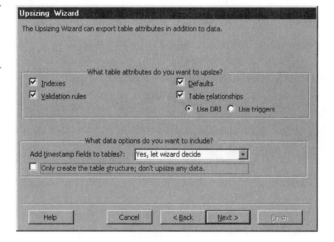

At the top part of the fourth dialog, select which field attributes you want to export to SQL Server. You can also select whether you want the Wizard to add timestamp fields to the SQL Server tables. Timestamp fields are used to indicate if a record has changed, not when it was changed. This information is then used by Access to determine whether a record that is being updated has changed.

You can also select to only upsize the table structures without any data. Press the Next button to move on to the next step of the Wizard displayed in Figure A-5.

Figure A-5

Upsizing Wizard
step 5

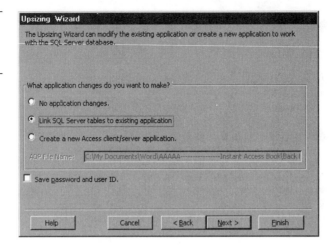

This dialog enables you to decide if and how you want to set up the front-end of the database. First, you can select to make no changes to your Access database that you are upsizing from. The second option modifies the Access database so that the new tables appear in the Tables tab of the database window as linked tables. The third option is to create a new Access database, an .adp file that contains all the forms, queries, reports, macros, and modules of this database with links to the SQL Server database, giving you a true front-end and back-end design.

Note that you can also select to save the SQL Server user name and password with the Access database so the user does not have to type it in each time they open the database in Access. Press the Next button to see the dialog displayed in Figure A-6.

Now press the Finish button and the Wizard will make the changes you selected in the previous steps. The Wizard then displays a report showing you the action taken by the Wizard.

Figure A-6

Upsizing Wizard
step 6

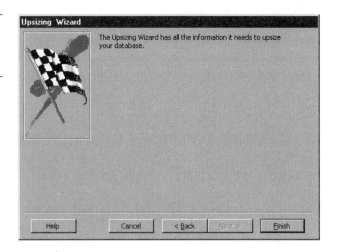

Index

About the CD

The CD that comes with this book contains all the Access 2000 databases and other files used in Chapters 2 through 18. Each of those chapters has its own folder on the CD. In that folder you will find the files for that chapter.

WARNING: BEFORE OPENING THE DISC PACKAGE, CAREFULLY READ THE TERMS AND CONDITIONS OF THE FOLLOWING COPYRIGHT STATEMENT AND LIMITED CD-ROM WARRANTY.

Copyright Statement

This software is protected by both United States copyright law and international copyright treaty provision. Except as noted in the contents of the CD-ROM, you must treat this software just like a book. However, you may copy it into a computer to be used and you may make archival copies of the software for the sole purpose of backing up the software and protecting your investment from loss. By saying, "just like a book," The McGraw-Hill Companies, Inc. ("Osborne/McGraw-Hill") means, for example, that this software may be used by any number of people and may be freely moved from one computer location to another, so long as there is no possibility of its being used at one location or on one computer while it is being used at another. Just as a book cannot be read by two different people in two different places at the same time, neither can the software be used by two different people in two different places at the same time.

Limited Warranty

Osborne/McGraw-Hill warrants the physical compact disc enclosed herein to be free of defects in materials and workmanship for a period of sixty days from the purchase date. If the CD included in your book has defects in materials or workmanship, please call McGraw-Hill at 1-800-217-0059, 9am to 5pm, Monday through Friday, Eastern Standard Time, and McGraw-Hill will replace the defective disc.

The entire and exclusive liability and remedy for breach of this Limited Warranty shall be limited to replacement of the defective disc, and shall not include or extend to any claim for or right to cover any other damages, including but not limited to, loss of profit, data, or use of the software, or special incidental, or consequential damages or other similar claims, even if Osborne/McGraw-Hill has been specifically advised of the possibility of such damages. In no event will Osborne/McGraw-Hill's liability for any damages to you or any other person ever exceed the lower of the suggested list price or actual price paid for the license to use the software, regardless of any form of the claim.

OSBORNE/McGRAW-HILL SPECIFICALLY DISCLAIMS ALL OTHER WARRANTIES, EXPRESS OR IMPLIED, INCLUDING BUT NOT LIMITED TO, ANY IMPLIED WARRANTY OF MERCHANTABILITY OR FITNESS FOR A PARTICULAR PURPOSE. Specifically, Osborne/McGraw-Hill makes no representation or warranty that the software is fit for any particular purpose, and any implied warranty of merchantability is limited to the sixty-day duration of the Limited Warranty covering the physical disc only (and not the software), and is otherwise expressly and specifically disclaimed.

This limited warranty gives you specific legal rights; you may have others which may vary from state to state. Some states do not allow the exclusion of incidental or consequential damages, or the limitation on how long an implied warranty lasts, so some of the above may not apply to you.

This agreement constitutes the entire agreement between the parties relating to use of the Product. The terms of any purchase order shall have no effect on the terms of this Agreement. Failure of Osborne/McGraw-Hill to insist at any time on strict compliance with this Agreement shall not constitute a waiver of any rights under this Agreement. This Agreement shall be construed and governed in accordance with the laws of New York. If any provision of this Agreement is held to be contrary to law, that provision will be enforced to the maximum extent permissible, and the remaining provisions will remain in force and effect.

NO TECHNICAL SUPPORT IS PROVIDED WITH THIS CD-ROM.